THE COLLEGE THAT WOULD NOT DIE

THE FIRST FIFTY YEARS OF
PORTLAND STATE UNIVERSITY, 1946–1996

THE COLLEGE THAT WOULD NOT DIE

THE FIRST FIFTY YEARS OF PORTLAND STATE UNIVERSITY, 1946–1996

Gordon B. Dodds

Oregon Historical Society Press

In collaboration with
Portland State University

Frontispiece: Stephen E. Epler

Published by the Oregon Historical Society Press in collaboration with Portland State University

Distributed by:

Portland State University
Post Office Box 751
Portland, Oregon 97207-0751

The paper used in this publication meets the minimum requirements of American National Standard for Information Sciences—Permanence of Paper for Printed Library Materials, ANSI Z39.48-1992.

Printed in the United States of America.

First Edition

Library of Congress Cataloging-in-Publication Data

Dodds, Gordon B. (Gordon Barlow), 1932-
    The college that would not die: the first fifty years of Portland State University, 1946-1996 / Gordon Dodds.
        p. cm.
    Includes bibliographical references and index.
    ISBN 0-87595-274-7 (cloth : alk. paper)
      1. Portland State University–History. I. Title.

    LD4571.P4 D63 2000
    378.795'49–dc21   99-051802

Dedicated to the memory of

STEPHEN E. EPLER

founder and savior of the University

CONTENTS

PREFACE

The origin of this book goes back a decade or so, when I was appointed university historian. My general charge was to prepare a history of Portland State University in time for the fiftieth anniversary, which at that time lay ten years in the future. Then president Natale A. Sicuro and Vice-Pres. Michael F. Reardon did not burden me with explicit directions about the form or content of the work, but rather let me shape it as I desired. Indeed, neither then nor later did any officer of the University provide any limitations or restrictions on what I was to write.

Given this freedom, what I have attempted to do is to furnish both a description and an interpretation of this remarkable institution's first fifty years. Even though Portland State's history is short, no single-volume account can be comprehensive. Presented, as are all historians, with the problem of selection, I decided on four principles.

I have chosen to emphasize the formative period down to the year 1969, when Portland State formally became a university, although I have not neglected the subsequent years. This provides perspective but also recognizes that in this first era emerged most of the subsequent patterns of the University's life, such as its urban focus; its difficulties with the chancellor, the state board, and University of Oregon; and its diverse student body. Secondly, I have attempted to say something about individuals and events that have had long-range influence (such as the contributions of Stephen E. Epler, the founder) and about the developments, although perhaps not so influential, that captured public attention (such as the Park Blocks "riot" of 1970). Thirdly, I have tried to include all significant aspects of the University community: administration, faculty, staff, and students, and their respective interactions with non-University forces such as the Portland metropolitan area, the State System of Higher Education, and its board and chancellor. Finally, out of the necessity to make this book most useful to a larger audience, I have focused on the major deci-sion-making bodies such as the president, faculty senate, student sen-ate, and the chancellor, rather than on more "local" units such as the academic departments, student organizations and publications, and athletic teams. In taking this "centralized" approach, I realize some-thing is lost in terms of flavor and color and, indeed, of complete accuracy, but consideration for readers requires not everything, even of note, can be included, or the book would grow to unmanageable proportions.

ACKNOWLEDGMENTS

The principal individual responsible for the creation of this history was former Portland State University provost Michael F. Reardon. Dr. Reardon created the position of university historian and arranged for me to occupy it. He also made possible travel money, three summers of unfettered research time, and funds for the preparation of the final manuscript.

The heart of the research materials for this book is the University Archives. Established by the first librarian, Jean Black, they have been superbly maintained and organized by Jerome DeGraaff, university archivist. He has been unfailingly cheerful and cooperative in making these indispensable materials available to me. Other members of the library staff who have also provided invaluable assistance are Kathy Greey and Rosalind Wang; they have put up with much from me, yet survived. Brent Schauer, Inge Wortman, Kathryn Kirkland, and Jean Tuomi kindly helped me and my assistants in locating photographs and photographic negatives for this book. The archives staffs of Oregon State University, the University of Oregon, and the State System of Higher Education were very helpful as well.

The written history of Portland State University also depends on unwritten materials. The thriving organization of Retired-Emeriti Professors of Portland State suggested its members form a volunteer corps to interview fellow members. Most of these volunteers were expertly trained by James Strassmaier, oral historian at the Oregon Historical Society, who contributed his most capable services to the University history. Those who conducted the interviews were Clark Brooke, Carleton Fanger, Ross Garner, David Newhall, Robert Tuttle, and Forbes Williams.

Faculty members and others connected with the University who were interviewed by the retired professors or by me contributed information available nowhere else. I am pleased to list their names here as a small indication of my gratitude toward them: Homer Allen, John Allen, Bernard Baumgartner, Alma Bingham, Jean Black, Joseph Blumel, Mabel Cramer, William Cramer, John Dart, Andreas Deinum, Brock Dixon, Arthur Emlen, Stephen Epler, Margaret Gottlieb, John Hakanson, Richard Halley, Hugh Hinds, Leonard Kimbrell, Charles Le Guin, Ella Litchfield, Ralph Macy, Grant Mumpower, Laureen Nussbaum, Rudi Nussbaum, Donald Parker, May Putnam, Eleanor Rigdon, Lucille Walker, William Walker, Hildegard Weiss, Howard Westcott, Charles White, Asher Wilson, and Loren Wyss.

Although in no way responsible for any mistakes in this manuscript, I am grateful to the following men and women who, by reading all or portions of it, kept many errors out. I hope their unrewarded tasks were in some ways satisfying. I know they made the book infinitely better than it would have been otherwise. These diligent readers number Carl Abbott, Whitney Bates, Oma Blankenship, Joseph Blumel, Bernard Burke, Marjorie Burns, George Carbone, John Cooper, Margaret Dobson, Stephen Epler, Kathy Greey, Richard Halley, Philip Harder, Jim Heath, Roger Jennings, Robert Lockerby, Hugo Maynard, Donald Moor, Frederick Nunn, G. Palmer Pardington III, Thomas Pfingsten, Nancy Porter, John Rosenberg, Charles Tracy, Hildegard Weiss, and Charles White.

Many others also were helpful in bringing this work to a conclusion. Lorin Anderson of Clean Copy made a most generous gift in kind. Information from personal experience or the provision of documents came from Barbara Alberty, Duncan Carter, Patricia Carter, Marc Feldesman, Joanne Gornick, Oliver Larson, Thomas Morris, Richard Piekenbrock, Raymond Rask, Amy Ross, Larry Sellers, Joy Spalding, Clark Spence, Ann Weikel, James Westwood, Don Willner, Barbara Winter, and Sharon Wood. I am grateful to them all.

I have been fortunate to have had the intelligent, resourceful, and energetic help of several graduate research assistants from the Department of History at the University. Without the aid of Shari Anderson, Katherine Huit, Katherine Moon, Malcolm Ringo, Theresa Theissen, and Douglas Will, this book never would have been completed on time. The last and indispensable stage of this lengthy project was expertly completed by Tina Hendricks, who prepared the final copy of the manuscript.

"We are starting from nothing."

ONE

The Years at Vanport · 1946–1948

t was a strange sentence to include in a letter welcoming a new
employee: "As you know we are starting from nothing." Yet this
description of the origins of Vanport Extension Center—the pre-
cursor of Portland State University—was an accurate one, for no
modern American university began in less promising circumstances
than Portland State. There were no students, no faculty, no staff. What
passed for a campus was the remains of a dilapidated Second World
War housing project that had been happily deserted by most of its residents as the war wound down.[1]

This uninspiring site at Vanport City presented little to lift the hor-
izons, either literally or figuratively, as the compact town—located between Portland and Vancouver, Washington—was completely surrounded by dikes ranging from fifteen to twenty-five feet in height. Although
citizens could see little beyond these massive barriers, their senses of
smell and hearing were tested from all directions. A Swift and Company
meat packing plant sent its aromas from the north. Westerly winds carried the din from the whistling locomotives and clattering freight cars
of two railroads. To the south lay four unlovely prospects: the turbid
waters of the Columbia Slough; more railroad tracks; the odoriferous
smokestacks of a carbide factory; and the pervasive effluvium of a "dead
animal processing plant." On the east lay the peeling, gray buildings
remaining from the wartime housing project. In this unlikely spot,
assaulted by its air, its geography, and its past, Portland State began its
beleaguered history, which produced in only fifty years Oregon's
urban university and a major force in the intellectual life of the state.[2]

Two men—one a symbol, one very real—were the founders of this
remarkable institution: Uncle Sam and Stephen E. Epler. The gov-

ernment of the United States contributed the campus, the buildings, the equipment, and the students to Vanport Extension Center. Stephen Epler contributed the institution itself. By 1946, when the Center was created, the federal government had a long history of support of education, which antedated the Constitution of the United States. Milestones measuring this progression included the Land Ordinance of 1785, which dedicated a portion of the national domain for public education; the Morrill Act of 1862, which did the same for higher education; the Hatch Act of 1887, which granted federal subsidies for the creation of state agricultural experiment stations; the Swift-Lever act of 1914, which gave grants for a system of agricultural extension work; and the Smith-Hughes Act of 1917, which financed instruction in agriculture and the skilled trades.

By 1946, the federal government also had a long tradition of rewarding its military veterans. After every conflict since the Revolutionary War, Congress had awarded land, money, or other benefits to servicemen and women. In 1944, Congress passed the most imaginative and comprehensive of these measures: the GI Bill of Rights. This enormously important statute, piloted through Congress via the collaborative efforts of the Roosevelt Administration and the American Legion, included a section that revolutionized higher education in the United States by providing tuition and maintenance allowances to veterans. In effect, it opened college and university study to millions of working and middle class Americans who never would have considered pursuing post-secondary education before the war. Opposed by some academic administrators who did not believe such students would be capable of university work, the GI Bill proved them wrong. By the fall of 1955—a decade after the end of the war—7.8 million veterans had embarked on education or training under the GI Bill, a total of 50.6 percent of all Second World War veterans then in civil life.[3]

The United States government also had another momentous effect on Portland State's origins: Vanport City itself. In 1945, Vanport was the world's largest housing project, built to help house the 160,000 defense workers who poured into the Portland metropolitan area to work in the Kaiser Company's three shipyards in Portland and Vancouver, Washington. Kaiser built Vanport, although it was financed and administered by the Federal Public Housing Administration and its subsidiary, the Housing Authority of Portland. Preliminary work on the 650-acre site began on 21 August 1942, and a little less than four months later the first residents moved into the two-story frame apartment buildings on 12 December 1942. At its peak of population in January 1945, Vanport numbered approximately forty thousand residents, making it the second largest community in Oregon. The men and women who lived at Vanport helped to make Henry Kaiser's shipyards the most efficient in the nation, establishing a record for productivity that won them a host of awards from the United States Maritime Commission. Coming from across the nation to temporary jobs in an evanescent community, Vanport's residents helped turn out hundreds of "ships for victory."[4]

As in the shipyards, life in Vanport City was regulated, noisy, and busy around the clock. The rhythm of the community matched that of the yards. Overseeing the hive of activity that was Vanport was the board of commissioners of the Housing Authority of Portland, which provided and maintained the apartment buildings, collected the rent from the tenants, and offered an array of services—some innovative and imaginative. Vanport had its own shopping centers (leased by the commissioners), a hospital, a jail, daycare centers, a library (furnished by the Library Association of Portland), recreation buildings, and a fire department, although police protection was provided by Multnomah County. There was a separate Vanport School District that provided—in two shifts daily—education from kindergarten through junior high. The school district also made daycare available throughout the school year, as well as during summer school sessions. All of these facilities and services came from the Housing Authority without the participation of Vanport's citizens. The "city," which was never incorporated, had no elected officials whatsoever. There were no political parties, no public discussion of the issues affecting the community, no elections. No one paid taxes; no one owned homes. All residents lacked the privilege, duty, right, and responsibility of governing their own affairs. Vanport, indeed, has been aptly likened by its historian to a city ruled by a benevolent "Big Brother."[5]

In spite of this paternalistic environment where everything was furnished, or perhaps because of it, the Vanport years did not compose a happy chapter in the lives of its residents. Problems abounded, ranging from inadequate heat in the apartments to fear of fire in the wooden buildings to continuous noise from workers coming and going from their round-the-clock shifts. There were no recreational facilities for adults, except for the movie theater—no tavern, nightclub, or dance hall. Juvenile vandalism, arising from unsupervised children, was a running sore. Vanport's population included Oregon's first sizable contingent of African Americans, who resented being shunted off to their own residential areas (although racial incidents were surprisingly few). Above all—in this transitory place—the gravest problem of all was that little community spirit developed; few ever took pride in living in Vanport.[6]

The unhappiness of Vanporters contributed to the bleak picture of the city painted by citizens of Portland and Oregon. Although it began in an atmosphere of pride, optimism, and patriotism, the city's reputation degenerated throughout the war until "during the first half of 1946 [when Vanport Extension Center was being planned] Vanport's image hit bottom, and bottom was a long ways down." By this time, Vanport was seen by outsiders as a mainly black project, as a target for arson and vandalism, and as the ultimate destination for welfare recipients. Although these images were wholly or partially untrue, they were compelling enough to make many Portlanders want to close Vanport and level its buildings to make way for industrial development.[7]

What gave the decaying city a new beginning, however, was the building of two communities—the first real communities in Vanport's history—the "Veterans' Village" section, allocated to returning servicepersons who could get no housing elsewhere, and a special group of them, those who attended Vanport Extension Center through the educational provisions of the GI Bill. What brought about this union was the Center's founder, Stephen Epler.

Epler was born in Brooklyn, Iowa, on 5 October 1909 to a young Christian (Disciples of Christ) minister and his wife. The influence of this socially conscious, activist denomination was a powerful one on Stephen Epler—and thus indirectly on Vanport Extension Center—throughout his life. The Disciples not only furnished his boyhood environment in the parsonage but also gave him his undergraduate education at Cotner College, a denominational institution in Lincoln, Nebraska, where his parents had met. The Reverend Epler held a succession of pastorates in small towns in Iowa, Nebraska, and Kansas, while Steve and his brother, Bruce, and sister, Irene, were growing up. Later, Epler remembered his parents' values as being powerful forces in his own life: their belief in independence and hard work supplemented the traditional moral values of the church. After graduating from high school in Norton, Kansas, in 1928, Epler enrolled at Cotner, where he underwent several experiences that changed his life.[8]

At Cotner, he met his future wife, Ferne Misner, a music major from Lincoln. He played on the football team along with his older

brother and developed a lifelong interest in sports. Through the influence of a chemistry professor, Joseph Moss, and of his own brother,
Epler majored in chemistry but also studied a good deal of education,
sociology, and history. One of the history faculty introduced him to
the progressive historians and to Lincoln Steffens, the famous investigative reporter, all of whom were examining with a critical eye the
strengths and weaknesses of American society and making suggestions
for its improvement. These readings convinced the young man to try
to help make his country one that would afford greater opportunities
for the common man. Finally, his Cotner years gave Epler a vocation,
teaching at a teachers college. He began training for it at the University
of Nebraska, which he entered in January 1932 after completing Cotner's graduation requirements a semester early.[9]

At the university, Epler fell under the influence of Prof. Knute
Broady, who directed his career in two ways: by giving him the ambition to pursue doctoral work at Teachers College of Columbia University and by recommending him for a job at the high school of the
small town of Chester, Nebraska. While at the University of Nebraska,
Epler's athletic talents paid his way as he was given the job of supervisor of physical education at the university's high school, where he also
coached basketball and track. Taking his MA degree in the summer of
1933, Epler began work at Chester High School in the fall.[10]

Chester High School, during Epler's first months there, gave him
the opportunity to display one of his greatest talents: innovation. The
high school and many other schools in rural communities were too
small to field the traditional football team of eleven players and sub-
stitutes. Rather than abandon the game he and the players loved,
Epler invented the sport of six-man football, which quickly caught on
in rural America. In time, he wrote a book on the game and formed
the national rules committee of the sport.[11]

After a year at Chester, Epler then taught for two years at the high
school in Beatrice, Nebraska before moving to New York City in the
fall of 1936 to study for the Ph.D. degree at the Teachers College of
Columbia University. Teachers College and New York City were exciting places for the Eplers (who had married in 1935) and far different
from rural Nebraska or even its capital city of Lincoln and its state university. They were in a minority, as most students at "TC" were from
the Northeast. More important, they enjoyed the cultural bounty of
the great city: museums, opera, and theater. Ferne paid most of their
expenses with her job as secretary to the mathematics department,

but Steve also had jobs on the information desk of the college and in its secretary's office, as well as working at Macy's department store. Teachers College was in constructive ferment during the years the Eplers were in New York. Founded in 1894, it quickly became the most famous teachers college in the nation. Its faculty was renowned and represented every political view on the American spectrum, from communism to conservatism. Faculty and students wrangled over the desirability of organizing a chapter of the American Federation of Teachers and argued over the degree of authority to be given to the dean as opposed to faculty. Their most momentous debate, however, was over the nature of the American public school curriculum.[12]

There were two schools of thought regarding this issue. The newer "experimentalists," influenced primarily by John Dewey, argued public schools should accord the teaching of initiative, responsibility, and discipline almost as much respect as traditional subject matters. The traditional "essentialists" maintained schools should recognize that subject matter, discipline, and obedience were requisite for adult responsibilities. Another divisive issue was the role of the teacher outside the classroom. One group, led by George S. Counts, Epler's major professor, asserted that since society affects the educational process, educators should be active in trying to improve society by "formulating desirable societal goals and then consciously seek to attain them." Others regarded this social engineering as dangerous, as educators could easily delude themselves into becoming creators of a utopia, a condition not only impossible to attain but one—in sinister hands—that could lead to fascism or communism.[13]

Whatever George Counts's influence was in American educational circles, and it surely was great, Epler saw little of his major professor. Counts was far too busy to read dissertation chapters thoroughly or even to talk frequently with his students, and his influence on Epler's personal intellectual development was not large. However, in 1943, Counts finally got around to approving Epler's dissertation—three years after Epler had left. The work was a study of the awarding of honorary degrees by three hundred institutions of higher learning in America. Epler's major conclusions were that businessmen—at least in the twentieth century—had been the principal recipients of these distinctions and that many of the honorees, regardless of their occupation, were persons of no particular intellectual distinction. The work, summarized in both *Time* and *The New York Times* in 1942 and published the next year by the American Council on Public Affairs, revealed

Epler's personality not only in its laborious, careful research but in its dry humor (he found the most ludicrous degree was that given by Newark University to Bonzo, a seeing-eye dog: Doctor of Canine Fidelity) and its democratic conclusion that university faculties and accrediting agencies, rather than presidents or boards of trustees, should recommend candidates for these degrees.[14]

Following his course work at Teachers College, Epler moved to Washington, D.C., in 1940 to take a job as a staff assistant at the American Council on Education, where his principal task was to create a bibliography on education and the community published later by the Council under the title of *The Teacher, The School, The Community*. The position with the Council was only for three months, so Epler immediately began casting about for a permanent position. Although offered a job at Limestone College in South Carolina, he decided instead to accept the post of dean of men at Southern Oregon State College (SOSC) in Ashland, one of the three institutions of the Oregon State System of Higher Education dedicated to the training of teachers. After arriving in Ashland in August 1940, Epler later learned teaching responsibilities were to be added to his administrative duties, especially after most male students had departed for the service following Pearl Harbor. His classroom commitments were varied, comprising courses in mathematics, education, and chemistry, but he enjoyed the work and the setting until he himself was caught up in the war.[15]

Epler joined the navy in the spring of 1943, taking basic training at the University of North Carolina. He then was assigned as a physical education instructor for pre-flight cadets at St. Mary's College in California. Subsequently, he served at the Jacksonville Naval Air Station in Florida, where he spent the rest of the war. Discharged from the navy with the rank of lieutenant, Epler had originally planned to return to SOSC, but something else had turned up over the past few months. Toward the end of the war, Epler had been contacted by John F. Cramer, dean of the General Extension Division of the Oregon State System of Higher Education, about a position counseling returning veterans in Portland about educational opportunities. When Epler showed interest, Cramer worked to get him released early from the navy. For Epler, a counseling job was ideal, providing the individual attention to students he had come to realize was the part of teaching he relished most. Quite simply, he believed he was needed more in counseling than in teaching.[16]

The Eplers moved to Portland on 1 January 1946. Like many other returning service families, they found housing almost impossible to obtain, so they moved to Vanport, where an apartment could be rented for less than $50 a month. Working downtown in the office of the Extension Division meant a daily trip from Vanport, but Epler entered into his new duties with enthusiasm. Yet, shortly after assuming them, his imagination, as in the case of the creation of six-man football, produced an innovative solution to a social problem. The GI Bill had provided money to fund a college education for veterans, but they needed more than their tuition and subsistence payments. Many were married; many had children. Few existing colleges had housing for this flood of veterans eager to take advantage of their new educational opportunities. And since the supply of veterans would be exhausted in a few years, officials of traditional colleges were understandably reluctant to build dormitories and married student housing for the returning servicepersons. As a result, veterans moved about the country, an army of nomads, looking to settle near a college where housing was available.[17]

As he later recalled, Epler was "slapped in the face" by his new idea. Fittingly, for an avid golfer, he remembered the idea probably came to him on the links, while he was playing with a colleague, Henry Stevens, the assistant director of the Extension Division. Why not, Epler asked Stevens, begin a new school where the housing existed and then bring the veterans to it? He proposed creating a branch of the General Extension Division to be called Vanport Extension Center. Stevens was impressed and, with his encouragement, Epler investigated obtaining facilities with officials from the Vanport School District and from the Housing Authority of Portland (HAP). After obtaining their consent, Epler and Stevens took the plan to Dean Cramer, who approved it and, without apparent difficulty, had it accepted by the chancellor and the State Board of Higher Education on 24 March 1946. All were enthusiastic because Vanport City could contribute not only apartments but community services and buildings (such as the hospital) that were lying idle, white elephants for the federal government and its local affiliate, the Housing Authority of Portland.[18]

Despite little time for preparation, Epler's plan was to open the school with a summer session, which meant that between 24 March and the meeting of the first classes on 18 June, everything had to be done. In order to translate the promise of buildings into reality, Epler had to make arrangements with the Vanport school board and HAP.

Faculty and staff had to be hired and the program announced to prospective students. To begin this complex task, Epler hired his first employee, Margaret Holland, as office manager and secretary. (Holland was actually Vanport's first employee, as Epler continued for a few weeks in the position of veterans' counselor.) Holland, a member of Phi Beta Kappa and an instructor in English at the Portland Extension Center, was a superb organizer who was blessed with charm and patience in abundance. Vanport's first office was a small one in the Portland Extension Center headquarters at 220 S.W. Alder Street in downtown Portland, where on her first day Holland found Epler interviewing veterans, working on Vanport planning, and typing his own letters. Holland took over the typing, put together the first brochures, and mailed them with application forms to prospective students. On 3 June, the entire office—including all files, supplies, and equipment—was carried in the back seat of Epler's car to Vanport Junior High School.[19]

Before Epler moved his office to Vanport, he hired the third member of the founding administrative triumvirate. He selected Phil Putnam, who was still in his army lieutenant's uniform at the time he was interviewed, as the Center's assistant director. Putnam, the nephew of Rex Putnam, state superintendent of Public Instruction, was born in South Dakota and graduated from the Black Hills Teachers College at Spearfish in that state. He later did graduate work at Stanford, the University of Oregon, and the University of Southern California. Put-

PSU Office of Publications

nam's administrative skill derived from his experiences as a teacher and public school principal and superintendent in South Dakota and Oregon. He was a superb choice who complemented Epler's skills in every respect and who made it possible to bring to fruition the institution "starting from nothing" Epler described in his letter of appointment. A man of energy, warmth, and organization, a master of the humorous anecdote, Putnam's main task was to deal with the "outside world"

Phil Putnam, indispensable assistant director of Vanport Extension Center

by obtaining buildings and equipment from government agencies and the Vanport School District; cultivating public relations through speeches, news releases, and correspondence with editors and radio station managers; and by organizing politicians and influential citizens to support the institution. Long before Putnam left Vanport in 1952 to become president of Palomar Junior College in California, his services were summarized succinctly by Epler, who said, "probably no man contributed more to the program than Dr. Putnam."[20]

The first summer school session went very well. Registration day was 11 June, with William Walker, a military veteran, the first to enroll. Joining Walker were 220 others in fourteen courses covering nine disciplines taught by seventeen faculty members. (The disciplines were Business Administration, Chemistry, Economics, Engineering, English, Mathematics, Physics, Psychology, and Sociology.) Of these pioneer students, 94 percent were veterans, including eight women; 46 percent were married; and their ages ranged from eighteen to forty-seven years, with the average being twenty-four years. If full-time students, they paid $50 per term to cover tuition and incidental and laboratory fees. (Non-resident students paid $95.) For returning servicepersons, these expenses were paid by the government, which also furnished monthly subsistence allowances of $65 for single—and $90 for married—veterans. Besides attending classes, summer students were offered social options under the direction of John Roberts, Epler's former football coach at Cotner College, which included picnics, fishing outings to the Oregon coast, and golf and tennis tournaments. Study and research beyond the classroom were confined to the Portland and Vanport city libraries, as the Center had no separate library building. Overall, the success of the first summer session proved the validity of Epler's plan for veterans' education and even earned a favorable notice in *Time* magazine.[21]

Success produced not only praise but problems, for while the students tackled their first assignments, the Center's administrators began the complicated preparations to accommodate the increased enrollment expected for the fall. Since the school district would need many of its classroom buildings for elementary and secondary students, Phil Putnam had to obtain other facilities. Although Epler had written to other colleges to help him estimate the number of potential students for the fall, his estimate of five hundred proved low, as actual fall-term enrollment turned out to be 1,410 students, far too many to be crammed into the eleven classrooms the school district initially promised for the term.

PSU Office of Publications

BEGIN YOUR COLLEGE WORK THIS SUMMER

DON'T WAIT!

VANPORT CENTER.

of the General Extension Division of the
Oregon State System of Higher Education Representing

UNIVERSITY OF OREGON • OREGON STATE COLLEGE • OREGON COLLEGES OF EDUCATION

Billboard advertising first summer session at Vanport Extension Center

Putnam finally secured the required space from several sources. Most important was the Housing Authority of Portland (HAP), which provided two nursery school buildings, a shopping center, and a recreation building that were converted into classrooms. HAP also provided the use between 7:30 AM and 3:30 PM of another recreation building where chairs and portable blackboards were set up and taken down daily before Vanport citizens took it over for recreational purposes for the balance of the day. In time, the Extension Center had six, one-story gray wooden buildings acquired from one agency or another. The Portland school board provided classrooms and laboratories at Grant, Jefferson, and Lincoln high schools, while the University of Oregon dental and medical schools contributed some of their facilities. Many students were nomadic, traveling around the city by car or bus almost around the clock from 7:30 AM until 10:00 PM, Monday through Saturday.[22]

The Vanport School District did provide some classroom space but not nearly enough in the eyes of the Center's administration. This discrepancy between need and reality produced the only major controversy of the Vanport years. It arose when Vanport School District superintendent James T. Hamilton maintained he could not release sufficient space to satisfy the needs of the Vanport Extension Center and still take care of his own students. Specifically, Epler had asked Hamilton for the use of Roosevelt School, with its twenty-three class-rooms. Hamilton refused because of his plan to add a ninth grade now required by state law and, perhaps (although he did not mention it publicly), the increasing number of children of Center students. Epler tried to outmaneuver Hamilton by appealing to public opinion through the issuing of press releases to newspapers and by trying to persuade Rep. Homer D. Angell and Sen. Wayne L. Morse to get Jesse Epstein, the regional director of the Federal Public Housing Admin-istration, to pressure Hamilton to release the space. Both the *Oregonian* and the *Oregon Journal* supported Epler editorially. As the issue heat-ed, representatives of the agencies involved met publicly on 29 Aug-ust, only two weeks before fall term registration was planned. Students organized to attend this meeting but not, as one of them was quoted in the *Oregonian*, as "a pressure group." At this meeting, an irate Hamilton denounced the "irresponsible, high pressure methods and the distor-tions of facts in recent college news releases." Furious school board members supported their superintendent by passing "a resolution asserting the board would have no further dealings with the college."[23]

To break the impasse, Hamilton retreated from the school board's position, asserting that since representatives of the state system and the federal government were present, he would try to reach an agree-ment. A compromise followed. The Center agreed to postpone the opening of the fall term for two weeks until 7 October. The Federal Public Housing Administration and the school district both agreed to make additional facilities available. Although there was a fear these arrangements still would not permit all prospective students, almost all were accommodated in the day and evening classes offered in the institution's varied regular and "loaned" campuses.[24]

In the 1947–48 academic year at Vanport (its last), Putnam and Epler were successful in adding eighteen thousand square feet of build-ings to the thirty-five thousand previously available by obtaining addi-tional surplus buildings from HAP. Indeed, by the end of its first year, Epler gratefully commented in his annual report that "the Housing Authority by its foresight in providing buildings for use by the college and furnished apartments to veteran students made it possible for Vanport College to function." Presumably for morale purposes, sever-al building names were changed over the years from the prosaic num-bers of the housing project era to names such as Pacific Hall, Cascade Hall, and Multnomah Hall.[25]

Fallout from the Center's 1946 dispute with the school board was evident in the summer of the next year. Hitherto, Vanport residents had taken little interest in school board elections, but Center students organized to elect two of their own, William McLeod and Herman Zukerman, to the board. At the same election, voters chose a (non-student) Vanport businessman—who was in sympathy with the students—to give them a temporary majority on the five-man board, although he soon was dismissed for non-attendance at meetings. What the motives were of the student members and their ally is unclear. Their election was a shock to Superintendent Hamilton and the school district teachers who apparently regarded it as the result of a conspiracy. Hamilton implied the election of the students was revenge for the classroom controversy the year before. Although Herman Zuckerman explicitly denied this motive, Hamilton asked the student directors to resign. When they refused, the teachers threatened to postpone the opening of fall term. Phil Putnam said the Center carried no grievance, but the controversy continued and was aired in the press.[26]

Finally, the Housing Authority appointed a committee of distinguished citizens, headed by the former president of the Portland Chamber of Commerce, to investigate the controversy. Its report said there was no legal basis to make the student directors resign, that poor judgment had been displayed all around, but that good will could prevail. The conclusion of the whole unhappy contretemps came at the school board meeting on 24 February 1948. At this crowded meeting, Hamilton's supporters were prepared and in the great majority. When McLeod's motion that Hamilton not be rehired for the following year was voted down, he and Zuckerman resigned on the spot. Whatever still festered from this dispute, which remains clouded in mystery, became largely moot when a flood washed Vanport away three months later.[27]

Although there was controversy over buildings, it was surprisingly easy to hire a faculty for a college without a past and without a future. It was easier to acquire a faculty, indeed, than buildings for them to teach in, for Vanport Extension Center had many attractions for prospective teachers. Some came for the same reason many married students did, the availability of cheap, furnished housing. Others liked the sense of adventure of beginning a new college. Still others found Portland an appealing city in which to live. Some prospective faculty first approached the director on their own initiative, while Epler (described by a colleague as "very persuasive in a kindly way") recruited others on the advice of those nominated by the faculty and staff of the University of

Vanport Extension Center campus

Oregon, Oregon State College, and the General Extension Division. Other names came from teacher placement bureaus and from the colleges of education. Some faculty members were already employed in non-teaching jobs in Portland, and many of the part-time instructors came from their ranks. One of the most beloved teachers in the history of Portland State, George C. Hoffmann, applied for a job after reading the article about Epler and the Center in *Time*.[28]

For the academic year of 1946–47, the faculty averaged thirty-seven years of age (coincidentally, the age of Epler), was 75 percent male, and 50 percent military veterans. Forty-five were full-time. They averaged three years of teaching experience at thirty-eight institutions of higher education, although more had degrees from and had served at the University of Oregon and Oregon State College than any other institution. Three were members of Phi Beta Kappa: Jean Black, librarian; Arthur J. Dowling, instructor in English; and Margaret C. Holland, office manager. By the next year, eight new full-time and eleven new part-time faculty members had been added, largely to replace those who departed. Turnover was a problem at such an evanescent institution, even though many were originally happy to be employed there.[29]

Working conditions were arduous. The standard teaching load was five, three-credit courses, although some faculty taught a sixth course at extra pay. Makeshift classrooms were always filled, and some were scattered about the metropolitan area. One economics instructor averaged 250 to three hundred students per term. Most teachers employed essay questions on their examinations, which they graded themselves

as there were no assistants. Library holdings were minute, and there
was a textbook shortage after the war. Coupled with large classes that
inhibited discussion, these conditions forced instructors to rely on lectures and textbooks as their teaching techniques. Exacerbating the
problem was the fact that—for lack of space—many classes at Vanport
were three hours in length. Almost every faculty member had additional responsibilities as adviser to one or more student organizations, and
every member was reminded in an editorial in the student newspaper
that they had at least an informal commitment to attend college social
functions. Faculty also served the metropolitan and scholarly communities by organizing a series of lectures on the implications of atomic
energy; a Great Books discussion group; and the Portland-area English
Association. However, they were neither blessed nor burdened with faculty self-rule. Governmental decisions were made by the director and
conveyed to faculty in weekly meetings. This system was not authoritarian, however, for Epler was always eager to listen to faculty (and student)
suggestions, either informally or in faculty or committee meetings.[30]

In spite of this enormous workload, faculty morale was high. In
part, the times were responsible for this satisfaction. Many were pleased
to have a job after the unemployment of the Great Depression. Others
were delighted to have a home after wartime instability, while still others were happy to have survived combat. Above all, faculty admired the
character and qualities of the students, most of whom were hardworking and intelligent and whose academic work reflected and represented these attributes. (Vanport students, as evidence of this, did well
after transferring to four-year institutions.)

The college community was also pleasant and secure. Students
and faculty were close in age and, in their youth, brushed off irritations
that might have driven older persons away. (Again, students averaged
twenty-four years of age and faculty thirty-seven.) Many faculty had
shared the war with the great majority of the students. Faculty and students, including Epler and Putnam, lived together in Vanport, jointly
struggling with the fluctuating temperatures, uncertain appliances,
and disintegrating furniture of their apartments. Teachers participated with students in intramural basketball games and in other recreational activities. Many instructors liked being pioneer faculty, some
even savoring the precariousness of their institutional situation.[31]

Greatness in teaching is an elusive quality to describe. Yet among
the hard-working men and women who made up the original Vanport
faculty, both contemporary documents and historical memory bring

certain instructors to the fore. It was perhaps their respect for the students that made faculty, in spite of their crushing teaching load, spend many extra hours teaching in a one-on-one situation. One able student remembers: "I learned more having coffee with Dixon, Hoffmann, Holland, Parker, etc. than in the classroom." Certainly, the most famous scholar among the pioneers was biologist Clarence A. Hubbard, a world authority on the bubonic plague, who had published *Fleas of Western North America*. The faculty member best-known in the community was Jessie May Short, instructor in mathematics. Short, in just a few months, endeared herself to the Vanport community before her death in February 1947. A retired professor from Reed College, Short was one of the few women listed in *American Men of Science*. She had worked in the Kaiser Company's engineering department during the Second World War and had been an active member of the housing commission in Portland, drawing up a new city housing code in the months before her death.[32]

One of the best teachers was George C. Hoffmann, instructor in history and political science, whose humor, charisma, extensive knowledge of literature, and dedication to students was acknowledged frequently in articles and letters in the *Vanguard*. One anonymous student, noting the reasons why she liked Vanport College, echoed the sentiment of many throughout the years: "Our 'Halls of Learning' may not be ivy-covered but neither are our teachers, and for that, Deo Gratias. I've got Mr. Hoffman [*sic*] for History and that's enough to make happy the heart of any struggling student. Hoffman is God's gift to students."[33]

As the faculty expanded in numbers, so did the range of courses. Thirty-six courses were offered in fall term 1947 and eighty-eight a year later. The courses were the usual liberal arts courses, supplemented by professional offerings in business administration, engineering, forestry, home economics, and journalism. As Vanport was principally designed to be a "feeder" school for the state system's four-year institutions, the courses had the same numbers as those of these colleges and universities. Indeed, the older schools shaped the course content by sending outlines and suggested textbook titles to the Vanport faculty.[34]

Students and faculty also were bound together in their frustration with the library facilities. Because of the shortage of space, students had no separate library facilities whatsoever until December 1946, when a room in Columbia Hall, a former recreation building, was opened under the direction of a remarkable woman, Jean Black. The college's first librarian, Black held four degrees, including a doctorate in history

Jean Black, the librarian, in the Vanport Extension Center Library

awarded by the University of Michigan. A colorful woman who had traveled extensively abroad (and had once interviewed Mussolini), Black was hired by Epler in September on the recommendation of William H. Carlson, the director of libraries for the State System of Higher Education. Almost immediately, she assembled a small reference collection in a twelve-by-fifteen-foot office she shared with the director of student activities; this office served until a more adequate library was opened at the end of fall term. By the date of the flood that ended Vanport, she had amassed a collection of 3,461 books and 151 periodicals in a thirty-six hundred-square-foot room. Along with offices and classrooms, the library was situated in Columbia Hall, the former Shopping Center No. 2. The library part of the building was "the whole northern wing of the L shaped building, its length running almost directly east-west." The room was well-lighted and seated 184 patrons at its wooden tables. The tables and chairs for the approximately 10 percent of the student body the library could accommodate were donated by the War Assets Administration or loaned by HAP. Other institutions generously aided the Center's library and its readers. The University of Portland library staff provided bibliographical assistance, and books were lent by the Oregon State Library and by the libraries of the University of Oregon and Oregon State College. Black was also responsible for distributing to veteran students ten thousand surplus books donated by the Library of Congress on condition they become the personal property of the students.[35]

One of the most surprising characteristics of the unusual institution that was Vanport Extension Center was that it had no budgetary problems. This was surely one of the sources of its early popularity with taxpayers and the State System of Higher Education. Epler, indeed, wrote proudly in his second annual report, "Vanport Extension Center has been entirely self-supporting in its first two years of existence." This delightful (although short-lived) situation resulted from the donation of the grounds, buildings, and equipment by the federal government and by the Housing Authority of Portland, and by the policy of the Veterans Administration to pay a higher fee for each veteran enrolled than was required from the non-resident student who had not seen military service. In its financing, as in all other respects, Vanport Center was not threatening to any established group or institution in the state, a condition of these halcyon years that was never repeated or even approximated in the years ahead.[36]

For the moment, however, as the end of the second academic year approached in May 1948, students and faculty could take pride in, and feel optimistic about, their fledgling institution. Although those in authority never contemplated that Vanport Center would be permanent, it was functioning more than adequately and seemed to have at least a few more years to devote to its unique mission within the state and city. In order to mark its progress, students, staff, and faculty planned an anniversary day celebration late in the term. As proof of their pride in the institution, more than five hundred members of the Vanport Center community turned out to weed lawns, prune shrubs, and paint parking strips and the facades of the college buildings. When the work was completed, members of the local fraternity Delta Tau Rho presented Epler with a plaque commemorating the occasion. Mounted on a stone base, the monument stood on a greenspace south of Columbia Hall, but only for a short time. (Like the college, it survived the flood, holding its ground after the water receded, and today stands outside Lincoln Hall on the Portland State campus.)

The most dramatic event in the Center's history was its last one. There had been a heavy snowfall throughout the watersheds of the Columbia and Snake rivers in the winter of 1947–48, which light spring rains did not dispel at the normal rate. May was both warm and rainy, and the Columbia reached its greatest heights since the flood of 1894. Worried by the rising waters, HAP officials at Vanport began patrolling the dikes on 25 May. Convinced they were inexperienced in such a crisis, the Housing Authority officials turned to the United States Army Corps of Engineers for advice. On 28 May, some HAP officials were placed on twenty-four-hour duty, and, on the 29th, a meeting was held among Corps, HAP, Red Cross, city, and county representatives. The Corps assured them the housing project was in no danger, although, apparently, HAP would have evacuated it anyway if it had been assured of adequate housing elsewhere. By this date, many residents were away from Vanport, either taking advantage of the Memorial Day holiday or because they distrusted official reassurances. The forebodings of the suspicious were proved true the next day.[37]

Early on the morning of Memorial Day, HAP distributed flyers to each Vanport residence, assuring citizens they were in no imminent danger:

DIKES ARE SAFE AT PRESENT.
YOU WILL BE WARNED IF NECESSARY.
YOU WILL HAVE TIME TO LEAVE.
DON'T GET EXCITED.

None of these predictions came true. At 4:17 PM, the dike supporting the railroad track on the west side of Vanport gave way. The first, six-foot break soon widened to five hundred feet. A ten-foot wall of water rushed through, sending spray fifty feet high as it met the waters of the low-lying sloughs. The sloughs filled in about forty minutes. The water then rose throughout the project, reaching to the second floor of the apartment buildings. In a few hours, the city was dead. That only fifteen persons were dead out of a population of approximately nineteen thousand was due to the presence of mind, resourcefulness, and heroism of officials of public and private agencies and of ordinary citizens alike. In their display of courage and unselfishness, members of the Vanport College community stood second to none.[38]

In spite of the assurances given by authorities in the early hours of the day, Epler and other officials had decided in the afternoon to remove the essential records and other materials of the Center. About thirty students and faculty—including Cramer, Epler, Putnam, Lester Egleston, Richard Halley, and William Walker—were engaged in loading records on the college truck. Transcripts, paychecks, and the library card catalog were loaded onto a truck and an old Studebaker bus (the college's best bus would not start). In the midst of the loading, Dean Cramer shouted the news of the bursting dike, which was within one

Aerial view of the Vanport flood, showing the break in the dike

PSU Office of Publications

hundred yards of Columbia Hall, where the records were kept. Epler drove off to warn his wife and children and others in the housing unit. After seeing his family off, Epler returned to the apartment to pick up his insurance policies, the key to his state car (which he gave to a student neighbor to escape with), and his golf clubs. He then was able to maneuver the book-laden truck through the fleeing refugees to Jefferson High School, where the principal and a number of boys who were playing tennis helped him unload it. He tried to take the truck back to Vanport but was unable to reach the Center before the water covered the roads.[39]

Others responded as courageously as Epler. Although the student and faculty apartments were nearest the broken dike, their tenants did not seek to save themselves first but instead warned others of the danger. As Epler remembered:

These initiated a warning system by word of mouth, since the warning sirens failed when the power was cut off, and, with no regard for their own possessions, moved rapidly through the immediate area aiding those who were helpless or who did not comprehend the danger....Many students carried on rescue work, traffic direction, and first aid. One of the students carried or led to safety a dozen people, three of them invalids who had given up hope of escape, two elderly women too frightened or sick to wade out, and children who, separated from their parents, were unable to keep ahead of the onrushing water. Similar instances of rescue work by students were common in

PSU Office of Publications

A resident tries to recover his property after the flood.

the sixty minutes during which the flood reached its peak of fifteen feet. The death toll would have been much higher had it not been for the valiant work of the college students.[40]

Almost nothing was saved. In addition to what was carried out before the dam broke, officials later salvaged some microscopes, a library book truck, and three books Epler later found floating in the water (a history of England, one on the mathematics of investment, and another on personal health). In his characteristically dry way, he wrote of these three works to the college librarian: "So you see we have the nucleus of a library." (The library also possessed ninety-two books that were checked out at the time of the flood.) Joseph Holland, the athletic director, used a boat to rescue $100 worth of football helmets and shoulder pads that were supported in the water by their foam rubber construction. Phil Putnam saved his wife, baby, and uncompleted doctoral dissertation, after warning the residents of his apartment complex. He later walked back to the flooded area, dove into the waters to rescue a dog, wrung out his clothes as best he could, and then tossed his soaked shorts into the slough remarking, "I've plenty more at home." It took him a moment to realize that his only remaining clothes were those on his back. Epler lost practically everything, including a grand piano belonging to his wife, an accomplished musi-

Flood scene at Vanport

cian. Others, including some of the 390 student families who lived in
Vanport, lost far more. Few Vanporters received monetary compensation for their losses, as national, state, and local governments and the
insurance companies were not held liable for them. All the college
buildings were destroyed or unusable. The only bright spot was that
no member of the college community lost his or her life.[41]

Nor did anyone at Vanport College believe the institution would
die. The night of the flood, the administration began checking for
missing students. The next day, the Portland Teachers Credit Union
and the General Extension Division provided a temporary office for
the college in downtown Portland. The following Wednesday, a college
assembly was held at Grant High School—the best-attended assembly
of the year—where all students were finally accounted for. At this gathering there was also expressed, fervently and repeatedly, the sentiment
the college would not die. The gathering became a pep rally, with Putnam's anecdotes leaving the audience in tears of laughter.[42]

TWO

The Center Becomes Permanent · 1948–1952

F ive days after the flood, Epler wrote to the Federal Works Agency (FWA) in Washington, D.C., seeking new buildings and equipment. Everyone connected with the Center—faculty, staff, and students—as well as a substantial portion of the community, hoped it would continue. The state board, responsive to this desire and to the continuing high enrollments at the traditional institutions, voted to give the Center another year of life on 8 June 1948. As Epler put it in a private letter: "the State Board took time from its discussions of sidewalks and cow pavilions to consider the Vanport problem and decided, against the recommendation of the Chancellor [Paul C. Packer] to close us as of September 1, to let us continue at least another year if we pay our way." The chancellor's argument was that "inasmuch as Vanport Extension Center was established temporarily, to be closed when the emergency passed, and inasmuch as it had been established at Vanport because the housing facilities were furnished, this would be a good time to close the facility." Given this reprieve, Vanport supporters not only talked but acted. The Center soon found temporary offices at the downtown headquarters of the Portland Extension Center, when W. T. Lemman, a student (and, many years later, chancellor of the State System of Higher Education), located temporary offices on S.W. Eleventh Avenue, the abandoned site of the regional Veterans Administration building. Many students, fearing Vanport would die, made plans to attend summer school at Lewis and Clark College, the University of Portland, or one of the state schools, but Epler was able to secure facilities at Grant High School, and the summer session opened as scheduled on 14 June. More arduous, however, than providing a summer session was the task of locating quarters for fall term.[1]

Epler, Cramer, and Putnam canvassed various possibilities for a new campus. They considered using the Odd Fellows and Elks buildings in downtown Portland, the Willamette Iron and Steel Company in Northwest Portland, and the Commercial Iron Company near the Ross Island Bridge. The most distant facility they considered was the Multnomah County Fairgrounds in Gresham. In the end, as at its beginning, the Center was saved by Uncle Sam: the new campus was to be another abandoned Kaiser shipyard site, the Oregon Shipyard Corporation's administration building at St. Johns. Yeoman work in arranging the leasing of the site to the state system was accomplished by officials in the federal Office of Education, the FWA, and the War Assets Administration, and by Oregon senators Wayne Morse and Guy Cordon and Rep. Homer Angell. The state board recommended the Oregon Shipyard site at its 6 July 1948 meeting and decided, in spite of the move, to continue the name Vanport Extension Center to simplify legal procedures and to honor the memory of Vanport.[2]

In nearly every respect, the new campus was superior to Vanport. Most of the college's work could be accomplished in a few adjacent buildings, rather than in many scattered ones. The buildings also were of better quality, and there were acres of parking lots. (Epler later said, "we are fortunate in having probably the largest single college parking lot in the nation and perhaps in the world.") Faculty appreciated sharing offices with only one or two others, and, since there was no longer competition with the Vanport School District for facilities, it was now possible to have one-hour daytime classes and two- or three-hour ones at night. The only serious drawbacks were the lack of housing facilities and the slightly longer distance from downtown Portland. A temporary difficulty was cleaning the basement of the administration building, which had been damaged in the flood, a condition that required Chancellor Paul Packer and other state system officials to use a temporary foot bridge to the building when they were inspecting it.[3]

Cleaning and remodeling were pushed rapidly, and Putnam scoured the country to obtain furniture and equipment to supplement that left by Kaiser, with most of it coming from the FWA. As the yearbook noted a year later: "When September came, much work was still to be done. We sat on chairs without writing surfaces; there were no blackboards or any of the other classroom conveniences; the building was filled with the smell of fresh paint and the noise of hammering, sawing, and other construction work. No one complained, however, and school started as though nothing had happened." The partnership of

Columbia Hall, Oregon Shipyard campus

college, government, and community had worked a miracle of restoration, its spirit captured by a Vanport student in the December 1948 *Christian Science Monitor*: "A College Comes Back."[4]

The new campus consisted of five buildings. The heart of the campus was a three-story administration building that had been rebuilt after a fire in 1945 and christened Columbia Hall to maintain continuity with Vanport. Its white exterior stucco walls, striped with black flood lines, enclosed classrooms, the library, offices, laboratories, a cafeteria, and a dining room. Two buildings, a barracks and a recreation center, were refurbished for men's athletics and physical education. A small office building, renamed Oregon Hall, was used for art and drama, student publications offices, clubs, lounge, and a snack bar. A third office building was too severely flood-damaged to be used for anything but storage. An old athletic field was reworked into a football practice field. Although the campus did not have either an auditorium or a gymnasium, all Vanporters were pleased the new campus afforded about twice the floor space as the original site—one hundred twenty thousand, as opposed to sixty thousand square feet. Lack of a gymnasium was compensated for in part by the presence of a Portland Parks Bureau recreation center six blocks away, which offered games and crafts for adults and pre-school and kindergarten classes and after school programs for children. Swimming classes used the Northeast Branch of the YMCA, while women's physical education and men's varsity basketball took place in the St. Johns Community Center.[5]

At the shipyard facility, the library was in much better quarters. It had a capacity of 210 students in the reading room, which was well-lighted and ventilated. The office and the workrooms were superior to those at Vanport, although the wall space for bookshelves was less generous. A study room to supplement the reading room was added in 1950–51.[5] Into this facility poured a stream of books, many of which were donated by institutions and individuals shocked by the library's destruction in the great flood. The most famous donor was Pearl S. Buck, winner of both the Nobel and Pulitzer prizes, who favored Vanport due to a fortuitous encounter with the Center's librarian. At the time of the flood, librarian Jean Black was three thousand miles away in Atlantic City reading a paper at the annual meeting of the American Library Association. The delegates were agog with news of the flood's destructive power. Walking in the corridors, Buck, a speaker at the convention, noticed Black's nametag and drew her into a conversation that resulted in her presenting the school library with autographed copies of each of her twenty-one books, with the provision they be placed on the shelves for student use, rather than under lock and key.[6]

Many other individuals and institutions also made contributions. The Los Angeles Public, Oregon State, and Oregon State College libraries, as well as the Library Association of Portland and the Library of Congress also contributed from their duplicate collections. Publishers, too, were generous, especially the H. W. Wilson Company and Prentice-Hall, both of which replaced all their books. Overall, 1,669 books were received as gifts by 30 June 1949. (At the time of the school's move downtown, the library had accumulated holdings and had increased services and staff beyond the capacity of the old Lincoln High School library.)[7]

In September 1949, librarian Jean Black, for a time the library's only employee, received an additional appointment as librarian of the General Extension Division, an assignment that was a mixed blessing for Vanport Center. The new position diverted part of Black's energy from Vanport, but she comforted herself with "the knowledge that the Vanport library will be used by other extension students in upper division and graduate classes…[justifying] the purchase of additional and specialized material, especially in such fields as education and literature."[8]

Fortunately, at this same time, the college was able to hire a second professional librarian, Elizabeth H. Hill, who wrote new book notices for the student newspaper, organized the pamphlet collection, and prepared indices to materials. As for services, students and faculty returning for fall term 1950 found the library had added a record collection and assumed responsibility for visual aids. Movie, slide, and filmstrip projectors and a tape recorder were now available. By 1951–52, there was also a civil service employee responsible for audio-visual aids and two assistant librarians.

In any case, on the new campus there were sufficient facilities so that everybody could get down to the business of learning. As Epler said in welcoming the first students to the new campus: "You will have the experience of turning a shipyard into a college." When the alumni returned for a weekend in November, the *Vanguard* editor reassured them: "Personality is the essence of immortality and Vanport's personality has survived the flood unaltered."9

Revived Vanport (usually called "Oregon Ship"), however grateful its adherents might be for its resurrection, was not without problems. Nature remained an unpredictable and uncanny threat. A small earthquake struck in April 1949, although it was minor enough to be laughed off in the *Vanguard*. Sometime in spring 1949, a faculty flood committee was appointed. Headed by Phil Putnam, it was "to be prepared if flood should threaten the college buildings." What exactly this committee did is unclear, but in May 1949, a year after the great Memorial Day disaster, whatever flood-prevention measures were taken proved insufficient to prevent the flooding of the recreation building; high water also came within a few feet of Columbia Hall. Later, the volunteer fire department saved Columbia Hall in September 1948, after a tar pot exploded, spraying flaming oil outside the building. In August 1949, students extinguished a grass fire that burned within fifty feet of the same building. And despite the move of some six miles, Vanporters at the new campus, did not escape the fumes of the carbide and other industrial plants. As a student poem declared:

Yes, other schools, the lucky dogs,
Have ordinary shrouds.
But here we have those carbide plants,
Prefabricated clouds.

When, in a period of two days, seven students were sent to physicians for foreign bodies in their eyes, Phil Putnam sought help from the

State Board of Health to abate the air pollution. Two engineers were sent to the campus to take dust samples, but nothing was done. Other inconveniences at Oregon Ship included the narrowness of some class-rooms, glass walls between classrooms that reduced privacy, and the noise created by the concentration of all classrooms in one building.[10]

Much more than an inconvenience for some students and faculty was the outbreak of the Korean War in June 1950. The war was not pop-ular with the American public, and there was a good deal of resent-ment about the revived military draft. By October 1950, Vanport stu-dents learned that for some college students there was a way to escape—temporarily—selective service. The government proposed a draft defer-ment plan that would allow students to postpone military service. To obtain deferment, a student had to obtain a certain score on a special multiple-choice intelligence test. This score would enable all first-year students to be deferred; deferment would be granted to second-year students in the top half of their first-year class, to third-year students in the top two-thirds of their previous year's class, and to fourth-year students in the upper three-quarters of their class. After considering the plan for several months, President Harry S. Truman approved it on 31 March 1951.[11]

Students who wished to volunteer for service, rather than be draft-ed, had the opportunity to listen to on-campus recruiters for the air force aviation cadet pilot training program, which led to a commis-sion after a year's training. The college also applied for a satellite unit of Oregon State's Navy Reserve Officers Training Unit. Phil Putnam made the application after a poll of male students showed 74 percent favored a permanent reserve unit at the college. Of the faculty polled, 91.2 percent favored the unit. Nothing came of the application, how-ever, nor was there much interest in starting an army reserve unit as proposed in September 1951.[12]

Students who would not, or could not, be deferred were granted tuition concessions by the Center. Those withdrawing before the last four weeks of the term gained a full refund; those who withdrew dur-ing the last four weeks were allowed either to receive credit (provided their grades were C or better) and no refund or given no credit and no refund. The Korean War also touched the lives of Vanporters in other ways. The staff prepared for air raids. There were air raid warning tests in May 1951 and November 1953; during the last exercise (after the move downtown), all faculty, staff, and students gathered in the gym-nasium "within five minutes of the sounding of the alarm." The Center, in cooperation with Lewis and Clark College and the University of Portland, conducted a civil defense public education program in the city, and a civil defense course was instituted in February 1952.[13]

Faculty and students who were reservists wondered if they would be summoned back to service. Several faculty members were active in the navy reserve unit, including Epler, Putnam, John Dunn, Donald Parker, Arba Ager, Brock Dixon, and George Hoffmann. But only two members of the faculty were called to active duty: Robert Merz, a sociologist, and Leroy Pierson, of the guidance department. Pierson left in October 1950 and Merz, to the tune of an appreciative editorial in the *Vanguard*, in January 1951. Assistant Librarian Elizabeth Hill left Vanport to accompany her husband, who had been recalled to service, and Lyle Massey, a local actor and stage designer who had given much help to the college players, was called up by the air force.[14]

So far as the Center was concerned, the most interesting aspect of the service of Pierson and Merz was its aftermath. Both men returned safely from the war, but one amidst controversy and contention. Pierson had no trouble gaining re-employment, for there was an understanding that he would have his position restored.[15]

But Merz was treated differently. He wanted to return to the Center after completing his military service in 1954, maintaining he had been on military leave. Center authorities refused to take him back, however, insisting when he was asked in January 1952 if he wished to return to Vanport after his military service, Merz indicated he wanted to continue in the navy and that this letter was tantamount to a resignation. In March 1954, Dean Cramer wrote to Luther Cressman, the distinguished anthropologist, for advice. Cressman replied that Merz would never complete his doctoral studies (which he had begun at the University of Chicago before the Second World War) and that Vanport would need someone with a doctorate when it became a degree-granting institution the following year: "You have no legal or moral obligation to him," he concluded. In April, Cramer conferred personally with Merz, who insisted he was going to see the chancellor. Cramer wrote Chancellor Charles D. Byrne, summarizing his view of the case. He cited Cressman's letter and added that George Hoffmann, "de facto head of social sciences here," also did not want him back.[16]

The final authority in the matter seemed to be the State Department of Veterans Affairs, which concluded in August 1954 that the Center "is not legally bound to re-employ said veteran, but that you have a moral right...to offer such employment." Apparently, the end of the affair was a letter Epler was asked to write to Merz indicating he would not be asked to return. Explaining in his diary why this was so, Epler wrote: "Cramer doesn't want him."[17]

The Korean War affected student enrollment to a degree. Enrollment was 1,624 in the fall of 1949 but fell to 1,349 a year later, the first full term after the war began. It dropped to 1,025 in the fall of 1951, rose to 1,357 by the next year, and reached 1,629 in the fall of 1953, after the war concluded. A GI Bill of Rights adopted after the Korean War included educational benefits, and the first veterans appeared in the fall of 1952.[18]

Except for those in the military and their relatives and friends, the great uncertainty for Vanporters in the early 1950s was not the war, but the questions of when and where the college would move next. And it surely would move, for out of the travail of the early years, it had been so successful that many in the Portland metropolitan region wanted to make the temporary institution a permanent part of the State System of Higher Education. Accomplishing this was a far more formidable task than overcoming the vagaries of nature had been.

So far as anyone knows, the first person to propose publicly that Vanport become a permanent institution was a student councilman, Richard Meigs, who wrote a letter to the Center newspaper on 6 December 1946. His letter made several points advocating a four-year, permanent institution. First, Meigs contended the state's population and that of its institutions of higher education would inevitably increase in the coming years, and that Oregon State College and the University of Oregon had already reached optimum size. Next, he pointed out there were students who could not leave Portland, who needed housing, or who required employment while attending college who would be best served by a permanent institution in their home community. Finally, Meigs did concede "Corvallis and Eugene will continue to have their attractions for people seeking the traditional 'Joe College-raccoon coat' education."[19]

Such a future was definitely not anticipated by John F. Cramer, dean of the General Extension Division and Epler's supervisor. A few days after Meigs's letter was published, Cramer spoke at a faculty dinner at Vanport. There, he first uttered what would anger faculty, students, and their community supporters for years: his belief Vanport would always be temporary and would be closed when the post-war veterans disappeared from campus. On this occasion, he predicted the school's demise would occur in 1950 or 1951.[20]

Coincidentally, on the same day as Cramer's talk, another speaker who would have a long connection with Portland State came to Vanport with a different vision of its future. Richard Neuberger was a nationally famous journalist who was also one of the few Democratic members of the Oregon legislature. The theme of his student assembly talk was the erroneous political priorities of Oregon voters and their willingness to be swayed by pressure groups. One of his illustrations was the hope citizens would make the Vanport Center permanent when he declared "it is ridiculous that the state-sponsored institutions of higher education are located in small towns." Portland offered housing and part-time jobs, he proclaimed, "which are a requisite for most students." These remarks were the first public expression of what would become Neuberger's enthusiastic, sustained, and ultimately successful support of the Center's permanency. And one month later, in anticipation of what was hardly a certainty, the first proposal was made for a campus other than at Vanport. A member of the student council proposed the campus be located on the site of a projected civic center on Portland's east side.[21]

However enthusiastic proponents of a permanent school were, Dean Cramer was a major obstacle. He had both a vested interest and a constitutional position to support his opposition. If Vanport became permanent, it might break away from his Extension Division and become a separate and flourishing unit of the Oregon State System of Higher Education. One argument he could make against the Center's independence was legitimate: the Oregon Constitution required the passage of a constitutional amendment to establish a state institution outside Marion County. Regardless of these objections, students began to agitate for a permanent college. Cramer opposed this advocacy and "made it crystal clear to Epler that the students' activities were unacceptable and that it was Epler's responsibility to make them stop." But Epler—although not leading the cause—was available to assist students who were.[22]

Although Epler certainly helped advertise the Center (he sent about five hundred copies of the "First Annual Report" to prominent Oregonians and to some national figures, such as Pres. James Bryant Conant of Harvard) there was little evidence of a groundswell of public support to make Vanport permanent. (Some of the reports were accompanied by copies of Epler's case study comparing the grades of veteran and non-veteran students at Vanport in its first academic year. It concluded veterans made better grades than non-veterans, and married veterans made better grades than non-married ones.) One prominent exception to the lack of public interest in Vanport's future was Mayor Earl Riley, who wrote a guest editorial for the *Vanguard* declaring enthusiastically "no institution of learning in Oregon has ever grown so quickly to leadership." This development, the mayor wrote, determined "the venture has been so successful that the institution is destined to a permanent place in the educational system of the state."[23]

In February 1948, Portland's citizens first became acquainted with the educational plans of John Hakanson, who would become a powerful leader in making Vanport Extension Center permanent. Hakanson had graduated from high school in Oakland, Oregon, in 1937 and had attended Southern Oregon State College before the outbreak of the Second World War. During the war, he served four years in the army, including two-and-one-half in the South Pacific theater, and was discharged with the rank of captain. After the war, he enrolled at Oregon State, but when his wife entered nurse's training at the University of Oregon Nursing School in Portland, he transferred to Vanport, where he became an able, enthusiastic, and loyal student who served on the student council and on the staff of the *Vanguard*.[24]

On 1 February 1948, the *Sunday Oregonian* carried a long article by Hakanson that was an effective statement of the case for Vanport Center's permanence. In this essay, Hakanson argued that Portland deserved a permanent publicly supported institution of learning because of its size, changing trends in American education, and housing and employment opportunities in the Portland metropolitan area. He began his article by stating "Portland is the only major metropolitan area in the entire West which does not have closely available a publicly supported institution of higher learning." He then went on to cite two recommendations from the recent preliminary report of President Harry S. Truman's commission on education: the number of college students should be doubled by 1960 and free public education should be extended through the first two years of college. Applying these recommendations to Portland, Hakanson argued they could not possibly be carried out without establishing a permanent public institution in the city.[25]

Hakanson moved on to restate the by now familiar arguments about the availability of jobs and housing in the metropolitan area and then turned to matters of politics and law. Originally, he admitted, he favored a four-year institution, but "because of long-standing tradition and sentiment, because of vested interests and our well-known conservatism, in short, because it is politically impossible at this time to obtain

a four-year college, I believe we should concentrate on a junior college."
Hakanson recognized the constitutional barrier to a new institution
outside Marion County without a popular vote, but he met it by arguing the legislature should simply authorize Vanport as a permanent
part of the Extension Service, part of the already established State
System of Higher Education. He also recommended legislators appropriate funds for a new building for Vanport, suggesting a portion of
the proposed new state office building in Portland might suffice. In
publishing this article, Hakanson became the first person to bring
together in writing the ideas of a permanent institution, a new building,
and a downtown campus. He concluded his plea by assuring downstate readers a permanent Vanport would not reduce enrollment at
lower Willamette Valley institutions because there would be a substantial increase in the population of the southern part of the state as well
as in Portland.[26]

How formidable downstate university opposition might be was
presaged in a matter arising in early 1948 that was only indirectly connected to Vanport College. Administrators at Oregon State College
planned to develop some business administration courses to supplement those already provided at the University of Oregon. The University alumni sensed trouble at once. The Executive Committee of the
University of Oregon Dads Club passed a resolution deploring the
move, asserting "we cannot help but feel that to embark upon any single deviation from its established basic policy would lead to a long continued period of conflict between the member institutions of the system over additional proposals to permit the duplication of educational functions among the various member institutions." The resolution was sent to Gov. John H. Hall, to the Board of Higher Education,
and to the chancellor. In the years ahead, "duplication" would be a
word that would echo repeatedly to help justify Eugene's opposition
to expansion, not only at Oregon State but also at the state's other
institutions of higher learning, especially at Portland State.[27]

More positively for the fledgling college, about a month later,
Edgar W. Smith, president of the State Board of Higher Education
and also, significantly, president of the Portland Chamber of Commerce, promised Vanport students that veterans' enrollment would
be substantial for another ten or twelve years, and that as long as
Vanport had a student body of one thousand, he believed the school
would remain. But he did not promise permanence. Two months later,
the Great Flood occurred.[28]

The Vanport community was relieved to hear the state board had given it another year of life after the flood, but this did not satisfy most students and faculty, nor many Portland citizens. The indefatigable Stephen Epler and the irrepressible John Hakanson, undiscouraged and undeterred, continued to lead the fight for permanence. Hakanson wrote a letter to the *Oregon Journal* in June 1948 reiterating his earlier arguments about the necessity of a permanent institution. His task was even more difficult now, however, as Vanport, with the decline of veterans' enrollment and GI Bill funding, could no longer depend on the federal government for most of its financial support. Thus, Vanport's advocates not only had to deflect the fears of Eugene and Corvallis but also solve the formidable problem of obtaining tax dollars from Oregon's citizens.[29]

Hakanson did not stand alone, however. In the week after the flood, the *Oregonian*, the American Veterans' Committee, the Portland Chamber of Commerce, and the Multnomah County Young Republicans all came out for a permanent institution. The *Oregon Journal* carried an article by Phil Putnam describing the continuing functioning of the college after the flood. Some progress for the cause was marked in October 1948, when the State Board of Higher Education held its monthly meeting at Vanport. As Epler described it to Hakanson, "Most of the Board were impressed and probably left with a more friendly feeling." By the end of October, Vanport's crusade was shifting to Salem, where John Hakanson planned strategy.[30]

Hakanson was an able advocate. He was loyal to the cause, a great admirer and confidant of Epler, and now, as a student at Willamette University (having completed his studies at Vanport), he was strategically located in the state capital. He had also forged a few political connections. He was not, however, a mover and shaker in the state's dominant Republican party. Hakanson's activity at Salem on behalf of the Vanport Center turned out to be not only a testimony to his political skill but also a tribute to the openness of the Oregon political system to the influence of an ordinary citizen.[31]

Hakanson made an appointment to talk with Gov.-elect Douglas McKay in an attempt to persuade him to include Vanport in his legislative recommendations. He suggested Epler send McKay Vanport's second annual report and that students be encouraged to write their legislators supporting Vanport Center's permanence, adding "especially valuable would be letters from upstate students directed to their home county legislators." In December, the *Oregon Journal* continued its support by printing a plea written by the editor of the student newspaper. As the year 1948 closed, Hakanson reported to Epler that he had talked to McKay, but the governor had refused to include a college for Portland in his message to the legislature. Hakanson suggested it would be a good idea to have an interim legislative committee study the problem and report in 1951.[32]

Something must have changed his mind, however, for early in January 1949, Hakanson himself drew up a bill for the establishment of a Portland institution and for the purchase of a building. He had in mind Lincoln High School, a building constructed in 1912, which the Portland School District was planning to replace. He suggested to Portland Republican representatives John D. Logan and Rudie Wilhelm, Jr. that they introduce his bill. From his Salem base, Hakanson now began to direct the legislative campaign. Epler furnished information from Portland, such as reprinted copies of Hakanson's *Oregonian* article and the Center's annual reports and a brief to the legislature from the Young Men's Council of the East Side Commercial Club.[33]

At this juncture, a legislative bomb detonated. Two Democratic senators, Richard Neuberger and Robert Holmes, introduced a bill on 12 January. The terms of their Senate Bill (SB) 9 were blunt. The bill proposed the creation of a University of Oregon junior college at Portland that would be empowered to offer courses equivalent to "those now made available during the first two years of academic training at the University of Oregon and Oregon State College." The teeth in the bill provided that no building program in excess of $100,000 could be undertaken on any state system campus until the new junior college was established. Finally, the sum of $2 million was to be appropriated to carry out the provisions of the act.[34]

Epler and Hakanson had nothing to do with preparing SB 9, but both knew it could not pass because it was sponsored by Democratic representatives in an overwhelmingly Republican legislature. However, Hakanson saw at once its possibility as a stalking horse. As he wrote Epler: "I think what I will do now is...write a bill looking to an investigation [into it] in Oregon, work for Neuberger's bill and if and when it looks hopeless I'll try to get an upstate Republican to introduce my bill."[35]

Neuberger's bill attracted a great deal of attention while Hakanson and Epler laid their plans. Not unexpectedly, the *Vanguard* endorsed it, but so, too, did the *Oregonian*—with reservations. Both seconded Neuberger's and Holmes's arguments that Vanport enrolled fourteen hundred students while the other three major Pacific Coast urban metropolises had state-supported universities with far greater enrollments: 17,296 students in Seattle; 31,086 in San Francisco; and 46,243 in Los Angeles. Neuberger further argued, in an article in the *Oregonian*, that "40 percent of Oregon's population lives in a small area right around the smallest county in square miles in the state." At a Center assembly, Epler exhorted the students to support the bill. The *Oregonian* polled the members of the State Board of Higher Education about the Neuberger bill. None endorsed the measure, some opposed it, others said it had possibilities, while still others did not comment. In the same interview, Chancellor Paul Packer and the president of Multnomah College, a private two-year college in Portland, were noncommittal. The president of the private, four-year University of Portland declared the state's population did not justify spending taxpayers' dollars for a new institution.[36]

On 25 January 1949, the state board went on record concerning SB 9. Its members voted unanimously not to start a new institution, saying only the legislature had authority to do so. Rather, it proposed buying an existing building in Portland to house both the Vanport Extension Center and the Portland Extension Center. A few days later, state board president Edgar W. Smith said the building the board had in mind was the old Lincoln High School. Whether or not he and the board had planned it that way, Smith's proposal enabled the Multnomah County legislators to vote for Hakanson's projected bill, for they then would be doing college students and Portland taxpayers two good deeds for the price of one. Incidentally, while this maneuvering was going on, the Oregon State College student newspaper, the *Barometer*, editorialized in favor of greater educational opportunities in the Portland area and attacked the intention of the Corvallis Chamber of Commerce to "fight any legislative bill to establish a junior college in Portland." Indicative of the status of Vanport in another quarter was the state system's publication of a booklet by the chancellor, *The Needs of Higher Education*, that did not mention Vanport.[37]

While these arguments raged, Hakanson completed the bill introduced by Wilhelm and Logan on 31 January 1949. Hakanson's bill proposed a permanent (the word "permanent" appeared seven times in the bill) extension center in Multnomah County and appropriated $1.2 million for the acquisition of an appropriate building. The Wilhelm-Logan bill was a political masterstroke. Sponsored by Republicans, members of the majority party, it did not hold hostage the state

PSU Office of Publications

John Hakanson (l) and Stephen Epler at the signing of the Wilhelm-Logan bill

system building program on other campuses; it kept the permanent Portland institution under the control of the General Extension Division; and it helped resolve the problem of the disposal of the old Lincoln High School building.[38]

Students rallied behind the new bill. A delegation of Vanport students asked the city council to pass a resolution in favor of a permanent institution. Mayor Dorothy McCullough Lee promised the students she would report to the council on the matter. She never did so, and the council never passed the desired resolution. A student delegation testified before a legislative committee in Salem. The Vanport student council also obtained the support of the student council presidents and student editors of the Portland high schools to persuade their parents, parents' organizations, and the local Parent-Teacher Associations of the merit of their cause.[39]

Hakanson, meanwhile, was working in two other directions. He wanted Epler to find out specifically the price of the Lincoln High School building. Second, he wanted Epler to publicize his calculation that if there was no permanent Vanport institution, then 750 students would go to other state schools; if Vanport were in existence, then the cost of educating the students at home would save the state $37,500 a year.[40]

On 5 April came the culmination of all these months of work: House Bill (HB) 213 was endorsed by the Joint Committee on Ways and Means. The endorsement was accompanied by two changes in the original bill. The Lincoln High School building was specified as the building to be purchased, and the price for buying it was reduced from $1.2 million to $875,000. The amended bill passed both houses and was signed by Gov. Paul Patterson on 15 April 1949; the vote in the House was 46-10 and in the senate, 18-11. Reflecting on the legislative journey over a year later, Epler complimented Hakanson on "the major part [he] played in making Vanport permanent."[41]

On 20 April, a gala celebration was held at the Vanport Extenion Center to celebrate the legislation's passage. Representatives Logan and Wilhelm were honored at a luncheon, as was John Hakanson, whose work on behalf of the law was commended by Wilhelm: "This student's work shows what an aroused and active student interest can do for your welfare." Also present were Epler, Cramer, and representatives of the FWA and the Veterans Administration, the federal agencies that played such a crucial part in the brief history of the Vanport Extension Center. Fittingly, the Portland school board and the Housing Authority of Portland also were represented.[42]

THREE

The Center becomes a College · 1949–1955

The passage of the enabling legislation was an enormous step forward for Vanport Center, but it was hardly the final hurdle the institution would face. Still, overcoming obstacles was a way of life at Vanport, so it did not seem surprising there was trouble over moving into the former Lincoln High School building. It was originally intended that Vanport Extension Center would take over the structure in time for the opening of the 1951–52 academic year, but delays in construction of the new Lincoln High School forced the school board to ask the legislature for a year's extension. State board officials had no choice but to comply, however disappointing the delay was to those who had worked so long for the downtown permanent campus.[1]

A building no longer fit for a high school (one that opened in 1912) had to be extensively remodeled to serve as a college. The state board selected a distinguished Portland architect, Hollis Johnston, to take charge of the conversion of the building (Johnston had been chief consulting architect for Bonneville Dam, among other commissions). After the departure of Lincoln students for summer vacation in the summer of 1951, the Center finally could reshape the building. The cafeteria was remodeled with a new coat of paint, along with the lowering of ceilings, the installation of new lights, and additional dining space.[2]

To complete the work, the board accepted a bid from E. Carl Schiewe on 18 June 1952. Schiewe's bid of $93,190 was the lowest among nine competitors; the state board minutes noted happily that "bidding was close and was more favorable than expected; as a result, practically all of the alternate additions can be included." With architect's fee and a 5 percent contingency fee, the total cost of the remodeling was estimated at $113,000. In harmony with the traditional practice of requiring a 10 percent contribution from the student body, $13,000 came from student fees. For this expenditure, architects and contractors provided faculty offices by breaking down larger classrooms; remodeled and enlarged the library; improved some of the laboratories; established a paneled conference room designed for state board meetings; and created student offices.[3]

When 1,272 students enrolled for the first term downtown in September 1952, faculty and students gave the new facilities mixed reviews. With characteristic cheerfulness, Epler's annual welcome to students emphasized the advantages of a central location near jobs and cultural opportunities. He foresaw only two negative aspects: the shortage of parking spaces and the jostling for space with the three thousand students of the Portland Extension Center's night classes. Shortly, however, other problems became apparent. Interviewed in that year's first issue of the *Vanguard*, two faculty members pointed out undesirable features such as the small faculty and student club offices and inadequate room for music practice. But both saw advantages, as well: proximity to evening students made many day students aware of the existence of night school, locker facilities were now available, and the library and cafeteria were superior to those at Oregon Ship. The most vigorous complaint, later sustained for more than four decades, was paucity of parking. The *Vanguard* posed a riddle: "Vanport had the largest in the world and Portland State College hasn't any. What is it? You guessed it—'parking facilities.'" Students also complained faculty members were given exclusive use of one-third of the cafeteria space.[4]

The library staff also made several adjustments when the college moved downtown. The library itself was located on the second floor of the building, on the Park Avenue side, equipped with a reading room that seated 170 persons, and open from 8:00 AM to 9:00 PM, Monday through Friday. All connected with the school eagerly awaited the new library building, but it would be several years before that ambition was realized. When the time came, the library would be blessed with a small but expanding staff of competent professionals and clerical employees who had worked devotedly throughout the years under incredibly difficult conditions. In 1952, students were issued charge plates with which to check out books. In 1953, the state board included Vanport in a special library fund for the state colleges of education, and the sum of $5,000 was allocated. Yet the library remained inadequate in its holdings, illustrated by the mounting pressure from Vanport students on other Portland libraries, which, the faculty believed, these libraries would not—and should not—relieve. By the time the College achieved degree-granting status in 1955, there were four professional librarians on staff: Jean Black (head librarian), Kenneth W. Butler (visual aids); Theodore C. W. Grams (technical services); and Leora F. LaRiviere (circulation librarian).[5]

A glaring weakness of the new building, one foreseen from the outset, was the lack of an adequate gymnasium for intercollegiate athletics. The inherited gymnasium had a low ceiling. (Lincoln High basketball players had an advantage over their opponents—they were used to shooting horizontally at the basket.) Over Christmas vacation 1952, Epler and Putnam scouted gymnasium facilities at the Multnomah Athletic Club, the old American Legion building, and the Jewish Community Center, though they found nothing better than those at the Lincoln High building.[6]

All in all, however, Portland Staters took pride in the new building, as was expressed in a formal dedication ceremony and open house during Homecoming Weekend. Held in the auditorium, the 26 October 1952 event opened with an invocation by Myron C. Cole, the minister of Epler's First Christian Church, followed by speeches from Chancellor Charles D. Byrne; Edgar W. Smith, president of the state board; James Pinardi, president of the student body; Homer Allen, president of the alumni association; and Frank Roberts, assistant professor of Speech.[7]

By the next year, however, new problems appeared. The board in April allocated $95,611 for interior and exterior repairs, noting grimly in its "Minutes" that "Much of the work on the Portland State Extension Building is deferred maintenance. The building is over forty years old. The Portland School District had done no major maintenance work on the building for several years prior to the sale of the building to the State of Oregon." Work began in August and included interior painting, the installation of fluorescent lighting, and new showers in the women's locker rooms. The last of the renovation work, completed in April 1954, sacrificed aesthetics for utility: the twelve original exterior metal doors were replaced with lightweight aluminum ones. The old doors, proclaimed the *Vanguard*, took "more than a gentleman to open doors for the coeds. It took a Sampson. Usually persons had to compromise; one leaning, the other pushing to open them. To get out of the building was like trying to leave a bank vault." In December 1953, the faculty discussed the possibility of adding an elevator, but Cramer said whenever he raised the issue it was dismissed by the board because of the high cost.[8]

Space limitations became more apparent as enrollments rose, until the faculty at last debated the possibility of holding classes on Saturday, although this did not occur. One department that benefited from complaints about space was Engineering, which gained the second building on the downtown campus in the fall of 1953—a converted Safeway store at S.W. Sixth Avenue and Mill Street. By 1954, complaints arose about the faulty public address system, lectures floating through thin walls into adjacent classrooms, noise from ballplaying in the Park Blocks, and problems scheduling an assembly period and intramural sports.[9]

The move downtown coincided with the governmental reorganization of the college. No longer under the wing of the General Extension Division, it now needed a name. Although some wished to retain Vanport in the name for reasons of tradition and sentiment, most wanted to give the institution a new name. As was so often the case, Epler was the initiator. On 13 December 1951, the faculty voted to ask Dean Cramer and the board to call the new institution "Portland State Extension Center," a name that incorporated Vanport into the older Portland Center. On 6 February 1952, Cramer made a special trip to Oregon Ship to inform Epler the board had "approved his reorganization plans including [the] name." Many students, faculty, and alumni, however, began calling it Portland State College at this time.[10]

The name was but a part of the new institution. Far more important was the administrative organization of the Portland State Extension Center. In October 1950, Cramer had given Errett Hummel, an administrative assistant in the Extension Division, the task of drafting a plan for the new institution, which he presented to Cramer on 15 February 1951. Cramer also conferred with the chancellor during the next months, and the two men agreed on a course of action. Organization involved two, interrelated tasks: separating the former Vanport Center from the Extension Division while recognizing both institutions remained in some ways connected, as both used the same building and shared some of the same faculty members.[11]

Although the task was difficult, it was accomplished quickly. The Administrative Council of the Extension Division discussed reorganization on 18 January 1952. Cramer reported to Chancellor Byrne that the council had, "with some very minor modifications," accepted the proposal they had earlier discussed. Its salient points were to integrate

PSU Office of Publications

Lincoln Hall, first building on the downtown campus

the old Portland Extension Center and the newer Vanport Extension Center "into one single extension program, offering both day and night classes;" that the new program be named Portland State Extension Center, which also would be the name of the building (the former Lincoln High School); that the institution be headed by a single assistant dean, James C. Caughlan, a veteran of Cramer's Extension Division staff, who would supervise the directors of the day and night programs; that Stephen Epler be made director of day classes; that Caughlan also fill the role of director of night classes, with assistance from Hummel; and that the day and night programs remain in the Extension Division.[12]

The state board approved the Cramer-Byrne organizational plans on 11 March 1952. Although a sensible organizational structure in many ways, Cramer's personnel recommendations accompanying it eliminated the most imaginative administrator of the group, Stephen Epler, from his deserved position as head of the entire Portland Extension Center. Epler, however, accepted the situation with his usual graciousness and loyalty, although he confided to his diary that "I'm having a time getting over not getting Assistant Dean job given to Jim Caughlan but I'll make it." Epler was not the only disappointed Vanporter; Phil Putnam, who had been relegated to the positions of registrar and assistant to Epler, was "unhappy & looking for another job."[13]

Everyone knew the permanent two-year institution was but a way station to the destination of a four-year college. The exact date of the beginning of the journey is unknown but certainly goes back to Vanport's first year, when at least a few students were talking of this possibility. In 1949, the president of the state board had predicted a permanent four-year institution for Portland.[14]

In spring 1950, some educators began publicizing the need for additional teacher-training facilities in Oregon to prepare for the impending influx of post-Second World War "baby boomers." Both the president of the American Federation of Teachers and the secretary of the National Education Association raised the question of the state's teacher-training facilities in February and April, respectively, of that year. In direct response to this challenge, the state board decided to discuss elementary teacher training, and there was talk of adding elementary teacher training at Corvallis, Eugene, and Vanport to that provided historically only at Eastern, Southern, and Oregon colleges of education. In an article discussing this possibility, the *Vanguard* raised the question: "Would the addition of teacher training at Vanport lead the way for an eventual four-year state-supported college in Portland?[15]

In May, the *Oregonian* carried a series of articles on the national and state teacher-training situation. It pointed out there would be only 489 spring graduates trained to teach elementary students to fill the approximately eleven hundred teaching jobs for the fall. The state board did not seem willing to do anything but discuss the matter, however, for since January 1950 it had twice turned down adding elementary teacher training at Corvallis, Eugene, and Vanport, at the behest of the chancellor and the president of Oregon College of Education (who was also the director of elementary teacher training for the state).[16]

The board's actions were described in an *Oregonian* series by reporter Wilma Morrison, who wrote, "the addition of elementary teacher training to [Vanport's] unhallowed halls sounds too much like the start of a four-year liberal arts college in Portland to please some of the state's other schools." She continued by saying this field would be particularly "unwelcome...to the University of Oregon and, to a considerably lesser degree, to Oregon State. Both these institutions have fought a state-supported college in Portland in the past, but the university is the one with the real Portland allergy...and quite naturally, because the university has the most to lose in competition with another liberal arts school located in the heart of its heaviest enrollment source, Portland."[17]

On 23 January 1951, the state board made something of a concession to Oregonians who aspired to teach elementary schools but who did not wish to spend four years at a teachers college. It adopted a plan that allowed students to attend the school of their choice. Students would then do two to three terms of work at one of the three state system colleges of education, then return to the first school for the final term and graduation. At the same meeting, the board permitted another choice that especially would affect Portlanders. It would allow students to take two years at Vanport, one year at Portland Extension Center, and the final year at a college of education.[18]

These measures did not satisfy prospective education majors residing in the state's largest city, however, and they certainly did nothing for liberal arts students. Perhaps in frustration at the plan's inadequacy, someone—purportedly a Vanport student—circulated a mimeographed document entitled, "Vanport College, Its Story," to legislators in late February 1951. It was a plea for "immediate legislation" to create a four-year institution in Portland, a plea supported by comparative data on state distribution of funds; student-teacher ratios; and cost per student per year at Vanport, the three teachers colleges, the University of Oregon, and Oregon State. It declared a four-year Vanport would not draw students from the older schools but simply provide an opportunity for Multnomah County residents who would not have a chance to attend college otherwise. When the chancellor obtained a copy of this document, he became furious.[19]

Firing off a letter to Cramer, Chancellor Byrne declared: "I am sending you enclosed a copy of a mimeographed document that I understand is receiving quite wide circulation. I understand that it has fallen into the hands of some legislators....The statistics quoted, of course, are very inaccurate and leave entirely the wrong impression. Also, I am sure that the comparisons and interpretations made are odious and not in harmony with the policy of the State System. While the damage, whatever it may be, has been done, I would like to have you trace the origin of this document. It would appear that a student or layman would hardly be well enough versed in educational statistics to think up the comparisons made in the document without some assistance." Two paragraphs later, the likely source of assistance was not too subtly pointed out: "I also note a reference [in the document] to the fourth annual report of the Vanport Extension Center. As you know, no other unit of the System issues annual reports and to my knowledge there has never been authorization for a unit to issue such a report. I would suggest that before any annual report is circulated that authorization through regular channels be obtained. I am counting on you to handle these matters with your usual diplomacy and skill." Byrne hastily assured University of Oregon president Harry Newburn of his action, as a note from a subordinate to the president indicated: "This is a copy of a mimeographed sheet passed out to some legislators at least supposedly by a 'student' at Vanport. Chancellor Byrne has the original and indicates he is tracing it down."[20]

The "Fourth Annual Report," so galling to the chancellor, was surely designed to give Vanport the support and publicity Byrne was so reluctant to accord it. It was sent to about five hundred people, including members of the state board; academics at other institutions (both high school and college); federal, state, and city officials; and local and state organizations, including the American Legion and the Parent-Teacher Association. When requested, it was sent to other interested persons. One important point to be made about this controversy is that all of the "Annual Reports," although written by Epler, were read, approved, and signed by Dean Cramer.[21]

The result of the search for the chancellor's culprits is unknown, but Vanporters were not intimidated by opposition. By spring 1952, as students and faculty prepared to move from Oregon Ship to their new quarters at old Lincoln High School, an organized movement was underway to carry Portland State to college status. As in the founding of Vanport Extension Center and the creation of a permanent institution, Stephen Epler led the struggle for the next stage of development, but he had many allies. The Mothers Club, headed by Mrs. Clarence White, began looking ahead to the fall elections as early as March. "She is calling all the candidates here for the Legislature about a 4 yr. college," Epler recorded. Later in the month, a student committee headed by Bernard Zusman sent a letter to all legislators asking for a four-year school in Portland. On 26 March, four hundred Vanport students attended a mass meeting at the college addressed by White; Homer Allen, president of the alumni association; the editor of the *Vanguard*; and others. They decided to form a committee—later called the Advancement Committee—composed of mothers, students, and alumni.[22]

How difficult the political task would be was indicated in an exchange of correspondence between a Portland citizen and Gov. Douglas McKay in late March. In response to the request he support a four-year institution, McKay flatly declared "it would be impossible at present to finance a four-year university....We must not lose sight of the fact that we cannot sacrifice quality for quantity in education. In my opinion it is much better to have fewer institutions of higher quality than several mediocre ones."[23]

The annual meeting of the Oregon Education Association debated a four-year school in late March. In commenting on this meeting, the *Oregon Journal* came out in favor of a college only "eventually," but did condemn two opponents of the proposal at the meeting who declared it an example of "statism" and worthless because only 5 percent of the population was capable of a college education. In April, Epler received the happy news from James Goodsell of the *Labor Press* that the editor wanted "to crusade for a 4 yr state college."[24]

By late April, Epler and the Advancement Committee decided to appeal to the state board at its June meeting to ask the legislature to create the four-year school. Epler spent many days working up a bill and a supporting brief for a four-year institution to present to the board, noting in his diary that one day he "worked all evening & until 1:30 AM on case for 4 yr college." Epler gave the brief to Allen, who was to make the presentation to the board, on 29 April, and finished the final copy of the bill on 19 May. While Epler labored, the Advancement Committee compiled statistics, questioned candidates for the spring primaries as to their position on the Vanport issue, and organized a speakers bureau to address civic groups.[25]

The brief prepared for Homer Allen reiterated many of the points made three years earlier in the quest for a permanent two-year institution. It opened by saying a four-year college would serve the area where one-third of the state's population resided, enable students to save money by living at home, and save the state the cost of erecting dormitories. It continued by saying the college and the community would reciprocally benefit culturally; the metropolitan area would gain economically and in gaining leadership and vocational skills from the graduates; and that part-time specialized teachers could be hired. The brief maintained the state of Oregon could afford the new college, that Portland was the only Pacific Coast metropolis without a four-year public college, that private colleges would not be hurt by competition from an expanded Vanport, and that many more students wanted and should be educated in higher educational institutions.[26]

The supporters of Portland State spent a far greater amount of time preparing for the board meeting than the board gave Allen when it met on 18 June. He made his presentation, was asked a few questions,

Sen. Richard Neuberger, longtime and
effective supporter of Portland State

PSU Educational Media Services

and dismissed. In spite of this chilly
reception, Portland State did not
abandon hope. In the fall, Epler
and members of the committee
began a series of speaking engage-
ments and meetings in the community with members of the Optimist
Club, representatives of the Young
Republicans and the American Federation of Labor (AFL), and with
state senator Richard Neuberger.[27]

The case for Portland State's
"advancement" was helped immea-
surably as state education officials
finally responded to the looming problem of the supply of teachers
in Oregon. In the early 1950s it was evident that within a few years
there would be an enormous need for public school teachers as the
post-Second World War babies reached school age. Existing teacher
training institutions in Oregon—Eastern and Southern State Colleges,
and Oregon College of Education—had nowhere near the capacity
to turn out the new teachers soon to be required. To address the problem of providing a supply of teachers, the State Board of Higher
Education in March 1952 hired a consultant, Earl W. Anderson, a
professor of Education at Ohio State University, to prepare a set of
recommendations. These recommendations, announced in the fall
of 1952, affected Portland State, but also all the other institutions of
the State System of Higher Education. Anderson's recommendations were made with the support of an advisory committee of citizens
and educators representing such groups as the Oregon Congress of
Parents and Teachers, the Oregon Education Association, and representatives of the state system institutions. Dean Cramer headed the
advisory committee. The major recommendations, issued in December 1952, included granting Portland State the authority to provide
"undergraduate four-year programs for the preparation of elementary and secondary teachers" and allowing "secondary education
students to concentrate in humanities, social science, and science-
mathematics."[28]

Naturally, Portland State was pleased with the original recommendations and worked to implement them. On 18 December 1952, a special meeting of the Portland State faculty passed a resolution endorsing the Anderson report, which Epler labeled a "turning point" in the "battle" for a four-year college. Among other points, the faculty declared "we are almost daily reminded that in the Portland area many persons who cannot for a number of reasons attend college classes elsewhere in the state both want and need an autonomous, degree-granting institution here."[29]

A much more important resolution was adopted by the state board at its meeting in the Benson Hotel in Portland on 5 January 1953. After a public hearing with testimony from several witnesses, all of whom endorsed the report's recommendation, the board made its decision and issued a policy statement about "the future development of higher education in the Portland area." It said future expansion would be downtown near the Portland State Extension Building, rather than at a suburban campus. It decided the expansion should take place on the block south of the existing building rather than on the three-quarters of a block across Broadway Street currently owned by the State. This last plot (now occupied by the American Automobile Association), the report stated, should be sold to pay for land for the construction of an additional building that should be authorized by the legislature at least by its 1957 session. It was recognized additional funds might be required, if the sale price was not sufficient. The decision to sell this lot, rather than to seek additional funds, was an action that demonstrated the anti-Portland State sentiment of the chancellor and the state board and probably reflected the University of Oregon's desire to limit the growth of the College. Also reflective of this hostility was the state board's refusal to buy at a low price a vacant square block now occupied by the Ione Plaza.[30]

The board resolved that four years of instruction be made available for prospective teachers; the junior year of the elementary program would begin in September 1954 and the senior year one year later, while the junior year of the secondary program would begin in September 1955 and the senior year in September 1956. Presumably, students would take their formal degrees after transferring to another institution, as the board was vague about permitting majors in broad fields of humanities, social sciences, and science-mathematics that would culminate in a bachelor's degree, stating only that this option should be made possible at an "early date." Majors, that is, those in specific disciplines, were not to be permitted in the liberal arts fields "until such time as the need is definitely established in Portland or elsewhere." The board recommended a separate degree-granting institution be created in Portland through a referendum authorized by the 1955 legislature to change the state constitution. This last recommendation was based on the belief, referred to earlier, that a constitutional amendment would have to be passed because the state constitution (Article XIV, section 3) prohibited the creation of a new state institution outside Marion County.[31]

The board also voted to add elementary education programs at the University of Oregon and at Oregon State College and secondary education programs at the three colleges of education. The teachers colleges also were given the authority to grant undergraduate degrees in social science, humanities, and science-mathematics. Portland State, however, was not given degree-granting authority.[32]

The board's action was not taken without heated opposition from the faculty of the University of Oregon, who feared a loss of appropriations for their institution. Pres. Harry Newburn (masking the university's real objections) spoke against allowing the schools of education to grant disciplinary degrees on the grounds the matter needed further study, the proposed changes were too expensive, and the colleges' academic offerings would be of inferior quality. Over Cramer's protests that Newburn was drawing a "red herring," the board sustained Newburn's objections. As in the case of Portland State at the December meeting, the influence of the University of Oregon again prevailed.[33]

Board acceptance of the Anderson report was encouraging to Portland State officials and supporters, but while not fully satisfying, it did give them ammunition to fight for a four-year institution as soon as possible. Indeed, in anticipation of the board's action, Epler on 22 December 1952 drew up a proposal for a four-year college and sent it to Homer Allen and to Grant Mumpower, the new president of the alumni association, both fervent advocates for the cause. Their enthusiasm was not shared by the chancellor. Travis Cross, the information director for the state system, wrote to Gov. Paul Patterson's assistant to ask to discuss, among other matters, "Portland State pressure for an institution sooner than the Board recommends."[34]

Epler, the Advancement Committee members, and other supporters decided to speed up the process for the constitutional amendment to allow the four-year college. They wanted it passed by the legislature in 1953, in time to be referred to the voters in the 1954 election. Epler's inner circle of advisers for legislative strategy included Allen; Mum-power; Mrs. Clarence White (president of the Mothers Club); faculty members, such as Brock Dixon; and William Pilling, an alumnus. On 18 January, at a strategy session in Epler's office, it was decided that Pilling would go to Salem to try to persuade all the Multnomah County delegates to sponsor the bill. Mrs. White was assigned to contact the veterans' and women's organizations in Portland. Soon, Homer Allen was assisting Pilling at the capital, trying to gain sponsors, while Epler consulted with Kelly Loe of the AFL on legislative strategy, spoke to Rep. Maurine Neuberger, and kept in touch with his agents in Salem. All this furious activity paid off on 22 January, when Rep. Gust Ander-son, with most of his fellow Multnomah County representatives as sponsors, introduced HB 131. The bill provided for a referendum in 1954 for a four-year college to open its doors by September 1956.[35]

Before the bill received its hearing, Epler and his allies kept up the publicity. Epler phoned radio commentator Lawson McCall (the future governor, Tom McCall) and Sen. Richard Neuberger, and worked with Art Crookham, a writer for the *Oregon Journal* (and a part-time Portland State faculty member), on an editorial for his newspaper en-dorsing the bill. Crookham also arranged for the newspaper's cartoon-ist to draw a cartoon of a young man knocking on a door with the cap-tion reading, "He Wants a Four-year College." Epler was delighted to see that the ever-cautious Cramer, at least privately, seemed "more favorable" to the bill as time passed.[36]

The bill was referred to the house Education Committee, chaired by Rep. Maurine Neuberger, which conducted a public hearing on 9 February. Homer Allen led off the testimony and was supported by representatives of the AFL, the Congress of Industrial Orgnizations (CIO), the Oregon State Grange, the president of the Portland State student body, and members of the Portland Junior Chamber of Com-merce. The major point made was that students could afford an edu-cation in Portland that otherwise would be denied them if their only choice was to attend a downstate institution. The only opposition to the legislation was expressed by Pres. Robert H. Sweeney of the University of Portland, speaking for the Association of Independent Colleges, who argued a two-year delay in presenting the amendment would enable the private schools to adjust to competition from the new institution while awaiting the forthcoming wave of high school graduates. The preponderance of favorable testimony at the hearing, however, did not guarantee effortless passage of the bill.[37]

Morgan Odell, the president of Lewis and Clark College, made a public speech on 14 February, echoing Sweeney's earlier testimony in asking for a 1958, rather than a 1955, start for a four-year Portland State College. But the private Portland colleges did not represent the sentiment of the majority of the metropolitan-area citizens. Both major newspapers, the *Oregonian* and the *Journal*, supported the bill, as did the labor unions and the parents and friends of students. Most of the opposition came from outside Portland, principally from Eugene.[38]

On 4 March, the University of Oregon faculty, fervently and self-servingly, addressed the recommendations of the Anderson report and its implications. At this meeting, they unanimously condemned the January actions of the state board in permitting the colleges of education to expand their upper-division liberal arts courses; in considering general baccalaureate degrees at these institutions; in reconsidering disciplinary majors at these colleges; and in moving toward a four-year institution in Portland. On the last point, the well-worn argument of duplication of resources was once again employed: "It must be recognized that such an institution is bound to duplicate in an extensive and serious way the facilities for liberal-arts training existing both in the private schools of the Portland area and in the publicly supported units of the state system as a whole. House Bill 131...would, of course, carry this duplication far beyond anything that the Board has yet contemplated....The situation in Portland, with its pressures and ambitions, with its complex pattern of private and public institutions, with its confusion of extension and daytime programs, creates an atmosphere favorable to clever operators and local partisanship." To make sure its sentiments became apparent, the faculty issued them as a formal press release on 6 March.[39]

The Portland State faculty was angered by this action of their colleagues at Eugene. In morning and afternoon meetings on 8 March, they debated how to respond. Richard Halley and Frank Roberts introduced a resolution to be transmitted to the state board reaffirming the faculty's statement of 18 December; it called again for the board to endorse the teacher training recommendations of the Anderson report and for the legislature to provide citizens with the opportunity, via referendum, to vote on a proposal for a degree-granting college. But between the morning and afternoon sessions of the faculty meeting, the resolution became moot as the board voted to reaffirm its position of delay on the Portland State issue.[40]

On 4 March, the house Education Committee voted five to three to send HB 131 to the house floor with a recommendation to pass. Among those voting "no" was Rep. Mark Hatfield, a faculty member at Willamette University. But if the committee favored the bill, the state board did not. At a public hearing, its members presented a range of arguments against it. They declared Portland State needed more experience before the legislature made the financial investment required for a change. Oddly, for a member of a board of a public institution, Cheryl S. MacNaughton expressed sympathy for the position of the private colleges, saying existing legislation addressed the need for teacher training in Portland and asserting the educational facilities in Portland were "amazingly good." She concluded by proclaiming "most students who want an education get one. Lack of money doesn't stop them. I've seen many students work their way through the private colleges." Perhaps MacNaughton's opposition was not so odd; her husband had been president of Reed College from 1948–52.[41]

President Newburn of the U of O maintained making Portland State a four-year school would dilute resources and thus lower standards. He said no other state supported three institutions of higher learning and recommended a study be made of the state's educational needs for the next twenty-five or thirty years. Representative Neuberger challenged him on all points, particularly vigorously on his last recommendation, which she labeled as a delay tactic: "This is the third legislative session where this has been considered....There has been constant delay and stalling, and we need to do something now to get an expression from the people on this matter." Her comments in favor of the bill were supported by those of James T. Marr, secretary of the Oregon AFL, who said: "We want a school where children from working families can go to school and work part of the time."[42]

Epler recognized opposition by the state board was a serious blow to HB 131. Although he continued to rally support for it by assigning specific tasks to members of the Advancement Committee and by speaking personally to the representatives of organized labor, he was gloomy about its prospects. In spite of his fears, however, a compromise was reached in the Education Committee. HB 131 was adopted, but with the provision the new school would not start until 1958. The vote was five to two this time, with Hatfield and Rep. Charles A. Tom of Rufus voting "no." Apparently, this compromise was made to allay the established schools' fear of competition for students until the baby boomers arrived in the colleges in the late 1950s. An editorial in the *Oregonian,* prepared by Malcolm Bauer (who also taught journalism courses at Portland State) after consultation with Epler, refuted the fears of the older institutions that Portland State would be unduly competitive with them as unwarranted. None of this helped—the opposition was too strong. HB 131 was killed by the full house in a vote of 36-21 on 24 March. Almost all the downstate legislators voted against the bill.[43]

Epler, who never gave up a battle for Portland State, recuperated for five days and then called a meeting at the home of Political Science instructor Brock Dixon. There, Epler, Dixon, and Bill Pilling and his wife, Kathleen, decided to press for an initiative measure to obtain the four-year, degree-granting college. They prepared a press release to advertise this new strategy. Two days later, HB 713 was introduced, which would give Portland State four years of teacher education and four years of general education, but not the authority to grant degrees. Portland State students, presumably, would get their degrees if they took their last term at one of the other state system institutions. This time—on this measure—Portland State supporters would not be working alone, as the state board endorsed the measure. Travis Cross, indeed, called Epler to get him to line up support for HB 713 and its senate companion measure, SB 426, which would also give the three teachers colleges the right to grant bachelor's degrees in humanities, social science, and science-mathematics, as recommended in the Anderson report. The *Oregon Journal* also swung behind the measure in an editorial on 4 April.[44]

The *Oregonian* threw its weight behind the two bills editorially, pointing out the hypocrisy of the University of Oregon arguing for retaining institutional specialization when "a few years ago" it "resumed instruction in the physical sciences and gained a handsome new building to house its biology, chemistry and physics classrooms." This argument was unconvincing to a Eugenean who wrote a letter to the *Oregonian* declaring, "Portland gets more money for the medical and dental schools than all the other colleges combined—and how many doctors and dentists are we getting? Where are they? We wait months for a dental appointment in Eugene. Portland wants to grab everything. They've already got a large state office building which ought to be in Salem with the others." Throughout these months, Epler's diary entries were filled with notes of conferences with the Advancement Committee, legislators, and organizational representatives.[45]

These efforts were rewarded on 18 April, when the House of Representatives voted 50-9 for HB 713. A point that occupied a good deal of time in the debate was whether it was foolish to establish a three-and-two-thirds-year school, instead of a degree-granting college. To achieve a four-year school, Sen. Warren Gill suggested the initiative measure would be the appropriate method but apparently got little support for it. The following day, the senate approved the Portland State measure by a vote of 16-14 and the bill for the teachers colleges by a 19-11 margin. As soon as the bill passed, White called Epler from Salem and burst into tears of joy while giving him the news. About twenty other Portland State supporters also had been in the gallery watching the debate, including faculty members George Hoffmann, Ella Litchfield, Don Parker, and Hildegard Weiss.[46]

Epler and his fellow advocates took some pleasure from the victory of HB 713 but were determined to obtain the four-year institution. Epler thanked Homer Allen, especially: "In my opinion, no other alumnus has done as much for the school during the past year." Allen himself wrote a letter to the *Oregonian* thanking the groups besides his own Advancement Committee that made it possible: "The press, the business community, labor, agriculture, the Mothers' club, alumni, social groups." But he also noted students would have to take at least one term at another institution. Portland State, he concluded, "has a long way to go before the headlines can say with complete accuracy, 'Portland State Becomes a Four-year College.' But those headlines are inevitable."[47]

Perhaps they were exhausted from the struggle over HB 713, but the Advancement Committee was not energetic in campaigning for an initiative to amend the constitution to accomplish the four-year institution. On 19 May, the committee met but accomplished little in pushing for the measure. In June, however, the state convention of the AFL voted to continue its support of a four-year college.[48]

One obstacle that had been assumed since the beginning was suddenly removed on 7 May 1954. The issue arose in connection with the University of Oregon Dental School's wish to construct a new building in Portland. Apparently, there was an objection on constitutional grounds, for the state board, before calling for bids, asked the state attorney general if the creation of the school by the 1945 legislature had violated the constitutional prohibition against locating a state institution outside Marion County without a vote of the people by referendum. In response, Attorney General Robert Thornton ruled the dental school was not a separate "public institution" from the University of Oregon but rather a "department" of the State System of Higher Education. Thus, it had not been unconstitutional for the legislature to create it without a referendum. Since the same reasoning applied to Portland State, backers of the Park Blocks institution could now abandon thought of an initiative and focus on a law to be secured in the 1955 legislative session.[49]

This task was easier than anticipated and much easier than obtaining permanent status in 1949 and HB713 in 1953. One reason was there was a new president at the University of Oregon, O. Meredith Wilson, who attended his first state board meeting on 9 March 1954. Wilson was not the strong opponent of Portland State his predecessor, Harry Newburn, had been. The second reason was the state board had changed its mind and was now willing to support the independent four-year institution.[50]

On 8 March, the board in committee, and, on 9 March, in regular session, declared it would recommend to the 1955 legislature that Portland State become a degree-granting institution. The board explained its reversal by saying preliminary planning had been completed to accomplish this change. An *Oregonian* editorial also noted President Wilson had abandoned the University of Oregon's traditional opposition to the change. These encouraging developments spurred a flurry of activity by Epler and the Advancement Committee, whose optimism was increased further after the Thornton opinion obviated the necessity of an initiative and shifted the battlefield to the legislature.[51]

The new campaign received support from old allies using familiar arguments. The AFL endorsed legislation, and the *Oregonian* editorialized in favor of it (also declaring Portland State's funding should be made commensurate with the institutions at Corvallis and Eugene.) By the time of the annual convocation that opened the fall term, Portland State had—numerically, at least—justified the support of its backers over the years. (Significantly, U of O president Wilson was the main speaker.) Registration was up 20 percent over the preceding year, the largest increase of any of the state's public educational institutions. Put another way, the final registration gain at Portland State of 716 students was almost equal to the combined increases at Oregon and Oregon State.[52]

The state board continued its support of the fledgling institution by voting unanimously on 14 December 1954 to accept a draft bill prepared by the chancellor's office to create a degree-granting institution.

Epler commented in his diary on this action: "My work here may be done." At the same board meeting, Chancellor Byrne resigned to be succeeded by John R. Richards. Two days later, after a meeting in Portland with the new chancellor, Epler declared, "He seems in favor of PSC." But Epler took nothing for granted. After the Portland State bill—SB 1, prepared by the state board—was introduced into the senate by the school's old friend, Rudie Wilhelm, and a comparable bill (HB 27) into the house by former Portland State student Bill Grenfell, he kept busy. He wrote legislators, urged the Portland City Council to support the Portland State bill, and phoned labor leaders to gain their endorsement. It should be noted as a testimony to Epler's character and to his loyalty to Portland State that this remarkable man never slacked off, in spite of his awareness that Dean Cramer not only wanted to become the president of the new college for which he had demonstrated so little support, but that he wanted to give no administrative position at all to Epler. Cramer told him bluntly his future at Portland State would be teaching education courses.[53]

The Portland State bills had relatively smooth sailing through the legislature. The major difficulty was the two bills differed on the location of the proposed degree-granting college. The senate bill proposed it be located in its current building (the Extension Center building) and adjacent property. HB 27 gave greater scope, stating the college could be located anywhere in the city of Portland. During the course of the legislative process, the senate bill was the one supported by the backers of Portland State. There were few hostile questions raised at the legislative hearings, although two supporters of Willamette University and the University of Oregon fired their last shot before the senate Education Committee on a minor issue.

Although no one intended Portland State would have its own dormitories, the "statement of one student that as student co-operative housing is added at Portland State, more students will come from out of the area," was quickly picked up by Senators Mark Hatfield (Salem) and Donald R. Husband (Eugene). Hatfield questioned whether "it was the thought of students that housing would some day be added to the urban school." Husband believed "if we were to stop this thing, it should have been done long ago—the bill will hurt private colleges. ...Portland State is going to become big and powerful and will hurt the quality of education in other institutions." But both senators agreed it was too late to block the bill. The president of the state board, and its chancellor-elect, representatives of the AFL, CIO, Oregon Education

Association, and Portland State students spoke in favor of the bill. The
senate passed it on 21 January by a vote of 24-2, the negative votes
coming from Truman A. Chase and Don Husband, both of Lane
County. Cramer noted with surprise in a private letter: "Even Hatfield
of Willamette voted Aye."[54]

The house Education Committee took testimony on 27 January
and on 1 February. Arguments made and organizations represented
at these hearings were similar to those before the senate committee,
except political commentator (and future governor) Thomas Lawson
McCall also spoke for the bill. The difference between the senate and
house bills regarding the proposed college's location was easily resolved
in favor of a downtown site. Cramer was confident the bill would pass
if it got to the floor but feared machinations in committee from Lane
County. "The Lane county delegation," he wrote, "does not hope to
beat it, but they hope to add a preamble to it which will tie the college
more closely to a downtown site and which will spell out the present
restricted curriculum." But all difficulties were overcome, and the bill
passed the house on 8 February by a vote of 58-2, the two negative
votes cast by Portland Democrats Jean L. Lewis and Walter J. Pearson,
who thought the bill weak because it limited Portland State to a downtown campus in the vicinity of the Extension Center Building.[55]

Gov. Paul Patterson signed the bill into law on 10 February, but
the official recognition of this milestone in Portland State's life came
on 11 February, with a campus celebration. There was a special assembly held at noon; Cramer, Epler, and student body president Ron
Denfield spoke, and all three were given pens used by Governor
Patterson in signing the bill the day before. There was a lunch in the
cafeteria, and then, according to the *Vanguard*, a student, "cheered by
the crowd, climbed a ladder and took down the bronze-lettered sign
'Extension Center,'—leaving on the brick wall only the words 'Portland State.'" Jubilant Portland Staters then participated in a six-block-
long parade of automobiles, horns blaring, and a large truck carrying
the school band. The procession began at Broadway and Mill streets,
proceeded along Sixth Avenue to Oak Street, thence to Broadway,
and back to the College. The *Vanguard* article concluded saying, "Many
of the cars bore signs expressing thanks to the legislature and the state."[56]

The legislature did deserve much credit for both the creation of
Portland State Extension Center as a permanent institution in 1949
and for the establishment of the degree-granting college six years later.
Work of the Multnomah County delegation was a tribute to non-par-

Students celebrating authorization for the creation of the four-year college in 1955

tisan efforts for the benefit of the region. One reason for the strong regional support was the steady and persistent efforts of organized labor, which recognized the sons and daughters of the working class had little opportunity for higher education without a state school in Portland. The *Journal* and the *Oregonian* were alike consistent advocates of the institution, devoting much space in both editorial columns and news accounts to the cause. Parents, especially through the Mothers Club, and alumni, through their association, stayed the course. The Advancement Committee drew on students, alumni, parents, and citizens throughout the years.

Underlying these efforts was the unprecedented growth in national prosperity, the enormous number of post-war "baby boom" children ready for school (which necessitated training teachers for them), and the desire of many students to take degrees outside of teaching fields to improve their intellectual and material welfare. When these conditions became apparent, the anomaly of the state's largest metropolitan area lacking first a permanent and then a degree-granting institution became insupportable. By 1955, the opposition of the chancellor, the state board, and the University of Oregon and its alumni were unable to deny the logic for creating the urban college. Finally, but foremost, the individual who directed these groups, forces, and individuals through character, intelligence, and charisma was Stephen E. Epler, the real founder of Portland State—a man overlooked on the two occasions when he might have been given the direction of the College.

FOUR

Faculty and Government · 1952–1955

During the years after the Vanport flood, from the move to St. Johns and then downtown, the faculty underwent several changes in numbers, characteristics, and obligations. And their work came to be carried on in an atmosphere more like a high school than the original veterans' college at Vanport. The causes for this change were several. Of course, the Center facility after 1952 had been a high school building—it had lockers, a public address system, and synchronized bells to mark the end of classes. More important, students in ever increasing numbers—even at Oregon Ship—had come directly from high schools, unlike the military veterans who were the typical students at the original Vanport. To many faculty, the recent high school graduates seemed callow, less serious, and less focused on putting their education to work than their predecessors. Also, the administration remained exclusively in the hands of men oriented to the public schools. Except for Epler, who had a Ph.D., all the high-ranking administrators from Cramer down possessed doctorates in education. All had served as public school administrators or teachers, or both. Finally, many students who did have career objectives desired to become teachers, and the need for teacher training had been the element that broke the logjam for a four-year, degree-granting institution.

But by no means were all new or old faculty in the Education Department. Many came to teach the liberal arts courses that were made available in the 1953 legislation. In September 1953, the state board's Executive Committee, confronted with the news of an 18 percent increase in day students at Portland State, voted to add fifteen instructors at the college at an average salary of $4,000 per year. Of these newcomers, many held, or would soon gain, the Ph.D. in disciplines in the liberal arts and sciences. Some came directly from graduate schools, while others had previous college teaching experience.[1]

Sometimes hiring faculty involved delicate maneuvers. For example, Dean Cramer had to secure the permission of Pres. Henry Newburn of the University of Oregon before he could hire away two U of O faculty members, Will V. Norris in Physics and Thurman S. Peterson in Mathematics. Newburn's consent followed the guarded agreement of the University's dean of the College of Liberal Arts and the Graduate School, Elden L. Johnson, who consented regarding Norris and Peterson but added: "We may have many other inquiries of this sort as the Portland institution develops and we may have inquiries which raise serious questions for us."[2]

Working conditions for faculty continued to be as difficult as at Vanport. Hard work was expected of them by administration and students alike, and not just in their teaching obligations. One of the earliest editorials in the student newspaper mourned the poor attendance of faculty at social events: "There are approximately 40 instructors and it seems that many more, other than the same four or five, could and should attend these social events that they are supposed to announce in their classes." Perhaps not as chaperones or spectators, but all faculty performed non-teaching roles. They served as academic advisers (all students were required to have an adviser and to attend advising sessions), and every faculty member was assigned at least one "co-curricular" organization, ranging from the Science Club to the student council.[3]

The faculty spent an enormous amount of time creating and revising the curriculum as the school passed from a temporary to a two-year to a degree-granting institution in nine years. A great deal of work was required in 1953 and 1954 in laying the foundation for liberal arts courses and additional education courses, following the state board's decision to grant Portland State Extension Center authority in training teachers for certification and to permit it to offer programs that would lead to bachelors' degrees at the other institutions. In curriculum matters, Willard Spalding of the Education Department and chair of the Curriculum Committee took the lead, though most faculty, including Cramer and Epler, participated in the discussion of courses to be offered.[4]

The Curriculum Committee sent two important documents to the faculty on 7 December 1953. One was entitled "Principles Underlying an Effective Program of Teacher Education" and the other was labeled "Requirements for the Bachelor of Science Degree in Education (Elementary)." At the faculty meeting on 9 December, without much discussion, the faculty adopted the rather general "Principles" document. In discussing the "Requirements" proposal, much more attention was paid to details. Before adjournment, the lack of foreign language requirements, a compulsory speech course, the lack of required mathematics, and the minimum grade point average of 2.0 (a "C") for prospective teachers all received scrutiny.[5]

On 18 January 1954, the faculty returned to the discussion of curriculum requirements. A motion to raise the grade-point average for the certification of teachers was discussed at length but ultimately defeated. Faculty then debated the committee's proposal on "group" requirements in broad areas such as humanities, science-mathematics, and social science. The issue was what groups of courses, or what specific sequence of courses, would be educationally desirable and, perhaps more important, meet the certification requirements of the State Superintendent of Public Instruction. Ultimately, the Curriculum Committee proposals were adopted without dissenting vote and accepted by the state.[6]

In April 1954, the Curriculum Committee presented another "principles" document to the faculty. Entitled "Principles Underlying an Effective Education in General Studies," it was intended to be "a general guide for training teachers for the secondary system, and for general education." Some of the document's provisions remained in force for almost forty years. The curriculum in General Studies was "intended for students who wish to follow a program of cultural courses which, though broad in scope, are yet sufficiently concentrated in one area as to permit the proper development of individual interests and demands." These courses were grouped into three categories: humanities, science-mathematics, and social sciences. A student would choose one of these three areas. One sequence in each of three different subjects was required at the lower-division level (for example, a Social Science major might take a sequence in History, Political Science, and Economics), and sequences in two different subjects were required at the upper division level.

Beyond the major, students were required to take courses in the non-major areas, with at least one sequence in each. Other important requirements for the degree included 186 total hours, a minimum of sixty-two hours in upper-division courses, nine hours of English composition, and six hours of physical education. A minimum grade point average of 2.0 was necessary for the degree. Sixty hours of correspondence courses were permitted. The faculty adopted this set of requirements on 5 April 1954 as a group of working principles.[7]

Final discussion of the new curriculum took place at a special meeting of the faculty on 28 September 1954. A motion by Frank Roberts to require a basic course in speech was lost by a narrow vote, although supported by Hoyt Franchere of the English Department ("we have a large number of students who could not speak clearly—were, in fact, mumblers.") Other discussions followed, and, in the end, the requirements for the bachelor's degree in General Studies was adopted unanimously.[8]

At the same meeting, the faculty turned to the curriculum to be required of students who wished to teach in the secondary schools. On introducing the subject, committee chair Willard Spalding stated, "The Committee has tried to keep the list of required courses as low as possible....The committee had to keep in mind that, while majors are authorized only in general areas, certificates to teach [requirements for which were set by the State] are granted in subject areas like English, Mathematics, Physics, etc." Under these constraints, the faculty had little authority to design a Portland State curriculum in the area of teacher training, so discussion seemed desultory, and a motion to accept the Curriculum Committee report was carried.[9]

Although less time consuming—and less important—than shaping the curriculum, some faculty were concerned with student conduct. Faculty members were appalled at conditions in the cafeteria: "The floor is usually littered not only with paper but with actual garbage, such as orange peels." A student once hurled the cap from a fire hydrant at the door of an office, narrowly missing Carl E. W. L. Dahlstrom of the English Department. Smoking in classrooms was an endemic problem; although not permitted, it was practiced by students (and some faculty), creating a misery for non-smokers for many years.[10]

Another recurring problem that bedeviled faculty for years illustrated the institution's smallness and its resemblance, in some respects, to a high school. This was the time in the week's schedule for the assembly period (known as "Period X"), at which time no classes were to be scheduled. There had been an assembly period since Vanport began. Since moving downtown, the period had been scheduled at 10 AM daily; later, it was moved to 1 PM. Still, there were complaints, as students who had afternoon work schedules could not attend the assemblies or participate in club activities. In 1954, the faculty revisited the questions associated with scheduling this period. How could it be scheduled to disrupt the fewest classes, inconvenience the fewest students, and still accomplish its purpose of general edification?

In May, the faculty began considering the issue. The department heads and Epler met on 18 May to work out a proposal for the faculty to discuss. Apparently, it was contentious, for Epler wrote, "Dept hds meeting as schedul[ed] called Franchere's bluff after he obstructed action." The faculty met on 19 May for a lengthy debate filled with motions and amendments. At the end, the faculty voted for two assembly periods, 10 AM on Tuesday and 1 PM on Thursday. This vote did not settle the matter, however, for the student council asked that it be reconsidered. The faculty agreed to do so, and out of this decision grew one of the most interesting debates of the early years, one that presaged problems over the nature of the college. At the heart of the discussion was whether the larger institution could continue to maintain the ability, which had characterized the original Vanport, to please everyone and accommodate all interests.[11]

During the discussion, some faculty wondered if it was appropriate to take a popular period, such as 10 AM on Tuesday, and use it for other than formal classes. Others believed such a use was appropriate because it would foster the co-curricular activities essential in a college. Still others took the view that the academic schedule should take precedence and that the co-curricular activities should meet in the evening or late in the afternoon. Some, including Cramer, wondered what the state board's response would be to the college's request for space if a morning period were used for "activities"? Cramer said none of the other state system institutions had a morning activity period, but Epler replied that none of them had classes at noon (unlike Portland State). Another concern of some faculty, James Caughlin among them, was the effect of fifteen hundred unoccupied students milling about the building if they did not attend an activity period. In the end, the faculty voted to retain its original decision of the preceding meeting.[12]

In dealing with this range of issues, usually conscientiously if not always efficiently, the faculty spoke as members of an organized body after the decision to make the institution a permanent one in 1949. At Vanport, the faculty as a whole met rather frequently, though not to initiate action. Perhaps the small number of the faculty, the receptivity of Epler to anyone's ideas at almost any time, the prospect the institution would die, or the burdens of enormous class loads made a formal organization unnecessary or unfeasible.

By 1951, however, many junior colleges in the Pacific Northwest were facing the need to organize their faculties formally. At the first faculty meeting of the year in fall 1951, Director Epler asked if there should be regular faculty meetings and if the faculty should make formal decisions affecting policy. The response was positive: a committee was established under the chairmanship of Frank Roberts, and a draft constitution was presented to the faculty in November. The final document, approved in December, stated the faculty had jurisdiction over "matters of policy which are discretionary with the Vanport administration and upon which the recommendation of the Faculty would be appropriate. Appropriateness would be determined by the faculty, in consultation with the director."[13]

The linkage between permanent status and faculty government was further manifest at this general faculty meeting on 13 December 1951. George Hoffmann of the Social Science Department moved that the name of the institution be changed to Portland State Extension Center. His suggestion was adopted unanimously. Then began a discussion of government. Clyde Johnson of the Chemistry Department proposed there be established an executive committee to deal with matters not important enough for the concern of the entire faculty. It was then moved that the faculty elect a temporary chairman to preside at faculty meetings. Frank Roberts was chosen, and he replaced Stephen Epler in the chair.[14]

The faculty then adopted a motion that "the chairman appoint a committee to draw up a detailed plan for operation of a faculty council." Roberts appointed Clyde R. Johnson as chairman of this committee, with the remaining five members to be appointed later. The faculty then elected five members to a temporary advisory council to act until a permanent structure was established. The first members of an advisory council at Portland State were Brock Dixon (Political Science), Mildred Flanagan (Mathematics), Stanley Johnson (English), James A. Macnab (Biology), and John H. Stehn (Music). The records are not specific about how it came to be, but by March 1952, there was a committee on rules for a faculty council. The committee members were Dixon, E. Hugh Hinds (Business), Clyde R. Johnson (Chemistry and chairman), Ella G. Litchfield (English), Phil H. Putnam, and Stehn. On 25 March 1952, the committee presented to the faculty its suggestions for a permanent faculty council.[15]

This document created a body whose purpose was "to deliberate and make recommendations to assist the administration and faculty in the solution of mutual problems." More specifically, it was to be responsible for the scheduling of activities, the preparation of the academic calendar, and the drawing up of the agenda for full faculty meetings. Moreover, "it shall continually try to delineate the area of faculty jurisdiction. It shall be authorized to initiate and prepare legislation for full faculty vote." It also was to offer its counsel to the administration on a variety of specific subjects, such as changes in the curriculum and "other appropriate matters as may from time to time appear advisable."[16]

On 7 April, the faculty discussed a report of this committee that dealt with the question of who was a voting member of the faculty, thus presumably defining the franchise for the election of advisory council members and general business. It was an important issue that would arise again in the years ahead. One motion, although it received no second, was to define the faculty voting members as those holding academic rank and teaching six hours or more. This proposal, if adopted, would have eliminated all administrators and support staff, regardless of whether they held faculty rank. The motion that ultimately was passed was inclusive. It defined voting members as all members of the Portland State Extension Center with academic rank. With this thorny issue out of the way, the faculty approved the creation of the Advisory Council.[17]

The council was to consist of six members, only one of whom could be an administrator. The Center director and assistant director were ineligible for election, although they had a standing invitation to attend the second regular meeting of the council each month. No more than two members of any department could serve simultaneously on the council, which was to meet every two weeks, with the director authorized to call special meetings "as may be needed." The council would elect a chairman and a secretary. By 28 April, the new councilors were elected: Judah Bierman (English), E. Hugh Hinds, George C. Hoffmann, Clyde R. Johnson, K. Ellsworth Payne (Chemistry), and Frank L. Roberts. With this election, the temporary faculty committee on rules went out of business. It is interesting that, compared to other crises in the years ahead, no general complaint or specific faculty member's grievance initiated this change in the institution's government. Perhaps it was simply a reflection of what independent institutional status was assumed to bring.[18]

Faculty members interested themselves in professional organizations outside the college, but they had limited support through the middle of the 1950s. By 1952, there was a chapter of the American Association of University Professors (AAUP) established on campus, but it did little. The local chapter hosted a dinner for the faculty, at which Chancellor Charles D. Byrne spoke in September 1953, and another a year later, when Pres. O. Meredith Wilson of the University of Oregon spoke on the subject of academic freedom. Two faculty members made a presentation about the advantages of being a member of the "Teachers Union" in May 1953, but it is not clear what group this was, probably the American Federation of Teachers. In the fall of 1950, the "Faculty Bulletin" carried a short article stating the "Higher Education Department of the Oregon Education Association is earnestly soliciting the membership of college faculty." It was said low membership in this organization was responsible for the poor success of professors in obtaining benefits compared to those of public school teachers, who had joined the Oregon Education Association (OEA) during the past ten years. An OEA chapter finally was formed on 5 October 1954.[19]

There were some benefits available to faculty in the formative years. They could belong to the Portland Teachers Credit Union to obtain loans and to deposit savings at interest. Many faculty obtained medical coverage through the Northern Permanente Foundation (the "Kaiser Plan"). Faculty had always been under the state's retirement system, but these benefits were broadened in 1950. By December 1953, both the chancellor's office and the state AAUP were considering how to improve retirement plans. Parking was a pervasive and continuing concern that was discussed frequently. On 9 December 1953, faculty talked of acquiring a fifty-by-one-hundred-foot lot; the results of a poll of the faculty released at this same meeting showed 66 percent of them drove to work. By January 1954, the Faculty Parking Committee had located a "capitalist" who would loan the sum of $1,000 to buy a parking lot across from the school. Twenty-five members of the faculty were needed to raise the money. A lot was finally acquired by September 1954, with faculty charged the sum of $4 a month for using it.[20]

As the formal opening of the degree-granting institution grew closer, the faculty addressed other issues that accompanied progression to the new status. Some concerns were new; others, though old, were newly relevant. Some of these matters were obviously designed to protect the interests of faculty fearful the changing nature of the institution toward a liberal arts orientation would make them redundant and liable to discrimination. While discussing promotion and salaries on 6 April 1953, for example, Cramer tried to be reassuring when he stated, "The bringing of new people to the faculty will not in any way affect the promotions of those already here." He specifically stated he was "interested in protecting the rights of those already on the staff." Besides reassurance about their prospects, some faculty wanted assistance in improving their talents. At the same meeting, the inadequacy of travel money was addressed—there was only $1,000 available for this purpose in the entire state system—but Cramer gave some "suggestions [unspecified in the minutes]....to help solve this problem."[21]

Surprisingly, salaries were not a topic of much faculty discussion, and a wry resignation seemed to be the invariable tone when the subject was brought up. As early as the fall of 1948, the "Faculty Bulletin," in asking for contributions to the Community Chest, noted: "We have been asked to subscribe to the Community Chest fund. We realize that many of our faculty are more logically recipients than donors to this most worthy cause. However, if you do feel that you can make a contribution, it will be sincerely appreciated." By 1952, the state AAUP had a committee on salaries that met with the governor and the chancellor; its members were told "the matter of a salary increase will receive some consideration." In 1954, the state legislature hired a consulting firm, Barrington Associates, to study state salaries.[22]

On 6 December 1954, the faculty passed a resolution encompassing three recommendations to the administration arising from the enrollment increase at the college. One asked for more money to provide additional staff "to reduce teaching loads to those of faculty in comparable institutions" and to "make it possible to secure more professors and associate professors through promotion and through retirement." The second sought a policy of advancement based on merit, annual seniority increases in salary, and annual cost-of-living increases. The third requested faculty support for a "substantial increase in out-of-state travel funds comparable to that provided for staffs of other institutions." Again, during the debate on these resolutions, some faculty were fearful the veterans would be denied promotion or equitable salary increases, while others were afraid needed new blood would be discriminated against.[23]

The caliber of the faculty in the first few years is probably necessarily unclear, as the main assignment of faculty in this era was in the immeasurable realm of classroom teaching. To get a grip on this slippery matter, the *Vanguard*, as early as 1948, had suggested a system of faculty evaluations ("Startling revelations and rude awakenings would no doubt characterize a program of this nature."). A plan was actually instituted jointly by administration and student government in the winter term of 1950, with faculty members receiving anonymous evaluations by their students in sealed envelopes to be read by the instructors and no one else without their consent. Students seemed reasonably content about the quality of teaching over the years, however, for it was rare for administrators to receive written complaints such as the one Cramer got objecting to a teacher's requirement of memorization of her outline to receive a passing grade: "We have tried to discuss with her the reason for rote word memory, which is not educationally sound without purpose or meaning, and she becomes defensive and sometimes angered."[24]

Although badly overworked and underpaid, and disagreeing over many issues, faculty members were not without social pleasures and were not unappreciated by students. Many relaxed at private parties in each other's company and participated in social functions at the College. Bill Lemman of the business office played Santa Claus at the annual Christmas party. Appreciative profiles of faculty frequently appeared in the *Vanguard*: Historian George Hoffmann was admired for his range of reading ("from comic strips on up"), but, like Stanley Johnson of the English Department, was revered for his encyclopedic knowledge of movies. Hoyt Franchere, chair of the English Department, was praised for his enthusiasm and interest in students and his skill as a jazz musician; all in all, the arti-

cle continued, "Dr. Franchere might be called the typical modern college professor. He not only has the reserved dignity of an educator, but the practicality and friendliness so important in modern education." Ella Litchfield, also of the English Department, influenced many students through her rigorous teaching (especially of Shakespeare) and forceful personality.[25]

It was noted with amusement that Jesse Gilmore, historian and Berkeley

Hoyt Franchere, professor of English and later dean of the Humanities Division

PSU Office of Publications

doctoral graduate, was issued a University of Southern California robe at convocation. Judah Bierman's Shakespeare class gave him a surprise birthday party, although they were in doubt about how many candles to put on the cake. Don Parker of the Business Department was the subject of an "In the Limelight" column in the *Vanguard*. Alluding to his summer fishing business, the reporter noted: "Many a girl's heart turns somersaults when she sees him in his Tradewinds' sweater and jaunty Skipper's cap and for that matter many a girl finds it difficult to do her work in his classes for he is one of the best looking males at Vanport college."[26]

Faculty wives also received attention in the student newspaper: "Mona Albertson, a Vanport faculty wife, is doing well in her new gift shop in the Oregon hotel. Mrs. Albertson features Myrtlewood but has increased her stock to include many other items." Faculty also socialized with students. Kenneth Butler of the library staff brought his love of cricket with him from his native England and organized a faculty-student cricket team that handily defeated Reed College. Faculty played on their own volleyball and basketball teams against students; professors interpreted the rules liberally, sometimes using six players.[27]

By the time Portland State College met its first class of students who would be attending a four-year, degree-granting institution in September 1955, the faculty had proven itself to be a body of hardworking, competent men and women. Their morale was high. They had survived the destruction of one campus and the move to two others. They were beginning to govern themselves, and they had played an important part in laying the basis of an institution that was somewhat different from the original Vanport. They had become more diversified, representing a wide range of academic disciplines. They had played integral parts in the movements to secure institutional permanence and degree-granting status. Now, they were prepared to meet the obligations, frustrations, and opportunities of the new college.

"One babysitter equals no Sunday pot roast."

FIVE

Student Life · 1946–1955

B etween 1946 and 1955, the number of students fluctuated from a fall 1946 enrollment of 1,411 students to a 1955 high of twenty-eight hundred, with the low point being 1,025 enrollees in the fall of 1951. The appearance and subsequent departure of Second World War veterans, the uncertain prospects of Vanport Extension Center, the Korean War, the need for teachers, and, finally, the securing of four-year, degree-granting status all affected enrollment. In 1946, students were almost all male, veteran, and white. By 1955, few veterans remained, and most faculty members who had taught in the school's early days found these later-era students to be somewhat less serious and somewhat less mature than those who had first sought an education at Vanport in the summer of 1946.

Although neither immature nor frivolous, an increasing number of women was the most obvious change in the student body. At Vanport, women totaled seventy-four of the 1,411 students in the fall of 1946. Two years later, their numbers had almost doubled, to 145 of the 1,087 students enrolled. Their presence required changes in the physical plant and in attitudes. In August 1947, plans were laid to convert part of one of the Vanport City housing units to a women's dormitory. It was anticipated that, in time, an entire unit equipped with a dining room would be provided for female students. Nothing came of the idea, however, although in the fall of 1947 a women's restroom was added to Portland Hall, the student union building. Less tangibly, but still importantly, as the *Vanguard* later put it in a 1952 article: "With the addition of girls in classrooms, another problem arose for some [male] instructors. Many stories, anecdotes, and illustrative lecture material had to be deleted as sessions changed from just the boys to mixed groups."[1]

Women made better grades than men, were assigned news articles, columns, and offices in the *Vanguard*, and founded many organizations. In the student newspaper, regular columns and stories designed
to appeal to women appeared under titles such as "Listen to Crickets,"
"The Fashion Plate," "Co-ed's Corner," and "Girls Guff." In May 1954, a
women's style show was highlighted in the paper. In 1952, the first
female editors of the *Vanguard* were chosen, and, in the unenlightened
thinking of the times, were described in the news articles as "comely
misses." One was also described as "a pert, ambitious miss who stands
five foot two and three-quarter inches and has blue eyes."[2]

Women formed their own clubs and associations. During the
1947–48 academic year, they organized the Associated Women Students, open to all female students. During the year, the organization
sponsored two dances, conducted an orientation program for new
students, and published a "Vanport Student Handbook," which described the buildings, listed the staff, furnished a campus map, and
provided information about financial aid, college songs, and dress
codes for dances. Another service group was the Pep Club (for Pi
Epsilon Pi), organized during the winter term of 1951 by the female
physical education students. Its purposes were to promote school spirit and to give service to the school. During its first year, Pep's activities
included attending all intercollegiate games, selling candy at the
Homecoming game, and participating in the Noise Parade, another
feature of Homecoming.[3]

The first women's social club, the Crickets, originated in March
1947 as an auxiliary of the Bachelors Club "to prove that women too
can be proud of their independence and to promote sociability and
general welfare and all around good fellowship among single girls in
Vanport College." Members offered to teach women how to cook on
the uncertain stoves of Vanport City, helped faculty wives improve the
grounds with shrubs and flowers, and sought out a needy family to
assist. Other women's social clubs followed, such as Ami Kai in 1952
and Chi Gamma in 1955. Both engaged in a variety of social service
projects, although their primary purpose was recreational.[4]

Women did not have many athletic opportunities at the college in
the early years, except for five required physical education courses.
This was not due to lack of interest but rather for lack of facilities.
(One of the first clubs chartered at Vanport was the Women's Athletic
Association in November 1947.) Even a year after the move to Oregon
Ship, the only faculty member in women's Physical Education, Emma

V. Spencer, declared: "We just don't have enough room and proper facilities to start any inter-school sports for girls." About all she could provide, beyond the required physical education courses, were co-educational square- and ballroom dancing classes.[5]

By 1950, the situation was only marginally brighter. Although there were no intramural or intercollegiate sports, Vanport women participated in the sports nights held several times a year by the eight smaller colleges in the Portland area. Teams competed in swimming, badminton, table tennis, volleyball, and square dancing. Looking ahead did not seem to be encouraging either. When the Center moved to old Lincoln High School, the school would obtain a gymnasium, but Spencer saw no salvation there, even for intramurals: "I'm afraid that due to the facilities over there, the boys would probably be using the gym most of the time." This prediction came true, for when the move downtown occurred, the women's physical education program was not even located in the main building but two blocks away in the recreation hall of the First Christian Church. For the most part, female athletes had to be content with physical education classes, although the first woman to compete on the same intercollegiate team with men was on the rifle squad in 1951.[6]

Far more notable, however, was another intercollegian, Margaret Dobson. Dobson was an outstanding softball player, renowned throughout the West as a third baseman on a city league team. What made her internationally famous, however, was the decision in April 1951 by the Vanport men's baseball coach, Arba Ager, to ask her to play on his team. Dobson played in two games and acquitted herself competently, though the main result of her stint was publicity for the college. The Associated Press filed a story from Portland, and there was also an article and accompa-

PSU Office of Publications

Margaret Dobson, first woman to play on a college baseball team

nying photograph in *Newsweek* (significantly, in the "In Passing" section, not in sports) and a notice in the Paris tabloid, *France Dimanche*. Phil Putnam even got a letter from a friend on the faculty at the University of Minnesota-Duluth, who wrote: "I understand that you will have some applications for admission from the Midwest area as a result of national publicity. You will not need to worry about a declining enrollment if you can come up with a few more projects like this." Dobson was also an excellent student who, in 1955, became the first Vanport graduate appointed to its faculty, and, in 1986, became Portland State's executive vice-president.[7]

The mores of the era dictated, of course, how women were perceived outside the classroom, not only in sports, but in all dimensions of college life. For example, noting the changes at Vanport after a semester of graduate work at the University of Southern California, historian George Hoffmann remarked: "The scenery—number of girls—has improved a great deal since last year." During the 1946–47 academic year, the *Vanguard* carried a column detailing the activities of the Bachelors Club. Entitled, "The Wolves' Den" and written by "A Nonomous Bachelor," one of its features was a section called "Whistle Bait of the Week:" "This week's honors go to a cute li'l chick from Anchorage, Alaska. She is 17 years old, blonde (real), and definitely whistle bait."[8]

Women's admiration for men was also public news. On the same page of this issue of the student newspaper, a woman reporter wrote in the "Meet Joe College" column: "One of the nice, attractive fellows who are attending Vanport college is George Van Bergen, business administration major.... George, who has dimples when he smiles, is not allergic to women, but has no immediate matrimonial plans." The matrimonial focus of some students was reflected in the title of the student directory, which was called "Date Bait" for several years. In 1954, when published by the Association of Women Students, the directory indicated which students were veterans and which were married. For 1954–55, the title of the directory was changed to "Dial-Logs."[9]

Female students did have a number of older women (connected with the college) with whom they could identify. Women were on the teaching faculty from the beginning, and Epler was known for his equal treatment of them. However, the librarian and the social director were for many years the only women in the administration. In addition, there were faculty who were assigned specific responsibilities for women students, the first being Katharine M. Rahl, who carried the title of Women's Adviser. Rahl had been a navy officer who had served with Epler at Jacksonville Naval Air Station, where she invented six-woman soccer. The wives of students also occasionally got together for social occasions, sometimes including female students. The faculty women had their own organization, the Vanport Faculty Women's Club, now the Portland State University Women's Association. Over the years, the club has engaged in a variety of social activities and service projects, including a tea for female students, lectures for its members, potluck dinners for family members, and book groups. Club activities also included fundraisers for scholarships for women (and later, men), the most successful of which was an art festival in the early 1970s under the direction of Emery Savage. The Women's Club also organized a Mothers Club, which raised money for scholarships and helped with the political campaigns for permanency and, later, four-year college status.[10]

There were few African Americans at Vanport, but there was at least one black faculty member and several prominent black students. In the early years, racial statistics were never systematically compiled, but in the fall of 1948, there were twelve African American students out of a student body of 1,232. The first black faculty member—indeed, the first black faculty member in the Pacific Northwest—was Edwin C. Berry, who began teaching a sociology course in the fall of 1947. Berry was the executive secretary of the Portland branch of the National Urban League. He had come to Portland from Pittsburgh in 1945, after ten years' work for the League in various positions. Since arriving in Portland, Berry had given guest lectures at most universities in the Portland area, but his Vanport position would give him a permanent base to demonstrate what he regarded as the "direct relationship between his teaching job and his league work,...as the Urban League is a practical application of sociology in the field of race relations."[11]

Several black students were chosen for, or elected to, positions in student organizations. Within one week in May 1948, William A. Hilliard, a Journalism major, was elected to the student council and promoted from sports editor to news editor of the *Vanguard*. In an interview for the paper, he described his life ambition: "The American newspaper is one of the greatest propaganda machines and I hope to use this machine for the unification of the American people." In time, Hilliard became editor of the (Portland) *Oregonian* and president of the American Society of Newspaper Editors.[12]

In 1950, two blacks were elected to positions in student government: Sadie Grimmett, secretary of the student council (and also a

member of Pleiades, the women's service organization), and Art Shep-
erd, vice-president. Grimmett, the daughter of Josephine Grimmett,
one of the first black public school teachers in Portland, later became
a public school administrator in Tennessee. Another African American
student, Milton Emanuel, was a member of a local fraternity, Alpha
Phi Omega. In the fall of the same year, Richard Bogle, a transfer from
Oregon State College, was named editor of the *Vanguard*. His activities
at Oregon State as a student senator, a disk jockey for the college radio
station, and on the college paper, in addition to his endeavors at
Vanport, suggested to someone he be nicknamed "Duz" Bogle because
"he does everything." In later years, Bogle became a television news
reporter and a city councilor in Portland.[13]

There was African American representation on the college athletic teams: Bill Carrington, in football, and Emery Barnes, in basketball, were two stars of the early 1950s. Barnes was especially popular,
evidenced by a lengthy feature story on him in the *Vanguard* praising
his industry and personality, as well as his athletic ability. These qualities helped Barnes in later life, as he became a professional football
player, social worker, and politician who became the first African American speaker of the British Columbia Legislative Assembly.[14]

The late 1940s and early 1950s were times of both progress and
setbacks for those advocating racial justice in Oregon. The state legislature passed fair employment laws in 1947 and 1949. In 1949, Portland mayor Dorothy McCulloch Lee appointed a citizens advisory
committee on race relations. The committee recommended—and
the city council passed—a public accommodations law for Portland in
1950, but it was defeated by voters in a referendum in the fall of the
year. Also in 1950, the council established a permanent advisory commission on inter-group relations, of which Epler was a member and,
later, its chair. In 1953, the state legislature did pass a public accommodations law and, four years later, adopted a fair housing statute.
During these exciting years on the civil rights front, Vanport students
and faculty were active in the cause for racial justice.[15]

Concern was first reflected publicly in the spring of 1947, when
there was an attempt to organize a local chapter of the fraternity,
Delta Tau Rho, which had a racial exclusion clause in its charter. The
student council first approved, then revoked, permission for the fraternity. Delta Tau Rho was eventually approved in the fall, but without
the discriminatory clause. The Vanport administration and faculty saw
to it that constitutions of student groups and college catalogs made

explicit statements prohibiting discrimination on the grounds of race, color, or creed. The 1950–51 *Catalog*, for example, described Vanport as "a friendly college," in part because of "the absence of racial and religious discriminations" and because students were assured "organizations with charter restrictions against race, creed, or color are not permitted."[16]

Vanporters not only talked about instances of racial discrimination in the larger community, they responded to them. A letter to the *Vanguard* described one incident: "Tuesday evening, January 16, five Vanport girls, on their way home from a play entered the Town Tavern at S.W. 9th Avenue and Stark street around ten thirty. One of the girls, colored, was refused service. Her friends, of course, walked out too." The administration had responded to the situation even earlier in the *Faculty Bulletin* of 18 January, summarizing the incident which, it said, "may be of interest to faculty members who do not wish to patronize businesses which practice racial discrimination."[17]

That spring, Vanport students, modeling their actions on the "Fair Bear" campaign begun by students at the University of California at Berkeley, started a "Fair Rose" movement in Portland. Its purpose was to obtain promises from places of public accommodation that they would not discriminate. The symbol of that promise was a decal placed in the business's window. By February the next year, after hours of going door to door, Vanport students—in cooperation with other area college students—were able to see the campaign they had begun was paying off. On the twentieth of the month, the *Vanguard* published an article containing the names of scores of Portland restaurants that "have agreed to accept certificates stating that they do not discriminate and 'serve all Americans.'"[18]

Richard Bogle summarized the state of race relations at Vanport at this time in an article in the *Vanguard*. He praised faculty as well as students. "The faculty here at Vanport," he wrote, "is more than just fair minded about racial matters as evidenced in Dr. Epler's appointment as chairman of the mayor's commission on intergroup relations....Vanport's students seem to be keeping pace with the faculty as is shown by the amount of interest in the current Fair Rose program. This is due in part to the lack of enforcement of a rigid mode of thought as some 'national' social fraternities and sororities encourage. The organizations here don't repress the students' natural sense of fair play which allows Vanport to continue on the path of progressive thought and action."[19]

On a less serious level, there was an organized social life for Vanport students, although many were not able to take advantage of it because of family obligation, jobs, or a feeling (especially among veterans) that they had outgrown such activities. Yet, the students and administration did provide an increasing array of social, professional, and special interest organizations. Befitting the times, the social lives of students were somewhat regulated by the institution. Faculty members were responsible for supervising men's and women's activities since Vanport days, although their titles varied over the years.

Epler himself was involved in student problems, as well as general supervision of the school. After the Center moved to the former Oregon Shipyard campus at St. Johns, for instance, a larger number of younger students entered the classroom. Some of them—even though underaged—also entered the taverns in the surrounding neighborhood. The owner of the Ranger Tavern on North Jersey Street wrote to Epler for a list of Vanport students and their ages so he could keep the underaged out. He promised to send duplicates to other taverns in the vicinity of the institution. Epler obliged him. A similar problem with underage drinking arose in 1954 on Anniversary Day, the school's traditional spring holiday. As Epler noted in his diary: "Dick [Halley, the Men's Adviser] and I drove to Roamer's Rest park for picnic. Students drinking beer—so we sent them home."[20]

One of the first students Epler encountered at Vanport asked him if there was a student newspaper. Epler responded in the negative, and the student promptly declared: "Fine, I'll start one." The founding editor's name was Don Carlo, a military veteran, who had been blinded in combat. Before military service, Carlo had worked on the newspaper at Washington High School and on the University of Oregon *Emerald;* while in the military, he served on various service newspapers. The first issue of the student newspaper was prepared in Carlo's apartment on Cottonwood Avenue and was published on 15 November 1946.[21]

The name of the newspaper was *Vet's Extended.* It was to be a temporary name until a more suitable one was chosen. But "Stooge," which one student wanted to call it, and "Aspect," which the staff had almost decided on, were rejected, when Vaughn Albertson of the English Department, the faculty adviser, hit on the name *Vanguard,* which met universal approval. The lead article in the first issue was a report on the student council elections. The initial editorial, entitled "The Spirit of a Student Body," declared:

We, as students, are helping to start a new idea for colleges. For it is true that there was no school here before, and it is also true that this organization was only started to alleviate the congestion created by the emergency....and though the only romantic thing around here is the cinder path from Portland to Oregon Halls, we do have the proper spirit of...a University. But even without all of the atmospheric attributes, we have within us the insatiable search for knowledge that was born while waiting for the end of the war. Many of us waited years so that we might have an opportunity to attend such a school.[22]

The first issue of the paper under the name *Vanguard* appeared on 14 January 1947. As with its predecessor, the paper was published weekly, on Wednesday afternoons. It was given free rein by the administration, which never censored it, but its life was not without problems. Frequently, there was a need for workers, with the paper on the verge of closure after reaching a staffing low point of two persons in April 1947. In November 1948, the paper decided to reduce the amount of space devoted to national issues in its editorial columns and to concentrate on "issues which directly affect Vanport college and its student body." Foremost among these was the crusade for a permanent institution, an issue pursued until the goal was attained.[23]

Student newspapers are episodically controversial, and the *Vanguard* was no exception. Complaints built up during the spring of 1949, culminating in a mid-May meeting of newspaper staff, faculty, Publications Board members, and student councilors. Many interested students also appeared for the meeting. A variety of opinions was presented, with one student's major complaint being "the Vanguard had printed a story about Vanport janitors next to the play review." He also said many students refused to work on the newspaper because it had "red ties." Administration representatives said the *Vanguard* was "not censored at all."[24]

After objections to the work of particular staff members were aired, members of the student council made suggestions the editor agreed to accept. Among them were promises to attempt to keep in closer contact with the paper's adviser; to increase the number of staff members; to publish a student directory; and to completely eliminate the discussion of national political issues. Editor Ray Bouse defended his staff and spoke particularly about "the red label thrown in the editor's face." Bouse "defied the council to find 'party line' stories in the last several issues and 'denied adherence to lines of any party.'" The dis-

Vanguard staff at Vanport Extension Center

pute evaporated as the school year closed. In the 1950s, some changes were made. Judah Bierman of the English Department became second adviser to the *Vanguard* in 1950, succeeding Vaughn Albertson and, in turn, being replaced by Alexander Scharbach, also of the English Department. Publication day was changed to Friday in November 1953. After seven years of publication, the *Vanguard* added its first page of photographs in the 5 February 1954 issue. In January 1954, the Publications Board was reconstituted to include seven persons: four students appointed by the student council and the three faculty advisers of the student publications, *Vanguard* and *Viking* (the student yearbook). The *Viking* began publication in 1947 and contained the typical group photographs and annual reviews of the genre.[25]

The first student organization chartered by the student council was the Bachelors Club on 23 November 1946. A social club for single male students, it sponsored dances, a co-operative study program, and also worked for a permanent Vanport College. Another social organization was the Barons, organized in the fall of 1949, which was heavily involved in intramural sports. The Barons also sponsored stag parties, beach trips, and a "Joe College and Betty Co-ed" dance. The college also saw the rise and fall of local social fraternities such as Delta Tau Rho and Sigma Delta Omega.[26]

Some student groups were at least nominally pre-professional. One was the Barristers Club, encompassing almost entirely pre-law

PSU Educational Media Services

Anniversary Day, the annual holiday at Vanport Extension Center

majors. Although the club was founded to promote good citizenship, good government, and good scholarship, it soon came to include good times (as in sponsoring dances). Those interested in public speaking had the Debate Club and Speakeasies, and student journalists organized the Press Club (one of its early presidents was Rodney Minott—later, a member of the History Department, chronicler of Shirley Temple, and United States ambassador to Sweden). Musicians formed a Choral Union, and, as early as 1948, there were two theater groups on campus. There always had been a lot of bridge played in colleges, and Vanport was no exception. In the fall of 1947, this activity was somewhat regularized with the formation of the Bridge Club. "At any time after that moment," the *Viking* recorded, "no one could enter Portland Hall and not encounter these rabid devotees hunched over the tables marred by signs of lusty kicks, grasping the worn cards in their sweaty hands, or wandering vaguely from person to person asking in quizzical tones, 'Fourth for bridge?'"[27]

Besides their own special organizations, Vanport students had college-wide functions. Every spring, there was Anniversary Day, which had begun at Vanport as a work party, followed by food provided by the college. In time, Anniversary Day came to incorporate entertainment, a picnic, games, and sometimes, swimming and boating. Occasionally, there was trouble. For instance, the 1950 celebration was canceled because, according to the dean of men, the students failed "to obtain the proper approval from the administration and because of the bad reputation of past student picnics."[28]

There were rally squads, talk of electing class officers, and student-sponsored dances, such as the one in September 1951 attended by one hundred students and fifty faculty members. Homecoming was an annual fall event, with the Noise Parade on Thursday preceding Friday's football game. In 1953, after the move downtown, a parade of flatbed trucks carrying floats and convertibles bearing the queen candidates, all accompanied by the noise of wailing sirens, blaring horns, and ringing bells, proceeded up Sixth Avenue to Duniway Park. Here, the Sigma Delta Omega fraternity had made a bonfire, and the five hundred students yelled cheers and sang songs before moving back down Broadway Street to the cafeteria for an informal dance.[29]

Almost all American colleges and universities make available opportunities in intercollegiate sports, and Vanport Extension Center was no exception. The first intercollegiate team fielded was basketball during the 1946–47 season, with John Jenkins as coach. The team compiled a credible record and won fifth place in a sixteen-team Western States College tournament at Compton, California. During the first academic year, Vanport also had teams in baseball, boxing, golf, and track. Football became a sport in the 1947–48 season; the team lost its first game to Pacific University, and, indeed, won only one game during the season, its last one, over the Sand Point Naval Air Station. Joseph Holland, among other duties, filled the position of coach. Wrestling also joined the ranks of intercollegiate sports in this year.[30]

There was an intramural program from the first year, although it became more formally organized in 1949, under the direction of Jim Vitti, instructor in Physical Education. He arranged the first competitions in touch football, basketball, softball, handball, and volleyball. Women's physical education classes in swimming and modern dance also were popular.[31]

In 1949, Vanport joined its first athletic conference—the Oregon Collegiate Conference—which was formed that year to include all of the state's public colleges. In addition to Vanport, the members were Eastern Oregon College of Education, Oregon College of Education, Oregon Technical Institute, and Southern Oregon College of Education. Vanport finished second in basketball in its first year of conference competition, but the institution's greatest success in its two-year college years before 1955 came in the 1954–55 basketball season. That year, the team won the conference championship, the National

Association of Intercollegiate Athletics District Two championship, and most of its games in a tour of Asia, where it played American military teams and national teams from Singapore, Hong Kong, Malaya, and the Philippines.[32]

Student government, at least in theory, included all students. During the nine years from the founding of the Vanport Extension Center to the opening term of Portland State College, there were four student government constitutions. Student government itself, called the Associated Students of Vanport College, was launched during the school's first fall term. On 6 November 1946, at an assembly of the student body, fifteen candidates were nominated from the floor, and the names of twenty-five others were added by petition the following week. The election was held on 14 and 15 November, under the supervision of the student body presidents of the five Portland high schools or their representatives. Fifteen candidates were to be elected under the preferential ballot method, and Bob Taylor won the most votes to become president. The next fourteen with the highest number of votes became members of the student council.[33]

New constitutions were adopted in 1949, 1951, and 1955, though they differed little in their provisions. Always, student governments held advisory powers, subject to the ultimate authority of the dean of students and the president. They had the delegated power to distribute student funds, but, if decisions fell afoul of administrative choices, they were overruled.[34]

Most students seemed to display relatively little interest in the workings of student government, but those who did often had an enjoyable and raucous experience. Objects of contention included the charge that the Engineering faculty had interfered in student elections, that the elections were conducted incompetently or corruptly, and that student government was in the hands of an "active minority." Periodically, editors, letters to the student newspaper, and student councilors castigated the students as a whole for complacency or indifference to their own government. These charges echoed on through the years, often with an uncanny similarity in content and tone.[35]

Students did take pride in the college but perhaps did not express it frequently in the manner of their colleagues at the traditional, ivied institutions. There were, of course, college songs, a mascot, and instant "traditions," some imported from older colleges. The first college song was "Here's to the Vikings," copied from the coast guard tune "Semper Paratus." It was replaced in 1952 by "Men of Portland State," sung to the tune of "Men of Ohio." The mascot was always the Viking, chosen because the school, just as with the Vikings, was breaking new ground and opening up new territory. College colors have always been forest green and white, a selection made by Joseph Holland, the first director of athletics, and his athletes. The college celebrations Anniversary Day and Homecoming were a recognizable part of collegiate Americana that did demonstrate pride and morale.[36]

For some critics, however, Vanport students did not display sufficient school spirit. In the student council elections of April 1947, only 249 students out of more than a thousand voted. The next month, lack of interest forced the cancellation of a variety show and a softball league, as well as the resignation of the president of the Girls Club. Apathy continued into the fall term, as a *Vanguard* article noted the lack of interest in women's sports. One student calculated about 20 percent of the students participated in school activities, plaintively querying in a letter to the *Vanguard,* is it "asking too much of any one student to come out and show a little of the 'rah-rah' spirit that is lacking at Vanport?"[37]

A response came three weeks later. "Believe me," a student wife wrote, "we wives would love to dance our little shoes off to the nylons, and to yell our curly heads off at the games. Our husbands envy you comparatively carefree bachelors your freedom to take up those exciting but time and energy-consuming sports, and hobby clubs. Since a large percentage of the V. C. students are married, and in their respective homes a large percentage of those are affectionately called "Daddy" your chances of creating a throaty "rah-rah' chorus are about the same as finding a pewter dollar in a mud hole. Face the facts,...Life is real, life is one heck of a struggle, and one baby sitter equals no Sunday pot roast."[38]

The move to Oregon Ship did not increase student interest in organized activities. *Vanguard* articles estimated in June 1950 that 20 percent of the students (as in 1947) participated in activities and that there was a general lack of interest in extracurricular activities in November 1951, although Homecoming that month did involve hundreds of students. The move downtown to the old Lincoln High School building did not allay the worry of those who feared the absence of school spirit. Yet the *Vanguard* editor in October 1953 saw this as a misperception. It was true, he wrote, the older or part-time student did not have the enthusiasm of the high school or established college student. But this was not a weakness, for "it is this very diversity of backgrounds and attitudes which make attending Portland State a much richer experience than that felt by students at older, more settled institutions....So let us not mourn the absence of homogeneity and 'spirit' based on what is past and gone. Our school is a new one, but unconquerable, lacking in tradition and history, but full of opportunity for establishing them; heterogeneous in student body, but united in determination."[39]

Some blamed the lack of school spirit on the move downtown itself: "I loved our home in 'Oregon Ship.' It was not beautiful; it was not even attractive. But you see, even after travelling an hour and a half to that paper-mache building that could burn down in thirty minutes, you found something that our present building lacks.... Students and faculty were friends and everyone helped when something needed to be done. I said that Vanport and its spirit has died. That it has." The issue of school spirit was raised again and again, until one engineering student, Wallace S. Priestley, declared in a letter to the editor of the *Vanguard*: "I am disturbed by the perpetual bombardment of those concerned with the school spirit of our college. Portland State is neither a high school where group activity is an expression of youthful conformity nor a campus college where the student sphere of activity is somewhat dependent on school regulation. Portland State is a city college."[40]

Priestley was right. Vanport was a different kind of college, and the students' pride in it was best expressed not in traditional ways but in admiration for its tenacity in cherishing educational opportunities in the face of enormous obstacles. As always, academic work was not a full-time pursuit for most students but had to be juggled with personal, family, and work responsibilities. "Life was real" for most of the students and faculty. "Life was a heck of a struggle," and students expressed their pride and spirit in satire, irony, and wryness. As one student wrote in a poem about Oregon Ship:

> Most colleges have shrubs around, that get damaged by the freeze. But we have sturdy derricks here, Just swinging in the breeze. Most schools are made of bricks and stones, Of laths and lots of mortar. But ours is made of plaster-board, With tooth picks for supporters.[41]

Students referred to their institution as the "U by the Slough, where Culture Meets the Sea" and as the "College without a Future." Someone suggested the school song, set to the music of "Sioux City

Sue," be entitled "Slu City U." One alumnus's most vivid memory of Oregon Ship was "the sight of a skeletal carp stuck in a wire fence...six feet up...being gnawed by a cat...." But he also remembered "a no-nonsense, purely educational institution that did unbelievable things in probably the most sorrowful physical plant and surroundings possible." The true spirit of the students, in the end, was their pride and pleasure in the gift of educational opportunity that Vanport and Portland Extension provided.[42]

"Wasteful duplication? We think not."

SIX

Organizing the New College · 1955

As the day drew near for Portland State College to become officially independent—separate from the old Evening Division of the Portland State Extension Center —administration and faculty had to address important matters of faculty organization, curricular changes, and the psychological burden of freedom. (The Evening Division was renamed the Portland Extension Center. For years thereafter, many faculty taught both at Portland State College and Portland Extension Center.) In January 1955, even before the legislature had established the College, Dean Cramer appointed a committee on faculty organization for the simple reason that, as he put it, "usually institutions of higher learning have faculty organization particularized in a constitution and bylaws." From his remarks at this meeting, Cramer specified only two questions a faculty constitution would address: Who belongs to the faculty, and what is a quorum for doing business? The members of the committee were Errett Hummel, Cramer's assistant chair; Thurman S. Peterson, Mathematics; Harold W. Bernard, Education; Carl E. W. L. Dahlstrom, English; and Warren W. Wilcox, Psychology. Like the plan for the constitution, the committee members bore Cramer's stamp, as all had been hired by him; none were Vanporters.[1]

The committee gave progress reports to the faculty on 7 February and 4 April, and released a draft of the constitution on 14 April. Consideration of the draft took place at a special faculty meeting on 18 April and at a second meeting on 2 May, when it was adopted. In introducing the constitution on 18 April, Hummel stated the committee had investigated the operations of the state system institutions and of those of "about thirty large urban schools in the western part

of the United States." The main purpose of its deliberations, he asserted, was to "look into the future so that it might formulate not a makeshift document of temporary and doubtful assistance to the faculty
but a constitution that would make possible the effective operation of
a rapidly growing college. The committee felt that it had to think in
terms of a school having an enrollment of thousands of students and
a faculty ranging from four hundred to six hundred members."[2]

The constitution was divided into five articles. The first dealt with
the powers of the faculty. Essentially, this meant the faculty had the
authority to determine educational policy and the procedures required
to carry it out. Article Two defined the faculty as all whose teaching or
administrative time at Portland State constituted at least 30 percent. It
limited, however, the right of instructors to vote to those who had two
years of service. Article Three, the longest, dealt with the organization
of the faculty. It set up its officers: the president of the college was
chairman of the faculty and also appointed its secretary. There was a
senate composed largely of elected members, but with some ex-officio
administrators. The senate had the power to represent and act for the
faculty, although the faculty could review all its actions.[3] There was an
Advisory Council to the president, elected by the faculty. There were
fourteen standing committees appointed by the president from recommendations of the Advisory Council. Each of the four divisional
faculties had authority over educational policies solely affecting that
division. Article Four prescribed the number and nature of faculty
meetings, and Article Five contained the procedures for amending
the constitution.[4]

In the two meetings during which the constitution was discussed,
four matters received the most attention. The first was the rights of those
holding the rank of instructor. The proposed constitution, while making instructors members of the faculty, prohibited them from voting in
faculty meetings until "after the satisfactory completion of two academic years in the service of the College." When questioned, Hummel defended this prohibition on the grounds most new faculty members thereafter would be coming from graduate school without prior teaching
experience. "Stepping from the role of student into the role of instructor does not automatically mature a man; it is through association with
other members of the faculty that he will develop the maturity needed for voting. That is why the provision is in the constitution."[5]

Judah Bierman of the English Department moved to amend the
provision so instructors could elect three of their number to serve and

vote in the senate and nine in the faculty meetings. Morton Malter, Education, declared those who teach should have the right to vote on policies affecting them. After some discussion, Hoyt Franchere, chair of the Humanities Division, persuaded Bierman to withdraw his motion; Franchere then moved to delete the provision prohibiting the instructor franchise, a motion that was carried. But the matter arose again at the 2 May meeting.[6]

New objections were that some employees who would not be employed for more than two years—such as glass blowers or laboratory assistants in the sciences—were classified as instructors. It was felt that as they were not real teachers, they should not have the right to vote in faculty meetings. Even the teachers should have to wait, Warren Wilcox (Psychology) maintained, for "there is more to being a teacher than being in the classroom, for many questions about educational policy arise that only experience can answer." Yet no one moved to reintroduce the ban on instructor voting.[7]

Of even greater concern was the provision for an elected faculty senate of twenty-four members, six each chosen from the four divisions. Some faculty opposed creating one, arguing it would be an elite body making decisions without the consent of the full faculty; that attending faculty, divisional, and senate meetings would require too much time; that the demarcation of authority between faculty and senate was unclear; and that those not in the senate would lose interest in college policies. Those favoring the senate remarked the faculty could review or repeal any measures adopted by the senate and that the senate would lift the burden of detail from the full faculty and leave most free for teaching and research. The provision for a senate remained in the constitution.[8]

The third important issue was that of a six-person Advisory Council, elected by the faculty, that would function as a committee on committees and as "an advisory body to the President on all policy matters on which he seeks their counsel." Hoyt Franchere wished to delete the Advisory Council from the constitution, preferring the divisions be the small, representative bodies that would communicate with the president. Hummel argued the council would be useful as a small group during the summer months, when most faculty were away from the college. When some suggested the relatively small senate could also function during the summer, Hummel replied that it contained one third administrators and was thus not as representative of faculty opinion as the council. A motion to delete the council was defeated.[9]

A final serious issue was the definition of membership in the faculty, which the proposed constitution delineated as all who were employed 30 percent as teachers or administrators at Portland State College. When asked how this figure was arrived at, Hummel's answer was, essentially, that "the figure of thirty percent was arrived at because probably nobody would fall exactly in that class; he will be either over or under." What he meant was that many faculty would be teaching part of their time in the night school and would be paid by the Extension Division. For most of these people, presumably from past experience, no less than 30 percent of their work would be at Portland State. A motion to raise the figure to 50 percent was lost. Final adoption of the constitution took place on 2 May.[10]

Many of the provisions of the 1955 constitution were continued in its 1961 successor and in the later amendments to that document. What was done in 1955 served throughout the years as a competent framework for the government of the institution. Senate, Advisory Council, committees, and occasional faculty meetings have met, discussed, moved, adopted, amended, and adjourned hundreds of times since 1955, carrying forward the business of College and University in response to internal and external pressures.

Dean Cramer also contributed to the organization of the faculty in a more formal way. Establishment of the College meant breaking away from the evening program. Popularly known as "Operation Siamese Twin," it involved some administrative readjustments and scheduling problems but also the creation of formal academic divisions. On 7 February 1955, Cramer announced the Division of Humanities with Hoyt C. Franchere as chair, the Division of Social Studies with George C. Hoffmann as chair, the Division of Science-Mathematics headed by Will V. Norris, and the Division of Education led by Willard B. Spalding.[11]

Of great importance was the choice of Portland State College's first president. Unlike the process used in all later presidential appointments, the initial one was made without faculty consultation. Only two candidates were ever mentioned: Cramer and Epler. Both desired the position. Cramer represented himself as unconcerned about the matter in a letter to the head of the Science-Mathematics Division:

> Nothing very new to report. The underground is still at work,
> but I refuse to be excited about it. I am not in competition
> with anyone, and refuse to be put into such a position. The
> student council, after a lot of finagling, has finally sent in a let-

John Francis Cramer, first president
of Portland State College, 1955-58

ter to the Chancellor commending the Board on its support of
the College, and also commending the Dean and the director
of day Classes, 'the man with
whom the students come in
closest contact.' Some people are
more excited than I. One faculty member, the rumor is that it
was a woman, and not the librarian, approached Maurine Neuberger on the matter but apparently got little encouragement.

This student council action may have been the final outcome of an
earlier one in which it passed a resolution recommending Epler for
the presidency. Somehow, Errett Hummel, Cramer's faithful assistant,
got word of this action, and he and Cramer quashed the resolution.
One faculty veteran who knew both men well said that in a vote of the
teaching faculty Epler would have won an overwhelming majority.[12]

Epler certainly had his advocates. Grant Mumpower, the former
head of the Alumni Association and a proponent of the four-year college, wanted Epler to become president. Phil Putnam praised Epler in
a letter to the state board, declaring "the establishment of a four year
college in Portland is a tribute primarily to the vision, dedication and
dynamic leadership of Dr. Stephen E. Epler....Oregon is particularly
fortunate to have an educator and an administrator of Dr. Epler's
stature available to head this newest addition to the Oregon State
System of Higher Education." But these tributes, and others, were not
sufficient to gain Epler the presidency.[13]

Cramer was always the favorite and, except for the occasional case of
nerves, probably always counted on getting the position. In an article
in February 1955 on the signing of the Portland State bill by the governor, an *Oregonian* reporter commented, "It has generally been assumed
that Dr. J. F. Cramer, dean of the general extension division of the system of higher education, will have his choice of continuing in that
office or of assuming the Portland State presidency." On 1 March, the
Oregon Journal commented Cramer had "the inside track" over Epler

for the position. Cramer was older than Epler, had the ear of the state board and the chancellor (to whom he had made many reports), and was known about the state in his capacity as dean of the General Extension Division. As Epler's superior officer, he seemed to many who did not know the two men to be the natural choice for the job. Epler, on the other hand, although well-known and widely admired by Portland citizens, the faculty, and all those who had worked for Portland State throughout the years, did not have support at the state board level, was far younger than Cramer, and was a liberal not a conservative.[14]

Although Epler could hardly have been surprised by the news of Cramer's selection, his diary entry was poignant: "Cramer named Pres of PSC by bd (as I expected). But it is a blue day for me." So disappointed was Epler that he and his wife, Ferne, discussed leaving academic life and "investing in a motel & operating it in So calif—perhaps San Diego." Fortunately, he did not leave academic life and was appointed superintendent of the Reedley School District in Fresno, California, a position that also included the presidency of Reedley Junior College. Later, Epler continued his distinguished career as president of the College of Marin in Kentfield, California, and became the founding president of Ohlone Junior College in Fremont, California.[15]

On 15 June, three days before his departure for Fresno, Epler was honored by the Alumni Association at a farewell dinner at the Bohemian Restaurant. Alumni, faculty, and friends in attendance presented him with an air conditioner for the California climate and listened to speeches by Epler, Margaret Holland, and Stan Dean, former student body president at the college. When he left three days later, Epler could assuage his disappointment at not obtaining the Portland State presidency, which he undoubtedly merited, by the knowledge his work had confirmed Emerson's declaration that "an institution is the lengthened shadow of one man."[16]

The new president, John Francis Cramer, was a veteran of the Oregon public school system who had become dean of the General Extension Division in 1944, two years before the creation of the Vanport Extension Center. In that position, he had authority over the new institution but rarely interfered in its operation. In its formative stages, Cramer assumed the Center would disappear with the decline of the supply of military veterans. After it became permanent, he took a greater, although guarded, interest in its future.[17]

Cramer was born in Kansas City, Missouri, in 1899. Just before his sixth birthday, his family moved to the state of Washington. After graduating from Wenatchee High School in 1916, Cramer entered Oregon's Willamette University, then served briefly in the Washington national guard and in the army during the First World War. He received his bachelor's degree from Willamette in 1919 and his master's degree in 1920, both in Chemistry. The next fourteen years saw him through positions as teacher, principal, and superintendent at Milton-Freewater, LaGrande, Coquille (where he sang in a group called the Corn Fed Canaries and was adjutant of the local American Legion post), and Grants Pass. At Grants Pass, Cramer became a victim of a power struggle on the board and was dismissed from his position. In 1932, he acquired his Master of Education degree from the University of Oregon.[18]

In 1934, Cramer became an officer in the Civilian Conservation Corps, in which he served until 1935, when he was selected as superintendent of schools in The Dalles. Before taking up this position, Cramer obtained a Carnegie Institution Traveling Fellowship to Australia for four months in 1935. After returning, he discovered "the Dalles Board was very different when I came back, and badly split. Two new members had been elected. This meant constantly walking a tight rope, although I never had any real trouble. But the strain was always there."[19]

Cramer became superintendent of schools in Eugene in 1937 and, in the same year, became the first person to receive the Doctor of Education degree from the University of Oregon. In Eugene, he established a vocational school that trained skilled workers, a school especially useful in producing welders during the Second World War. In 1943, Cramer was chosen president of the Oregon Education Association. The following year, he was selected by Chancellor Frederick M. Hunter to be dean of the General Extension Division, a position that necessitated a move to Portland.[20]

Over his long career in the public schools, Cramer was on many occasions caught between contending factions in small-town Oregon. The largest community he had served in before coming to Portland was Eugene, which had a population of 20,838 in 1940. Experience in these jobs had deepened a conservatism in him, a sense of caution, that earlier manifested itself when, as a member of the Washington State National Guard, he helped confine members of the Industrial Workers of the World in stockades during the First World War and by his membership in the Republican party. In Grants Pass and in The Dalles, he had discovered what happened to administrators who were too outspoken.[21]

A fine raconteur with a genial personality, Cramer, by the time he had become a college president, had successfully headed the second largest school system in the state and gained valuable experience in dealing with the state board and the chancellor as dean of the Extension Division. He had testified before legislative committees and had traveled abroad, in addition to publishing a book on Australian education. But his presidency of Portland State College always was shadowed by the belief of most faculty members that he had become the institution's supporter only after others had gone through the risks to establish it.[22]

Shortly after Cramer's selection as president, he had to forward to the chancellor a list of proposed courses for the new college. This list was then sent to the University of Oregon and to Oregon State College for their comments. It created an uproar, predictably, at the University of Oregon, which had always feared "duplication" of its efforts by the institution in Portland. One of the objections made by the department heads at Eugene was a legitimate concern that the numbering of courses at Portland State conform to those at the other state system institutions.[23]

The other, greater concern was that Portland State faculty were attempting to prepare a list of courses far in excess of those required for divisional majors. U of O faculty feared the list was the first step toward departmental majors. As the head of the Eugene Chemistry Department wrote: "It may not be for us to say whether or not Portland State should lay the groundwork for specific departmental majors, but we should be aware that is what is being done." The head of General Science wrote: "It is difficult to make comments concerning the proposed science program...it seems to me it is organized in such a manner as to 'bootleg in' departmental majors as general science majors or as part of the teacher training program." U of O president Wilson summed up the objections by stating Portland State should confine itself to its mission of teacher training and general concentrations, while the Extension Division "still exists and can still perform professional and upper division functions that are required in Portland." He continued: "The curriculum requests of Portland State college do not show evidence of careful examination in the interests of a balanced curriculum for what is, of necessity, a relatively small faculty and a somewhat larger but still small student body."[24]

Not surprisingly, given the influence of the U of O with the chancellor, Portland State was forced to back down. This was accomplished by the chancellor appointing a committee of faculty members from the University of Oregon and Oregon State University to pare the

Portland State courses. The committee represented the sciences, humanities, and social sciences. The result of their investigation was a report from the chancellor to the state board Curriculum Committee, which accepted it (with the addition of one course in Physics), as did the full board. The result was as follows: of the original 1,573 credit hours submitted by Portland State for its new college curriculum, "Dean Cramer withdrew 81 credit hours and following conferences with the reviewing committee, withdrew a further 159 credit hours." After these reductions, the chancellor unilaterally eliminated still another sixty-six hours.[25]

At the same meeting that it approved the curriculum, the state board directed its officials to take the final steps to implement the opening of the College on 3 August, as required by the enabling legislation. Portland State was now officially organized. Its first students would arrive in September, and those with sufficient transfer credit would graduate in June 1956. The faculty had a constitution and the College its first president. But its problems were just beginning.[26]

One amusing difficulty, reflective of the conservative political climate of the 1950s and the fact that Portland State was a state institution, emerged from a May 1955 *Oregonian* article stating that Democratic congresswoman Edith Green's administrative assistant, Donald R. Larson, was to resign from her staff and become assistant to the dean of the Extension Division. Alarmed (and confusing the Extension Division with Portland State, as so many did), the chairman of the Republican State Central Committee wrote a letter that was passed on to the chancellor's office: "The attached clipping has caused numerous calls to this office. The general thought being the Republicans supported Portland State as a community spirit project, now it will be turned into an institute of New Deal teaching, guided by Larson." The letter was accompanied by a letter from a Republican physician: "I don't know Don Larson—but his future political activities should be watched." Travis Cross of the chancellor's office smoothed it over by pointing out that Portland State was not the Extension Division; that the state system loaned "men for all sorts of government work in the executive branch, why not one in a generation to the congressional;" and "fear of Portland State becoming overly Democratic can be somewhat subsided in the fact that the new president, J. F. Cramer, is an avowed Republican."[27]

The long struggle for college status came to a symbolic end with the double ceremony of the College dedication and the inauguration of John F. Cramer as its president at Portland's Civic Auditorium on Sunday, 23 October 1955. A traditional academic procession of the Portland State faculty and representatives of 140 colleges and universities opened the ceremony in the afternoon, followed by addresses by Gov. Paul L. Patterson, R. E. Kleinsorge, president of the state board (who also administered the oath of office), and Mayor Fred L. Peterson, representing the city of Portland. Cramer delivered his inaugural address reviewing the short history of the institution, noting the increasing significance of urban universities in the United States and emphasizing the importance of close links between the urban university and the larger community in which it resides. In the evening, the principal address was delivered by J. Paul Leonard, president of San Francisco State University.[28]

The happiness of the occasion was somewhat marred by low attendance from Portland State students and from the citizens of Portland. The *Vanguard* attributed the seeming lack of interest to poor publicity, but it may have been caused by factors that would long remain: the many interests of students of a commuter college and the ignorance of Portlanders about their college. Also unsettling to the Portland State audience were the remarks of the president of the state board. Although Kleinsorge was in many ways complimentary to the new institution, he made it clear Portland State should not be overly ambitious when he proclaimed that one challenge for both the College and the board in the future

> is not the expansion of the curriculum into a cafeteria of courses just to fill the catalog. The goal is and must continue to be a strengthening of standards and the production of alumni who are equal to or superior to those from longer-established institutions—both public and private—in this state. To withstand the pressures for a glorified, suburban campus and to provide only those courses which meet a definite need, which do not wastefully duplicate, these are the problems of the future with which our successors on the board will be faced.

As so often before and after, the code word "duplication" was used to make sure Portland State was kept in its proper, subordinate position to the University of Oregon and Oregon State College.[29]

Kleinsorge's speech began a journalistic war of words. In an editorial entitled "Halting Start," the *Oregonian* condemned Kleinsorge's comments. It noted there would be no attempt at Portland State to duplicate the expensive professional training in engineering, medicine, dentistry, or advanced sciences but asked "is it possible to have 'wasteful duplication' in liberal arts, which must be the core of the program in Portland State and in the regional colleges that were once colleges of education? We think not!" An angry student, who could not obtain a major in History at Portland State, concurred with the editorial in a letter to the paper: "I was informed that Portland State college could not give a degree in history because this would be a duplication of a program in the state system. About the only duplication required would be to substitute Portland State on the top of my degree in place of University of Oregon."[30]

Defending the interest of the University of Oregon, a *Eugene Register-Guard* editorialist, in "Solemn Words at a Love-Feast," upheld Kleinsorge's remarks. Noting Kleinsorge was being criticized in Portland for his remarks, the paper saw it otherwise: "At the dedication of Portland State College, featured by the grandiose dreaming of promoters of that institution, it was Dr. Kleinsorge who brought the crowd back to earth." The board president's cautionary words, continued the editorial, "were not pleasing to the group which has dreams of a vast UCLA in downtown Portland." It commended the state board for having "shown remarkable courage in holding back the empire builders and in insisting on orderly development, on one step at a time."[31]

In spite of this carping, motivated by fear and envy of the inevitable growth of a public college in the state's greatest metropolitan area, Portland State could take pride in its nine-year history. Starting from nothing, it had advanced to a college strong enough to inspire dismay in Eugene, however unfounded that dismay might be. Far more important, while many of the other temporary post-war institutions disappeared with the military veterans, Portland State survived and took root. It was well-grounded for the years of growth and expansion that lay in the decade ahead.

"They're nothing but a bunch of hogs."

SEVEN

Buildings and Grounds · 1955–1969

After Portland State became a four-year college in 1955, the campus expanded rapidly. Both the number of buildings and the size of the grounds increased in the period before university status was attained in 1969. In the fourteen years between 1955 and 1969, the College added twenty-six buildings to Old Main by erecting several new structures and acquiring many older buildings. The total building space expanded from the 135,052 square feet of Old Main to 1,985,366 square feet at the close of the period. The College was freed from its original boundaries along the Park Blocks and was enabled to build westward, as the state board and the legislature came to realize the College was not only permanent but growing.[1]

Portland State College's original campus plan was drawn up under the leadership of President Cramer and Will V. Norris, professor of Physics and chair of the Science Division. They asked the state board to sell five-eighths of a block east of Broadway (currently occupied by the American Automobile Association) to buy property south of Old Main (now Lincoln Hall). On the first four blocks of this new acquisition, four-story (later to be expanded to seven-story) buildings were to arise, with a tower to connect the parts of the center two blocks. The next two blocks, the site of Shattuck Elementary School, and the adjacent block to the south also were acquired. At the suggestion of Errett Hummel, his administrative assistant, Cramer toyed briefly with the idea of building a heliport atop one of the College buildings, but the plan came to nothing. At this time, there was hope the campus would be enhanced by the City of Portland's construction of an exposition-recreation center nearby that could be used by Portland State for an

Will V. Norris, professor of Physics, principal architect of the first campus plan

auditorium and—at least some of the time—for parking facilities. The city's voters dashed these hopes, however, when they turned down the project in November 1956.[2]

The state board authorized the construction of the first classroom building, State Hall (now Cramer), in 1955 and a bond issue for the construction of the Student Center building (now Smith Center) in the fall of that year. While State Hall was rising, Cramer decided he needed additional assistance from Norris in the planning process and in March 1956 asked him to take the full-time position of assistant to the president in charge of buildings and planning. By September of that year, Norris announced to the faculty that the Student Center had joined State Hall under construction and that preliminary plans for the library portion of another structure (now Neuberger Hall) had been completed and accepted by the state board, as well as those for the second unit of State Hall. Even before he had officially assumed his new duties, Norris plunged enthusiastically into a tour of

thirty-five college and university campuses to see how urban institutions had grappled with problems of expansion.[3]

On the opening day of spring term 1957, the first unit of State Hall went into full use. The quarter of the building students and faculty entered that day contained fifty thousand square feet of teaching space, including a large room in the basement seating two hundred students and an acoustically engineered music auditorium on the

Cramer Hall under construction

Smith Center under construction

top floor. Although students, faculty, and staff were relieved to have the new building's modern facilities and equipment, historic college building traditions were not forgotten, as members of the senior class planted ivy on either side of the Park Avenue entrance to Old Main at a ceremony in November 1957.[4]

The presidency of Branford P. Millar, who succeeded Cramer in 1959, saw the completion of the first building program and the development of geographical expansion west of the original spine of structures along the Park Blocks. Additional parts of Smith Center and Cramer Hall were completed in 1966 and 1969, respectively, and Neuberger Hall was finished in 1968. Millar recognized, however, that the College could not flourish in its original confined location. Others had recognized these limits before; indeed, the new president inherited a campus planning committee that had been formed in the fall of 1958. Millar encouraged this body to continue its work and welcomed their report in June 1960. In their conclusions, the committee members emphasized two points: a growing college needed more facilities, and there was no way to acquire them in any direction except westward. It recommended the "campus boundaries be expanded to include the four blocks lying between Montgomery on the north, Park on the east, Hall on the South and 11th on the west."[5]

But before he could do much about reshaping the old plans, Millar and the College community were caught up in the construction bond campaign of 1960. As early as February of that year, at a special faculty meeting with Chancellor John Richards, the faculty pledged to assist in publicizing the forthcoming November election, when Ballot Measure 6 would be voted on by the electorate. The measure would raise by $40 million the ceiling for the state system's bonding capacity. Of this amount, Portland State's share would be $1.5 million, to be used for athletic facilities and additions to the College Center. Millar successfully urged students to participate in the campaign, and many faculty and staff also worked hard for the measure, which the voters approved by an overwhelming majority.[6]

While the bond issue campaign was being waged, other developments affecting campus planning occurred in 1960. To direct the planning of facilities growth, the College hired Cyrus R. Nims as director of physical planning. Nims was an architect and city planner who had recently served as acting director of the Portland City Planning Commission. The College also employed Walter Gordon, dean of the School of Architecture and Applied Arts at the University of Oregon, as a planning consultant. The planners did not work in a vacuum, of course, but were constrained by decisions made by two other governmental bodies. The State Highway Commission in July 1960 decided to build a freeway south of the Park Blocks, and the Portland School District decided to retain Shattuck Elementary School, which occupied the two blocks directly south of Neuberger Hall. The Shattuck property had been included within the College boundary in 1954, when the school board had plans to close the elementary school. These two decisions necessitated any further expansion be west of the Park Blocks.[7]

On 13 September 1960, the state board, after considering proposals of thirteen firms, accepted the recommendations of College officials to employ the architectural firm of Skidmore, Owings, and Merrill to draw up a master plan for development. The plan presented by the architects in 1961 outlined new boundaries for the College. The new freeway would mark the limits to the south and west; Market Street was to remain the northern boundary, and Sixth Avenue would be the eastern limit. Within this area, the planners anticipated that by the year 1991, a student body of twenty thousand men and women would need to be accommodated. The buildings they would require, according to the plan, included two large science buildings, a health education and gymnasium building, three parking structures, a physical plant building, five classroom buildings, an auditorium, and three library buildings. As in the case of all plans, architectural or otherwise, not all that was projected was attained.[8]

In the 1960s, in addition to the completion of Cramer, Smith, and Neuberger halls, the College acquired three private residences across the Park Blocks by 1965, the first of which was Harder House in 1961. These structures, although in some ways antiquated (two are more than one hundred years old) and somewhat distant from the classroom buildings, have served a variety of College departments and offices to the present time.[9]

In the mid-1960s, the federal urban renewal program was one impetus for the College's new master plan, a task assigned in 1966 to the firm of Campbell, Michael, Yost of Portland. Its plan, both completed and approved by the state board in October 1966, assumed the 52.3 acres available for College development would permit the growth of an institution comprising 27,500 persons (23,500 students—twenty thousand full-time equivalent students—and four thousand faculty and staff members). Under the new plan, the campus boundaries were the freeway to the south, Sixth Avenue to the east, Thirteenth Avenue to the west, and Market Street to the north. When the plan was completed, there would remain only three existing privately owned buildings within the campus boundaries: the Campus Christian Ministry Building, then under construction, and two apartment buildings, the Ione Plaza and the Park Plaza.[10]

The development plan included other features regarded as appropriate to an urban university, especially in an era in which architects liked to design large structures for campuses, such as Simon Fraser University and the University of Illinois at Chicago. There was to be one parking space for each full-time equivalent student, although this feature of the plan seemed more appropriate for a suburban, rather than a city, campus. The plan proposed a system of above-grade pedestrian walkways, a series of covered bridges that would connect the buildings on the Park Blocks with those on the west. The bridges were necessary, as the plan anticipated there would be more than one hundred thousand pedestrian trips across the Park Blocks during the course of a single day. The architects, indeed, considered the walkway system over the Park Blocks to be the "backbone of the Development Plan," which formed the "basic element which relates the part to the whole. It is this system which will become the basic continuity element of the future physical development of the College." (As it turned out, however, the overhead pedestrian bridges were never constructed because the Park Blocks between Market and Mill streets and Ninth and Tenth avenues were ultimately closed to vehicular traffic, a closure originally proposed in an article in the *Vanguard* by Portland architect Wallace Huntington.) A Park Blocks area free of excessive student traffic was needed not only as a safety measure and to keep vehicular traffic flowing, but also to maintain this park area for the convenience and pleasure of both the students and the community as a whole. The plan was a sensible one that tied the campus into the urban renewal plans going forward along with it, although, as is inherent in even a good plan, circumstances forced alterations in the years ahead.[11]

Portland State's participation in urban renewal began in September 1964, when the state board approved the preparation of a survey and planning application to the federal Urban Renewal Agency. This decision began a complicated process that proceeded through several bureaucratic steps before land could be cleared and new buildings begun. The federal government first inspected the area to see if 50 percent of its buildings were sufficiently dilapidated and unsafe to meet urban renewal criteria for redevelopment and if it contained at least two environmental deficiencies, such as inadequate street layout. Then would follow a detailed plan for campus growth provided by the College (ultimately, the 1966 architectural plan alluded to previously). The Portland Development Commission would then purchase the land and clear it, while relocating its original residents and businesses. The state system would then buy back the land from the Commission. The federal government would pay two-thirds of the project cost—estimated at $15,709,130, less what the College would pay for the cleared land. Buildings would be constructed within the area as enrollment demanded and state funds permitted.[12]

The urban renewal grant proceeded as hoped. In November 1965, the College received money from the government for the preliminary survey. In September 1966, the state board made its vital commitment to buy the land from the Portland Development Commission after it had been acquired and cleared. At the same meeting, it authorized the sale of $6 million in state bonds to pay its one-third of the project cost. The Portland Development Commission approved the arrangements the same day the board acted. In September 1968, the Commission agreed to start the actual process of acquiring land, relocating its residents, and beginning construction. At the College's request, the first properties to be developed were the block west of the Ione Plaza bordered by Tenth and Eleventh avenues and Montgomery and Mill streets, to be used for the second science building, and the block across Broadway Street from Cramer Hall, to be used for a parking and public services building.[13]

As in the case of most large enterprises, the urban renewal plan was a mixed blessing. Certainly, it was beneficial to Portland State in a variety of ways. Indeed, without it, it seems impossible a university could have emerged. There was no land for a campus anywhere else in the metropolitan community to be acquired at a price the state board could pay. The original land on the Park Blocks could never contain the buildings necessary for a growing college, let alone the university that would arise in the future. Only expansion within the area surrounding the Park Blocks, and only expansion with the aid of the federal government, was possible. Portland State would either grow, or wither, downtown.

The price of growth, however, was high. One of the amenities of the old, cramped campus with its inadequate buildings was the community surrounding it. Set on the fringes of the old South Portland neighborhood—a historic region with a cosmopolitan community of Jews, Chinese, African Americans, and members of other ethnic groups—the core of the College's buildings on the Park Blocks contained many of the amenities of a "traditional" campus. Although there were no College-owned dormitories, there was a range of lodgings from squalid rooming houses to luxury apartments. The local fraternities had their own quarters, more or less dilapidated, more or less permanent. There were retail clothing stores, such as Mr. Al's for men and Young's Gown Shop for women. The thirsty gathered at the Montgomery Gardens and the Chocolate Moose. The hungry ate in Laddies or bought their groceries at Papa John's across Broadway from the College Center. The all-time favorite coffee shop was Bianca's, whose warm and colorful owner endured several moves as the campus expanded.[14]

"Counter culture" students, and non-students who eschewed the intellectual work of a traditional college (the "fringies"), founded a Bohemian neighborhood in Cable Alley, in the Lair Hill region, and on Hall Street ("the Village"). There were no parking meters to deter shoppers then, and no automobiles were required for commuting, anyway. The residential neighborhood, with its inexpensive housing, coupled with the College's low tuition rates, made Portland State an institution open to students of all income levels. Of equal importance for some, it gave them a cultural community to supplement the lack of gathering places dormitories and fraternity and sorority houses furnished at traditional residential colleges.[15]

Urban renewal would destroy all of these buildings and create a kind of wasteland around the College. What remained was necessary, but the students did not let the old order go without protest. A symbol of their sympathy for the unwillingly displaced was a stand taken on behalf of "Papa" John Vlathos, owner of the City Grocery. A merchant for fifty years, Vlathos had been moved by Portland State once before, when Cramer Hall was constructed; not surprisingly, he was bitter toward the College officials, lambasting them in an interview with the *Vanguard*: "They're nothing but a bunch of hogs, they just condemn your place and take it to build another school building, and there isn't anything you can do." Students urged that an exception be made and that he be allowed to stay. To dramatize his cause, they painted a mural on his store's exterior wall, but all in vain. Papa John was gone.[16]

From the mid-1960s on, more buildings were constructed or acquired so that in 1969, when the school achieved university status, it had quite an impressive physical plant. The major new buildings were Science Building I, the Physical Education Building, Parking Structure I, the Heating Plant Building, and the Campus and Grounds Building, all completed in 1965; Millar Library in 1966; and the President's Residence, located in Dunthorpe near Lewis and Clark College, in 1969.[17]

EIGHT

Government of the New College · 1955–1969

Three men presided over Portland State College in the years
before university status was gained in 1969: John F. Cramer
(1955–58); Branford P. Millar (1959–68) (a triumvirate was
in charge for one year before he became president); and
Gregory B. Wolfe (1968–74). They were very different men in background and personality but what held their careers together at
Portland State were the myriad implications of the institution's quest
to become a university.

The irony of Cramer's administration was that it proved disappointing to the man who had so desired the presidency. Cramer entered upon his new duties shadowed by the belief of most faculty that
Stephen Epler deserved the job. Once in office, Cramer pushed forward with the building program and the curricular readjustments in
the liberal arts and in business administration required by the advent
of college status. But he did not have a happy time as president and
resigned the office on 7 March 1958. As he described the situation in
an autobiographical essay later in the year: "The presidency became
more difficult in 1958, largely due to the difficulty in getting along
with the Chancellor. He has been increasingly dictatorial, and the
strain has increased. The local Portland community—faculty, students,
parents, newspapers, legislators, employers, trade unions—all wanted
faster development and expansion of curriculum. Chancellor and
Board wanted to hold this down, to slow down enrollment and budget increases. So, as the man in the middle, I was never quite right. I
was not aggressive enough for the faculty, and did not hold things
down enough for the Chancellor [John Richards]. So I decided that
it wasn't worth it, that I would live longer as a teacher. I asked to be

relieved of the presidency." Cramer's assessment of his presidency is an accurate, if poignant, description of his service.[1]

The *Vanguard* quoted Cramer in an article on his resignation as saying, "Six years ago I had a coronary attack, and have learned to adapt myself to it. Physically I am very well, but the pressure and tension are very hard on me." However, in explaining the reasons for his resignation to the faculty, Cramer denied his health had anything to do with his resignation, leaving his listeners to read between the lines, as a report in the "Minutes" of a faculty meeting suggest: "He spoke of the excellence of his health, and referred to problems arising not within the faculty but within the state system which inevitably led to his resignation. It is his impression that closure of pathways of communication within the OSSHE hierarchy would have had a deleterious effect upon development of the college had he continued longer as its president."[2]

Following his retirement, Cramer became professor of Education. Members of the faculty and other friends raised money for his portrait, painted by Florence Heidel, which was presented to the College in 1959. But the former president did not wish to be relegated to the status of museum artifact. He took his new position seriously, rather than treating it as a sinecure, taught faithfully, and when called on by his successor, fulfilled a variety of assignments, including acting as temporary chairman of the Education Division in 1963. Cramer served as visiting professor in Hong Kong, was a consultant for the six state departments of education in Australia, and helped conduct a study for the Portland City Club. He worked almost to the day of his death, which occurred from a heart attack in October 1967. Following Cramer's resignation, a triumvirate composed of John M. Swarthout, dean of the faculty (chair), Errett Hummel (Cramer's administrative assistant), and John H. Stehn (professor of Music) directed the College for seven and one-half months.[3]

Unlike Cramer's appointment, that of his successor was made after a systematic national search by a College committee. A *Vanguard* columnist suggested the faculty Advisory Council, six professors elected by the faculty, compose the search committee, but the chancellor was not ready for that much democracy. Instead, a joint faculty-administration committee was appointed. The search committee was made up of seven faculty members (representing the ranks of assistant professor on up), the chairman of the Education Division, and the dean of students. Its first chair was Ralph Boyd, professor of Business Administration, but he withdrew when he was nominated as a candidate for the presidency. He was replaced as chair by Willard Spalding, chairman of Education. The committee organized its task into three components: a search for candidates, development of criteria and of a job description, and the final selection of persons to recommend to the chancellor. Chancellor Richards promised the Portland State faculty he would "not name or even suggest anyone for the position as president of Portland State College," saying he interpreted his role as that "of review for and recommendation to the state board." The committee hoped to have its decision by 1 June.[4]

The committee insisted the chosen candidate have a doctorate and both teaching and administrative experience, be "a recognized scholar in a subject matter field," be able to work with the faculty, and be able to "work in a metropolitan community with the people and organizations of the community." Faculty were encouraged to make nominations (as were the various learned societies) and were promised progress reports by the committee.[5]

The committee's choice for president was Branford P. Millar, a student of English literature with a doctorate from Harvard, who most recently was on the faculty of Michigan State University. Millar was an excellent choice. He was intelligent, unpretentious, principled (he had been a conscientious objector during the Second World War), and was devoted to the liberal arts as the foundation of a college or university. Able as Millar was, the College would have to wait for him, for his commitments at Michigan State did not permit him to come to Portland until the fall of 1959. In the meantime, the triumvirate who ran the College did not, unsurprisingly, launch the institution upon new waters.

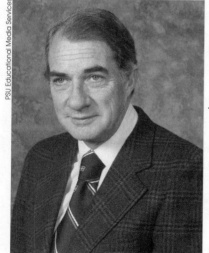

Millar's principal assistant was John M. Swarthout, the dean of the faculty, who arrived in Portland in early 1958, before Millar had been selected. Coming to Portland from Oregon State, where he had been chair of the Political Science Department, Swarthout was an intelligent, bluff, slightly world-weary adminis-

Branford P. Millar, President, 1959-68

John M. Swarthout, dean
of the College, 1958-67

trator who combined the qualities
of encouragement and gentle discipline to gain the faculty's respect on
most issues. Mildly cynical, he once
relayed to Millar a comment that
stood for his assessment of administrative duties: "The relationship of
a president to his faculty is less that
of a general to his troops; it is more
like that of a watcher at the end of a
dock to a group of seagulls circling
overhead." In turn, the faculty found Swarthout's varied business
interests a matter of amusement (or perhaps envy), especially his and
his wife's ownership of Bonnie's Burgers, a fast food business in
Northwest Portland.[6]

Swarthout's years as dean did not go unnoticed outside the institution. He was offered the opportunity to be considered for college
presidencies elsewhere, but he always declined because he wanted to
complete his work at Portland State. By July 1966, however, he had had
enough and resigned as dean, although he agreed to stay on a year
while his successor was selected. Writing to a fellow administrator shortly after his resignation, Swarthout declared: "In part I want to get back
to being a political scientist, but in all honesty to you, if not to everybody else, I have got to add that I am sick and tired of what I am doing."[7]

Another important administrator, one who bridged the Cramer-
Millar years, was Willard Spalding. A former superintendent of the
Portland public school system (1944–47) and dean of the College of
Education at the University of Illinois (1947–52), Spalding came to
Portland State in 1952. He served as chair of the Division of Education,
acting dean of the faculty, and chair of the search committee that
selected Millar. Indeed, it was he who had submitted Millar's name to
the search committee. Two years after Spalding resigned in 1963 to
become associate director of the Coordinating Council for Higher
Education in California, Swarthout summed up his contribution to the
College (and something of his personality) in a letter of recommendation: "Old Willard was known hereabouts as the gray fox during his
tenure locally, and he earned it." More important as a contribution to

the College than his wiliness was Spalding's insistence the teacher-training curriculum be made a College-wide responsibility, rather than simply that of the Division of Education. During his tenure at Portland State, Spalding's distinction as an educator was recognized, among other ways, as Inglis Lecturer at the Harvard Graduate School of Education (1953) and as visiting professor at that institution in 1963.[8]

To succeed Swarthout, Millar chose Howard Boroughs as dean of the faculty in February 1967. Although he had not taught much during his career, Boroughs had held a range of administrative and research positions at the University of Hawaii, the Institute of Agricultural Sciences of the Organization of American States, the National Science Foundation, and the U. S. Office of Education. Beginning his career in the last year of President Millar's regime, Boroughs continued as dean into the presidency of Gregory B. Wolfe. Boroughs's title, dean of the faculties, was slightly different from that of his predecessor; a change, he said, "indicative of our becoming a university." In an early interview with the *Vanguard*, the new dean proclaimed one of his ambitions was to tear down walls between divisions and departments with a "bulldozer," figurative destruction that would also help the institution attain university status. He also wanted to break down barriers between students and faculty, regretting that "only now the students are getting involved in faculty committees." As it turned out, however, Boroughs was remarkably ineffective in his tenure in office. As the College expanded its student enrollment and diversified its curriculum leading to university status, presidents shuffled the structure of their executive councils. When Millar was inaugurated, he inherited an Administrative Council composed of the deans, the business manager, and other high administrators. But on 30 October 1963, he decided to abolish it: "The Administrative Council henceforth will cease to exist. The meetings of the president with his staff members representing the various service and academic areas shall be known as the Executive Committee." In the realm of administration, rather than advice and counsel, Millar also rearranged and added personnel to the executive office by dividing authority among the dean of faculty, the dean of students, and a new business manager (former Vanport student and future chancellor, W. T. Lemman, Jr.), and by appointing E. Dean Anderson as his executive assistant.[9]

In early 1960, Millar began to shape the academic direction of the College by appointing an Educational Policies Committee. This was a high-level body (known somewhat cynically to the faculty as "the blue ribbon committee") that was to chart the course of the curriculum for the decade ahead. Composed of Millar, Swarthout, the four division chairmen (Arts and Letters, Education, Science, and Social Science), and four faculty members appointed by the president from nominations made by the divisional chairs, it demonstrated the interest and personal commitment of Millar to the institution's basic academic purpose.[10]

Deliberations of the Educational Policies Committee were one source of the academic reorganization of the College that took place during the 1964–65 academic year. But the roots of it went deeper in time, probably as early as there had developed any realistic hopes of Portland State becoming a university. For example, in a thoughtful letter to Dean Swarthout in June 1962, Willard Spalding argued the structure of the College should not be the result of hasty decision but rather of wide reading and deep thought to attempt to relate structure to some or all of the following: the object and process of academic study; the social institutions served by the College; and the fundamental attributes of mankind, e.g., language. In addition to considering the specific bases for any decision about structure, Spalding made an even more important point for the shaping of Portland State:

> Despite a brief recent history of battle, with consequent psychic scars, we must begin to act like what we will become, a great university guided by our sense of purpose. We cannot continue to act as less than the equal of OSU and the University of Oregon, suspicious of them at all times, fearful that they will outwit us. We need to think of OSSHE as in truth a system, with responsibilities to the metropolitan area, and welcome the System's strengthening of graduate work in it. Our internal structure as a university must reflect our new perceptions.[11]

Not until more than two years after Spalding's letter was written did the College conclude anything about governmental reorganization. After long discussions, the Educational Policies Committee in June 1964 approved a position description for a "dean" of a division or school (to replace the title of "chairman") and another for a "head" of a department (to replace the title of "executive officer"). This allocation of responsibility under the new positions represented a compromise between those on the committee who wished to retain a divisional structure without departments and those who wanted to abandon the division without giving up departments.[12]

In a letter to Millar in August, Swarthout accepted and broadened this compromise. He proposed a school of liberal arts to include divisions of humanities, science, and social science, each headed by a dean who would report to the dean of the faculty (there would be no separate dean of this school). The professional divisions (business and education) would attain the status already possessed by social work, that of a "school." Swarthout made his case for this arrangement on several grounds. First, it was practiced at such institutions as Washington State University, the University of Chicago, and several of the California state colleges, such as San Jose State College. Second, it was preferable to eliminating divisions, because the loss of them would make administration unwieldy. And thirdly, the absence of divisions was contrary to Portland State's history. "I also believe," he wrote, "that the elimination of divisions, to leave all liberal arts departments directly responsible to a single official, would be unwise in view both of the large problem of span of control that would appear and of the historical legacy established here over many years and now pretty well embedded in our people." Finally, he maintained when the College became a university, it might be desirable to make the "schools" into "colleges."[13]

A month later, Swarthout summed up the purpose of the position descriptions agreed to by the Educational Policies Committee in June. In general, he wrote, they "call for increased decentralization of authority from the College administration and a commensurable assumption of increased responsibility at both school and department level." But how, he wondered, to shuffle the departmental blocks into the appropriate school or divisional building? Swarthout's answer was to bring together the liberal arts and the professions related to them (for example, political science and public administration) into three schools: the humanities and fine arts; the sciences, basic and applied; and the social sciences, also basic and applied.[14]

Although a powerful figure, Swarthout did not get his way in this matter. At a meeting on 22 April 1965, the Council of Academic Administrators recommended, and President Millar subsequently agreed, that the liberal arts and the professional programs were not to be combined into the three schools Swarthout proposed. The familiar was to continue; the old divisions remained and social work, business, and education units were to remain in separate bailiwicks. The divisional chairmen were retitled deans and were required to consult "with appropriate faculty members" before appointing the department heads, an increase in the powers of the teaching faculty over the position descriptions of June 1964.[15]

Although when Millar presented the plan to him he "detected a little squirming on Lew's [Chancellor Roy M. Lieuallen] part—I hope we don't have a problem." The chancellor did not object to the reorganization, which went into effect in June 1965. The only remaining business was to rename the assembly of academic administrators that now comprised the deans of schools and divisions, the dean and the associate dean of the faculty, the graduate dean, and the directors of international programs and program analysis. Swarthout's nomenclature proposal was accepted: "I propose that the groups be called henceforth 'Council of Academic Deans,' in short, CADS. This name would seem to be both descriptive in its full form and peculiarly appropriate in its short form in view of the normal attitudes of college faculty toward the authority represented individually and collectively by the body's membership."[16]

As the administration reorganized to meet the needs of growth in these years, so, too, did the faculty strive to enlarge its authority. In 1960, responding to this pressure, President Millar appointed a committee under the chairmanship of David Malcolm, professor of Biology, to revise the constitution. The charge of this committee was, as quoted in the faculty minutes: "To clarify passages in the constitution regarding faculty committees, the faculty senate, and the Graduate Council. Provisions for a graduate faculty must be considered in view of the changing character of the college. The areas of apparent overlap between committees and councils will receive serious attention." The committee asked the members of the faculty senate for their suggestions for revising the constitution, and a questionnaire for this purpose was later distributed to the entire faculty.[17]

In May 1961, a draft of the revised constitution was ready for study by the faculty, which held open hearings on it. It took several months for the revisions to make their way through the Advisory Council and to the floor of a special faculty meeting in January 1962. Here, it was discussed at some length, with the major point of contention being who was a member of the voting faculty. The draft had defined faculty members who could vote and be eligible for election to the senate as all those who did "at least fifty percent teaching, research, or administration." This definition excluded the librarians (except for the head librarian, who was specifically included). Naturally, they objected to their second-class status and were able to get a motion passed to drop the exclusionary definition. On 28 February 1962, in another special meeting, the faculty adopted unanimously the revised constitution.[18]

Constitutional revision next came to the fore in 1966. It arose out of a discussion in the faculty senate about the role and function of the Scholastic Standards Committee that led to consideration of "giving the committees more responsibility on policy formulation and less responsibility in the area of doing detailed clerical work." In turn, faculty began talking in the senate of revising the constitution to accomplish this purpose. The faculty voted to ask the Advisory Council to suggest the president appoint an *ad hoc* committee to be responsible for recommending constitutional revisions. In the course of the discussion, Millar suggested an all-university conference—based on one recently held at the University of California—at which position papers would be presented for general discussion on such topics as: "(1) An analysis of faculty governance at selected colleges and universities; (2) A constitutional history of faculty governance at Portland State College; and (3) Desiderata for a new constitution and system of governance."[19]

The next month, Millar wrote to the faculty explaining his reasons for calling the all-university conference—reasons that included all of the internal problems associated with growth, the increased size of the administrative bureaucracy, and the consequent loss of intimacy related to a college that only recently had no departmental majors, no organized departments, and no graduate curriculum. Millar also declared there were external reasons for rethinking the governmental structures, such as demands for services from the outside; faculty mobility in an era of great demand for faculty; and a national concern about the role of higher education. More specifically, the president called attention to the need to address such problems as the infrequent meetings of the entire faculty; overrepresentation of ex-officio administrative officers in the faculty senate; the lack of definition of the responsibility of certain committees (such as General Student Affairs); the immense load of detailed work laid on other committees (such as Academic Requirements), which prevented them from turning attention to policy-making; insufficient communication among faculty and between faculty, administrators, and committees; and lack of encouragement of students to contribute to College decisions. In a second letter to the faculty on 25 January 1967, Millar announced he was calling an all-university conference, with student participation. He appointed committees, under the general chairmanship of Gordon Hearn, dean of the School of Social Work, to prepare for the conference.[20]

The conference was taken seriously, and many faculty and staff members put a great deal of work into it. Perhaps the most important committee was that on Constitutional Goals, which called for faculty comment on the matters of faculty powers and authority; academic freedom and faculty rights; faculty organization; and faculty-student relationships. The College librarians, always fearful of exclusion from voting membership in the faculty, were delighted with the choice of one committee member. As librarian Jean Black put it: "Ed Gnoza was elected as one of the five members of the constitution committee....The perennial tendency of 'classroom' faculty to consider themselves as something special and to desire to discriminate against other faculty has again reared its ugly head. With Ed on the committee we know that our interests will be protected there, whatever may come when the constitution comes up for vote." Although a useful idea, the conference got off on the wrong foot when an article appeared in the *Oregonian* reporting on a press conference Millar had held to announce it. The lead paragraph stated the conference's purpose was "to head off Berkeley-type student riots at Portland State College." The *Oregonian* story said nothing about revising the constitution.[21]

Preparation for the conference was thorough and inclusive. The student government chose fifteen students to participate. To focus conference discussions, four position papers were presented on: the history of faculty governance at the College; patterns of faculty governance in general; goals and issues for the College; and on the decision-making process for choosing the architect for Science Building II, presumably a case study of college governance. The conference was opened by a panel discussion of the topic, "The System of External Constraints within which Faculty Governance Must Operate in a Public University." The following day, the position papers were discussed in nine separate groups, and, on the last day, resolutions were adopted to establish a Constitutional Drafting Committee.[22]

The Constitutional Drafting Committee, under the chairmanship of Frank Giese, professor of Foreign Languages, moved quickly. In October 1967, it provided an amendment to the current faculty constitution that would change the definition of voting faculty. Voting in faculty meetings would now be confined to those actually engaged in the teaching of at least one course. It would also remove non-teaching administrators from eligibility to serve in the faculty senate. But the amendment was tabled by the faculty.[23]

The draft of the full constitution was released to the faculty in April 1968. On the contentious issues of faculty membership and voting privileges, it defined voting faculty as those "whose major function is the teaching of courses...or the conduct of scholarly research." The existing constitution gave the franchise to all who held the rank of instructor or above and were engaged in teaching, research, or administration at least half time. Under the new proposed constitution, the faculty senate would consist of thirty-five members, one for each twenty members of the faculty. The existing constitution included the major administrators as voting members of the senate and had based teaching faculty representation on a figure of one for each ten members of the faculty.[24]

Besides trimming the voting power of administrators, the major change in the new constitution was to take formal note of the rights and responsibilities of students. Two student representatives were permitted to sit on all committees, except for the Graduate Council. In terms of committee structure, the new constitution contained six regular committees and two special committees (the existing constitution also had eight committees). There were four councils in the new document (instead of three in the old) and three boards (instead of none).[25]

One who was not impressed with the new constitution was Howard Boroughs, dean of the faculties. After looking over the draft, Boroughs wrote to Millar stating his objections: the top administrators would lose power to the faculty councils; the administrators would be left with diminished duties and, thus, might resign and their replacements might be hard to find ("Portland State College would have to get another Dean of Faculties"); the new powers of the faculty would take time away from their teaching and advising; it would also increase faculty workload, as the constitution required "faculty" approval for any contracts with outside agencies; and a two-thirds majority of the senate could create or abolish a school or division.[26]

The faculty began considering the constitution on 16 May 1968. Frank Giese, chair of the drafting committee, moved for the adoption of the constitution. He began his defense of it by admitting the entire process of presenting a new constitution—as it was based on the election of the drafting committee at the informal constitutional conference of March 1967—was unconstitutional, since it was not based on any provision in the existing constitution. Nevertheless, Giese continued, the committee accepted its "wide-open charge to produce a draft constitution for this institution." He added the committee had pro-

duced a realistic document, not a utopian one, a document that did
not attempt to give all power to the faculty or define community-col-
lege relationships or deal with the general good of higher education.
Giese stated the committee's awareness of the binding constraints of
the *Administrative Rules* and of state law. And although he disclaimed
any desire to "seize power" for the faculty, he did state "an effort has
been made in the general direction of increasing the faculty voice in
the governance of the institution."[27]

The drafting committee, Giese reminded his listeners, worked
mainly from experience, not from theory, holding hearings open to
all faculty; examining other constitutions (those of Southern Oregon
State College, the University of Minnesota, and the University of Ohio
at Bowling Green were the most useful); consulting recommendations
made by the national office of the American Association of University
Professors; and scrutinizing conditions at Portland State. On the basis
of this testimony and study, Giese reported the principal changes from
the current constitution: a senate reduced in number from sixty to
thirty-five members; a steering committee to organize senate business;
a better-defined sense of responsibility for faculty bodies (the senate
would make most decisions, leaving the faculty as a review body).[28]

Turning to structure, the major change was in creating four councils based on the model of the existing Graduate Council. These bodies—the Graduate Council, the Undergraduate Council, the Council
of Student Affairs, and the Council of Administrative and Institutional
Development, and their subcommittees—would recommend policy to
the senate. There were also three boards that handled student funds
and eight committees of the senate. Of the last, the two most important were the Budget Committee and the faculty Welfare Committee.
The Budget Committee was proposed by the AAUP, modeled on a
committee at the University of Washington. The Advisory Council was
abolished, although one function of it—recommending members of
committees to the president—would be given to a new "Committee
on Committees." The presidential advisory function of the Advisory
Council would go to a new committee composed of the heads of the
four councils and the elected chair of the senate. Giese then reviewed
the criticisms of the draft that maintained both too much and too little had been changed. The most contentious issue was the definition
of the faculty; he said it had been discussed extensively by the committee for several months. Other criticisms were that the faculty was
usurping administrative power; that there would be too many faculty

on committees; and that it did not spell out carefully enough the manner of electing departmental chairs.[29]

When the actual debate opened after Giese's preliminary remarks, the librarians were soon able to get themselves defined as faculty members by amending the constitution to include certain staff members within the definition of faculty. The faculty at this meeting also decided to keep faculty meetings open to the press, unless closed by a two-thirds vote. The faculty resumed deliberations on 21 May. It first decided to provide for mail ballots on any main motion if requested by two-thirds of the faculty. The faculty agreed to the election of departmental chairs (or their selection after consultation with departmental members in special circumstances). The faculty met again on 28 May and on 8 October. By this time, there was a new president, Gregory Wolfe, who took a somewhat more optimistic view of the constitution than had his immediate subordinate, Howard Boroughs. In his inaugural speech in September 1968—while the new constitution was still being discussed—Wolfe praised the section that prohibited the president from presiding over the senate but expressed a concern that if the faculty is "to remain the center of gravity in matters of learning,...it must seek ways of allowing the college community into the orbit of judicial and political power." Presumably, he meant to permit students more authority, but this was not spelled out. Regardless of anyone's intentions, however, what came of all this was a bit anticlimactic. The new constitution was never adopted by the faculty (although portions were accepted at this time and through the years), and the University still functions under the constitution of 1962.[30]

As the College changed its curriculum during these years, the governmental structures below the faculty level needed to be reshaped. This meant the creation of departments within the divisional and school structures that were the original administrative organizations beyond the executive branch. The departmental structures were first authorized in 1960, with eight departments serving as the pioneers: Biology, English, Foreign Languages, Geography, History, Mathematics, Physics, and Psychology. They were joined in 1961 by Art, Chemistry, Economics, Music, Philosophy, Political Science, and Sociology. In 1962, Earth Sciences joined the ranks; Speech and Theater Arts attained departmental status in 1964; and Anthropology in 1965. (The unusual name "Earth Sciences" was necessitated by the University of Oregon's objection to having two "Geology" departments in the state.) All these structural changes followed, it should be emphasized, the creation of departmental majors.[31]

Not until January 1962 did anyone grapple with how departments should conduct their affairs and what powers they should possess. This first attempt was a discursive discussion by the Educational Policies Committee that was frankly summarized by its secretary: "There was a certain lack of focus throughout the whole discussion and the meeting ended on a questioning note." After discussing other options to the existing departmental arrangements (giving greater power to the department head; preserving the status quo; and de-emphasizing the department by concentrating greater power at the divisional level), "there seemed to be general agreement that such departmentalization as we have already experienced here at Portland State has been desirable, and that it has in fact facilitated the ends and objectives of administration." The discussion also touched on subjects that would become perennial: the perhaps artificial distinctions between fields of knowledge; the desirability of joint listing of courses between or among departments; and the matter of joint appointments.[32]

The same committee returned to the matter of departmentalization in two further meetings, with the conclusions being that distinct fields of knowledge required departments—that, in effect, departments were here to stay—but that they would not replace divisions. So far as their authority was concerned, the Educational Policies Committee agreed informally that departments would "bear primary responsibility for" recruitment of staff; origin of recommendations for promotion and pay raises; development and maintenance of standards of productivity and welfare for its staff; curriculum development; and encouragement to carry on research.[33]

In fall 1962, the Educational Policies Committee returned to the discussion of the department when it received a paper written by Willard Spalding entitled, "The Place of the Department in the University." This thoughtful essay assumed the continuation of the department as an administrative unit although, as Spalding wrote, this may be "an assumption which may prove to be incorrect in view of the innumerable institutes, centers, and other units which are flourishing in other universities." But if the department was to continue, then—according to Spalding's plan—it would have to be modified so that the heads of divisions and schools would assume additional administrative responsibilities (although he did not specify what they were), leaving the department head with three charges: "stimulating faculty scholarship;" "recruiting and employing faculty;" and "promoting and dismissing faculty."[34]

The importance of the role of the department and its head is indicated by the time it took to reach any conclusion about them. Over a year after the presentation of the Spalding essay, a majority of the Educational Policies Committee agreed on at least one other matter: the department should have full responsibility for appointing new staff members below the rank of associate professor but that "associate and full professors should require prior approval at the school and college level."[35]

In February 1964, the same committee wrestled again with the place of the department. It began with a historical survey of how the current department heads (who were called "executive officers" at the time) had assumed their positions. Some had been appointed by deans; some had been elected. Most department heads held office at the pleasure of their division heads, but some were elected for two-year terms. Committee members then grappled with what title should be given to the chief administrator of a department ("head", "chairman," or "executive officer"); how and by whom they should be selected; their responsibilities; and how they were to be evaluated. There was great concern—and the only one about which a clear conclusion was reached at the meeting—about how to choose a department executive: "It was felt that in no case should a faculty recommendation be considered an 'election'"—only so far should democracy be carried. By June, a draft statement for a department head had been put together. The establishment of departments had other than structural results. It tended to restrict curricular innovation by making it more difficult to develop inter-disciplinary courses and to discourage other pedagogical experiments. Tradition and the desire to organize like a "real" university prevailed over innovation. There were changes in the faculty senate in the 1960s also. As with his predecessors, Millar had always presided over the senate. Although popular with most faculty, Millar's loquacity sometimes impeded the progress of senate business. Soon after Gregory Wolfe became president, Whitney Bates (History) suggested to him the senate elect its own presiding officer. Wolfe considered the matter. Finally, the same proposal came from the AAUP chapter and Wolfe agreed. Later, to expedite its business, the senate in 1971 adopted a suggestion by James Hart (English) to form an elective steering committee.[36]

One of the attractive features of university life, although sometimes a confusing one to both academics and outsiders, is the blurring of roles among faculty, administrators, and students. Their work is not neatly compartmentalized, respectively, into teaching, administering, and studying. Nowhere is this overlapping more evident than in the committee structure, which involves both housekeeping and policy making. In the years now under discussion, committees did an enormous amount of work as enrollments increased, graduate work was added, and new programs begun. The Curriculum, Teacher Education, and Scholastic Standards committees, and later the Graduate Council, were heavily overburdened. And although this work was arduous and important—and often insufficiently recognized when tenure, pay, and promotion decisions were made—it was work that always had been expected.

The most controversial dimension of committee work was not policy, but structure. This was the question of whether or not students should serve on committees. It arose in the late 1960s due to the conviction of students around the world that they should have more influence on shaping their societies, including the university. Beginning in the United States with the civil rights movement, flaring spectacularly with the student demonstrations at the University of California at Berkeley in 1964, and inflamed by the Vietnam War, the student as "activist" became a national type, familiar to viewers of television news and denounced by many as a "potsmoking," destructive anarchist. (For the opposition of Portland State students to the war, see chapters fourteen and sixteen.) Part of that story was the desire of students to assume places on committees at Portland State.

Indeed, students had served on committees as early as 1958, when they took their places on the Assemblies, Convocation and Forum; Intercollegiate Athletics; Student Affairs; College Center; and Publications committees. These committees were open to students, presumably because they affected the extra-curricular realm where students were judged competent to have a say. But committees affecting curricular matters were not open to them. A student gained a committee assignment through appointment by the dean of the faculty. In 1960, Asher Wilson of the Theater Arts Department suggested students be made "consulting" (presumably, non-voting) members of the Library Committee, but its members, after discussing his proposal, concluded: "Though there was some difference of opinion, the Committee was rather convinced that little was to be gained by student representation. Since student interests generally could be expected to fall within the area of library practices (which are within the province of the Librarian), the contribution of students to the policy-making functions of the Committee was questionable."[37]

A turning point on this issue came when Portland State was accredited in 1965. The accrediting team faulted the College for not having students on faculty committees. Alluding specifically to "the lessons" of Berkeley, the accreditors asked the College "to carefully review the possibility of students as members of selected college communities." Based on experience elsewhere, the report stated, "there will be disappointment at times over individual students' performances as committee members but the general experience in this area suggests that benefits sharply outweigh any potential disadvantages."[38]

Student interest in influencing curricular matters through committee membership was manifested in the next month with a request for membership on the Curriculum Committee. As in the case of the Library Committee six years earlier, the committee's response was not positive: "The committee was not ready to ask representatives of the student body to sit in Committee meetings; however, when the Committee felt it advisable to gain student point-of-view on specific questions, the Committee would extend an invitation to student representatives to appear before the Committee to provide pertinent information and answer questions." In April 1966, the School of Education chose (by members of its faculty) a forty-member "council" of students, a plan initiated by Walton Manning, a professor in the school. The council was a recommendatory body, whose suggestions would be regarded as advisory, but not binding.[39]

The breakthrough for students came on 3 October 1966, when the faculty senate opened committees to them. The vote was the culmination of deliberations by the General Student Affairs Committee (GSAC). In its report to the senate, GSAC recommended students be made voting members of all existing committees (a total of fourteen), except the Elections and Research and Publications committees (since they dealt only with faculty matters) and—though temporarily—the Scholastic Standards Committee and the Graduate Council, committees apparently judged unsuitable for student participation without further discussion. Since the faculty constitution was in the process of revision, GSAC recommended an *ad hoc* committee of an equal number of both students and faculty be formed to consider the question of student participation on committees. In the meantime, students would be appointed to committees in much the same manner as were faculty members. They were to be nominated by student government officers and by school and department heads to the Advisory Council, which in turn made recommendations to the president, who made the appointment. After extensive discussion, the senate voted to accept the committee recommendation by a vote of twenty-five to fourteen, adding to the committee recommendation only that the number of students on the *ad hoc* committee be limited to two, thus ensuring the faculty of majority status. Joe Uris, president of the Associated Students, was clearly delighted with the outcome, labeling it as a "major breakthrough" and a "wonderful opportunity."[40]

This did not end the matter, however, for it proceeded to a special meeting of the full faculty. It remained a live issue because Marjorie Nelson and Arthur Boggs of the English Department convinced enough of their faculty colleagues to sign a petition to call for the special meeting. Some faculty members who signed the petition believed the senate action went too far; others opposed it completely; while still others wanted to define differently the committees for which the students were eligible. Boggs, for example, had two objections to students serving on committees: "On principle, I feel that most faculty committees are not the place for students. Secondly, I feel that I could not express myself frankly and honestly in a committee where students were present."[41]

The special faculty meeting took place in November. The meeting opened with consideration of a request—passed unanimously—that Associated Students president Joe Uris be allowed to address the faculty. The chairman of the Student Affairs Committee then presented his recommendations, as modified by the senate. Uris spoke, as did several of the faculty. The faculty then passed by voice vote a motion (modified in two ways from the one the senate had adopted) permitting students to serve only on "some" committees and giving the student government officers the sole right to nominate student members for committee service.[42]

Whether students in the years ahead found committee membership as satisfying and effective as its proponents had hoped in 1966 is an unanswerable question. In later years, not a great many students rushed to serve on committees, and, at times, there were vacancies. But in the context of the 1960s and early 1970s, as dissent and protests reached unprecedented heights, the presence of student committee members was probably a force in helping to solve the problems of the University community.

At the departmental level, students also expressed a desire for involvement. In 1967, the Speech Department was the first to permit students to serve on its committees. The English Department followed in 1968, when it opened three of its five standing committees to voting students members: the Curriculum and Undergraduate Requirements, the Composition, and the Departmental Activities committees. The History Department took a slightly different approach in November 1969, by naming a committee of five faculty to investigate how it could involve students in its operations. The committee held an open hearing and follow-up discussions, and, in time, students did attend departmental meetings.[43]

"I'm busy even when I'm depressed."

NINE

The Undergraduate Curriculum · 1955–1969

Regardless of college government structure, no one could gainsay the fact that the main responsibility of most faculty was teaching. And among the most arduous of the many heavy tasks of Portland State College faculty after 1955 was to shape a curriculum that would somehow meet the needs of an emerging college and a prospective university. What they accomplished was remarkable. Teaching a twelve- to fifteen-hour load, advising numerous students, and carrying heavy committee assignments, the faculty developed a curriculum for undergraduate departmental majors, established programs for Middle East studies, created a separate school of business administration, began a study-abroad center, trained students for the Peace Corps, and assumed College-wide responsibility for the training of elementary and secondary teachers, all at the undergraduate level, while at the same time seeing the College through three accreditation reviews.

Pressure for departmental majors came from students and faculty alike. Although the many students who were going into teaching were satisfied with the broad divisional majors, others wanted the depth provided by traditional liberal arts majors. The first step toward this goal was taken at a faculty meeting on 6 November 1957, when the faculty was preparing a discussion statement for a forthcoming meeting with Chancellor John Richards. Among its requests for the development of Portland State was a "half loaf." This would be a divisional major with a subject matter emphasis. For example, a student might be awarded a bachelor's degree in humanities with a major in English. Nothing came of this idea, but, the following April, Willard Spalding, acting dean of the faculty, wrote to the chancellor asking for departmental majors in fifteen areas. He was willing to delay the request for two of them—Art and Music—for a reason of expediency by now familiar to supporters of Portland State: "Though no evidence that we can find supports the claim that Portland State College diverts students from two of the specialized schools of the University of Oregon [presumably, the Schools of Music and Architecture and Allied Arts at Eugene], we shall not press for immediate authorization to offer majors in art and music."[1] In May 1958, Spalding did represent the College before the state board. He made the point that his colleagues were continuing the broad mission of general education by developing additional divisional courses at the upper as well as lower divisional levels, but he also reiterated a point he made in an earlier letter to the chancellor—the time for departmental majors was at hand. More specifically, Spalding asked the board to develop a chronological schedule of appropriations so the College could plan its future in this area as well as others.[2]

The board concurred, and planning for departmental majors began during the 1958–59 academic year. The first disciplinary majors were in Business Administration, English, Foreign Languages and Literature, Geography, History, Mathematics, Physics, Psychology, and Teacher Education. The faculty senate approved the creation of a major in Anthropology and another in Speech-Theater Arts in May 1961. President Millar remarked, "With the passage of the two majors the college has reached the point where it had most of the liberal arts majors in its total program. Perhaps the goal now should be to think about refining the programs that are in existence instead of adding new curricula." This suggestion was followed as the curriculum continued to expand (as will be noted later), especially in the graduate realm.[3]

In addition to moving in traditional curricular directions with the establishment of liberal arts majors, the College began to innovate. The first important step in the study abroad program was the establishment of the Middle East Studies Center. This institution demonstrated the continuing interest of the federal government in Portland State; was the first step in including "exotic languages" in a student's program; and initiated academic "centers," rather than the traditional departments or divisions as foci of intellectual endeavor. It was also important in demonstrating the influence of Frederick J. Cox, professor of History, as an astute and crafty academic entrepreneur. The Middle East Studies Center was one of innumerable results of one of the most influential laws in the history of American higher education.

Stung by the Soviet Union's success in rocketry and weaponry (first demonstrated with the lofting of Sputnik in the fall of 1957), the American public demanded Congress and the president do something to catch up. One response was the National Defense Education Act (NDEA) of 1958, drafted with important contributions by two Oregon legislators: Sen. Wayne L. Morse and Congresswoman Edith Green. A portion of Title VI of that act provided for the establishment and operation of language and area centers to accomplish two objectives: the teaching of "uncommon" languages, and the understanding of those areas of the world where such languages were used. Presumably, Congress was thinking of competing more vigorously with the Soviet Union for the allegiance of nations and cultures uncommitted to either side in the Cold War struggle and of creating experts for work in those countries, including the gathering of intelligence.[4]

Professor Cox seized this opportunity. In November 1958, a representative of the Department of Health, Education, and Welfare (HEW) came to Portland to hold a conference with those interested in establishing NDEA language centers. Several faculty and administrators, including Cox and Frank Eaton, executive officer of the College's Foreign Language Department, attended the meeting. Events moved rapidly after the conference. In January 1959, the College established a committee under Cox's chairmanship to explore the possibility of establishing a Middle East Studies Center at Portland State. In June, the College obtained the consent of the chancellor for the first course to be offered—first-year Arabic—in order to justify the grant application to HEW for a center. Later in the month, Dean Swarthout appointed Cox as acting director of a Middle East Studies Center at the College for the purpose of planning its activities. Neither the College's Curriculum Committee nor the faculty as a whole had anything to do with these developments. Although this may have reflected the pressure of time, rather than administrative Machiavellianism, it became a precedent for the creation of future centers and institutes by administrative fiat without faculty participation. In spite of the hurry, the work was in vain, as the government turned down the College's request.[5]

From the summer of 1959 to February 1960, Cox worked with the Curriculum Committee, the chancellor, and other administrators to prepare another application to HEW. Hoyt Franchere, chair of the Division of Arts and Letters, conferred in Washington, D.C., with HEW officials and with Congresswoman Green and Sen. Richard L. Neuberger. By the end of February, the College's proposal was accepted by HEW, and $25,019 was granted for the first year of operation. Portland State was one of three undergraduate centers announced at this time, the others being the University of Arizona and the University of Iowa. In July, Cox was appointed director of the Center.[6]

During the first year of operations, 1960–61, the Center program enrolled fifty-two students in the Arabic language; instruction in Hebrew was also provided. There were visiting lecturers brought to Portland; a workshop was held for high school social studies teachers; and an eight-week summer session took place. A student organization was founded, books, periodicals, and newspapers were added to the College library, and four undergraduate scholarships, funded by members of the Portland community, were established. There were five faculty members on the area side of the program and four faculty teaching languages, although not all were full-time appointees in the Center. Twelve courses were offered in area studies (from the disciplines of Anthropology, Geography, Economics, and History) and twenty-three in languages.[7]

While the Center was getting underway in Portland, Cox had greater ambitions. He drew up a proposal for an American Universities Center for Middle East Studies in Cairo and arranged a conference on that subject in New York City in the fall of 1961. Dean Swarthout was enormously impressed with this proposal and with Cox. If the Cairo center was implemented and financed with federal and foundation funds, he wrote to Millar, it would cost Portland State little money ("chicken feed"), but the gains would be great in prestige, contacts with important persons, support in materials, and opportunities for Center staff to spend time in the Middle East. Swarthout concluded his letter with a tribute to his fellow academic imperialist: "Godamighty, what imagination, energy, and willingness to leap can do for an institution! The amount of mileage we're getting out of practically no cost except in the blood, sweat, and tears of a few of our better guys is astronomical. Sir Hamilton Gibbs [director of the Middle Eastern Studies Center at Harvard] no less, was in New York for a short spell of the Conference, and all the Big Boys wanted to get at him. They couldn't; he was closeted with Fred Cox, finding out all about Portland State instead."[8]

The American Research Center in Egypt was established in July 1963. The purpose of the Research Center was to provide funds for faculty to study all phases of Islamic history and culture. Portland State was a member of the original consortium of universities that founded it along with Columbia, Harvard, Michigan, Princeton, and UCLA.

The consortium's representatives worked on a proposal in 1961 and 1962, and in the latter year requested funds from the State Department to fund the Center. The State Department agreed to expend approximately $500,000 over a five-year period for the consortium's use.[9]

By the end of the 1967–68 academic year, the Middle East Studies Center had become an important component—perhaps the most important component—of international education at Portland State. The graduating class of 1968 included eighty-six students who had taken some Middle Eastern work during the course of their undergraduate studies. More than half of them were majors from three departments: Foreign Languages and Literatures; Political Science; and History. In a longer perspective, since the Center had opened in 1961, twenty-nine students had been awarded competitive grants or scholarships or Peace Corps assignments in the Middle East. The Center cooperated with the staff of Woodrow Wilson High School in Portland in teaching Arabic; Wilson was one of only eight high schools in the United States offering instruction in this language. What became, in time, a program for instruction of foreign students in the English language began in the Middle East Studies Center. The Center cooperated with five other universities in offering on a rotating basis an intensive summer program in Arabic studies. The Center established in 1964 a summer program in Cairo to enhance the Arabic language capabilities of American scholars.[10]

The successes of the Middle East Studies Center were based on the availability of government funds, the interests of students, and the energy and astuteness of Frederick Cox. There was another ingredient in its success. This was the fact that the Center did not have courses or teaching faculty separate from the academic departments. It was not a rival of them; it offered no degree, although students could take a certificate to complement a degree in their own discipline. The Center, in other words, was not regarded by faculty as a threat to their traditional domains.

Another curricular innovation of the 1950s was the honors program. On 5 November 1958, the faculty established a committee to plan an honors program. Chaired by Carl E. W. L. Dahlstrom of the English Department, the committee moved with speed unusual for a faculty committee and gave its first report to Dean Swarthout in May 1959. After considering three types of honors common in American colleges and universities—grade distinctions; accelerated and intensified specialization in specific disciplines; and "a program of acceleration with additional special curricula for the achievement of intellectual excellence and maturity but with a general or broad 'liberal arts emphasis'"—it recommended the third type of program, adding prudently for a financially short institution, "providing adequate faculty time is available and administrative policies are favorable."[11]

The committee noted the importance of admitting only intellectually capable students into the program; furnishing them a broad program of studies, but one studied in depth; and encouraging the honors students to pursue graduate degrees. Sophomore students with a minimum cumulative grade-point average of 3.0 would be admitted to the program if they possessed "those personal and intellectual attributes conducive to the successful completion of the Program." The program was to be established and guided by an Honors Program Council headed by a director. The committee report was transmitted to the faculty in November 1959.[12]

Two days later, the Honors Committee met again. It decided, in order to maintain momentum, to recommend to Swarthout and President Millar the appointment of a director of the honors program. This individual—with the consent of the College administration—would then appoint the members of the council, who, in turn, would develop the program. Work on an honors program, incidentally, produced one of the rare instances of willingness of the University of Oregon to cooperate with Portland State. At this time, the U of O was contemplating founding an honors college, and Robert D. Clark, dean of the College of Liberal Arts, was happy to send information to Portland State because "if all of us can develop special programs and present a united front to the board and the legislature, we may be able to get the extra funds that we shall so much need."[13]

The strategy for gaining an honors program soon changed. Hoyt Franchere, the dean of the Arts and Letters Division, wrote to Dahlstrom saying, in effect, the committee had the cart before the horse. Franchere recommended the committee work out an honors program in some detail—in regard to both cost and curriculum—before the president could go to the chancellor to gain approval for it and its director. The example of the University of Oregon was invoked, as Franchere concluded his letter: "I understand that this is precisely what President Meredith Wilson did at the University of Oregon which now has an honors college." By this time, the hope for some type of honors program had enough life that—on Dahlstrom's recommendation to Franchere—Frederick Waller of the English Department was given released time during the 1960 spring term to plan an honors program and an advanced placement system. Waller was chosen because he seemed to be the only faculty member with actual experience in an honors program. In March, the Dahlstrom committee was discharged from its responsibility.[14]

At the end of the month, a new five-person committee was assigned to study an honors program. Brock Dixon, the assistant dean of the faculty, and Waller were to conduct an investigation into "a way to meet the needs of our superior student." Their report was to become the basis for some kind of honors program. John F. Cramer was also appointed as a consultant to the committee. By May 1960, this committee had developed some points for discussion by the division chairs and their faculties. It suggested a four-year program, based on existing courses at the lower division level, the upper division work being in a major field of study, and the emphasizing of the vital role of the adviser in the program. These suggestions, of course, were the best possible ones, given the usual financial constraints.[15]

The Honors program began on an experimental basis during fall term 1960, with five courses offered. The choice of these courses reflected the connection between scholastic achievement and subject matter content—more specifically, the connection between the Honors program and the Advanced Placement program of the College Entrance Examination Board (CEEB). The courses themselves (Appreciation of Literature, English Composition, History of Western Civilization, History of the United States, and Differential and Integral Calculus) all represented fields of study in the CEEB program. None of the courses was new, but each would now include a special honors section requiring higher quality work from the students. The initial year went so satisfactorily the faculty senate took up the creation of an honors council in April 1961.[16]

The debate on creating an Honors Council was vigorous. Waller moved that a permanent honors council headed by a director be created. The program was to encompass a two-year honors sequence in each of the three academic divisions; a third-year, all-college honors course; and special departmental work leading to honors degrees in each department. In speaking for the motion, the committee noted that, although its report had been distributed to the faculty earlier, "there had been practically no response." But "spirited" response came in the faculty meeting. The report and the motion were assailed in a variety of ways. It would restrict the best students to track courses; a better program could be developed in each department; the program would create an overload for those teaching the courses; it would compete with departmental courses; and the proposed honors council should not be created by the dean of the faculty. A major argument in favor of the program was that special programs for intellectually gifted students had been established for years in high schools and that graduates of these programs would expect similar experiences in college. In the end, the original motion passed by a vote of sixteen to four.[17]

The first year of the regular Honors program was 1961–62. The program, now out of the experimental stage, included two-year sequences in science, social science, and humanities during both freshman and sophomore years. In the humanities division, for example, freshman took a combined appreciation of literature and composition course, while sophomores had a sequence in tragedy, comedy, and satire. The program, under Waller's direction, was open to 10 percent of the freshman class, based on scores on the College Board examinations, on a first-come, first-served basis. It should be noted that, although the original committee had considered this approach, no inter-disciplinary courses were offered. Further courses were added in the years ahead, including (beginning winter term 1964) an independent reading program where students would read eight to twelve books per term and be examined on them at the end of three terms.[18]

The Honors program proceeded quietly for two years, until Dean Swarthout decided it should be given a routine evaluation. He asked the Honors Council to review the program and to establish evaluative standards for it. The senate's interest was reflected when it held a full-fledged discussion of it in May 1966. By this time, it was clear the program—in terms of student enrollment—was not popular. President Millar mentioned the costs of upgrading the program to an institution-wide (rather than a departmental) level would require "large amounts of special funds for support." He also pointed out he "had the impression that honors programs might be something of a fad, beginning several years ago, but now there was a lessening of appeal for this type of academic endeavor."[19]

The apparent demise of the honors program occurred later in the year, when the last meeting of the Honors Council took place. By this date the Council had found no way to maintain the program, and, in April 1967, Waller (now associate dean of the faculty) announced the honors sections were being discontinued for financial reasons. The program was soon resuscitated, however, by Judah P. Bierman of the English Department.[20]

Bierman, who was given released time to work on honors in the fall of 1967, worked rapidly and obtained faculty senate consent for an experimental honors program to begin in September 1968. In arguing for the program, he assured the senate it would require no additional funds. Perhaps for this reason, Millar now changed his tune from two years earlier, maintaining "the entire institution benefits" from "the mental stimulation provided by the challenges posed and met in an honors program." Twenty-eight students enrolled in the program, which began in the fall of 1968. Actually, the "program" at this time was a single course, carrying eight hours of credit, that Bierman himself taught. The students were all freshmen who were invited to join the class based on their high school rankings. By the following year, Honors had been renamed the University Scholars Program, presumably to clear up any confusion with graduation honors based on grade-point average.[21]

Another curricular experiment came with the advent of study abroad. Portland State's first study abroad program derived from one for high school students called the American Heritage Association, started in 1958 by a Lake Oswego High School teacher named Felix Calkins. Originally a summer program that sent students to the East Coast, in 1962 it was supplemented by a European dimension for college students. In that year, Calkins and Charles M. White (History) created a program for students from Portland State, Willamette University, and the University of Washington. In the fall and winter, students studied Western Civilization and World Literature (along with elective courses) at their home institutions and, in the spring, studied in London with a summer continuation in Paris.[22]

The administration of the program was institutionalized in 1963, when the Northwest Interinstitutional Council for Study Abroad was organized, with Oregon State joining the agreement. Participating schools were admitted to the arrangement if they agreed the instructors of one school were to be accepted by the others; the two above courses were required of each student in the program; and that the teachers were appointed by their home departments. The coordinating body (the "Council") consisted of the academic representatives from the participating institutions. Over the years, several schools have joined and then dropped out for a variety of reasons. But in 1996, the Council numbered Portland State, Oregon State, Central Washington,

Washington State, Western Washington, the University of Washington, Alaska Anchorage, and Alaska Fairbanks. Over the years, the study sites have varied, but Avignon, Koln, London, and Siena have been sites for many years.[23]

This educational consortium is one of the oldest in the United States. It has been so successful it has been emulated in a Midwestern Interinstitutional Council for Study Abroad and a Pennsylvania Council for Study Abroad. Success has been built on the cooperation of the institutions involved, especially the objectivity of its faculty-selection procedures. No school is "entitled" to a professor in any given year; merit is the criterion for choice. Over the thirty-three years of its history, the merit-selection process has resulted in the choice of over fifteen Portland State professors representing at least nine disciplines to participate in this program.[24]

By the early 1960s, study abroad was part of a nation-wide movement in American higher education, evidenced at such institutions as Stanford, Harvard, and Antioch. It next emerged at Portland State in the form of a program in Italy. Brock Dixon, associate dean of the faculty, headed a study abroad committee that reported early in November 1961, but the moving spirit in what became the Italian Studies Program was George Carbone, who had joined the History Department in September 1961. Dixon's committee, through Carbone, made contact with the University of Pavia and the Italian government and received preliminary assurances of cooperation from both. Swarthout was so taken with the reports of these conversations, as he had been in the case of similar discussions about the Middle East Studies Center, that he wrote Millar the time had come to discuss the proposal at the administrative level: "God knows a college like ours has no strength as great as that of its limited number of driving staff people sold on what they're trying to do, and I strongly hesitate to extinguish the flame as long as a proposal has reasonable prospects for success."[25]

The study abroad committee certainly drove ahead. By late November, it had worked out a plan to cooperate in a program with the University of Oregon and Oregon State College. It was the first major cooperative venture with other institutions of the state system. The reason for cooperation was that Portland State alone could not provide enough students to justify paying the salary of the resident director. Portland State thus lost exclusive control of the program (officially named the Oregon State System of Higher Education Program in Pavia) but, in return, received enthusiastic support from Gordon Gil-

George Carbone, professor of History, founder of the Italian Studies Program

key, the dean of the Liberal Arts College at Oregon State, and good support from the Department of Foreign Languages at the University of Oregon. Swarthout noted there were weaknesses in the plan: "While I must admit to a feeling that we would by this sharing lose control, I think that the prospects for success would be enlarged." What he meant, of course, was the chances for getting the program supported by the chancellor would be improved if the two larger schools were incorporated into it. At this time, Swarthout outlined the steps necessary for getting the chancellor's approval in time, he hoped, to begin the first year of the program in September 1963. Included in his suggestions was one to send Carbone to Italy in August 1962 to make the local arrangements in that country. Swarthout recognized fully the pathbreaking nature of the venture: "We are treading new ground both in the establishment of an overseas campus and in the development of such a program as an interinstitutional undertaking, a part of the curricula of several colleges, and there is no procedural precedent that I can discover."[26]

Carbone did go to Italy (his airfare and expenses covered by a Portland businessman, Al Giusti); the administration worked with officials at Oregon and Oregon State; and a cooperative plan was prepared for the chancellor's consideration by September 1962. A little later, Carbone outlined to the faculty senate the steps taken to form the Italian program. The courses would be produced at the University of Pavia; instruction would be given in the Italian language; and the subjects taught were to be History, English, Economics, Political Science, Philosophy, and Art. At the same faculty meeting, Dean Dixon revealed a similar program in Germany soon would follow. Dixon also stated the College Curriculum Committee would get the details of the program at its next meeting. This last remark indicated that, as would happen again, the faculty was being asked to approve arrangements that—for lack of time— had been arranged by the administration or through informal explorations by faculty members. The following month, the senate approved the new program unanimously, after being reassured students would, after the first year when intensive language courses were being instituted, be required to demonstrate language competence before acceptance into the program. As it turned out, almost all the courses were taught in English. A formal proposal was sent to the chancellor on 9 January 1963, and the state board approved the Pavia program on 21 January, with the proviso that the cost of educating the student be no higher than at home.[27]

Clearance by the state board, however, did not mean an effortless path to Pavia. In March 1963, only five months before the students were to begin work, Carbone received a grant to do research in Rome. Since he had been scheduled to be the resident director in Pavia, the program had to find a substitute. Fortunately, Carbone remained available during the planning months and, even more fortunately, a capable replacement was found in Frank Vecchio of the Portland State Foreign Languages Department. Fluent in Italian, Vecchio had "excellent rapport with students, and was to be accompanied by his wife, a school teacher." Carbone was also on call for assisting while he was in Rome.[28]

Carbone did continue to share much of the planning burden. He made another trip to Italy in March and returned home with the happy news the Pavia Chamber of Commerce and the Italian Ministry of Foreign Affairs had promised the sum of $3,300 in scholarship aid to the visiting American students. He also provided details about the academic and living arrangements at this time. The classroom work was from Monday through Thursday, "to provide long weekends for study and touring." Except for the language and literature courses, the classes would be conducted in English. Students would live the first year in the Pavia Palace Hotel, have free memberships in the local tennis and rowing clubs, and receive special rates for the LaScala operas in Milan, which was only twenty minutes away. Carbone indicated that when the program became more fully established, the students would live in Italian homes. Students had to be at least sophomores and would carry a course load of fifteen to eighteen hours per week. Students were "to elect a president and other officers to carry out student activities and to confer with staff members on administrative problems." They were more tightly regulated in their personal behavior than at home. Attendance was required at all classes and field trips; no student could operate a gasoline-powered vehicle nor house a visitor; and "woman students could not travel alone or singly with men, but should be accompanied by at least one other woman."[29]

By May, eleven Portland State students had found these prospects appealing enough to be accepted into the program. At this time, Carbone could also report that a dinner dance at the Eagles Hall, sponsored by the Portland Italian community and spearheaded by Anne Chiotti and Don Casciato, had raised at least $500 for scholarships for Portland State students going to Italy. The remaining arrangements moved smoothly, and most students seemed to profit from their year abroad. One of them wrote enthusiastically to one of her professors in Portland: "I have meant to write to you for a long time—but Italy is so full of exciting things to do that I'm busy even when I'm depressed (which I rarely am)....Besides being surrounded by erudite minds, I'm in the center of Renaissance art, close to LaScala and have unlimited opportunities to speak Italian." As the first year wound down, five other students wrote an evaluative letter to President Millar. Their only criticisms were the program's cost (they suggested a program of financial aid) and difficulty in communicating with Portland State officials, as in the case of determining their graduation requirements. These complaints were far outweighed by their compliments about the course, the field trips, and the proximity of Pavia to other sites for vacation travel.[30]

The new program was not without difficulties, however. About Christmastime, Carbone and his wife, Margaret, had to come to Pavia from Rome to take over as resident directors while Frank Vecchio returned home for the holidays. At this time, Vecchio reported to the Italian Studies Program Committee that the hotel facilities were not ideal. For example, "the marble floors and the [resident] professor's dog created noisy problems." He suggested a joint Portland State-Pavia University commission be established to work on housing problems so the state system students might stay in university dormitories. A more serious problem, Vecchio declared, was the linguistic preparation of the students: "Many of our students," he declared, "are in danger of failing their courses owing to language difficulties." Better professors were also needed: "Many of the Italian professors are in their twenties and, in order to overcome their language difficulty, are resorting to the reading of their lectures from textbooks, which is, of course, not very stimulating to the students." Two Oregon State students wished to return home early: one to become president of his fraternity, and the other because of financial difficulties. The complaint about inadequate language preparation was also echoed by returning students and passed on as a warning to those going the next academic year. It was still being made in the 1968–69 academic year and was largely responsible for the elimination of the program in 1973.

Other causes of its demise were student drug use, rising costs in Italy, the transfer of Italian language courses taken in Portland from Portland State to the Division of Continuing Education (DCE), and the difficulty of staying neutral in the Communist-Non-Communist struggles in the city and at the University of Pavia.[31]

A major administrative difficulty was working out an agreement between the state system administration (represented by Portland State) and the authorities of the University of Pavia. To start the process, Malcolm McMinn of the Portland State business office drew up a "proposed constitution of a Joint Italian American Committee" for the "Italian Studies Center at Pavia, Italy." Such an agreement was necessitated to remove the program from "visitor" status to a permanent administrative structure, operating in Italy according to local law. Negotiations did not go well with the Pavia representative, Angelo Grisoli, a professor of Law at the university. He wrote to Portland making suggestions about the American draft proposal but did not take kindly to modifications proposed from the Portland State administration, regarding them as personal criticism. He also found the Portland State officials to be dilatory in their communications, and he insisted in a letter to McMinn the College assume "a more definite and responsible course of dealing." President Millar responded for McMinn in a long, flowery letter insisting on the College's commitment to the joint enterprise and accepting Grisoli's draft of the constitution.[32]

The state system's irritation with Professor Grisoli came to a head in the next year, when he had a showdown with Sidney D. White (Oregon State), the resident director for 1964–65. Swarthout maneuvered to have Grisoli replaced (or at least supplemented by another Italian to be appointed to the commission) as a member of the joint commission. Referring in a letter to Carbone to a visit he had made to Pavia in the preceding year, Swarthout wrote: "For your secret eye, of course, Bre'r Grisoli was the one bloke in Pavia who aroused my ire pretty consistently when I was there. He seemed to have all the arrogance of a natural-born four-flusher, and I'm not at all surprised that he came to blows with old Sid at last. I think he would have done so with any Director we had abroad. Help us slap the bloke down, as I know you will, with that iron hand in the velvet glove." This matter was resolved by the addition of another Italian to the commission to supplement Grisoli, but other administrative problems remained.[33]

One was a dispute with Piero Bolfo, the proprietor of the hotel where the students were housed. The cause of it was a decision made by the resident director to allow male students to seek their housing else-where for the 1965–66 academic year. Bolfo appealed the decision to Swarthout in Portland, but the dean supported his director, and the contract was signed for the new year with a somewhat disgruntled hote-lier who had to be content with housing the female students. On a hap-pier note concerning housing, the College was delighted to hear Carbone had worked out an arrangement with the City of Pavia to use free of charge the historic Eustachi House in the city. The city agreed to remodel and rehabilitate the house for the use of the students and faculty for a conference center and for living quarters for the director. After rehabil-itation, the house was first occupied during the 1967–68 academic year.[34]

In spite of these difficulties, the program was fundamentally so successful that Carbone tried to work out a similar one with the Uni-versity of Trieste. The thrust of this program would have been in Slavic Studies. Although Carbone's preliminary soundings were received positively in Trieste, nothing came of the idea.[35]

By the close of the 1967–68 academic year, the director could right-fully declare "the center has definitely come out of the 'struggling child' stage that we have been accustomed to viewing it." Indeed, the program had come a long way in five years. It was the first state system study abroad program. As such, it had required negotiations among three academic institutions, delicate discussions with the University of Pavia, the city of Pavia, and the Pavia business community, and super-vision of the academic and social lives of young American students, many of them abroad for the first time. That the program had worked so well was a tribute to George Carbone, its founder; Dean Swarthout; Oregon and Oregon State administrators; and John Dart, director of International Programs at Portland State.

A much smaller program than the Middle East Center and the Italian Studies Program that was started in these years is the Sapporo program in Japan. Begun in 1967 as a proprietary dimension of the Port-land Summer Term (a part of the DCE) by Robert Dodge of the Business School, it became a regular program of the summer session after Charles White became summer session director. The heart of the program is the homestays of PSU students in Sapporo, but many exchanges have fol-lowed from the original plan, in addition to fostering harmonious rela-tions with Japan and providing gifts to the University.[36]

"A wise decision not to scrounge and expedite ourselves into mediocrity"

TEN

The Origins of Graduate Education · 1958–1966

Besides innovations in the undergraduate curriculum, the decade of the 1960s saw the beginning of Portland State's own graduate programs. The first graduate degree program was in social work, a program that—while worthy in itself— also revealed conditions the College would encounter for a long time: the desire to provide a professional service to the community, the support of state legislators from the metropolitan area, and the opposition of the University of Oregon.

The roots of social work education, indeed, were at the university at Eugene. From 1919–32, the University of Oregon had operated a Portland School of Social Work, but, in 1932, the state legislature had closed the school due to lack of funds and because of the reorganization of the State System of Higher Education. Social workers were aghast at this development, and, in 1934, the Portland chapter of the American Association of Social Workers, as recorded in its minutes, "raised the question of how to proceed to have a training center started in Oregon, or at least somewhere on the Pacific Coast." In the 1930s, the chapter contacted the Sociology Department at the University of Oregon and also raised the possibility of a school jointly supported by the states of Oregon and Washington. Nothing came of these efforts, however, perhaps because of the Great Depression and the Second World War that followed it. The Portland chapter of the Social Workers Association persisted, however, and, in 1956, it produced a thorough study, detailing the need to professionally train social workers in Oregon.

The next year, it organized a special committee to secure the objective of a professional graduate school in Portland. The committee gathered an enormous amount of community support from a range of organizations. Members of the committee met with the secretary of the State System of Higher Education, who suggested they talk with the president of the University of Oregon before approaching the chancellor. In July 1958, after the committee had provided additional information to him, Pres. O. Meredith Wilson recommended to the state board that a graduate school of social work be started in Portland as a part of his university. In September, Chancellor John Richards "appointed an inter-institutional committee to study the possibility for the establishment of a graduate school of social work in Portland." The committee reported in April 1959 in favor of a school in Portland but could not agree under whose auspices it should operate. Later in the year, the chancellor gave President Wilson the authority to appoint a committee to settle the matter.[1]

This committee, composed entirely of faculty members from the UofO, suggested three courses of action, all more or less beneficial to their university. The school could be located at Eugene, under the aegis of the UofO; it could be located in Portland, as part of the University of Oregon Medical and Dental schools; or it could be at Portland State, with students taking their first four years of work in Portland and the last year in Eugene.[2]

While these committees were deliberating, the social work community began gathering support to persuade the state legislature to authorize a school, although its institutional connection was not yet clear. The legislature in 1959 did pass Senate Joint Resolution 36, which provided for the opening of the school by fall term 1961. Community pressure had done its job. In 1960, Portland State College was asked by the chancellor to submit a proposal to establish the school. This was accomplished by a social work planning committee chaired by George C. Hoffmann, chair of the Division of Social Science, and including President Millar, Dean Swarthout, other faculty and administrators, and consultants from the social work community.[3]

The request to Portland State that led to the appointment of this committee was presented in June to the state board's curriculum committee by President Millar. He said Portland State would be hard pressed to complete the report by the deadline imposed by the resolution and under even greater time pressure (assuming the report was accepted with a recommendation the school be at Portland State) to get the school into operation by the 1961–62 academic year. He believed the opening might have to be postponed one year. The president also reported—in a move to assuage concerns of the University of Oregon—that "it would be very beneficial" to have some joint faculty appointments with the University.[4]

The Portland State committee's final report suggested a "Social Service" training program that would deal with a broader range of human problems—such as corrections, family counseling, mental health, and vocational rehabilitation—than had traditional "social work." The name of the program was to be the Division of Social Service, headed by a chairman under the dean of the faculty. The students would have a six-year course of training, four years at the undergraduate level and two years at the graduate. The graduate degrees offered would be the Master of Arts (MA) and the Master of Science (MS) in Social Work, while undergraduates would take a bachelor's degree in the field of General Studies. A search for a highly qualified chairman would be conducted nationally.[5]

The state board accepted the committee's report in the fall of 1960 but added the requested year of grace for preparations; the school would open in the fall of 1962. The next year, the legislature approved funds to begin the school, and the search for a chairman proceeded to a successful conclusion. Neither was controversial. The legislature passed the bill, which the governor signed on 24 May 1961. The search committee for the chair was headed by George Hoffmann and was provided excellent staff support by Brock Dixon, the assistant dean of the faculty, who winnowed the candidates to a small pool of excellent talent for the final choice. Millar played a delicate role well: he was a member of the search committee in fact if not in name, but he also had the final say on the selection. After the search was completed, Swarthout relayed to Millar the committee members' appreciation of his willingness "to confuse your role as president by serving also as a pro tem member of the selection committee, while still maintaining your independence as the recipient of the committee's recommendation."[6]

The first chair of the School of Social Work was Gordon Hearn, whose appointment was confirmed by the state board in October 1961. The new chair had been on the faculty of the University of California at Berkeley since 1948 and was currently professor of Social Welfare and assistant dean of students. Hearn's Berkeley commitments prevented his moving to Portland until January 1962, but he began

Gordon Hearn, founding dean
of the School of Social Work

PSU Educational Media Services

work at once from his home in Berkeley. Needless to say, a great deal needed to be accomplished in a short period of time to launch Portland State's first graduate program.[7]

Two matters of nomenclature had to be settled. Contrary to the recommendations of the organizing committee, the title of the school was changed to the School of Social Work from the suggested School of Social Service. And the name of the degree earned by its graduates was to be, at Hearn's request, Master of Social Work ("the recognized professional degree given by the great majority of institutions that have programs in the field, and people in the profession have strong feelings about it."), rather than Master of Arts or Science in Social Work.[8]

The dean's most important task, as in any academic endeavor, was to hire excellent faculty. From Berkeley, Hearn set the recruitment process in motion, and, ultimately, seven faculty were appointed for the first year, including Rose C. Thomas, Portland State's second full-time, African American faculty member. Under great time pressure, other tasks were accomplished: brochures were mailed to prospective students, field placements were arranged, and the initial curriculum was devised. The College had hired a social work librarian in the summer of 1961, who had secured the essentials of a professional library. A minor task devolving on the school was the design of the first academic hood given for a graduate degree at Portland State. This task was completed in March 1964 by a committee composed of Hearn; Hoyt C. Franchere, chair of the Division of Arts and Letters; and Frederick H. Heidel of the Art Department. (Unfortunately, the committee did not know Portland State's colors; it recommended the hood be kelly green and white, rather than the proper forest green and white.)[9]

Throughout all this intensive labor, the dean and faculty also had to keep their eyes on the 1964 accreditation visit by the Council on

Social Work Education. The accrediting team's visit took place from 22-26 March 1964. Its job was difficult, because of the newness of the school (the last term classes of the two-year program had not yet been taught) and the youth of the college of which it was a part. Nevertheless, the team did recommend Portland State's new venture receive accreditation, though it did find areas needing improvement. It wanted faculty members to be clear about its objectives: were they to educate undergraduates, sub-professionals, or post-graduate students? In conversation, the faculty stressed the graduate training of social work caseworkers as its primary goal; the team was in agreement with this emphasis. It also recommended the hiring of additional faculty—there were not enough at the present time, and with a growing number of students to enroll in the years ahead, several more faculty were needed. Physical facilities, although not crowded, would need to be upgraded shortly through the addition of more classroom space. The team spent most of its evaluative efforts on criticism of the curriculum. Essentially, its report asked the school to improve its teaching in the area of social welfare policy.[10]

On the positive side, the accrediting team praised the quality of the faculty, though faulting its size. The school was administered well, it concluded, and possessed the support of the College administration. For the moment, both budget and physical facilities were adequate. Field instruction was good, and the admissions policy and academic standards sound. All in all, the team's conclusions could be welcomed by Portland State. Indeed, they were so received, although Dean Swarthout complained to Hearn that "so much time and space went into the discussion of the specifics of the curriculum." But accrediting by the Council on Social Work Education did follow the team's report, and the school was well-launched when its first class graduated in June 1964.[11]

Although the creation of the School of Social Work was Portland State's first venture into graduate courses and the granting of degrees, it was not the first graduate program authorized. As the need for teachers of the post-war generation of children was a major cause for granting Portland State first permanency and then four-year status, so teacher education was the first step to graduate work. The State of Oregon increased the requirements for secondary teachers in the late 1950s, and many Portland teachers wanted to take this additional course work in the Portland metropolitan area, rather than traveling to a distant residential campus.

Portland State's opportunity to plan graduate work arose in the summer of 1957, when Chancellor John Richards asked the presidents of Oregon State College, the University of Oregon, and Portland State College each to appoint three members to a committee to advise him about allocating resources to state system institutions. The time was ripe to do so, the chancellor said, because the work following on the Anderson report concerning teacher education had been completed. Now, it was important to decide what role each institution would play. President Cramer appointed Hoyt Franchere, George Hoffmann, and Willard Spalding as Portland State's representatives on this committee.[12]

Willard Spalding made a preliminary report to the Portland State faculty on 24 September 1957. In it, he outlined possibilities for the institution's future growth. His third priority was to provide MA and MS degrees in General Studies and Master of Arts or Science degrees in Teaching (MAT and MST) for teachers. Many courses that might be developed, he said, would be applicable to each of these four degrees. He implied there would be a demand for all of the degrees, because few students in the state system availed themselves of General Studies degrees, and, if Portland State adopted a "distinctive degree" in this area, then it would draw this clientele. Similarly, if the teaching graduate degree were offered, it would fill a niche in Oregon higher education. As ammunition for this last point, Spalding concluded by emphasizing that the secondary education accrediting team that had recently evaluated the teacher education program "noted that it did not culminate in a Master's degree."[13]

On 20 May 1958, Spalding made a major presentation to the state board that dealt with all aspects of the Portland State curriculum and the institution's plans for its expansion. In this presentation, Spalding noted the need for improving teacher education. Among the ways to do so, he argued, was to "propose that Portland State College be authorized to develop five-year programs for preparing elementary and secondary teachers which will terminate in the degrees of Master of Arts and Master of Science in teaching, to be completed prior to certification and employment."[14]

A follow-up to this presentation came in June 1958, when Hoyt Franchere introduced a motion in the faculty senate to create a graduate council. He stated this body was necessary "in view of the need for a longer period of reflection looking toward a well-integrated program for graduate studies." The purpose of the council, as voted by the senate, was two-fold: to help place alumni of Portland State in graduate schools and to plan for master's degrees at the College. The council was composed of the dean of the faculty, one member from each of the four divisions, two members of the general faculty, and the dean of the General Extension Division. The specific duties of the council were to recommend requirements for the master's degrees; to recommend additional library facilities and the strengthening of areas in which books were needed to support graduate work; to recommend admission and graduation requirements for degree students; and to approve instructional staff for graduate studies. The role of the council was obviously based on two assumptions: that many of the degree students would have some of their work transferred from the Extension Division and that there would be a two-tier faculty, with some not considered qualified to teach graduate students.[15]

Various College officials and faculty worked for the next three years to garner support for the MAT-MST degrees (the idea of a General Studies degree was dropped along the way, as there was never any enthusiasm for it on the part of either administrators or faculty.) In January 1958, Spalding, in his capacity as chair of the Committee on Teacher Education, presented a proposal for the MAT-MST degrees to the state board. He made three main points to justify the degrees. One was that in the national discussion of proper teacher preparations "the most important factor" was "increasing emphasis upon academic content." Subject matter, as well as techniques, were seen as important for the teacher. His second point was that teachers now needed five, rather than four, years of preparation. Third, the developing trend to have teachers certified in subject areas required graduate work. Spalding predicted the legislature would pass a five-year requirement for teacher certification during the current legislative session. On 22 July 1958, the state board authorized (although it did not fund) a five-year program at Portland State leading to a master's degree. Spalding described the detailed degree programs developed by the faculty and concluded his plea by offering three reasons for the board to adopt them: teachers with advanced degrees earn higher salaries; beginning teachers—whose pay is low—could not afford to attend a residential university for an advanced degree; and graduate advisers needed to be in close proximity to graduate students.[16]

The College's request to the board for funds to start the program was not included in the board's request to the legislature in 1961, although it supported the program in principle. In reporting this blow to the faculty senate, President Millar glimpsed a silver lining: "The College has not lost ground, for the program is good, has been re-affirmed in principle by the Board, and additional education offerings on the undergraduate level will also strengthen the case for graduate work at Portland State College."[17]

As Spalding predicted, the legislature did pass the bill requiring five years for certification, effective 1 July 1965. It gave urgency to Portland State's desires. Spalding pled in a letter to Dean Swarthout for him to try to get the board to reconsider its funding decision, as "the need for immediate reconsideration is urgent. Portland State College is the only collegiate institution in the Oregon State System of Higher Education which cannot offer Master's Degrees to graduates planning to teach." He even raised the question of whether Portland State could remain an accredited institution in the realm of teacher education without these degrees. The Committee on Teacher Education continued to work on a time schedule for the MAT-MST degrees, in the hopes that somehow funds would turn up to support the program. But finally, Spalding and Swarthout temporarily gave up the cause in August. The reason was that Chancellor Richards would soon retire, and it might be wiser to wait to see how his successor viewed the matter, perhaps in a more favorable way.[18]

The new chancellor, Roy M. Lieuallen, did decide to ask the 1963 legislature to make the Portland State degree program a high priority. In the meantime, displaying their usual ingenuity in the face of budgetary hardships, Portland State administrators, with the chancellor's approval, decided to seek a grant of $97,543.45 from the Ford Foundation's Fund for the Advancement of Education to initiate graduate work in teacher education. If funds were made available from the Foundation, it was hoped the program would begin in September 1962. This hope seemed justifiable, for it had been suggested by representatives from the Foundation itself. But hope was dashed in February 1962, when the Foundation refused support. The reason was its focus was on "experimental and demonstration programs likely to have value for other institutions which observe the experiments in a given place."[19]

While awaiting approval of the MAT-MST program—and to accommodate the authorized social work degree (MSW)—the Graduate Council proceeded to develop rules and regulations for graduate work. Discussed in three meetings of the faculty senate in spring 1962, they were approved on 4 June 1962. These requirements were noncontroversial and unsurprising for the most part. The Graduate Record Examination was an option but not a requirement for admission; there was a language requirement for the MAT but not for the MST, unless a department required it; and none for the MSW. To maintain good standing, a student had to maintain a cumulative grade-point average of 3.0 and was not allowed to have more than nine hours of work below the B level. For the degree, a thesis, written examination, or both were required. Up to fifteen hours of transfer credit could be applied to the Portland State degree, and twelve hours of graduate credit could be reserved by undergraduates. The normal load was set at fifteen hours. Twelve of the thirty hours of residence credit were required to be in 500-level courses (those open to graduate students only). Most of these regulations laid down by the Graduate Council and adopted by the faculty at the beginning of the graduate program have remained in effect as subsequent master's degrees were added.[20]

Finally, the realization of many hopes and the many hours of planning were justified in 1963, when the legislature voted funds to begin the master's degree programs. In September 1963, the first students were admitted to the MAT and MST programs. As the pace of graduate work, authorized and projected, picked up, the need for a leader to direct it became apparent. In December 1963, Dean Swarthout announced his intention to seek a part-time director (not dean) of Graduate Studies. In February 1964, Swarthout returned to the subject in a meeting of the Academic Council, when he called for the appointment of an assistant dean of the faculty for Graduate Studies. In September, the title was revised and an incumbent selected to fill the position, when Frederick J. Cox, professor of History and director of the Middle East Studies Center, was appointed Portland State's first dean of Graduate Studies. Cox was given responsibility for program planning, policy development, administration, staff consultation, and College representation to outside agencies.[21]

Later in the year, the state board passed a resolution concerning graduate work in the Portland area. It promised to strengthen the MAT and MST programs at Portland State with a request for another legislative appropriation of $152,700. It also promised to strengthen a wide range of disciplines at the College in anticipation of offering MA and MS degrees in them later. The sum of $700,000 was to be requested for this purpose.[22]

The preparatory work for the MAT/MST degrees was not simply a matter of waiting and hoping for the legislature to fund the program. Administrators and faculty, correctly assuming it would be launched eventually, struggled with a variety of problems before the first students appeared in the classrooms. In January 1963, the Graduate Council called for the divisions and departments to submit courses for graduate credit, revalidating them from January 1962, for the 1963–64 College catalog. In March, it asked for revalidation and new graduate course requests for 1964–65. On 14 June 1962, the College requested the sums of $109,445 for 1963–64 and $208,428 for 1964–65 to mount the MAT/MST program.[23]

The chancellor finally approved the program in early May 1963, but serious problems, mainly financial, remained. Given the reluctance of the legislature to appropriate money for Portland State's MAT/MST work, Millar and Swarthout had grasped at the straw of at least partially funding it by taking over some evening classes offered by the Extension Division's Portland Continuation Center (which carried Portland State credit but for which the College received no revenue) and by moving some College classes from day to evening to increase the pool of students. This idea of shuffling existing resources was abandoned in May 1963, when Millar made a principled decision to delay the program until a clear commitment of additional money was made by the legislature. In summing up a conversation with Swarthout, the president wrote to the dean:

> I think we made a wise decision not to scrounge and expedite
> ourselves into mediocrity by the avenue of overcommitment.
> In the medium and short run we shouldn't sell ourselves short,
> but seek to do well those things which we have already under-
> taken as basic commitments. If this is tough on students and
> the metropolitan area and the state, so much the worse. But if
> the State Board and the legislature can be tough about resources,
> I am sure it behooves us to be tough about the quality and
> character of the programs for which we are responsible.[24]

Problems of status and institutional rivalry continued. One petty matter was whether Portland State graduate courses could carry a large or small letter (G or g) after the course number. Oregon and Oregon State wished to retain the upper case designation for their courses and relegate Portland State to the use of the lower case. This was part of a larger concern; as Swarthout reported to Millar after a conversation with a member of the chancellor's staff: "The University [of Oregon] is becoming immensely defensive again, and frightened at the role that may be left for it if other institutions begin to give departmental graduate work in the Liberal Arts fields."[25]

Much labor was expended by the Graduate Council in dealing with the indispensable minutiae of the new program. A style manual for the graduate thesis was written, and course offerings carrying graduate credit had to be expanded. The question of whether the Graduate Council, because of its increasing press of business, would meet in the summer was discussed. Faculty for graduate courses were approved. This last matter required both Graduate Council and senate action and involved the Council's establishment of criteria for instructors of these courses. Essentially, what the Council would normally require of instructors was possession of the doctoral degree and achievements ranging from previous teaching at the graduate level to scholarly publications. Graduate advisers were appointed for the departments.[26]

Not only were there many decisions to be made, they had to be decided by September 1963, when the new program admitted its first students. To help in the preparations, the College appointed graduate teacher education coordinators, one for each of the four divisions. These coordinators were to ensure the department executive officers understood their role in the MAT/MST programs and were also to serve as advisers for those who wished a divisional, rather than a departmental, degree. It was decided not to use either the lower or upper case G but to note that any course, when taken by a graduate student, carried graduate credit. Separate sections of courses dedicated primarily to the needs of public school teachers would be offered two days a week, either Monday and Wednesday or Tuesday and Thursday, at the hours of 4:30 PM to 5:45 PM, 6:00 PM to 7:15 PM, and 7:30 PM to 8:45 PM. Dean Brock Dixon addressed the last matter in a sensible memorandum to advisers: "The important thing to note in this connection is that no MAT course will meet only once a week. We have been talking for years about the difficulty of maintaining high standards of performance among tired faculty and students in long sessions at the end of a long day." He added another important point: the new program was intended to be College-wide in content and administration. Thus, each student's adviser was responsible for helping him or her in selecting the courses in both the liberal arts and education portions of the program. In concluding his memorandum, Dixon captured the flavor of the moment: "Let us admit to one another quite frankly that this is a new experience and be prepared to tolerate some delays and false starts. On the other hand, let us all remember that fall is approaching and that about 600 school teachers expect us to be ready to roll in September."[27]

By August, the registration and advising procedures had been worked out. The timing was unusual, for students would be admitted to graduate work only weeks before classes began, although all involved could take comfort that this compressed schedule only would be for the 1963–64 academic year. But the novelty of the program and the difficulty of getting it established in the teeth of indifference or opposition required Portland State to insist that a high quality of advising and instruction be established at the beginning. It was essential, above all, that the new graduate degree be distinguished from the collection of courses teachers had formerly taken under the aegis of the Extension Division. As one of the new guidelines put it: "We want to avoid any impression that we are continuing the catch as catch can registration without faculty control which has of necessity characterized Extension procedure."[28]

The new program had at least two potentials for faculty grievances. If six hundred students were intending to take courses at the unusual late afternoon or early evening hours, it was probable that an occasional teaching assignment at one of these hours might be required. A more likely cause of complaint was the creation of the graduate faculty. This was a ramification of the Graduate Council proposal that it approve certain faculty to teach graduate courses. The Academic Council saw the danger in this proposal, which "suggested a separate 'graduate faculty' or suggested that undergraduate teaching was of lesser status than graduate teaching."[29]

The movement for liberal arts and sciences MA and MS degrees—although long at the back of everyone's mind concerning graduate education—followed the establishment of the MAT/MST program. Most faculty wanted to see advanced degrees given in their disciplines, but they wanted the program to be developed under fewer time constraints and with greater faculty participation than the hurried (and largely administration-sponsored) process of authorizing the MAT/MST degrees. Even Hoyt Franchere, usually the most authoritarian of administrators, wrote to Swarthout about the need, where the selection of master's degrees was concerned, "to err on the side of the faculty, who are our peers after all, than on the side of mere haste." President Millar was of the same mind and told the Academic Council members a month later, "There must be faculty participation in establishing priorities for new graduate programs or at least in determining the procedure which must be followed."[30]

The roots of the issue of faculty participation in establishing graduate programs went back to the approval of the first eight MA or MS
programs in 1964. They were presented to the Curriculum Committee
in November, after their earlier approval by the administration and the
state board. Time had been of the essence earlier in the spring, when
the degree programs were incorporated into the College budget—indeed,
such pressure of time as to prevent senate consideration of them. The
administration did consult the faculty informally, but the proposals
were not considered through normal channels. A week later—after the
degrees also had been approved by the Graduate Council—they were
approved by the senate. Final faculty action on the first eight degree
programs in liberal arts was completed in May and June 1965.[31]

When the next biennium's allocations were at hand, the senate did
take a more thorough part in the deliberations, culminating in the
passage of a resolution in March 1966 that the priority list for 1967–69
graduate programs be prepared by the College administration and then
presented "to the Graduate Council for its information and to the
Senate for its action." Faculty members now hoped the reason (or excuse)
for unilateral administrative action in graduate matters—in this case,
constraints of time—would no longer pertain.[32]

An issue relating to which disciplines would offer graduate degrees,
and when, was the matter of permitting departments without graduate-
degree authorization to offer some graduate credit courses. The issue
first arose in November 1964, when the Education Division asked that
certain psychology courses (in individual intelligence testing) be given
emergency approval to carry graduate credit to support the projected
MA degree in Education. George Hoffmann, the dean of Social Science,
assented, but it was turned down by Frank Roberts, the associate dean
of the faculty. President Millar also was suspicious of such proposals,
raising the question of whether they could "possibly become a bit of
elaborate log rolling for building up graduate course work in advance
of institutional commitments and intentions? Under certain circumstances that might be imaginable, this could parlay into a situation
where practically every department had enough courses for a master's
degree and so ought to be authorized to offer one."[33]

The Graduate Council and the graduate dean, as graduate programs were authorized, also conflicted over their respective powers.
The essential difference was that the Council wished the power to establish requirements for graduate work and admissions, to approve or dis-
approve graduate programs and the assignment of graduate credit to

courses, and (on the recommendation of Division Chairs) to designate graduate faculty. Dean Cox saw the Council role as recommendatory in these matters, although he would grant the Council authority to act on all matters of policy referred to it by the dean of Graduate Studies.[34]

Making decisions about graduate offerings also was one of the range of problems affected by Portland State-Portland Continuation Center (PCC) relations. Not only was this a problem for finances—as Portland Continuation Center was supported almost entirely from tuition fees—but the program was confusing for almost everyone who participated in it. The Continuation Center had its evening classes in the Portland metropolitan area and its own summer school. Until Portland State was given graduate degrees, Continuation Center students had to finish their degree work at other state system institutions. Thus, there were two institutions, two administrations, two faculties, and two student bodies. But the situation was made more complicated by the fact that students often enrolled in both institutions simultaneously, and Portland State faculty often supplemented their incomes by teaching PCC courses as overload at night. As Portland State built its graduate offerings, this complicated situation of overlapping student and faculty bodies had to be clarified. Cox and George Timmons, the associate director of the Portland Center, took the first step in doing so by completing a census of all those taking post-baccalaureate courses at PSC or PCC, whether part-time or full-time, degree or non-degree, certificate, regular, provisional, or special students. In late September 1964, there were 1,344 Portland State graduate students (1,027 degree and 317 non-degree) and 1,082 Portland Center (Portland Campus) students (197 regular and 885 non-degree). The number of Portland Center (outlying, non-Portland district) students was not available. There were 216 students who defied the ingenuity of the census takers and were classified as undetermined PSC or PCC. The data supplied ammunition for Portland State, as it began to build its graduate programs, since many PCC students would transfer to Portland State when degrees were offered. The College needed to be financially prepared for them in staff and facilities when they arrived.[35]

In the next year, Cox pressed his quest for equitable funding with the College business manager. He noted in a memorandum that Portland State did almost all the counseling, scheduling, and advising of students, and the preparation of their graduate forms, "without adequate compensation," as PCC received a portion of tuition money equal to that of Portland State without performing any of these labors. Cox hoped to count all students in PSC graduate programs—regardless of how many courses they also took at PCC—as Portland State students. On another financial matter, the enterprising Cox noted the College was excluded from a lucrative federal program, Title IV of the National Defense Education Act, which provided fellowships for doctoral students in many disciplines. Portland State had no doctoral students, but Cox, based on a talk he had heard recently by the Commissioner of Education, thought he detected a "slight loophole through which we might qualify." The commissioner had stated planning for implementing doctoral programs would suffice to ensure fellowship awards. Cox maintained Portland State was engaged in such planning through offering courses in conjunction with doctoral programs at the Oregon Medical School (in Psychology) and at the Oregon Graduate Center (in certain fields of science). If the chancellor could be persuaded to pursue the matter, then the College would benefit to the amount of $2,500 per fellowship, money that could be used for any purpose. Although nothing came of this idea, Portland State did get federal money for graduate fellowships (totaling $64,800) in 1966, awards for education students who were studying to teach the "visually handicapped and mentally retarded." These were the first federal fellowships after those granted to the School of Social Work, whose students had held them since the beginning.[36]

The question of how graduate students were admitted also proved a problem, particularly with the School of Education. The school wished to be empowered to admit as probationary graduate students those whose undergraduate grade-point average fell below 2.75. If these students did satisfactory work, then they could be admitted to regular academic status. Cox objected to this arrangement, arguing the Office of Graduate Studies should make the decision on admitting all graduate students, including those who did not meet the regular admissions standards. Cox commented bitterly, in a letter to Swarthout, that "over the past year the Graduate Office has noted that the one school, division, or department that consistently pleads for admitting every student who applies is the School of Education." He said this easy standard gave poor publicity to the graduate programs of the College as a whole.[37]

All in all, however, in spite of the pressures of time and limited resources, the College administration and faculty had made an excellent start in launching its graduate-study programs.

"You may find the hair rising upon
the back of your neck a bit."

ELEVEN

The Quest for University Status · 1959–1969

T he struggle for graduate work at the master's level was
time-consuming, arduous, frustrating, but, ultimately, successful. The same was true for doctoral degrees, although the success was more limited. The College eventually obtained some
but always had to struggle against the combined forces of the chancellor, the state board, the University of Oregon, and Oregon State
College. In the end, Portland State had to be satisfied with doctoral
degree programs that did not "duplicate" those at the two, older graduate institutions. The difficulties of gaining doctoral programs first
manifested themselves at Portland State in the late 1950s and the early
1960s, at a time when developments in business and government,
ironically, seemed to promise happier outcomes.[1]

The most important factor in instigating Portland State's doctoral quest was Sputnik. The Soviet Union's lofting of the first artificial
satellite in the fall of 1957 set off a determined effort on the part of
the United States to catch up to the Russians in space exploration.
Sputnik forced the creation of the National Aeronautics and Space
Administration (NASA) and the National Defense Education Act, both
in 1958 (the latter was amended in 1962.) The education statutes
poured millions of dollars into universities for curricular improvements, fellowships, facilities, and equipment. It was obvious Portland
State would attempt to obtain its share of the federal largess, a desire
many individuals and institutions in the Portland metropolitan area
heartily supported.[2]

The problem was there was no research-oriented university in the
community. Portland was probably the only city of its size in the U.S.

without such an institution. It had, besides Portland State, Lewis & Clark College, Reed College, and the University of Portland. But almost all of Oregon's research work, and all doctoral programs, were carried on at Eugene and Corvallis. The lack of a Portland research university seemed a deficiency to many, not only for pure scientific study, but for economic development as well. The governor of Oregon, Mark O. Hatfield, was pressing to develop the state's economy in directions other than the traditional agricultural, forest products, and tourism bases. There were promising developments in the electronics industry, beginning with the founding of Electro Scientific Industries and Tektronix in the 1940s, but the link between higher education and high technology was far from being exploited fully. A Portland business organization, Downtown Portland, Inc., supported such a linkage. Its executive secretary wrote a long report urging the establishment of a graduate center at an already-established university or college, mentioning specifically Reed College, Portland State, Lewis & Clark, and the University of Portland as possible hosts.[3]

The response to the perceived need for graduate education in science and technology in the Portland area came from four institutions working sometimes in harmony, sometimes at cross-purposes: the governor's office, Portland State, the chancellor, and the state board. Governor Hatfield moved first, asking the State Department of Planning and Development in 1959 to appoint a committee on Science, Engineering, and the New Technologies (SENT). Chaired by Walter Dyke, a Physics professor at Linfield College, the committee included John Swarthout, Portland State's dean of the faculty, as a member. The committee reported in May 1961.

Its main recommendation called for a new, independent (of the state system or any existing institution) graduate university in the Portland area to "serve all resident industry as well as new and prospectively new science-based industry." Dean Swarthout was not pleased with the report's conclusions. He wrote President Millar, who was to discuss the report with the governor, that he should emphasize to Hatfield the importance of building a graduate school on the base of an existing undergraduate college working to get MA/MS degrees established and of associating the graduate center in science with the humanities and social sciences. He concluded darkly, pointing at the interests of private industry, that "much of what's happened has resulted from personal efforts to promote personal ends, in part at state expense and the expense of adequate development of graduate edu-

cation in the Portland metropolitan area." What Portland State needed was to make sure the autonomous university did not delay the
adoption of the master's degrees in science—or other fields for that
matter—at the institution, and that Oregon and Oregon State did not
fish in the waters to expand their offerings in the metropolitan area.[4]

How dangerous this last possibility was became clear in a joint proposal drawn up by the graduate deans at Oregon and Oregon State in
October 1961. It was a response to the proposal for an autonomous
university in Portland and was to be discussed by the presidents of the
two schools and Portland State before they were to discuss the proposed university with the governor. This document began forthrightly
with an attempt to undercut the autonomous center, stating "a
Portland Graduate Center should be established under the aegis of
the Oregon State System of Higher Education." It gave Portland State
the position of director of the center, saying the three institutions plus
the medical and dental schools should pool their resources to provide
unified admissions, registration, library, and business office facilities.
But it also declared each institution would have its own courses that
would be credited at their own institutions and applicable to their own
degrees. Portland State would thus not get all the courses to be
offered in Portland, nor would it be permitted to give doctoral
degrees. The suggestion was a clever plan for the older institutions to
meet the demand for graduate work in science and engineering in
Portland, while throwing a sop to Portland State by letting it have master's degrees. Millar was not to be outmaneuvered, however. In
December 1961, he discussed the idea of a Portland graduate center
in a faculty meeting, asking the dean of faculty to develop a program
of courses and fiscal support for them that would be compatible with
the center.[5]

While the state system institutions planned what to do about the
proposal for an autonomous university, Governor Hatfield in January
1962 appointed a second committee to further advise him on the
issue. So far as Portland State was concerned, the composition of the
committee was a slap in the face, for it included the chancellor; Pres.
Richard H. Sullivan of Reed College as chair; Howard Vollum, president of Tektronix; and the presidents of the two universities. President
Millar—through insult or oversight, both equally reprehensible in the
eyes of Portland State—was excluded from the original committee.
After protests by influential citizens and an angry editorial in the
Oregonian, Millar was put on the committee.[6]

The state board was not idle while the Sullivan committee was organizing. After gathering data from the individual institutions, the board established a Coordinating Council for Graduate Work in the Portland Area on 13 March 1962. It beat the Sullivan committee to the punch by issuing its recommendations six weeks before the governor's committee made its report. The Council disingenuously declared its "proposals will in no way impede the activities of the governor's committee headed by President Sullivan of Reed College but, rather, will supplement the eventual action of that committee." The Council proposed a person be appointed to further study a possible course of action for system graduate work in Portland; that Portland State be given funds to hire a person to help develop graduate study, recognizing that "initially only selected graduate efforts should be initiated;" that "salients," such as an Institute for Applied Mathematics, might be established; and that system institutions formulate budget requests for the 1963–65 biennium.[7]

At the same time as the Sullivan and state system bodies were meeting, Portland State was refining its own contribution to the graduate work controversy. This was a proposal for an Institute of Applied Mathematics, worked out in the spring of 1962 by the executive officers of Applied Engineering and Science, Harry White and Thurman Peterson, respectively. This proposal began by repeating the general knowledge that there was little graduate work available in science and engineering in the Portland area, except for courses offered by the General Extension Division, many of which were "handled by one-shot-a-week commuting staff, an onerous assignment hardly calculated to attract senior faculty who normally would give these courses." Although the two men recognized the long-range solutions would involve a great deal of money for buildings, library acquisitions, and staff, in the interim, additional courses in mathematics and physics could be given by existing faculty at Portland State. Concerning the long range, White and Peterson advocated preparing at once for master's degrees in science and mathematics. The heart of the proposal—and its immediate response to community needs everyone from the governor on down was talking about—was to create an Institute of Applied Mathematics. The authors discussed the need to understand that "economic development is now generally recognized to be inseparably linked with scientific research and technological advance" and that "in the research and development process, applied mathematics is assuming a dominant position." White and Peterson also advocated the creation of a

Portland Research Foundation, which would be privately supported. Its tasks would be to focus on scientific and technological projects in the "most urgently needed areas of science" and to support the Institute of Applied Mathematics. The institute would be a part of Portland State College (the authors likened it to the Middle East Studies Center), which would be supported by the foundation and by state and federal monies. Institute faculty would be made up of two current Portland State faculty and four new appointees from outside the College. A computer center would be part of the institute.[8]

Millar transmitted the components of the institute proposal to the chancellor's Graduate Center Committee, which showed a "strong interest" in it. The committee members were receptive, Millar reported to the College Executive Committee, in terms of both economy and expediency. But its fate awaited the Sullivan committee's report.[9]

The Sullivan committee worked rapidly throughout the spring and early summer. Its main focus, of course, was on scientific and engineering education in Portland, but that charge meant it necessarily became involved in the older issue of all master's degrees anticipated at Portland State. At the 22 June meeting, several important issues were decided, and some victories for the state system and for Portland State were achieved. U of O president Arthur Flemming and Dean Swarthout (sitting in for President Millar) successfully argued for a clear statement that the proposed graduate center would never be permitted to offer degrees on its own. A quid pro quo was worked out, and, here, Swarthout was hardly leading from strength; the committee would support the authorization of Portland State to offer full graduate work as soon as possible, in exchange for the assurance that the entire center would not become "an organic part of a single urban university" (which Portland State had no possibility of becoming). Swarthout was so pleased with these developments he closed his memorandum to Millar reporting on the meeting by saying, "God knows this is a different group from the one that dominated the original SENT Committee, and the holdover members have either been educated (like Howard Vollum) or chastened (like Sullivan). I almost envy you the chance to meet with them again."[10]

The Sullivan committee delivered its report to Governor Hatfield on 30 July 1962. After surveying the historical background of graduate work in the nation and in Oregon and after reviewing the state's economic developments, the committee made its recommendations. Bowing to the need to develop existing colleges and universities, it also recommended the creation of a new graduate institution in the Portland metropolitan area, to be called the Oregon Cooperative Center for Graduate Education and Advanced Research. The assumptions underlying this proposal were that it would obtain private and public support from the citizens of the state; it would provide excellent programs; it would attract funds from private sources because it would render particular services (meaning to high technology); and that it would be of such quality it would attract national funding sources. The center would be a legally autonomous institution, with support from the existing public and private institutions of higher learning. According to the report, the new center would not injure, but assist the growth of existing institutions. One sentence in it, however, was a blow to Portland State: "Foreseeing such long-range changes does not lead to the conclusion to create the Center within the purview of a single existing institution." Only a sop was thrown to Portland State when the report asserted: "The committee believes in the likely growth of the Portland urban area and in the likely emergence of one or more urban universities within the metropolis. The committee welcomes the possibility or indeed, as it expects, that probability. Reference has already been made to the rapid growth of Portland State College; its further evolution would appear inevitable and desirable. Private institutions may follow the same course."[11]

The committee reiterated the point that "in all of this range of educational offerings the degrees can be in fact conferred by one of the existing colleges or universities in Oregon." However, in the indefinite future, it realized the center might offer degrees in its own name in two situations: if the institutions decided their own programs did not justify them or if there was disagreement between the older institutions and the center over what degree programs might be offered. It summarized the point: "The committee does not, therefore, recommend that degree-granting by the Center be foreclosed; it does urge caution and restraint, and it recognizes that it may prove to be never necessary or desirable in any particular application." The conclusions of the Sullivan committee, in the eyes of the state system, were a great improvement over those of the first SENT committee, which had recommended the autonomous institution. That last possibility was put off indefinitely, while system schools would develop the Center's precedent-setting programs with what little help the private liberal arts colleges could contribute. For Portland State, the conclusions of the Sullivan committee, while hardly ideal, were about all it could get.[12]

While the Sullivan committee was making its final report to the governor, the state system's Coordinating Council, under the direction of Miles C. Romney of the chancellor's staff, continued its work. It issued another preliminary report on 29 November 1962 and a final report on 4 March 1963. The final report, entitled "Planning for the Development of Graduate Education in Oregon," began by frankly noting there would be an autonomous center for graduate education in Portland and that state system institutions would be glad to cooperate in its development. Romney could not be specific about how this cooperation would develop, as the autonomous center was just then being organized, but he did say, "Perhaps the best that can be done at this stage is to consider how most effectively the state system can strengthen the programs that are being extended to the Portland area from campuses outside the area. " More specifically, his recommendations gave little comfort to Portland State. In the areas that Romney declared had the "widest appeal to the business and industrial community of Portland"—the off-campus master's degrees in business offered by the Uof O and in engineering by OSU—he recommended greater appropriations to maintain and increase them. He concluded, ominously for Portland State, that it did not seem feasible at present to offer these two programs in Portland "through any other State System auspices."[13]

Romney gave lip service to the importance of developing graduate work at Portland State by citing the master's degree programs that had been authorized in social work and in teaching (the MAT/MST degrees), but, throughout the report, he poured cold water on the idea of developing Portland State as a distinguished graduate institution. He did so in several ways. Portland State's development, he wrote, must occur with due regard to "the total graduate education commitments of the State System and the economic factors that impinge upon the development of higher education in the State System." He argued for time: "Experience in other metropolitan areas has demonstrated," he conceded, "that inevitably one or more urban universities rises to meet such [graduate education] needs. But such developments are the work of neither a day nor a decade." Romney also spent time attempting to refute the argument that graduate programs furnished off-campus by Oregon and Oregon State were a burden on faculty and of less benefit to students than on-campus programs at Portland State. He raised the stumbling block used in earlier years to attempt to prevent Portland State from becoming both a permanent, and then a four-year, college—duplication of resources. While admitting duplication was unavoidable—and, indeed, desirable—at the under-graduate level, he said "the hazards of duplication at the graduate level become more real…the more advanced and more specialized the program." These hazards included the higher costs of graduate education, the difficulty of recruiting a graduate faculty, the relative fewness of students, the lesser number of vocational opportunities, and the fear of staff at existing institutions that duplicate programs would diminish their legitimate aspirations.

Romney laid down some general principles governing the range of graduate programs, one of which, striking as it did at Portland State's aspirations, deserves quotation at length:

> The financing of new programs of graduate education should not be permitted to interfere with the effective development of programs already in existence. It will be the policy of the Council to give first priority to strengthening existing programs of instruction and research, remembering, however, that the interests of the state as a whole have precedence over the interests of a given institution. Where choice must be made between quality and accessibility, however, quality must be given pre-eminence.[14]

In the appendix to his report, however, Romney attempted to undermine the autonomous university and in so doing gave some comfort to Portland State. He stressed the inter-relationship between a strong undergraduate liberal arts education (which the autonomous university would not provide) and graduate work. Further, he stressed the advantages of basic graduate research rather than that applied to specific concerns of specific industries (as the autonomous university would do): "The faculties of high-quality graduate schools are a resource which science-based industry feeds upon. These faculties and their research, both basic and applied, are significant factors in creating the climate in which science-based industries are germinated and thrive."[15]

The effect of this report on Portland State administrators and faculty can be easily imagined. When Romney circulated the "general principles" portion of his report to the system institutions, Swarthout asked the division chairmen to comment on it, warning them that "as you read through the several pages, you may find the hair rising upon the back of your neck a bit. Please try to guard your emotions, since it is imperative that we approach the question here involved in a cool and collected way, undisturbed by choler." Swarthout's injunction to calmness was justified, as he spelled out his gratitude toward Romney for doing what he could. After the dean perused the final guidelines, he commented on them in a note to Millar: "This guidelines statement seems to have come about as far toward what we would like it to say as we have any reason to expect it could." He was particularly heartened by Guideline 3-e, which proclaimed:

> Provision must be made for the orderly and sequential assumption by Portland State College of an increasingly important role in graduate education in selected fields and at selected levels, as the resources of Portland State College and the State permit. As Portland State College's role in graduate education in the Portland area expands, a fundamental reappraisal of the roles of graduate programs 'extended' to the Portland area by the other state system institutions will be required....I believe we ought to settle, and happily, with this statement as it is, thanking Miles Romney for bringing a beam of reasonableness and a ray of logic to bear on what could have been a chaos of conflicting interests and points of view.[16]

What could not be looked at so happily, however, was Governor Hatfield's antipathy toward Portland State, based on an ideological commitment to private colleges and universities and his belief that an independent graduate center should concentrate on "practical" solutions to the state's economic problems, rather than on basic research. The governor, acting on one of the proposals made by the Sullivan committee, appointed a board to establish an independent graduate center in Portland. The board was composed of educators (from both public and private institutions) and businessmen, and it included one representative from Portland State, Willard Spalding. The governor attended the initial meeting of the board for what was first called the Portland Graduate Center and made several points it should follow in designing the center, including "no funds for the Center to be requested from this legislature." The charter of the new institution was conveniently vague in its purposes, although the name was changed to the Oregon Graduate Center for Study and Research. The charter said nothing specific about granting degrees, although that could be inferred from its history and from one of its purposes: "To enlarge the opportunities, especially in the metropolitan area of Portland, Oregon, for graduate education for men and women of high promise."[17]

The Oregon Graduate Center (OGC) began precariously. Its first president, Donald Benedict, formerly of the Stanford Research Institute, had trouble raising money, and the new institution was only sustained through the contributions of businessmen, including Howard Vollum of Tektronix, John Gray of Omark Industries, Ira Keller of Western Kraft, and a physician, Samuel Diack. But even they could not raise enough money, a condition that may have forced (or it may have been his intention from the beginning) Governor Hatfield to ask the legislature to appropriate funds for the Center in the 1965–67 biennium. However, he was unable to provide it, even though he tried to hold the state system hostage by remaining neutral on its attempt to raise money for its own program in Portland. Deprived of legislative aid, the Oregon Graduate Center continued thereafter on its uncertain course, sometimes flourishing, sometimes declining, but never reaching the status of a major university in any respect. Although Portland State did cooperate with the new institution in the years ahead, there is no doubt the presence of OGC (now the Oregon Graduate Institute) has diluted the efforts to develop strong graduate programs in science and engineering in the Portland area.[18]

While the governor was pushing OGC forward, Sen. Don S. Willner of Portland was making one of his many contributions to Portland State. Impatient with the foot-dragging of the state board and the chancellor on graduate education in the metropolitan region, Willner introduced Senate Joint Resolution 8 on 25 January 1963. The resolution's preamble declared Portland was the only metropolitan area in the West without a graduate school of arts and sciences; that many students could not take up residence in Eugene or Corvallis; and that the existence of graduate education would both attract new, science-based industries and aid existing businesses in the area. It concluded by resolving, "The State Board of Higher Education shall establish a quality program of graduate education in the arts and sciences in the Portland metropolitan area" and that the board should plan such a program in time to make budget requests to the legislature for the 1965–67 biennium. The resolution passed overwhelmingly in both houses of the legislature. While it was being debated, President Millar hailed it, emphasizing the economic potential of the program endorsed in the resolution, which "serves notice that Oregon intends that its economic growth shall keep pace with the rapid advances in modern technology." Willner was careful to state that his center would not detract from the private graduate center simultaneously being created. The main effect of the resolution, which received extensive coverage in the Portland press and produced much favorable publicity for the College when its spokesmen testified for it in Salem, was to focus attention on the paucity of graduate offerings in Portland.[19]

One prominent supporter of the resolution was the City Club of Portland, a prestigious organization that debates public issues, usually on information gathered by its Research committees. A City Club committee (which included Willner and E. Dean Anderson of Portland State) had been considering the state of graduate education in Portland since 1961. It issued a full report in May 1963, which made a three-fold recommendation to solve the problem of the lack of science and engineering education in Portland. The recommendation held something for, and required something from, everyone. Portland State was given a request to the state board to build it up to full university rank. Second, the Portland business community was asked to support an institution that would provide facilities for post-doctoral research in the physical sciences, engineering, and the life sciences. Third, business was further requested to support a second institute, one for applied research in various areas that would stimulate industry.[20]

By late spring 1963, it was clear Portland State would not gain university status without surmounting additional difficulties. Supporters of advanced science and engineering education had splintered their efforts because of the necessity of compromising among the demands and aspirations of the state board, Portland State, Governor Hatfield, and the business community. As earlier noted, the governor and OGC were unable to obtain public funds for the Center in the years ahead, and Portland State had been able to take advantage of the discussion over scientific education to secure board commitments and legislative promises that made clear that MAT/MST and MA/MS degrees would soon be forthcoming. These were gains, to be sure, but they fell short of the creation of a first-class metropolitan university, such as the University of Illinois (Chicago) would become.

Portland State's chances of obtaining this status were slightly muddied in 1964, when Reed College announced plans for a private graduate center under its auspices. Although Samuel Diack of OGC did not see these plans as competitive with his new institution (he was "very enthusiastic" about the Reed plan, according to a *Vanguard* report), Senator Willner was careful to tell the state board the Reed graduate program "does not relieve the State System of Higher Education of its responsibilities for graduate education in the Portland metropolitan area." In April 1964,the state board adopted a preliminary report on graduate study. It was helpful to those at Portland State who wanted the graduate programs of the institution to develop slowly and carefully, which was essentially Millar's view, but it disappointed those who wanted an immediate, large-scale build-up to full university status. The report favored the "evolutionary" development of the College into a university, while recommending the institution's graduate offerings be developed over the next decade. Millar took comfort from these conclusions; as he told the *Vanguard,* "I would say that the board's agreeing to these basic assumptions was a major milestone." The board made their recommendations more specific in December.[21]

The legislature did its part to fulfill these recommendations by voting in its 1965 session for a special allocation of $789,683 to enhance both undergraduate and graduate work at the College. The graduate portion was to be spent on developing master's degrees in Physics, Chemistry, Engineering, and Applied Science. Working with the chancellor's office, Portland State was able to enhance its graduate offerings by obtaining approval for ten additional master's programs in 1966, contingent on the legislature funding them in 1967.[22]

This pace, although promising, was not rapid enough to satisfy Senator Willner, Portland State's main legislative champion. Willner wanted Portland State to be called a university but, more important, wanted the state system to develop an "immediate program" to provide "advanced education and research to the Ph.D. level and beyond in selected scientific fields." Help for doctoral work also came from Tom McCall, Republican candidate for governor, who promised, if elected, he would support Ph.D. programs at Portland State. Once elected, McCall did honor his promise by asking, in his inaugural address in 1967, that the legislature fund the planning of doctoral work at Portland State.[23]

Willner immediately moved to implement this request by introducing Senate Bill 31 on 17 January 1967, a measure that was a significant departure in content from his earlier plans based on a state system-operated, cooperative doctoral-granting institution. In contrast, SB 31 dealt only with Portland State, calling for the beginning of doctoral programs no later than the fall of 1969 and providing the sum of $2 million to bring these programs to realization. Portland State was ready with ammunition for the senator. In February 1967, the Office of Graduate Studies had recommended it would be feasible to begin doctoral studies in four fields in the fall of 1969: Biophysics, Environmental Science, Mathematical Statistics, and Urban Affairs. Willner endorsed these proposals in speaking for his bill and tried to defuse criticism by noting the four selected degrees were not competitive with Oregon or Oregon State and were interdisciplinary in nature.[24]

Senate Bill 31 did not pass, but it did keep the issue alive for another session. The final breakthrough came in the 1969 legislative session. But before it was attained, Portland State had to prepare a detailed set of recommendations for doctoral programs based on internal discussion and had to convince the chancellor and the board to accept them. In November 1967, the Graduate Council reported to the faculty senate in favor of adopting the following doctoral programs: Mathematical Statistics; Urban Studies; Biophysics; and Environmental Sciences and Resources. This selection of doctoral programs had real advantages to the emerging university, especially because they were all interdisciplinary in nature. This was advantageous, as Millar told the senate at the time, because "it is a political judgment and should be treated as such." The components of the judgment were the support for additional educational facilities in science in a metropolitan area traditionally starved for them, a need recognized since the late 1950s; the necessity of moving more quickly than Portland State had anticipated in developing new programs; and the fact that the failure of SB 31 did not leave a great deal of money for doctoral work.[25]

In response to whether the Ph.D. programs were required to be interdisciplinary, Millar responded they need not be, either in guidelines laid down by the board or by the College. Other speakers suggested the Graduate Council might set up priorities for the program, but this was refuted by the chairman of the council, who believed it might select the wrong political priorities and that the OGC program might overlap Portland State offerings. The speaker who made the last point, a sociologist, said the College's focus might be better on urban, rather than scientific, problems.[26]

Interdisciplinary doctoral programs had other advantages for Portland State. In the first place, they seemed on the "cutting edge" intellectually and socially. As the director of Program Analysis pointed out in regard to environmental sciences (and his remarks also were relevant for other doctoral programs): "Nationally a number of new proposals are currently being implemented through the development of Environmental Center Programs at colleges and universities; ...in addition other institutions have developed, or propose to develop, programs in one or more interdisciplinary areas such as Urban Studies, Biophysics, Environmental Science, Systems Science."[27]

Secondly, many of these programs could be presented as being of direct, practical community service. Those who advocated this view hit on a historical analogy they hoped would be appropriate. This comparison was the model of a "city-grant" college that would be analogous to the land-grant university that had been a feature of rural America since 1862. This model had been used by Frederick Cox in 1965, at the time the autonomous university was being discussed. Cox quoted President Millar as one who foresaw Portland State as a city-grant college that would "bring the maximum of its resources to bear on its urban community with a total impact somewhat akin to that which the land-grant college had on our rural and agricultural life and economy." Two years later, in the College's proposal to the state board for a doctorate in Urban Studies, the same note was struck: "Portland State College should, as rapidly as possible, develop its facilities, programs, and curriculum in relation to the Portland metropolitan area in much the same manner that, in the past, land grant colleges developed their resources with respect to an agrarian society." The Division of Science presented its proposed doctorate in Biophysics as politically palatable also: "The obvious appeal of the problems of living systems to everyone, coupled with the certainty of practical applications to human welfare, generates sustained public support." Similar statements appeared in other doctoral proposals.[28]

Thirdly, and no one mentioned this publicly, the Portland State doctoral programs would enable the school to circumvent the older institutions' monopoly on Ph.D. degrees. As interdisciplinary degrees, they could not be challenged as duplicating the existing programs in individual disciplines at Oregon and at Oregon State. A Physics doctorate could be presented as part of an Environmental Sciences program or a Sociology doctorate under the umbrella of Urban Studies. Whatever merits there were in the interdisciplinary approach belong to the initiator of the idea: Karl Dittmer, dean of the Division of Science. Coming to the College in 1966 from Florida State University, "King Karl" was a forceful and effective advocate of the interdisciplinary doctoral programs through his testimony before legislative committees and his connections with scientific and business groups in the Portland community.[29]

The new doctoral programs were discussed extensively, but almost always favorably, in the faculty senate in November 1967 and in January 1968, after Dean Cox reported to the body that four doctoral programs had been submitted to the chancellor. These were Environmental Science and Resources; Mathematical Statistics; Systems Science; and Urban Studies. In the end, the board approved the programs, except for Mathematical Statistics (significantly, the only one not interdisciplinary and, thus, threatening to the two older universities). After the usual hearings by the board and its committees, the board approved the recommendations for the three programs in June 1968. Urban Studies and Environmental Sciences would begin in 1969–70 and System Science the following academic year.[30]

The final stage for the doctoral programs was a part of the last leg of Portland State's quest for designation and funding as a university. Both depended on the actions of the state legislature. As in the case of the permanent institution in 1949 and the four-year college in 1955, the legislature led, and the chancellor and board followed, although this time not nearly so far behind nor as reluctantly as in the earlier campaigns. Indeed, an aura of inevitability now attached itself to the cause of changing Portland State to a university, so that only token resistance was left. The more difficult of the two issues was the question of appropriating money to fund the graduate programs, not the inexpensive matter of the name change. This distinction was typical in Oregon, a state historically reluctant to fund programs in the realm of higher education.

In spring 1968, the campaign for the two objectives opened. Sen. Ross Morgan gave a thoughtful talk at Portland State, during which he endorsed the idea of university status but recognized both the difficulty in finding funding for it and the danger that doctoral work could de-emphasize undergraduate work. On 11 November 1968, the faithful champion, Senator Willner, announced he would introduce a bill in the next legislative session to obtain university status for Portland State. Willner tried to dramatize his cause by making his announcement on Veterans Day, to connect with the memory of the first Vanport student body and by promising to attempt to have the bill signed by 14 February 1969, the perceived fourteenth anniversary of the College. At this time, Willner made two arguments of substance for his measure. He declared assuming the name of university would make Portland State eligible for additional federal aid and that Portland State was one of three universities (the other two being the branches of the

Governor Tom McCall signing bill creating Portland State University

University of California at Santa Cruz and Irvine) using interdisciplinary programs "to emphasize urban involvement."[31]

Willner was as good as his word. Indeed, political realities dictated he introduce two bills for Portland State early in the 1969 legislative session. The first bill simply changed the name of the college to a university. The second would require the state board to initiate doctoral programs beginning in the fall of 1969 and appropriated the amount of $891,000 to mount them. Willner, aided by information furnished by the new president of Portland State, Gregory B. Wolfe, had little trouble getting the name change adopted; it passed in the senate by a vote of twenty to five and in the House by a vote of fifty to four. Wolfe, John Nolan (president of the Associated Students), and representatives from the Port of Portland, Pacific Power and Light, and the Portland Chamber of Commerce all testified for the bill before the senate Education Committee. Many faculty and students also attended the hearing, riding in a bus chartered by the Dan Davis Corporation, the builder of a large private dormitory (now called the Ondine) adjacent to the campus. Gov. Tom McCall signed the bill into law on 14 February, the day Willner had promised. The second bill, as it involved money, took more effort.[32]

Although there was no question Portland State would get some money for its support, there was no certainty it would be adequate. But the measure was not necessary, as it turned out. The governor had

Students changing sign on Lincoln Hall after Portland State becomes a university

included enough money in his own higher education requests to begin the new programs. Still, Willner's second bill gave publicity to the College, and when it was defeated, no harm was done.[33]

Portland State became a university in the absence of much public controversy—and with such overwhelming support in the legislature—because of a favorable combination of developments and personalities that made the time auspicious for it, a mere fourteen years after the institution obtained the right to grant any degrees at all. In 1949 and in 1955, the struggle had been sharper, with both antagonists and proponents more clearly defined and far more numerous. Furthermore, in those earlier campaigns, Portland State advocates were working in a less complex bureaucratic and social environment, which made the task of obtaining recognition both simpler and harder. In the late 1960s, the rise of public interest in a host of urban problems from air pollution to drug use to race relations caused some to turn to the urban university as a problem solver to a far greater degree than in earlier years. The ideal of a public service institution, always present at Portland State since the 1950s, now became more and more significant, and a greater and greater asset to the institution as it strove to expand and develop. By this time, also, the opposition of the older institutions was less formidable than in the past, simply because they and their supporters knew Portland State was here to stay and that growth at the institution was inevitable. More was to be lost than gained in fighting its development openly and vigorously.

Finally, the 1960s were a time in which, although there was great criticism of specific actions of government, there was still hope political action could solve public problems. After all, the 1960s was the time of national civil rights and environmental and social legislation, such as the epochal measures of the Lyndon Johnson administration (the Civil Rights Laws of 1964, 1965, and 1968); the various components of the War on Poverty; Medicare and Medicaid; and the Environmental Protection Act. At the state level, the era was marked by the governorship of Tom McCall (1967–75) under whose leadership Oregon passed a Willamette River Greenway, the Bottle Deposit Law, a Land Conservation and Development Act, and a Wild Rivers Act. Furthermore, it was relatively easy to enact sweeping legislation, because this was a prosperous era in the United States, and social change was not as threatening as in more parlous economic times.

Against this background conducive to governmental action, the particular leaders of Portland State's cause advanced it as skillfully as Stephen Epler and John Hakanson had done in earlier times. One scholar has identified six groups as contenders in the struggle for university status. The first of these, and the most important because it was the dynamic group, was President Millar and his fellow Portland State administrators. Millar skillfully moved the development process forward by applying three strategies. First, he came to recognize the enormous importance of community support for Portland State. Like Epler before him, he cultivated the powerful groups in the Portland metropolitan area and helped them see the compatibility of their interests with the quest for a public university in the only city on the West Coast without one.[34]

This strategy marked Millar to be a quick learner, for when he first came to Portland State, he did not initially exploit the connection between mortarboard and metropolis. Indeed, a report of his first remarks to the faculty after his appointment stated he was "not sure what…the distinctive nature of an urban college" was, though he suspected "a good college is a good one anywhere." Finally, the report stated one of Millar's main tasks would be "to interpret to the public what a college ought to be. It should be a secular sanctuary rather than a market place. It is fundamentally concerned with 'learning' rather than 'know-how.'"[35]

But Millar soon recognized the values of developing and publicizing the connections between the College and the community. He was

also skillful in dealing with the chancellor and the board, and he possessed a valuable sense of the moment. Although he preferred the
College develop into a university in a careful, step-by-step manner, he
realized this ideal was impossible to realize in an environment in
which community and faculty were pushing hard for development.
Millar did not make the mistake Cramer had of compromising, of trying to please both board and chancellor on the one hand and the faculty, students, and community on the other. Cramer pleased neither
group; Millar led the Portland State partisans, but in a quiet and non-
confrontational way that was ultimately effective in turning the College
into a university. "Millar not only possessed skill as an academic leader and manager," one scholar concluded, "but had a finely honed
political sensitivity which he brought to bear in his dealings with the
Board and its staff, members of the Legislative Assembly, and Portland
business and industrial leaders."[36]

President Millar also had allies in the business community of the
Portland metropolitan area. These men and women again and again
pointed out that Portland was the only large city on the West Coast
without a research-oriented public or private university. When this deficiency first was recognized, one group of businessmen followed Governor Hatfield's lead in pushing for a private graduate center (aided
by the State), while another favored building a public institution
(either a greater Portland State or a state system co-operative institution). After the Oregon Graduate Center was denied state funds in 1965,
the two business groups coalesced to assist Portland State's push to
become a university.[37]

Neither the College nor the business community, however in agreement they might be, were working in a vacuum. The legislature was
the decisive element in determining the speed of Portland State's progress. This influence was recognized, although no one said anything
about it publicly, not only as a matter of the legislature's power but of
how that power had been used historically in the realm of higher education. What had made Portland State permanent and what had given
it college status was the legislature, which had acted in both instances
against the wishes of the chancellor and the board who, in turn, were
responding to the power and tradition of the University of Oregon.

In the struggle for university status, the most important of all leg-
islators was Sen. Don Willner, who played the role earlier designed by
Rudi Wilhelm, John Logan, and Richard and Maurine Neuberger.
Willner introduced bills, testified for them before board and legisla-

tive committees, and spoke for them outside the legislative chambers. Of equal importance, like Millar, he was able to build consensus both within and without the legislature. Willner was an active member of the board of directors of the Portland Chamber of Commerce, which gave him access to the organization's executive director, Oliver Larson, and other leaders of the city's business community. The linkage between community and college was the confidential communication between Willner and Millar (often through Dean Anderson, Millar's assistant). Millar could not openly oppose his employer, the state board, while Willner could. As Willner remembers the situation: "I basically made the political judgments and Bran and his group made the academic judgments."[38]

The political judgments involved gaining the support of the downstate legislative leaders for a measure that would enhance the metropolitan area and was believed—although erroneously—to diminish the futures of the University of Oregon and Oregon State University (Oregon State became a university in 1961). This support was gained through the statewide support of the Portland business community, working through the Portland Chamber of Commerce and by a political alliance worked out in the 1969 legislative session between Willner, a liberal Portland Democrat, and Stafford Hansell, a conservative Hermiston Republican, whereby the Portlanders supported programs for Eastern Oregon and Hansell backed making Portland State a university.[39]

Willner, of course, could not carry the cause himself, but he was the most prominent and effective advocate. Pro-Portland State legislators, in turn, were not the whole government of Oregon. Their powers were shared with the governor. Oregon's governors of the era held differing views of the future of Portland State. Mark Hatfield had long been cool toward Portland State, dating to his opposition to a four-year college in the mid-1950s, when he was a state legislator. As governor, he favored a private, autonomous university in the Portland area and was the moving force in starting the Oregon Graduate Center. He tried to get state funds for this institution, but when he could not do so, lost interest in public graduate education in Portland. By contrast, his successor, Tom McCall, was very helpful to Portland State and took pride in the role he played in establishing the institution. In the end, President Millar and his successor, Gregory Wolfe, were able to mobilize enough interest groups to win the coveted university status.[40]

Although Portland State expanded mightily during the 1960s, the College was not an imperialistic monster eager to grow in all directions

at any price. The experiences with a law school indicate the limits—
some external, some self-imposed—of the opportunities for growth.
In a way, given Portland State's eagerness to identify with the greater
metropolitan community, it would have been appropriate for the
College to acquire a law school, but it was not to be.

There was an opportunity to do so. There was a law school in Portland, one with a long and colorful history. This institution was Northwestern College of Law. It had derived from the first law school in the
city, that of the University of Oregon, which founded it in 1884. It was
a proprietary branch of the University, dependent solely on student
fees for its expenses and offering night classes only. In 1913, the University decided to move the Law School to Eugene, an unpopular move
with many students, who could not leave the metropolis. In 1915, Calvin
Gantenbein, the dean, changed the Portland school into the Northwestern College of Law by buying the institution from the University.
The school had never been accredited, but enough of its graduates
passed the bar examination to keep it going for several decades.[41]

In 1958, John Gantenbein, son of Calvin, converted the school
from a family business to a non-profit corporation. The trustees, all
prominent members of the bar, soon recognized the lack of accreditation and poor facilities in a downtown building were serious obstacles
to making the school a continuing success. By 1960, they were actively
seeking to reorganize the school, perhaps by having it taken over by
the State System of Higher Education. When the board took up the
matter, it referred it to Pres. O. Meredith Wilson of the University of
Oregon. Wilson was not enthusiastic about the University assuming
this responsibility but said it could be done, although "he discussed
the possibility of the law school being attached to Portland State College
or the University of Oregon." He further stated the proportion of Washington students attending law school was far greater than in the state
of Oregon and implied there were enough opportunities at Eugene
for aspiring members of the bar, although he did remark the residents
of Portland might need a school for the sake of convenience.[42]

In February 1962, the Oregon State Bar informed Chancellor Roy
E. Lieuallen it was studying the situation at Northwestern College of
Law and asked if the chancellor were interested in being informed of
its progress. Two months later, the bar committee investigating the
matter asked him "if there is anything that can be done by the State
Board of Higher Education to meet the present and future needs for
proper legal education in the Portland area."[43]

The chancellor took up the matter with Gov. Mark O. Hatfield in 1963, who cautioned that nothing be said about expanding the University of Oregon to Portland until after the legislative session for fear the legislators would regard it "as an effort to add to our 'empire,'" but it was then decided to have the University develop a plan to acquire the Northwestern Law School as a branch of the University of Oregon Law School. The chancellor consulted Pres. G. Herbert Smith of Willamette University (which also had a law school), who opposed the move, fearing competition, even though the chancellor had threatened that unless the University of Oregon were allowed to have an evening law school in Portland, then the (obviously undesirable) possibility would arise of "the pressure to become so great that a law school would be established in connection with Portland State College."[44]

Officials of Northwestern wrote to the chancellor and to the presidents of the University of Oregon and Portland State urging a merger on the state system "provided, of course, that reasonable terms can be agreed upon for this purpose." In response, Branford Millar said he would be glad to discuss the matter with the Northwestern and state system officials. How seriously he hoped to be taken is unclear, but, in any case, the chancellor and the board agreed "the University of Oregon is in the most advantageous position to establish appropriate relationships with Northwestern College of Law." If the chancellor had shown interest, Millar would certainly have backed off, for he had no intention of pursuing the matter. Although urged by Business Manager Lemman and Dean Dixon, who saw a Portland State law school as a source of future legislators and, hence, alumni allies, Millar wanted to concentrate on developing the College. He firmly declared Portland State needed a "third-rate" law school like a "hole in the head."[45]

Portland State was out of the picture, but not for long. Northwestern officials became disappointed with the progress of the negotiations with the University of Oregon and, in April 1964, asked the chairman of the state board if they could discuss a "possible merger or affiliation with Portland State College." No progress had been made with the University of Oregon by July, so, again, the merger possibility with Portland State was raised. The president of the board poured cold water on this prospect, however, by declaring "it is my conviction that the Board of Higher Education would strongly resist identification of Northwestern College of Law with Portland State College. As you may know, we are not ready to expand course offerings at Portland State College in the graduate area. We and officials of that institution are acutely aware that much, much strengthening of the undergraduate structure must be accomplished before we superimpose further graduate responsibilities upon it." Negotiations then began with the University of Oregon, but they broke down over a variety of matters. In the end, the Northwestern Law School merged with Lewis & Clark College on 13 September 1965.[46]

The state system had one last flurry of activity concerning Northwestern. The Northwestern Law School had not prospered satisfactorily after its merger with Lewis & Clark—the school remained unaccredited, and its first dean resigned because money promised for development had not materialized. In 1968, during these discouraging times, Keith Skelton, a state legislator and a Portland State faculty member, urged the state board to "either purchase and operate Northwestern as a separate law school or as an adjunct to the law school at the University of Oregon." Perhaps Portland State might have fished in these troubled waters, but it did not do so; the unhappy situation at Northwestern cleared, and any chance for Portland State to add a law school evaporated. Probably, the chances never had been great, and, most certainly, they had not been pursued vigorously by Millar.[47]

While the colorful struggle for graduate work and university status was taking place with all the intermittent progress and reversals that accompanied it, Portland State faculty members and administrators were working in other directions they conceived universities should work. One of these areas was the creation of institutes or centers, academic entities separate from, although dependent on, traditional departments but often focused on "practical" issues of interest to the community. Institutes, at least in theory, could contribute to the community, publicize the College, attract funds, and give prestige to faculty. They seemed like university, rather than college, bodies, and thus desirable to ambitious faculty members.

The first proposal for an institute at Portland State came originally from a letter sent by the United States Public Health Service in Portland to Dean Swarthout in July 1960. Swarthout turned the matter over to the fertile brain of Brock Dixon, one of that galaxy of academic entrepreneurs that included George Carbone and Fred Cox, men who were able to do much with little in publicizing the College by involving it in new ventures. In September 1960, Dixon, who was assistant to the dean of the faculty, contacted Edward Eldridge of the United States Public Health Service and arranged a luncheon with him that included members of the College's Biology and Chemistry departments. The Public

Health Service had funds available to finance research projects in a variety of academic disciplines. Some Portland State faculty members already held such grants. But future Health Service funds could be doubly valuable to Portland State. Faculty would be able to work in stimulating areas of research, and the College might be able to use some of the money to improve laboratory and other facilities at the College.[48]

Dixon consulted Clyde Johnson, a respected faculty member from the Chemistry Department, and Johnson, in turn, consulted his colleagues in the Science Division, who proposed a committee to look into the matter. Dixon endorsed the idea in a memorandum to Swarthout. Swarthout appointed Johnson to head such a committee to accomplish three purposes the scientists had already proposed to Johnson informally: encourage faculty to apply for Public Health Service grants; plan a long-range program in public health research; and "explore with the administration and building planners the possibility of requesting considerable sums of money from the Public Health Service to help finance research facilities in the new science building." (A building that had been authorized but not funded at this date.)[49]

Johnson's committee, the Public Health Service Relations Committee, completed a rough draft of its report in February 1961, requesting $250,000 from the Public Health Service. On 10 May, the committee completed the final version of its report, recommending a request to the Health Service for $237,000 for equipping 10,580 square feet in the new science building. This money was to be provided under the Health Research Facilities Act. In the next three weeks, the pace quickened, as Swarthout and the committee pulled some threads together and the legislature made a decision. In early June, Swarthout was able to inform the Public Health service the College would soon apply for money to establish an environmental public health research unit at PSC. Both the administration and about thirty members of the Science Division supported the idea of requesting the funds. Best of all, Swarthout wrote, the legislature had just provided the sum of $2.3 million to build the science building. The plan was for the Health Service money to be used to place the health research unit on the entire fifth floor. Two days before the deadline later in the month, the administration, after working with the committee and a local representative of the Public Health Service, mailed off the final application for the grant. Although sent at the last minute, the application was successful, a labor indicative of the ingenuity of Portland State faculty in trying to build their institution.[50]

Sources for other institutes popped up over the years, often to answer the demands of some non-university interest. The city of Portland initiated one such request in 1962, when Mayor Terry Schrunk suggested something be done at the College to develop a curriculum in municipal planning. The mayor's interest accelerated a plan the dean of the faculty had been working on for two years. Swarthout and his staff had been considering how to get the College involved in teaching urban affairs but had come to no conclusions about what should be done. Now—after Schrunk's show of interest—Swarthout told Millar it well might be time to bring together under one administrative "roof" a curriculum in planning; a set of research activities; and an "institute, workshop, or what have you for appropriate people in Portland, like that for which a couple of colleges have gotten whopping grants....given the right dynamic and respectable leadership, we could attract both money and local attention in quantity....knowing the college, I suspect we could do it with a lot of sweat and not very much money." Nothing came of this particular institute—not because it was a poor idea—but because the urban studies constituencies came to focus on a graduate program, including a doctoral degree, which they were able to achieve in 1969.[51]

A type of institute that indicated the interest of the liberal arts disciplines in such structures was one that never accomplished much. This was the Psychological Research Institute, created in 1965. It was to be an agency staffed by members of the Psychology Department that would conduct research projects of use to the community. The Institute obtained a director, Morris Weitman, and account numbers but never any money to spend. Its hope of obtaining funds by contracting with non-university entities was also not realized. In his letter authorizing the Institute, in terminology all too familiar to Portland State faculty, Swarthout wished it "every success" but stated "it cannot at this time be assured of financial support from state funds." Not surprisingly, given blessing but not funds, the Institute faltered.[52]

Another institute arose out of the blending of community need and the desire to advance the College drive for graduate status. This organization, as we have seen, was the Institute of Applied Mathematics—the idea of Thurman Peterson, the head of the Division of Science and Mathematics. When Peterson conceived of it in May 1962, he anticipated the usual financial difficulties in effecting any program at Portland State. Peterson's solution was to establish a private foundation at the same time as the institute. The institute itself would be "split between graduate teaching and research roughly half and half, and its support accordingly divided in the same ratio between state funds and foundation-furnished funds." The foundation, it was projected, would raise money initially from "local private sources" and then branch out into the raising of grant money. To avoid charges of departmental parochialism (presumably, although this was not stated in the documents), "the foundation would be expected to expand into other areas than math as rapidly as feasible." Also looking to the future, Peterson intended to rent space for the institute for several years, until it could be fully developed, instead of trying to raise money for a building at the beginning.[53]

In January 1965, Prof. Harry White of the Engineering Department drew up a formal plan for the Institute of Applied Mathematics. White set his plan in the context of the need for graduate education and research in the fields of engineering, science, and technology, a context familiar to everyone who had been caught up in the struggle for graduate work at Portland State; the institution's quest for university status; and the rise of the Oregon Graduate Center. The plan made the familiar point of the lack of advanced scientific training in the metropolitan area and urged the institute as a means to fill that gap. It said "mathematical institutes are appearing on the national scene," mentioning those at the University of Wisconsin and the University of Maryland. The plan made the point that "economic development is now generally recognized to be inseparably linked with scientific research and technological advance." The institute would have a computer center, faculty from within and without the College, a director, and an operational budget for 1965–67 of $491,896, in addition to capital costs of $446,570.[54]

The plan was submitted to the newly created Applied Mathematics Institute Committee, chaired by Dean Swarthout, which decided to hire two consultants to advise about its contents: Thornton Fry, consultant to the National Center for Atmospheric Sciences at Boulder, Colorado, and Carl Kossack, the director of the Graduate Research Center of the Southwest in Dallas. Fry visited Portland State in February 1965. In his report, it was clear he had grasped the essential point that institute and university status were intertwined. He said the Portland State community must decide if it wished the College to become a university: "Unless the College is to escalate to full university grade I would not recommend the establishment of an Institute of applied mathematics; *if the College is to become a university the proposed Institute is the log-*

ical first step." If the College decided to take this step, then Fry saw no problems with the details of the proposed plan such as the budget.[55]

Carl Kossack visited shortly afterward. Kossack raised some warning signals in his report. He said prospective faculty might be in short supply, since so many "emerging institutions" were entering the field of Applied Mathematics. He felt a more detailed plan would have to be drawn up to gain the attention of "the highest governing group in the state, including the Ways and Means Sub-Committee of the legislature." He recommended cooperation with other institutions in the area and suggested an "interim arrangement" be made with Oregon State so that Institute faculty members who were without the doctorate could take their advanced degrees at Oregon State.[56]

After digesting the comments of the consultants, Cox, Peterson, White, and Dean Frank Roberts revised the original proposal for the Institute. It was decided to produce scaled-down budgets for the next two biennia. The operating budget for 1965–67, for example, was reduced from the earlier draft's $491,896 to $288,180. Although Swarthout continued to encourage the proponents of the Institute, it eventually came to naught for the same reasons as had the later-proposed doctorate in Applied Mathematics: the belief on the part of the state board that it duplicated graduate offerings at Oregon and at Oregon State.[57]

Another institute proposal showed the perils of becoming involved in community-desired—and, in this case, community-funded—appendages of the College. This enterprise was called the Investment Analysis Center. The history of this proposal is important, because it set off a discussion—on the eve of Portland State's becoming a university—of the place of institutes and centers within the university structure. The idea of the Investment Analysis Center had originated in the School of Business Administration. It was to be a body supported financially by the investment community of Portland to use computers in investment analysis. The center, according to its advocates from the Business School, would be useful to the public; it would be a teaching and research device; and it would provide favorable community visibility to Portland State.[58]

Howard Boroughs, dean of the faculties, was suspicious of this proposal, specifically, and of institutes and centers, in general. He had the topic put on the agenda of the Council of Academic Deans in May 1968, where it was discussed fully. At this meeting, Boroughs outlined his objection to both centers and institutes, noting he "had been reluctant to encourage the development of centers and institutes, and indicated that he was not sure that institute status would make the activity more valuable or aid in fund raising." Besides their uncertainty as fundraising vehicles, Boroughs also was critical of institutes on other grounds. He said they weakened a department by creating internal problems between the faculty in the institute and those not—they could well create a two-tier faculty, with one group having a lower teaching load than the other. Another way the teaching load might be circumvented, he said, was "the creation of institutes provides an easy route for the faculty to become directors of centers, and thus ignore teaching requirements."[59]

Dean Donald Parker of the School of Business, ignoring Boroughs's objections, stuck to his proposal by assuring the deans there would be a continuing infusion of funds from the Portland investment community. It was this point Dean Dittmer of Science feared. He wanted to make sure the money flowing to the university be unrestricted and "not controlled by industry." When Boroughs commented the Institute might become a service bureau, Dean Hoffmann picked up the point, saying if a service bureau was the institute's function, then "he was not convinced that we should become involved." Although lukewarm on the institute, Hoffmann would accept it if the purpose of it were principally educational. He and Dittmer agreed any institute must be for the benefit of, in this case, the investment community as a whole and not an individual company.[60]

The Council of Academic Deans (CADS) discussed the matter at two other meetings. Parker maintained the proposed director of the Center, Shannon Pratt of the Business School, would quit the faculty if the Center were not formed. CADS remained divided, opponents fearing the danger of the Center becoming a tool of the donors and that it might create a two-class faculty. The Council discussed the matter again a week later. Many of the same arguments were gone over, with Boroughs raising a new objection: the problem of administering the control of expenditures by the Center. Parker also revised his arguments by this meeting. He now formally proposed the creation of the Center, "primarily as a vehicle for attaining outside funds." Dittmer was by now more positive, stating the Center might be able to make joint appointments to its faculty (presumably, businessmen who would teach part-time), attract "outstanding" faculty, guarantee summer employment to faculty, and produce overhead that could be spent for general College purposes. Parker tried to assure his skeptics the Center would be educational, that it would serve the community, and that it would not provide counsel about investments. Entrepreneurial as always, Cox argued circularly that "all college activities are public, and that there are many publics to be served." And, he added, "academia must put the resources where the need is." By the end of the meeting, Boroughs was weakening in his opposition, as was Hoffmann.[61]

Boroughs, a few days after this meeting, asked President Millar if he advised the faculty senate vote on the proposed center, but that route was dropped. In the end, Boroughs's objection was overcome, and the plans for the Center went forward. The Investment Analysis Center was formed in June 1968, with Shannon Pratt as director. By October, it was announced that seventy-six students had completed research projects under the Center and that twenty-nine students were working in non-credit, work-study projects. Commercial sources had donated $14,000 in cash and $56,000 worth of [unspecified] "material." There would soon be appointed an advisory board from various College departments and from the investment community. There was a bit of a dispute over how much time the Center had used on the College computer. Boroughs pointed out it had used almost all the College's research time. Parker tried to counter by saying most of the Center's computer use was during off hours, and, he claimed, "the income derived from [the] Investment Analysis Center computer use has kept the Computer Center alive." In any case, the Center was in business.[62]

Almost all the virtues and deficiencies of the university's institute component were to be found in the proposal for the Institute for Social Innovation, headed by George Fairweather. Fairweather was a psychologist who had come to Portland State in 1967, along with five associates: four psychologists and one social worker, all of whom were supported by a large grant from the National Institute of Mental Health. These researchers were all housed in the Psychology Department and had faculty appointments, although their funding source was elsewhere. In 1967, amidst much controversy, the faculty had rejected Fairweather's proposed degree program for a doctorate in the field of experimental social innovation. Fairweather came before the Council of Academic Deans in October 1968. He stated he did not want to become involved in obtaining new courses because "such involvement would impede the institute." He said he needed to know the fate of the institute one way or another, as he was negotiating with other universities to transfer his grant. Somewhat pathetically, he noted, his group "had been rebuffed by the faculty and the administration, and some-

Final examination of first doctoral graduate

times by both." Most of the deans were in favor of establishing the institute, Hoffmann carefully distinguishing his support for it from his disapproval of the Center for Investment Analysis on the grounds Fairweather's institute would serve the community, not a special interest group. Other arguments in its favor were that it would complement the impending doctoral programs in Urban Studies, Environmental Sciences, and Systems Science; provide opportunities for the faculty to engage in research in social problems; help the developing programs in special education in the School of Education; and attract outside agencies to Portland State (Dean Cox mentioned a show of interest by the Department of Psychology at the Medical School).[63]

The debate over this institute when it was presented to CADS was over two major issues. The first was substantive: Dean Dittmer asked if the work could not be carried on within the different departments, and Joseph Blumel, the dean of Undergraduate Studies, asked if the research opportunities arising from the institute might be made available to several departments. Fairweather assured them they would. The second issue was whether faculty approval would be required before the Institute could begin work. Hoyt Franchere argued this would be desirable. Boroughs attempted to dispose of the issue summarily: "Dean Boroughs asked why this was necessary. It had not been done in the past when similar institutes were established." Blumel supported him, stating the program did not involve curricular proposals, although he did say the faculty should be kept informed of developments in this area. Fairweather tried to pressure CADS to decide immediately, reportedly stating his group "would need more than approval in principle." He went on to say he was "negotiating with other Universities and [needed] a firm decision one way or the other." The meeting closed with CADS asking Boroughs to discuss the matter with President Wolfe.[64]

CADS soon received another description of the Institute from Fairweather, which they considered two weeks after their initial discussion of his proposal. This second document was a cause for confusion, because it contained a list of courses and programs that would definitely carry academic credit. It seemed to emphasize, as Blumel noted, the "teaching and training of graduate students and suggests a degree type of program instead of the multi-disciplinary research activity presented in the original program document." He insisted if the original proposal were now expanded to include courses, then the Institute must be taken to the faculty for its approval or disapproval. Franchere agreed, observing correctly "the faculty would view this program as a backdoor approach to curricular offerings without faculty approval." Dittmer recalled to his fellow deans the statement of the original proposal that said any courses developed by the Institute faculty would be developed within the departments concerned. He feared the second proposal would permit the creation of separate graduate degree programs in the Institute.[65]

A lone dissenter argued the Institute's programs could be carried out by existing departments, but the principal disagreement was not over whether the Institute was meritorious or not but how it should be created. Franchere argued the faculty should decide on the creation of the Institute, but most of the other deans said this was unnecessary, as other institutes had simply been established by the administration. As Cox put it: "Other than faculty interested in social research, the general faculty does not care about the establishment of such an institute" and that he "encouraged the CADS to get on with business." Boroughs suggested the faculty be at least informed formally of whatever was done, a proposal seconded by Caughlan, who said the faculty usually first heard of such innovations through the media. Boroughs took this suggestion to heart and made somewhat of a point of it in a memorandum to Wolfe, in which he conveyed the unanimous recommendation of the deans that Fairweather's institute be created.[66]

In the end, the whole discussion became meaningless, as Fairweather decided to move his institute, now incorporated into the Psychology Department and renamed the Institute for the Psychological Study of Living Systems, to Michigan State University in 1969. Reasons given by the chair of the Psychology Department for this move included Fairweather's inability to initiate graduate work in the areas of his scholarly interest and the rather vague "they couldn't get the sort of working arrangement they wanted." Fairweather's authoritarian and secretive personality also did not assist his cause, nor did his personality conflicts with members of his own institute. In any case, the controversy over this particular institute did force a discussion of the role and function of institutes in general, useful in light of the growth of the university in the years ahead.[67]

*"Those damn Mosser Plan cards
cluttering up my office"*

TWELVE

Curricular Innovations,
Teaching Evaluations,
and the Library · 1955–1969

hile many in the college community planned and
struggled to create a university curriculum complete
with advanced degrees, including doctorates, research
institutes, and federal grants, many did not abandon
interest in what the undergraduates were learning. They were concerned the undergraduates might lose their way in the wake of two
otherwise desirable developments taking form in these years: the addition of departmental majors to serve the cause of specialization and
the effect this more specialized curriculum might have on the general education of students. These concerns became apparent shortly
after Portland State received college status in 1955.

The new college was originally permitted to offer only two degrees:
a baccalaureate degree in Education and one in General Studies. The
only specialization permitted was that the General Studies student—if
desired—could specialize in humanities, science, or social science,
but there were no departmental majors. As the faculty pushed for
these disciplinary fields, there was concern general education might
become a casualty of specialization. President Cramer was one of those
worried about this possibility, and he was able to persuade Chancellor
John Richards to assist him in doing something about it. Cramer
appointed a General Studies Committee, headed by Philip Hoffman,
dean of the faculty. The committee included two members from each

of the divisions and a liaison to the Curriculum Committee. The committee was appointed on 2 October 1956 and met weekly from the fall of 1956 to the spring of 1958. One committee member from each division was also the chair of the three divisional subcommittees on General Studies.[1]

Unlike many college committees, the General Studies Committee had financial assistance. It was given $15,000 by the Fund for the Advancement of Education and another $15,000 by the chancellor. Through its own research, talks with colleagues at other institutions, and the hiring of a consultant, the committee first set about defining the terms "general studies" and "general education." Working mainly from experience, rather than from theory, the committee found three possible models in use throughout the United States: a core curriculum in which each student took certain courses; a program in which students were required to pick from a set of courses within each division; and a combination of the first two. The committee also decided early in its deliberations to concentrate on designing an upper-division program, as the College already required work of each student in the second model in the freshman and sophomore years. Progressing rapidly by meeting once a week for two hours, the committee made some preliminary recommendations in a report to the College community in January 1957.[2]

The committee began its report with a definition of the purpose of general education: to develop "inquiring, philosophical minds— with the development of students who are educated rather than merely indoctrinated." "The term general education," it continued, "suggests breadth of inquiry without sacrifice of depth in the thoroughness of understanding required of the student." After its decision about definition, and after some preliminary research, the committee drew up a tentative plan of study that would require each student to take one, three-hour general education course outside his or her division during the junior year. Choice was to be limited at the beginning, as there was only one course in each division: a science course entitled "The Living Cell;" a social science course called "The City;" and a humanities course entitled "The Creative Process." Juniors also would be required to take one course outside their own division, selected from a list of three or four provided in each division. The committee suggested, as examples of such courses, topics such as "Problems of Earth" and "The Ethical Basis of Economic Theory." Seniors would be required to take nine credits of General Studies courses in their own divisions. These divisional courses were required to offer insights from at least two departments within the division and "some considerable relation with a discipline from another division."[3]

By the fall of 1957, the hardworking committee had reached some other conclusions. On the negative side, its research in the experiences of other colleges and universities showed, it believed, that a separate faculty for general education courses was "almost always" a failure. It said General Studies courses, in searching for breadth, usually became superficial in content. It found courses taught by teams were more expensive than conventional courses and that "students in such courses become confused by the parade of instructors passing before them." And the committee recognized frankly the political dimension of introducing a General Studies program, the fear of some faculty that it stood for "innovation, for uncertainty, for threat to the present power structure; that it suggests the possibility of institutionalizing errors demonstrated by unsuccessful programs that are well-known."[4]

The committee—besides discerning error elsewhere—also began to implement its own ideas. It had agreed to arrange three experimental junior-level General Studies courses (one in each division) during the 1957–58 academic year, courses that were to emphasize independent work and subject matter bridging two departments and divisions. The committee obtained permission from the chancellor to teach these courses on an experimental basis and consent from the faculty senate to allow students to count them as one of the course sequences required for graduation. The courses were publicized to all faculty and junior students in time for fall term, and special books were ordered for the library to be used in them. Plans were made to develop senior-level courses as well. Meanwhile, in the midst of all these labors, the chair of the committee, Dean Philip Hoffman, moved to another institution. Willard Spalding, his interim successor as dean of the faculty, replaced him.[5]

The committee made further proposals to the faculty senate in December 1957. These encompassed a set of requirements somewhat reduced from those discussed earlier by the committee. The junior requirement became one, three-hour course from each of the three divisions, and there was now to be one, three-hour senior course in the student's major division. The recommendations were to go into effect on 30 June 1961. In presenting its proposals, the committee tried to reassure the faculty the regulations would not apply to students taking departmental majors when they were offered; that there would be no separate faculty or administration for General Studies; that no faculty members would be required to teach more than one General Studies course per term; that added funds would be requested for the new courses; and that the requirements in upper-division General Studies courses would only constitute 8.25 percent of the total credits required for graduation.[6]

In spite of these assurances, the report was discussed carefully by the senate, although the General Studies Committee did report "comments and criticisms were directed mainly toward important items, even when couched in somewhat heated language." There was a fear that General Studies courses would use up allocations needed for other areas or somehow delay progress toward departmental majors or both. The senate changed the effective date of the new courses to 30 June 1962 and narrowly defeated an amendment that would have made the proposed courses an alternative, rather than a requirement. In the end, the new courses were adopted. The opponents did not give up, however, and the proposals were referred to the full faculty in a meeting on 12 February 1958.[7]

At this meeting, the conservatism of the faculty in curricular matters was openly and overwhelming demonstrated. By a vote of 74-22, the proposal was watered down to an additional option to the existing graduation requirements in General Studies. The element of compulsion was abandoned. The major reason for the opposition, in the minds of the committee, was the fact that any new general education courses would get in the way of the possibility of departmental majors. The committee made its final report on 7 April 1958, summarizing its work, asking that the experimental courses be studied by the Curriculum Committee and recommended for permanency, and recommending the divisions create other General Studies courses. By the time of this final report, the committee not only had seen the issue of general education thoroughly ventilated but also had seen nine experimental courses—six junior courses and three senior ones—in the process of preparation for the 1958–59 academic year. The brochure sent to students describing the new General Studies courses stated their purpose: "To show relationships between ways of thinking that are usually considered different merely because they are applied to the study of different subjects. The intention of such courses is to liberalize, in the best sense, the educational program at Portland State College."[8]

When the departmental majors were authorized in 1960, interest in general education courses continued. Departments established their own requirements, of course, but students were also required to take classes outside their majors across the liberal arts divisions; if they so chose, students could meet a part of this requirement by enrolling in the special general education courses. By this time, general education and General Studies had become confused and conflated. The General Studies degrees continued after the introduction of departmental majors, but they—as more courses were added to the pool available for the degree—became little more than a collection of courses suitable for any degree. Only a small number of students who took the special, interdisciplinary General Studies courses were getting the type of general education the special committee had envisaged. Faculty fears had scuttled required general education in the quest to preserve existing courses and to hasten the development of departmental majors.

The general education program went largely unchanged for a decade. When it was again considered, it was in the context of the academic and social ferment of the 1960s that had been touched off by the Berkeley "Free Speech" movement, beginning in 1964. Demands for a "modern" curriculum "relevant" to contemporary individual and civic needs merged into the national civil rights and anti-Vietnam War movements in which students and faculty were figuring so prominently. What many commentators in the media labeled "The Age of Permanent Protest" had arrived. In 1968, the critics of tradition who concentrated on curriculum focused on "general education," but they divorced the term from its traditional use.

Although hardly a revolutionary, Frederick Waller, dean of undergraduate studies, initiated the idea of reforming general education. His tack was to call a university-wide conference, based on the format of the preceding year's one on government, to reconsider the program. Waller initiated the conference in a memorandum to the faculty on 23 February 1968. What he wanted the conference to do, he explained, was not simply to reshape the existing general education program or add new courses to it. He had something larger in mind for "general education." He wanted the faculty to suggest at conference end "what sort of school or curriculum within the college might best meet the needs of [certain] classes of students...'the locked outs,' the 'flunk outs,' and the 'drop outs,' but in an experimental setting involving the wide spectrum of students characteristic of an urban, public institution." "The faculty," he said, "will have an opportunity to plan an experimental program from scratch, within the larger college but with no holds barred."[9]

In other words, the outcome of the conference was programmed before it opened. It was to create an experimental college or program mainly to appeal to three groups of former students or prospective students. The conference deliberations were designed to discuss the nature of the proposed college, not its desirability. It also was clear there would be difficulties in creating a true "general" education program if it were tailored to fit a small segment of the student body, not its generality. In spite of these contradictions, Waller was so confident of his desired outcome that he was quoted in the *Vanguard* as already having written "to a number of foundations for possible support of the experimental program if interest is shown at the conference."[10]

Confusion as to its purpose aside, preparations for the conference went forward. As before the governance conference, discussion papers were circulated in advance. They dealt with the current experiments in American higher education; with the history of general education at Portland State; and with the study of some characteristics of the contemporary student body. Especially helpful was the essay written by Robert Tuttle of the English Department dealing with the pedagogical assumptions that had undergirded general education curricula over time.[11]

The conference met on 4-6 April 1968. Classes were canceled so all faculty and students could attend. Students, indeed, were invited to participate in all aspects of the conference, and the *Vanguard* editorialist declared it provided "an excellent opportunity for students to become involved in planning the college curriculum." The conference opened on Thursday night with a faculty panel discussion that dealt with the pre-conference essays; on Friday, there were two panel discussions in the morning (one composed exclusively of students) and small group discussions in the afternoon. In the evening, there was a banquet address at the Benson Hotel by the dean of undergraduate studies at San Francisco State College, who spoke of that institution's experimental college. Saturday morning saw a general faculty discussion and the passage of a resolution.[12]

After its careful preparation and wide publicity, the conference itself was rather anticlimactic. Only about seventy-five participants attended the discussions, and only a few students were on hand at the Friday banquet address. Waller's resolution on the final morning "to undertake a committee investigation and evaluation of an experimental program" at the College was watered down into a resolution (which passed) "to encourage further study into the possibilities of an exper-

imental college by independent groups and interested persons at Portland State."[13]

The conference outcome, however disappointing it might have
been to the advocates of an official experimental college, raised the
hopes of those who wished for an informal, unstructured experimental
institution. What they spoke of was a "free university," an autonomous,
ungraded, college without requirements within the umbrella of the
official college. They were encouraged by the conference resolution
as a spur to carry on their plans. Some, in contrast, were disillusioned
by the outcome of the conference, regarding the concluding resolution
as a stalling tactic: "Maybe in a few years," one disappointed student
wrote to the *Vanguard*, "you will decide to approve experimenting with
some of the new concepts in general education. Maybe. Of course none
of these ideas will be new then; they will be safe." Others confessed
hope there were enough reformers—a small but growing number of
faculty and students—who really could create reform in what they
described as "this ancient classical education system which has served
us for centuries—but now [is] completely irrelevant." Indeed, some
faculty and student groups did begin to meet immediately after the
close of the conference to plan an experimental college.[14]

President Millar also tried to salvage something by suggesting curricular reform need not await a full-blown experimental college. He
said experimental courses could be offered as early as the fall term
under existing "omnibus" course numbers and be taken along with
those existing courses that "offer present relevancy" by students who
wanted an education reflecting immediate concerns. (The use of omnibus numbers had been, and would continue to be for many years, a
strategy to escape the state board's curricular restrictions.) A leader of
the group of twenty students discussing the experimental college (the
small number is significant) agreed with Millar about the need for publicizing the "relevant" courses and in keeping student interest alive
until an experimental college might be funded (which the student
hoped would be in time for fall term 1969.) Millar further demonstrated his interest by suggesting these courses might be graded on a
pass-no pass basis, carefully adding only if the Curriculum Committee
and the faculty agreed. Yet the final result of the all-university conference was the realization that general education and an experimental
college held little interest for most faculty and students.[15]

The faculty of Portland State College increased in number and
variety from 1955 to 1969. Its numbers rose from 108 to 624. The per-

centage of women faculty increased in these years from 14 to 18 percent. The first two full-time African American faculty members were appointed: George V. Guy in Education and Rose Thomas in Social Work. Although the research dimension of faculty work became more important, in the sense that more faculty had time to devote to it, the focus of faculty life remained the classroom.[16]

Traditional teaching methods of lectures, assigned readings, discussion, papers, and examinations continued, but they were joined by a new device. Its use reflected the advance of technology, the desire to save money, and the assumption there would not be enough new faculty to maintain the existing faculty-student ratios in the years ahead. The innovation was educational television.

Portland State took its first tentative step toward the new medium on 15 December 1955, when President Cramer wrote a memorandum to members of the Administrative Council. The memorandum was in reaction to the appointment by the chancellor of an interinstitutional television committee that, in turn, was the response of the state system to the appropriation by the legislature of $5,000 to study the feasibility of educational television in Oregon. The responsibility of conducting this study had been turned over by the governor to the state system. A second source for Cramer's memorandum was Willard Spalding and Hoyt Franchere's suggestion that Portland State apply to the Ford Foundation Fund for the Advancement of Education for an experimental program in the use of closed-circuit educational television.[17]

Cramer's response to this situation was characteristically reactive. He said it would be purposeless to approach the Ford Foundation for a grant, as the state system intended to do so. He wanted instead for Portland State to cooperate with the state system by presenting the chancellor with a list of courses that might be used for experimental purposes on educational television. Cramer emphasized these courses would not be taught by Portland State faculty but rather by professors from Oregon or Oregon State, although they would be received on several campuses. Second, the president wanted Portland State to prepare to become more directly involved in educational television, although he did not say how this would be accomplished.[18]

The state system did receive a $200,000 grant from the Fund for the Advancement of Education in May 1956, which was matched by the system. Committees were established at each institution, and, in the spring term of 1957, closed-circuit experimental courses were taught at Oregon and Oregon State. In the 1957–58 academic year, six courses were taught on an interinstitutional open-circuit network. In the 1958–59 academic year, four courses were taught. None of these courses in the first two years were taught by Portland State faculty nor were they received at the College.[19]

In February 1960, President Millar created an institutional television committee of one member from each division, chaired by Lester F. Beck, a psychologist from the Division of Social Science, with Brock Dixon as an ex-officio member from the dean of faculty's office. The committee's charge was "to generate institutional commitments to the State System's institutional TV program." By the time the committee held its first meeting later in the month, Beck's own course in General Psychology had been tentatively chosen for Portland State's first originating course over the state system network.[20]

During March, the committee gathered responses from each of the divisions regarding the desirability and feasibility of television teaching and also sent three faculty members to discuss this type of instruction with colleagues at other institutions whose disciplines had been involved in interinstitutional television courses. As might be imagined, the responses of both those who had and had not experience with educational television varied widely, from it being flatly labeled "dehumanizing" to practical concerns about agreeing on a reading list to serve students at different institutions.[21]

In early April, the committee made a progress report to Dean Swarthout in which it said "the general conclusion reached by the Committee is that PSC should cooperate to the fullest in the use of TV for inter-institutional teaching." It gave the dean a list of twenty-one courses whose instructors had shown an interest in experimenting with television teaching. Whatever programs were transmitted would be sent over Channel 7 from Corvallis and linked with Channel 10 in Portland by relay. (At this time, public broadcasting in Oregon was the responsibility of the General Extension Division of the State System of Higher Education.) The interinstitutional television committee and the institutional executives finally agreed there would be four courses presented on public television stations in the fall term of 1960: Constructive Accounting, History of Western Civilization, Foundations of Physical Science, and General Psychology.[22]

The Western Civilization course for the 1960–61 academic year serves as an illustration of the challenges and successes of the first television instruction. The course was presented by three historians, Basil Dmytryshyn, Charles Le Guin, and Charles White. They prepared the

Instructors in the Western Civilization televised course

course outline and the visual materials themselves, with minimal assistance from a student, cutting up books and films (probably illegally) for illustrative still shots. They recorded the programs in the KOIN-TV studios in the fall and winter terms and then in the KOAP-TV (public television) studios in the spring—a cold, drafty, and temporary shack wrapped in chicken wire to minimize an electrical interference problem and located atop Healy Heights in Southwest Portland.

For the academic year, student enrollment averaged sixty-three students per term. Although the program aired at the unusual time of 6:30 AM (5:30 in areas not on daylight savings time), the students' work was comparable in quality to that in the traditional Western Civilization sections, and few dropped the course. (The early class time once occasioned an embarrassing incident for one of the instructors, when one of his students sat down next to him at a bar and remarked in what seemed to be a rather loud voice: "I feel so strange sitting by you without my pajamas on."[23]

In May 1961, Portland State's television committee, now headed by John Allen of Geology, made a comprehensive report to the faculty about the instructional television situation. It reported that, in January 1961, Portland's Channel 10 had begun broadcasting from a makeshift facility on Healy Heights: There was talk its permanent studio would be in the fifth floor of the new classroom building arising south of the College Center (now Neuberger Hall). This possibility was a bit ominous for the College because the studio had been intended for closed-circuit television, but a way out was that most of Channel 10's morning and afternoon programs would be devoted to courses originating in Corvallis on Channel 7 and thus would not preempt the closed-circuit courses. The committee concluded its report with a proposal to equip a certain number of classrooms with television sets and to hire personnel to operate the closed-circuit facility.[24]

By November 1961, the problem Allen mentioned had magnified and seemed to threaten the whole interinstitutional television program. As the chancellor's representative in charge of the program, John E. Lallas, put it in a letter to the institutional executives: "The single most important problem...is to select courses that are mutually acceptable to all institutions. At first glance, considering the substantial number of lower-division, large-enrollment courses, such a task might seem relatively simple. In fact, however, reluctance by the respective institutions to receive telecourses that are originated at other campuses has been far greater than acceptance of such a procedure." Lallas pleaded with the presidents to take a personal interest in moving the program forward or at least in deciding whether such courses were worthwhile.[25]

The presidents were galvanized sufficiently by this spur from the chancellor to meet a month later. Their conclusions, not surprisingly, favored development of each institution's facilities and balked at pushing for interinstitutional courses. The language of self-interest was classic: "Continuing effort should be made to develop interinstitutional televised instruction. In addition, careful study should be made of the potential of closed-circuit, intra-institutional television to determine its potential. There was general consensus that effective development of interinstitutional television would require a fairly long period of time." The presidents requested no additional legislative funds and concluded happily that the chancellor's office "assumes that responsibility for the initiation of teaching practices and the use of the newer media is the prerogative of the respective institutions." Finally, "processes for the selection of courses are to be developed within the institutions on the basis of procedures most acceptable to the executives."[26]

Portland State's Lester Beck was one who actually did develop a successful television course. In collaboration with colleagues from Oregon, Oregon State, Oregon College of Education, and the General Extension Division, Beck's General Psychology course was taught over the public broadcasting system to about sixteen hundred students during the 1961–62 academic year. The lectures in the course, given by about thirty-five psychologists chosen by the interinstitutional committee conducting the course, were pre-recorded. The initial response of most students was favorable, especially from those given the chance to supplement the televised lectures with sessions with instructors.[27]

The first Portland State department to make a systematic examination of televised instruction was the English Department. A committee of six, under the chairmanship of Philip Ford, investigated the possibility of teaching certain courses in the department and examined various ways they could be taught. After gathering data from various institutions, including Oregon College of Education (where English composition had been taught via television), the committee concluded educational television "probably has considerable though not altogether measurable value as a means of extending the range and increasing the flexibility of English teaching." It vetoed the idea of teaching composition on television but did say it would be worthwhile to experiment with the survey course on World Literature. In methodology, it favored using live or taped televised lectures as supplements to regular class lectures. The committee not only feared the watering down of standards and the loss of the student's faculty of independent thought through televised lectures but also found that instructional television did not save money. Nevertheless, it did suggest offering the one open-circuit course and supplementing certain conventional courses with closed-circuit television. Hoyt Franchere, chair of the Arts and Letters Division, took this report to the Educational Policies Committee where it was discussed, but no action was taken.[28]

By fall term 1962, Portland State's Philosophy Department was offering a section, which enrolled 120 students, to supplement the inter-university television course in introductory philosophy, but its professors were not compensated. The state system, however, did become interested in closed-circuit television, and the chancellor requested in November 1962 a report from each of the institutions on the status and future needs of closed-circuit television. Kenneth Butler of the library prepared the bulk of the Portland State report in response to this memorandum, stating the institution's use of closed-circuit television depended on the acquisition of a videotape recorder. If that was accomplished, then the College might be able to give some or all of the seven courses its television committee was interested in presenting. The system did ask the institutions to request funds to buy a videotape recorder to use in conjunction with closed-circuit television whenever they were made available. Needless to say, the request, in the amount of $58,500, was promptly forthcoming.[29]

With the promise of equipment for the 1963–64 academic year, the dean of the faculty in January 1963 spurred the divisions to begin thinking seriously about what courses they might offer on closed-circuit television. After due consideration and careful planning, Portland State stepped into the electronic world of closed-circuitry in the winter term of 1964, nine years after the Administrative Committee first took up the matter of televised learning. The first courses were Beginning Health and Western Civilization. If they proved to be successful, other courses were to follow in the spring. A great deal of care went into establishing and evaluating the validity of the courses and in creating the facilities necessary for their presentation.[30]

Each classroom in South Park Hall (Neuberger) was equipped with reception facilities, as were four rooms in State (Cramer) Hall and six in Old Main (Lincoln Hall). There was also the recording studio on the top floor of South Park Hall. The Western Civilization course was a hybrid of the old and the new. The television lectures were broadcast twice a week, while a third hour was reserved for discussion with the instructor. There were also to be three control sections taught in the traditional manner. To justify the television teaching experiment, Frank Roberts, the assistant dean of the faculty, explained in the *Vanguard* that there were three main advantages to the new approach: better use of visual aids, more economical use of visiting lecturers, and better utilization of faculty time (he gave as an example an instructor with three sections of the same course who needed only to give one lecture).[31]

After the first one-year term, the Western Civilization course was abandoned because the heavy teaching loads of its three instructors precluded their continuing the extensive preparation required for continuing success in the new medium. But the health education course continued and was joined by an Introduction to Business course. A poll of students in the seventh and eighth week of fall term found a majority in the health course favorably impressed by it. In the spring term, the number of on-air hours had grown to sixteen, and there was a formal Instructional Television Department organized under the supervision of Kenneth Butler, the audio-visual librarian. By fall 1964, the number of hours in televised courses had almost doubled as business, health, and geology courses were presented on closed-circuitry and World Literature and Introduction to Philosophy came on the interinstitutional network. The literature course was produced at Portland State. In time, David Newhall of the Philosophy Department produced his own courses in Introduction to Philosophy, Ethics, and Logic for open-circuit television. By this date, the interest among faculty and students in television had also produced a television workshop class under the auspices of the Theater Arts Department.[32]

In two more years' time, there was enthusiasm for instructional television on the part of a few faculty, indifference on the part of the majority, and a well-publicized controversy running in the *Vanguard* about one of the closed-circuit courses. This class was Geology 202, Introduction to Geology, taught by John E. Allen, one of the early proponents of instructional television. Its format comprised two televised lectures per week and a third hour in which Allen appeared in the auditorium of Old Main to answer questions from the 223 students enrolled in the class. In March 1966, toward the end of the winter term, a petition, ultimately signed by eighty-nine students, was presented to Allen. The petition contained various complaints about the course, ranging from objections to the length of the exams to concern about questions not covered in class. Criticism regarding the television lectures found that too much information was conveyed too quickly and that it would be desirable to have an informal seminar with the instructor once a week, in addition to the large, question-and-answer session. It is apparent that most of the criticism had nothing to do with the fact that the course was televised and almost everything to do with its large size.[33]

Allen took the criticisms raised in the petition in good spirit. He recognized the validity of some of the remarks and responded in the weekly open session that much of what he did was required by necessity. He would have essay examinations and more personal contact, he asserted, if money was made available for teaching assistance. He also remarked, to cheers from the students, that he wished they had taken their petition to the state legislature. Instructional television, in spite of studies and controversies, remained a small part of the teaching and learning processes at Portland State, if the term is used to define teaching by the College's faculty. If it refers to the use of materials prepared elsewhere—films and videos—then their use on closed-circuit television has expanded enormously over the years.[34]

Besides the traditional lecture, other aspects of conventional teaching were challenged in the 1960s. One of these was the grading system. The principal change advocated was the substitution of pass-no pass grading for the five-grade (A-F) method used on most campuses since time immemorial. The issue first arose at Portland State in 1966, when some students petitioned the Physical Education Department to introduce pass-no pass grading in compulsory physical education courses. The department considered the matter, brought it to a vote, and decided not to agree to the change unless the College as a whole did so.[35]

Although nothing was decided at this time, the petition concerning grading in physical education was taken up the following year by the Curriculum Committee, which decided to broaden its study of the issue to encompass grading across the disciplinary spectrum. In spring 1967, the committee issued an interim report based on a survey of Portland State departments and other institutions using pass-no pass grading. It summarized the arguments in favor of the change as an attempt to reduce the emphasis on grading; encourage students to take courses outside their field of specialization without fear of lowering their grade-point averages; make it easier to grade courses where performance was based on innate ability or where formal grading practices were inadequate (such as internships); and to better evaluate students in courses lacking "adequate intellectual content" (e.g., physical education, typing, and shorthand) without distorting the grade-point average.[36]

One year later, the Curriculum Committee formally recommended to the faculty senate on 30 April that the divisions and departments be permitted to experiment with pass-no pass grading. It proposed the new grading system be permitted in courses graded exclusively on a pass-no pass basis and in those where it was an option along with traditional letter grades. The recommendations were debated throughout almost an entire senate meeting in May 1968. Joseph Blumel of the Economics Department, chair of the committee, spoke for the motion and clarified various points such as that the proposed system applied to undergraduate students exclusively and that it was of an experimental nature only. In the end, the senate decided to approve courses to be graded exclusively on a pass-no pass basis, but not those where students would have a choice between a pass-no pass or conventional system. The first departments to use the new format were Geology and History. Beginning with winter term 1969, almost all geology courses and about twenty history courses were to employ the new grading system. In time, most other departments provided the pass-no pass option. Another grade-related issue to come to attention at this time was—as in the Korean War—the linkage of grades with draft deferments. In order to protest the Vietnam War, or to keep some students from being conscripted into it, some faculty began to give all students in their classes the grade of "A."[37]

Other teaching experiments were not as well publicized as instructional television or pass-no pass grading, but they did demonstrate the ingenuity and dedication of the faculty in improving their classroom performance at a time of rising student-faculty ratios. Jerome Leavitt of the Education Division had an interest in experimenting with teaching machines (devices popular in the 1960s because they theoretically both improved learning and cut costs) for the use of elementary, secondary, and higher education teachers. Leavitt and Swarthout sent a request to the Ford Foundation for a grant to support Leavitt on a half-time appointment for one year so he could study the literature of the field and visit some of the manufacturers of teaching machines. The College had the interest, but the foundation did not, as it rejected the application.[38]

Another faculty member interested in teaching experiments was Walter Nunokawa of the Psychology Department, who, in the spring term of 1965, conducted experiments in his general psychology and personality courses. In the first course, 25 percent of the course was devoted to lecture and textbook coverage of content, while the remainder was devoted to independent investigation. The pressure for independent thinking was too much for the 50 percent of the course members who dropped out. Nunokawa redesigned his personality course to be almost entirely independent study, with occasional instructor consultations. Although initially a painful experience, in the end, all the students asked Nunokawa to use the technique in other courses.[39]

As always, even in a time of ferment such as the 1960s, the faculty was reluctant to abandon traditional teaching methods for new devices that, while perhaps useful, might be simply novel. There was a fear, too, that the administration might be interested in instructional television, teaching machines, and other experimental devices not to improve knowledge but to be modish or to avoid hiring new faculty. Administrators, for their part, feared faculty conservatism and its parade of excuses to avoid trying anything new. In May 1965, for example, the Advisory Council asked President Millar to develop a program to experiment with ways to improve teaching. When asked by the president to comment on this request, Dean Swarthout replied cynically, "It has always seemed a little humorous to me when a body of chosen representatives of the faculty urged the administration to take action to change the direction of the faculty they represent, because the faculty they represent won't get on the ball to do the things the faculty representatives think the faculty they represent either wants to do or ought to be doing."[40]

Outside the classroom, the faculty carried on the important advising dimension of teaching and in this area also strove for improvement. By the late 1950s, advising had come under increasing criticism because it had not reached all students. Although individual advisers might be more than competent, there was no systematic plan to see that all students were advised. To rectify this weakness, in the winter term of 1957, it was made mandatory for each student to have an adviser and for the adviser to sign each student's program of studies before he or she could register. This plan, laudable in intent, failed. Students who knew what they wanted forged advisers' signatures on their registration forms. Second, students who needed help were often given short shrift because their advisers' time was taken up with counseling students who did not want or need it.[41]

In early 1960, Dean Swarthout asked Brock Dixon, his administrative assistant, to conduct "a general review of our advising program." To help accomplish this purpose, Charles Bursch II, dean of students, proposed the signature control system be strengthened. He recognized this system placed a burden on the registrar, but he hoped it could be improved to become less troublesome to that official. Bursch himself made some suggestions to that effect.[42]

Although Dixon moved forward with his assignment, mistakenly hoping signature control would be in effect by fall 1961, criticism of advising continued to be reported in the *Vanguard*. The accrediting team specifically criticized the advising system in 1965, a fair recognition, in Millar's mind, of a "glaring" deficiency in the College program. In the fall of 1965, Channing Briggs, the new dean of students, proposed a summer advising program for entering freshmen. He suggested high school counselors—not regular faculty—be hired to do this work. In a significantly altered form, this suggestion was ultimately implemented, but through the use of faculty not high school staff. Again, advising, like teaching and research, was a matter no amount of good intentions could handle satisfactorily in an era of enrollment growth without compensating funding.[43]

Another matter difficult to handle satisfactorily, although grappled with throughout the era, was the evaluation of teaching performance. The theory went that if teaching were the most important function of the university, then it should be measured frequently and accurately and the best teachers rewarded both materially and in prestige. Like most theories, the problems were not in the assumption but in the application, but not for lack of trying.

In 1963, Tau Kappa Epsilon, a social fraternity, instituted its Professor of the Month award "to bring attention to the notable and commendable aspects of outstanding PSC teachers' work and life." The first winner was H. Frederick Peters, professor of Foreign Languages and Literatures. Although dispensed on rather unscientific grounds, the fraternity award did call attention to a matter that awaited further study.[44]

In the mid-1960s, as part of the criticism of American institutions, the university naturally fell under fire. One assault was the growing public belief that universities emphasized publication over good teaching as a means to determine merit salary increases and to decide the award of tenure and promotion. The old saying, "publish or perish," became a byword of these critics. Although this aphorism never had been true at Portland State, it was to be expected the institution could not escape its application. A *Vanguard* columnist made the assertion in February 1965, and an instructor in philosophy ruminated on it, pointing out—not unsympathetically—the pitfalls of the various means proposed to rectify the problem. In April, the *Vanguard* polled students to see if they wished faculty evaluations, and, in May, a member of the student senate suggested students participate in a confidential survey of each faculty member; folders would be made available to students but not to faculty.[45]

The student senate did not follow up on this suggestion, however, asserting the questions were unfair, but its major proponent attempted to carry out a revised version anyway. He formed a group called Student Services, intended to pass out an evaluation questionnaire to students waiting in lines during fall term registration. A booklet containing the results was to be compiled and sold. The plan failed when only two hundred of the six thousand questionnaires distributed were returned. The student group blamed the low rate on the unwillingness of the dean of students to permit them to be placed in collection boxes in the College Center. What may have foiled both student efforts was a far more comprehensive and controversial plan for evaluating teaching passed by the state legislature earlier in the year.[46]

This plan was proposed by Rep. John Mosser. Although well-intentioned, the Mosser Plan became a source of numerous difficulties and heated contention for over two years. Mosser's intent was to reward good teaching with a special monetary grant from the legislature for the most effective teachers in the state system, a grant that would be in addition to the faculty member's regular salary. When the bill was introduced, Chancellor Lieuallen, for one, did not expect it to get much attention and thought it probably would not pass; after it began to receive publicity, he asked each of the institutions to develop a response.[47]

At Portland State, the Academic Council decided if the bill passed, then three responses were in order: the College would accept the money, even if strings were attached; the money should be built into the existing salary of the meritorious professor; and students should make quantifiable recommendations, but not be allowed to be "on joint committees dealing with the subject of awards or increments for good teaching." When the institutional executives met, the situation had clarified to some extent, but one complicating factor had not been resolved. Mosser's original plan was to appropriate $1 million for his awards, but the salary subcommittee of the education subcommittee of the Ways and Means Committee reduced the amount to $500,000.[48]

More serious than this reduction, however, was the entire proposal's effect on salaries. The chancellor had been pressing—as always—for salary increases. This was his major priority, far more important than the Mosser Plan. But he noted with alarm that the salary subcommittee had recommended the Mosser money be taken out of the salary improvement funds. The chancellor told the institutional executives the Mosser award money must be in addition to the salary budget and that the individual awards must be a permanent addition to the professor's salary. As Dixon summarized this part of the meeting for Millar: "Lew [Chancellor Roy M. Lieuallen] does not want to reject money and at the same time label us as reactionary opponents of all change and reform, so the question of the most painless method for implementing the Mosser Plan was before us."[49]

What the institutional executives finally agreed to do was to recommend to the salary subcommittee that the Mosser funds be set at $250,000 and all dispensed in the second year of the biennium so there would be time for a careful plan of faculty evaluation to be worked out. They also concluded each institution should be permitted to decide for itself whether to reward teaching with a cash grant or to give it to individual faculty members to buy equipment or develop plans to improve teaching. The committee of institutional executives also recognized another problem in the Mosser Plan, an implication that good teaching was not already being recognized; Chancellor Lieuallen's solution was to try to arrange a hearing for the institutional executives before a legislative subcommittee to explain what was already being done "to recognize and reward good teaching."[50]

The Mosser Plan was adopted by the legislature with an appropriation of $500,000. The appropriation came with accompanying guidelines from the Ways and Means Committee that the fund should be divided between the two academic years of the biennium; that it should be $1,000 per faculty member; that to be eligible, faculty must have taught an average of two, three-credit courses during at least two terms of the academic year for which they were being considered; and that "students should be involved in either the nomination or selection of grant winners, and could be involved in both." It required that faculty members be involved in the implementation of the plan and allowed plans to "vary among institutions." The deans of faculty of the institutions and the Portland State Council of Academic Deans considered the specifics of implementing the Mosser Plan, and President Millar, after these deliberations and after receiving a set of guidelines from the institutional deans, appointed a committee from faculty recommended by each of the schools and divisions, the Department of Health and Physical Education, and four students appointed by the student government.[51]

The Portland State committee plan (approved by the state board in early October) applied only to faculty and students who wished to participate; included faculty who were at least .50 full-time equivalent and had taught at least six credits per term for two of the three terms during the academic year in which the award applied; and was based on an IBM card system. The method of evaluation, as might be expected, proved the most troublesome of any of the elements associated with the plan. Each student received a card to rate instructors on a five-point continuum in regard to six qualities: stimulates thinking; shows a confident attitude toward students; organizes and prepares course content well; explains and illustrates clearly; inspires confidence in knowledge of the subject; and is willing to listen to and consider differences of opinion. The plan was announced to the College community in the *Vanguard* in October 1965.[52]

It caused a bit of a stir and was the subject of discussion at the regular fall faculty meeting in early November. Although only seventy-five members of the faculty were present, they raised several questions for the Awards Committee. Millar was rigid on one point: the College would participate in the plan, though he was willing to see the faculty debate the mechanics of participation. No one wanted to engage in such a debate. When Dale Courtney of the Geography Department and president of the local American Association of University Professors (AAUP) chapter suggested a dialogue with Representative Mosser, only three faculty members supported him. The most interesting remark came from Dean Swarthout, who said the administration had raised objections to the plan when it was under legislative consideration. "We tried to fight it before it got through, and we lost." Like many others, Swarthout knew trouble lay ahead.[53]

The problems initially were more evident at other campuses than at Portland State. The Oregon Technical Institute and the University of Oregon refused to participate. Oregon State agreed to be included only after a relatively close, 35-24 vote in its faculty senate. There were three main objections to the plan raised elsewhere: it was an implicit condemnation of publication by implying publication was at the expense of good teaching; it was a legislative intrusion on the classroom; and the money for the awards was drawn from salary funds, so it really offered no extra money. An informal survey of the faculty, conducted by a *Vanguard* reporter, found the expected range of opinions. John Hammond, Philosophy, and Joseph Blumel, Economics, regarded it as a good first step toward evaluation of teaching. Judah Bierman and Florence Riddle, both of the English Department, objected to student participation in the plan, while that department's Thomas Burnham objected to merit plans on principle: "If I want a Christmas bonus, I could go into some other line of work."[54]

Early the following year, when the first term opened in which Mosser awards would be made, the issues surrounding them were heatedly debated. President Millar suggested to the faculty senate it might now wish to discuss the plan in light of the changing circumstances. He referred to the Emergency Board's reduction of the amount of money available in the biennium from $500,000 to $200,000 and to the opinion of George Layman, member of the State Board of Higher Education and former legislator, that the Ways and Means subcommittee directives about the methods of distributing the awards might not have the force of law. What this last opinion might offer would be a way to use Mosser funds not for cash awards determined by student vote but rather for a system of faculty applications for grants to improve their teaching or for other alternatives. Representative Mosser was not pleased with the idea of debating his plan further, insisting it was "clear" the system of cash grants was at its core, and that changing the central element "might be a possible device for eliminating everything from the plan but its name."[55]

The faculty senate discussed the Mosser Plan on 17 January at the close of a long meeting devoted largely to dealing with regulations for graduate study. Some senators said the reduction in money for the awards justified abandoning the whole program; others said it was too late to stop participating, but that the matter could be reviewed for the following academic year, perhaps by a faculty committee that might devise superior selection methods. Still others said those nominated for the awards should be required to present plans outlining how their money would be used to improve teaching. Senators then began to depart the meeting, and a lack of a quorum was noted. In an informal poll, fifteen senators voted in favor of proceeding with the agreed on plan: only two voted no. There was no consensus in favor of having the president call a special meeting of the entire faculty to consider the plan (and Millar did not do so) nor was there any subsequent attempt by the faculty to petition him to take this action.[56]

In the end, the awards were made at the end of winter term 1966. They were not made without controversy. It had been intended to distribute the cards prior to "Deadweek" (the week before examinations), but the cards were defective and had to be reprinted, so the evaluation was rescheduled for Deadweek itself. Then, there was a computer delay in evaluating the punch-card data. One faculty member wanted the list of winners published with an addendum indicating some faculty on leave were not eligible for the competition; others were doing administrative work; while still others chose not to participate. The omission of their names should not be, he said, the basis for invidious comparison.[57]

The most evident controversy was touched off by a letter to the *Vanguard* by Donald Moor of the Philosophy Department. In it, Moor said the manner of conduct of the evaluations had "publicly humiliated" the members of the faculty. He suggested "those administrators who are responsible for the disgraceful bungling of the Mosser evaluations put their raises for the coming year on the line." When Millar, bemused by this letter, wrote to Moor for an elaboration of his points, he responded that the method of administering the punch cards was done contrary to what had been promised. Moor had understood that faculty members who did not want to participate in the plan need not do so in any way whatsoever. What he discovered was that on evaluation day, he was expected to present the cards to his classes, even though he did not care to participate. He also had expected some person assigned by the administration would administer the evaluation in the professor's absence. Millar responded by thanking him for his constructive criticism, saying, in essence, that his and Moor's understanding of the matter differed.[58]

Ultimately, thirty faculty members received awards, although they were not notified until June. At the end of the long process, many surely would have concurred with Swarthout's anguished comment: "If I ever see another bunch of those damned Mosser Plan cards cluttering up my office again I'm going to flip." There was some consolation for all involved in the arduous process, however: more than four hundred faculty were on the payroll in the winter term—seventy-five of them were ineligible, and fifty chose not to participate. Of the remaining 275, only seven instructors received an average score below the midpoint on the rating scale, while more than 50 percent ranked between good and outstanding.[59]

The following academic year, several changes were suggested for administering the Mosser awards. The Awards Committee itself proposed some revisions at the faculty senate's October 1966 meeting. The first recommendation was that the senate, and then the full faculty, vote on whether or not the College should even participate the next year. The second was that, before voting, the senate and the faculty should be given the results of a questionnaire distributed to the first year's participants. The third was that the data on the IBM cards should be more precise so that the Awards Committee need not make as many subjective judgments in determining the recipients. The last was that the exact weight given to each question should be decided before the cards were distributed.[60]

The faculty senate "discussed at length" the report and then sent it on to the full faculty. Before doing so, it also voted to ask the dean of the faculty to appoint a committee to study and evaluate the Mosser Plan. Morris Weitman of the Psychology Department, an expert on surveying, was appointed to head this *ad hoc* committee. After surveying the faculty by questionnaire, Weitman's committee reported to the faculty in November with a motion that "the Mosser Award idea be accepted and approved with no condition attached." Hoyt Franchere moved for an amendment requiring faculty members to apply for a Mosser Fellowship award and to demonstrate the money would be used for an imaginative project for the improvement of teaching. The idea was suggested by Karl Dittmer, the dean of science, who had encountered such a plan at Florida State University. Those granted fellowships would spend spring or summer term using them. The substitute passed by voice vote. The faculty then narrowly defeated a motion (97-91) to "reject the Mosser money." The amended motion then was passed by a large margin.[61]

Dean Swarthout transmitted the results of the faculty's deliberations to Chancellor Lieuallen, changing the title of the program to Mosser Fellowship Awards for Distinguished Teaching. He summarized the faculty discussion of the awards ("one of the most spirited and interesting of any I have heard at general meetings of the College faculty") and pointed out to the chancellor the final vote was 62 percent in favor, while the questionnaire distributed by the Evaluation Committee indicated only 29 percent favored continuing the cash awards. Swarthout urged the chancellor to accept the revised standards for the award, saying their spirit was in keeping with Mosser's original intent. Mosser himself, however, did not see it that way, declaring the revised award did not meet the specifications of the legislature "in so far [sic] as it departs from judging teaching excellence and judges teaching proposals instead."[62]

Lieuallen agreed with Mosser, rejecting the fellowship proposal on four grounds: the legislature required the award must be given in cash; it must reward past teaching performance; it must not be accompanied by conditions on future performance; and students must be involved in the selection process. With the ball back in its court, the faculty held a special meeting to discuss the future of the Mosser Plan at Portland State. Morris Weitman moved to reject the Mosser Plan for the coming year. An "extensive discussion" then took place, resulting in the faculty rejecting Weitman's motion by a vote of 52-43. A motion then was adopted that the president appoint a committee to evaluate teaching excellence, with the purpose of applying these criteria to the Mosser Awards. In effect, this action meant Portland State would again participate, a position that placed them with Oregon College of Education but not with the other institutions in the state system, which declined to participate in 1966-67.[63]

Karl Dittmer was appointed to head the student-faculty committee charged with developing the instrument to evaluate faculty the coming year. The committee delivered its report in May 1967. It addressed many of the objections raised against the procedure the previous year. The most important recommendations required summary ratings based on the number of students taught by a professor regardless of classes (provided he or she taught six hours of classes in at least two of the preceding three terms); equal weight be given to all questions on the evaluation card; and the creation of a system for breaking ties (junior faculty would receive preference, but if two faculty of the same rank tied, the instructor who had taught the most students would win). There were to be fifteen questions, each of which would be answered on a five-point scale. The committee also tested the evaluation in twenty-six classes comprising 1,037 students. The committee report was discussed carefully, and the evaluation procedure was adopted by a vote of 83-49. The revised evaluation was held late in May but for the last time. The legislature, doubtless discouraged by the indifference or hostility of the faculty at the state system institutions, did not renew the appropriation.[64]

A far more important and enduring problem than the Mosser awards was the state of the library. On the eve of four-year status, librarian Jean Black pointed out three great problems that harassed library patrons: there were too few trained librarians; there was inadequate storage for periodicals and inadequate funds to bind them; and there was crowding in the reading room, where students maneuvered for passage between shelves and tables ("a hereogeneous lot, battle scarred and ugly"). Black obtained no secretarial help until fall 1954 but received support in the form of the first faculty library committee, which relieved her of the burden of selecting all the books herself. Even when the hiring of library personnel was authorized, it was difficult to obtain them as librarians were in short supply.[65]

Relief from some of these problems appeared in the mid-1950s, when the legislature authorized both the four-year college and buildings to help implement that mission. Amazingly, the library (which was to share space in one of the new classroom buildings), was planned by its architects without the consultation of either librarian or Library Committee. The architects plan called for a five-story building that had service areas and an audio-visual department in the basement, technical services and the librarian's office on the ground floor, the reserve room and the education books on the second floor, and the remaining books on the top two floors.[66]

When Black was called on to fill out the details of the structure, she had little time to devote to them because staff constraints forced her to assume duties other than architectural consultant: "I walk a pre-

Jean Black, first head librarian
and first woman administrator

carious path trying to take care of
the essential current duties of my
position and to give attention to the
proposed building." The arduous
nature of her work could be appreciated fully only by those who knew
she was not only librarian for the
College but also for the Portland
Extension Center, which had its
own separate budgets for its evening courses and summer sessions.[67]

Not only Black, of course, but all of the library's small staff had to
be energetic and resourceful in order to handle staffing the existing
library while planning for the new one. Those who lagged were dismissed. As Black wrote of one: "Fundamentally, however, there was a
general lack of 'snap' which unfits her for our service. You have to
catch on quickly and be ready to take on something new at a moment's
notice to keep pace here." Among all the other changes in 1958, the
library took on the task of shifting the book classification system from
Dewey to Library of Congress.[68]

In planning the new library building, Black received invaluable
assistance from a new addition to the staff in August 1958: Edmond
Gnoza, who had worked at the University of Idaho library when it was
planned and completed. As Black wrote: "I do not see how we could
possibly have achieved the work but for his previous familiarity with
this process." A highlight of the process occurred on 25 March 1959,
when Gov. Mark Hatfield, at a ceremony in Salem attended by Black,
President Millar, and Chancellor Richards, signed the appropriations
bill providing the funds to complete and equip the library.[69]

The move into the new building took place over Christmas vacation 1959–60, under the supervision of Gnoza. The five-level building
seated seven hundred persons and had the capacity for 130,000 volumes, compared to the Old Main library, which could seat two hundred readers and house sixty thousand books. Although the new
library was vastly superior to the old one, it was not without problems,
some of which were endemic to its sharing a building with the College
Center, a handicap necessitated largely by the inadequacy of building

PSU Educational Media Services

Groundbreaking ceremony for the first library building

funds approved by the legislature but to some extent caused by limited consultation by the architects and facilities staff with the librarians and the Library Committee. As Black put it: "When persons coming from the noisy precincts of the College Center where 'live' music, piped music, conversation at a level to hold its own above clattering dishes and broadcast announcements prevail, plunge directly into the lobby with no 'cooling off' area, they play hob with the library atmosphere."[70]

Noise also came from the two-story lobby, which served as an echo chamber, and from the lack of a barrier between the elevators and the stair landings and the reading areas. A grave, seasonal problem also afflicted the new library's patrons. For, one supposes, reasons of economy rather than an inexcusable oversight, the new library was equipped neither with air conditioning nor windows that could be opened. In the fall of 1961, students and faculty petitioned the state board for air conditioning, citing a variety of statistical indices, including a mid-day average temperature of eighty-six degrees on the third floor during one thirty-day period the past summer. Black wrote bluntly: "The library building has proved to be a regular hell-hole whenever the outside temperature is even mildly warm."[71]

Conditions in the new library perhaps could be endured, however, because by 1963 there were plans for an even newer building. The

College was able to secure board permission to acquire a block west of the Park Blocks—at Southwest Tenth Avenue and Harrison Street—on which to build the new structure. The architects, Skidmore, Owings, and Merrill, for economic reasons, were able to building only one-half of the planned structure in the 1960s. This meant the building would be taller than originally projected but with fewer floors of larger area, an inconvenient arrangement the librarians protested in vain. The state board, however, approved the building plans in 9 March 1964 for a five-story building to be completed in 1967. The remaining four stories to what became Library West (and subsequently by state board decision on 16 June 1969, the Millar Library) would be added later.[72]

The major difficulty with the planned two-stage construction of the library was that its services would be divided between two buildings until its completion. The audio-visual and technical services areas would remain in the College Center building, divorced by two blocks from the main building. Everyone found this inconvenient, and it was sharply condemned by the library specialist on the accrediting team in 1965. "I think," Black later wrote, "that he really considers I have been remiss in not making violent formal protest to the President. Perhaps I am; but after being on the ground and necessarily conditioned by the realities of life within the State System for nineteen years, I cannot believe that it would have been possible for me to have any success in this line."[73]

Meanwhile, patrons and staff continued to suffer in the old library. Next to the reserve room on the ground floor were the map collections, established at the end of the bowling alleys of the student union. "No one could be expected to work there for any length of time," the librarian reported, "because of the awful racket of the striking balls and falling pins." The most "unbearably crowded" working area was Technical Processes, where conditions were so bad they created a personnel problem. Black reported, "Some Civil Service applicants have surveyed the area and promptly announced they would not work under such conditions. Two professional resignations were greatly influenced by the situation." Portland Community College students housed in the old Shattuck School building next to Portland State, without paying state system tuition, used the library for a study hall, complained about the inspection point when leaving the building, and even asked for library cards.[74]

With all these crowding problems, students and faculty recognized the new library building would be worth waiting for. Although the

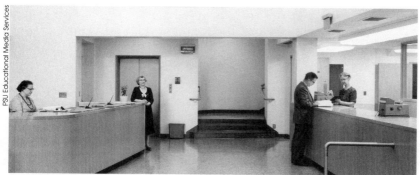

PSU Educational Media Services

The library in the College Center Building

physical division from Technical Services was as serious a problem as anticipated, another division was looked on by the library staff more positively. This was the decision to leave the reserve room in the old building, where it not only served its stated purpose but also that of a study hall, thus freeing the new quarters for students who wanted to use library materials, rather than to study. Indeed, Black hoped when the second part of the new building was constructed the reserve room would remain in the original building, although this did not happen.[75]

The new building had, it seemed, hardly been opened when it began to be overcrowded. By November 1969, the *Vanguard* carried a story with the headline: "Library running out of space for books, students." Frank Rodgers, Black's successor, was even more blunt, declaring: "Right now this library is inadequate." The pressure of additional students and more books (which required more shelves that in turn reduced seating space) meant that soon it would be impossible to move the reserve library and the audio-visual department to Library West to join the rest of the collection. At best, if the state board acted with the utmost speed, the second part of Library West would not be completed until 1974.[76]

"The business of a college is responsible inquiry."

THIRTEEN

Faculty Life · 1955–1969

B esides evaluating its curriculum and teaching, the faculty and administration strove to improve other working conditions. Grievance procedures, methods of evaluating faculty for promotion and tenure, and salary increases all took up a good deal of time as the College changed rapidly into a university. The College, of course, did not operate without the external constraints of legislative appropriations, the advice or requirements of chancellor and state board, and public opinion, but the fifteen years after the attainment of college status were generally optimistic ones—years in which faculty members gained a greater degree of authority, using it to attempt to regularize procedures that formerly had been somewhat (usually benignly) authoritarian.

Although it is somewhat ironic to characterize "public service" as a special dimension of the work of men and women whose entire working life is devoted to public service, tradition nevertheless does have a separate category for faculty beyond that of teaching, research, and university service. Portland State faculty have always been involved in service to the metropolitan area and to the state, and their interest in these communities expanded after the institution became a college. Perhaps those whose service was recognized farthest afield in these years were two professors of German Literature, Frank Eaton and H. Frederick Peters, who received the Cross First-Class of the Distinguished Service Award of the Federal Republic of Germany in 1960 for their organization of the Deutsche Sommerschule am Pazifik, a branch of the College, and for their contribution of books in the German language to the College library.[1]

Another group served by the College in a unique way was the Finnish community of Portland. President Cramer had heard of nationality rooms at the University of Pittsburgh, which were furnished in the cultural style of a particular nation, although they were used for regular classroom purposes rather than for courses about specific ethnic groups. Cramer took the idea to the state board, which originally discouraged the idea, as it feared such rooms might rouse nationalistic spirit or invite vandalism from rival national groups. In April 1956, however, the board relented, and the way was clear for the new classroom building (now Cramer Hall) to be equipped with nationality rooms furnished by local communities. The only group that rose to the opportunity was the Portland Finns, led by the local chapter of the Finlandia Foundation, which raised $60,000 to equip a room with handmade articles, including wood paneling, fabric wall hangings, a wooden map of Finland, and a blackboard with a special screen. The room was dedicated in 1959 in a ceremony that featured a talk by the Finnish ambassador to the United Nations.[2]

Other attempts at community outreach were not as successful. One of these efforts occurred in 1959, at the time of a strike of the employees of Portland's two daily newspapers, the *Oregonian* and the *Oregon Journal.* With the consent of the faculty adviser, *Vanguard* editor Doug Porter and his staff decided to publish a fifteen thousand-copy special edition containing national and international news, to fill the void while the major papers were not publishing. The special edition was not intended to make money, for it would be given away, but rather to provide a public service. Porter also said the service would bring favorable publicity to Portland State by making citizens "realize that Portland State is more than an extension center affiliate or a correspondence school." Staff members of the *Vanguard* (and also of the *Viking,* the College yearbook) obtained the consent of the two dailies and the typographical unions and were poised to prepare the first edition when College administration vetoed their plans. President Millar and Charles Bursch, dean of students, forbade the venture, fearing it might injure Portland State's image and, as the *Vanguard* reported, "could be considered opportunistic and quite justly could be deeply resented by our friends in organized labor."[3]

Far less controversial was the creation of an institution unique among the state system schools. The Portland State College Speakers Bureau, established in December 1956, was designed to ease the pressure on faculty members, many of whom were in constant demand to speak to community organizations. Although this demand was a tribute to the College, it also could be taxing for the faculty members

PSU Educational Media Services

Frank Roberts, professor of
Speech and public servant

involved. The bureau, under the
direction of the director of public
services, provided a listing of faculty
members available to speak to organizations on topics in their expertise.
It served to match speaker to audience in a regularized manner, high-
lighting an important dimension of
the College—the human aspect—
to a public usually apt to think of
Portland State as a large, impersonal institution.[4]

Faculty members also served
the community by participating in
political life. Frank Roberts of the Speech Department was elected
chair of the Multnomah County Democratic Central Committee, and
Markko Haggard of Political Science was a precinct committeeman
and a member of the same body. In 1966, Roberts was elected to the
lower house of the state legislature and later became a state senator.
Haggard also studied the community as well as attempting to mold its
political life. His Political Research Bureau engaged in studies of
Oregon political life, evaluating election results in races for political
office and ballot measures, including a statistical study of the voting
returns of Multnomah County. How political participation aided the
College was demonstrated when Haggard, as a member of the Democratic party's platform committee in 1960, was instrumental in getting
the party to support a forthcoming state bond issue for college and
university buildings and for an increase in faculty salaries.[5]

In time, Haggard assumed a larger role in public life when Gov.
Tom McCall appointed him in 1969 as the first state ombudsman. This
position was a delicate one that involved serving as the citizens' representative in dealing with state agencies. It had no power but that of
publicizing and settling by persuasion complaints of citizens who had
become caught up in the state bureaucracy and knew of no one to turn
to to help them with their problems. McCall appointed Haggard, he
later wrote, because "he was a man of great humanity, yet streetwise
enough to know the structure of government and devise answers to

most of the problems that were brought to him." James Hart of the English Department was one of McCall's campaign workers. Other faculty members who plunged into politics included Margaret Clarke of the English Department, who served as campaign manager and, later, research assistant for Robert Holmes, who was elected governor of Oregon in 1956. G. Bernhard Fedde, a lecturer in the Department of History and a lawyer, often volunteered his legal services to those who were seeking exemption from military service as conscientious objectors.[6]

In the realm of the arts, John Trudeau of the Music Department founded in 1963 the Peter Britt Music and Arts festival at Jacksonville in southern Oregon. Trudeau and Sam McKinney, director of Portland State's outdoor program, had been talking of the idea of an outdoor musical festival and were approached by the Ashland Shakespeare Festival to hold a musical series complementary to the plays. When the facilities at Ashland proved to be inadequate for the music project, Trudeau and McKinney turned to Jacksonville. Trudeau became musical director of the popular festival, which has continued to present—in conjunction with the Peter Britt Institute—a workshop in musical techniques. Public service in this case, as in that of Haggard's position, took on a scope far broader than the Portland metropolitan area.[7]

Within Portland itself, the oldest community festival is the Rose Festival, established in 1907. It draws thousands from around the Pacific Northwest for a series of events spread over the month of June, including the Grand Floral Parade. The opportunity to participate in such an event to publicize the College was not lost on Portland State. The student government discussed the idea of entering a float in the parade in 1959, but the plan died for lack of money. Two years later, there was a float sponsored by the Viking Vets organization, "a Viking ship in dragon form floating on an ocean of flowers." President Millar had hesitated about approving the venture, fearing the construction of the float would cut into study time for final examinations, but when assured otherwise, gave his consent.[8]

Other endeavors had greater intellectual content as the College reached out to community institutions. One of these was a joint venture between the Oregon Historical Society (OHS) and the Department of History that began in the 1964–65 academic year. The program provided OHS staff members as instructors of four courses (such as historical museums or regional, state, and local historiography) for students interested in careers in public history. The public history course, the first offered west of the Mississippi, was clearly of benefit to the two institutions, especially as OHS was soon to build its new facility just three blocks north of the College on the Park Blocks.[9]

Also connected with history was the College's participation in events commemorating the centennial of the Civil War. The Theater Arts Department put on a play, *The Octoroon*, while the Music Department contributed a band concert of music inspired by the war. Several movies were shown, and panel discussions were held on "The Civil War Amendments" and "Strategy of Desegregation." Dean Swarthout and George Hoffmann, chair of the Social Science Division, presented a slide lecture on four major Civil War battles, each personifying the Union or Confederate commanders in each struggle.[10]

The most publicly visible of Portland State's faculty was Ben Padrow, professor of Speech. Beginning in June 1962, Padrow became the moderator of a television program, "College Opinion," produced by a Portland television station. The program consisted of local college students discussing topics of current interest, such as religion on the campus or the Vietnam War. Portland State, one of eleven colleges featured on the program, appeared three or four times a year. The advantage in publicizing the College was obvious; as Padrow said, it gave the audience a chance to "see the oncoming results of a college education."[11]

The working conditions of faculty, so onerous both within and without the classroom, generally changed for the better after 1955. One issue that engaged administrators and faculty was the devising of a grievance procedure. The issue arose at this time because the chancellor and the State Board of Higher Education were preparing to adopt new provisions in the Administrative Code concerning tenure and termination and called for local contributions to their discussions. The Advisory Council took up the matter in the fall of 1962. Before this time, there may have been grievances, but there was no systematic procedure for resolving them. But as the Council remarked in presenting its recommendations for a grievance procedure, "It seems idle to hope, on a campus the size of our own, for a decision-making system from which no grievances arise." Well aware that not all complaints were worthy of being dealt with as grievances, the council tried to draw a line by first deciding to which cases the formal grievance procedure might apply. The best it could do was to assume the formal procedure must be used for the urgent case, "one in which alleged administrative ill will or ill judgment brings serious consequences in its train."[12]

The Council then went on to establish criteria for the grievance procedure: to recognize an urgent case and to treat it with fair play;

to assure consideration of an aggrieved faculty member's complaint by an appropriate group of his colleagues; to encourage the settlement of a case at the earliest stage; and to provide procedures flexible enough so that steps in resolving the case be appropriate to it. The Council concluded its report with a series of recommendations for the procedure. The grievant could appeal successively to the executive officer of his department, who would consult a departmental committee for advice; appeal would next go to the chair of the division, and then to the dean of faculty. The dean of faculty, on receiving an appeal, was then to ask the Advisory Council to consider if the case were "sufficiently serious or sensitive to warrant further faculty review." If the Council so decided, then the dean would request the president to appoint a faculty consultation committee to advise the dean. From the dean's decision, the appeal could go to the president, and then—under the Administrative Code—to the chancellor.[13]

While the Advisory Council was working on its report, President Millar gathered data from the national office of the American Association of University Professors and from other sources. He worked closely with the local chapter of the AAUP, as well. Simultaneously with these deliberations on grievance procedures, the Advisory Council was dealing with a procedure for settling a specific type of grievance: the dismissal of a tenured faculty member. It made recommendations in this area also.[14]

By late November 1962, the new grievance and dismissal procedures were available for circulation. While generally approving them, the local chapter of the AAUP did raise some objections. It said there should be an established committee, not an *ad hoc* one, to evaluate grievances, and that this committee not function at the departmental level. It also wanted to guarantee that when faculty members filed grievances they not be subject to the filing of a termination notice. This last reservation arose not from the realm of abstract rights but from an immediate case.[15]

In August 1962, a faculty member protested his teaching schedule in a letter to his departmental executive officer. In October, he was told by his superior that he could file a grievance before a departmental committee but that the chair would also ask that same committee to consider that he be terminated. Besides the conflation of these two matters, a further complexity was that the faculty member had for years been in conflict with his departmental executive and his divisional chair. It looked suspiciously like the termination action was in retaliation for the filing of the grievance.[16]

Furthermore, both the faculty member and the AAUP were disquieted by the initial handling of the case. While it was sensible to set aside the grievance while the dismissal action proceeded, it was not suitable for the departmental executive to fail to present specific charges before the departmental committee, leaving it to the committee to do so and thus putting itself in the position of being both prosecutor and judge. When the matter was transmitted to the division chair, he was unable to discover the explicit charges, and, thus, the faculty member was in no position to file a specific rejoinder to them. At this juncture, the local AAUP conveyed its unease to President Millar and to Dean Swarthout. Fortunately, the next stage of the process, the appointment of the consultative committee by the president, was done according to the procedures. In the end, the faculty member was not dismissed. Portland State tried again to deal with grievance and termination procedures in 1966, when a College arbitration panel was instituted to deal with these matters; in 1967, a grievance procedure for non-tenured faculty was adopted.[17]

The College took the initiative in 1962 to develop a procedure on the related matter of termination procedures, as distinct from grievances, as the Administrative Code of the State System of Higher Education did not address this matter. The College administration, in consultation with the Advisory Council, promulgated a termination procedure in October 1962. In February 1963, the institutional executives decided to consider the matter and drew up a set of procedures for state board consideration. Most of this document was based on a draft recommended by the state federation of the AAUP, in whose deliberations on this matter James Hart of Portland State's English Department played a significant role. As the Code document left some provisions for local variations, the College administration and the local chapter of the AAUP began discussion of them in February 1963.[18]

Not until almost two years later, however, did the matter move forward, when the Advisory Council, in conjunction with the help of a special faculty committee, began to draft a set of procedures governing termination and grievances. The reason for doing so at this time was a set of recent changes in the Administrative Code that required local action. President Millar wisely turned this matter over to the faculty bodies rather than having the administration prepare a draft document. When the faculty committee went to work, it was faced with two options: either leave the Administrative Code as the sole procedural system or supplement it with local revisions. It chose the second option.[19]

The major issue to be resolved was the nature of the various committees that would deal—from departmental to presidential level—with the termination procedures for tenured faculty. More specifically, there was disagreement over when the consultative phase between the faculty member and the departmental chair (an informal discussion of the problem) would advance to the formal stage of the administration bringing charges against the faculty member. By 1 February 1966, the committee had worked out its internal disagreements and released a draft of its procedures to the faculty. The document was drawn carefully, with the heart of it being an *ad hoc* hearing committee appointed by the Advisory Council to hear the charges for dismissal brought against a faculty member. At the hearing, the faculty member was guaranteed a series of rights (such as to be represented by counsel). All in all, the procedures met the requirements of the national AAUP. The faculty, after brief discussion, adopted the procedures on 16 February 1966.[20]

Few tenured faculty were dismissed, but almost all faculty taught. The teaching load, with some exceptions, dropped from twelve hours in 1955 to nine hours in 1969, although most faculty in Foreign Languages and Literatures continued to carry twelve-hour loads. This was a welcome change and hardly controversial. Indeed, the only contentious issue regarding teaching loads in these years arose in 1966, when Leroy Pierson, the director of the summer session, imposed a five-day, rather than the traditional four-day, week for summer school classes. Pierson instituted the change after consultation with various deans and department chairs, rather than with the faculty involved. His argument for the shift was that it provided fuller utilization of College buildings during the term. He expressed disappointment, for example, that students did not use the library on Friday, as the building was almost entirely vacant on that day. The summer school catalogs, however, stressed the recreational opportunities of Oregon. Pierson reminded one veteran faculty member of a high school principal who wanted to maximize the use of faculty and facilities throughout the week.[21]

In January 1966, the five-day week became an issue, as several summer school faculty signed a petition to the dean of faculty protesting the decision. They argued Fridays could be used for preparing examinations, writing lectures, and grading papers and that the imposition of a fifth day of classes was injurious to morale and harmful to students who wished to work on Friday, rather than attend classes. Dean Swarthout responded to the petition with a long letter to its signatories. He supported the director of the summer term by refusing to abandon the five-day week. Swarthout maintained the College was moving to make the summer term as close to a normal term as possible and that "summer teaching properly should become a normal full-time obligation, and the instructional week should reflect the fact." He rejected the argument that Friday was spent for academic pursuits ("the only thing which is significantly interfered with by the five day week is recreation") and tried to soften the dissenters by reminding them that air conditioning would be available in most of the classroom buildings by the coming summer. He said the extra day would make it more convenient to advise students. He concluded by stating, "Admittedly, if we could—or should—consider only the wishes of students and faculty, we would continue the short week and long weekend." Although these arguments were not convincing to the complaining faculty—and at least one faculty member declined to teach during the summer term—the new policy was kept in force, even though it was a classic illustration of what faculty always resented: the imposition of an academic decision by the administration without consultation with teaching faculty.[22]

Those faculty looking ahead to retirement were pleased with one major change in fringe benefits instituted in this era. This was the option of accepting an alternative to the State of Oregon's retirement plan, which was sponsored by the Public Employees Retirement System (PERS) organized in 1946. This plan had been welcomed by faculty members, but, by the early 1960s, there was criticism of it—criticism that might well be noticed by administrators, as it was difficult to recruit and retain faculty in that period of rising college enrollments and subsequent national competition for faculty members. Improved fringe benefits could well enhance the quality of Oregon's faculty.

The state federation of the AAUP became interested in retirement benefits in 1959, establishing a retirement committee whose chair reported to the Portland State faculty in February 1960. The report was a comparison between PERS and that available through the Teachers Insurance and Annuity Association (TIAA), a national corporation organized in 1918. The AAUP report found the TIAA program far superior to that of PERS. Contributions to TIAA were fully vested in the employee immediately, while PERS required ten years of service before vesting. The TIAA plan thus permitted faculty mobility to institutions outside the state system. The returns on TIAA's investments to this date were higher than those of PERS. Unlike PERS, which invested only in fixed-income securities, TIAA permitted investments in stocks of up to 50 percent of the member's contributions. TIAA allowed contributions after the age of sixty-five, and it permitted the retirement payment option to be taken after the age of sixty-five, if the employee continued to work. Neither of these options was available under PERS.[23]

Convinced of the desirability of the TIAA retirement program, the state AAUP pressed the legislature in 1961 to permit state employees to separate from PERS and join TIAA. This was not to be accomplished quickly, however, although it was ultimately achieved. By 1965, Gov. Mark O. Hatfield endorsed the idea of the TIAA option, as did the legislature (the governor apparently wanted to find an issue that would appeal to the higher education community), and, in May 1965, Governor Hatfield signed into law the bill allowing the option. Portland State and the other state system institutions now joined twelve hundred other colleges and universities in this plan.[24]

Other fringe benefits were also obtained in the 1960s. Although free tuition for faculty members' families was rejected by the state board in March 1961 (on the grounds it preferred to seek salary increases rather than fringe benefits), other benefits did become available later in the year. W.T. Lemman, Jr., the director or business affairs, surveyed various major medical coverages and suggested Blue Cross would be the recommended one for Portland State faculty. He also favored a group life insurance program offered by Standard Insurance Company. The state system also planned by 1965 to propose to the state legislature a list of benefits to which the system would make a partial contribution, including group life insurance, disability insurance, and group health and accident insurance.[25]

In the important matter of salaries, Portland State continued to lag behind other state system institutions and well behind comparable institutions in the United States. Various attempts were made to redress this situation by the College's administrators, but their arguments, which ranged from justice to the fear of losing faculty to other colleges, usually fell on deaf ears, even in an era when faculty were in a seller's market. Needless to say, this failure was not due to administrative incompetence or lack of zeal but rather to the two towering barriers to Portland State's advance at almost any time and on almost any issue: the opposition of Oregon and Oregon State (always influential in the offices of the chancellor and the state board) and the unwillingness of taxpayers to spend money for public purposes.

A few instances of these difficulties will suffice to illustrate. A typical, evasive political response came from Gov. Elmo Smith, who wrote to President Cramer in 1956 in response to his request for salary enhancement for the faculty. Smith's letter stated, in part:

> I realize that many friends of higher education would like a flat, unequivocal statement on this matter. I must in good conscience and being aware of the total responsibilities of my office, however, qualify my stand. I will tell you that my sympathies and my judgment go along with the program of the Board, and I shall do everything in my power within the limits of sound economics and good government to remedy a serious situation with respect to the faculties in our state institutions of higher learning.[26]

Portland State's position as a salary "stepchild" was indicated in 1963 by a small but significant gesture on the part of the chancellor. For some time, the salaries of Oregon and Oregon State had been combined to measure against nineteen comparable institutions for salary purposes. These data had been used to inform the legislature and the public about the salary situation in Oregon. Then, in early 1963, the salaries at the Oregon colleges of education were measured against their opposite numbers elsewhere. As Millar put it in a letter to the chancellor, "This leaves Portland State unaccounted for," because it was not on either of the comparator indices. Millar asked the chancellor if he intended to develop comparators for Portland State, asked to be consulted if he did so, and concluded: "The key questions would be with what other institutions Portland State College should be compared, both in respect to its current condition and to its intended stature and objectives in the future."[27]

Administrators, the local AAUP chapter, and the AAUP state federation continued to press the case for decent salaries throughout the 1960s. Portland State faculty were active in the work of the state federation, compiling data and testifying before legislative committees. The information they unearthed was discouraging. Whitney Bates of the History Department, for example, testified before the legislature's Joint Ways and Means Committee in 1967, showing that faculty of the state's institutions of higher learning, compared to similar institutions elsewhere, were paid nearly $800 less in salaries and $500 less in fringe benefits. Although salaries rose in the years after 1955, they never approached the top of the comparator institutions at any time. As in the case of fringe benefits, salaries alone would never bring or retain faculty in these years.[28]

The rather perverse silver lining in these material aspects of faculty life was that, if one found them unsatisfactory, there were plenty of chances to go elsewhere, for these were the days of the seller's market in academe. This was not only useful to faculty, but it was an argument for administrators in attempting to gain salary increases as well as a challenge to fill vacancies. Ingenious attempts were made to supply or retain faculty in these days. In 1962, the executive officer of the Mathematics Department suggested to President Millar the department set up internships to hire as part-time faculty graduate students at Oregon and Oregon State who had completed all of their studies but their dissertations. Although President Millar showed some interest, nothing came of the idea. In 1963, in a plea to obtain higher salaries, Millar attempted to show how desperate the problem of faculty retention was. He said if the legislature did not increase salaries significantly, "the result could well be tragic for us." Millar documented his case by pointing out that faculty resignations that year were running 50 percent ahead of normal and that in one department with five members (Social Science), three faculty had resigned for the second year in a row. Ten members of the Science Division had resigned. There had been four rejections for one position offered in Business Administration, and seven for one position in Foreign Languages, Anthropology, and Sociology, respectively. Of the 270 faculty, one third were in correspondence with other institutions; of these, thirty-six had received firm offers, and sixty-one more were in the process of negotiations.[29]

The supply situation was not entirely gloomy, however, for some faculty still wanted to come to Portland State. The excitement of building a new college, the opportunity to be influentially involved in setting its course, congenial colleagues, the attractions of the metropolitan area, and the natural environment of the Pacific Northwest made it possible to replace most of those who departed.

Indeed, hiring posed a subsidiary problem of offending institutions who lost faculty to Portland State, especially those in the nearby geographical area. The situation was so prickly Swarthout was impelled to write to the division and department chairs that they should inform their opposite administrative numbers whenever they were negotiating with one of their faculty to come to Portland State. In the case of the state system schools, he continued, the permission of the institutional president must be secured before beginning negotiations. "A couple of cases occurring very late in the hiring season," Swarthout admitted, "have aroused some pretty intense irritation, stimulated by the

difficulty that is always involved in finding replacements for unex-
pected vacancies when the market has been nearly exhausted." The
cause of late hiring was frequently due to the fact that authorization
to hire, because of the date of legislative appropriations, was close to the
beginning of the academic year. Another dimension of hiring that differed from later years was its informality. There were no national searches or even systematic local ones. Rudi Nussbaum of the Physics Department had come to Portland for an interview at Reed College; he was
offered the position, but refused it. While still on the Reed campus,
he phoned the Portland State Physics Department whose chair, Mark
Gurevitch, came over to Reed and hired Nussbaum on the spot, the
contract being notarized by a Reed official in a Reed building.[30]

But such measures were the exception to the rule; the main problem facing administrators was retention caused by lack of money, not
hiring. In 1965, as a measure of desperation, President Millar took the
unprecedented step of appealing to the chancellor as he was "faced
with an extraordinarily difficult problem, beyond our solving in the
normal way." The president wanted the chancellor to take to the board
his request that three faculty members be given substantial salary
increases beyond the norm—and also before the usual date of notifi-
cation—so they would not leave. If the raises were granted, they would
be sufficient to hold the faculty members, even though their salaries
would still be $1,500 to $3,500 short of what other schools were offering. "We cannot expect to hold them," Millar emphasized, "unless we
take immediate and fairly drastic action." In this case, the three faculty members stayed, but many others were lost along the way because
of the lowly position of Portland State in the hierarchy of the state system, not only because of inferior salaries but also because of the large
numbers of students, many courses, inadequate library and laboratory facilities, and cramped offices.[31]

A crucial ingredient in a college or university is academic freedom,
a condition indispensable for the life of the mind. It is far more significant than income or fringe benefits in appealing to faculty. Freedom had been well-rooted during the Epler years, when a range of
controversial visitors had spoken freely and the McCarthy period of
the 1950s had claimed no victims at Portland State. One lingering
remnant of McCarthyism, however, was the loyalty oath, a component
of the National Defense Education Act of 1958 that, among other provisions, provided loans to students. Indeed, under this statute, two oaths
were required—one saying the loan's recipient was not a member of

a group dedicated to the overthrow of the United State government and one promising support of the United States. The faculty was dismayed by this aspect of the statute and took it up in its quarterly meeting in February 1959, voting its opposition to the loyalty oaths as "impugning the honor of the intellectual leadership of the country." The issue of refusing to accept the grants under the act until the oath was repealed was discussed, but this action was too drastic for passage. (Swarthout argued expediently that a concerted protest campaign involving all universities would be more effective than would "a refusal to accept benefits of the act as an isolated gesture of protest.")[32]

One faculty member did more than pass resolutions against the loyalty oath. Florence Brush, assistant professor of Physical Education, refused to sign the state's loyalty oath for teachers in 1965, along with five other members of state system faculties. Her October paycheck was not issued, but she and the other objectors—assisted by the Oregon chapter of the American Civil Liberties Union (ACLU)—went to circuit court, asserting the oath violated the free speech and due process clauses of the United States and Oregon constitutions. Judge Edwin Allen agreed with them and declared the law unconstitutional.[33]

The issue of "controversial speakers" always dogged colleges and universities as members of the public were wont to take umbrage when spokesmen of minority views appeared on campuses or when faculty members advanced unpopular views outside campus. In the face of efforts at repression, Millar and the faculty were consistent defenders of the freedom of speakers. In early 1962, the issue came to the fore as a result of a courageous public statement by President Millar. Alarmed by complaints to him about the political speeches of faculty members, Millar issued a statement assuring faculty "their right of free speech is one that the College takes for granted," regardless of the content of their views. A pleasant surprise for Millar was that his statement was widely requested from "colleges, private organizations and businesses throughout the state" and that it had been enthusiastically received by them.[34]

Millar took up the other side of the question, that of outside speakers brought to the campus, about a month later. The issue arose when students invited Gus Hall, the general secretary of the American Communist Party, to speak on campus. There were the expected complaints from members of the public, complaints that had been responsible for the barring of Hall from speaking at Oregon State, Washington State, the University of Washington, and (by city council vote) the Portland Public Auditorium. Millar issued a statement firmly supporting the students and explaining why the College approved the invitation: "The approval is based entirely on the belief that if the business of a college is responsible inquiry, then the prohibition of inquiry, the closing of books, the muffling of speakers in matters of legitimate concern is contradictory to it." Herbert Aptheker, the Communist historian, spoke on campus in April 1962. Two years later, the College's speakers forum invited Hall's successor, Henry Winston, to speak on campus. The Executive Committee discussed the request and gave its approval, and Dean Briggs made a public statement explaining, "It is the policy of the college not to bar any speaker on the basis of his beliefs if he will submit to questioning and present facts to his audience."[35]

When Frank Wilkenson, an alleged Communist, was invited to speak at the College by the Young Democrats in 1965, the chair of the Counter-Subversives Committee of the Oregon American Legion wrote to Chancellor Lieuallen demanding he prohibit Wilkenson's appearance. Lieuallen responded, "The issue at stake as I interpret it, is not the right of Wilkenson to *speak*, but the right of students to *hear* a controversial point of view. Only through exposure to such controversial points of view will our young people be able to evaluate them and defend adequately our prevailing ideology."[36]

In the early months of 1967, the College, not without some trepidation, opened its platform to three especially controversial visitors who drew enormous crowds on the college and university lecture circuit: Timothy Leary, advocate of the legalization of LSD, dismissed member of the Harvard faculty, and co-founder of the International Federation for Inner Freedom, came in February; two weeks later appeared Stokely Carmichael, chair of the Student Non-violent Coordinating Committee and coiner of the phrase "black power," who packed the two thousand-seat gymnasium; and, in April, Allen Ginsburg, the *avant garde* poet, one wont to disrobe during his public appearances, read (fully clad) from his works.[37]

This openness to all ideas on the part of Portland State and other state system institutions twice produced legislative responses in the decade of the 1960s. In 1965, at the request of the American Legion, Sen. Eddie Ahrens of Salem introduced a resolution calling for a legislative study committee to investigate Communism in the state. "Sen. Ahrens stated that the bill was prompted by recent student demonstrations at the federal building [in Portland] at the McCarran Act." The resolution did not pass.[38]

Two years later, Portland State's speakers policy was criticized indirectly by Rep. Leo Thornton of Clackamas County, who became alarmed at the speakers who had appeared recently at the University of Oregon. He introduced a bill into the legislature in 1967 to give the State Board of Higher Education the responsibility for campus speakers. In defending his bill before an audience at Portland State, Thornton said the purpose of the bill was to restrict the appearances of "known advocates of lawlessness and anarchy" on campus, specifying Leary as one he would proscribe. Nothing came of the bill.[39]

All in all, the Millar administration did an excellent job of resisting pressures on academic freedom. It defended the principles in a forthright manner, not hiding behind generalizations or tactics of delay and evasion. A vivid illustration of this approach is contained in a letter Millar wrote to a citizen of Sherwood, who objected to a faculty member's (Charles McKinley of Political Science) comments on a television program about the necessity of revising the state constitution; protested the appearance at the College of Martin Luther King Jr.; and condemned faculty and Millar as Marxists who were "indifferent to or unread in the Bible." The letter was accompanied by literature labeling prominent American politicians such as Presidents Eisenhower and Kennedy and Vice-President Nixon as Communist dupes worthy of impeachment. Millar responded to his critic frankly and forthrightly: "It is not possible for me to react to your charge with any other feelings but those of revulsion and pity. I am deeply disturbed when I find Christianity and the Bible used as a mask for slander and a platform for vilification." He refused to do anything about the charges versus McKinley: "On the contrary, it is my responsibility to assist the assurance of the right of professors of the College, and myself, to free speech, and to provide institutional protection against attempts at slander and intimidation such as have become recently more frequent."[40]

"Portland State is a fine little college but
I hadn't realized that smart students went there."

FOURTEEN

Student Life · 1955–1969

S tudent life did not change noticeably after Portland State
Extension Center became Portland State College. At a commuter college, most students had the pulls of jobs and families
and studies, all more powerful than extracurricular activities.
For the minority with the time and inclination, extracurricular activities flowed in accustomed channels for the most part, with a wide range
of opportunities available in music, theater, athletics, publications,
religious concerns, and many others. In three dimensions of student
activity, however, things were done and said that reached beyond the
boundaries of the campus to become matters of interest or concern
to citizens of city and state. The public became very much aware in the
1960s of the College's fraternities and sororities; the College Bowl;
and, most of all, student political activism.

Portland State's first national Greek organization was Tau Kappa
Epsilon (TKE), chartered at the school in March 1957 under its first
local president, Raymond M. Rask. Ironically, the chartering of this
fraternity was an example of the cart preceding the horse, for its establishment caused the administration to look into the matter of whether
or not national Greek-letter organizations should exist at Portland
State. In reviewing the question, the Administrative Council had to take
two other *faits accompli* into account besides the chartering of TKE.
The Council discovered representatives of several national fraternities
and sororities had asked Portland State what its policies were in
respect to their organizations because they wanted to organize chapters
at the institution. The College's response was that they could be organized according to the rules laid down for the organization of any

national or local student-interest group, under policies adopted by the faculty senate on 3 December 1956, which said, essentially, that the faculty Student Affairs Committee would make the decision. As the inquiries mounted after the acceptance of Tau Kappa Epsilon, the administration gathered data from other colleges and universities.[1]

Among the questions asked of other schools with a Greek system was their experience with the financial stability of national organizations, the university scholarship requirements for Greek students, whether or not the institutions imposed a probationary period before full membership, and, most importantly, in the light of future controversies at Portland State, the religious and racial discrimination clauses in the Greek organizations' national constitutions.[2]

In March 1959, the Student Affairs Committee notified the senate that it would bring the question of national fraternities and sororities before it, with particular attention to the matter of discrimination. The committee presented a motion at the senate's April meeting that the term "national organizations" in the 1956 resolution be applied to fraternities and sororities and that the national headquarters of these groups be told the Portland State chapters would be permitted to pledge any person regardless of race, color, and creed. The last requirement was an obvious attempt to overturn the national policies of many sororities and fraternities that prevented the pledging of African Americans, Asian Americans, and Jews as members. The motion, as amended to ask the president to appoint a committee to study the place of student organizations on campus, was adopted. While the committee was deliberating, it was agreed that no new student organizations could be created.[3]

The committee, chaired by E. Dean Anderson, reported in March 1960. It was a split report, six to six, on the most important question—the election of members of student organizations with national affiliations, the most controversial of which were, of course, sororities and fraternities. One group favored the automatic admission of any student who met published criteria of the group. The other favored the admission of members by the election of the local chapter. The entire committee agreed, however, that no one would be prohibited from joining a local chapter, regardless of its national organization's policies. This last standard would agree with that laid down earlier by the state board.[4]

The senate debated the report of the special committee at four meetings in March and April 1960. In the end, Millar assured the sen-

Sorority rush party

ate he "would reject any organization whose officers at national level required local chapters to adhere to practices of racial and religious discrimination." He said this was a matter of state law, from which he would not deviate, and insisted his position be included in the minutes. In the end, a compromise was passed that permitted local chapters of any groups to choose their own members, provided the national organization could still lay down standards in regard to field of interest, total credits, or academic honors. This compromise satisfied those who were concerned with national honorary societies, and the policy was adopted by the senate on 18 April. Although it had no effect on Portland State—because it did not permit such fraternities or sororities—the anti-discrimination forces at the College were heartened by a resolution passed by the state board on 24 January 1961 giving state system institutions two years to withdraw recognition from fraternities and sororities with restrictive clauses.[5]

In October 1961, charges of racial discrimination in sorority pledging appeared in the *Vanguard* and the *Portland Reporter*. An African American student, who had gone through rush, was reported to have been refused acceptance in a sorority because of her race. The *Vanguard* columnist maintained specious reasons were given for denying her admission (allegedly too low of grades to qualify; "she didn't fill out a card") and that sorority members had declared, "This is a social organization. We can exclude anyone we want," and that "we're not strong enough yet to try and pledge a Negro girl." Millar and Charles Bursch II, the dean of students, investigated the matter, interviewed the African American student involved (who said she did not believe she had been a victim of discrimination), and reported to the faculty senate that the story in the two newspapers had been based on hearsay. Millar, however, stated, "The institution will take action on complaints of discrimination and will be vigilant of the possibility of discrimination both in specific cases and in general results." The student government cabinet discussed the situation but did nothing about it.[6]

But the sorority discrimination issue did not die. The president of Alpha Phi sorority, Coralen Richardson, proposed a constitutional amendment to the sorority's national charter that would permit the local chapters to pledge students without an alumna recommendation. Her purpose was to strike at racial discrimination, for she believed the students would be likely to admit new members without racial or religious discrimination but that the alumni, products of another era, would hold to traditional prejudices. Richardson found little support for her suggestion and never attended another meeting of her sorority after making it.[7]

In January 1962, President Millar reported to the Advisory Council that there was still concern among faculty and students about sorority discrimination. He also mentioned the sororities had been accusing him of harassing them and that he "admits it if the 'steady beady eye' constitutes harassment." Millar felt that "there might well be discrimination among the Greeks and such testimony as [was] received from sorority members would tend to confirm such a feeling." The president also felt "the Greeks [sic] organization were antipathetic toward the academic goal of seeking truth through widening areas of knowledge." He promised to take action when needed.[8]

In one sense, the issue did not seem likely to appear again, as sororities were not terribly popular at Portland State. The national organization of Gamma Phi Beta removed the local colony (a probationary chapter) in the winter of 1962 because of a drop in membership and because it "could not find women students at PSC of the calibre desired by the national." In one sense, the action was historic, as it was the first colony to be removed from an institution in the eighty-seven-year history of the sorority. The *Vanguard* editorialist assessed the situation correctly in commenting, "We interpret calibre to mean sorority conscious. This type of woman is not noticeable here. She doesn't have time to join a sorority. The type of life she leads at PSC is considerably different from that of a U. of O. coed."[9]

The problems of the six national sororities at Portland State were revealed further in a two-part *Vanguard* series in May 1962. Of the sixteen hundred Portland State female students, two hundred were sorority members. The president of the panhellenic council ascribed this small membership to mistakes committed by the sororities, an unsympathetic student press, and to a College administration that has "not completely understood their problems or potential." Sororities had attempted to solve their own problems, such as taking measures to raise their grade-point averages when they were below the College average and providing a longer rush period for prospective pledges to get to know the sororities, but the difficulties for a Greek system at Portland State were great.[10]

In January 1963, the College made a decision regarding the place of sororities on campus. The Executive Committee was apprised of a straddling decision made by the state board that declared system sorority chapters could join national sororities with discriminatory clauses in their charter if the locals were given a waiver allowing them not to discriminate. The Executive Committee refused to endorse this possibility and demanded that until the nationals removed their discriminatory clause, the situation could not be resolved.[11]

The beginning of the end for old-style sororities at Portland State occurred on 26 September 1963 during the midst of rush, when President Millar temporarily suspended all six sororities. He did so because two African American students attended sorority open house, were asked to return by three sororities, and then were cut from the list of invitations at the next round. At the time of the suspension of rush, only four of 115 prospective members had been rejected, two of whom were the African American students. Millar, at the time of the suspension, announced the appointment of a faculty committee, headed by Richard Halley of the Economics Department (formerly dean of men), to investigate the role of fraternities and sororities at the College. The president said the committee would concern itself with not only the matter of race discrimination, but that involving Jews, Catholics, and those with backgrounds in various European countries, although a *Vanguard* survey at this time indicated there were Jewish and Catholic sorority members and no "indication of discrimination on the basis of national origin." David H. Newhall of the Philosophy Department had already made up his mind. In a letter to the student newspaper, he said the Greek system "has been tried and found wanting" because its "nationally controlled system...[was]...too rigid to adjust to the requirements of a young college whose roots are planted deep in the democratic demand for equality of opportunity, both social and educational."[12]

The suspended sororities did not disappear. Their members, acting as "individuals," continued to participate in College activities, such as assisting during registration and helping canvass neighborhoods for the United Good Neighbors Drive. The administration looked the other way during these activities, to the dismay of the *Vanguard* editorialist. But when the sororities proposed to hold formal rush activities off campus in January 1964 without the sanction of the administration, they went too far and decided, on second thought, to cancel their plans. They were torn between antagonizing the administration and a need for revenue (which came from pledge fees), as their coffers had become depleted. Without permission to advertise in the *Vanguard* and forced to hold rush events off campus, their income from their annual Pajama Dance, a popular event open to the whole College, fell off sharply.[13]

On 16 January 1964, President Millar released the report of the special faculty committee. The core of the report took the form of a resolution for the faculty senate. The heart of the resolution unequivocally declared:

> For each organization on campus, [the] autonomy to nominate and select members without regard to race, color, religion, or national origin shall rest entirely with those members who are currently enrolled students of the College and shall not be restricted in any way by...restrictions, written or unwritten, imposed from outside the College. Furthermore, this right to nominate and select members regardless of race, color, religion, or national origin shall not be restricted or modified by national officers, alumni, advisors, or others from outside the college through exclusive privileges of recommendation, approval privileges or veto power.[14]

The report also required representatives of the sororities to meet regularly with a student activities adviser to discuss policies for the organizations; a new, more leisurely calendar of rushing was to be instituted; each sorority would be required to make an annual report to the College of all its activities during the year; and it mandated the withdrawal of official recognition, if any of these terms were violated. If the sororities agreed to these conditions, Millar recommended they be reinstated.[15]

The faculty senate took up the proposed resolution on 20 January. During the discussion, a variety of concerns were touched on; some debated at greater length than others; and some returned to repeatedly. The major points made regarded the difficulty in proving discrimination, the educational value of sororities if carefully regulated, the fact that discrimination had been reduced in recent years for all groups but African Americans, the relationship of the local chapters to the national organizations, and the belief that more might be accomplished against discrimination by retaining properly supervised sororities than by abolishing them. President Millar said administering the proposed regulations would not be an onerous burden, and Dean of Students Briggs asserted the sororities had behaved circumspectly during their period of suspension. In the end, the senate voted thirteen to ten to adopt the committee report and its recommendations. A *Vanguard* editorial gave good advice to the sororities: "[They] have everything to gain and little to lose by accepting the recommendation's conclusions. If they do not choose to do so they can die willingly in protest, or attempt an off campus operation...and die slowly and painfully of attrition. Without college acceptance there is no justification for the existence of sorority groups."[16]

The response of the sororities to the faculty action and the newspaper editorial was prompt, clear, and shortsighted. One week after the faculty meeting of 20 January, Dean Briggs met with five of the six sororities (Delta Delta Delta did not attend) to develop regulations for the re-admission of the sororities to official status and to guide their future conduct. On the evening of the same day Briggs was conferring with the local representatives, the national officials of the five sororities mailed a letter to President Millar indicating they were not willing to follow the new procedures and were setting up an independent panhellenic office to function off campus. On 24 January, the national president of Delta Delta Delta wrote to Millar disassociating the sorority from Portland State. The student officers of the six sororities were in agreement with the positions of their national offices.[17]

Millar wrote back to the six national presidents asking for clarification of their positions and reported to the senate at its meeting of 3 February of the events that had transpired. After responding to questions and listening to senators discuss the matter, Millar concluded the meeting by commenting that the sororities would remain in suspension until they conformed to the rules of the College and the state board. The sororities' response was to go off campus as private organizations, gathering their prospective members from the *Portland Panhellenic Blue Book*. They withered without College support but did not disappear.[18]

In 1968, a national sorority, Phi Sigma Sigma, organized a colony at Portland State with the consent of the College administration. By this date, four sororities still hung on with Portland State students as members but without the support of the institution. Three had houses for meetings and one an apartment. In November 1969, four sororities were officially recognized at Portland State: Alpha Chi Omega, Alpha Omicron Pi, Alpha Phi, and Pi Beta Phi. All pledged to obey the University's guidelines, including freedom of the local chapters to select members without regard to race, color, or religion or without approval or veto by the national organization or alumnae.[19]

A much more satisfying and unifying aspect of student life than the sorority controversy was Portland State's appearance in the College Bowl. Sponsored by General Electric Company, the College Bowl was a national quiz program, originating in 1958, that matched teams from two colleges on Sunday afternoon television. A team victorious in its first appearance proceeded to its next opponent until defeated or until it had won for five consecutive weeks. The winning team's college received a $1,500 scholarship each week and an additional $1,500 if it won in all five weeks. The questions asked on the program ranged over all categories of knowledge from history to literature to religion. The program was popular, and it had by 1964 included three Oregon colleges: Reed and Lewis and Clark, which both lost in the first round, and Oregon State, which had been a three-time victor.[20]

The first advocate of Portland State's appearance on the College Bowl was Brian Fothergill, a Mathematics major, who began the process in 1962, when he persuaded student body president Dennis West to contact the program. Later, E. Dean Anderson, executive assistant to President Millar, took up the correspondence. Finally, in May 1964, the College was chosen as a participant for the 1964–65 academic year.[21]

Ben Padrow, professor of Speech and director of Forensics, was the coach of the College Bowl team, and four regular and four alternate students were selected. Padrow was aided by other members of the faculty: Ronald Glossop (Philosophy), the team's assistant coach; Morris Silverman (Chemistry); Arthur Boggs (English); Robert Crowley (Music); Freeman Anderson (Education); and Joseph Frazier (His-

Ben Padrow, professor of Speech
and coach of the College Bowl team

PSU Educational Media Services

tory). Brian Fothergill maintained his interest in the program by obtaining advice from the coaches of the teams from Lewis and Clark, Reed, and Oregon State. Although diligent in training, coaches and team practiced against a background of uncertainty because no one knew when the team would appear—the date depended on the progress of its predecessors on the program. Portland State had to wait until a team won five consecutive times before it could replace it. The suspense of waiting finally ended in January 1965, when the College was notified it would appear on 31 January against the University of San Francisco.[22]

The team left for New York on 29 January as the guest of General Electric, which paid for all expenses. The team consisted of Jim Westwood, captain, a junior in Physics; Larry Smith, a junior in English; Robin Freeman, a senior in Philosophy; and Mike Smith (no relation to Larry), a junior in Psychology. Al Kotz, the first alternate, was a senior in English. On Saturday, the team visited the Museum of Natural History and attended a Broadway performance of Edward Albee's *True Alice*. Padrow, overlooking nothing in preparing his team, forbade the consumption of carbonated drinks, milk, or coffee so that the team members' salivary glands would be functioning properly.[23]

The Portland State team won its first round handily against the University of San Francisco and was given a reception on its return by the alumni association, which was attended by students, faculty, and political and chamber of commerce officials. The only discordant note struck at this time was the seeming unwillingness of the Portland business community to emulate their counterparts elsewhere in matching the team's winnings. After their first appearance, team members received love letters, requests for autographs, and a copy of Ian Fleming's *Chitty Chitty Bang Bang* (which was then donated to the College library) for identifying the novel's author on the program.[24]

The second round produced a victory over Park College, attendance at Euripides' *Trojan Women*, a visit to Greenwich Village, and a trip to Washington, D.C., as a guest of United States congresswoman

Coach Ben Padrow (l) and the College Bowl team

Edith Green. When it was all over, Portland State had won five consecutive victories, adding Kent State University, Coe College, and
Birmingham Southern University to its first two victories and setting
individual game and series records in the process. The consequences
of this sweeping triumph were four-fold. The most obvious, although
perhaps most evanescent, was the national and local publicity received
by the College. On the eve of the third round, for example, Dean
Swarthout was able to convey to Padrow and the team a remark a
friend of Millar's made to the president: "I always knew that Portland
State was a fine little college, but I hadn't realized that smart students
went there." Swarthout continued with his own observations: "The
answer I give when people ask me how you were chosen for the squad
is an injustice to you, I know, but seems so appropriate for Portland
State. I just tell them that you were chosen by lot."[25]

The College also reaped a monetary reward for the victory, as various organizations contributed a total of $15,575, which was put into
a scholarship fund. Next to General Electric, the largest contribution—
$1,500—came from U.S. National Bank. Team members received the
gratitude of their fellow students and faculty members at a convocation at the College addressed by President Millar and the president of
the state board. On this occasion, each team member and Padrow

were presented with a replica of the silver bowl given to the College, and the alternates, Assistant Coach Glossop, and Brian Fothergill each were given a Portland State jacket and necktie. Later, the state board, the Oregon state senate, and the faculty of Oregon Technical Institute sent congratulations. Team captain Westwood addressed both houses of the state legislature; the *New York Times* and *Time* magazine reported on the victory; and Governor Hatfield proclaimed a Portland State College-GE College Bowl appreciation day.[26]

Spurred by Portland State's College Bowl success, Ken Lewis, a Portland citizen, led the effort to establish a High School Bowl, in which metropolitan-area students competed on a local television station program. Ben Padrow helped establish the program, and Portland State was cited as co-sponsor each week.

Finally, the most enduring consequence of all was a tribute paid to the memory of Michael Smith, a team member who died of cystic fibrosis in 1968. In spite of his disease, Smith lived fully and actively, graduating with a double major in Psychology and English, winning a graduate assistantship in the English Department, painting, and writing for all three College publications. As Padrow said after his death: "Several times during the nine months that I worked with him in preparation for the College Bowl he had serious illnesses and was forced into the hospital. Each time he called me to assure me that he would be back. Before the fourth game in New York he became seriously ill with pneumonia. Mike said that he was going to play the fourth game and he did. He played the game every time." It was entirely appropriate the state board named the College center after Smith in 1969.[27]

A more complicated dimension of student life, one that extended over several years, was student political activism, especially in protest against the Vietnam War. The Portland State movement, like those elsewhere, was triggered by the Free Speech Movement that began in the fall of 1964 at the University of California at Berkeley, when the university administration denied radical students a place to solicit volunteers and money for a variety of social and political causes. The students retaliated by occupying university buildings. Student activism became nationalized, however, not by free speech and free association issues but by the Vietnam War.

At Portland State, the news from Berkeley was received with interest but galvanized few people. Faculty members signed a petition in support of the action of the academic senate at Berkeley, stating: "The content of speech or advocacy should not be restricted by the University. Off-campus student political activities shall not be subject to university regulation. On-campus advocacy or organization of such activities shall be subject only to [reasonable regulation to prevent interference with the normal function of the university]." How many signed this petition is not clear, and it is significant that neither the senate nor the entire faculty took up the matter of supporting the Berkeley senate's position.[28]

The Executive Committee discussed the Berkeley situation at length during February 1965. Its consensus was that the appeal of the Free Speech Movement to a large number of students there was not the issue of making space available for causes but rather the impersonal nature of the university, about which the students had many legitimate complaints. To prevent a comparable protest from arising at Portland State, the committee recommended solving specific grievances such as long registration lines, paucity of parking spaces, lack of physical amenities, slowness of evaluating transfer credits, and impersonality in dealing with students. Essentially, the committee concluded the grievances at Portland State were compounded by "the inability of the PSC student to identify with the College."[29]

The Executive Committee discussed various ways to involve students effectively, including putting them on policy-formulating committees, listening to them when so placed, and involving them in College activities, such as the recent campaign for state bond measures for college and university construction. It recommended better advising of new students, both to help them with course planning and to show them there were faculty members who were personally concerned with their welfare. All of these suggestions were sound but difficult to implement.[30]

The student response to Berkeley, so far as official action was concerned, was the passage by a single vote in the student senate of a resolution supporting the statement of the Berkeley faculty senate. By March 1965, Millar assured the public it was unlikely a Berkeley situation would arise at Portland State. His confidence was based on the facts that Portland State had no censorship of student organizations, that its bureaucracy was small in size, and that faculty did not overemphasize research in comparison to teaching.[31]

The first real protest at Portland State arose over the Vietnam War, more specifically, over the "military-industrial complex." The protest occurred because the College and the Portland Chamber of

Commerce were sponsoring a national security seminar put on by the Industrial College of the Armed Forces, a branch of the Defense Department, to be held over a two-week period in April and May 1965. Several students and faculty scheduled a competing, week-long "insecurity seminar," with panel meetings on topics such as "the Warfare State" and "the Armed and the Disarmed Economy—Prospect for Peace." Panel members included Michael Reardon and Morris Webb from the History Department and Brock Dixon, dean of administration.[32]

Later in the spring and fall of 1965, there was a series of poorly attended events that showed the indifference of most students and faculty toward the war. In May, there was a nationally broadcast discussion between defenders and opponents of the war that was piped into the lounge of the College Center. In October, there was a "teach-in" from Toronto broadcast on television featuring representatives from South Vietnam, Cambodia, and the United States, followed by a local panel at Portland State. Not more than fifty persons attended this event. The College's Young Republicans held a meeting to support the actions of the Administration in Vietnam.[33]

In 1966 and 1967, in contrast to rallies, marches, and draft card burnings in many cities and universities in the United States, Portland and Portland State were relatively quiet. Professors David Newhall of the Philosophy Department and Laureen Nussbaum of the Foreign Languages and Literatures Department wrote articles for the *Vanguard* on non-violent resistance and opposition to the war, respectively. There was a forum at which Selective Service officials and draft resisters and pacifists appeared. There was a silent peace vigil in the Park Blocks outside the College started by Robert Crowley (Music) on Wednesday afternoons, which drew twenty to thirty persons for a period of several months. Three busloads of students attended a peace rally in San Francisco, and about five hundred persons, including some Portland State faculty and students, marched in a parade in downtown Portland supporting resistance to the draft.[34]

In April 1968, there was a nationwide strike against war and racism. Students were supposed to boycott classes to discuss these social issues. The strike at Portland State was handicapped from the beginning because one of the organizers suggested the striking students should go to the beach or mountains to discuss the issues, a proposal met with ridicule. Few students went on strike, although several supported the aim to discuss the issues but not the emptying of classrooms. Others said the strike had not been given enough advance publicity to be effective, while still others supported only one of the two goals of the strike organizers. In a *Vanguard* interview, one student "sympathized with the anti-war orientation of the strike but wasn't so sure about the anti-racism issue. 'I'm not sure I want Negroes to be equal,' she said, 'I'm afraid that they'll want to dominate.'"[35]

Individual acts of resistance to the war effort were also few in number. One faculty member who refused to pay his telephone tax, maintaining it contributed to the war effort, had it deducted from his paycheck by demand of the Internal Revenue Service. More spectacularly, Robert Williams, a member of the Philosophy Department, refused to be drafted into the armed forces in October 1968. He attempted to publicize his action by taking sanctuary in the College Center while awaiting the Federal Bureau of Investigation (FBI) to arrest him, but the agency refused to cooperate by coming to the College. Tired of waiting, Williams and 120 student and faculty supporters marched and sang their way down Broadway to the federal courthouse, where he was arrested. Later in the month, there were large demonstrations against the war in many American cities, as well as in Japan and London, but only one thousand people participated in an anti-war protest march in Portland. The march had been endorsed by Pres. Gregory Wolfe in a letter to the student newspaper, but apparently he was not persuasive in turning out members of the College community.[36]

So far as events at the College were concerned, there was a great deal more interest in recruiting by the military and by corporations than there was in marching against the war or participating in teach-ins. In October 1966, two students and Professor of Music Robert Crowley picketed a recruiting table on the overpass between State Hall (Cramer) and the College Center. They were ordered by Channing Briggs, dean of students, to set up a table a "judicious distance" from the marines, in lieu of picketing; they reluctantly agreed to do so. In March 1967, a student-faculty group picketed the recruiting efforts of the Dow Chemical Company because it manufactured napalm, a gasoline jelly used by American forces in Vietnam.[37]

Military recruiting became a truly inflammatory issue on 26 October 1968, when Gen. Lewis B. Hershey, the director of the Selective Service Adminstration (SSA), issued a directive to conscript men involved in illegal demonstrations against the service and military recruiters. Several colleges and universities barred military recruiters from campus until the directive was rescinded. The Portland State chapter of Students for a Democratic Society (SDS) circulated a petition asking the College to adopt a similar course. President Millar promised to take seriously any petition to the administration but said current policy was to leave the College open to recruiters from any legitimate organization. "Believe it or not," Millar said, "[some] students wish to seek placement in the armed forces."[38]

Although Millar rejected the SDS petition, the issue was far from over, as the Portland State chapter of the American Association of University Professors in late January voted to bring two resolutions to the faculty. One was to urge Hershey to repeal his directive and the other was to ask the College to suspend military recruiting until it was repealed. By the time the faculty met on 7 February, the SSA and the White House had issued letters in effect repealing the Hershey directive. At the meeting, the faculty voted overwhelmingly to censure Hershey for his directive but not to close military recruiting. The second measure to close military recruiting failed in spite of an effort by some of its opponents—who could not defeat it in a fair vote—to kill it by leaving the meeting in an attempt to lose the quorum necessary to conduct business. The maneuver failed. Most faculty believed banning the recruiters would deny students' right to information and, thus, their ability to accept or reject the draft.[39]

After the meeting, some faculty objected to President Millar not stepping down from the chair when he read the two letters from the SSA and the White House. They argued this action threw the weight of the Administration behind retaining military recruiting and was decisive in the faculty vote to uphold it. Nothing came of this protest.[40]

Dow Chemical returned to the attention of Portland State's antiwar protesters in February 1968. The protests were part of a national trend, for more demonstrations had occurred against the chemical company across the country during the preceding fall term than against military recruiting. SDS organized a protest against Dow on 21 February, picketing outside the door of the placement office where Dow was recruiting. Students proffered homemade napalm on ice cream sticks, tossed a couple of helium-filled balloons containing anti-napalm messages into the recruiting office, and tried (unsuccessfully) to march into the auditorium before a play was to be presented there. Earlier in the day, balloons had been released in the College Center, and some demonstrators milled around outside the placement office. A man tried to push one of the faculty members participating in this demonstration, tore up his sign, made obscene comments to him, and disparaged his masculinity. During the day there were also two quieter events: a panel discussion with a recruiter from Dow and a movie entitled *Napalm*.[41]

On 4 December, SDS returned to the charge when fifteen demonstrators, including a drummer, marched through Old Main (now Lincoln Hall) to the placement office. This time, the objection was to recruiting by the Central Intelligence Agency (CIA). John Jenkins, the director of the placement office, approached the demonstration in a relaxed manner, saying he approved of it but also asserting he did not object to the CIA recruitment as it was a legal organization. After lingering twenty minutes at the office, the demonstrators moved to the president's office, where Gregory Wolfe agreed to meet them on the following Saturday at an all-campus gathering to discuss recruiting, but the demonstration did not change the College's policies. The faculty showed little interest in the controversies over recruiting. It was only involved once, in 1968, when Dean Briggs reported in March to the faculty senate on the College's recruitment policies and procedures; presumably they were acceptable to that body, as no one moved to change them.[42]

In addition to protesting the Vietnam War, students became active in other causes in the 1960s. At least one participated in the great civil rights march led by Martin Luther King, Jr., in 1965 from Selma to Montgomery, Alabama. In April of that year, six uniformed members of the National Party of America (NPA) arrived in a pickup truck in the Park Blocks outside the College. The organization advocated deporting African Americans to Africa and testing all Jews "to see if they have a genetic problem that can be corrected." Those who "failed" the test would be deported to Israel.[43]

When a member of the NPA began making a speech from the truck, most in the crowd of 250 found his message distasteful. Some deflated the truck's tires; others leapt on its hood; and still others burned the organization's leaflets. At this juncture, John Stevens, a faculty member in the History Department, rushed to the truck's cab and tore down the Confederate flag. A fist fight erupted, and the police took the NPA members to headquarters. Afterwards, Stevens was contrite and apologetic: "It was unfortunate. I don't want students to idealize it. Groups like that will be around for a long time to come and we must put up with them."[44]

Even more sensational was an accusation by an undercover agent for the FBI, Russell K. Krueger, that three Portland State students were Communists. The House Un-American Activities Committee had been

Joe Uris, most influential student leader of the 1960s and 1970s

investigating the national movement against the Vietnam War and was allegedly concerned about Communist participation in it. Quickly, the College community rallied to the students. Ninety-seven faculty members signed a document protesting the allegations against the three students, and a group of students circulated a petition calling for a debate in Congress about the continuation of the Committee.[45]

The three students—Joe Uris, president of the Associated Students, Denise Jacobsen, and John Van Hyning—were given the opportunity to go to Washington, D.C., (at their own expense) to testify before the Committee to clear their names. Although, thanks to the intervention of United States representative Wendell Wyatt of Oregon, the Committee did finally offer to pay the students' travel expenses to Washington, all declined for a variety of reasons. Uris's statement was most eloquent: "I am not a Communist. But I will not dignify a committee which has abused the faith of the American people and misused the funds of the American taxpayers by making an appearance to attempt to clear myself of allegations made in the most unjust manner and in the most un-American of spirits." One of the least serious consequences of the blackening of the students' reputations was the refusal of radio station KISN to run an advertisement for a student dance that mentioned Uris would be the master of ceremonies. The reason for the refusal was the complaint of parents of three Portland State students.[46]

Student government election campaign

Uris's prominence at Portland State had arisen a year earlier when, as student body president, he presided over a strike called by the student government. The major issue was control of the funds for student activities, which were dispensed by student government with veto power by the administration. Uris wanted to change this: "We are striking to give greater representation to students. Students should have the end say in all their programs and final control of all of their funds." Until that happened, he and the Associated Students executive board asked students to boycott all student activities at the College. Other issues in the strike included demands for pass/no-pass grading in physical education courses; recognition by the administration of a new student constitution; student government's right to nominate all student members of faculty and administration committees; and creation of a joint faculty-student registration committee to address problems of registration.[47]

The strike lasted approximately three weeks. It ended after amicable negotiations between the student government and Millar's Executive Committee were completed. The two bodies exchanged memoranda over the proposed student constitution, with the students pressing for immediate recognition of the new constitution, student participation in resolving legal disputes over interpreting the constitution, and the creation of a joint faculty-student board of arbitration to deal with "all areas requiring legal consideration." The strike ended on 9 November, through action of the Associated Students executive board. Terms that made the strike settlement possible were the College administration's willingness to recognize the student constitution and agreement on the arbitration board composed of three faculty and four students, including the chair. Uris called the strike "a qualified success" but noted the students still did not have full control over the dispensing of the student activities fee.[48]

Although not his final moment in College affairs, Uris's last hurrah as student body president was colorful and controversial. When his administration was succeeded by one headed by a conservative, Tim Dorosh, Uris and his administration planned a pseudo-patriotic inauguration ceremony to mock his successor. There was to have been a color guard carrying the American flag, a band playing patriotic songs, the speakers' stand decked in patriotic bunting, and the sale of popcorn and strawberry pop, with proceeds going to the Oregon White Shield Home for Unwed Mothers. Millar heard of the plans beforehand and made his objections known to Uris. The president believed he had reached an understanding with Uris that patriotic symbols would not be used during the ceremony, but, if this was his impression, he was clearly wrong. For, as the ceremony opened, a woman sang "God Bless America" in a deliberately off-key manner, a red-white-and blue vest was awarded Uris, as was a broom draped in the national flag.

Whether the act of defiance was a joke or malicious provocation, Millar took it seriously. He threatened disciplinary action against some of the students and a crackdown on student government. He declared the administration had usually followed a hands-off policy regarding student affairs, but, hereafter, "there is no doubt that there will have to be a closer scrutiny and not more freedom but less freedom because of this incident." The context of his strong line, as he himself indicated, was the recent denunciation of Uris and the other two students as Communists by the House Un-American Activities Committee. "If we are to defend the fundamental legal rights of a person on the one hand...the college must not be guilty of confusing defense of rights and giving license to be irresponsible on the other." As it would do increasingly in the next few years, the College administration walked a thin line between antagonizing the public and alienating the students.[49]

The year 1969 was a kind of transition between the growing student restiveness of the late 1960s and the days of rage of the early 1970s. Many of the old issues, such as opposition to the Vietnam War and protests against corporate and military recruiting, continued, while new grievances arose concerning the internal operation of the College. The most publicized event of the year occurred early in the fall term, when the College community was divided over a national moratorium called to rally public opinion against the war. The plan, devised by the U.S. National Student Association (NSA), was for college classes to be canceled on 15 October and 14-15 November so students would go out into their communities and appeal to the public to join their protest. The hope of NSA was that the Nixon administration, which had not listened to students, would listen to the middle class working taxpayers they hoped would join in the protests.[50]

The student government at Portland State passed a resolution unanimously urging President Wolfe to cancel classes. The faculty senate then took up the matter. The meeting of the senate was unprecedented in one respect: it was televised by the Center for the Moving Image, although the vote to do so was by a margin of one, 25-24. The meeting itself, it is interesting to note, was not called by a member of the faculty but rather arose because the student government wanted it to pass a resolution.[51]

The resolution called for the cancellation of classes on 15 October and their replacement with "a variety of individual and group activity" to discuss and protest the war. There was a lengthy discussion of the resolution (which, in the nature of things, had been slightly amended by the senators). Representative sentiments expressed in the debate as recorded by the secretary were that the senate was obligated to support an official action of the student government; concern over who would be in control of the activities that replaced the classes; and a preference for voluntary decisions of students to attend class and outside events, rather than coercive ones. In the end, the amended resolution calling for the moratorium passed by a vote of 37-4. President Wolfe refused to cancel classes, however, preferring to leave the decision to individual departments, faculty, and students. In taking this position, he concurred with the actions of the presidents of the University of Oregon and Oregon State University. Wolfe, however, did urge the members of the Portland State community to participate in the events of the moratorium.[52]

When 15 October arrived, the day's events turned out to be only partly heartening to its supporters. The first major event of the day occurred in the ballroom of the College Center when Frederick Schuman, professor of Political Science, told the crowd that fascism in the United States would increase with the continuation of the war, and

Richard Forbes of the Biology Department spoke of the destruction the war was causing to the natural environment of South Vietnam. The crowd then moved to the Park Blocks, where it was joined by others to march, seven thousand strong, down Broadway. After a stop at noon for five minutes of silence, the marchers continued to the waterfront memorial to the battleship *Oregon*, where the memorial's American flag was lowered to half mast and a flag with a peace symbol raised under it.[53]

The marchers then moved into the industrial district of Northwest Portland, where they appealed to the workers to leave their jobs and join the march—none did so. The march then returned to Portland State. During the day, there were demonstrations at the Armed Forces Induction center and an attempt of five hundred people, led by state legislator Wallace Priestley, to "liberate" Lincoln High School by asking the students to leave classes to join the march. None did. In the evening, a meeting was held at Portland State to plan the November moratorium. Moratorium Day had a spectacular turnout in comparison to previous anti-war marches, but it picked up no support among the general public and certainly did not end the war. Essentially, it strengthened the resolve of those already committed to the anti-war cause. The University administration took the moratorium in stride for the most part, although Channing Briggs, the dean of students, reported to the Executive Committee in late October that "some executives at other institutions had received handbooks (printed in German) on revolution...[and] that administrators at PSU [should] be alerted to the possibility of such mail appearing here."[54]

The next step in the anti-war protesters' plan was to call for students to cut classes for two days in November, then a day more each succeeding month until the war ended. Plans for the November moratorium were laid by its organizers with the hopes that "most" students and "many" civil servants would not appear for classes or work. On 3 November, the faculty senate was asked again by the student government to pass a resolution urging the faculty and students to support the moratorium. This time, the resolution was presented in a provocative form: "Whereas Portland State University is part of the military-industrial complex, and whereas the Vietnam War is the most striking manifestation of the nature and functioning of that complex...PSU Faculty will join with students in a strike whose purpose is to disassociate if only briefly, PSU from the military-industrial university complex." Bill Nygren of Students for a Democratic Society, in supporting the resolution, "spoke at great length about the tiered hierarchy in higher education." The original resolution was amended twice to remove the inflammatory language, and the following resolution was adopted in the end: "The Faculty Senate of Portland State University urges the faculty and students of PSU to support on November 13 and 14, 1969 the National Moratorium on Vietnam." The resolution was adopted on a non-recorded vote but only the Philosophy Department canceled classes.[55]

On 7 November, disappointed by the toning down of the resolution as finally adopted by the senate, those wanting more militant action pressed at a general faculty meeting for a stronger resolution calling for a strike. The resolution was debated with arguments similar to those made in the two earlier meetings on the moratorium and, in the end, was defeated. The victorious opponents of the resolution argued the passage of the resolution would politicize the University, while its supporters argued it would do so in a rightful cause. One advocate assailed critics of the resolution by labeling them "Batmen:" "mild-mannered professors by day—peace workers by night." On the eve of the strike, Wolfe warned protesters who prevented students from going to class that they would be in violation of University regulations.[56]

On 14 November, there were about one hundred picketers outside College buildings urging students not to attend school. Attendance was down somewhat, but few students who came attended the moratorium events. Support of the moratorium was down from that of one month before. The march down Broadway this time had about three thousand people (led in their chanting by Wallace Priestley, wielding a bull horn) accompanied by an elderly woman in tennis shoes who repeatedly declared, "Every major, large-scale demonstration against the Vietnam war...has all-out Communist support." The march stopped at the Pioneer Courthouse, where several speakers denounced the war, and then proceeded toward the industrial district, but only about one hundred marchers actually bothered to get there. In the morning, a demonstration at the selective service induction center was broken up by police using clubs and mace after one policeman had been pushed through the glass doors of the Center by the protesters. On the following day, several students were in San Francisco to join a large march against the war.[57]

Intermittently during the war years, there were continued attempts to prevent military and corporate recruiting at the Placement Office. In December 1968, responding to the complaints about recruiting,

Demonstration against military recruiting on campus

President Wolfe and Dean of Students Briggs devised a compromise between those who wished no recruiting by these organizations and those who wanted to continue the traditional policy of welcoming representatives of all lawful institutions. The policy was to allow all recruiters but to require them to meet with students to discuss their corporate policies outside recruiting hours. The purpose of the policy was to legitimatize the dissenters, take the potential for violence out of their protests, and enable the recruiters to carry on their business. This stance was supported by the national ACLU, which declared "a decision to admit some [recruiting agents] and exclude others would be discriminatory and an incursion into the basic principles of academic freedom." But in February 1969, Students for a Democratic Society at Portland State charged Wolfe was ignoring his own policy.[58]

The SDS chapter demonstrated against navy recruiters in early November. The recruiters set up their tables in the placement office in Old Main, where demonstrators appeared. The navy then shifted tactically to Room 292 in Smith Center and then to Room 296. The twenty demonstrators milled about for two hours before dispersing. In mid-month, there was a demonstration against the marine recruiters, which did not prevent them from recruiting. In the afternoon following the morning demonstration, there was a panel discussion attended by a marine recruiter (an Oregon State graduate from Portland) and several of his opponents. The marine stated he was present on campus to "explain the Marine Corps in a meaningful and persuasive way" and would not return if the student body did not want him to, but he questioned whether the demonstrators represented the entire student body. At the panel discussion, David Horowitz, a member of the History Department, declared, "The controlling interests in the U.S. have become a polluted empire," and that he felt the military was "part of the empire and the university should break from the empire and the military."[59]

The year 1969 was an exciting year for student government in its personnel, as well as its policies. In February, Andrew Haynes, a graduate student and former employee of the Bonneville Power Administration, was elected student body president, the first African American student to be so honored in the state of Oregon. At the occasion later in the year of the joint inauguration of Gregory Wolfe and Paul Bragdon as presidents of PSU and Reed College, respectively, one of the Reed faculty remarked on seeing Haynes, "I see you put your token in the platform committee." He was told, "He's no token; he's our student body president." Haynes won 36 percent of the vote in a seven-person race. Immediately, his election became a matter of controversy, as an article in the *Oregonian* labeled him an "avowed militant." On campus, his constituents were surprised to find they had voted for a man who wished to abolish intercollegiate football because it was supported by student activities fees, though it did not have student support. Haynes also maintained student government was ineffectual and should be replaced by a joint student-faculty government that, at least as the student members of it were concerned, would develop a constructive relationship with the community. This last development, he said, would take the form of an experimental college through which students would do one term's work in the community during their academic careers, a requirement that would help them focus their educational and vocational goals (the example he gave was of a social work student who would find through field work in the experimental college whether he or she really wanted to become a social worker). Haynes argued liberal arts education had become traditional over the past seventy years and needed refreshment by exposure to the city as a learning laboratory.[60]

By late May, Haynes had become somewhat discouraged about realizing his goals of abolishing football, establishing a student-faculty government, and creating the experimental college through discussion with the administration. He called a press conference to announce he had some new goals and a new way to achieve them. He abandoned the student-faculty government plan in favor of a community government in which anyone affected by "the decisions of the university should have a say in the government." He also now called for the setting of a quota of "culturally deprived" students (whom he defined as "poor whites, Mexicans, the Indians, and the blacks") who would be permitted to enroll, even if they did not meet the normal standards of admission. Haynes admitted there already was a 3 percent quota for students who did not meet normal admission standards but said in practice the quota was always allotted to the Athletic Department. In order to gain these objectives, Haynes called for a student shutdown of the University in the coming September to give the student government a position of strength from which to negotiate with the University.[61]

Haynes's proposals were far from popular either with student government or with students in general. He presented the student senate with six proposals he did not want discussed but simply voted up or down. They included cutting money from the football budget and using it to install "black studies content as a departmental requirement for graduation in the appropriate majors;" placing the control of the dean of students in the hands of student government; and using some of the money cut from football for an addition to the work-study funds. The senate adjourned without making a decision on the proposals.[62]

Although student government did not respond, about three thousand students signed a petition protesting the idea of closing the school in September. Members of the football team also called a press conference objecting to the cutting of funds from their sport. A poll taken by the *Vanguard* in early June showed five of Haynes's proposals garnered little support. The only one that received majority support (60 percent) was the experimental college. The largest measure of disapproval was the 86 percent that opposed the idea of closing the school in the fall. The poll also asked if students wished to recall Haynes; 51 percent opposed the recall.[63]

The same week, a group called the Student Coalition was formed in opposition to Haynes and his supporters. Its aims were "to call Haynes' bluff" and "to propose alternatives to Haynes' demands." The

Student Coalition conducted its own poll, which indicated 86 percent did not favor the tactics of the Haynes group (presumably the boycott), and 87 percent wanted a direct student vote on Haynes's five proposals. By the end of the month, Haynes was losing hope that his plans would be carried through. Although he discounted both polls taken during the last week of the term, he said the state board had told Portland State's administrators "to hold the line" for fear that, if it accepted them, the ideas would spread to other colleges in the state system. When fall term opened, instead of conducting a shutdown in Portland, Haynes was at Syracuse University, where he had enrolled in a doctoral program.[64]

The subject of another student controversy was Peter Freedman. Freedman had been admitted to the School of Social Work in May 1969, but the decision was reversed, and he was denied admission by the school in September. At a subsequent hearing at his request, Freedman was told the basis of the action was his unstable work history. Although for privacy reasons the school did not give the basis for the decision, Freedman maintained it was unsolicited information provided to the school by the Oregon Department of Vocational Rehabilitation, which had fired him in June. Freedman maintained his dismissal was for not following the Department's rigid policies while working in an innovative manner in Portland's black ghetto.[65]

Freedman requested help from the Portland State chapter of the New University Conference, a radical faculty organization. The chapter took up his cause, disrupting classes in the School of Social Work by speaking and handing out leaflets. One conference member criticized the University for accepting the criteria of the state agency: "By endorsing the position of an outside agency which deemed Peter's work 'illegitimate,' the school has accepted the value-judgments of white, middle-class administrators far removed from the demands and needs of clients....This is an overtly political and repressive approach to the problems of our society and to the function of the university."[66]

Freedman took his appeal to the General Student Affairs Committee. The Committee explored the question at an initial meeting, and then, afterwards, most of its student members suddenly resigned. One who did, Lindsay Stone, asserted the "GSAC has no power and that faculty and administration 'don't want to cause any waves' since it might affect their academic futures." "Committees have become a mire of impressive words," he said, "but they don't do anything." All but two students returned for the next meeting of the Committee, when Freedman and his attorney appeared. Gordon Hearn, the dean of the School of Social Work, however, refused to appear before the Committee because he maintained admissions decisions should be made by an academic group and not the General Student Affairs Committee. The Committee, with twenty-one members (excluding the two students who resigned), voted with one dissenting vote to refer the case to President Wolfe with the request that "he conduct a full, impartial, objective review of the Peter Freedman case" and report back to the Committee. The Committee then moved to a discussion of its role in general and concluded its mission was to develop general policies, rather than to decide individual cases. This resolution seemed to satisfy all, including Lindsay Stone.[67]

It is not surprising that all the turmoil on the campuses of the state system (especially at the University of Oregon and at Portland State) attracted the attention of state legislators. During the year, the House of Representatives appointed five members, under the chairmanship of Rep. Robert G. Davis of Medford, to serve as a special house Task Force on Higher Education. Its mission was to look into the performance of the state system institutions and the goals for higher education in the 1970s. The task force took testimony at Portland State on 21 February, a week after its had visited the University of Oregon and two weeks after visiting Oregon State.

Contrary to what many academics feared and some ordinary citizens hoped, the report was sane and thorough. Its seventy pages did address the issue of campus disturbances but went to the root causes of them. It blamed the troubles basically on the inadequacies of undergraduate education, including the use of teaching assistants as instructors in lower division courses and overemphasis on research rather than teaching. It made some suggestions for fairly comprehensive changes in administering the state's educational establishment, including the merging of the State Board of Education (for elementary and secondary education) and the State Board of Higher Education. It said the new board and its chancellor should be moved from the University of Oregon to Salem and given a new building. It recommended excellence in teaching as well as research should be rewarded. It also recommended students be drawn into the university decision-making process in matters relating to their concerns. Finally, it proposed the creation of a citizens advisory committee to evaluate finances, classroom instruction, and faculty tenure.[68]

While some of these proposals were not popular in the universities, and some unwise, the task force was remarkable for what it did not suggest. It said neither special legislation nor legislative intervention were required to control campus disorder, although it did say the board should use its available powers more vigorously. Indeed, its conclusions concerning disorder were that "incidents of disruption thus far on Oregon campuses have been minor and that in general the administration of student conduct has been commendable." And the report spoke to public opinion: "The public should keep the size of the disruptive vocal minority in perspective—the one percent who attract so much attention and malign the campus's image while doing it."[69]

Many in the state legislature, including Representative Davis, did not follow the task force's advice. Later in the same month the report was published, House Bill 1880 was introduced. The bill authorized the governor to proclaim an emergency at any state institution of higher education in case of imminent danger to educational processes or to life and property of its personnel. During such an emergency, police could exclude nonstudents and nonemployees from campus and buildings, unless their appearance was authorized by the university president. The bill was apparently aimed at "outside agitators" designing to stir up trouble at the universities. The bill was introduced, considered, and passed by the House of Representatives by a vote of fifty to seven, all within a period of twenty-four hours. It was criticized by several legislators, the chair of the Oregon Civil Liberties Union, and by President Wolfe, but its proponents said it required immediate passage because of an upcoming, unauthorized "Renaissance Fair"—presumably controlled by radicals—to be held at Oregon State later in the week.[70]

In contrast to the house, the bill received a hostile reception in the senate. Testimony taken before the Education Committee saw only four witnesses in favor of the bill, and, outside the legislature, both Secretary of State Clay Myers and State Treasurer Robert Straub criticized it as unnecessary (in the case of Myers) and as giving too much authority to the police and bypassing the state board (in the case of Straub). Gov. Tom McCall, however, said passage of the bill was necessary to dispel "the panorama of paranoia" that surrounded the higher education system. The senate revised the bill drastically to require the governor to consult with university officials and state and local police before declaring an emergency; to describe the property involved (which would include all public buildings, not just those of the state system); and to give those arrested under the bill immediate access to the county circuit courts. In revised form, the bill passed both houses of the legislature and was signed by the governor on 6 June.[71]

An issue spanning the last half of the 1960s was that of the rights and responsibilities of students and their incorporation into some kind of constitution or bill of rights. Ever since the Free Speech Movement at Berkeley, student demands for rights forced themselves onto the academic agenda. As the Vietnam War intensified, student protests increased in number, size, and stridency. Opposition to the war and assertiveness on behalf of civil rights spilled over into movements on the campus for greater student rights. Partly out of belief that governmental concessions to students would quell or quiet these protests and partly because they believed modern students had greater interest in, and capacity for, responsibilities, faculty, administrators, and students held numerous discussions on college campuses about accommodating these demands.

At Portland State, the leader of the movement for student power was Joe Uris, the president of the Associated Students of Portland State College (the official name of the student government). In 1966, under Uris's leadership, the student government drew up a new constitution and a bill of rights. Uris saw the student government as a union that would bargain with the administration to attempt to secure its demands. The demands themselves took the form of a bill of rights, the heart of which stated student government would hire the student activities advisers so that they would have no conflict of interest with the administration, as they did at the present time. A "Freedom Constitution" was also drawn up by Rod Barrett, a sophomore student senator.[72]

Both the bill of rights and the student constitution ran into difficulties in the student senate and among students as a whole. Led by Sen. Bob Handy, the student senate refused to approve placing the documents on the ballot for a student referendum. When Uris tried to gather petitions from the student body to place the constitution on the ballot, he fell many hundred votes short. Handy's main objection was that Uris had tried to present a new constitution without properly amending the existing one. Uris responded that "both the Declaration of Independence and the Federal Constitution upon which our nation state is based were extra-legal documents." In time, however, these difficulties were overcome, and the constitution went before the voters in April 1967, when it was approved by a vote of 355-80, a small turnout that probably indicated the degree of student interest in the whole issue.[73]

In November 1966, students presented the new constitution and bill of rights to the administration. It was referred to the Executive Committee, which discussed it and responded to the Associated Students executive board. The Executive Committee stated it looked forward to the acceptance of the new constitution but needed clarification of certain provisions, particularly where it dealt with matters clearly the prerogative of the faculty and about which the faculty alone could speak. Dean Swarthout, for the committee, proposed a joint student-faculty panel to discuss clarification of the constitution. This discussion essentially came to naught, as did the constitution itself, when President Millar refused to accept the entire bill of rights because many of the rights contained within it "infringed on faculty rights." He also vetoed two sections of the constitution itself: those referring to the student-faculty appeals board (on the grounds there was no such body) and the responsibility of the student senate to initiate programs "of academic, community, social and recreational" nature because this provision suggested the student senate would have complete responsibility for these programs, rather than sharing them with the administration and the faculty. Millar referred the matter to the General Student Affairs Committee, which refused to discuss the matter.[74]

The whole matter became moot by September 1967, when Millar made his annual "State of the College" address to the faculty. In it, he recommended the College adopt an important document entitled the "Joint Statement on Rights and Freedoms of Students." This document, designed "to enumerate the essential provisions for students to learn," was the product of five national organizations: the American Association of University Professors; the U.S. National Student Association; the National Association of Student Personnel Administrators; the National Association of Women's Deans and Counsellors; and the Association of American Colleges. This product of laborious negotiation among the five organizations, agreed to in 1966, was regarded by Millar as not only theoretically desirable but one that was within the traditional practices of Portland State. He stated, "There is very little in the document which is startling for Portland State. It sets forth a series of topics and objectives which we should regard as minimal standards. The value of it lies in the fact that it covers the waterfront. It provides a working basis for the areas of vital concerns."[75]

Millar sent the document to the General Student Affairs Committee for consideration before bringing it to the faculty. The committee, even though it had not completed a detailed study of the statement, realized the administration needed interim guidelines for cases that might arise before its study was completed. Accordingly, it asked the faculty senate to approve the statement "in principle" on 8 January 1968; the senate concurred unanimously. The senate discussed the document on 20 May and 3 June 1968. At the June meeting, the statement was adopted, but it was discovered there had been no quorum present, and the action was accordingly held to be invalid.[76]

Student newspapers are noted for their contentiousness. It was no surprise the staff of the *Vanguard* participated earnestly and vigorously in the movement for student rights in the 1960s. In early 1967, the paper went on strike because of its editors' objections to the actions of members of the dean of student's staff, which had responsibility for supervising the newspaper's finances. What the editors objected to was a series of blunders, they claimed, by the dean's staff, which included "some of the most incompetent people ever to disgrace the academic titles they have wrangled [sic] for themselves." The specific actions objected to were the reduction in the editor's salary, a budget cut, and objections on financial grounds to a plan to put the paper out twice a week.[77]

The *Vanguard* editorial board announced it would publish no paper beginning in the spring term of 1967, unless certain conditions were met. These conditions included the auditing of the paper's books by an accountant from the College business office; the placing of the *Vanguard* fully under the Publications Board (a faculty-student committee with oversight of student publications), which would mean removing the dean of students from control of it; and a demand that the dean of students specify his intent to recommend to the president and GSAC that all responsibility for all publications be removed from his office.[78]

The strike was settled with the return to publication one week late in the spring term. The editor and President Millar agreed financial support of the *Vanguard* had not been adequate over the past two terms; that GSAC should recommend to the senate a "definition of the role of the paper;" and that the paper should be allowed to appear twice a week.[79]

Within a month's time, Millar turned from friend to foe of the *Vanguard*. In late May, the newspaper ran an article on the impending visit to the campus of poet Allen Ginsberg, accompanied by a photograph of him nude from the groin up. At least in one respect, the timing of the photograph was unfortunate, as it appeared at the exact

Vanguard photograph that caused President Millar to suspend the newspaper

time the legislature was discussing the state system budget. The *Oregon Journal,* one of Portland's two daily newspapers, reported critical reaction from some of the city's citizens to the publishing of the photo, to which the editor of the *Vanguard* replied: "Allen Ginsberg is not a conventional personality; the photograph which I ran reported a facet of his showmanship which readers have a right to know." He expressed confidence there would be no legislative reprisals against the College because of the photo, and he tried to distinguish the paper from the institution: "The college administration is in no way responsible for the running of the picture."[80]

Millar took no such sanguine view. He ordered the issue confiscated and withheld from circulation. He was concerned about the photo and wrote the editor expressing his disagreement with his prediction there would be no legislative disapproval of it: "I have never had such violent reaction from outside the College as in this instance, and it may well spill over." He asked the Publications Board to develop written standards for the newspaper. The president's ire was further displayed after he saw the next edition of the *Vanguard,* which ran a publicity photo for the musical *Archie and Mehitable,* soon to be presented on campus, which showed a rear view of a woman in tights bending over a garbage can with the caption, "Touching Bottom." The issue also contained a photo of a clown labeled John Mosser (an assistant to Governor McCall) and a tasteless letter to the editor.[81]

Millar felt the editors were out of hand, and he suspended publication of the newspaper (although the salaries of staff members would continue) until further notice. The order went forward even though the Publications Board had passed a vote of confidence in the editor before the paper was suspended. Millar defended his action, asserting there had "existed mutually understood criteria" of the standards governing the student newspaper but that "of late...there have been a number of instances which call these standards into question and suggest that other standards are being followed which are incompatible with or deliberately contrary to those which have prevailed."[82]

There was varied reaction to the suspension. Editor William Weissert blamed Millar for caving into a fear of retaliation based on the circulation in the legislature (and at city luncheon gatherings) of a reprint of the story and the accompanying photo, coupled with a collection of four-letter words from one of Ginsberg's poems. Four student groups wrote Millar supporting the suspension. A radical faculty group, the Society for New Action Politics, offered the editor its office and equipment to publish the paper. There was a threat to picket Millar's house. Letters pro and con appeared in the *Vanguard,* including one from the writer, Tom Gaddis, who declared, "The recent issues of the *Vanguard* are among the finest quality in a good, swinging college paper that I have ever seen" and another from a student assailing the Ginsberg photo "in a publication already famed for poor taste and indiscretion, this aesthetically offensive and ethically questionable photograph represents a new triumph." One faculty member, Donald R. Moor of the Philosophy Department, organized support from eighty faculty members for an *Independent Vanguard.* The paper published two editions, on 31 May and 2 June 1967. There also was a panel discussion on publications attended by about 350 students and faculty.[83]

The Publications Board unanimously passed a resolution asking Millar to reinstate the *Vanguard* immediately. It also adopted a statement containing journalistic standards for the newspaper, as Millar had requested, basing them on canons adopted in 1923 by the American Society of Newspaper Editors. The board also stated, "We do not feel any violation of these standards sufficient to warrant suspension of the *Vanguard* has been made." On the other hand, a group of ten faculty members circulated a memorandum supporting the president's actions in suspending the paper until standards for publication were clarified. One of them, Basil Dmytryshyn, professor of History, criticized the Ginsberg photo but considered the Mosser caption an "uncalled for insult...because Mosser was an advisor to a governor who has 'more than a casual interest in higher education and student welfare,' and because many PSC faculty participate in the Mosser plan and support the principle behind it." None of this group claimed a wish to censor the *Vanguard,* nor did any wish to discipline Weissert, but none thought an independent newspaper would solve any problems because the public would not differentiate between an independent paper and one sponsored by the College.[84]

An informal poll of twenty-five faculty members was divided over the wisdom of the paper's suspension, while 92 percent of fifty students polled opposed the suspension. Thirty-seven of the fifty students favored an independent student newspaper; one of them, Craig Wollner, a graduate student in History, proclaimed the newspaper's staff "must do something in the face of irrational action." When the faculty senate took up the matter in June 1967, it did not consider the Publications Board's statement of appropriate standards but, rather, recommendations by the Advisory Council as a set of interim policies until the Publications Board and GSAC could devise more permanent arrangements.[85]

The Advisory Council presented to the senate a document on "Policy, Statement of Taste, and Procedures for Review." The statement on taste required the most discussion, and, finally, the following resolution was adopted: "The faculty believes that under special conditions an editor may find sufficiently significant reasons to warrant the risk of offending even a large segment of his audience, but no editor may justify the risk of offending even the smallest segment of his audience without a reason relevant to the academic community the publication serves." Finally, all three parts of the document were adopted.[86]

The senate debate gave Millar an opportunity to address the faculty in a formal way. He denied the *Vanguard* had been suspended because of the two photographs but, rather, because of institutional confusions. He believed the role of the Publications Board was "ill-defined," as was evidenced not only by the latest controversy but by the strike of April and also a controversy over the literary magazine, *Yin-Yang*, which had been suspended by the Publications Board "for lack of editorial criteria and unsatisfactory organizational arrangements." Millar believed, however, the senate action of the day provided appropriate temporary guidelines for the board to supervise the operation of student publications.[87]

In the summer of 1967, the Advisory Council drew up a charter for a new Publications Board. It established a nine-person board that consisted of five faculty members and four students. The duties of the board were to "establish fiscal and editorial guidelines for all student publications, appoint all key personnel and review their performances." The board was held responsible by the academic community "for maintaining a free and responsible student press," and was expected to "develop a general statement on standards of publication to serve as a guideline to student editors." The first guidelines were unanimously adopted by the Publications Board in October 1967, and, there, the issue of student publications rested.[88]

The creation of Portland State College roughly coincided with— although it did not directly cause—some changes in the organized religious opportunities available to students. The most significant was the development of an ecumenical Christian Campus Ministry with its own interdenominational facilities and programs. This institution was one of the earliest of its kind in the United States and the first to include Roman Catholics, but it was not the first organized religious presence at Portland State.

Since Vanport days, there had been a chapter of the Inter-Varsity Christian Fellowship. Then came a Baptist Student Union, sponsored by the Southern Baptist church, and Chi Rho, supported by the Roman Catholic church. Most of the large churches located near or on the Park Blocks had organized groups for young adults or college students or both. There was a faculty committee on religion from the earliest days. But the originator of the ecumenical presence was William E. Hallman, a Presbyterian minister who came to Portland in 1955 to direct the activities of the Westminster Foundation of the Synod of Oregon, including exploring the possibilities of establishing a campus ministry at Portland State.[89]

Hallman spent one year in investigation, then, in 1956, he organized the Campus Christian Organization, locating it on S.W. Broadway in rented quarters. The importance of this organization was its ecumenical focus. Although Hallman's salary was paid by the Presbyterian church, he always made his ministry interdenominational. This experience was preliminary to an important step the churches took in 1957. In that year, Hallman became chair of the Committee on Campus Christian Life of the Oregon Council of Churches. In cooperation with the United Campus Christian Fellowship of the National Council of Churches, he persuaded this committee to sponsor an interdenominational conference at Western Oregon State College in Monmouth to discuss an ecumenical ministry at that institution. In the same year, a two-day meeting at Portland State brought together College faculty and administrators, Protestant leaders from the area, and the national secretary of the United Campus Christian Fellowship. This meeting was helpful in discussing what form or forms campus ministry should take at the College. Its report concluded the possibilities should be explored of founding a new type of ministry, "one which would be ecumenical in its thrust on this campus, but would provide opportunity for denominational expression." Representatives of the Methodists, Congregationalists, Episcopalians, Lutherans, Presbyterians, and American Baptists met through 1958 and much of 1959 to discuss this opportunity.[90]

In January 1959, with the aid of the Rev. Robert E. Rumer of the First Congregational Church, Hallman organized another conference at Portland State. Again, both College faculty and administrators and National Council of Churches representatives were present to discuss an ecumenical ministry. So, too, were representatives of the seven denominations that had been present at the Monmouth conference two years earlier. At the 1959 meeting, it was decided to ask the Christian education ministers of the downtown churches to form an interim ministry at Portland State and to appoint an advisory committee from the seven denominations to suggest a more permanent structure. A committee of four was later established to write a plan of operation; its report was completed on 30 September 1959. In February 1960, five denominations: American Baptist, Disciples of Christ, Methodist, United Church of Christ, and United Presbyterian founded the Cooperative Campus Christian Ministry (CCCM). Episcopalians soon followed. These groups already had a building to move into, as the Presbyterians had bought a house in 1959 at 621 S.W. Hall Street, which they named Westminster House, for the use of all the denominations. The philosophy of those who gathered in the building was that it would house programs conducted by the individual denominations but that it would also be home to a CCCM board of directors, chosen by all the denominations, that would present a common, "ecumenical" program supported financially by all of them.[91]

There were multiple sources for this unusual Campus Ministry. The most important was the dedication and patience of William Hallman, its moving spirit, and the relationships he had established since 1955 with Portland State faculty and administrators. Hallman believed his ministry to be not behind his desk but in the halls, offices, and coffee shops of the College, where his ebullient figure was well-known across campus. Other clergy, in this time of an emerging ecumenical spirit, felt rewarded by helping to form a pioneering institution that truly reflected this new philosophy. Hallman always took particular care to work with the downtown churches so that his program did not seem threatening to them. He was largely successful in allaying their fears, but he did not always succeed in gaining more than a token support of time from their clergy. House manager Kate Moore played a consistently supportive role in the establishment of the program. Finally, students of the various denominations were generally enthusiastic about the new venture.[92]

Enthusiasm was needed at times, as CCCM was not born without conflicts. After all, the 1950s was a decade of great religious "revival" in the United States, and many clergy were not willing to tamper with what seemed to be a success. Thus, it was not surprising that some of the downtown clergy were fearful a novel ecumenical program at the College might hamper them in two respects: by luring students away from their existing faith and by competing with the Sunday programs of the surrounding churches.[93]

The founders of CCCM decided in 1961 to change the name of their building from Westminster House to Koinonia (the Greek word for "community") House to better testify to their intention. At Koinonia House, each denomination had its own minister, some assigned full-time, some given part-time duties at Portland State. As the years progressed, structural changes took place in the administration of the Campus Ministry. In 1961, the Lutherans affiliated with CCCM, and, four years later, the Roman Catholics also joined—the same year the name of the organization was changed to Portland Campus Christian Ministry (PCCM). The building was also moved, continuing a peregrination that now took it to rental quarters at 711 S.W. Hall Street, near Neuberger Hall. In 1972, another change took place, when five of the denominations: American Baptist, Disciples of Christ, United Methodist, Presbyterian, and United Church of Christ decided to abandon their separate pastorates and together fund a single "ecumenical minister." The first person to fill this new position was Z. Arthur Buck, a United Church of Christ pastor, who knew the Portland State campus well, having served as associate coordinator of educational activities at the University.[94]

From the beginning, the programs of Campus Ministry have been both contemplative and activist, but most of the first programs were focused on the individual, not on the community. As the concerns of society have changed, the interest of Koinonia House staff, students, and faculty have followed, until over the years, an enormous number of courses, religious services, political programs, individual counseling sessions, and recreational activities have taken place. One of the early pro-

grams that bridged the gap between College and church was the new
student camp begun in 1957. The three-day orientation for incoming
freshmen was held at Camp Adams, a church-owned two-hundred-acre
site about thirty miles from Portland. Topics dealt with at the orientation
included the purpose of a college education, college work opportunities, and extra-curricular activities. There was a sermon preached one
evening, and recreational activities accompanied the academic programs. Hallman was the adviser, and he could be pleased with the success of the camp and with a laudatory editorial in the *Vanguard* that
followed it. Even by the early 1960s, the emphasis with Campus Ministry
remained on "inward-looking" programs, rather than on social action.
In the first year of the new CCCM organization, 1960–61, there was the
fifth orientation camp, a Tuesday night fellowship supper, study retreats,
two non-credit courses, faculty firesides, co-sponsorship of a College play,
and a lecture series on preparation for marriage, all worthy endeavors,
but not one activity directed to the non-College community.[95]

In the later 1960s and 1970s, Koinonia House reflected both the
"inward" and political side of student concerns. One popular facet of
CCCM was the Agora, a coffeehouse in the basement of Koinonia
House. Its focus was a "ministry of expression," in which students and
faculty gathered for art exhibitions, music, and conversation. The Agora
also served as a place of refuge for many individuals who were beaten
at the time of the Park Blocks "riot" in 1970. Although the Agora was
usually in financial difficulties, and was ultimately closed for lack of
funds, it served its purpose as a relaxing place where no overtly religious
programs were thrust on its patrons. For years, a brief, daily noon service was held by the PCCM staff, scores of students were counseled
about their personal problems, and hundreds availed themselves of
the quiet lounge for reading, study, and reflection. This campus "living
room" was also employed for a sherry hour after the monthly meetings of the faculty senate and served as the locale for retirement parties, wedding receptions, and other social occasions. In 1981, a rare
event occurred in American campus ministry, when PCCM staff sponsored a joint Protestant-Roman Catholic celebration of the Word and
Eucharist on the first Sunday in Advent, an event that was a far cry from
the tentative steps toward ecumenism that marked the early days of
Koinonia House.[96]

Campus Ministry has also been a center of social activism. As
would be expected, there was a great upsurge in social concerns in the
1960s and 1970s. When a repressive bill to limit the type of speakers

permitted on campus was introduced into the Oregon legislature in 1967 (House Joint Resolution 46), Campus Ministry staff condemned it in emphatic terms. In the same year, Koinonia House began one of its longest-running social programs, the Portland Draft Counseling Center, later called the Portland Draft and Military Counseling Center, and, still later, the Portland Military and Veterans Counseling Center. Beginning as a program of Campus Ministry whose staff trained the counselors and oversaw the program, it became an independent corporation in 1970, although always identified with Campus Ministry, not only through its location in the basement of Koinonia House and the funds donated to it by church members but also because of the moral support provided by the staff of "K-House" and the religious undergirdings of pacifism. Throughout its history, PCCM provided information about selective service and conscientious objection, pacifist theology, and military discharges. A thriving and flourishing institution with a staff of several workers during the Vietnam War, it withered after the end of the draft in 1972 and closed its doors in 1979.[97]

In the same era, Koinonia House was the sponsor of the In the Streets Volunteer Service Bureau, which coordinated social action volunteer opportunities for college students (a kind of local Peace Corps). PCCM also organized a Juvenile Detention Home project in which students visited the Home and organized a seminar program for those incarcerated there. Since the middle of the 1960s, the Portland churches had sponsored a Portland Youth Activities Contact Center that ministered to the needs of runaway children. It was never formally connected with PCCM in its personnel or funding, but Campus Ministry for a time provided it with a headquarters at Koinonia House. PCCM staff played an important role as a voice of peace in the tense years of the Vietnam War, especially in the confrontation of May 1970. Even in the conservative 1980s, Campus Ministry retained its social conscience as, for example, through its support of the "sanctuary movement." Concerned with the civil wars in Central America and the refugees who fled from them to the United States only to face deportation as illegal immigrants, the PCCM board in November 1986 declared Koinonia House a place of sanctuary for them. Although this declaration had no legal effect, and was not used by many refugees, it did give public moral support to the cause of the weak and oppressed.[98]

The setting for the exciting events of the 1960s and 1970s, and the less spectacular ones afterward, was a new K-House. Late in 1963, Portland State announced a plan to raze the block where the Koinonia

House stood in order to make room for what would become Neuberger Hall. By this stage of the ecumenical experiment, the participating denominations were confident enough of its success to commit themselves to a new structure. They came to this agreement in 1964, among themselves and with the College, an indispensable role in the negotiations played by W.T. Lemman, Portland State director of business affairs and sympathizer with Campus Ministry programs. It took somewhat longer to draw the plans and build the building, but the move into the new structure took place in February 1967. The new building was constructed efficiently and economically at a cost of $320,000. It consisted of three levels. The basement—called the Agora—was for a coffeehouse. The first floor contained a large lounge, kitchen, staff office, library, and seminar room. On the second floor was the Great Hall, which contained a small chapel and offices for the campus ministers and seated 175 persons for lectures, dances, and banquets. That the ecumenical movement had taken strong root at Portland State is evidenced by the denominations' commitment to the expense of a new building and to their promise to maintain their stake in it in the years to come.[99]

*"We win some and lose some,
but we have a chance."*

Fifteen

Athletics · 1955–1969

Turning from the spirit to the body, after college status was attained the institution grappled with the problem of developing intramural and intercollegiate athletics as enrollment steadily rose. When the period opened, there was a dearth of athletic facilities, a weak intramural program, almost no women's sports, and a men's intercollegiate program that was based on membership in the Oregon Collegiate Conference (OCC)—a financially sound program that had rough equality among its colleges but lacked in other respects, such as professional coaches. By the time university status was achieved in 1969, all of these conditions had largely changed for the better, with the exception of intercollegiate athletics, especially football, which had been cast loose into the limbo of independent (non-conference) status. With the changes, however, came the necessity for large-scale money-raising, the recruiting of students to play sports, and the foreclosing of opportunities for less-talented athletes to compete.

In 1955, health education, physical education, and athletics—both intramural and intercollegiate—were all organized under the Division of Education. Joseph Holland, who combined the duties of director of athletics and executive officer of the Department of Health Education and Physical Education, was responsible for men's and women's physical education, teacher training in both health and physical education, and intercollegiate and intramural sports, in addition to doing some coaching. Although it placed a heavy burden on one person, this structural arrangement had gone unchallenged for several years.

Joseph Holland, who laid the basis
for athletics at Portland State

The faculty had designed a set
of guidelines concerning athletic
policy in 1956 and 1957 that lasted
until the mid-1960s. Under the general supervision of the faculty senate, the principal policy-making
body was the faculty Intercollegiate
Athletics Committee (IAC), headed
by a chair who presided over its meetings and represented the College at
athletic conferences or other bodies dealing with intercollegiate athletics. In June 1956, the committee
presented a comprehensive set of
motions which—when adopted by the senate—established a clear philosophy for intercollegiate sport. The essential elements of this policy
were that teams could be fielded in any sport in which there was interest by an "adequate number of students," a provision that grounded
the program on student interest rather than on alumni or other
supporters. Coaches were to be regular members of the faculty, which
ensured they would regard themselves primarily as teachers, rather
than part-timers largely disconnected from academic pursuits.[1]

Students who participated in athletics were largely treated in the
same way as all others. To be eligible for intercollegiate competition,
athletes had to be full-time students (enrolled in twelve hours of classes and having passed in twelve hours the preceding term). There were
scholarships especially for athletes, but those receiving them had to
meet the same standards of the Scholarship Committee—which
administered them—as did all students. Athletes were given special
help in two ways. There were certain jobs normally reserved for them,
although the pay could not exceed that for other student work. The
director of athletics also had a fund from which he could make student loans according to the regular procedures of the faculty Student
Loan Committee. Although athletes were specifically denied a training table during the season, football players were given a free noon
meal during pre-season practice.[2]

In June 1957, the director of athletics organized a Booster Club.
The club was designed to raise money for scholarships or tuition

grants-in-aid for athletes. Safeguards were built into the club's activities. To obtain one of these awards, an athlete had to secure the approval of a coach, the IAC, and the Scholarship Committee. The Booster Club raised $2,400 for tuition grants-in-aid to help twelve athletes and an additional $600 for scholarships. By this time, in other words, the faculty had committed itself to treating the student athlete in a slightly preferred manner compared to the regular student.[3]

Since its Vanport days, the College had been affiliated with the Oregon Collegiate Conference. The first suggestion that this connection might not continue came from a sportswriter in the *Oregon Journal* in January 1956, at the time of the breakup of the Pacific Coast Conference. The writer speculated that Portland State might move up to a higher level of athletic competition by joining this conference. The idea was at once disparaged by a *Vanguard* columnist, who declared it was chimerical on the grounds of money. Without either a large alumni base or a large student population, he wrote, the College could not raise scholarship money in sufficient amounts to attract enough good athletes to field winning teams in a higher-level conference. He summarized the situation quite accurately: "All we would gain by such a move would be to make PSC the 'doormat' for the conference for years to come. We have a good conference now and we play teams of about equal caliber. We win some and lose some, but we have a chance."[4]

Four years later, talk of joining a new conference arose again at a lettermen's banquet on 28 March 1962. Frederick Cox, chair of the IAC, stated on this occasion that the College had been asked unofficially to join a new (unspecified) conference. President Millar confirmed such an approach had been made but said Portland State would not accept such an invitation for some time to come, mainly because of the lack of facilities. At this time, a new physical education building was nothing more than a priority of the state board in requesting funds from the 1963 legislature. The president commented, "We are just barely holding our own in the Oregon Collegiate conference. And in a new league, no one has an ambition to start out in the cellar."[5]

By May 1963, the conference situation had been clarified. The legislature authorized the construction of a physical education building, and it was confirmed the College had been asked to join at least two conferences. The offers had been declined, however, because of the lack of facilities and because the policies of these conferences were in conflict with the College's policy of "a fully-rounded athletic program." In this fluid situation, President Millar announced first to the IAC and then to the senate that he would undertake "a thorough review of fundamental athletic programs, policies, and administration." Millar assigned the task of conducting the review to the IAC.[6]

To deal with the problems associated with health education and physical education across the board, the College hired Harry A. Scott as a consultant in the summer of 1963. Scott was an emeritus professor of Physical Education at Columbia University, who had conducted several evaluations of physical education programs in the United States. His report was filled with suggestions for reorganizing the teaching of health and physical education, but only those pertaining to the future of Portland State intercollegiate and intramural athletics will be considered here.[7]

Scott's recommendations—based on solid evidence—were presented in a lucid manner and made sense in the context of the overall situation of Portland State College. He reported that, in the 1962–63 academic year, there were ten intercollegiate teams (all for men) involving 230 students in a total of 163 contests. Football had the most participants, fifty, and cross country the fewest, ten. Women had an "extramural" (not intercollegiate) program that was more a group of demonstrations and clinics than a set of competitions. In the 1963–64 academic year, for example, there was a "playday" at Lewis and Clark College; a track and field workshop at Eugene; field hockey matches with Lewis and Clark and Marylhurst; a basketball sports day at Corvallis; softball games with Marylhurst and Lewis and Clark; and a tennis sportsday at Willamette University. In the preceding year, about 150 women participated in intramural and extramural sports, but the report does not make a breakdown between the two. Scott's conclusions about women's sports were devastating: "No budgetary provisions for women's extramurals are made. Necessary encouragement and help is not generally forthcoming when new activities are proposed. The women's program does not meet the standards set forth by the Division of Girl's and Women's Sports, A.A.H.P.E.R. [the American Association for Health, Physical Education, and Recreation] or those of the Joint Committee on Extramural Sports Competition for Girls and Women."[8]

The intercollegiate athletics program was supported almost entirely by student fees. Estimates for 1963–64 were for $76,356 to be realized from these fees, against only $2,000 to come from gate receipts. Scott concluded that, so far as the purpose of its athletic program went, Portland State's aims were laudable and that the College was living up to what it said it was going to do. He enumerated the College consensus of those concerned with intercollegiate sports: that they should be educationally oriented, rather than "big time;" that there were problems with the affiliation with the Oregon Collegiate Conference; that the program was inadequately financed; that sports publicity should be improved; that if the OCC affiliation were abandoned, perhaps a period of several years of independence should be tried if a new conference affiliation could not be secured; and that the greatest problem was the lack of sports facilities. The only College building with any sports facility was Old Main, built in 1912. The College used ten facilities it did not own, the farthest being five and one half miles from Old Main.[9]

Scott furnished recommendations for the athletics and physical education programs. He suggested the Department of Physical Education be elevated to divisional status but still be responsible for intercollegiate athletics. He proposed the creation of a position, coordinator of intercollegiate athletics, that would be responsible for the management of this program. Scott wanted the faculty IAC to continue in structure and in responsibility. He proposed various ways to increase income, chiefly by raising the level of student fees. Scott also proposed a reserve fund for contingencies be taken from a portion of the student fees allocated to athletics.[10]

What created the most interest in the report were the options Scott laid out for the program. Although he said Portland State theoretically had a range of options from "big-time" status to pure amateurism and from independence to conference affiliation, basically he suggested Portland State pursue its old policy of "an educationally oriented program for student-athletes based on the principles and practices of amateurism, and taught by competent educators who are also expert technicians in the field of sports." He gave three reasons for continuing the status quo in policy: economy (the present system was functioning); educational soundness; and feasibility within "the present financial structure" of the College. Scott followed with a lengthy description of the characteristics of a sound amateur program and suggested San Francisco State College as a model. He stressed an educationally sound program would depend in part on paying coaches out of regularly appropriated College funds.[11]

Scott saw the College, without much of a tradition in athletics or anything else, as being in a favorable position to find its own way unbound by traditions or "vocal alumni." He urged the slow, patient development of a program, especially in football, and one based on providing scholarships and other financial assistance to athletes on the same financial eligibility standards as for non-athletes. Scott recommended seeking endowments and gifts to support athletic scholarships.[12]

On the thorny matter of the level of competition, the consultant strongly implied that conference membership, in an organization with colleges in the same region and of comparable athletic philosophy and financial situation, would be better than independent status. If the OCC did not satisfy, then Portland State should join another conference or establish a new one, but he did not recommend a specific course of action. He said it did not matter much if the College remained with a National Association of Independent Athletics affiliation or adopted that of the National Collegiate Athletic Association. The former had the advantage of being the affiliation of most Pacific Northwest colleges, while the latter was older and more influential, hence, prestigious.[13]

President Millar appointed a special committee to evaluate the recommendations of the report and to make further suggestions for future policy. The committee, chaired by Albert Dehner of the Business Administration Department, included members of the faculty at large, the Physical Education Department, and the Intercollegiate Athletics Committee.[14]

Millar also referred the report to Dean Swarthout for his comments. Swarthout's answer was revealing, not only of his views, but of what came to control Portland State athletics for the indefinite future. The dean of faculty characterized Scott's recommendation of continuing an "educational rather than a commercial" program as "a healthy starting position." Although, he continued, "I am not at all sure…it stands as a pinnacle of realism. The implications lead to an eternal small-time, or at least medium-time, program. There are a number of reasons for wanting to be 'excellent' in intercollegiate athletics as in everything else a college does, not all of which we might wish to discuss in public review." In other words, he implied, as many would do later, Portland State might be compelled to emphasize athletics more than would be justifiable on academic grounds, in order to obtain public support, although he might well have added there was poor attendance and little other support from the students.[15]

Conference affiliation was the main subject for discussion and action that resulted from the entire Scott report. Even while Scott was completing his report, the IAC voted on 30 July 1963 for Portland State to terminate its membership in the Oregon Collegiate Conference. The committee argued conference affiliation should be based on size of student body, geographic location, and type of educational programs and that, presumably, the OCC did not offer Portland State those conditions. The implication of this action was that Portland State would advance to a higher level of competition.[16]

One *Oregonian* sports writer suggested Portland State join the Big Sky Conference, which desired to expand from six to ten members. Certainly, some in the community favored "big-time" status, but another *Vanguard* news article pointed out that many of these individuals did not realize the financial costs of such a program. The reporter stated Portland State's current football budget of $17,000 would have to be expanded to $80,000 to be successful in a "big-time" program. Another who disparaged the idea, probably reflecting his institution's traditional anti-Portland State bias as much as objective analysis, was Arthur Esslinger, dean of the School of Health, Physical Education, and Recreation at the University of Oregon. In a panel discussion at Portland State, he said the only possibility for the College was to remain in the OCC. Esslinger ruled out joining another existing small college conference because they were little improvement over the OCC, and he said becoming independent, becoming "big-time," and joining the Big Sky were all too expensive either in traveling expenses, scheduling difficulties, or the cost of athletic scholarships.[17]

In spite of this suggestion, Portland State did examine the possibility of joining the Big Sky Conference. In November 1963, W. T. Lemman, the College business manager, attended a meeting of that conference. He reported to the Executive Committee, after which Millar announced he would turn the matter over to the IAC. Big Sky affiliation seemed more likely as a result of an important personnel decision, the hiring of J. Neil "Skip" Stahley as director of athletics in May 1964. Stahley was an experienced coach and administrator at the University of Idaho, who prided himself on being an English, rather than a Physical Education, major and on not having held an athletic scholarship as a student.[18]

In terms of Portland State's athletic future, Stahley's appointment was important in one other respect than his administrative talents. He had been the founder of the Big Sky Conference and presumably would be able to lead Portland State into that organization from his new position. Stahley's appointment was also important as a direct reflection of the Scott report. Scott recommended the separation of

J. Neil "Skip" Stahley, director of Athletics

the positions of athletic director and director of the physical education program, and Stahley was the first to fill the post of athletic director. That the coming of an athletic director did not presage "big-time" sports was emphasized in a statement on scholarships by the Executive Committee in June 1964. It said the director of athletics might raise money for athletic scholarships but the awarding of them should be left to the faculty Scholarship Committee, according to established standards for all scholarship students.[19]

In late spring 1964, the student senate heard testimony on the athletic program from the new football coach, Gerald Lyons, and other coaches, who recommended abandoning the OCC for the Big Sky. Lyons said the OCC posed scheduling difficulties, and its members were generally "undependable." He also asserted joining the Big Sky Conference would cost only about $10,000 a year more in expenses than was currently being spent. After the testimony and the discussion, the student senate gave a vote of confidence to the efforts to upgrade the athletic program. The sentiment of the senate was that of the College administration, which gave the OCC the required one-year notice of withdrawal in September 1964.[20]

It was easier to leave the OCC than to gain another conference affiliation, even one founded by Skip Stahley. The most important step was raising the money required for athletic scholarships. The Big Sky institutions awarded one hundred scholarships a year, sixty of which were in football. To help finance scholarships for athletes, the Big Sky schools used student fees ranging from $15.80 per term to $45 per term. Portland State gave $4.50 per term for athletics, and there was no possibility the student government would be willing to raise this amount. Thus, Stahley's challenge was to energize the Booster Club to make the major contribution to athletic scholarships. The chances of Portland State joining the Big Sky would depend on his ability to raise the money from the community.[21]

By early 1965, the pressure to join the Big Sky mounted. The possibility of joining the Northwest Conference was considered and rejected, as all the other members were small, private liberal arts colleges. Portland State also contemplated membership in the Evergreen Conference, but the schools' student bodies were smaller in number than Portland State's and its membership was shifting and, hence, uncertain. Further, there was talk of Arizona State being interested in Big Sky membership, which might make it necessary for Portland State to move quickly to preempt that school from gaining an open position in the Big Sky Conference. For whatever reason, a *Vanguard* reporter concluded optimistically: "PSC currently would have no problem entering the Big Sky. Portland would become the league's one big city—the backbone of the Big Sky."[22]

In February 1965, the IAC recommended to President Millar that Portland State apply for membership in the Big Sky Conference. The anticipated timetable was application in May, acceptance in November, and participation in the 1965–66 conference basketball season. The IAC, under the chairmanship of Jesse L. Gilmore of the History Department, had put in many months of study before making its recommendations. Its bases for the recommendation to join the Big Sky were that the goals of the conference were those of Portland State; the level of competition was above that of the OCC; the Big Sky had a full-time commissioner to assure compliance with the conference's standards of conduct; and the conference constitution guaranteed the control of athletics by the member schools' administrations and faculties.[23]

The committee admitted frankly a major problem in the new conference affiliation. It was "financially impossible" for Portland State to raise immediately the money to support one hundred athletic scholarships. However, the committee was optimistic the financial problems could be surmounted in the near future. Its hopes were based on the belief the Portland metropolitan area would provide enough local athletes so Portland State teams would be winners. Oregon and Oregon State were no longer going to be playing "home" games in Portland, and Portland State might well take up the entertainment slack by drawing many more spectators and, hence, gate receipts than in the past. Finally, donors in Portland were a "virtually untapped source" of funds. The committee suggested the projected athletic budget from all sources for 1965–66 would be enough to start competition in the Big Sky Conference.[24]

Portland State applied for membership in the Big Sky Conference in mid-May 1965. Everyone at PSC had assumed acceptance of the application would be a formality. A *Vanguard* sports writer, the month before application, reflected this optimistic view: "If Portland State applies for the Big Sky, Portland State will be accepted into the Big Sky. It's as simple as that. PSC has too much to offer the conference not to get in. One of the fastest growing colleges on the West Coast, definitely headed for university status, and surrounded by a metro-politan-cosmopolitan atmosphere, PSC would be a worthy addition to any conference." Indeed, some were wondering if Portland State were aiming too low in joining the Big Sky, fearing it would soon dominate the conference.[25]

Needless to say, it was an enormous shock to supporters of Portland State athletics when the Big Sky Conference decided not to act on its membership application (and that of Arizona State) on 22 November. The two applicants were not rejected, but their status was temporarily in limbo. Conference rules required unanimous support of all members to admit a new school, but two members abstained from voting on the grounds they lacked the time to study the strengths and weaknesses of the applicants. Stahley was shocked: "They gave us a great deal of encouragement," he told the *Vanguard*, "and led us to believe that we would be accepted without any trouble."[26]

In spite of this blow, Stahley continued to be optimistic about athletic progress. He said Portland State would remain an independent for some time but would eventually be able to join a conference as it acquired funds for more athletic scholarships. For example, he stated that in 1964 Portland State had only three football scholarships, but, in 1966, it would have a combination of twenty-five scholarships and jobs to offer football players. This was a far cry, however, from the 105 scholarships the Big Sky schools could now distribute among their teams. Portland State had a difficult task to demonstrate its athletic prowess as an independent, and conference membership seemed equally elusive.[27]

In 1967, the Intercollegiate Athletics Committee voted not to seek admission to the Big Sky Conference in the near future but to continue for at least one more year as an independent. The year ahead was not a happy one, however, as Jerry Lyons, the football coach, resigned. Whatever his personal skills and ambition might be, he based his departure on plausible reasons. Stahley had made a good start in raising football scholarship money, but the amount had leveled off to about

$9,900 in both 1966 and 1967. The College had—in effect, if not in words—been rejected by the Big Sky Conference, probably for this lack of financial support. Competition had gotten more difficult as an independent, because Portland State was playing schools with a much higher athletic budget. Finally, Lyons resigned because he had not been given a set number of assistant coaches he could count on and because he had too heavy a physical education teaching load to concentrate on coaching. He returned—apparently happily—to the world of secondary school coaching.[28]

The IAC seemed to reach a turning point also in the 1967–68 academic year. Given the decision of the previous year not to press for Big Sky membership, the Committee recommended (and Stahley agreed) adjusting the level of football competition downward for the next two or three years. The director of athletics continued to push for Booster Club contributions, four basketball games were televised, and for the first time admission was charged for faculty and student wives. But these efforts to raise income were not successful.[29]

Stahley's final effort to upgrade the status of Portland State athletics came in 1969, with a formidable attempt to raise the level of support from the Portland business community. Stahley asked Bill Moore, president of the Portland Bottling Company, to organize a committee to mobilize the financial resources of businesses behind Portland State athletics. The committee members were to ask their friends to join them in an effort to unite the business community in its fundraising efforts for athletics. To initiate this effort, Stahley and the committee planned a breakfast meeting at the Hilton Hotel on 15 May to publicize the campaign.[30]

The committee planned to obtain pledges of $100,000 a year for a period of five years for athletic scholarships. Stahley gathered a list of friends and former players to speak at the gathering. The attendance was high, two hundred people, including businessmen such as Al Giusti, the wine merchant, and Earl Chiles of Fred Meyer. They were addressed by dignitaries such as Jim Owens, the University of Washington football coach, who stated 90 percent of his university's athletic budget was generated by football, and by Jerry Kramer, the professional football star, who said Stahley's fundraising effort was a chance for the donors to become involved with youth. All was going well until Pres. Gregory Wolfe spoke. Whether they were his true sentiments or whether they were simply an illustration of his penchant for glibness, Wolfe dealt a severe blow to Stahley and his committee's appeal when he proclaimed to the booster meeting that the University did not "want to project an image of bulging muscles or suggest our students' interest is only pigskin deep," but that the scholar-athlete should be as much scholar as athlete. Whatever his point, the "pigskin-deep" phrase was taken to mean the president did not support the fund-raising endeavor. It never was successful, and it was many years before Portland State obtained a football conference affiliation.[31]

Stahley's life as athletic director in 1969 was made more interesting by three other movements. As mentioned earlier, Associated Students president Andrew Haynes wanted to abolish the football team and spend student activities fee monies elsewhere. This attempt came to naught for lack of student support, although the students had never supported athletics strongly either. Almost simultaneous with it arose a controversy at Oregon State University, where the football coach dismissed an African American player from his team for wearing a beard. The controversy escalated and culminated in many of the African American students leaving OSU. Stahley maintained there would be no such problem at Portland State, but he was wrong. One of the coaches ordered a black student to shave his beard or be cut from the squad. He reversed himself on second thought, however, and permitted the player to remain, ascribing the legitimacy of his beard to a cultural preference (presumably, a white student would be forced to shave.) The faculty senate debated the facial hair matter in April but were persuaded to issue no statement, as President Wolfe said he was working the issue out in quiet discussions.[32]

On 5 November, about fifty members of the Black Student Union staged a sit-in in President Wolfe's office to protest perceived injustices in the Athletic Department's program and to demand Wolfe remedy them in a week's time. Their five demands were that Portland State hire black coaches immediately; that it begin a program to recruit black athletes and give them equal treatment in housing and scholar-ships; that scholarships be provided to black athletes so they could graduate on an extended schedule (meaning, their scholarships would continue after their athletic eligibility ran out); that counseling be provided for black athletes to ensure they graduate, not simply main-tain their eligibility; and that the Athletic Department correct the (unspecified) racist attitudes and actions that pervaded it. Wolfe promised to look into the matter.[33]

The president assigned the investigative task to William A. Williams, associate dean of students, while Athletic Director Stahley dismissed the charges out of hand, stating they were "absolutely unfounded." After Williams concluded his report, Wolfe made some recommendations. He advised Stahley to arrange for adequate counseling for black athletes and asked the Intercollegiate Athletics Committee to devise a code for black athletes. He refused the demand that a black coach be hired immediately, promising only that when a coaching vacancy occurred, he would have Stahley hire a person who met the highest standards. He further stated there was no money to hire any coach immediately. He also refused the demand for equal recruitment and housing of black and white athletes and for financial aid for extended graduation schedules. The contretemps over the black athletes, like the other causes of the late 1960s, was but a mild prelude to those that would soon follow in a dangerous period that tested the University's capacity to sustain reason and civility as its hallmarks.[34]

"The University has no armament."

SIXTEEN

The Days of Rage · 1970–1974

The years 1970 to 1974, indeed, had a unity that set them apart from those that preceded and followed them. Although, of course, not disconnected from what went before and after, this brief era was marked by an unprecedented outbreak of violence on the University campus; by the demands for recognition of a variety of hitherto unacknowledged student groups; and by financial difficulties that surpassed anything encountered earlier in the history of the institution. While these events were often exciting and captured the attention of the media and the public, they should not be distorted to mean that those who played a role in them were typical members of the University community. Even in this time of spectacular developments, one unspectacular trend was manifest, even though easily forgotten in both the time of trials and its aftermath: most members of the Portland State community wanted to proceed quietly with the traditional purposes of the institution. One other matter must also be remembered. In spite of the noise and violence, the inflammatory rhetoric and the prognostications of apocalypse from right and left, the University was little changed in mission, structure, or personnel as a result of these four years, however important they seemed at the time.

The Vietnam War, of course, continued on into the 1970s, although the opposition to it at Portland State had declined, at least as measured in numbers of incidents and in attendance at protest rallies. The opponents seemed to have hit their peak of public support with the moratorium of October 1969; afterwards, although the war was hardly forgotten, it drew less attention on campus. Early in January 1970, Channing Briggs, the dean of students, placed five students on probation for blocking access to navy recruiters two months earlier. Quickly assuming a collective name (as was the custom of aggrieved groups in that era), the Portland State Five sought out allies in the faculty to assist them. First, they were successful in having their penalty temporarily suspended by Vice-Pres. Robert Low, who wanted to investigate whether the dean's imposition of it violated the Statement of Student Rights and Freedoms. Then, members of the faculty took up their cause.[1]

Michael Reardon of the History Department moved in the faculty senate on 26 January 1970 that the five students be removed from probation on the grounds the University had not followed its own procedures; the motion was defeated by a single vote. At the same meeting, Frank Giese of the Foreign Languages and Literatures Department, moved the senate recommend to the president the office of dean of students be discontinued because of "several happenings over the past three years where actions taken by the Dean of Students were abrasive and had resulted in a lower student morale." The motion was put over until a subsequent meeting. On 9 February, the senate voted to recommend restructuring the office of dean of students and to remove its disciplinary functions.[2]

Military recruiting remained a contentious issue. Both the administration and the opponents of recruiting (led by Students for a Democratic Society and the New University Conference) prepared for a visit of navy recruiters in late February. President Wolfe announced they would be permitted, arguing for the traditional University policy of tolerance and openness to conflicting views, and appealing also to the ACLU's position that all recruiters or none must be allowed. He also called for a referendum at the opening of spring term to see what student and faculty beliefs were regarding recruiting. When the recruiters arrived at the placement office in Smith Center, their opponents pushed them out of the building, the navy men not resisting the use of force.[3]

Before the recruiters returned, the University obtained a court order restraining thirty-six Portland State students from obstructing recruiting or engaging in anti-recruiting demonstrations. In spite of tensions when the recruiters returned, there was no violence, and the heat drained from the issue. The restraining order was dropped for four of the students in early March. In an effort to settle the matter once and for all, Wolfe and the faculty senate discussed recruiting policy at the senate meeting on 2 March. The president reiterated his policy of favoring open recruitment by all groups—the policy supported by

PSU Educational Media Services

Gregory Baker Wolfe, president, 1968-74

the ACLU and the American Association of University Professors—and announced to the senate there had been enormous pressure from various powerful groups in the metropolitan community to crack down on the anti-recruiters by using city police and criminal prosecutions against them. In spite of these pressures, Wolfe proclaimed his faith in reason remained unabated. He reported to the senate that he asked for the restraining order only to keep the University free to maintain its policy of open discussion of all views.[4]

When the senate, after sifting through routine matters, took up military recruiting, it discussed a motion from Stephen Kosokoff of the Speech Department that military recruiting be abandoned at Portland State. After lengthy discussion, and after defeating an attempt to amend the motion by requiring military recruiters to debate their opponents at the end of the recruiting day and another to offer recruiting facilities only to groups without facilities in the metropolitan area, the Kosokoff motion was defeated by a vote of twenty-five to seventeen. These votes indicated that, under extreme pressure on an emotional issue, the senate stood firm for the open society. The senate position proved to be that of the faculty and the student body, in general.[5]

This result was somewhat of a surprise to faculty members who had successfully petitioned for a special faculty meeting to discuss recruiting, the restraining order, and the referendum on recruiting that was held at the beginning of spring term. The petition asked also that the president not preside at the faculty meeting but that he be present to answer questions. Little happened at the meeting because Wolfe opened it by releasing the results of the spring referendum. A large percentage of faculty and students voted in the referendum (77 percent of the students; no percentage figures are available for the faculty). The results overwhelmingly confirmed Wolfe's actions and the policies of University, ACLU, and AAUP in favor of unrestricted recruiting. Of the faculty, 332 favored continuing recruiting for all employers; 105 supported selective recruiting; and 49 declared for no recruiting at all. Of the students, 4,868 supported all employer recruiting; 1,486 supported selective recruiting; and 429 wished for no recruiting. Various questions were raised, but no action was taken, and recruiting policies were settled for the indefinite future.[6]

Enforcing that policy was another matter, as became evident when demonstrators tried to break up a navy recruiting session in late April. Vice-President Low called Portland police to remove the disrupting demonstrators. There were some shoving matches between pro and anti recruiters, and an opponent tried to throw a smoke bomb into the room where the recruiters were stationed, but the bomb ignited his own hair, which he extinguished with a cup of Kool-aid. As a result of the potential for violence in the demonstration and to prevent it in the future, the administration decided to move recruiting out of the heavily used Smith Center into the placement office in Old Main and to make recruiting by appointment only. What was perhaps more significant was the decision to call in the police. It was the first time police had been summoned to the campus by University officials, and it divided faculty, at least those who were interviewed by the *Vanguard*.[7]

Until May 1970, the anti-war protests at Portland State had involved a minority of students and faculty and, in the case of the anti-recruiting protests, a small minority, indeed. What happened next involved almost everybody and became the most spectacular event in Portland State's history since the Vanport flood. It arose because of a change in American policy in the war. President Richard Nixon decided on 30 April 1970 to attack North Vietnam by means of ground and air strikes in neutral Cambodia, which military planners regarded as a conduit for the North's invasion of South Vietnam. The tactic worked—in that it relieved pressure on the South Vietnamese forces—but it was a political catastrophe for Nixon, as it reenergized opposition to the war at home. One of the many demonstrations against the Cambodian incursion occurred at Kent State University in Ohio, which led to the fire-bombing of an ROTC building. The state governor sent in national guard troops to quell the disturbances, and the guardsmen, taunted by students, finally fired into a crowd, killing four students and wounding eleven others. Two weeks later, two students were killed at Jackson

State College in Mississippi. Soon, there were demonstrations—some becoming riots—at more than four hundred campuses.

Before the deaths at Kent State, there were protests about the invasion of Cambodia planned at Portland State. A small group of activists phoned the national office of the U.S. National Student Association to ask what it suggested should be done. The answer was to be flexible in tactics but to attempt to secure the goal of closing the University in order to dramatize the protest in the widest possible way. But nothing had been determined until the news of Kent State horrified the campus community. After that, the Portland Five and other activists constituted themselves as a strike committee to close the University.[8]

The strike committee decided to focus their effort on a boycott of classes, in part, because they saw the tactic as effective, in part, because— unlike their counterparts elsewhere—there were no polarizing personalities or issues they could use locally. The University administrators were not unpopular figures and could not be demonized; the University was not involved in classified research for the Department of Defense or for corporations that were a part of the "military-industrial complex." Indeed, the main tactics used at Portland State at the beginning of the Cambodia strike were ones tried before: the class boycott, the speakers at community organizations, and the march to try to lure high school students and the industrial workers to go out on strike to protest the war. The strike locally was to be coordinated with a national strike scheduled for 6 May through 8 May.[9]

The strike committee moved quickly and effectively to organize the boycott. Beginning on 4 May from its headquarters in Smith Center, the committee members used telephones and duplicating machines in the offices of student government and the *Vanguard* to rally support for the cause. The committee arranged a noon rally on 5 May for the ballroom in Smith Center and advertised it by leaflet. At the rally, the organizers defined the strike's objectives, casting, wisely or unwisely, a broader net than the Cambodian incursion or even the war itself. The strike was to protest Cambodia, but it also was to protest the imprisonment of Black Panther leader Bobby Seale, the deaths at Kent State, and the projected shipment of nerve gas by the Defense Department for storage in Oregon. The last position was chosen, presumably, because there had been a loud outcry led by Gov. Tom McCall on the part of ordinary citizens against the movement of this dangerous substance. In a sense, it was a popular issue that might appeal to citizens not upset by the other causes.[10]

The committee was able, by calling each member of the faculty, to get 134 members of a total of 725 to support the strike to some degree, from discussing the strike issues with their classes to calling them off for the three-day period. This number was about one-sixth of the entire faculty. Other militants, calling themselves the Student Mobilization Committee to End the War in Vietnam (MOBE), tried methods other than persuasion to gain support for the strike. They tried to force Wolfe's hand. They demanded he close the school for the three days of the national strike. If he did not, then they would attempt to persuade students not to attend classes by picketing the entrances to the institution. Wolfe refused to be coerced, citing a state board policy that prevented "overt interference with the operation of the institution."[11]

Wolfe's position on the strike was taken not simply because he was carrying out state board policy. Rather, he had demonstrated a belief in the University as a place of reasoned discussion throughout the earlier difficult times of his administration. He argued discussion of the issues was much more likely to occur rationally in a university that was open than in a closed one whose students would then try to resolve the issues in arguments—or worse—in the streets. Also, as all his subsequent actions during the strike would indicate, Wolfe was dedicated to the peaceful exchange of ideas, committed to heading off violence at almost any cost.

In spite of Wolfe's opposition, a peaceful boycott of classes was held on Wednesday, 6 May. No one who wanted to enter the buildings was prevented from doing so, and many professors simply discussed their usual subjects, while others called off classes or used them to discuss the war or other contemporary issues. More controversial was the attempt by some of the protesters—students and faculty alike—to visit classes to discuss the issues. Almost all, when refused, left quietly, while a small group attempted to remain, even when asked to depart. All in all, about half the students attended classes on Wednesday. There was also a rally in the Park Blocks on Wednesday morning. Before it was over, the nature of the protest had been radically changed, with severe consequences.[12]

During the rally, a motorist hit one of the strikers, breaking his leg. In response, students and faculty constructed, from park benches and other materials, a series of barricades across the streets surrounding the campus. The administration, in a thoughtful move to head off violence, secured permits from city authorities to close the streets, thus legitimating the barricades and draining anger from the protesters. The barricades inspired the strikers as a symbol of their cause (the more historically minded likening them to the insurrections in France that have intermittently marked that nation's history), but they enraged the strike's opponents. To these men and women, University and community people alike, the barricades were symbols of defiance and, at worst, precursors of violent revolution.[13]

Whatever the barricades symbolized, they were a magnet. To the Park Blocks flowed a motley crowd that included curious citizens, students and faculty both supportive and opposed to the strike, students from other colleges, newspaper and television reporters, and members of the Portland police. The University had no control over most of these people—an ominous condition—for as Wednesday wore on, rumors of confrontation circulated. The strikers had organized opposition now from within the University, a group of faculty and students called the University Organization. Obviously, then, within this emotional and crowded scene lay the potential for violence.[14]

President Wolfe responded to the threat of violence by deciding to cancel classes for the following two days. But he declared the University buildings would remain open for the purpose of dialogue on the issues of the strike. On Thursday, the first day of canceled classes, the campus was quiet, and the number of people in the Park Blocks was considerably reduced from the day before, as most students, faculty, and staff stayed away. A few classes were held as scheduled. But the barricades were a symbol that was increasingly galling to ordinary Portlanders, especially the residents of the areas surrounding the University. They objected to the noise in their usually quiet park; they loathed the exhibitions of public sex; and they protested the lewd talk, drunkenness, and consumption of illegal drugs on the barricades.[15]

The most unseemly display by a small number of protesters occurred on property belonging to the University. On Thursday night, a dance not sanctioned by the University was held in Smith Center. It turned into a public relations fiasco for the strikers. After the dance was over, many remained for two days "trashing" the second floor of the building, whose floors became littered with vomit and excrement and some of whose occupants stole from the concessions stands, raced about unclad, and engaged in public sex. Naturally, the media made the most of this wild scene, and their attention gave most citizens, already irritated by the inconveniences and defiance of the barricades, a further cause for rage.[16]

President Wolfe was, of course, under enormous pressure from these outraged citizens and their elected officials to call the police to dismantle the barricades and to eject the occupants of Smith Center, a large number of whom were not affiliated with the University. Wolfe's primary purpose was to prevent violence, however, not to reclaim property. He was particularly appalled when Gov. Tom McCall, incredibly oblivious to what had happened at Kent State, threatened to send the national guard to the campus. If that happened, Wolfe told the governor, he would resign on the spot. McCall, either finally remembering recent history or impressed by Wolfe's firmness, did not send the guard. Local politicians also were intimately involved in the events at Portland State: Frank Ivancie, commissioner of parks, and Terry Schrunk, mayor of Portland, were both feeling pressures from angry constituents, and hardly pressures sympathetic to the strike or to its symbols.[17]

Thursday and Friday were relatively peaceful. On Thursday, there were agitated conversations, some fistfights, the continuing occupation of Smith Center, and a march of five hundred persons to City Hall. There was a memorial service for the Kent State and Jackson State students at noon on Friday. On Saturday, however, after a group of demonstrators climbed a fire escape and disrupted a meeting in Wolfe's office in Cramer Hall, the president declared a state of limited emergency, which authorized him to call on the police. He ordered all campus buildings closed, except for Smith Center, because he did not want to use force to evict the people camping out there.[18]

On Sunday night, 10 May, Mother's Day, Wolfe called a special faculty meeting in the University gymnasium to report on the past week and to help ease tensions for the opening of school the following day. He opened the meeting with a tribute to the Portland State students who had worked so hard to keep the campus peaceful. He then discussed "bases for more appropriate operating formats during what may become a prolonged period of frustration and ambiguity—not just for a week, not just for a month, but for the coming few years." In his belief that the campus would be troubled for a long time, Wolfe was wrong, but it reflected the sentiments of many faculty who gathered in the gymnasium that evening.[19]

Wolfe accordingly proposed, now that the strike presumably was over, that steps be taken to involve the University community in the troubled years he saw lying ahead. He suggested the establishment of "councils or centers of concern," where faculty would be available to talk with students and others about issues of community concern that lay within their specific competence, such as nerve gas storage or international affairs or the dangers of totalitarianism. He also urged those in quest of social justice not to tire in the pursuit of that cause and not to alienate by their tactics ordinary people who would be inclined to support their causes. Some members of the public, he said, were calling for repressive measures, but, Wolfe proclaimed, "I have never believed, and I do not believe now, that force has any place in the academic community. However, we must all recognize that if force should be employed or required because of a breakdown in the peace of the campus, that the university has no armament."[20]

After Wolfe concluded his remarks, twenty-one members of the faculty followed with their comments. One, representing the strikers and sympathetic faculty, asked faculty not to conduct classes until 20 May, when a national strike was set. Others objected to the president's action in closing the University for the past two days. Another asked for tolerance, allowing those who wished to strike to do so, while permitting the non-strikers to address their classes. Samuel Oakland of the English Department suggested, "Some of the faculty members who haven't talked to any of the kids at the barricades, they might come down with their campers and spend the night. They could go past the barricades, bring a load of oranges or apples or something to distribute. And then walk around talking to them." Some likened the actions of the federal government to that of the Nazis, others implied the strikers were using Nazi tactics to destroy the rule of law. In the end, no action was taken, and the faculty dispersed to prepare for classes the next day.[21]

Contrary to what many had hoped for, the next day was most definitely not a return to business as usual. Instead, it became the most dramatic day at the University since the Vanport Flood. The basic cause of the momentous events was the dislike of the barricades by the public and city officials. The barricades themselves were more symbolic than anything else, for it was possible for pedestrians to walk around them, although vehicular traffic had to be diverted a few blocks out of its ordinary course. Of much less public concern, there was also in the Park Blocks a first aid station known as the "Hospital Tent," although it was not really a hospital. Both barricades and tent were, it need be emphasized, on city property. Thus, they were not structures over which the University had legal control.

As classes proceeded on Monday, President Wolfe and the strikers agreed the barricades would be removed later that day. Some could not wait, however, to remove the hated objects. In the morning, fifty to one hundred students tried to destroy one of the barricades but were held off by the strikers. Frustrated by this rebuff, the attackers went to city hall and demanded that Mayor Terry Schrunk remove the barricades immediately. The mayor agreed and worked out a plan for city sanitation workers to remove the barricades, supported by unarmed police. Ominously, however, the mayor also ordered a special forces unit, the Tactical Operations Platoon or "Tac Squad," to stand by on the Park Blocks. The barricades were removed without violence, although during the process the strikers hurled obscenities at the police.[22]

Only the hospital tent remained standing. The strikers had a valid permit allowing it to remain until the next day, and they insisted it be honored so that the tent could stay as long as possible as a final symbol of defiance. The police officer in charge of the operation, Capt. Norman Reiter, agreed with the strikers about the permit. So, too, did President Wolfe. Both men advised Mayor Schrunk and Parks Commissioner Ivancie not to have the tent torn down. Wishing for a symbolic victory to appease their angry constituents, however, the two officials ordered the tent torn down. The decision, in any context except pandering to a segment of the public, was unnecessary. The campus was quiet, classes were meeting, all buildings were open, and the barricades were gone.[23]

About 5:40 in the afternoon, the Tac Squad members marched from their station behind Shattuck Hall down the Park Blocks to the tent. They ordered the strikers to disperse from around the tent, but they remained, arms locked together. The Squad then attacked with billy clubs. In two minutes, thirty strikers were beaten to the ground, and twenty-seven people admitted to Portland hospitals. After taking the tent down, the Tac Squad dispersed, leaving shock, horror, and anger in its wake.[24]

The consequences of the police beatings were innumerable. In the short run, many students and many non-Portland State students met Monday night in the ballroom of Smith Center. Some wanted to rebuild the barricades, but it was decided that would antagonize many who converted to the strikers' cause because of the police attack. This was an important consideration for, as one strike leader asserted: "Now instead of a few militants striking with 2,000 sympathizers, we have 2,000 militants." The meeting called for an investigation of the police and for a more representative leadership of the strike steering committee (presumably, to include members of the now sympathetic, former

PSU Office of Publications

Police beating citizens in the Park Blocks

silent majority). The strike committee published a pamphlet containing photographs of the attack and statements of eye-witnesses.[25]

President Wolfe and Vice-President Low, both exhausted from the
week's events, condemned the police action. Wolfe told the mayor,
"The circumstances did probably more to create a sense of bitter reaction among students who had been hitherto uninvolved, than anything else that could have happened." Low stated he "would denounce
the unnecessary violence." In the early hours of the next morning,
Wolfe was admitted to the hospital, struck down by an inner ear infec-
tion and exhaustion, after seventy-two hours of sleeplessness. He, thus,
was unable to lead, as he had intended, the great march of three to five
thousand people on city hall later in the morning. The march included some citizens, faculty, administration, and students from both pro-
and anti-strike factions. The marchers carried five demands to city
hall, which were presented by Joe Uris, now a graduate student in Sociology. They wanted an investigation of the police attack, the abolition
of the Tactical Operations Platoon, the resignation of city officials who
sent the police, the prosecution of police officers, and a discussion with

Mayor Schrunk. Although city hall was filled with armed police, Schrunk refused to address the marchers, who then returned to the Park Blocks, most to resume the routine of classes.[26]

In order to head off further violence, some faculty did more than march and teach on that day. Jacob Fried of the Anthropology Department, David Newhall of the Philosophy Department, and two members of the English Department, Robert Tuttle and Frederick Waller, formed an Ad Hoc Group for Campus Safety. Its members were to act in times of campus crisis to observe events at the crisis location, interpose themselves between parties who threatened to conflict physically, report their observations to the University and the community, and be willing to testify to their observations. The same day, the faculty met for an extended session.[27]

The faculty meeting adopted a series of resolutions looking to the past and to the future. It condemned the use of violence by the police. It regularized a roster of faculty dedicated to protecting campus safety and established an emergency speakers bureau. It authorized the publication and distribution of eight questions and answers that showed the police intervention was unnecessary and brutal. It stated the campus community could keep order in the future without outside intervention, unless asked for by the president. It called for an investigation of the police intervention on campus and called for American academic communities to devise ways to end the Vietnam War. It wished President Wolfe a speedy recovery, condemned the Mayor's refusal to meet with the marchers earlier in the day, asked that classes be kept open for the remainder of the term, except in "exceptional circumstances," and declared that faculty should make alternative arrangements for students to make up work missed for whatever reason during the term.[28]

During the following week, there were several aftershocks to the police action. The Oregon State Federation of the AAUP on 16 May passed a powerful resolution originally drafted by the PSU chapter: "We condemn alike the tactics of those few within our schools who attempt to coerce by threat, intimidation, and sometimes violence, and of those outside who would resort to repressive measures or excessive response in the quest for social peace....We reject the view that the classroom has suddenly become 'irrelevant' and the notion that professors and students must choose between their public concerns and their academic obligations." In subsequent weeks, faculty members met with church congregations and other groups to explain the University's position. Their efforts helped to defuse the anger of many cit-

Pickets during the 20 May 1970 strike

izens toward Portland State. Other conciliatory actions taken by the University included a meeting between President Wolfe and several legislators and members of the governor's staff on 19 May, an effort to encourage a large faculty attendance at commencement in June, and an attempt by the deans to gather names of crucial outside decision makers, presumably to inform them of what had really taken place during the days of turmoil.[29]

On 20 May, the day of the national strike, classes were held, and one thousand persons marched downtown from the Park Blocks. The march stopped at the *Oregonian* building on Broadway, where a "die-in" was staged to simulate deaths caused by nerve gas. The march then proceeded to Pioneer Courthouse, where a mock trial was held convicting Mayor Schrunk, Commissioner Ivancie, and the Tac Squad for the bloodshed in the Park Blocks. The marchers then delivered the guilty verdict to police headquarters before returning to city hall.[30]

Chancellor Roy Lieuallen felt obligated to investigate the disorders at the state system institutions (although there were disorders only at the University of Oregon and at Portland State). Commissioner Ivancie, who was in a campaign for reelection, asked the state senate to investigate both the disorders at Portland State and the Portland State administration and faculty. Senate president E. D. Potts, although disapproving of the demonstrations, said an investigation could not be conducted immediately because of the "atmosphere of the times." The General Student Affairs Committee adopted a Harvard University statement on the rights and responsibilities of the members of a university community, the core of which was a declaration of academic values: "Among these are freedom of speech and academic freedom, freedom from personal force and violence, and freedom of movement. Interference with any of these freedoms must be regarded as a serious violation of the personal rights upon which the community is based." A student filed a disorderly conduct complaint against David Horowitz of the History Department for disrupting two classes during the strike. Horowitz pleaded not guilty to the charge.[31]

Convicted in Multnomah County district court, Horowitz received a suspended sentence, although he did suffer for the actions he took during the strike. The History Department had recommended he teach a fall term course for the Division of Continuing Education. This type of recommendation was routine and was almost always followed by DCE, but, in this case, Horowitz was rejected as the course instructor. At first, Leroy Pierson, DCE director, would give no reason for rejecting Horowitz, an evasion that fueled speculation he had been turned down for his participation in the May strike. Later, Pierson stated vaguely and fatuously, "We do not feel in our professional judgment that Mr. Horowitz is a person to be teaching adults. This does not have anything to do with his political views." A replacement instructor was secured from Oregon College of Education, after the PSU History Department refused to recommend a substitute. The department and the local chapter of the AAUP intervened on Horowitz's behalf but to no avail. A petition asking the DCE to hire him and improve other facilities in the extension program was delivered, but none of the demands were met.[32]

After the strike, community members opposed to campus disruptions formed a Citizens Coalition for Responsibility. Its spokesman, William Moshofsky, outlined in July the Coalition's plan to prevent future disturbances. It called for a volunteers corps to infiltrate state system campuses to find out who made administrative decisions at the universities; study the political balance of outside speakers invited to the institutions; review policies on tenure and discipline of faculty members and students; and investigate student newspapers. Essentially, the committee was proposing a witch hunt, but it also offered assistance to those on campuses who wished to institute legal action to ensure the rights "of responsible students and faculty members."[33]

The committee was widely publicized but not always favorably. It was attacked in an August television editorial by Floyd McKay, a prominent news analyst on KGW-TV in Portland. In March 1971, the committee issued its report. It called for legislation to strengthen the power of state system university presidents, declaring their authority had been "eroded because of excessive domination by faculty and students in decision-making and administration." In an interview after the report was issued, Moshofsky stated he did not recommend the abolition of tenure at the moment but said tenure policy should be reviewed as the danger of arbitrarily firing faculty if it were abolished was "a lesser risk than having it." The report also called for reducing the influence of faculty and students in the selection of university executives. But as public passions cooled, the committee faded away, its significance being simply one measure of some citizens' discomfort with the events of the days of May.[34]

Adding to these interesting times, though not directly involving Portland State, was the prospect of a September confrontation between the American Legion, which was holding its annual convention in Portland, and the People's Army Jamboree, a crowd of political radicals, counter-culture people, and curious onlookers that descended on Portland to protest the war, specifically, and American values and institutions, in general. Against the background of May's national and local unrest, authorities believed the prospective confrontation held enormous potential for conflict on the streets of downtown Portland. Although the event was discussed on campus and in the *Vanguard* and the public media, and the University had made preparations to hold the final weeks of the term at Portland Community College, nothing happened at PSU except the breaking of a window at Smith Center. In one of his finest hours as governor, Tom McCall defused the impending crisis by sponsoring a rock festival well outside the city that drew many of the People's Army away from Portland, thus, according to critics, underscoring the fact that most of the young were less committed to their cause than to having a lark. There was no violence and little property damage.[35]

In November, two events occurred that marked the ending of the events of May. Early in the month, fifteen hundred persons assembled in the Park Blocks next to Smith Center to march downtown to Pioneer Courthouse to rally against the war. Only one person was arrested (for discharging fireworks). Significantly, there were no large-scale meetings, no moratoria, no heated discussions at the University. It was as though the community had been largely drained of a will to protest after the May strike was over. (In February of the next year, the will to protest was even weaker. Radical students found no support for a strike, and only three hundred persons marched downtown, in spite of increased military activity in Laos.)[36]

As for the aftermath of the strike violence itself, a Multnomah County grand jury, impaneled in July to investigate the Park Blocks confrontation, took testimony from more than two hundred witnesses and made its report in November. Its principal conclusion was that the police had used excessive force in dispersing the students guarding the hospital tent. But it also stated the photographs and testimony of witnesses did not reveal any specific officer who could be charged with brutality. It also said it could not conclude whether or not the strikers had a valid permit to keep the tent up at the time of the attack. Thus, no individual, whether police officer or politician, was made to bear the consequences of the beatings. And the reaction to this surprising conclusion was muted at the University, limited to some critical comments in the *Vanguard*.[37]

Many gained some satisfaction, however, if not for the past, at least for the future. In July, the ACLU filed suit on behalf of several citizens, including Portland State students and one professor seeking an injunction to require police not to use "unreasonable force" while arresting members of crowds or while dispersing them. The case was finally settled with the issuance of a consent decree in which the ACLU agreed to drop its class-action suit in return for the police department revising its manual for the Tac Squad. The new manual included the provision that "peaceful, but unlawful assembled demonstrators must be afforded the opportunity to submit peacefully to arrest before the riot baton or night stick might be employed to subdue them." This revision was really an admission by the city that the police had used excessive force, an admission that might provide some consolation for its victims.[38]

The May strike was put to good use by a range of persons from right to left who attempted to use it for their or their causes' benefits. The most colorful was Mario Fenyo, assistant professor of History. Fenyo was denied tenure by the History Department in the winter of 1970–71. Throughout the ensuing controversy, the department maintained, as was universal in American higher education, it was not required to give Fenyo the reasons for its decision. Contrary to what many asserted on Fenyo's behalf, department members argued he was not

Prof. Mario Fenyo of the History Department

"fired," which implies incompetence, but rather was not awarded tenure. They said it was to his interest, however, to blur this distinction. The award of tenure, maintained department members, requires a positive act reflecting the judgment that a person awarded it is not just adequate but a solid choice. Tenure is, thus, not based on the assumption that once hired one is entitled to it unless a case is proven against him or her. Proprietary rights, in other words, do not accompany an appointment. Fenyo maintained the University administration "needed a scapegoat for the May strike troubles," and, thus, he was denied tenure for political reasons. This assertion was heatedly denied by Jesse Gilmore, department chair, who declared: "In my opinion, Fenyo is naive, immature, childish, and uncooperative. I have 20 or more applications sitting on my desk right now from people who could take his place."[39]

Before the matter had reached this impasse, Fenyo had appealed his case at several levels. Fenyo and his supporters always maintained, first before two review committees of the College of Social Science and, later, before the full faculty, that the History Department had treated him unfairly in refusing to tell him the reasons for its decision not to continue his employment. They advanced two arguments in support of this claim; one was a moral argument, and the other a "legal" one.

In support of the fairness claim, Fenyo and his advocates cited the independent judgments of the College of Social Science Promotion and Tenure Committee and the national council of the AAUP. They did not cite the AAUP policy statement as a regulation by which the University was bound, however, because the policy statement had been promulgated in an advisory letter after the actions by the History Department and the dean of the College of Social Science had been taken but before the committee review. Although the policy in this circumstance could have no binding effect, its moral authority was unaffected. The claim was that what was fair was fair, regardless of whether there was a ruling requiring it.

The "legal" argument was a procedural one. PSU procedures required a dean to act on the advice of the College review committee. In this instance, the dean had gathered, from conversations with members of the History Department, information regarding the reasons for the department's action, but he did not offer this information to his College advisory committee with a request for reconsideration, thereby depriving himself of the benefit of the committee's informed advice. This seemed to Fenyo's supporters an unacceptable undermining of the established procedure. Deans, they believed, are not entitled to make use of information denied their faculty advisory committees. A Division of Social Science committee upheld Fenyo's claim he was denied tenure for an improper reason (because it was not based on substantive grounds), but the dean of the Division overruled the committee. President Wolfe then appointed a committee to advise him about the decision; it upheld the Department of History. Fenyo then appealed to the state board, which also decided against him.[40]

Fenyo and his supporters did not give up. His principal ally was the Radical Social Science Union, a group of faculty and students that placed orange and black stickers around campus with the inscription "Rehire Fenyo" and circulated petitions at spring term registration demanding he be appointed for another one-year term. The Union also published a four-page pamphlet on the affair entitled, "Why Fire Mario Fenyo?" The situation then took a comic turn as Fenyo announced he would file a civil suit against Basil Dmytryshyn, senior professor of Russian History, for "malicious interference with contract." The grounds for the suit were that Dmytryshyn, according to Fenyo, had called a secret meeting of the History Department over a year before to prepare the way for his dismissal. Fenyo also charged that Dmytryshyn had "vetoed his participation in two national meetings of historians, presumably because it would give him too much prestige." The allegations were preposterous. Gilmore and Dmytryshyn denied the whole thing, and Fenyo never proceeded with the litigation.[41]

Fenyo's last endeavor was to appeal successfully to his faculty colleagues to keep his case alive. A sufficient number of them signed a petition demanding the faculty take up the Fenyo case in a special meeting. The faculty met on 12 May, with about seventy-five faculty and two hundred students in attendance, and passed a resolution asking for a special committee "to investigate the firing of Mario Fenyo." The committee was supposed to obtain from the History Department a written statement detailing the reasons for Fenyo's non-reappointment (which the resolution called a "firing"). Wolfe refused to appoint the committee because Fenyo's appeals had been exhausted under the procedures, properly applied, of both the faculty constitution and the state board's Administrative Rules.[42]

This was the end of the trail for Mario Fenyo, but not for the Fenyo family. Ileana Fenyo, Mario's wife, was in the news in January 1971, when she sued President Wolfe for her degree in U.S. district court in Portland. This novel cause arose from her suspension by a student-faculty committee in 1970 for disrupting marine recruiting. Subsequently, she audited classes while on suspended status. In a later term, she enrolled in these courses *in absentia.* Fenyo maintained her First Amendment rights were violated because the University did not inform her of one of the committee hearings where she was found guilty of disruptive activity. Proper redress, she claimed, would be for the court to require the University to award her the bachelor's degree, $30,000 in damages, and impose an injunction against other such penal suspensions. When the case came to trial in March 1972, Fenyo had revised her requests to simply her bachelor's degree, based on giving her academic credit for the courses she had audited. In rendering judgment, district judge Gus Solomon dismissed her case as "without merit." He said, "Her rights were meticulously protected," and the court had no right to order the University to give her a degree.[43]

A more enduring result of the years of protest were the "conduct codes." These were rules and regulations designed to guide the behavior of students and faculty and provide fair procedures for sanctioning those who violated them. The codes came from both the faculty and the state board, with members of the faculty attempting to modify in a more precise and objective manner the codes adopted by the board as a response to demands of many citizens and some faculty and students that it do something about preventing disruptive behavior on campuses. The idea of a conduct code was first introduced by Howard Boroughs, dean of the faculties, at an Executive Committee meeting in late December 1969. The committee concluded the problem was "touchy," and the faculty must be involved in the preparation of the code. Later, as a sort of preemptive strike before the board acted, Boroughs appointed a faculty committee in March 1970 to draw up a faculty conduct code. Before it finished its work, however, the board issued its conduct code as a revision of the Administrative Rules of the state system in September 1970.[44]

The Faculty Conduct Committee, under the chairmanship of Roger Moseley of the School of Business Administration, met regularly and completed its report on 24 March 1971. The committee was constrained in its deliberations by the fact the board rules took precedence over whatever the University chose to do. Nevertheless, the committee hoped its rules would be sufficiently persuasive to the board to allow them to take effect at Portland State. The faculty committee report, unlike the board document, was distinguished by a long and eloquent statement of the purpose of the University and procedures indicating how, if at all, conduct could be regulated in attaining that purpose. "The purpose of the university," the committee document proclaimed, "is to improve the human condition through proper nurture of the intellect. Members of the academic community have long stressed the principle that the common good depends upon the free search for truth and its free exposition....It follows that for any restriction upon speech or action to be justified in a university the offense must be so severe that the attainment of the purpose of the institution is frustrated by permitting the freedom to indulge in it."[45]

The major difference between the faculty and the board codes was in how personal misconduct liable for sanctions was defined. The board code stated "moral turpitude" was sanctionable. The faculty committee believed this charge was so extremely vague as to be dangerous. It could cover unlawful actions; it could cover unpopular opinions; it could cover actions lawful but distasteful. What the faculty committee wished to substitute for "moral turpitude" was "gross personal misconduct," which it defined as "behavior that is so utterly blameworthy that in the extreme it makes a person unfit for association with the academic community. The standard is not that the moral sensibilities of persons in the community should be affronted, but that the conduct should, by its very nature, render the person who engages in it unworthy of membership in the academic community." While still somewhat vague, this definition was far clearer and far less dangerous to the purposes of the University than the board's standard.[46]

The faculty senate first discussed the code on 5 April 1971. After discussion, the senate voted to refer the conduct code to a special committee to be selected by the presiding officer of the senate from among its members. The special committee, chaired by David Smeltzer of the Political Science Department, reported to the senate on 1 June. His committee's report was an attempt to weave its proposed code with the state board's conduct code into a coherent document acceptable to the senate. It retained, for example, the board's dangerously vague term of "moral turpitude." The committee compromises caused some discontent. The members of the senate could not decide whether its incorporation of the board code meant an endorsement of it. In the end, the senate evaded the issue by voting that its inclusion of the Administrative Rules in the senate document did "not imply either approval or disapproval by the Portland State University faculty of the board's *Administrative Rules.*" The code was then carried unanimously, an expedient decision that overruled the thoughtful and careful work of the Moseley committee. The senate's code came down to an attempt to preserve the principles of academic freedom by not challenging the board's narrowing of them. At the same meeting, the senate voted to establish another of its committees to study the relationship between the University's conduct code and the Administrative Rules.[47]

This new committee, chaired by Howard Dean of the Political Science Department, reported in February 1972. The heart of its recommendations was to eliminate conviction of a crime or felony involving moral turpitude and others of the board's proscribed conduct as cause for imposing sanctions. Instead, they were to be regarded as "evidence to demonstrate cause for the imposition of sanctions." The senate adopted the recommendations of the Dean committee for transmission to the state board on 6 March 1972.[48]

While the faculty was drafting a conduct code for its own members, it was also engaged in developing one for the student body. A student conduct code, the result of deliberations of the General Student Affairs Committee, a committee of the student senate, the faculty senate Steering Committee, and the faculty senate, was passed by the senate on 24 May 1971. It was an unremarkable document, one that conformed to the Administrative Rules.[49]

The war protests—as did the war—ran down in 1972. In January, Students for a Democratic Society vacated their office at Portland State. In early May, there was a march against the war in Portland, but the organizers realized the tactics of barricades and sit-ins were now counterproductive. The march itself drew only 250 participants. A rally at Portland State was also poorly attended. The end of the use of selective service may have been the major cause in defusing protests against the war in Portland, as it was nationally, but, by 1972, the antiwar movement as a mass movement was over.[50]

Individuals and small groups still took action, however, and one of these protests marked the end of spectacular activities at the Univer-

sity in the Vietnam War era. In early March 1974, the Portland State
community was shaken at hearing the news of the indictment of one
of their colleagues, Frank Giese, of the Foreign Languages and Literatures Department. Giese was a respected faculty member, a scholar
of French literature, former chair of the Graduate Council and of the
constitution drafting committee. The federal indictment charged Giese
on six counts ranging from unlawful possession of a destructive device
to conspiracy, all in relation to the bombing of two military recruiting
stations in Portland in January 1973. A Portland State student, James
Cronin, and three other persons also were indicted. For a time, Giese
could not be found, and rumors spread that he was a fugitive from justice, but his attorney speculated he had not known about the indictment. Several of Giese's colleagues, eager to set the record straight,
testified he, indeed, had not known of his indictment because he was
on a business trip to Canada when it was issued. In any case, Giese sur-
rendered to authorities on his return. Both Giese and Cronin pled not
guilty, were released on bail, and their trial was scheduled for the fall.[51]

Giese argued the prosecution was a political one. A long-time man
of the left who had supported the Progressive party in 1948 and 1952,
worked for civil rights, and opposed the Vietnam War, he was currently the co-founder of the United Front Bookstore in Portland, which
sold left-wing books and periodicals. He argued he had nothing to do
with the bombings but had been arbitrarily arrested by the federal
government for his radical activities. His supporters organized a Giese-
Cronin defense committee, with about eighty members attending the
first organizational meeting. The trial was scheduled to begin on 30
September. Whatever its outcome would be, it was the closing of the
times of turbulence.[52]

No one knows what all the results were of the antiwar protest at
Portland State. It is impossible to prove their effect on the course of
the war. Only those caught up in the events of the six or seven years of
protest know the individual effects on them. Yet two conclusions about
these fevered years seem clear. There were little long-term, and only
brief short-term, effects on the University in terms of its structure and
purposes. There was definite short-term resentment against the University. A development officer who contacted forty Portland corporate
leaders in January 1971 reported "great concern to businessmen is the
upheaval on campuses. Long hair is continually mentioned as preju-
dicing them against our students and the names—Waller, Fenyo and
Horowitz came out continually. Several businessmen felt we should

have been more strict in dealing with faculty and students who disrupt the campus."

Twenty years after the event, Joe Uris declared: "In the end, as in its beginning, the student strike at PSU changed little." Joseph Blumel remembered when the University opened in the fall: "It was as if we had returned almost to a situation of normality. There was little remaining student activism....From one spring term to the following fall term, the atmosphere had completely changed." If the protesters were attempting to change the University as a symbol of the military-industrial complex or of capitalism, as well as to stop the war, they were unsuccessful. Although attempts were made to do so, no one could show the protests caused any enduring public backlash against the University, although—for unrelated reasons—there were troubles lying ahead for it. Faculty and student government did not change much because of the protests, the curriculum was not altered, and the type of student admitted changed little, if at all. Most faculty and students throughout these years wanted business as usual. Except for about a week in May 1970, they got it.[53]

The second clear conclusion about these years is that Portland State's president, other administrators, students, and faculty did an outstanding job in preventing violence, injuries to persons, and destruction of property. President Wolfe, students such as Joe Uris, and campus pastors such as Rodney Page, were only three of hundreds of people who, in a perfervid time, kept the peace. The context for the Portland State peacekeeping was the most emotional era in American history since the Great Depression. More than twenty-five hundred campuses were shut down in 1970. Students were killed and injured at Kent State, Jackson State, and the University of Wisconsin. Bombs were detonated in federal buildings and on campuses, including one at the University of Oregon on 2 October that caused more than $50,000 in damages. At Portland State, the only damage was in Smith Center, amounting to $14,150, most of it wreaked by outsiders. The real damage, the beatings in the Park Blocks, was entirely the result of outsiders. Although Gregory Wolfe did not have the happiest presidency in Portland State's history, he was a tireless (and within the University community, an almost completely successful) advocate of peace and the rational settlement of controversy.

"It's a matter of money."

SEVENTEEN

Student and Faculty Concerns · 1968–1974

S tudent life in the early 1970s was not all disrupting recruiting on campus or protesting the Vietnam War. But neither was
it all going to classes and writing papers and taking examinations. Indeed, student life was one of unusual ferment in these
years, and in ways unconnected with the war. New groups emerged,
and old issues took on new dimensions. The times were ones of
decreasing national idealism, after the enormous social accomplishments of the Lyndon Johnson presidency, but concerns for the disadvantaged elements of society, for justice, and for the natural environment were still issues that stirred consciences at PSU.

One of the first causes to arise was that of the physically disabled.
Those who made it an issue, more than anyone else, were two students: Art Honeyman and Mike Goldhammer. Honeyman, a graduate
student, affixed a sign to his wheelchair proclaiming, "Spastic power is
an irrational feeling but then, so is love." He was an activist on campus, helping teach Prof. Earle MacCannell's sociology course entitled,
"Relations with the Handicapped." He also ran for the state legislature.
In November 1970, Goldhammer founded a group called College
Resources Information Program (CRIP) that was designed to provide
an information center in Smith Center and to foster resources for disabled students, such as providing information on housing and working to improve the physical facilities at the University.[1]

There was much for this group to do. When it was founded, there
was no wheelchair access to the second or third floors of Old Main; it
was impossible to get through the turnstile in the cafeteria; doors to
offices and restrooms were difficult or impossible to negotiate; there
was only one elevator in Neuberger Hall, and it did not stop at mez-

zanine offices; and many sidewalk curbs were not wheelchair accessible. More important, the majority of the campus community regarded the disabled uneasily. One student in MacCannell's class played the role of a wheelchair student for several days. One of his observations was: "Wheeling your way through crowds, you notice people looking at you just a little longer than with the usual glance. That is if they look at you at all. For the most part it's impossible to hold eye contact with a healthy young member of the opposite sex. You often wonder as you sit in the chair if perhaps they are a little scared to look you in the eye."[2]

CRIP sought to redress some of these difficulties. It published a wheelchair guide for disabled students that listed accessible facilities. It worked at the state legislature in favor of a bill that would require state-funded buildings to be designed to meet the needs of the physically disabled. It sponsored CRIP Day, when chairs were loaned to nondisabled students to get them thinking about the daily difficulties encountered by the handicapped. Best of all, the disabled were overjoyed to hear of the University's plan to close the Park Blocks to vehicular traffic, the heart of the campus improvement project. The plan would eliminate dangerous crossings and enable students to proceed directly to buildings on both sides of the Park Blocks.[3]

In the next year, CRIP worked to persuade facilities planners to install elevators in the Shattuck building and in Old Main. In the meantime, if disabled students had classes in these buildings, their instructors would try to change the classes to another site. When all else failed, students would be carried to class. While Goldhammer and his allies worked through CRIP, Honeyman's main contribution to the cause was through his teaching. In the fall term of 1973, he taught a course in the College of Arts and Letters entitled, "The Cripple as Symbol in Literature," which he maintained would fulfill a unique gap: "There has been no literary study of the cripple as far as I know," he told a *Vanguard* reporter, "this is the only class like it." Through these efforts and those of others, Goldhammer, who became student coordinator of CRIP, was convinced Portland State was the four-year college in Oregon most accessible for wheelchair students.[4]

Hispanic students also became a presence at Portland State in these years, although their number was small compared to their place in Oregon's population as the state's largest minority group. One militant student, Ileana Fenyo, in a letter to the *Vanguard* in 1970, said there was no active Hispanic group because of discrimination. She maintained the University administration was either apathetic or opposed to admission of Hispanics and that it would "not grant Chicanos financial aid,...unless and until the Chicanos are prepared to use force." Although neither advocating nor employing force, Hispanics did became more militant the following year.[5]

In August 1971, Hispanics from within and without the University issued President Wolfe a three-point ultimatum asking for a full-time director of Chicano Studies; for fifty Chicano students admitted by the fall term; and for a variety of housing, tutorial, and financial aids. When Wolfe refused the demands on financial grounds, a group of about fifty Hispanics marched around three Portland State buildings in mid-August. The person who spoke for the group declared if nothing were done, then litigation would begin. Vice-President Blumel requested Wolfe create a half-time position in the admissions office to recruit minority (but not especially Hispanic) students. However, about all that was done specifically for Hispanics in these years was the offering of a course in Chicano literature at the PSU Education Center in Northeast Portland. The University did make a financial contribution to this program, but only community members, not students, were allowed to enroll.[6]

Students of a minority sexual orientation also made themselves known in these years of student and social ferment. In the fall of 1970, a homosexual student wrote a letter to the *Vanguard* announcing gays were applying for organizational status at Portland State. The purpose of the group, he said, was to provide a panel of students who could speak in classes about homosexuality; to promote public understanding of it; and to furnish a positive self-image for gays.

The first organizational meeting of the Gay Liberation Front was held on 4 November 1970. It was not a placid event. At this session, Guy Everitt was elected president. His first action on assuming office was to threaten a march on the *Vanguard* office to "scare" the editor into devoting more space to gay liberation and to women's liberation. Some of those attending the meeting planned to ask President Wolfe to fire the editor of the newspaper and, if that was not done, to "do something" (unspecified) to the editor. The secretary of the new organization assailed the director of the University Counseling Center for allegedly suggesting he engage a female prostitute to straighten out his sexual orientation. A gay commune in Lake Oswego was publicized, an offer of support from the University's Young Socialist Alliance was made, and an alternative newspaper was discussed. In spite of these hopes, Everitt told the fifty to sixty persons attending the meeting the Gay Liberation Front was not effective and needed more members.[7]

The follow-up to this initial meeting was a denial by the director of the Counseling Center that its policy was to change a person's sexual orientation and a capacity turnout at a public meeting in Smith Center that featured a panel discussion by five members of the Gay Liberation Front. The panelists called for education to break down the stereotypes about gays and, again, denounced the student newspaper. It is significant of the fears of the times that none of the panelists would give their names or permit themselves to be photographed for the *Vanguard*. In April 1971, the Gay Liberation Front called for a boycott of a Portland State theatrical production, Mort Crowley's *Boys in the Band*, maintaining the play stereotyped homosexuals by implying they could never be happy in any situation. Play director Jack Featheringill of the Theater Arts Department insisted the play had artistic merit, even though its characterization of gays was negative. Many students, he informed a reporter, told him they were pleased to see a play on a once-forbidden topic.[8]

By the fall of 1972, the gay liberation movement was in the doldrums. The Gay Liberation Front had disbanded, and an October meeting of homosexual students, which drew only about thirty men and women, proved discouraging: the cause was not being pushed effectively on campus, speakers declared, because of its advocates' lack of visibility, caused by the unwillingness of men to admit women to the cause, by the prejudice of the vast majority of the student body, and by the discrimination in the classroom against homosexuals by professors. Meetings and rallies were possible ways to break through the encircling prejudice, members asserted.[9]

The next month, action followed talk with the organization of the Gay People's Alliance (GPA). The first objective of the new group, it was proposed, should be to question faculty members about their willingness to teach "homosexually oriented classes." Interest on the part of faculty members, it was hoped, might in time lead to a gay studies center at the University, a program that might begin to dispel stereotypes about gays. When he was approached by gay students about a center, Ronald C. Cease, dean of undergraduate studies, said he doubted if the state board would approve one for lack of financial resources. Besides working for the center, other projected activities of the GPA were to confront the Counseling Center, participate in a peace march on 18 November, and sponsor discussion groups.

In 1973, the first openly lesbian speakers appeared at Portland State, Phyllis Lyon and Del Martin, authors of *Lesbian/Woman,* who spoke about sex stereotypes. They also urged members of the audience to support a bill before the Oregon legislature that would extend the state's civil rights laws to homosexuals. The issue of stereotyping in the Theater Arts Department arose again, when the GPA criticized the presentation of *Staircase,* a play about two homosexual barbers.[10]

On 6 February 1974, the Gay People's Alliance made front-page news in the *Vanguard,* which reported a meeting between President Wolfe and Jerry Gayken of the Alliance. As was customary in those days of confrontation, Gayken presented an indictment and a list of demands to the president. He claimed Portland State discriminated against homosexual students and faculty across the board: in admissions, in course content, and in hiring, promotion, and tenure policies. To redress these grievances, Gayken demanded Wolfe issue an executive order prohibiting discrimination against gays, endorse a program of gay studies, and hire a gay person to counsel faculty, staff, and students.[11]

Wolfe denied there was any real evidence of discrimination against gays, but he asked Vice-Pres. for Administration Robert Low to develop a policy stating that no decision of the University would be based on sexual orientation. Low said he had no objection to such a policy but wondered if the University could issue one in light of the defeat of a bill in the legislature that would have mandated such a policy. Low also was skeptical about gay studies, saying, "What is there to study? There is no similar content to black or women's studies. Gay people are identified as an interest group, not an ethnic group. They have no history in that sense." Dean of Students John Evans recommended the GPA, hitherto unfunded, be funded out of student incidental fees. Wolfe and Vice-Pres. for Academic Affairs Joseph Blumel said there was no evidence to prove discrimination without someone testifying to it, but Gayken pointed out no homosexual student would risk penalties by denouncing discrimination.[12]

Wolfe left office late in February 1974, but in May, Acting Pres. E. Dean Anderson issued a statement incorporating gays into the University's policies against discrimination. Portland State, through Anderson's courageous decision, became the first public institution in the state of Oregon to adopt such a policy. It did not create a stir on campus, nor in the larger community.[13]

African American students continued to voice their concerns in the 1970s. Unlike the gay movement, black students did not begin their quest for inclusion in the new decade but continued a movement started at least two years earlier, as in the case of Andrew Haynes's student government policies and the protests against the Athletic Department. Also, unlike members of some other student groups, African Americans worked closely with the Portland community in the development and administration of programs of interest to the black population. And in some cases, programs that benefited blacks also encompassed other groups, so it is difficult to determine exactly what the forces were behind each group's objectives.

In the history of the African American community at Portland State, the year 1968 was a pivotal one. It was also one of the most turbulent in American history, marked by the assassinations of Martin Luther King, Jr., and Robert F. Kennedy; the raucous Democratic national convention in Chicago; protests against the Vietnam War; and race riots in hundreds of communities across the country (although disturbances in Portland were mild). Americans groped for solutions to both the underlying and superficial causes of these discontents, and some of them concentrated on bringing the long-desired goal of the civil rights movement—integration—closer to reality. For these men and women, education and access to education were fundamental. Portland State's small contribution to this endeavor began in the spring of 1968, with the appointment of a student-faculty Task Force on the Disadvantaged.

Under the chairmanship of Ronald C. Cease of the Political Science Department, the task force met weekly through the summer of 1968. It had one means at hand to facilitate whatever it decided to do, a program announced by the chancellor that would permit the enrollment—of up to a limit of 3 percent of the student body at each state system institution—of students who did not meet the ordinary standards for admission. Although not confined to black applicants, the program was of assistance to them. The task force first devised what it came to call project TEACH. Portland State allocated $50,000 for the full tuition costs of those admitted to this program, which enrolled thirty-six students for fall term 1968.[14]

Of these thirty-six men and women, about two-thirds were African American, with the remainder being Hispanic, Native American, or white. What students, who worked with departmental advisers, gained from TEACH was an individual counselor, housing (in the case of eleven), and the opportunity to enroll in a three-term course specially designed to orient them to the College. Other than the orientation course, which also included remedial work if needed, the students in project TEACH took regular college courses. The program was an act of faith in both University and students, for 50 percent of the students had not completed high school, and 50 percent had a high school grade-point average well below that of regular admission requirements.[15]

By December 1968, several other programs of the task force were underway or in the planning stages—unusually speedy action for a university body—speed occasioned by the tact of Chairman Cease, the diligence of the members, and the pressures from a society wracked by racial strains. The first of these additional programs to get under-way was called the Portland State College Albina Education Center, which began in September 1969, under the direction of Harold Williams. The Center was an attempt to reach out into the neighborhoods of Northeast Portland with a program of both credit and non-credit courses. Although most anticipated the program would be largely for blacks, it turned out half the students in the first term were white.[16]

There was a small paid staff for the center, but the faculty were all volunteers from Portland State. There were student tutors also, who worked for course credit but no pay. In spite of little financial support, the center was popular, as the student body crammed into an old store front at 2611 N.E. Union Avenue (now Martin Luther King, Jr., Blvd.)

rose from fifteen students in September 1969 to five hundred students in February 1970. A year later, enrollment was up to seven hundred persons, but the racial composition had changed to 85 percent white. In a way, the Albina Center was like the original Vanport Extension Center: it was informal; its students were low income, for the most part; and it provided—for some—a chance to go on to a more typical institution.

Portland State College
Albina Education Center

Unlike Vanport, however, there were no admissions requirements at Albina, the instructors were not paid, and many classes were not for credit. The center was a notable experiment in community outreach, but it foundered for lack of monetary support. It could not carry on long with unpaid instructors, and this precarious financial situation caused its demise.[17]

More enduring for African Americans was another product of this turbulent era. In 1968, Gregory Wolfe asked Frederick C. Waller to head an *ad hoc* student-faculty council to develop an academic program in Black Studies that might take one or all of three dimensions. It might become a certificate program like those already established at Portland State; it might incorporate Black Studies into the existing curriculum; or it might work with other colleges in the Portland area to develop a Black Studies program. The council organized quickly and was able to report to the faculty senate on 13 January 1969 that it was moving along the three lines suggested by the president.[18]

The next step was the creation of an experimental Black Studies Center headed by W. Philip McLaurin. Essentially, the first center was a collection of courses funded by individual departments, a small beginning, but not a program with much cohesion and not one that could offer a certificate, let alone a degree. By 1970, PSU was ready to press for a regular Black Studies certificate program. In January, the faculty senate approved it, and, in April 1970, the state board adopted the program, which the University hoped would begin in the fall term. As always, there was hope the state legislature would appropriate the needed $187,000 to support the program. As always (especially in these parlous economic times), President Wolfe stated the University would try to find the money elsewhere if it did not.[19]

The new program, under McLaurin's leadership, was ready on schedule. In fall term, students could choose from a range of courses presented to them in a nineteen-page booklet, including "Peoples and Cultures of Africa," "Introductory Swahili," and "Afro-American Poetry." The program was interdisciplinary in that a student's certificate program was drawn from courses in various departments, instead of solely from Black Studies, although McLaurin hoped that, in time, an MA degree—or even the Ph.D.—would be offered. For the moment, however, a student would leave PSU with a degree in a particular major and the new certificate.[20]

The program had varied objectives these courses were to support. The principal one, McLaurin told the *Vanguard*, was to develop a "black intellectual group" that would provide leadership for the mass of the people. A second goal was to inform white students of the sources and costs of racism and thereby to persuade them to work with African Americans to eliminate it. The problem with implementing the program, however, was not its goals or its course content but rather in obtaining financial support for it. In the turbulence of the early 1970s, social change was not a popular cause for the great mass of Americans, and McLaurin feared the legislature would never dare appropriate enough money for a program dedicated in part to reform society.[21]

About six months later, McLaurin gave up the battle of getting financial support. He resigned as director of the program in April 1971, stating the University was not committed to giving it enough money to make it effective. Although he believed a solid academic foundation had been laid, as reported in the *Vanguard*, McLaurin reasoned that "by bringing in a new director with higher credentials, the program would have a better chance of receiving the money needed to fully develop Black Studies." He himself hoped to remain in the program as a connecting link between Portland State and the African American community.[22]

McLaurin's successor was Lenwood G. Davis of the History Department, who took over as acting director in September 1971. Davis hoped that during his temporary tenure the University would recruit additional black faculty members and that he could persuade more black students to include work with public agencies in their curricular choices. Davis's successor, appointed a year later, was Almose Thompson, who promised to try to provide two new directions for the program. He believed it lacked "academic credibility" because there was no coherent structure to the requirements, and he vowed to help give it order. Second, he wanted the program to take on a research and service dimension in support of its activist objective. He proposed the program staff provide—through their studies—solutions to community problems and assistance in such matters as writing grant applications for community agencies.[23]

Thompson also developed other proposals as he settled into his new position. One was to change the name of the program to the Northwest Institute of African and Black American Studies. This was not intended as a cosmetic change but one he believed would have substantial value. He believed the new name would reflect a prospective broadening of the program to include African as well as African American and white American students so that the Americans would learn of African culture and so that the Center would be of assistance to African students living in Portland. Thompson also believed funding agencies would be more willing to grant money to a program with a broader focus than simply African Americans. But the name change never occurred.[24]

A second innovation Thompson proposed was the publication entitled *Northwest Journal of African and Black American Studies.* Its purposes were three-fold: to reveal various aspects of black culture and history; to serve as a vehicle explaining what the center was doing; and to give African American scholars, especially those in the Pacific Northwest, an opportunity to publish their work. Thompson was to be the managing editor, supported by a board of black scholars from around the nation. In April 1973, the first number of the new journal appeared, containing contributions from authors throughout the United States, although Thompson hoped in time to publish more contributions from the region.[25]

In spite of his high hopes, Thompson was plagued with continuing financial problems. In February 1974, James Rogers, an English professor who taught two-thirds time in the Black Studies Program, resigned because of "lack of University support for the program." His resignation triggered a student petition drive to persuade him to change his mind and to get a larger budget for the program, but Rogers departed in spite of this show of support. In an attempt to alleviate the paucity of funding, the center was transferred to the School of Urban Studies in the spring of 1974 and, in August, obtained yet another director. William Harris, most recently director of a center in Seattle comparable to Portland State's Albina Center, assumed the leadership of the Portland State Black Studies program.[26]

During the years of growth and changes in the center, other developments affected African American students. One was a program launched by the State of Oregon called Operation PLUS (Paced Learning for Urban Students). Begun in the fall of 1968, the program was intended to accomplish three objectives: to provide the opportunity to attend college for students coming from economically disadvantaged backgrounds; to remove the barriers impeding successful work by these students once admitted to college; and to improve curriculum planning for courses for them. The students accepted into Operation PLUS were given full financial assistance. In July, Julius "Bill" Wilkerson was appointed director of the program, which had enrolled seventy-eight students by winter term 1971. But by this date,

Wilkerson was disturbed by the usual concern of Portland State programs, lack of money. With more money, more staff could be hired and more students recruited to the program.[27]

Black students also had their own voluntary programs. One was a Black Cultural Affairs Committee (BCAC)—a branch of the Educational Activities Committee, a branch in turn of the Dean for Students Office—which sponsored visits of black speakers, artists, and films to the campus. In 1971, at the request of BCAC, the program council of Educational Activities voted to allow it to become an independent board. The following year, the new board assumed responsibility for Black Culture Month. It sponsored a range of speakers and artists from the Portland community and beyond throughout the month of February. Although the turnout from the largely white Portland State student body was not overwhelming, the board's adviser said: "We're patient. We would hope that there would be more response from the PSU student body. It is a black thing, but it is also an educational process for everyone."[28]

Native Americans also organized at Portland State in this era. In January 1971, the American Indian Action Group held its first meeting. Its purposes were to preserve the cultural heritage of Native American peoples, foster closer relations between other groups and Native Americans, create unity among the Native Americans at PSU and help them to adapt traditional culture to modern life. In November 1971, Native American and Chicano students objected to a Theater Arts Department's production of a play, *Indians*, because it contained a religious ritual scene and because there were no Native American or Hispanic cast members and some of the costumes and drumming practices were not authentic. The play's performance was postponed one week so that the ritual scene might be deleted and non-white actors permitted to audition.[29]

One vivid instance of the problem of acculturation took place in October 1972. Nine Native American students entering the University from a reservation in Montana arrived only to discover their anticipated financial aid was not forthcoming. There had been a mix-up because of errors on the admissions and financial aid forms, which temporarily precluded their receiving financial assistance. After a delegation of local Native Americans walked into President Wolfe's office, the problem was quickly straightened out by the University, which arranged for alternative funding sources. Native Americans organized a chapter of the United Indian Students in Higher Education at Portland State in 1973. Its first major activity was to attempt to find funds for a Native American person to counsel Native American students, especially those who were coming to the urban university from a rural reservation. Its best-known campus activity was joining with the School of Social Work's Indian Education Project to sponsor an annual Pow Wow at the University (begun in 1971), which included native foods and dances for the enjoyment of the participants, Native Americans, and others.[30]

Foreign students had always been present at Portland State, but their numbers rose to record heights in the 1970s and early 1980s. While their presence contributed to the diversification of the University, their fluctuating numbers posed a problem for institutional revenues, and their preparation in the English language at times was inadequate for success in their studies.

Two of the great, enduring national issues of the 1960s and 1970s were the environmental and consumer movements. Ralph Nader was the symbol of both and their principal spokesman on the national scene. His institutional legacy was the Public Interest Research Group. In October 1970, two of Nader's employees from Washington, D.C., visited Oregon campuses. Their mission was to get students in state system institutions to pay a mandatory $1-per-term fee to support and finance firms of professional lawyers and researchers to investigate and litigate "public interest" matters. Later in the month, Portland State students helped organize the Oregon Student Public Interest Research Group (OSPIRG) and set up their own chapter of the organization at the University.[31]

The first wave of enthusiasm for OSPIRG was temporarily checked when the chancellor and members of a state board committee objected to a clause in OSPIRG's mission that permitted it "to defend human and civil rights secured by law, such as those relating to environment and justice in the marketplace." The objection was that student groups were not permitted by state board rules to engage in legal action under its umbrella. One board member, Elizabeth Johnson, feared state money (the mandatory student fee) would be used "to bring legal suits in the market place." After the state board removed the offending clause, it voted to leave the fee collection for OSPIRG up to individual institutions.[32]

A student petition in the winter term of 1971 showed overwhelming support at Portland State for a fee increase devoted to OSPIRG. President Wolfe originally thought of holding a formal student referendum on the proposed increase in fees but decided not to bother with it and to move directly to working out with the group some form of funding. This was done at Portland State, not through a special additional fee but through the usual process of allocating existing incidental fee moneys to student groups. Any funding of OSPIRG, however, raised objections by some students and by some members of the business community. Their pressures made the state board on 22 May 1972 repeal the $1 additional charge option (which had not been employed at Portland State) and also permit students who objected to OSPIRG to obtain a refund of that part of their student fees. This decision was prejudicial and unfair, as no other student group was required to refund any of its fee support.[33]

In spite of this decision, OSPIRG and its Portland State chapter carried on their work, but they were not free of business hostility. Its next critic became the Foundation for Oregon Research and Education (FORE), a group founded in 1971 to prevent disorder on campuses and supported by almost every major business in Oregon and numbering prominent businessmen and other citizens on its board. E. Dean Anderson, longtime Portland State administrator and acting president in 1974, tried to use his FORE board membership to educate the group about the real workings of the University. FORE had "investigated" state system management and business practices in 1973 and was engaged in 1974 in studying Portland State's use of incidental fees. This last investigation reflected not only a concern about permitting student fees to go to OSPIRG but also use of these fees in recent years to support radical, and seemingly radical, activities. It planned to move its investigation to Oregon State and the University of Oregon next. In the end, OSPIRG continued to be funded and continued to expose environmental malpractices by business, agriculture, and government.[34]

Student publications, especially newspapers, are almost always controversial. Their editors, for a variety of reasons—desire for attention, a fit of impishness, a concern to reveal truth—have stirred administrators

PSU Educational Media Services

E. Dean Anderson, long-time and faithful administrator

and community from time to time. To grasp the latest "controversial" issues at Portland State, it is necessary to first review the supervisory agency of student publications. In the beginning, there was a Publications Board that met once a year to select the editors of the student publications. Whatever supervision of newspaper or yearbook there was came from its faculty adviser. In 1962, Wilma Morrison of the Journalism Department was given the responsibility of broadening the composition and duties of the board to include students; it was also made directly responsible to the dean of students. After President Millar suspended the *Vanguard* in the spring of 1967, a new faculty-student Publications Board was created in the fall that was directly responsible to the president. Its duties included monitoring the finances of student publications, selecting their editors, disbursing funds, and determining policies. In the spring of 1971, President Wolfe appointed a committee to reevaluate the Publications Board and its relationship to the University.[35]

Whoever was on the board, as well as others in the University community, received quite a surprise when the 7 January 1972 issue of the *Vanguard* appeared. It contained a frontally nude photograph of John Lennon and Yoko Ono as part of an advertisement for some of their films to be shown at PSU. Portland's district attorney, Des Connall, made a television appearance indicating state law prohibiting the furnishing or sending of obscene materials to minors might have been violated. There were a number of complaints about the photo received at city hall, although few at Portland State, and one of the district attorney's staff met with members of the University administration and the *Vanguard* staff to discuss the matter. In the end, nothing punitive was done, as the University was able to convince the prosecuting attorneys Portland State was an adult community in which the laws concerning minors were not applicable. Throughout the controversy, the administration supported the newspaper, Vice-President for Administration Low commenting, "I feel the *Vanguard* made a careful and responsible judgement."[36]

In terms of organization, Wolfe floated a trial balloon in March 1972 that the *Vanguard* might become independent from University control, as it had briefly after Millar had suspended it. An impetus to do so came from the University of Oregon, where its student newspaper, the *Emerald*, had received largely independent status in recent months. There were real advantages for both newspaper and administration, theoretically at least, in such an arrangement, as the paper would be free from the threat of censorship, and the administration would not be blamed for the contents that caused public complaints. The problem in working out such a mutually beneficial arrangement was financial—it would be difficult for the newspaper to become self-sufficient by furnishing news only to a student body audience.[37]

The type of problem a student newspaper could cause the administration was again vividly revealed in an edition of the *Vanguard* published on 30 October 1973. In the paper that day, there was a satirical supplement, entitled "The Papal Bull," designed to mock the Roman Catholic church on the eve of the great church festival of All Saints Day. There was an outcry within and without the University, and the Publications Board decided to determine if editor Scott Cline had violated the section of the board's charter prohibiting offensive material unless the newspaper could show "the public interest and welfare can best be served by a breach of some people's taste and can defend that position."

On 16 November 1973, the Publications Board held a public hearing on the charge that Cline had violated the charter. There was a ninety-minute hearing, ably conducted by the board's chair, Bernard V. Burke of the History Department, followed by a one-hour executive session, after which the board announced its conclusion. Cline was reprimanded for his action, and the board issued a public apology to those "who were offended by *The Papal Bull*." At the hearing, Cline denied he had violated the charter guidelines but admitted an "error in judgment." He said in the future the *Vanguard* would publish parodies "but of not the same nature as *The Papal Bull*."[38]

An equally troublesome matter for the Publications Board concerned the *Review*, the University literary magazine. The problem was that about three hundred copies of a press run of one thousand had disappeared and that the editor, E. G. White-Smith, had spent the entire year's budget for one issue of the journal when it had been intended to produce three. The Publications Board charged the editor with mismanage-

Bernard V. Burke, professor of History and chair of the Publications Board

ment, and he accepted the responsibility stating, "I made a lot of mistakes and it didn't work out." The board dropped the matter, since it could do nothing further about it, and moved on to try to find funding sources for the year ahead.[39]

In the realm of athletics, a continuing issue was whether or not the University should join an athletic conference, the same issue that had been discussed in 1963. In a *Vanguard* interview in early March 1970, J. Neil "Skip" Stahley voiced the hope Portland State would eventually reach athletic parity with the University of Oregon and Oregon State. But he stated Portland State did not have the financial resources at the moment even to compete on a regular basis with the Big Sky schools. And as Stahley correctly pointed out, the funds would come only when the community (meaning the business community) decided to commit itself to raise the money.[40]

Portland State did try once again to join the Big Sky Conference. On 9 November 1972, the Intercollegiate Athletics Committee recommended the University join this conference. The committee reached this conclusion by first finding the current status of intercollegiate athletics at PSU to be "unacceptable" because of instability in the program (for example, frequent turnover of personnel), lack of faculty and student interest in intercollegiate athletics, and the necessity of drawing financial support from student incidental fees, which caused resentment among the students. Conference membership, the committee reported, would alleviate some of these conditions because it would require no additional funding, would increase revenues from gate receipts and television broadcasts, enhance student and community interest (and, hence, revenue), and further the institutional image by gaining the University greater publicity throughout the Pacific Northwest.[41]

On 20 November, Portland State representatives attended a meeting of the Big Sky Conference, and, afterwards, Roy Love, the new athletic director, expressed himself confident the University would be accepted for conference membership. In February, President Wolfe approved the plan of applying for conference membership, an action taken in spite of the low level of student interest in football. Indeed, a few days after Wolfe's decision, results of a student poll appeared in the *Vanguard* indicating 57 percent of the students who responded wanted to see no, or reduced, incidental fee funding for football. One major reason for the students' hostility to the program was the ever-increasing deficits for football. Since 1967, the deficit had been growing; it was $260,650 in 1972.[42]

In spite of these concerns, PSU applied for Big Sky membership at a conference meeting in May 1973, where the faculty representatives of the eight schools of the conference voted unanimously to admit Portland State. The only remaining hurdle was approval by the conference presidents, an action the University confidently anticipated. But it was not to be. In November, the presidents voted to table Portland State's application. The reasons given were "lack of student support, lack of support from the school's administration, and lack of evidence that PSU can finance a competitive program." One specific cause of the tabling may have been a resolution by the Portland State student senate opposing conference membership, a resolution conveyed to the student body presidents of the Big Sky schools, who relayed it to the institutional presidents before the meeting.[43]

There was one other disappointment for Portland State athletics advocates who were worried about finances. In late October 1973, a plan was worked out by Portland State, Oregon State, and the University of Oregon, and by Chancellor Roy Lieuallen and Gov. Tom McCall to request direct legislative support for intercollegiate athletics in the form of payment of salaries in the athletic departments and the expenses of women's athletic programs at the three state universities. If forthcoming, this funding would relieve the pressure on gate receipts and incidental fees to carry the costs of the intercollegiate program. The plan died, however, when it was killed in a legislative committee in February 1974.

A more pressing matter than long-term athletics policy was racism, this time not at Portland State but at one of its rivals. As a small part of the civil rights revolution of the times, some African Americans were demanding university sports teams not compete against Brigham Young University (BYU), an institution of the Mormon church, because of the theological principle of the church that blacks not be admitted to one of its orders. Stanford University, among others, broke athletic relations with Brigham Young, and athletes from other schools wore black armbands when competing against it. The Portland State student senate raised the issue in late October, when it passed a resolution that "Portland State University have no further athletic relations with Brigham Young University."[44]

The issue was an immediate one at PSU because its wrestling team had competed for many years against Brigham Young. On the day before the 1971 annual match, there was a forum organized by Karen Stoner, a student, to discuss the forthcoming match. One of the pan-

elists, Skip Stahley, said the Portland State black wrestlers had no complaint about competing against the Mormon institution and pointed
out that one of BYU's football players was black and that the Department of Health, Education, and Welfare had investigated Brigham
Young and found no evidence of racism at the institution. A black student present, Cliff Walker, declared black athletes were keeping quiet
for fear of losing their scholarships, and he passed out leaflets at the
meeting calling for a protest at the following day's match. Although
asked to stop the match, President Wolfe refused to do so.[45]

The day of the match itself was more exciting than its preliminar-
ies. Although there had been talk of a demonstration by black athletes, none was held. Before the match started, the chairman of the student senate said a few words condemning racism at both schools, then
the match began. Midway through it, however, a bomb threat was
phoned to the gymnasium. The nearly eight hundred persons attending were evacuated temporarily, but, when no bomb was found, the
match continued without further incident.[46]

Later in the month, the athletic program became embroiled in
another controversy, this one also involving Cliff Walker. Walker was
convinced Stahley was going to resign in the near future and that the
Intercollegiate Athletics Committee, of which Walker was a member,
was going to hire an associate athletic director to groom for the succession. This candidate, rumor had it, was Don Read, the football
coach. Frederick M. Nunn of the History Department, the committee
chair, refused to comment on the allegations, maintaining committee
deliberations were confidential. In any case, Walker was on the right
track, and Read was hired for the associate position effective 1 April.[47]

Upon his appointment Read, like many before him, exuded optimism about Portland State's athletic future. He stated PSU had the
use of a large stadium and was located in a large population center,
two essential ingredients for success. If properly developed, these
advantages might propel the University into heights of athletic
prowess comparable to that enjoyed by San Diego State University and
the University of Washington. San Diego State's athletic program was
so successful, indeed, that President Wolfe hired its athletic director,
Ken Karr, to study Portland State and to recommend a direction for
the athletic future of the institution.[48]

In November 1971, Stahley had had enough. He resigned effective 15 December to be succeeded by Don Read. Stahley's tenure had
been a success in many ways. He had made arrangements to use Civic

Stadium for football and had contracted with the City of Portland for the use of Duniway Park near the campus for track and field. Three new intercollegiate sports were added—gymnastics, soccer, and swimming—and Portland State won its first National Collegiate Athletic Association Division II championship (in wrestling) in 1967. But football remained the great unresolved problem. It was needed to raise enough revenue to support most of the other intercollegiate sports but was not in itself profitable. Stahley had proposed the years 1968–71 be a test period to see if football could escape a deficit, but in only one of those three years did it do so.[49]

During these years, great gains were made in women's intercollegiate athletics. Under the direction of Oma Blankenship of the Health and Physical Education Department, whose title was women's sports director, women's sports (called "extramurals") expanded from two to ten sports, and its budget increased almost four-fold, although it was small in comparison to that dedicated to men's athletics. Blankenship got PSU affiliated with the Association of Intercollegiate Athletics for Women, a national governing body, and with the Northwest College Women's Sports Association. These achievements were gained in the face of many obstacles: no athletic scholarships for women; difficult scheduling, as Portland State was not in a conference; and the enormous dedication demanded from coaches, as their coaching duties absorbed at least twenty hours per week. All that the coaches received in compensation was release from one of their five regular courses.[50]

PSU Educational Media Services

Other problems were the traditional societal images of women: women were, by nature, not supposed to be interested in sports or very well coordinated, and those who were interested and competent were usually labeled "tomboys." Furthermore, not only was there no money available for athletic scholarships, but the petty amounts dispensed from student incidental fees

Oma Blankenship, professor of Health and Physical Education, the moving spirit in women's athletics

never covered trips to out-of-state schools. Finally, in regard to intramural athletics, there was the lack of distinction between physical education and competitive athletics. This hurt the athletes because there
was no intramural program as such. If a woman wanted to play sports
but was not good enough to compete at the varsity level, then she had
no choice but to take physical education courses. For those who wanted simply to compete at the intramural level, there was no opportunity. When Lee Ragsdale, the head of the Health and Physical Education
Department, was questioned by a *Vanguard* reporter about this lack,
he responded in an accurate and characteristic assessment of many situations at Portland State: "It's a matter of money."[51]

While few recognized at the time what all its great ramifications
would be for women's athletics, Congress passed a significant civil
rights law in 1972. Title IX of the Education Act of 1972 declared: "No
person in the United States shall, on the basis of sex, be excluded from
participation in, be denied the benefits of, or be subjected to discrimination under any educational program or activity receiving federal
financial assistance." This provision applied to women's athletics, and
although its full implementation lay in the future, it opened the door.[52]

Portland State sports made a breakthrough in another area when
it hired a new football coach in 1972 to succeed Don Read, who had
moved to the University of Oregon. His replacement was Ron Stratten, who had formerly been on the staff of the U of O. Stratten was one
of the first African Americans appointed as a head football coach at a
predominately white university. His problems, mainly the inter-related
lack of conference affiliation and lack of financial support, were insu-
perable obstacles, however, and he resigned in 1974.[53]

The most far-reaching changes in the student life of PSU in the
early 1970s came in the lives of its women students. Many of the
changes that took place also involved faculty and female staff, and
these intertwined causes will be discussed here together. As was to be
expected, many Portland State women participated in the feminist
movement begun nationally in the 1960s. The movement was multi-
stranded, with a variety of goals and tactics, and many women at PSU
declared it was badly needed. At the heart of the problems of women
at the University, as elsewhere, was the persistence of traditional attitudes toward women. News articles, letters to the editor, and other
pieces in the *Vanguard* reflected older beliefs that were now contested.
One of the most-hated articles in the student newspaper representing
sexist attitudes was an essay published in November 1970 entitled

"Geography of a Woman," which equated spans of a woman's age and sexuality to the characteristics of world geography. Denounced in a letter to the editor as both racist and sexist, the editor apologized for the essay, blaming its publication on a "bureaucratic mix-up."[54]

To combat this type of attitude, a Portland State women's union was founded in 1970. Its original purposes were to raise the consciousness of the University community about sex discrimination and to develop programs to meet the needs of female students. It intended to deal with issues such as the neglect of the study of gender roles in academic courses, insensitive language used by professors about women students, failure of women to graduate at the same rate as men, why women entered certain disciplines at a higher rate than men, and the relatively small number of women faculty members and administrators.[55]

Even before the founding of the women's union, female students had taken concerted action to solve one of their problems. The first sit-in experienced by president Gregory Wolfe was by a group of fifteen female students with children on 29 September 1969. The purpose of the visit was to obtain childcare facilities on campus. Wolfe took the request seriously and acted almost immediately. He assigned the task of developing a facility to a committee of faculty, staff, and students headed by Arthur Emlen, professor of Social Work, which surveyed PSU students about their need for childcare facilities. The committee reported in November 1969 that they had located a place for the center in Smith Center and that it should be instituted by the winter term of 1970.[56]

This schedule was not adhered to, as the University found neither sufficient funds for the program nor an acceptable facility. What it did do almost immediately was start a childcare referral center that provided information on facilities throughout the city. The University made attempts to locate space for the center, investigating Shattuck School, the Jewish Community Center, and an office of the Portland Development Commission, but nothing was accomplished. Parents' frustration at the slowness of progress in starting the center led to what the *Vanguard* called a "baby-in" in September 1970, almost a year after the issue had first been raised. During the course of a faculty reception at President's Wolfe's house, students showed up—uninvited— bringing with them seventy-seven children aged two months to ten years. Wolfe had learned of what was planned two days earlier and had arranged for the children to be diverted to the lawn and their parents sent out the back door.[57]

Finally, in January 1971, President Wolfe signed a charter for the Portland State Child Care Center. Sheltered under the office of the dean of students, the center was governed directly by a board of nine members, eight to be chosen from the University community and one to be the president or his representative. The location of the childcare center was in a former Portland Development Commission building at 1025 S.W. Harrison Street. Although originally scheduled to open in early April, it was delayed first to May and then until 19 July, when the first day of school was held. The repeated delays were caused by the need to repair the building and accomplish myriad other tasks, such as hiring staff, gathering toys and furniture, determining a priority list for admissions, and deciding how many children could be admitted (the original number was approximately fifty). Diane Duveneck, who had headed a day care center in California, was the first director.[58]

Under Duveneck's leadership, the center quickly involved a great many parents, who donated time and equipment and served on the board and its committees. The start was so promising, indeed, that by October, Wolfe was writing to the Portland Development Commission to see if PSU could secure another building to accommodate the many who had been turned away for lack of space. In January 1972, the commission agreed to sell Portland State the Fruit and Flower building at 1609 S.W. 12th Avenue. Fruit and Flower was a private charitable organization that had provided child care in Portland since 1885. It had now moved its school to Northwest Portland and had disposed of its old building to the Development Commission. What it had discarded was a useful structure, a tasteful Georgian building built in 1928 for the specific purpose of the care of young children. Several of its rooms were child size, and it had the great advantage of having a kitchen.[59]

The original intention was for the center to operate both the Harrison Street location and the new building simultaneously, with the offices and the five-year-olds in the new building and the infants through age four at Harrison Street. However, this arrangement proved to be costly and inefficient, and, by April 1973, all operations were consolidated in the Twelfth Street building. That building, and the center itself, by this time had acquired a new name: the Helen Gordon Child Development Center, honoring one of Portland's (and the nation's) most distinguished advocates of child care, a woman who had given generously of her advice during the early days of the Portland State Child Care Center.[60]

Helen Gordon Child Development Center

Not all moved along smoothly at the center, however, even after the acquisition of the Fruit and Flower building. A funding crisis arose in early 1973. The center by this date was financed by parents' fees, support from the federal government, and Portland State student incidental fees. In January 1973, the Oregon Children's Services Division announced new regulations. To take effect on the first of February, they were to cut off federal funds to children of married university students and to those who had less than twenty-four months remaining in their University program. Application of these regulations was delayed by protests, but they were implemented in late spring. Although shifting federal monies indicated the precarious nature of center funding in the early years, the Helen Gordon Center continued moving forward on the basis of support from incidental fees and parental tuition payments.[61]

The Helen Gordon Center's history is a further illustration of the abilities of Portland State students, staff, and faculty to cooperate successfully in filling a community need. Like the campaign for a two-year, and then a degree-granting, institution, and as with the movement to provide student housing (to be described shortly), the Gordon Center was a result of local initiatives that succeeded in the face of adversity and resulted in one of the finest institutions of its kind in Oregon.

The establishment of the Women's Studies program at Portland State is another example of a cooperative endeavor that prevailed because of imagination, tenacity, and hard work. It became the first one established in Oregon and one of the first developed in the United States. Beginning in the fall of 1970, Nancy Hoffman of the English Department and Nona Glazer Malbin of Sociology designed a plan for both a research institute for the study of women and a program of Women's Studies. Implementation began in the winter term of 1971, with a set of courses taught under omnibus numbers and with a series of lectures (funded by the Educational Activities Office) by speakers from beyond the campus. From its beginning, the focus of the program was to involve community members, students, and faculty in its operation. For example, Hoffman decided to plan her new course, "Literature by Women," with the cooperation of its prospective students and saw that a notice was placed in the *Vanguard* indicating the time and place where students could meet to do so.[62]

During the summer of 1971, advocates of Women's Studies determined, in the words of one of its founders, "to build a university institute that could provide funds for students, faculty, and community people to teach in the program, office space and supplies adequate to our burgeoning needs, secretarial help independent of established departmental budgets and official course designations in the university catalogue." The Women's Institute and Resource Center, as it came to be called, had a well-organized component called the Women's Study Collective, which had developed a proposal for a full-fledged academic certificate program comparable to the Middle East or Latin American studies certificates and to the one proposed at this time for Black Studies. The program was rewritten in the spring of 1972. By then, at least forty courses were given in Women's Studies, almost all in the Colleges of Arts and Letters and Social Sciences, but they had no common institutional focus or academic pattern. A certificate program, in contrast, would provide a typical academic "credential," and, also, it was hoped by its proponents, justify the University providing—even in difficult financial times—at least minimal funding for office workers and community lecturers. At this stage, no support was asked for additional faculty.[63]

The proposal for the certificate went to the curriculum committees of the two colleges in the fall of 1972. Both approved the program in principle, although the matter of financing it at a time of financial constraints was raised in both bodies, and the Social Science committee also wondered about its organizational structure. Financing was indeed uncertain, for the funding was coming from Educational Activities, a branch of the Dean for Students Office, and thus dependent on the shifting annual allocations of the incidental fees. Another difficulty was convincing faculty that credit courses should be given by students and community residents. Finally, the proposal faced opposition in that it suggested the coordinators of the program be selected by participants in it, rather than having a chair appointed by a dean.[64]

Discouraged by the hesitancy of the two committees to move forward with the proposal, the Women's Studies Union reconsidered it at a retreat in February 1973. It was at this time decided not to give up but to push for acceptance of the program through the usual channels of approval by the PSU Curriculum Committee, faculty senate, vice-president for Academic Affairs, and state board. Vice-Pres. Joseph Blumel, although approving the content of the program, felt it would never be accepted with the elective coordinator as a part of it. The Women's Studies Union was reluctant to give up the elective principle. As one spokeswoman said: "Basically, Women's Studies is against hierarchical systems because women have traditionally ended up at the bottom of the ladder." Nevertheless, to get the program accepted, it was willing to compromise. The resulting compromise was to create a faculty-student steering committee that would appoint, monitor, and replace the director of the program. Blumel accepted this arrangement, and the curricular approval process was underway.[65]

In these early years, Women's Studies advocates had problems with others than University administrators. Some feminists wanted them to be more assertive, to demand a full-fledged department with additional faculty and financial resources. Some in the program wanted to do research work as individuals or in small groups, while others favored small group dialogue about their individual concerns. It was difficult to avoid disturbing otherwise sympathetic women if a too-radical educational model was being followed. Another concern was whether the program should focus on the career needs of individuals or on the student and community constituencies. Some feared the first two coordinators, Nancy Hoffman and Nancy Porter, were too authoritarian. There was a dispute over what students would be hired for work-study jobs. And those aggrieved, for one reason or another, ascribed their plight to "a gay-straight split, an academic-political split, a working middle class split." Problems in any organization are inevitable, success is not. But Women's Studies did succeed, both in the short and long term.[66]

One success was gained in the faculty senate. On 4 November 1974, the Women's Studies certificate program was debated. There were objections the program was "political," not objective, and that it was too expensive at a time of financial emergency. One faculty member thought there would be insufficient interest to sustain the program. But at the close of the debate, the senate voted by a large majority to approve the program, which, in turn, was approved by the state board in September 1975.[67]

One University development that was of interest to the entire PSU community, though with a special dimension for women, was the creation of a security force. President Wolfe had discussed the creation of a security force with Portland's chief of police in October 1968, when a regular police officer was tentatively assigned to the College. What was created, however, was a University agency with its own employees. Organized in 1969 as the Community Relations Office, the force was named the Campus Safety and Security Office (CSSO) the following year. Its officers were not armed but worked closely with the city's police department. One reason for creating it, in addition to stopping drug sales and trespassing and to protecting life and property during the time of antiwar protests, was to halt the molestation of women, which was a continuing—perhaps growing—problem. The notorious murderer, Jerome Brudos, who already had killed three people, attacked a departmental secretary in a University parking building in April 1969. She fought him off heroically. A female student was gang raped in the Park Blocks on 19 January 1970; another fought off an attacker in Cramer Hall on 28 January; and two students were assaulted on 1 February, one in Cramer and one in Smith Center.[68]

In spite of these attacks and PSU's response, some faculty members assailed the creation of a University police force. The New University Conference (NUC), a faculty group dedicated to radical change in the University, maintained in a letter to the *Vanguard* the security office "will find it impossible to provide the kind of security people wish and it will become frustrated and resentful of being saddled with unreasonable demands; it will probably demand more staff and resources to do the job. If it got adequate resources that would be a disaster to the university since it would mean a force of dozens of police and a huge budget. The school would be an occupied zone." NUC proposed, instead, that PSU hire students to patrol the campus and to study on stairwells and in hallways. Their effectiveness would be as witnesses who would saturate the institution and, by their presence, deter crime.[69]

The security force, in spite of these misgivings, proved to be effective. The number of indecent exposure incidents declined, and, by July 1970, the number of drug sales and trespassing in Parking Structure I had been reduced almost to zero. In October, the CSSO added to its arsenal of protection by hiring its first woman officer, Beatrice Appleton, a Portland State art graduate, who previously had been trained as a security officer by the United States Navy. Appleton declared, "I can go into areas that men can't and also handle complaints from women that men can't."[70]

In the early 1970s, the major change facing the faculty was the requirement to face up to the matter of achieving equality of opportunity in the hiring, tenuring, and promoting of faculty. The issue arose at Portland State early in 1970, when the Ad Hoc Committee on Sex Discrimination of the State Labor Commissioner made its report. The committee found "discrimination in employment based on sex exists throughout all levels of the Oregon economy." While the committee did not investigate Portland State, the *Vanguard* was curious. It interviewed John W. Raynor, the University's personnel director, who proclaimed "as far as I know there have been no cases of female discrimination in employment at PSU." He said there was equal pay for equal work and no discouragement of women from applying for traditional "men's jobs." Raynor also declared if employees or prospective employees believed they were discriminated against, then they could have recourse to his office, the Oregon State Employees Association (the civil service union for classified employees), the Department of Labor, and the Equal Employment Opportunity Commission.[71]

All of these points may have been correct, but they were not the entire story of equality of employment. A month later, an article appeared in a campus newspaper that took another tack. It pointed out there were ninety women on the entire faculty, only eleven of whom held the rank of associate or full professor and none of whom was a department head. Additionally, only thirty-four women sat on the forty-nine University committees and sub-committees, and no woman ever had served on the prestigious Advisory Council. Finally, 90 percent of all courses were taught by men.[72]

President Wolfe was not unaware of the current place of women and minorities in the University and was determined to do something about it. What brought it forcefully to his attention was a report by the federal Department of Health, Education, and Welfare, which had investigated the University of Oregon and concluded the institution was guilty of gender discrimination in its hiring practices. In April 1971, Portland State's affirmative action program began when Wolfe appointed an affirmative action committee headed by Orcillia Forbes, director of the health service, whom he charged with developing policies in four areas: equal opportunity for all students in all University programs; equal opportunity in employment; the investigation of complaints of discrimination promptly and impartially; and the compliance of any contractor with the University with equal opportunity laws. When the Forbes committee began work, it was given data from the Office of Institutional Research as a basis for its labors. Some of the most interesting were those revealing a collective portrait of the instructional staff: 606 were men, 105 were women, thirteen were Asian Americans, five were African Americans, and none were Hispanic. The 18 percent of the instructional staff who were women were paid lower salaries than were the men (except for graduate assistants, who were paid the same), although they held a similar percentage of advanced degrees and had the same average of years of service. Concerning the administrative faculty, there were eighty-seven men and thirty-five women. Eleven were Native American, two Asian American, and one Hispanic.[73]

In the same issue of the *Vanguard* that carried the news of the appointment of the Forbes committee, an editor reviewed the statistics from the Office of Institutional Research and demanded "the administration should take immediate steps to stop this flagrant discrimination against women." This suggestion drew a letter to the editor from a female faculty member who interpreted the statistical data in another way. She argued the data did not prove "flagrant discrimination against women" but rather that "familiar as I am with the traditional role which most women are still inclined to accept, I was surprised and favorably impressed that as many as 180 of about 880 academic staff members are women." Although granting the existence of prejudice, she said women often failed to qualify themselves for senior academic positions. It was this deficiency, not prejudice, that accounted for their disproportionate numbers in academe.[74]

While the Forbes committee got down to business by meeting with department heads and with other administrators, the personnel office began a program for minority persons who did not qualify for civil service jobs. They were to be hired at a lower starting salary than the civil service usually permitted, then trained until qualified and, at that stage, appointed to civil service jobs at a regular pay scale. In early

May, the Forbes committee issued a report to the president. It recommended a special fund be established to upgrade women's salaries for the coming academic year and that the committee searching for candidates for the vacant position of dean for students choose a woman or a minority person for the opening.[75]

Wolfe accepted the committee's report in its entirety but hired John Evans, a white male, as dean for students. The report noted that besides the low percentage of women and minorities in the workforce, and their lower pay, there were no women in administrative positions beyond one department head, and that among the civil service (composed 65 percent of women), there were no women in the top managerial positions. Using the forum of his annual "State of the University" address at the opening convocation, Wolfe agreed to the committee's plan for hiring over the next four years. He, thus, committed PSU to hiring new employees in the same percentage as they were represented in the national labor force: women, 30 percent, and minorities, 14 percent.[76]

The president also accepted the objectives of the committee's plan. It recommended that in hiring additional minority faculty, care should be taken to include all three groups: African Americans, Hispanic Americans, and Native Americans. It also wanted 80 percent of the new minority members hired to be instructional, not administrative, faculty and that, between 1971 and 1973, a specific pool of raise money should be set aside for minority and women employees. In the classified ranks, the committee suggested (and Wolfe agreed) efforts should be made to train minority members in the classified and service jobs for managerial positions and that one woman or minority person should be placed in a managerial position in each of the next two biennia. Wolfe not only talked, he acted, and, by late October, twenty-two faculty had received pay adjustments for 1971–72 to correct inequities.[77]

Regardless of what had been done and what was being projected at Portland State, the University faced another inquiry into its personnel policies. In October 1971, HEW announced that, beginning in December, it would conduct a routine investigation of employment practices at Portland State as part of a survey of employment in Oregon colleges and universities. In March, it had investigated the University of Oregon and now it was to examine Oregon State as well as Portland State. While the investigation continued, in November 1971, all working on employment equity received a discouraging blow. Because of the financial problems facing the University, Wolfe called a

meeting of the Portland State women employees to give them the un-
pleasant news that budget cuts would prohibit the hiring of additional women and minority group members as proposed in the Forbes
committee recommendations.[78]

The HEW investigating team arrived at Portland State in January
1972. It issued its report on 26 February of that year. The report contained a list of deficiencies and a set of requirements for future actions—requirements Wolfe said he and other University officials concurred with "in general." HEW faulted PSU for not developing an
aggressive program for University employees; for underrepresentation of minorities in high administrative positions and in graduate
assistant positions; for underrepresentation of women in instructional positions, in high administrative positions, and as members of all-
university committees; for salary disparities between male and female
faculty; for lack of a maternity-leave policy; for underrepresentation of
minorities in higher-level classified positions, including officials, managers, professionals, and craftsmen; and for concentrating female civil
service workers in the lower-paying positions. Wolfe appointed an
Affirmative Action Committee in Faculty and Staff Employment to prepare a compliance statement for HEW, which it completed in late
March. The committee was also charged with monitoring the progress
of the University in its hiring practices.[79]

While organizing the long-term responses to the HEW requirements, Wolfe also took some immediate actions. He sent Clarence
Porter, his executive assistant, on a nation-wide recruitment tour to
seek women and minorities who might be interested in applying to
Portland State for employment or graduate work. Porter's trip was
also to take him to foundations and government offices in an attempt
to raise money for developing programs for minority students. The
results of his trip to nine predominantly black colleges and to Washington, D.C., to confer with representatives of thirteen others included developing a pool of African American men and women who were
potential faculty or graduate students. Porter also searched on the
tour for funds to create an administrative internship program for
women and minorities and for a "desegregation center" at Portland
State. Porter hoped the center, designed to train educators to deal
with the problems of desegregation, would be financed by a grant
from the Seattle office of HEW.[80]

In August 1972, the University appointed an administrative assistant to the Affirmative Action Committee to "recruit and work with

women and minority classified staff members." By this time, also, seventeen faculty were approved for affirmative action salary raises. In September, Orcillia Forbes was appointed to the position of assistant dean of student services. In October, Shirley Kennedy of the Anthropology Department attended a national meeting of the American Council on Education on the subject of "Women in Higher Education" and returned convinced Portland State "'is ahead of the game' in establishing an equality-oriented university." This estimate was seemingly confirmed in April 1973, when HEW accepted Portland State's first annual report on the progress it was making toward the objectives set forth in the compliance document.[81]

Toward the end of President Wolfe's tenure, the Affirmative Action Committee reported further progress. In the two years since 1972, reported its chair, Orcillia Forbes, the female instructional faculty had increased from ninety-seven members to 104 and the minority representation from four to sixteen. She could also state the number of minority persons in office and clerical positions had increased from 10 to 27 percent and, in the category of service worker, from 25 to 36 percent. The percentage of female graduate assistants increased from 27 to 41. However, the percentage of females in academic administration had fallen, and the number of minority graduate assistants had increased at a rate below the University's goal. All in all, in spite of PSU's difficult financial picture, some progress had been made on the affirmative action front.[82]

In reflecting on this progress, it is clear it had been brought about not only by the Wolfe administration but by one of the great constant factors in the growth of Portland State, the United States government. As in the case of the creation of Vanport Extension Center; the Middle East Studies Center; research grants, student loans, and fellowships; and the Vietnam War, Uncle Sam was an influential figure in the quest for equal rights at PSU.

Regardless of their race, color, creed, national origin, gender, or sexual preference, an increasing number of Portland State students needed housing near the University. The number of students enrolled at PSU was increasing, while the supply of affordable housing was in decline. To fill this need, there arose a remarkable institution, Portland Student Services (PSS), a valuable joint contribution of students, administration, and city to the welfare of the University community.

Portland State always had been consigned by state officials to be a stepsister of the University of Oregon and of Oregon State University.

In 1955, the legislation creating the four-year institution had declared that Portland State College would be "a downtown city college, which shall not be a college of the campus type." This policy was reaffirmed by the state board implicitly in 1962 and explicitly by the College in 1965. In 1966, however, the board changed its mind and decided to provide "residence halls for single students" at Portland State. But President Millar was unenthusiastic, and nothing was done, even though the Portland Development Commission was demolishing buildings near the campus—some for College purposes—including those used for student housing.[83]

Students, however, did not placidly accept the destruction of housing stock. Their response was an intriguing blend of academic research and social activism, the community service dimension of the University at its best. Several students, led by Stan Amy, John Werneken, and Anthony Barsotti, persuaded an Urban Studies professor, Sumner Sharpe, to set up an independent research course, entitled "The College Housing Project," in the spring term of 1969. The purpose of the course was for the eight or nine students enrolled to determine if there were a need for student housing at Portland State.[84]

The class's report indicated a serious need for student housing near the University and suggested the institution persuade the Portland Development Commission not to destroy, at least for a temporary period, nine apartment buildings near Portland State that were scheduled for demolition as part of urban renewal. The problem was what to do with the buildings if they were saved. The state board would not allow Portland State to be the landlord because it had already been agreed by the University and the Development Commission that any buildings turned over to PSU by the Commission could be used only for educational purposes. The students' solution to the problem was to propose a non-profit corporation that would act, instead of the state board, as the landlord and administrator of the apartment buildings. The plan was for the Commission to transfer the buildings to the state board, which would then lease them to the corporation.[85]

Portland Student Services, Inc. was the result of this suggestion. To make it a reality required a great deal of work on the part of the students, in cooperation with local businessmen, University officials, the Portland Development Commission, and the state board to give the proposal credibility and authority. Director of Business Affairs W. T. Lemman was particularly helpful in advising the students about preparing their case. Portland State, in making its presentation to the

Commission, declared the two-year trial period would be a test, not just for the nine apartment buildings but for the idea that there could be created four or five "enclaves" of student housing scattered about the city. If the enclaves worked, then the rentals from them would be used to buy other apartments for student housing, mainly in the southeast part of Portland.[86]

In June 1969, the Portland Development Commission approved the proposal. On 21 July, the state board unanimously approved the lease arrangements. While the preparations were being made for these meetings, the students were also filling out the structure of PSS. As a reflection of the times, with its emphasis on "participatory democracy," the articles and by-laws of PSS gave the student tenants a good deal of authority over the housing project. Each building would elect representatives to a tenant council, which would present tenants' views to the management of the corporation and which would have the power to elect annually four of the seven directors of the corporation. The remaining three directors would be non-tenants chosen by the other four tenant directors. The tenants also had the power to call special meetings to depose any director by majority vote.[87]

All was going well until the question of money arose. In order to renovate the buildings so they could be properly occupied, and also so they could be demolished at the end of the trial period, the state board had requested the sum of $205,373 from the state legislature. Since the legislature was not in session, the request was referred to the emergency board, a continuing legislative committee used in Oregon to distribute funds not previously authorized by the biennial legislature. The board initially refused to grant the money, arguing it would get Portland State into the dormitory business to the detriment of the residential universities—a change of policy of such magnitude the entire legislature should decide it. The state board got around this position, however, by taking advantage of a state guideline that permitted it to approve expenditures not in excess of $50,000. Accordingly, it leased the nine apartment buildings for $49,500. The lease would be paid back from student rents.[88]

With the last major roadblock removed, renting and other administrative procedures were worked out, and the first students moved in during the fall term of 1969. But while they were doing so, PSS directors also were looking at the calendar while worrying about finding facilities for after the two-year trial period expired and new buildings were needed. This search resulted in the greatest controversy in the

history of PSS, before or since, and again reflected the spirit of civil
activism of the times. It was ironic this conflict pitted a student-run
institution against neighborhood activists, who argued PSS was trying to
destroy their low-income housing.

The search for new facilities was grounded on the decision it
would be wiser to build new housing than to rehabilitate older stock.
Governed by this assumption, the directors first looked at a property
immediately south of the University but rejected it because it was too
expensive to build on the steep hillside terrain there. It then turned
to Mountain Park, several miles south of the campus near the Sylvania
campus of Portland Community College. Cascade College, in North
Portland, also wanted to sell a dormitory. By the time the search was
over, twenty sites had been surveyed. What was finally selected, however, was a neighborhood that would be the place of controversy—Goose
Hollow—a site located between Market and Clay streets and Fourteenth and Seventeenth avenues.[89]

The site was within walking distance of the campus, the real estate
firm owning the land was willing to sell, and its price ($336,950) was
reasonable, but there was one major problem: many people were
already living there, including some Portland State students. The
neighborhood earlier had been damaged by the construction of a freeway, but it was still viable, and the rents were cheap, although the buildings were dilapidated. When the residents heard the apartment buildings and houses in which they lived were to be sold and the land
cleared for a sixteen-story apartment building for student housing,
they were frightened and angry. Their concern led to a struggle, from
August 1970 to March 1972, among the neighborhood residents, PSS,
and the city bureaucracy to see if the new structure would be built.[90]

The neighborhood fought against the PSS project in an attempt
to save its housing. Given the times, it had the expected allies—an alternative newspaper, *The Willamette Bridge*, and radical students who had
been part of the anti-war movement at the University—but also a seemingly incongruous one, Commissioner Frank Ivancie, who earlier had
given the order to clear the protesters from the Park Blocks that resulted in the bloody confrontation of May 1970. Ivancie's opposition was
to non-profit housing, not to displacing neighborhoods, but he was a
political force in the city the radicals had to accept as an ally. The strategy of the opponents was to attempt to link the Goose Hollow proposal with the Portland Development Commission, which had been the
agency of clearing the land (and, hence, people) around the University.[91]

After listening to a great many protesters who wanted the city council to stop the project, raising objections from its supposedly dangerous terrain to a purported linkage between PSS and big business, the council unanimously voted to approve the new apartment structure, declaring it was a lawful venture the city had no power to halt. Opponents of the project fought on, however, using litigation, arson, and vandalism as their weapons, but these tactics failed, and it was granted the requisite $3,193,000 government loan to construct the building on 30 March 1970. The building was virtually completed on 28 April 1972. By this date, the work of Portland Student Services was so successful that not only was the struggle over the Goose Hollow building resolved, the state board extended its lease to PSS on the nine apartment buildings for another ten years on 22 May 1972. Although in the years ahead many of the idealistic features of PSS disappeared—such as the participatory role of the tenants, tenants who increasingly complained about a variety of matters—there was no question the corporation provided better and more numerous housing spaces than were available before its creation. Its creation was one of Portland State's great success stories, largely accomplished through student skill and determination.[92]

"We're gonna fight you about it."

EIGHTEEN

Curriculum and Government · 1970–1974

I n a period of contentiousness, it is not surprising much of the faculty's time devoted to curriculum and government involved controversial matters. One issue of a great deal of interest to many students was the fate of the General Science Department. This department provided less-technical scientific courses than those offered in the other science departments, courses designed to appeal to students who wished to take them to meet their general education requirements in science and to those preparing to teach in elementary and secondary schools. The courses were popular and enrolled almost three times as many students as did those of the largest specialized science department.[1]

In spite of these enrollment figures, Karl Dittmer, dean of the Division of Science, was not impressed with General Science. Indeed, in the summer of 1970, he told the department head the department no longer existed. Departmental faculty responded with a position paper to Vice-Pres. for Academic Affairs Joseph Blumel urging the department be retained. In October, Blumel agreed with them in stating a dean could not abolish a department unilaterally. Everyone involved in the controversy agreed it came down to money and educational theory. Dittmer maintained money flowed from national and state governments and from private foundations to departments with scientists engaged in research, a task in which those in General Science did not engage. Its critics also said if the enrollment from General Science were incorporated into the "regular" scientific departments, then they would receive more state monies, as they were distributed on the basis of enrollment.[2]

Deciding the fate of General Science involved a long and emotional process. In February 1971, Dittmer again recommended the

Karl Dittmer, dean of the College of Science

department be abolished and its courses distributed among the other science departments. At this time, Glenn Murphy, the acting chair of General Science, was quoted as saying Dittmer would not be successful in eliminating his department because the dean's arguments were not convincing and because he did not have the right unilaterally to disband a department. To resolve the matter, Vice-Pres. Joseph Blumel appointed a committee headed by Bruce Brown, assistant dean for academic affairs, to study the issue and make a recommendation to President Wolfe.[3]

Although the testimony before the Brown committee was given in private, Dittmer gave an interview to the *Vanguard* in which he elaborated on the reasons he favored abolishing the department. He said its elimination would create a larger pool of faculty to teach non-science students; mingle the non-scientists with science majors and graduate students, whose research interests and skills would influence them; give the College of Science a greater interest in, and responsibility for, training teachers; break the isolation of General Science faculty from their colleagues in the specialized fields; maintain standards in courses by giving the generalists an occasional chance to teach advanced specialty courses; and, finally, the move would save money. Those testifying on the other side before the Brown committee and other fora argued students would learn more from professors interested primarily in teaching rather than from those for whom research came first; that their grades would suffer in competition with science majors; and that specialized professors would be likely to take for granted a greater scientific literacy than they possessed.[4]

The Brown committee reported in April the General Science Department should be maintained but with substantial revisions in the curriculum. This action did not save Glenn Murphy, however, who was dismissed as acting chair by Dittmer. The department, after considering other candidates, voted to recommend him as permanent head. Dittmer refused to accept the recommendation. The victory in the conflict was seemingly Dittmer's, when the department was abolished on 28 December 1971 (effective 15 June 1972) as one of the reductions made under the state board's declaration of financial exigency on 14 December. Dittmer had anticipated the state of exigency and had recommended the abolition of the department on 7 December. The controversy then moved to the faculty senate.[5]

The senate was concerned not about the wisdom of the decision to abolish the General Science Department (at least officially) but about the method by which it was done. On 7 February, the senate addressed this concern by taking two actions. It passed a resolution, introduced by John Hammond of the Philosophy Department, stating the abolition of a department should follow the same channels as creating one, that is, by beginning with the Curriculum Committee and finishing with the senate. In the case of time constraints that precluded this process, the administration should consult with the senate or one of its committees. The second senate resolution rather vaguely asked the senate president to "implement the Hammond Resolution as it applies to the General Science Department."[6]

The presiding officer of the senate implemented this instruction by appointing a committee consisting of Vice-President Blumel; Dennis Boddy, chair of the General Science Department; and Dean Dittmer to form a committee to implement the Hammond resolution by looking into the status of the department. It reported to the senate on 6 March. Blumel and Dittmer said the department was being eliminated mainly for reasons of financial emergency, while Boddy declared other reasons were predominant. The special committee recommended no action, and the senate took none other than to accept the report, although its acquiescence may have been in part because Blumel promised in the future he would handle departmental abolitions in accordance with the first senate resolution of 7 February.[7]

By the next month, the senate had become more aggressive. It passed a resolution on 3 April asking that "an appropriate Faculty body consider" whether the abolition of the department had met both the institutional guidelines and the terms of the Hammond resolution and whether the Department of General Science should be reinstituted. The senate presiding officer appointed a committee headed by David Wrench of the Psychology Department to implement the resolution. The Wrench committee reported on 1 May. It concluded the decision to abolish the department did not violate institutional policy concerning budget cuts in an emergency, but that the decision "was not reached by a procedure in accordance with institutional policy of significant consultation."[8]

The committee further recommended that PSU procedures concerning financial exigency, which it concluded had "not been thought out," become the concern of the senate. It also recommended a senate committee on educational policies be established and there be created an all-University committee on General Studies. Obviously, the debate over the fate of General Science had plucked deep chords among the senate members, touching on faculty security, general education, the fate of particular colleagues, and University government. During the senate's discussion of the report, John Hammond moved that the General Science Department be reinstated while a special senate committee looked into the matter, but senators tabled action on the motion until the following week.[9]

On 8 May, the General Science issue was partly concluded. The senate voted to substitute a motion made by Judah Bierman of the English Department for the Hammond motion. It then passed the substitute, which required the vice-president for Academic Affairs and the dean of science to look into the teaching of science for non-majors. It passed a second motion deploring the lack of consultation in the abolition of the General Science Department and asking for consultation in "future administrative actions involving academic program changes."[10]

On 4 June of the following year, the matter was finally concluded with the report of the senate's *ad hoc* committee, which concerned the teaching of science in general education. The committee was established by the Bierman motion and chaired by John Allen of the Earth Sciences Department. Its conclusions were based on a great deal of work. The committee took testimony from seven faculty members who had once taught in the General Science Department, questioned the one student who appeared in response to invitations to testify publicized in the *Vanguard*, and studied enrollment data since 1970. The committee's conclusions vindicated the decision of Dittmer to eliminate the department: The "committee found no evidence that the needs of the non-science students have been neglected as a result of the elimination of the General Science Department." Except for the dropping of a single course, there was no change in the number of courses formerly offered in the General Science Department. Enrollment in these courses had fallen off but probably because students had heard—contrary to fact—the courses had been eliminated. Indeed, they had been incorporated into other departments. The controversy over General Science had engendered publicity, but, in the end, relatively little curricular harm had been done. The students were being offered almost as many courses as before, and the gains and losses of amalgamation projected by Dittmer were now possible. Those who suffered the most were the General Science faculty, one of whom was terminated under the declaration of financial exigency and the rest dislocated to new departments.[11]

Two other curricular controversies developed at the same time the arguments over General Science flew back and forth. These debates concerned the Law Enforcement Assistance Administration (LEAA) and the Pacific Rim Center. Both programs involved grants from governments, both were assailed by some faculty and students as instruments of the "ruling class," and both were attacked for being instituted without faculty participation in the decision to accept them. In other words, the opposition to the two programs was very much a product of the mindset of the past few years.

The LEAA was a part of the Omnibus Crime Bill passed by Congress in 1968, which attempted to deal with crime in a variety of ways. Portland State's first connection with the program came when it helped fund the expenses of police officers who took courses at the University to improve their vocational capabilities. It did not make much of a stir, except for an attack by a small group of radicals from Students for a Democratic Society and the Friends of Progressive Labor, who castigated the program in declaring the police only serve the ruling class and that, being "basically repressive," educating them in college for their profession only "makes it even worse."[12]

Portland State began taking steps in the spring of 1972 to become more deeply involved with LEAA. The director of the law enforcement programs (part of the College of Social Sciences) wrote a grant proposal for a criminal justice center of excellence at Portland State, which would improve the offerings in the program and also link PSU with other universities in a regional consortium of LEAA-funded institutions for research in criminal justice. For lack of funds, nothing came of this application at this time.[13]

By September 1973, however, funds became available and officials at LEAA asked Portland State (not the reverse) if it was interested in submitting a proposal for a program of study that would lead to doctoral-level research and education in criminal justice (although not for a new doctoral degree.) Portland State would be a part of a consortium of universities offering doctoral work in criminal justice and related areas. Vice-President Blumel stated there was support for the proposal among the faculty of the Urban Studies and Systems Science doctoral programs but was advised by the Council of Academic Deans and the Advisory Council not to go ahead with it before full scrutiny by the faculty senate. Nevertheless, the University did apply for the funds without consulting the senate when, in mid-October 1973, Charles Tracy, the head of the Administration of Justice program at the University, announced an application to LEAA for a $600,000 grant to develop or strengthen doctoral programs related to criminal justice. This news caused an uproar, although the proposal had been officially supported by the Graduate Council and discussed informally on the campus shortly before, and a small group of faculty had met with, and written to, Vice-President Blumel to protest the plan. Some of the protesters also signed a letter to LEAA, written by Rupert Buchanan of the Philosophy Department, requesting it not consider the application until it had been considered by the faculty senate, a request characterized by Tracy as a "low blow."[14]

On 5 November, the faculty senate did meet to consider the matter. The meeting was initially disrupted by a member of the National Caucus of Labor Committees (described in one of its statements as an organization "attempting to mobilize the working class as a united front"), who denounced LEAA as "a domestic counter insurgency program." When the senators got down to business, they heard Blumel review the history of the LEAA grant application and address four issues revolving around it, issues that might well pertain to other grants from outside agencies. First, on the matter of requiring faculty approval of the grant before the application was made, he said it would be unfeasible to do so because of timing and because certain grants were simply extensions of existing programs already approved by the senate. Second, he said law enforcement education was a legitimate function of an urban university, one that fit the mission of the institution. Third, Blumel maintained a grant from a federal agency would not limit the freedom of the University by imposing conditions inappropriate for an educational institution. Finally, he said when the federal money ran out, PSU would have to depend on state funds to continue it but had no legal obligation to do so.[15]

The senate then proceeded to debate a motion introduced by Anthony Wolk of the English Department that would have the University not join the LEAA consortium project. If adopted, this motion would have been a recommendation to kill the grant application, as the grant money was contingent on PSU's joining the consortium. Those who supported the motion stated it was a faculty governance issue and that the senate should approve the principle of the program before the money was applied for, rather than discussing its details after it was received. Supporters also asserted LEAA money would give the agency certain authority to shape the program and thus undercut the senate's control over the curriculum; that the University would be forced to continue the program, because of its momentum, even after the federal money ran out; and that it would require a new doctoral degree program (a point denied by Blumel, who said all that was required was doctoral work, which could be carried on under the existing Systems Science or Urban Studies doctoral programs).[16]

In the end, the Wolk motion was defeated by a vote of 45-11, with one abstention. Shortly thereafter, President Wolfe traveled to Washington to sign the consortium agreement on 16 November 1973. It established a seven-university organization consisting of the University of Maryland, the University of Nebraska, Arizona State University, Northeastern University, Eastern Kentucky University, and Michigan State University, in addition to Portland State. During the following thirty-three months, PSU would receive $600,000 to develop a program for doctoral work in criminal justice that would begin admitting students on 1 July 1976. However valuable it was in the long run, the LEAA grant had proved to be an abrasive issue, mainly because it antagonized some faculty, not only for its content and its source of funds, but because it was initiated by the University administration without prior faculty consent, the same issue that was offensive to some faculty in the abolition of the General Science Department and in the creation of the Pacific Rim Center.[17]

The history of the Pacific Rim Study Center is another illustration of the difficulties in creating an institute in response to community demand but without faculty participation from the beginning of its planning. Both as a governance issue and as a body perceived as serving a "special interest," the Pacific Rim Center raised issues that produced sufficient rancor and misunderstanding to destroy a plan with a good deal of potential. The center's origin—in the longest view—was the hope, dating to the nineteenth century, that Oregon's economy would grow mightily if trade with Asia somehow were to be increased.

Gov. Tom McCall shared this hope of tapping the "limitless markets of Asia" (as was said in the earlier century), and, when he returned

from a trade mission to the Far East in February 1972, he recommended the establishment of a Pacific Rim Center in Portland that
would be under the aegis of the State Board of Higher Education. He
asked the board to submit a report on the feasibility of such an institution, and the chancellor called for information from all system
institutions to include in the report. At Portland State, Vice-President
Blumel asked all departmental chairs to contribute to the report.[18]

Data from the institutions were coordinated by Miles Romney, vice-
chancellor for Academic Affairs, who presented a formal proposal for
a Pacific Rim Center that was approved by the state board in late March
1972. The report offered a plan for a rather nebulous institution.
What was clear at the beginning, however, was that the center would
serve both community and the university. Romney recommended the
center should provide research and consultation to businessmen and
government officials interested in the nations of the Pacific Rim; proph-
esied it would foster exchanges between Oregon and Pacific Rim
nations among businessmen, governmental officials, and academics;
and predicted it would initiate degree programs in Asian studies. The
location of the Center was to be in Portland, but the board did not
commit itself to siting the institution at Portland State. Final action on
the proposal was to be taken at the board's May meeting.[19]

Locating the proposed center at PSU was far from the wishes of
certain faculty members. At its 3 April meeting, the faculty senate passed
a resolution introduced by Stephen Kosokoff of the Speech Department declaring, as the senate had the "right to review all new university programs," it should do so in the case of the Pacific Rim Center.
The presiding officer of the senate appointed a committee to look
into the matter. Other faculty and student opponents, organizing as
the Anti-Imperialist Movement, presented a public forum in early May,
at which Kosokoff said, "The main aim of the center was to study and
stabilize the governments in the Pacific Rim area, in order to maintain
the exploitation of natural resources by the American industries."
Gary Waller of the Sociology Department saw the center as a part of a
plan he claimed was intended to make Oregon the light metals refining capital of the world, in conjunction with a nuclear power plant
and the construction of a freeway through the African American ghetto in Portland.[20]

In spite of these protests from the left, the board moved ahead. In
early May, it appointed an inter-institutional Pacific Rim Study Center
Committee to plan the details of the center. The committee comprised

mostly representatives of the Portland area, with Portland State represented by Donald Parker, dean of the School of Business, and by Charles M. White, who was both a member of the History Department and assistant dean for international studies. White served as the committee's secretary. The chair of the committee was William F. Lubersky, the chairman of the board of the Portland Chamber of Commerce, although he rarely appeared at meetings. On 22 May, the board again discussed the center; at this meeting, it heard opposing testimony from Kosokoff and Waller, the latter reiterating defiantly that the Third World would not accept the Pacific Rim Center: "They're not gonna have it, we're not gonna have it, and we're gonna fight you about it."[21]

While the opposition protested, Portland State attempted to obtain the center for its own. Kee Kim of the Economics Department made a formal proposal to the state board to obtain the center at the university. Kim designed a program, with an annual budget of $407,000 (most of which would come from private contributions), that would concentrate on three areas: research; workshops, symposia, and seminars; and curricular coordination and development. To prove the center's worth to the community, Kim recommended it begin with research, then "demonstrate its usefulness to its sponsors and contributors by performing practical service functions which will meet immediate needs;" and only as the last stage develop new degree programs. Vice-President Blumel also set up a Pacific Rim Studies Center Advisory Committee, which had four subcommittees ranging from research to symposiums to curriculum. These subcommittee reports were digested by the full committee, which issued an interim report on 26 June 1972. This report was passed on to the inter-institutional advisory committee, which recommended to the state board on 29 August 1972 that it establish the Pacific Rim Center, although it did not specify where.[22]

In recommending the center, the state system advisory committee took pains to assuage some faculty concerns that had arisen in the past months. Each state system institution would continue to offer Pacific Rim courses, results of research projects would go into the public domain, and no project results would become the property of any funding organization, a policy initiated by Charles M. White. The funds for the center were to come from new sources, rather than be transferred from existing funds—an important consideration at a time when the state system was under severe financial constraints. The system would pay the administrative costs of the center, but all other expenditures, such as conference costs and research grants, would come from outside fees or gifts. The state's contribution to the center's 1973–74 budget would be $148,000. On the potentially explosive matters of location and governance, the advisory committee recommended the center be an autonomous agency of the state system located "on or adjacent to the Portland State University Campus."[23]

When the state board's Academic Affairs Committee took up the Pacific Rim committee's recommendations, it made only one important change: it placed the center at Portland State University. This decision was reached only after the presidents of the University of Oregon and Oregon State University "spoke strongly" in favor of the institution being at Portland State, assuring the committee there would be no lack of cooperation among state system institutions if the program were located there. When questioned about the opposition to the center from Portland State students and faculty, President Wolfe sidestepped the issue, saying only that he had graduated from the Fletcher School of Diplomacy, an institution that "did not step back from assumption of public responsibility." Another positive note was sounded when a message from the governor was conveyed stating he was requesting the sum of $20,000 from the Emergency Board for the balance of the 1972–73 year to employ a temporary director to begin the program as soon as the board approved it. In the end, the committee voted unanimously to approve the center.[24]

On 26 September, the full board approved the Academic Affairs Committee's decision. Its support was even more enthusiastic than that of the committee, for in the interim the emergency board had been persuaded by McCall to give $100,000 (rather than $20,000) to the center. A few days before the board's approval was given, Wolfe tried again to reassure the faculty the primary purpose of the center was academic, not economic—that it was not, in other words, to make the University a handmaiden of the business community. With the center authorized, C. Easton Rothwell, a former president of Mills College from 1956–65, and, most recently, regional director of the Asia Foundation, was appointed interim director. Before his self-imposed deadline of June 1973 to turn the job over to a younger person, Rothwell had much to do to overcome lingering distrust of the center's purposes among faculty and students, to ensure the "soft money" from business and foundations flowed in, and to help design a curriculum.[25]

The residual opposition gained another chance to attack the project when the senate's *ad hoc* Pacific Rim committee reported in October, raising grave concerns about the center. It objected to the center being authorized without having gone through the usual curricular channels, and there was concern about its purposes. Accordingly, it recommended the senate try to determine what its proper role was in creating departments, centers, and programs, including the Pacific Rim Studies Center. Second, it recommended the senate not consider the center for approval until its members were furnished documents that included clear statements about proprietary research, academic as opposed to economic emphases in the program, and faculty influence in determining educational policy in the center. The senate adopted the two committee recommendations after a good deal of debate.[26]

In November, the administration provided answers to some of the questions raised during the preceding month's meeting, and, in December, the presiding officer of the senate appointed a committee to explore the senate's role in developing new instructional units. This committee issued a report one year later that drew conclusions about the legal basis for developing these units, and President Wolfe's interpretation of this authority. This report marked the end of the faculty's concern about the formation of the center. What is clear in all the debates over the Pacific Rim Center is that the faculty's role in the controversy was reactive, that the center's origin was in business and government and the University administration. As in the case of the creation of the LEAA program and the abolition of the General Science Department, the faculty was confronted with a *fait accompli*. The faculty was also offended by the fact that Rothwell was an old friend of Wolfe, that he traveled to Portland from San Francisco only two days a week, and that he was a relative of Helen Wilderman, the registrar.[27]

By January 1973, Rothwell, the acting assistant director, Frederick M. Nunn of the History Department, and Charles R. White of Political Science, had prepared a tentative plan for a certificate program in Pacific Rim Studies. The program was further refined in late February to be sent on to the vice-president for Academic Affairs, but its progress was overshadowed by news from Salem that, unbeknownst to the Portland State administrators, Sen. John Burns of Portland was planning to introduce a bill authorizing a private firm to develop a $50- to $60-million-dollar complex for an international trade center on the west bank of the Willamette River between the Marquam and Hawthorne bridges. Part of Burns's plan was for the Pacific Rim Center to be located in one of the complex buildings, a building financed through higher education bonds.[28]

While the University administration did not object to having the center thrust on it by state government, it quickly concluded it did not want a building forced on it. William Neland, the director of the physical plant, told a *Vanguard* reporter there were more pressing University building needs than for the Pacific Rim Center, and that in any case the state board should not be in the business of constructing buildings for private land developers. A bit later, President Wolfe was even more blunt: "Research centers are not located in commercial facilities....Scholarship belongs on the campus," he told the *Vanguard.* The Burns bill came under heavy fire also from Ed Westerdahl, state board member, director of the Port of Portland, and former assistant to Governor McCall. Westerdahl stated he approved the trade center but not the plan of financing it with funds from the State System of Higher Education. The Burns bill eventually died in the Economic Development Committee.[29]

All of this concern over the building paled in comparison to the next crisis, that of founding the center itself. Rothwell and Wolfe had always insisted the center not be a fly-by-night operation funded at a starvation level. For 1973–74, PSU's request was for a legislative appropriation of $435,000. The Education Subcommittee of the Joint Ways and Means Committee originally proposed an appropriation of $200,000. When a motion by the chair of the committee to raise the amount to $350,000 was defeated, he moved to cut the appropriation to zero, assenting to the Portland State view that a small appropriation for an inadequate center was not worthwhile. The legislature then turned to a plan to fund the center on a contractual basis through the Port of Portland and the State Economic Development Commission. Its appropriation of $375,000 was contingent on these two bodies drawing up a plan for the center acceptable to the legislature's Emergency Board.[30]

These conditions were completely unacceptable to Portland State. Rothwell resigned almost immediately after they were revealed, and, on the following day, Wolfe announced the center had been dismantled. It was impossible for the University to have the fate of one of its components determined by state agencies that had no connection with higher education. As Wolfe put it to a reporter, "Support for the center from faculty and foundations was threatened by...an uncertain commitment from Oregon's public leadership." Although there was discussion later in the month of a plan to revive the center as an independent agency of the state board, and further discussion in April and

May 1974, it never came to fruition. The rise and fall of the Pacific Rim Center is the story of a potentially worthwhile project caught between two ideals of a public university: scholarship and public service. In time, what doomed the center was not faculty complaints about its method of creation but rather the fear the public service dimension was outweighing the academic side and that even the service rendered was more for select private interests than for the community as a whole.[31]

During the early 1970s, PSU concluded another matter of academic government of greater importance than the structure of departments and centers. The ties with the Portland Continuation Center (PCC) of the Division of Continuing Education (DCE)—which began to be cut in 1952, when Portland State obtained its administrative separation from the Division—were further loosened as the College planned to take over the credit offerings of the DCE. This was an arduous process to unlink a historical connection not fully understood by many faculty and students. Over the years it had developed, the faculty of Portland State were paid salaries—that of DCE wages—which were considerably lower (except for the several faculty who were full-time DCE who received comparable salaries). Portland State students had to be admitted to the College to take a full load by meeting certain standards, while anyone could enroll in DCE courses; Portland State students could take DCE courses but not the reverse; Portland State faculty, when teaching DCE courses as overload, received wages—not salaries—for teaching them (except for those with a split appointment). The Portland metropolitan community was confused as to the difference between the two institutions, even their abbreviations were similar: PSC and PCC. The College was supported by legislative appropriations and student tuition fees, while PCC depended solely on student fees. Administrators also were confused over the missions of their respective institutions.[32]

The efforts to untangle these snarls began in earnest in 1968. On 5 February, the faculty senate passed a resolution asking the president to appoint a special committee to provide recommendations "concerning the present and future relationships between Portland State College and the Division of Continuing Education." Others, too, were concerned about this matter, as the chancellor had already appointed an inter-institutional committee concerning continuing education in the state system. The faculty senate held a special meeting on 15 April that was solely concerned with DCE. At this meeting, W. T. Lemman, Jr., the director of business affairs, reminded the senate state appropriations were based on student credit hours. He noted that, during the 1967–68 academic year, if the credit hours of the PCC courses Portland State students were taking (Portland State received no compensation for these credit hours) were allocated to the College, they would support twenty-five to thirty Portland State faculty. A major concern expressed by the senate in this discussion was the fear evening and Saturday classes would become part of the regular teaching load.[33]

Bernard Silverman of the Chemistry Department was asked to chair the special PSC-PCC Relations Committee. The committee discovered, to no one's surprise, there were "several very complex aspects" of the relationship and asked, in November 1968, for further time to study it. The committee reported orally to the senate in June 1969. It recommended that over the next four years the University should add as many Section 91 and Section 21 courses (evening and Saturday credit courses) as currently offered by PCC; that students enrolled in these courses should meet the entrance requirements of Portland State; that all credit courses should be taught by Portland State faculty and be counted as part of their load; and that non-credit courses should be taught by DCE faculty. The report was briefly discussed and then referred back to the committee with instructions to report again in writing.[34]

In February 1970, two proposals for reorganizing the evening classes at Portland State were presented to the faculty. One was written by James Ashbaugh of the Geography Department, the other by Leroy Pierson, the director of PCC. The essential difference between them was that Pierson favored, as would be expected, the retention of continuing education courses within DCE. His main argument was that this arrangement would provide an extra income for faculty members, as they would be paid overtime wages for teaching them. The senate decided to send both proposals to the Academic Requirements Committee. The Budget Committee also became involved, and each committee presented a written report in November 1970. A motion was made to merge Portland State and the Portland Continuation Center and to work out the details of the merger at the level of the departmental curriculum committees. The motion was tabled, but another was passed to ask the Council of Academic Deans (in consultation with the department heads) to prepare a detailed plan for the merger.[35]

The Council of Academic Deans reported in March 1971. The questions that had been discussed for years were raised again in the discussion of its report. Would teaching evening classes be required?

Would new faculty have to be hired? Would not a merger reduce faculty supplemental income? Answers were given, but they did not fully satisfy the senate, which voted to create a select committee of its own to take up the matter of the proposed merger. Branford Millar, former president, accepted the position of chair of this committee. The select committee reported in May. It recommended, effective fall term 1972, all University credit courses, day or evening, be offered by Portland State; that in order to accommodate evening and part-time students, registration and transfer privileges should be simplified; equivalent funding should be provided for both day and evening courses; and evening classes would not be a part of normal teaching loads for current faculty, although they could be required of any new faculty. After little discussion, the motion was adopted unanimously.[36]

Leroy Pierson attempted to pour cold water on the senate's action. In a *Vanguard* interview, he stated the merger, for financial reasons, was "a long ways away" because of the fiscal crisis in higher education in Oregon. Only when it cleared, he predicted, would Portland State be able to pay faculty for teaching the former DCE courses. He admitted there was no question PSU faculty were better paid for their University work than in their earlier capacity as PCC instructors (an annual average of $12,000, as opposed to $4,450 for three courses per term per academic year at PCC). Pierson also stated his concern that Portland State would not serve adults as well as PCC had and that PSU "wanted to stamp out all part-time teaching." In the same article, Blumel was quoted as saying Portland State's goal in the whole affair was "primarily educational rather than the building up of faculty," citing the confusion among students as to which of the institutions they were actually attending.[37]

In September 1971, anticipating favorable action on the merger by the state board, Portland State began administering the credit evening classes. The most evident effect on students was that instead of being allowed to take a full load of DCE classes as before, now students taking more than two undergraduate courses (or one graduate course) had to be admitted to the University. Faculty still would receive "wages," rather than "salary payments," for teaching overload courses in the evening. One administrative result of the merger was that Pierson and his assistant director, Clark Spurlock, assumed positions within the Portland State hierarchy. In November, the state board approved the merger and gave Portland State $124,076 to pay for assuming the DCE courses. This was an effective and expedient action, for enrollment at

Portland State had fallen badly, and the chancellor as late as October had recommended the University budget be reduced by $230,000 because of it. Throughout the course of the negotiations between PSU and DCE, W. T. Lemman provided one of his many services to the University over the years. His knowledge of finance, his diplomacy, and his devotion to Portland State helped bring them to fruition.[38]

DCE was in the same year taken off general fund support by the state legislature and required to become self-supporting from tuition fees. By 1974, Portland State and the University of Oregon were suggesting they be permitted to give their own courses, not only on campus, but at off-campus sites, formerly the bailiwick of DCE. Such an arrangement would add to enrollment and, hence, to the amount of state aid flowing to the universities, and, perhaps, enable their faculty (many of whom were teaching these off-campus courses) to receive salary rather than wage money for them. Needless to say, DCE opposed the arrangement.[39]

Also at this time, the Division of Continuing Education lost one of its functions, the Portland Summer Session, to the University. First headed by Leroy Pierson, then James Lill, the summer program took on new life under Charles M. White, who became its director in 1970. During the twenty years of White's leadership, the summer session grew into one of the twelve largest in the United States. White made several changes in both the administrative procedures and academic content of the program that were both sensible and imaginative. He removed an uncertainty for prospective students by making a rule that no class would be canceled because it did not enroll a minimum number of students. Students enrolling for a few credits did not subsidize those enrolling for a greater number. The rates per course were constant—in contrast to other terms, when students enrolling in thirteen or more credits paid a lesser rate than those enrolling in twelve or fewer. Concomitantly, if no student enrolled in a course, then the professor might be assigned alternative duties by an appropriate dean.[40]

Faculty salaries, if calculated on a per diem basis, were always equal to, and generally above, the compensation professors received for comparable work of comparable length in other terms of the school year. The summer session—because it advertised its courses widely, as well as having an attractive program—enrolled a high percentage of persons who were not regular Portland State students. This meant that, since summer courses are not subsidized by the state, the University did not lose state aid for the credits taken in the summer rather than in other terms. If PSU students took summer classes, then they would take fewer in other terms, with a consequent reduction in state aid. White also introduced in 1985 the option of students paying for their courses by credit card, a practice later followed by the University for other terms.[41]

White turned the emphasis of the curriculum from those courses that appealed mainly to teachers to a far broader range of selections. Foreign languages, for example, came to be emphasized and were frequently presented in conjunction with foreign-area studies courses so that students would be immersed in the culture as well as the language of their studies. In 1970, there were three languages offered. By White's final year as director (1990), twenty-one languages were offered in the program. White also added non-credit courses to the summer session program and provided courses in a variety of schedules, in addition to the traditional four- and eight-week sessions. It became possible, for example, to complete a year's study of a subject through the intensive courses in summer session.[42]

Students, although not faculty, were pleased with White's decision to tell faculty what times the courses were scheduled, because this enabled them to take more courses throughout the day. Summer session administrators encouraged innovation. They authorized "special programs" planned by faculty with their department's approval. Summer session funds were allocated to these programs. Often, after several years of a successful summer program, the "special" money was added to the department's regular summer allocation to continue the program. The summer session added to its academic strength when it made a point of hiring visiting professors and foreign professors, in particular.[43]

The summer session also has served as an effective part of the University's mission to the community. It was the moving force in starting Chamber Music Northwest, a program of string concerts that at first lost quite a bit of money. But White did not give up, and the concert series (although no longer at Portland State) is now a major attraction in the Pacific Northwest. Another appealing facet of summer session for the community is the "Tour the World at Home this Summer" program that began in 1985. It is a series of free public lectures given by visiting professors, each of whom must agree to give a lecture as a condition of employment.[44]

Finally, all of these possibilities were presented in an attractive format in the annual summer school catalogs, which set such a high standard that the National Council of Summer Schools decided to name its award for the best catalog in White's honor: the "Charley." Summer session itself won other honors, such as the "best program" award of the Western Association of Summer School Administrators (representing about one hundred institutions) and the North American Association of Summer Sessions (encompassing more than three hundred schools).[45]

A minor variation in the theme of university structure and government, comparable to the talk of acquiring the Northwestern School of Law in an earlier day, occurred briefly in 1970 and 1971. The Oregon Graduate Center (OGC), founded in Washington County in 1963 as a private university to carry out practical research to benefit Oregon industries, was in financial trouble. There was talk of spending state money to save the institution, but Sen. Don Willner led the opposition, fearing "if the Oregon Graduate Center becomes a separate school in the State System of Higher Education it will probably have the effect of killing off quality graduate education in the sciences at Portland State University." Willner instead proposed that OGC be made an "autonomous part" of Portland State. Nevertheless, Rep. Hugh McGilvra of Washington County introduced House Bill 1480 to appropriate $950,000 from the general fund to allow Portland State to take title to the land and buildings and to run the enterprise. Reaction at Portland State to this proposal was guarded, as it was no secret that about one half the center's operating budget came from private funds, and much of its income, even after a merger, would still have to come from the private sector. In any case, at a time of financial austerity, there was no realistic hope for the appropriation, and HB 1480 died in the Joint Ways and Means Committee. There were some negotiations, anyway, between the administrations of the Graduate Center and Portland State, but they came to nothing.[46]

"What really galls me is to see
the guts of this university ripped out."

NINETEEN

The First Retrenchment Era · 1971–1974

Overhanging all the struggles and triumphs of the
early 1970s—from the Division of Continuing Education
merger to the Pacific Rim Center to the Big Sky Conference—was the University's precarious financial position.
From 1971–74, there was almost constant discussion of retrenchment,
dismissals, and budget reductions. Serious cutbacks were implemented, and even when they were not, stress and fear took a toll on morale
and energy.

The crisis began in the spring of 1971, when the state legislature
reduced the governor's request for the state system budget for 1971–73
by $6.5 million, of which $2.5 million was to come from reducing
operating expenses. Portland State's share of the reduction amount-
ed to $210,000, which translated into the loss of fifteen full-time equiv-
alency (FTE) positions for 1971–72. This loss was grave, but it was not
all the financial unpleasantness the University had to face. The legislature had already reduced Portland State's budget request by $80,000,
and the University lost another $136,000 when the legislature elimi-
nated almost all state contributions to DCE. Thus, when faculty members assembled to begin fall term in September 1971, President Wolfe
not only greeted them with this bad news but also with his response to
it. He announced a freeze on new hirings, another on equipment pur-
chases, and the release of only one quarter of the 1971–72 student fee
monies.[1]

Gloom was magnified by the possible defeat at the polls in November of a cigarette tax and by President Richard M. Nixon's recent
wage-and-price freeze prohibiting salary increases for faculty not teach-

ing during the summer term, when the wage freeze went into effect. In October, the administration extended the registration deadline in an attempt to enroll more students and also froze 25 percent of the library's book-purchase funds. On 23 November 1971, the Finance Committee of the state board recommended the state system declare financial exigency at its December meeting. It also authorized the presidents of the individual institutions to declare exigency in the interim. On the same day, President Wolfe did so for Portland State. On 17 December, the state board declared a state of financial exigency throughout the state system. The decision's most dramatic effect was that it gave university administrators the power to dismiss tenured faculty members without following the usual procedures. In reporting this news to the faculty, Wolfe also said that for the 1972–73 year, there would be a loss of 22.6 instructional positions, resulting from lower-than-predicted enrollment in 1971–72 and from board projections of continued low enrollment for the following year.[2]

To meet the crisis, Wolfe first urged the faculty to help seek ways to attract additional students. As possibilities, he suggested increased class sizes and additional evening sections taught as part of the faculty's regular load. With the counsel of Vice-President Blumel and the deans, Wolfe developed six principles to guide the University during its economic crisis: no across-the-board reductions; an insistence that categorical reductions (e.g., library books) only should be used as temporary expedients; instructional programs involving students should be cut last; the availability of programs at other institutions in the Portland metropolitan area should be taken into account when cutting Portland State programs; cost effectiveness of a program would be considered; and state system guidelines would be taken into account. In developing these criteria, Wolfe rejected more drastic measures, such as the suggestions of one of his administrators, Mark Howard, that all existing library book orders be canceled and that faculty teaching loads be increased.[3]

Wolfe hoped, he told the faculty, for a solution to save at least some of the 22.6 positions. If the Portland State students at the Portland Continuation Center were credited to the University, then its income would be proportionately increased. Fortunately, another solution appeared in January, when the chancellor agreed to recognize Portland State's fall term 1971 enrollment as the projected—rather than the actual, unrealized one—a decision that reduced the number of faculty positions to be eliminated from 22.6 to five.[4]

By May, the state system's financial picture cleared sufficiently so that it was able to repeal the state of financial exigency. Yet PSU had been injured by the cuts imposed under exigency for the 1972–73 academic year. Wolfe, Blumel, the Advisory Council and the budget and senate steering committees determined the reduction should be 29.3 faculty positions (nineteen teaching faculty and ten administrators with faculty appointments) and a base, 1-percent reduction in the overall budget. The faculty reductions were accomplished through retirements, non-renewal of non-tenured faculty, and resignations. No tenured faculty member was dismissed. In November 1972, the news came that the state board had given permission to the University to absorb all but a few of the DCE night classes taught in Portland. This transfer allowed Portland State to wipe out its budget deficit in a single stroke.[5]

The elimination of the deficit also quieted a brewing controversy in the Division of Arts and Letters. When the budget news was grim at the beginning of fall term 1972, Wolfe had asked each department to submit a contingency reduction of 3 and 6 percent. Those in Arts and Letters refused to do so and were supported by their dean, William Hamilton, arguing their programs would be drastically cut while more popular programs, such as Business and Engineering, would be reduced at a lesser rate. Division members also were afraid those advising the president were not representative of the liberal arts.[6]

For about thirteen months, financial matters seemed reasonably normal, but a financial crisis appeared again in December 1973. Because of underrealized enrollment in the fall term 1973, the 1973–74 University budget was reduced $323,000. On 18 December 1973, further bad news followed when the state board's Business and Finance Committee projected its enrollment estimates for 1974–75. For Portland State, it estimated a decline of 1,081 full-time students from the previous year, a decline translating into a $1,510,000 cut in PSU's budget for the year. The administration was now placed in the position of giving one year's timely notice (as required by the board's Administrative Rules) to those it might have to dismiss. The dubious distinction of the first to receive this notice was Katherine Corbett, director of the Office of All-University Events, whose position was eliminated in December 1973.[7]

In the crisis, various solutions were proposed—some more reliable than others. Portland State had always been allocated funds on the same basis as the other state system institutions: fifteen credit hours

equaled one full-time equivalent student. But unlike residential institutions, Portland State enrolled many part-time students, as most of
the student body worked. In 1973–74, for example, Portland State's
students averaged 10.36 credit hours per term. Some at the University
wanted to lower the numbers required for one FTE at the institution.[8]

Another ingenious solution was developed by some graduate students in the Department of Geography. They proposed each student
help solve the financial crisis by participating in a painless solution.
Since audit courses required no work but were counted by the University as part of the student's credit-hour load, why not have each student
enroll in one, three-hour audit course each term? This action would
raise the number of hours PSU was credited with and corresponding-
ly increase its income based on the FTE formula.[9]

As the budget-cutting process proceeded, the person ultimately
responsible for making the difficult choices on termination became E.
Dean Anderson, who took the position of interim president on 1
March 1974, after Gregory Wolfe resigned. He would have to issue the
required one-year's notice on March 15 for faculty who would be terminated the following year. In preparing the list, Anderson relied
heavily on the counsel of Vice-President Blumel, who was in a doubly
uncomfortable position. Not only would he have to make the recommendations, he also was a candidate to succeed Wolfe as president.
Anderson and Blumel's task was to cut twenty-eight FTE positions,
which would translate into fourteen that would require termination
notices—because the other fourteen positions were held by faculty
members on fixed-term appointments that expired.[10]

When the 15 March deadline was met, the faculty to be terminated were informed properly, but the University community was left in
the dark as to who they were. The administration did not release the
names of those being terminated because of a ruling by an assistant
attorney general that to do so would violate state law protecting the
privacy of individuals. Thus, students were uncertain about how to
anticipate their fall course schedules because they did not know who
would be teaching their desired classes. Although some of those terminated made the news public, not all cared to do so.[11]

The next deadline that loomed was 15 June. On that date, the
notices for the 1975–76 academic year had to be sent out. This was
also the date when program eliminations or reductions had to be made.
On 6 May 1974, Vice-President Blumel told the faculty senate of the
amount of the reductions, reductions worked out in close coopera-

tion with the senate budget committee. A total of $888,588 was to be trimmed from the teaching areas and $683,000 in the non-teaching areas. Blumel said three principles underlay the reductions: to minimize the effect on the University's enrollment; to retain as many programs as possible that fit Portland State's special role in the state system; and to avoid undue disruption of programs.[12]

The points that stood out in Blumel's report, and which were the subject of a good deal of comment, included the fact there were no faculty cuts in the schools of Business Administration, Education, or Social Work. When questioned in the senate on this point, Blumel responded there was growing enrollment in all three of these areas and if any cuts were made in Social Work, then that program would have to be discontinued. Other notable points in the report were the discontinuance of Black Studies as a separate department and its incorporation into the School of Urban Affairs; the transfer of English as a Second Language from the University budget to a self-supporting basis and the removal of its courses from credit status; and the elimination of the administrative paid component of the Central European Studies certificate program.[13]

The cuts were protested, as would be expected. A statement issued at a student forum contended certain cuts were a "racist attack on blacks, foreign students, and other oppressed nationalities." The Environmental Sciences doctoral program would suffer, its proponents declared in a *Vanguard* article, and other programs also had their de-

PSU Educational Media Services

fenders. The most vigorous comments on the situation came from George Hoffmann, dean of Social Science, who protested that the liberal arts and sciences were bearing the brunt of the cuts. In his usual forceful language, he told a *Vanguard* reporter: "What really galls me is to see the guts of this University ripped out....A university is a tremendously important institution. I put its value above the church and above the family....I don't want to see this University become a Portland Tech,

George Hoffmann, professor of History and dean of the College of Social Science

but at this rate it will become nothing but a training facility." Although he had nothing against training accountants and engineers, Hoff-mann said without strong liberal arts and sciences programs, "when these people go home [after work] they won't know what to do with themselves except sit in front of the damned idiot box." He particu-larly mourned the necessity of releasing younger faculty who were bright and aggressive, for their departure would leave the University "with nothing but a bunch of deadheads who just meet their classes and sit on their rumps."[14]

In mid-May, the list of terminated faculty was released, the attor-ney general finally deciding it need not be protected under privacy statutes. Besides complaining about the list and its perceived injus-tices, some departments did something to save their members. The History Department, for example, formulated an ingenious plan that would hurt some of its members financially but would hold the de-partment intact. The normal teaching load under its new plan would still be three terms a year, but summer school would be taught as a regular term instead of as one of the others. Since summer term al-ways paid less than a regular term, this plan would save money to save faculty.[15]

The most controversial reduction came in the College of Arts and Letters, after the other cuts had been announced. The acting dean of the College, Frederick Waller, decided unilaterally to eliminate the teaching of Russian language with its two faculty members. Faculty protested he had no right to cut Russian because it was a department, and departments could not be cut without consulting their members. Waller responded Russian was a program that could be eliminated without consultation. He argued each language was a program, and Russian was the area that drew the fewest students.[16]

On 15 June, termination notices were sent to sixteen faculty mem-bers, three of whom were tenured professors. This was the final list, one completing a reduction—counting those who had been given notices earlier in the year—of about fifty-seven full-time equivalent instructors. One faculty member presented a unique defense against his dismissal. Marc Feldesman of the Anthropology Department argued he could not be terminated because he was indispensable. He appealed his dismissal, arguing he was the only physical anthropolo-gist in the Portland metropolitan area, and, without anyone to offer Physical Anthropology, the result would be "the destruction of the Anthropology department at Portland State." The hearing committee upheld Feldesman on procedural grounds, but Joseph Blumel, the new University president, overruled the committee.[17]

In the end, there was a happy outcome for Feldesman and all others given their one-year notice. Funds were found as enrollment increased, and the termination notices were recalled. The exigency and retrenchment years were disheartening and destructive in some respects and, certainly, an indicator of the difficult financial times that would lie ahead for the next twenty years. That they were not even more difficult was almost certainly due to the early and deep involvement of the faculty and its committees in the discussion of where, what, and whom to cut. In contrast to the battles over General Science, LEAA, and the Pacific Rim Center, in this case the administration consulted the faculty early and frequently, listened to its suggestions, and thus helped it more easily bear the harsh results of the retrenchment process. All in all, it was a remarkably unacrimonious process, proved so by the faculty's insistence that the chief architect of the response to retrenchment, Vice-President Blumel, be appointed Gregory Wolfe's successor as president.

But it was not one without institutional effects. The most important result was the fillip it gave to the movement to organize the faculty into a collective bargaining unit. Since the middle 1960s, talk of collective bargaining had been rife among American academics. In a turbulent era of higher education marked by riots, demands, protests, strikes, and sit-ins, the issues of rights, responsibilities, and university governance equaled, if not surpassed, the traditional faculty concerns of academic freedom and salaries. The oldest professors' organization, founded in 1915, the American Association of University Professors, struggled to keep up with the changing times and only with great reluctance swung behind the idea of collective bargaining. It did so under the blunt threats of the American Federation of Teachers, the National Education Association, and state civil service unions. When it did grasp the nettle, the AAUP issued two powerful documents that provided an undergirding for the proper way to bargain and govern. These landmarks were a "Statement on Government of Colleges and Universities" (1966) and a "Statement on Collective Bargaining" (1973).[18]

During the winter of 1971–72, an informal group of Portland State faculty members began discussing the ramifications of collective bargaining. The group had no agenda and was not the creature of any organization but was primarily a study group determined to inform itself about the issues. As the group delved deeper into the issue, it decided to involve the entire faculty in its deliberations. Christine Thompson of the English Department, one of the study group, accordingly presented a motion at the meeting of the faculty senate on 6 March 1972 addressing the question of collective bargaining. The motion, passed by voice vote, asked the presiding officer to appoint a special committee to investigate the process of collective bargaining and to assess its strengths and limitations.[19]

Richard Halley of the Economics Department was chair of the committee. It presented a preliminary report in May that consisted of an informative essay by Hugh Lovell of the same department entitled "Faculty Collective Bargaining under Oregon Law." This document described the steps that would have to be taken before a union was officially established at a state college or university. Throughout his report, Lovell had to conjecture what might happen, rather than appeal to history, because there had never been a faculty union with collective bargaining power in the state and not many throughout the nation.[20]

The committee made its final report on 8 January 1973. It was a model of its kind. The twenty-nine page document dealt concisely and objectively with all aspects of the question of collective bargaining. It reviewed the major provisions of several collective bargaining contracts then in effect at several American universities and compared them to existing procedures at Portland State and to the rules of the State System of Higher Education. It then took up the "intricacies of collective bargaining and the collective bargaining unit," which was an elaboration and extension of the preliminary report of the year before. It devoted a good deal of attention in this section to the matter that would become most important in a few months time, namely whether a faculty—assuming it wanted to be represented by a union—would be better off represented by a local union at one institution (such as at Portland State) or by one that attempted to include all the units of the state system.[21]

The report included the results from sixteen questionnaires received from those sent to twenty-eight institutions currently involved in the collective-bargaining process. Most of the questionnaires were favorable to collective bargaining, indicating it made faculty-administration relations more clearly defined and enabled "scholars to function more effectively." The report concluded with some general observations from the committee. First of all, it stated collective bargaining in higher education was apt to be a more complex process than in the private industrial sector. Working conditions, for example, included a greater range of items. Dependence on the legislature was a complicating factor. And the lack of experience with the process made for uncertainty about its results. Second, concerning future prospects, it stated it would be difficult for Portland State's faculty, acting as its own union, to gain much in bargaining with the unified state system board. It also predicted there was little interest by other state system institutions in collective bargaining at this time. It predicted union groups at Portland State would not get the support of 51 percent of their members for collective bargaining, let alone a majority of the entire faculty favoring it. Finally, the committee said if any group wanted to take steps toward collective bargaining, it should be one of the professional associations or unions, not the faculty senate itself or any committee thereof.[22]

In one major respect, the committee members erred. There was interest in the state system in collective bargaining, at least at one other institution. In March 1973, the faculty at Southern Oregon State College (SOSC) formed their own union and petitioned the Oregon State Public Employee Relations Board (PERB) for a collective bargaining unit to be formed at their college. The question before the board was whether it should permit a single institution of the state system to have a separate bargaining unit or whether it should require the entire system to compose one large bargaining unit. Only after that question was resolved would an election be held to determine what union would represent the faculty in the bargaining unit.[23]

The situation at SOSC caused a great deal of discussion at Portland State. Representatives of the AAUP and the Oregon State Employees Association (OSEA) presented their views at campus meetings on the questions associated with collective bargaining. Waiting in the wings were the Oregon Education Association and the American Federation of Teachers, also potential candidates to organize the faculty. The faculty senate took up the matter on 23 April, when it passed a resolution to be sent to PERB supporting the position of the SOSC faculty in seeking a separate bargaining unit and also requesting it to reach the same conclusion if and when the question of collective bargaining came up at the other state universities and colleges.[24]

In the debate on the motion, the senate focused on whether or not the single-campus or the statewide unit would be preferable, not only at SOSC but also at Portland State. Hugh Lovell of the Economics Department was the main spokesman for the local unit, while Robert Williams of the English Department was the principal advocate of the statewide unit. Lovell said a statewide unit would be difficult to escape from if any single institution wanted to change its mind about either the desirability of a statewide unit or the particular union chosen to represent the faculty in such a unit. Williams argued the main focus of bargaining would be salaries and that a statewide unit, because of its greater numbers, would have more influence on the salary matter than a local unit. Some faculty, especially Gary Gard of the Chemistry Department, tried to delay the vote, but he was countered by those who said it should be taken so Portland State's sentiment could be given to PERB by the time of its hearing on SOSC on 1 May.[25]

Several faculty, supporters of the OSEA position for the most part, were disappointed with the result, but they were able to secure the necessary signatures for a special faculty meeting to reconsider the matter. When the faculty met, it devised a mail ballot that asked two questions: whether faculty were in favor of the local or the statewide unit and whether the faculty wanted collective bargaining at all. The discussion was entirely irrelevant, however, as ten days before the faculty met, the PERB hearings officer had decided in favor of the local unit. For the record, the PSU faculty did vote, 187-137, in favor of the statewide unit, and the SOSC faculty chose an independent union to represent its bargaining unit.[26]

In January 1974, against the backdrop of grave financial difficulties for PSU, the first union tried to organize at Portland State. This was the Independent Association of Professors (IAP) founded by two members of the Economics Department, Hugh Lovell and John Walker. The IAP began gathering signatures to place it on a ballot as a choice for union representative and to have a collective bargaining election at Portland State. The overwhelming emphasis of IAP was on economic matters, a focus disconcerting to some faculty who took a broader view of faculty concerns. Whitney Bates of the History Department, vice-president of the local chapter of AAUP, spoke for many in and out of his organization, stating, "Sometimes in collective bargaining there is a chance of selling academic freedom for economic gain. I would be wary of that."[27]

By 1 March, the IAP had been joined by OSEA and AAUP in the task of gathering signatures to represent the faculty. By now, momentum for some form of collective bargaining had picked up around the state. There was a meeting sponsored by the Interinstitutional Faculty Senate at Corvallis on 2 March that reviewed the collective bargaining activity at the state system campuses. Those faculty present noted there was "a lot of action" at all of the institutions except Eastern Oregon State College and the University of Oregon Medical School. They also passed a resolution declaring, "Collective bargaining has now become an indispensable tool in maintaining and improving the position of faculty members of the Oregon State System of Higher Education, as well as in strengthening the quality of education offered by these institutions." E. Dean Anderson, the new interim president, who took office on 1 March, also foresaw that "we will be in a bargaining position very soon and the changes will have a profound effect on the University."[28]

In early April, OSEA filed a petition with PERB asking it to rule in favor of a statewide collective bargaining unit. The hearings examiner ultimately decided in favor of local units, a decision that certainly strengthened the power of the faculty. For if a vote had been taken on a statewide basis for or against unionization, the UofO and OSU would almost certainly have defeated it. The chancellor also favored the statewide unit because it would be easier to defeat unionization at that level and, if unionization were accomplished, easier to block faculty objectives. Although the new University president, Joseph C. Blumel, was convinced collective bargaining was possible in the near future, its advent lay three years ahead.[29]

When Gregory B. Wolfe resigned as the second president of Portland State University, he left an institution that had done surprisingly well in accommodating the great divisive issues of the early 1970s. The enormous potential for violence and permanent intellectual and social scarring arising out of the antiwar movement was largely avoided. Members of minority ethnic groups, women, and homosexuals made their case as equal members of the academic community. The case was not always assented to, but far more than at other Oregon public institutions, Portland State led the way in the quest for equality. The era was marked by severe financial pressures that would not lift thereafter. Never again was there optimism about PSU's economic future. Yet, in coping with financial constraints, the faculty was feeling its way toward unionization as a constructive means to share more effectively with administration the burdens imposed by parsimonious taxpayers skeptical of the benefits of higher education and by the continued lack of support of the state board, which favored the University of Oregon and Oregon State University. Throughout its history, Portland State always had been assailed by adversity from one quarter or another. By the middle of the 1970s, its experience in fighting challenges had become a valuable asset as it entered the less spectacular but even more gravely troubled next two decades.

As any president must do, Wolfe both initiated and reacted to events. He was a courageous man who faced hostile crowds in the days of rage. He was intelligent and often personable. But what got in his way was his clever tongue and his condescension toward his constituents and their perception that he was contemptuous of the institution he headed, as evidenced by his account of the Pacific Rim Center, prepared with a collaborator after his departure from the University:

> Many faculty...saw him as an interloper from the East into their preserve [and] were put off by his style and elegance, his tastes and his friends....He never served beer at parties, they complained, only wine and champagne; he did not associate with the "jocks" either at the university or in the Portland community; he insisted on academic excellence, on developing programs that were competitive with the best in the country when, in the opinion of some commentators at the time, the protesters were content to do their classroom chores and spend as much time as possible skiing, fishing, and running their small businesses in Portland.[30]

"Many smiles and tired faces
and some friendly handshakes"

TWENTY

The Second Retrenchment Era • 1974–1996

F ollowing the resignation of President Wolfe, E. Dean Anderson assumed the presidency as acting chief executive while a search committee headed by Robert Rempfer, professor of Mathematics, sought a permanent replacement. A long-time servant of the University dating to the presidency of John F. Cramer, Anderson was assistant to the president from 1955–71, when he became vice-president for University Relations. The new interim president had no ambition for the permanent position (alluding to Harry Truman's famous statement, he said he always wanted one more desk to pass the buck to), yet he took the job seriously and served capably until his successor was chosen in 1974. The obvious choice to become the new president was Joseph Blumel.[1]

Blumel's candidacy was supported by many faculty, including Rudi Nussbaum, professor of Physics, who wrote a letter to the *Vanguard* urging Blumel as "the one candidate on this campus whom I would support if he would want to make himself available." The *Vanguard* itself endorsed Blumel for the position, arguing his knowledge of the financial situation at Portland State, his backing of a base funding level and equitable financial treatment for the University, and his desire to awaken community support gave him the advantage over his competitors. In a later editorial, it also commended Blumel's handling of the financial crisis of the past six months, especially his saving of positions in the liberal arts. Besides Blumel, the other candidates for the position were Dixy Lee Ray, chair of the Atomic Energy Commission, and Phillip Sirotkin, vice-president of Academic Affairs at the State University of New York (Albany).[2]

The state board selected Blumel on 21 May 1974 to provide, he later conjectured, the "stability and continuity" an experienced "inside" administrator could contribute after a time of searing troubles. Blumel was born in Kansas City, Missouri, but spent his formative years in Nebraska City, Nebraska, where he graduated from high school. The child of working-class parents (his father was a carpenter) who insisted their children attend college, the young man was also encouraged in his educational and cultural ambitions by two of his teachers and by a Catholic priest who befriended him early in his life. After attending the University of Nebraska, he dropped out for financial reasons to teach in a country school for one year. Upon completion of his bachelor's degree in Business Administration from Nebraska, he served in the Korean War and then used the GI Bill to take his advanced degrees in Economics at the University of Oregon.[3]

The new president had long service at Portland State. Coming to the department of economics in 1956, quickly earning a reputation as one of the best teachers in the institution, Blumel gained administrative experience as a member of several committees before becoming dean of undergraduate studies and associate dean of the faculties (1968–70) and, most recently, as vice-president for Academic Affairs. On one occasion, Congresswoman Edith Green, a former schoolteacher, visited Blumel's class and proclaimed him the best teacher she had ever seen. Blumel's many years at Portland State had confirmed him in the correctness of his decision to join the faculty in the early days of the College, based on his belief it was a promising institution. He was taken with the morale of the faculty members and their enthusiasm about the future of the institution, even though they had enormous teaching loads and cramped offices. In addition to his long service and loyalty and hope for a college open to the student of modest circumstances, Blumel had earned his new position because he was a humane and intelligent administrator who had already made many difficult personnel decisions during the time of financial exigency.[4]

Upon the assumption of his position, Blumel remained in the midst of attempting to resolve the institution's financial difficulties. Indeed, the gravest problem facing the University for all its later history, overshadowing events in every realm of its life from curriculum to athletics to facilities, was the financial crisis caused by the unwillingness of the citizens of Oregon to recognize and support its institutions of higher learning. This was not a new challenge, but its effects had been in the past felt cyclically, with the University community confident in the periods of especially low support that conditions would improve in the future. This, indeed, always had happened, but optimism would never in the future be as great about the prospects of Portland State as it had been in the 1950s and 1960s.

In the short run, in the early months of the Blumel presidency, there were new solutions offered for the financial difficulties. One was a bill introduced in the legislature by Sen. Ted Hallock of Portland that would have made budget allocations on the basis of actual students enrolled in institutions, rather than on a full-time equivalent (FTE) basis. The plan was received neutrally by the chancellor, whose representative stated it was developing its own plan on allocations. Naturally, Hallock's bill was hailed at Portland State, but a proposal of its administration to help solve the financial difficulties ran into a good deal of opposition.[5]

Faced with the FTE allocation system and confronted with shifting student demand in different academic areas, the administration suggested a certain number of full-time faculty be appointed on fixed-term appointments that would never carry tenure. Another element in the discussion of tenure was the chancellor's concern that so many faculty at Portland State (about 65 percent) were tenured. The administration argued that by adopting a voluntary target of tenured faculty, it could avoid having a fixed quota imposed by the state board.[6]

The opposition to a tenure quota was led by the local chapter of the AAUP. It argued the use of fixed-term appointments to ensure tenure quota was justifiable only in extreme cases and that the administration had not shown the financial situation was grave enough to justify hiring what would be, in effect, a group of second-class faculty. The plan was discussed in the March 1975 faculty senate meeting, and President Blumel was able to assure the senators these were not valid concerns, that the necessary degree of flexibility for adjusting faculty numbers to shifting enrollments could be met without using fixed-term appointments to limit the number of tenured faculty.[7]

The budget crisis of the early 1970s was what finally pushed Portland State faculty to collective bargaining. For many faculty, collective bargaining had been a kind of theoretical ideal, interesting to discuss but unlikely to adopt, until the University's financial difficulties made it a possibility to help foster faculty contributions to the difficult decisions that the times demanded. The AAUP moved more effectively than its competitors among the aspiring unions to translate this growing sentiment into action. In the spring of 1977, it conducted a survey of its members to assess the chapter's sentiment and discovered that 60 percent were in favor of collective bargaining. Over the next months, the required number of signatures were gathered to place the questions of collective bargaining and determination of the bargaining agent before the full faculty. The contenders for bargaining agent were AAUP, the Oregon Federation of Teachers, and the Oregon State Employees Association (OSEA).[8]

Under the leadership of Pres. Bernard V. Burke (History) and assisted by Peter Arum of the AAUP's western regional office, the chapter worked efficiently to advance its cause. It formed a task force to determine positions to be placed before the electorate in the forthcoming election. It set up a liaison committee with representatives in as many departments, programs, and schools as possible to carry the AAUP position to the voters. These men and women, in conversing with individual faculty, as well as the publicity committee in its literature, had to concentrate on making one point: the AAUP was an association of professionals and not an industrial union that conjured up for white-collar professors' images of smokestacks, strikes, and industrial violence. To do so, the AAUP representatives stressed its long history (founded in 1915) and the range of its professional concerns, beginning with the defense of academic freedom and tenure and carrying through with the financial and personnel assistance provided by the national and regional offices in other areas, from governance to salaries to the working conditions of women faculty members.[9]

AAUP's main rival was OSEA, bargaining agent for the state civil service employees. The principal faculty member who supported OSEA was Daniel Scheans of the Anthropology Department. A devoted teacher and forceful advocate of faculty rights, Scheans became convinced of the need for collective bargaining at the time of the faculty terminations in 1974. He regarded the cuts as being made without regard to either the welfare of individual faculty members or to the welfare of the departments losing members. His preference for OSEA as a bargaining agent may have been influenced by its director, Mort Shapiro, whose contempt for administration and management matched Scheans's. In any case, OSEA's main argument in the campaign was that it was a knowledgeable and experienced organization whose staff could relieve faculty of the heavy labor of the collective bargaining process. The Oregon Federation of Teachers (a branch of the American Federation of Teachers) mounted a low-key campaign. During the campaign, the administration, although making its oppo-

sition to collective bargaining clear, presented its arguments in a rational and restrained manner. Typical of this stance was President
Blumel's comments in September 1977 that the collective bargaining
election was "a matter of great importance, one that could have profound implication for the future of the university and one that deserves
careful and sober consideration." As would be expected for a venture
into the unknown, collective bargaining was widely discussed on campus. Much of a faculty senate meeting was devoted to the topic. The
senate arranged for a debate on the issue. AAUP sent representatives
to department meetings and sponsored an open house.[10]

AAUP's electoral campaign was successful, and the faculty voted
in favor of collective bargaining with the AAUP as its agent in March
1978. Fifty-nine percent of the faculty voted for collective bargaining
and 71 percent voted for AAUP. Of the 660 faculty members eligible,
544 voted. Little time was spent in celebrating the victory, however, as
preparations for the first round of collective bargaining began almost
at once. The chapter council appointed its bargaining team: David
Newhall (chair), supported by Bernard Burke, Barry Anderson (Philosophy), John Erdman (Mathematics), Ansel Johnson (Earth Sciences),
Donald Moor (Philosophy), and Ann Weikel (History). As in the election campaign, the chapter used committees to develop its bargaining
positions. Study committees prepared position papers on issues across
the board of academic interests. These drafts were then reworked by
members of the negotiating team before being presented at the bar-

gaining table as the chapter's positions.
The chapter council worked hard to invite the individual faculty members to
contribute their suggestions to the fram-
ing of the bargaining issues. The council also instituted a membership drive to
strengthen the hand of the union at the
table, rewrote the chapter constitution
to accommodate collective bargaining
requirements, and appointed Marilyn
Engdahl as its first office manager.[11]

That there would be obstacles ahead
was always anticipated by chapter mem-

David Newhall, professor of Philosophy and chair
of the first faculty collective bargaining team

bers, as the new venture in collective bargaining began. The first snag was an adversarial position taken by the administration before actual bargaining opened, a refusal to allow the department heads—who were not members of the bargaining unit—to call department meetings to elect liaison committee members from their departments. President Blumel took an uncharacteristically belligerent position on the issue, stating he was "astounded" the AAUP would request "excluded personnel assume union duties." Another vexing matter to be decided at this time was whether or not the AAUP should engage in a contest with the American Federation of Teachers to represent the graduate teaching assistants. It decided not to do so because of the need to marshal all the chapter's resources to make the first contract successful and because the AAUP national office would not offer financial assistance in the campaign.[12]

In spite of these distractions, a list of negotiating positions was approved by the chapter in time for the first bargaining session on 24 August 1978 in Room 326, Smith Center. Across the table from Newhall and his team were the representatives of the administration and the state board, led by Vice-Chancellor W. T. Lemman and also including Michael Corn (legal adviser to the president), Kenneth Harris (budget director), Leon Richelle (vice president for Academic Affairs), and James Todd (vice president for Administration and Finance). Lemman headed the team because, technically, the AAUP was negotiating with the State System of Higher Education and not with PSU. In the first bargaining session, the AAUP made thirty-six proposals covering a wide area of concern. The administration took a narrow position at the beginning, asserting its willingness to bargain only the minimum topics required by law, rather than any permissible subjects. This adamant position was not the choice of Portland State administrators but that of the state board.[13]

An early indicator of the administration's tactics concerned a proposal presented by the AAUP about retirement benefits. The proposal was discussed during two, three-hour meetings, but, at the end of the last session, Lemman announced the administration would bargain no more on the topic since the subject was preempted by law. Lemman declared PSU could not negotiate on the subject of pensions since the state pension law covered employees at other state system institutions for which PSU had no right to negotiate. The conclusion AAUP drew, perhaps unfairly, was that the administration was trying to wear down the faculty negotiators, who were not compensated for the

W. T. "Bill" Lemman, student, faculty member, chancellor, who did much for Portland State

long hours they spent in preparing for and conducting negotiations.[14]

What had been suspected as a delaying tactic became evident by mid-March. By this date, only one substantive agreement had been reached in the many months of bargaining. The lone success was an agreement to exchange information, an innocuous measure chapter negotiators believed might have required at most an hour's time. The nadir in this posture of adamancy came with the administration's proposal on retrenchment, presented on 14 March. In essence, this proposal would have permitted the University president to lay off tenured faculty members without declaring financial exigency, thus circumventing the process of faculty consultation such a declaration required. What the administration seemed to want was to eliminate tenured faculty when it was financially expedient to do so, rather than financially necessary to do so.[15]

By early April, the normally soft-spoken David Newhall was writing an article in the AAUP's newsletter expressing his concern about the administration's obduracy. By this date, not only was he disgusted with the matter of the perceived assault on tenure but also by the announcement by Lemman on 3 April that the administration had no intention of discussing any matter of faculty grievance whatsoever, arguing it would interfere with their "management rights." This assertion was especially puzzling to the AAUP team, as the administration had itself—earlier in that very meeting—placed a governance proposal on the table. Newhall concluded his reflections: "I hope that the sad revelations of today's bargaining session are temporary obstacles and not rigid positions....a feeling is beginning to spread amongst the faculty that the State Board of Higher Education intends to *delay* fruitful negotiations, *demean* the faculties (three of them) that have had the courage to say that the time has come for collective bargaining, and *destroy* a legally sanctioned procedure lest it spread to more campuses of the System."[16]

By the end of the academic year in June, there was still no contract. The AAUP by this time had made forty-seven separate proposals, while the administration had made ten. The AAUP team was fully convinced the administration approach was almost completely negative, that administrators were trying to sabotage the collective bargaining process at Portland State so that the other state system institutions would conclude it was futile, and that the Lemman team was not negotiating with AAUP in a spirit of solving common problems. Things were moving so slowly that, in June, Newhall felt obligated to tell the chapter it might have to face an impasse at the bargaining table, followed by mediation and factfinding.[17]

This gloomy prediction did not come true. Chief negotiator Lemman got into the spirit of constructive collective bargaining and helped move the process forward. Both sides grew weary. Their constituents wondered if the process would ever end. Finally, on 3 August 1979 at 3:02 AM, the two teams reached a tentative agreement on a contract, after eleven months (190 hours) at the negotiating table. "At the conclusion," so the minutes recorded, "there were many smiles and tired faces and some friendly handshakes." Both chapter president Ralph Bunch (Political Science) and Joseph Blumel praised the agreement, and "both sides commented on the professional and responsible manner in which the negotiations were approached." The chapter members could take pride in the agreement and those who negotiated it for them, especially David Newhall, the chair of the negotiating team, whose knowledge of the issues, sense of timing, and patient good humor were exemplary throughout the arduous months at the table. Proof of the team's success was that the contract was adopted by an overwhelming margin, 127 in favor, one opposed, with three invalid ballots. Approval was the final step in the long process that made the PSU chapter the largest bargaining unit exclusively represented by AAUP in the West.[18]

It was, indeed, an excellent first contract. What was most remarkable about it was not that it was done well, which it was, but that it was done at all. Its content in and of itself protected favorable past practices and made some gains for the future. The contract, among other provisions, formalized the traditional participation of faculty in University government, guaranteed it a role in the declaration and terms of financial exigency, and separated promotion raises from across-the-board increases. The negotiations set a valuable precedent for both sides that would be followed in nine subsequent ones—some

University President Joseph Blumel (l) and Ralph Bunch, president of the AAUP, shake hands at the conclusion of the first collective bargaining agreement.

difficult, some easy. With each negotiation, the University community became more accustomed to the process and, vastly more important, accustomed to the AAUP playing a significant role in governance matters under the principle of shared authority. From settling grievances to advising in financial retrenchment to shaping post-tenure review, the AAUP chapter has been an important factor in PSU community life. Not all faculty drew this conclusion, however, and in 1986, an attempt to decertify the union was defeated in a reasonably close vote. In the same election, oddly, the faculty rejected a "fair share" agreement, whereby all teaching faculty would have had to join the union or contribute a portion of their salaries to the cost of union activities. Indeed, a majority of the faculty has never joined the AAUP, preferring to enjoy the benefits of the contract without material costs to themselves, but in 1995, during the presidency of Craig E. Wollner (Urban Studies), the faculty voted that all members of the bargaining unit must participate in a "fair share" agreement. In time, two members of the chapter, both of the History Department, gained national office in the AAUP. Ann Weikel served on the national council from 1984–87 and was a member of the executive committee of the Collective Bargaining Congress (1980–86), while Thomas D. Morris was a member of the national Committee A on Academic Freedom, the Association's most important committee, from 1986–92. In 1982, the PSU chapter won the Beatrice G. Konheim Award, given to a chapter for "outstanding achievement in advancing the Association's objectives." The citation accompanying the award praised the chapter "for its strong and positive role in defense of faculty threatened by a major financial crisis at the institution."[19]

Although the budget and its implications were never far from anyone's mind at Portland State from the early 1970s forward, the next grave crisis occurred in the 1980–81 academic year. Conditions were so bad that President Blumel, on 17 February 1981, informed the faculty and its bargaining agent (the AAUP), pursuant to the collective bargaining agreement, that it might become necessary to declare financial exigency or program reduction. Oregon was in economic depression, the worst since the Great Depression of the 1930s. When the legislature met in January 1981, it had to confront the implications of this condition, including severe trimming of the budget for the State System of Higher Education, but it wished to delay its decision as long as possible to see if the economy might turn upward.[20]

This strategy of delay, however justifiable it might be on economic and political grounds, created a dilemma for the Blumel administration in living up to the terms of the collective bargaining agreement. The contract required the full involvement of the union and the faculty in effecting the retrenchment processes. But these processes would require several months to complete and might well be impossible to finish in the period between the legislature's adjournment and the time required to give timely notice to those faculty who would be laid off. On the other hand, the procedures could be invoked immediately without knowing what amounts of money would eventually be made available by the legislature. President Blumel asked the advice of the senate as to how to proceed.

During the last part of the preceding year, the president had asked the Budget Committee (on 10 October and 22 December) to draw up contingency plans for the 1981–83 biennial budget, based on whatever information was available to it. This "information" might better be labeled "conjecture," as no one knew what the governor would propose or what the legislature would do with his proposals. Accordingly, the committee planned for reductions in Portland State's annual budget, ranging from $1 million to $10 million per year. In December, the governor's budget did become available. It constituted a $1-million reduction from the 1980–81 budget, adjusted for inflation.[21]

Lacking historical precedents, the Budget Committee devised its own set of techniques in an attempt to find a fair way to distribute the budget cuts. By the March senate meeting, it had developed a set of ten values by which to measure these cuts and was then prepared to move on to make recommendations for specific reductions. Its most important value was to "provide programs in selected professional fields," a controversial decision that antagonized many in the liberal arts disciplines who had to be content with the second-place value, "programs in arts and sciences that are generally recognized as essential to a university." The Advisory Council also reported at this meeting, making as its first priority for avoiding cuts—if cuts were necessary—to protect the library. Its second place went to "the traditional liberal arts curriculum." The senate considered these various recommendations and then adjourned to await further developments from Salem.[22]

In April, Steven Brenner (Business Administration), chair of the Budget Committee, made an additional report defending the committee's recommendations and stating there had been "no conspiracy" against the liberal arts and sciences in its previous recommendations. He stated the committee's remaining work would be planning the criteria for elimination of programs (defined by the University attorney as units, departments, or units within departments) and then the decision of what programs to eliminate. The Advisory Council also made a further report at this time, again making the salvation of the library as its first priority but also making a variety of other recommendations, such as making cuts that would be visible to the public, e.g., no commencement exercises, undertaking a more vigorous fund-raising campaign, and allowing faculty the option of reducing FTE voluntarily. At this meeting, also, the Educational Policies Committee made its report. This committee's ranking of values closely resembled that of the Budget Committee, with the exception of placing liberal arts first and professional schools second.[23]

The AAUP Budget Committee made the final report at this meeting. After commending the administration for bringing about "an unprecedented amount of communication between the faculty and the administration," its report separated the goals and values to be used during the retrenchment process into seven categories, with the highest ranking being morale, followed by academic quality. Specifically, it insisted notice of dismissal be given during the fall quarter, to be effective the following fall quarter. Second, it hoped that if the choice had to be made between the termination of some faculty and short notice or placing all faculty on 0.96 FTE, then the second option was preferable. Third, those who were to be terminated should have the choice of being given one year's notice at full time or two years' notice at one-half time. Program reductions were to be avoided if at all possible. If reductions were required, then it would be best to eliminate the graduate program or some other aspect of a department's activities, rather than an entire unit.[24]

At the next week's meeting, Blumel tried to clarify the procedural steps. He began by pointing out that program reduction or elimination under the collective bargaining agreement would require a twelve-months' notice to affected faculty. This would make it impossible to accomplish termination by the fall of 1981, and possibly by the fall of 1982, since notice would have to be given by 15 June 1981 for the 1982 academic year, and the legislature might not have settled on the budget by that date. The president thus declared the only option was—if faculty were to be terminated—the declaration of financial exigency, which did not require as long an advance notice. The essential question thus became whether or not exigency should be declared. A factor adding to the uncertainty was that a specific plan for reductions—even a tentative one—could not be offered until exigency was declared. Another of many uncertainties was whether the state board would declare the entire system in exigency or whether Portland State would be the only institution placed in that embarrassing situation.[25]

Later in the meeting, Donald Moor, representing the AAUP position, counseled delay before taking the drastic step of declaring exigency. He moved that the president neither declare exigency nor the need for program reduction "until final legislative action determined the budget for the next biennium." His argument was in part based on what had happened in 1971 and 1974, when faculty were told they would lose their jobs before the full nature of the emergency became known. As it turned out, they did not lose their jobs, but the damage to morale had been considerable. In such a situation, Moor implied, there would arise the problem of certain departments, or certain individuals within departments, being singled out as in some way inferior to those chosen to remain.[26]

The counter-argument was that exigency and the specificity that would follow from it would be more helpful in that it would provide certainty for faculty members, rather than keeping them in the dark until the legislature made its decisions. When the legislature did act, probably by mid-summer, there would be so little time to make program cuts with any faculty input that it would be—in Thomas Buell's (English) words—"madness" to do so. Moor responded that the AAUP would bargain for the .04 reduction, perhaps accomplishing it before mid-summer, which could give two months to decide who would receive notice. Others countered that the Association of Oregon Faculties (a system-wide, faculty organization dedicated to salary improvements), the Interinstitutional Faculty Senate, and a survey of PSU faculty all opposed the 0.96 plan. The Moor motion was defeated in a close vote—twenty-two no, nineteen yes, and one abstention. A motion that the president not declare exigency until the May revenue projections were made was also defeated. What the senate finally passed was a motion that stated if financial exigency became necessary, then the president should declare it at the "earliest possible date." What the debate revealed was that senior faculty were unwilling to cut their own pay to save junior colleagues.[27]

By August, the situation had cleared somewhat. The legislature had adjourned after adopting a budget for the first year of the 1981–82 biennium. This budget made it possible to save all tenured faculty and all those on tenure track. Wage savings, temporary-leave savings, energy savings, and the non-renewal of a few fixed-term positions combined to accomplish the required reduction. This was reasonably positive news, but the negative was that the legislature had asked the state system to make program reductions or eliminations, in Blumel's words, "to accommodate on a permanent basis the budget reductions expected to be on-going." Various faculty committees had already set to work on this task to assist the president to prepare a specific plan for the senate meeting in September and the state board meeting in November.[28]

By the time the senate met for its first faculty meeting of the new academic year, President Blumel had declared financial exigency on 16 September 1981. The decision was not popular, although most faculty agreed the president had made it in good faith, as he discerned the financial situation. Nevertheless, the AAUP asked the senate at this meeting to rescind the declaration of financial exigency. Rudi Nussbaum of the Physics Department, who presented the chapter resolution, was careful to stress it was not aimed at the president but rather at the state board, which it asked, in effect, to look at the whole system and not treat Portland State differently from the two other major universities. President Blumel said he had no objection to the resolution, which also was supported by the Associated Students of Portland State University.[29]

Although some argued the rescinding of exigency would be a confession of unwillingness to face financial reality and an unwillingness to make up the senate's mind, the motion passed. So, too, did a motion sponsored by the AAUP dealing with early and partial retirement and the benefits associated with them. But the final motion of the day failed. This was an Advisory Council proposal dealing with the problems in some of the departments that had to undergo reductions or eliminations. Although sensible and humane in its provisions, the motion could not prevail against the opposition of those led by the Business School's Steven Brenner, who argued cushioning the pain of those terminated would be too high a price to pay for the large classes and inadequate salaries that would follow. Some faculty members, however, sacrificed themselves for the sake of their colleagues by taking early or phased retirement, which they had not planned to do in normal circumstances. The final plan for layoffs was completed on 18 January 1982, and layoff notices were issued on 21 January, which ended the condition of financial exigency. During and after the formal period of exigency, the administration established a Task Force on Emergency Services, which was somewhat successful in extending University privileges and obtaining new positions for laid-off faculty. Faculty members also arranged for the establishment of a faculty support fund within the PSU Foundation to receive money for faculty to help support their laid-off colleagues.[30]

Two years later, financial crises again were the talk of the University. On 16 September 1983, President Blumel sent a letter to the faculty advising it of "the possibility of the necessity to make a declaration of financial exigency or the need for program reduction." He elaborated on this matter at a convocation five days later. The situation was grim. In 1983–84, PSU would have to absorb $750,000 of temporary reductions in order to avoid layoffs. In 1984–85, Portland State would have to identify permanent savings of $748,000 remaining from the previous fiscal year and an additional $1,015,000 on a permanent basis. Making the situation even more difficult than in the last retrenchment, the president declared, was the legislature's mandate prohibiting raising of tuition and the political impossibility of cutting legislative appropriations for plant maintenance, library, and programs associated with economic development.[31]

On 3 October, Blumel formally asked the senate to advise him whether or not to declare financial exigency or the need for program reduction, and, if so, as to which mode of retrenchment it preferred. Because it was so likely some type of retrenchment would be required, Blumel stated he had already asked the Council of Academic Deans and the Budget Committee to propose a provisional plan for it. The senate decided to sponsor a faculty forum on 10 October for a full discussion of the University's financial condition and what could be done about it.[32]

The AAUP presented a proposal for solving the financial crisis that included reducing administration positions, sale of real estate, and greater use of sabbatical leaves, educational leaves, and early and phased retirements. However, when the senate resumed its deliberations on 7 November, President Blumel reported he had considered carefully the AAUP suggestions but found them insufficient to solve the crisis and to justify his rescinding of the retrenchment statement. He maintained the cumulative effects of the union proposals would simply not be enough to overcome the financial crisis of the biennium. Blumel also rejected a proposal not raised by AAUP—the closing of the University during August, Thanksgiving week, or December—measures, he said, which were unpopular with students.[33]

When the senate considered the president's provisional plan for retrenchment, there was a good deal of discussion of the symbolic value of closing the University, if not for a month, at least for a day. Speeches were made urging small programs be maintained because they performed essential functions of an urban university not performed elsewhere. The Public Health Studies Center, for example, was defended vigorously as an example of an urban function, while the Middle East Studies Center's demise would, some argued, lose the University support among a section of the larger community. A question was raised about what the University of Oregon was doing, but the president had no information on that subject. Others feared some faculty would be pressured into retirement against their will to save colleagues. But the senate debate, considering the importance of the subject, was not lengthy, and no course of action was suggested, let alone agreed on. Discouragement probably precluded any specific proposal after the AAUP proposal had been rejected. On 2 December 1983, President Blumel issued the proposed final plan for retrenchment. When the senate met three days later, only three questions were raised when the floor was opened to discuss it.[34]

The only other official faculty response made to the financial crisis came in February 1984 in a matter reminiscent of the disputes over the Mosser awards in the mid-1960s. In 1983, because it would not or could not raise faculty salaries in general, the legislature became alarmed when some distinguished faculty began to leave the state system for other universities. In order to stanch this flow of talent, legislators voted the sum of $200,000 in 1983 to supplement the salaries of faculty who were being recruited elsewhere. Instead of calling the fund what it was, a retention device, it was named the Faculty Excellence Awards Program. Five awards were given to Portland State. When the awards were announced, there was a faculty outcry on both procedural and substantive grounds.[35]

The words describing the criteria for the award, as well as its title, were also ill-chosen: "Candidates should be in a field or program of excellent quality or one which should be of excellent quality at your institution." One question immediately raised was how could one determine excellence? Another was how the University had chosen its candidates, as they were recommended through different procedures across the University, rather than through the standard procedures for recognizing merit. Some senators saw an anomaly in the state system raising the salaries of some faculty at the same time retrenchments were occurring. Still others predicted the awards would have a different effect from that anticipated by the legislators: those who did not receive the awards would be so disappointed they might resign. To focus the opposition, the AAUP introduced a motion passed by the senate congratulating the Portland State winners, opposing the raising of salaries for the few while the state system was dismissing faculty, and urging—if they were to be given again—that the awards be based on the usual procedures for granting merit pay.[36]

All of these crises, those of 1971, 1973, 1981, and 1983, reflected the parsimony of Oregon taxpayers in supporting public services, especially higher education. The only positive result of the turmoil over retrenchment was the development of mechanisms based on the principle of shared authority, that faculty union and faculty committees assist the administration in dealing with the financial difficulties.

These mechanisms would be most severely tested after 6 November 1990. On that date, less than two months after Judith Ramaley took office as president, the voters passed a constitutional amendment (Measure Five) limiting the rise of property taxes. For higher education, the consequences of this amendment were grave, and perhaps in time, disastrous. The amendment limited property taxes but also guaranteed state funds would make up the difference in funding lost by public elementary and secondary schools through the lower property taxes. The only way this could be done was to reduce appropriations devoted to other state services, such as higher education.

By January 1991, it was clear 2 percent would have to be cut from the current year's budget, one half of which could be made up by raising tuition and fees, the other half by reductions in faculty, staff, or other budget items. It was hardly the most propitious circumstance for a new president to begin her career. One certainty in the financial situation was that Chancellor Thomas Bartlett did not want to employ across-the-board cuts in making these reductions. President Ramaley promised, in dealing with the crisis, to cooperate with faculty committees and the AAUP and to "do her best not to lay off faculty." She unveiled a process that involved the administration gathering data about enrollment targets and depth of the required reductions; senate Budget Committee development of criteria for budget review; senate response and adoption of criteria; administration creation of a provisional budget plan; senate Budget Committee response to it; state system testimony before the legislature's Ways and Means Committee; board instructions for the final 1991–93 budget; and final budget preparation by the president. Throughout this lengthy process, the AAUP would be consulted.[37]

At a special meeting on 25 January, the faculty senate addressed a document prepared by the administration entitled, "Criteria for the Allocation of New Resources, Reallocation of Existing Resources, and Reduction and Elimination of Programs." It was a ten-page document compiled by the administration from an Oregon State University proposal and a 1991 Portland State planning document, which twice had been revised by the Budget Committee, that was the most comprehensive framework for retrenchment worked out in the history of the University. At this meeting, Ramaley conveyed the sense of urgency under which PSU was working when she explained that a provisional 1991–93 budget had to be submitted to the chancellor in two weeks, a document cutting 6.5 percent ($8.2 million) from the University's original budget. To prepare several options for retrenchment, Ramaley announced a "transition team" made up of six administrators, six faculty members, and headed by Interim Provost Robert Frank.[38]

The "Criteria" document was discussed briefly in the senate, with most attention paid to its extremely broad definition of "programs." Underlying everyone's considerations was the clear realization some people would be cut. There was no hope the economy would improve sufficiently, that the legislature would become more generous, or that the citizens would oppose retrenchment of State expenditures. Given these circumstances, it was hardly surprising that the "Criteria" document was approved by the senate.[39]

President Ramaley announced a plan for retrenchment following the adoption of these criteria, a plan the senate addressed on 11 February. The most spectacular element of it was the elimination of the School of Health and Human Performance. The most innovative feature of the plan was to "suspend" (not admit students for one year), rather than eliminate, certain programs. The two most vehement objections to the retrenchment plan was the fear it was an attempt to "restructure" the University, to downgrade the liberal arts in the guise of meeting financial problems, and that it was prepared without consultation with faculty committees. By 4 March, Ramaley assured the faculty a tentative budget had been established for 1991–93. She also attempted to be reassuring in stating that other institutions in the state system were "suspending" programs and that the suspensions could be lifted at any time without seeking approval of the state board. She promised no tenured or tenure-track faculty would be laid off and that all positions to be eliminated would come from administration, classified service, and non-academic areas of the University—a position gratifying to faculty but hardly morale-building for the underpaid civil service employees. The president also announced four constitutional committees—Budget, Curriculum, Educational Policies, and Graduate Council—were reviewing the work of the transition team and offering "a legitimate second opinion" on its decisions.[40]

By the end of March, twenty-five persons had been notified their jobs were being eliminated: eight tenure-track faculty, eight classified employees, three non-academic personnel, and six unranked faculty. At this time, the four constitutional committees made preliminary reports to the senate on the transition team's work. Again, as so often in the past, the proper constitutional processes for curriculum adjustments were not followed for lack of time. By this date, it was too late to bother with the committees' views about program elimination, as the state board had already acted on programs. The AAUP on 1 April submitted a motion for the record, which was adopted, protesting the by-passing of the senate in the retrenchment process, but the protest was a formality. At this meeting, however, female faculty had somewhat greater success in getting a motion passed that asked all program and personnel cuts be reviewed carefully so campus diversity could be maintained.[41]

By early May's senate meeting, the constitutional committees were still reporting on the work of the transition team. The Curriculum Committee disagreed with the transition team's decision to suspend the bachelor's degrees in Philosophy, Physics, and Health. Since the suspension of these programs had saved no money, there was nothing to be lost financially by restoring them. The senate accepted this recommendation. The graduate council's recommendation that the master's degree programs in Health Education, Political Science, Sociology, and Fine Arts be restored was also approved by the senate. Although the programs were restored, it took over a year to do so, and, of course, suspension of programs for any length of time was damaging. However, the senate did not seek to overturn the council's support of the transition team's recommendation to eliminate the doctoral options in Criminal Justice and Electrical Engineering and the MAT/MST degrees in Physics. The Budget Committee reported it had disagreed with many of the recommendations of the transition team and would now coordinate the recommendations from the other three committees and present them to the senate.[42]

President Ramaley's first academic year concluded in June. At this month's senate meeting, the Educational Policies Committee, the fourth of the constitutional committees dealing with retrenchment, made its report. It made recommendations concerning program review procedures, but the senate ignored them. The senate did, however, accept the Budget Committee's recommendations for the 1991–92 academic year. For this year alone, as an emergency measure, departments were to maximize student credit hours by offering more late afternoon and evening sections and by using any carryover monies and one-time savings to employ part-time faculty to increase enrollment.[43]

By early winter 1992, the budget crisis was again the foremost concern of the University community. Measure Five was to become effective in stages. To address the first stage of tax reduction, Gov. Barbara Roberts had to propose a reduced budget that would probably amount to $138 million for higher education. She would then meet with the chancellor who, in turn, would confer with the system presidents. At an unknown time in the future, each institution would have to decide how it would meet its share of the reduction for the 1993–95 biennium. To prepare for this reduction, President Ramaley planned to appoint a fifteen-member budget reduction team, with representatives from the administration, the AAUP, the Associated Students, the Oregon State Employees Association, and the chair of the Budget Committee, among others. The new committee was to follow the criteria for budget reduction adopted by the faculty senate on 25 January 1991. Again, this approach seemed sensible on the surface, but, in following these criteria, the committee was furnished no effective guidelines for distinguishing which programs were indispensable for a university curriculum from those that were not.[44]

Portland State faculty responded to the budget crisis in another way, by attempting to collaborate with its colleagues at other state system institutions. On 8 February 1992, the Interinstitutional Faculty Senate recommended to Governor Roberts that she call a special meeting of the legislature to do something to cover the cuts required by Measure Five. The letter to the governor stressed that faculty and maintenance had been cut back, tuitions raised, and more than three thousand students excluded from state system institutions because of enrollment limitations due to the property tax limitation measure. The governor did nothing.[45]

By May, the state system had prepared budget guidelines, and the University administration had announced a schedule of meetings at Portland State to discuss them. The president also announced she would appoint a campus budget reduction team. On 1 June, Ramaley announced formally she was invoking the relevant article of the collective bargaining agreement in order to initiate the program-reduction process. The task of reduction was formidable, to trim 20 percent of the forthcoming budget. At a continuation of this meeting two days later, the senate came to grips again—as it had in January 1991—with how to justify program reductions. What it had before it now was a statement, euphemistically entitled, "Resource Allocation Criteria," prepared by the University Planning Council and the Budget Committee. The tenor of the senate debate was favorable to the new criteria, at least in the sense they were superior to the earlier ones, and they passed with minor amendments.[46]

The budget reduction team, composed of faculty, students, and staff, considered a retrenchment plan proposed by the provost and the vice-president for Finance and Administration. The plan was considered by the deans and in a public hearing. The comments were, in turn, considered by the president before she made her final decisions. Although no tenured faculty member was dismissed under this plan, many positions made vacant by retirements were not to be filled. The cumulative effects of Measure Five were disastrous, and until some method of adequately financing the university was acceptable to Oregon's citizens, the state's future in the higher education realm was bleak indeed.[47]

One financial matter did give some hope, at least temporarily, to Portland State administration and faculty. It was the promise of the chancellor to design a fairer mode of distributing money to system institutions than FTE. In the 1983–84 academic year, this new formula was instituted. Called the Budget Allocation System (BAS) Model, it was designed "to permit allocation of funds on a basis that recognizes differential costs of various fields of study rather than rely on State System average costs by lower division, upper division, and graduate levels of student populations." The ingredients to be factored into the BAS model included instruction, research, academic support, student services, physical plant operations and maintenance, and institution support.[48]

The BAS model was more beneficial to Portland State than the earlier formula, but it was not completely fair. Although still driven by FTE count, it did recognize the difference between FTE students and head-count students, an advantage to PSU, which had so many part-time students. It also was helpful—as it was to all the institutions—in that it did not depend on slight variations in enrollment but rather on broader "corridors" of enrollment. On the other hand, the BAS model granted more money for doctoral education than for undergraduate or master's, a disadvantage for Portland State, which was restrained by the state board and the chancellor—reflecting the fears of the University of Oregon and Oregon State University—from offering a broad range of doctoral programs. Other disadvantages were that the BAS model did take account of equipment replacement, but this was of little help to Portland State, which had little equipment to replace. The model also shorted the University in its allocations for library funding.[49]

TWENTY-ONE

Curriculum, Teaching, Students · 1974–1996

T he major curricular change in the realm of graduate education was a reprise of the struggle over graduate scientific and
engineering education that had first arisen in the 1960s. This
time, the motivating factor was not the space race with the
Soviet Union but the severe depression that struck Oregon in 1979
and lasted until the next decade. As forest products slumped as the
state's leading industry, many in the public, education, and in politics
(but, to their credit, not many in high technology itself) saw the high-
tech enterprise as a "golden boy" that would furnish the economic
opportunities that would substitute for declining traditional industries. High-tech industry would not only profit the state economically,
it would do so via clean, non-polluting enterprises that would spare
the state the ravages of environmental destruction. Those who placed
their faith in high technology also realized it came with a price—the
development of an education system that would bring and retain the
new enterprises from elsewhere in the United States and from around
the world.

By the 1960s, the Oregon Graduate Center was the only university in the Portland metropolitan area dedicated principally to this type
of education, but it was not a major university and its focus was applied, not theoretical, science. Portland State had graduate programs
in Science and Engineering, but its only scientific doctoral work was
in Environmental Sciences. Oregon and Oregon State had doctoral
programs in Science and Technology, but their campuses were distant
from the Tualatin Valley of Washington County, where the base of high
technology had been located since the 1950s.

In this hopeful yet anxious situation, many attempted to become the leader in providing the advanced scientific and technical education the region required if high technology was to be its savior. There were three or four eager candidates for this role: The Oregon Graduate Center had location and experience but was short of resources; Oregon and Oregon State also had tradition and the advantage—such as it was—of being publicly supported institutions; Portland State furnished a downtown location that was partly advantageous (in the cultural amenities provided by a large university) and partly disadvantageous (not being in Washington County). OGC and Portland State might ally against the lower Willamette Valley institutions. The three state system institutions might cooperate against OGC. Oregon and Oregon State might seek to develop programs—even entire campuses—in the teeth of each other's opposition and that of Portland State. Portland State, being the largest urban university, might become predominant.

The sorting out of these educational contingencies began in the legislature's 1982 special session, which Gov. Victor Atiyeh had called to make cuts in programs in view of the $314-million shortfall in revenue projections for the coming biennium. During the session, Rep. Vera Katz of Portland introduced a bill to establish the Oregon Consortium for High Technology Education. It was a bill favored by the Oregon Council of the American Electronics Association (AEA), a national, high-technology trade association. The Oregon Council in 1982 was the first state affiliate of the AEA to engage formally in political lobbying and support of candidates and governmental measures. Katz and the council were able to persuade the governor to make the consortium plan a part of his economic development program and, thus, to unite formally high technology, higher education, and economic progress into an appealing political triangle. With this support, the bill became law.[1]

The legislature appropriated $500,000 to fund the consortium. Katz, never a strong supporter of Portland State and only a slightly stronger advocate for the state system as an entity, saw to it the money was funneled not only to state system institutions but also to private schools, such as OGC, and to the community colleges (e.g., Portland Community College, of which she was an employee). The allocation of funds, according to the law, was to be by the Educational Coordinating Commission, a state agency created in 1975 to plan, coordinate, and evaluate education from kindergarten to university within the state. Its role was mainly advisory in fact and mischievous and confusing in practice (the commission was abolished in 1987), but, in this case, it had real authority. Katz wanted it to spend the consortium money because she did not trust the separate institutions to do it, and she believed if the state system alone were given the disbursement power, it would distribute the money equally among its component institutions, rather than giving it to exceptionally promising programs.

The consortium, whose members were appointed by the governor, consisted of ten business, political, and educational leaders but not the chancellor nor any president from a state system institution. These appointments were a sharp and apparently intentional slap in the face of the state system, in general, and of its only Portland institution, in particular. As it turned out, the workings of the consortium vitiated Katz's ostensible purpose of concentrating resources on promising programs. Instead, it became an academic pork barrel. The consortium dispensed its money (ultimately increased to $3 million) in two phases from 1983–85. Thirty-two projects were funded, distributed among six community colleges, one private college, two private universities, and three public universities. Portland State obtained funds for two laboratories (computer vision and laser system) and for some electrical engineering and research equipment.[2]

Largely shut out of the consortium, the state system began its own campaign to gain a greater share of state support. Under the leadership of Chancellor William E. Davis, appointed in 1982, the board adopted a "Proposal for a High Technology Engineering/Computer Science Program for Industry." The heart of Davis's plan was a Council for Advanced Science and Engineering Education/Research for Industry (CASERI). This council would be headed by a director responsible to the chancellor. As with the consortium, it would have representatives not only from the state system institutions but from private universities and the high-tech industry, as well. The purposes of the council were to identify the needs of industry and to match them with the resources of universities; to strengthen academic and research programs "in areas essential to high-technology industry;" and to develop educational programs to serve industry.[3]

When this program was translated from the general to the specific, Portland State got a bit more than one third of the loaf. PSU was to play "a central role" in a state system program of electrical and computer engineering in the Portland metropolitan area, which required the creation of nine new full-time faculty positions distributed, how-

ever, among Portland State, the University of Oregon, and Oregon
State University. That Portland State was not to have all of these positions made no sense intellectually or geographically, but the power of
the two older universities gave them a strong foothold in this promising endeavor.[4]

Both CASERI and the consortium, however, remained more promising than successful, largely because of interinstitutional rivalry, their
cumbersome bureaucratic structure, and insufficient state funding.
But not all supporters of scientific and technological engineering gave
up, however, especially as a potential new source of funding emerged.
This was the state lottery, approved by voters in fall 1984. With this
money supply at hand, the 1985 legislative session saw the introduction of another measure conceived by the Oregon Council of the
American Electronics Association and sponsored by Representative
Katz. This bill was to create the Oregon Center for Advanced Technology Education (OCATE). OCATE was allocated $500,000, plus the bal-
ance of the monies as yet unexpended by CASERI. In order to eliminate interinstitutional struggles during the legislative process, the
precise goals of the law were left to a new governor's Commission on
Technical Education, which was to be an advisory body to the new center. (There was also a sub-body called the Advisory Committee to the
Commission on Technical Education, made up of various public and
private university presidents).[5]

Portland State's response to the creation of OCATE was probably
best expressed by President Blumel, who saw it as possibly beneficial
but feared "if it proves to be a device for bringing ordinary advanced
work from Oregon and Oregon State and for supporting the Oregon
Graduate Center with public funds, or if it means a new institution of
higher education, the consequences could be serious."[6]

OCATE's first program was to establish master's and doctoral programs for the benefit of the high-tech community. It was also to develop a master's degree in Business Administration, sponsored jointly by
the three state system universities. The faculty for these programs
would be drawn from the state system institutions, Oregon private colleges and universities, and institutions from outside the state. The site
of OCATE was the Washington County campus of Portland Community College (PCC). Portland State and PCC, as well as other private and public institutions, also became involved in a program at
Portland Community College to furnish high-tech training for students
who did not want to take an undergraduate degree. Supposedly, this

arrangement, coupled with OCATE, would furnish the equivalent of a technical university, but this dream was only realized on paper.[7]

Although none of these graduate programs were very successful because of their late start compared to other states, interinstitutional rivalry, and the fluctuating condition of the state's economy, talk of expanding doctoral programs in the Portland area continued into the late 1980s. Natale Sicuro, Joseph Blumel's successor as president, asked the chancellor and state board to consider a proposal for a Vollum Graduate School of Science, Engineering, and Technology (after Howard Vollum, founder of Tektronix) at Portland State. It would have created an institution that would complete the graduate research and instructional programs in Science and Engineering at Portland State and OGC; include OCATE; and be housed both on the former Graduate School campus in Washington County and downtown at Portland State. Not many of those who spoke said much favorably about PSU's role in these programs. Usually, it was quite the reverse, with the University of Oregon, Oregon State, and their supporters in the media assailing any such plans. In interpreting the decline of higher education in Oregon, a Eugene television editorial (KVAL-TV, March 1987) stated, "Perhaps the most debilitating practice has been the effort to bolster Portland State University by taking money away from Oregon and Oregon State and financing duplicate programs in Portland." By this time, years of experience in being slighted made the PSU faculty wary about proposals for new programs. Their suspicions were reconfirmed in December 1988, when Paul Bragdon, Gov. Neil Goldschmidt's assistant for education, spoke to UofO faculty members. Among other points, Bragdon said, "It's important to make a distinction between the two major research universities in the state—University of Oregon and Oregon State University—and the rest of the system's schools. The educational needs of the greater Portland area could be served better, especially at the graduate levels, but that should be accomplished by cooperation with the larger schools, not by establishing a third major university."[8]

When Governor Goldschmidt in 1989 talked of improving doctoral work in the Portland area, he also suggested the need for it to be examined once again. (It would be the ninth study of this issue.) The policy of delay was annoying but more so was the governor's plan to raise tuition in the state system. This may have been an economic necessity, but what antagonized PSU faculty and administration was that their institution would receive a lower tuition increase than the

Oregon and Oregon State and that Portland State would not be permitted to retain any of the tuition increase to improve its programs.
The governor's budget proposal also included $6 million in matching
funds for Oregon and Oregon State but only $3 million for Portland
State. Furthermore, the governor was simultaneously proposing tax
monies be spent on new programs at other colleges and universities
(including private ones) in the Portland area.[9]

The faculty senate could at least complain about these proposals,
although its influence would be minimal. It passed a strong resolution
condemning them and, in the resolution, had the pleasure of turning
the old "duplication" argument back on the University's traditional ad-
versaries. "Duplication of facilities and equipment within a few miles
of each other is costly and impractical," it declared and suggested in
conclusion that "this legislative session should continue to build on
the existing facilities and personnel of PSU, rather than divert educational funds and energies elsewhere." The following month, the senate invited Paul Bragdon to speak on the future of higher education
in the Portland area. Bragdon, the former president of Reed College,
was suspect in the eyes of many at Portland State because private education was to be a beneficiary of the governor's plan. His remarks and
his response to questions at this meeting confirmed this suspicion.[10]

Essentially, Bragdon told the faculty the governor thought well of
Portland State and of higher education in general—particularly as an
engine of economic development—but that the new study was necessary because it was to be done (unlike the previous eight) by an outside group. He further said that the lower tuition increase was to maximize access to Portland State and that the matching-funds differential (in a masterpiece of obfuscatory phrasing) had been misread at
Portland State: "It was not the governor's intention," Bragdon declared,
"to give a signal that PSU should be downgraded or that graduate
programs should be stripped; rather, PSU should continue on its mission." Bragdon also repeated the true-but-timeworn bromide that the
state budget had other calls on it than higher education and that,
accordingly, the faculty should publicize its case for funds among the
public and legislators. The governor's attitude should not have come
as a surprise to the PSU community, for in a campaign speech at Portland State the year before, he had declared Oregon could afford only
one first-class university.[11]

Other curricular issues, like graduate education in the Portland
area, had lives of their own; they arose, disappeared, then reemerged.

One important development that institutionalized Portland State's old community service role was proposed by Pres. Joseph Blumel in 1974. This was a School of Urban Affairs that brought together six curricular or research programs: Administration of Justice, Institute on Aging, Black Studies certificate program, Urban Studies certificate program, the Urban Studies Center, and the Urban Studies graduate programs. A joint university-community committee approved the plan for the school in 1974, and the faculty senate endorsed it in November 1975. In April 1976, the state board gave final approval. A proposal from the Foreign Languages and Literatures Department to change thirty of its courses from four to five hours per course was discussed. Although the argument here was to reward students for large amounts of work, the idea of having courses carry more credit hours would arise again in the context of a proposed change to the semester system in the 1980s and the revamped general education program in the 1990s. The issue of general education made its periodic appearance. At Portland State, the general education program had never, from its beginnings, followed the Columbia-Harvard models of broad surveys of literature, history, art, and music. Rather, because of departmental rivalries, "general education" was erroneously defined as a collection of courses, some of which—by no stretch of the imagination—met any definition of general education. From time to time, this state of affairs called forth reformers, but none was very successful.[12]

In March 1975, the Academic Requirements Committee, under the chairmanship of Charles M. White (History), proposed all courses offered by the Colleges of Arts and Letters, Science, and Social Science be acceptable for meeting the general education requirements (except for two required English composition courses). The proposal was discussed at length but almost entirely on technical grounds (e.g., how would it apply to transfer students?). Only one senator, Whitney Bates of the History Department, objected on the grounds of content, arguing the proposal diluted the general education requirement to "anything goes." The committee knew Bates was right and that what he was criticizing—the "anything goes" principle—was not true general education. But it also knew the faculty, in practice, was comfortable with this evasion. It knew whenever students petitioned for exemptions from the rules to allow them to count courses excluded from the general education roster, the departments almost in every case approved the exemption. The committee knew, also, that the list of eligible courses for general education was always out-of-date, as new courses were never on the list. Finally, departments never admitted any of their courses were unacceptable for the general education of students. Fear of losing departmental credits, in other words, overrode devotion to the general education of students. The proposal passed.[13]

In 1979, a general education committee tried again to define general education, its purposes, and how to design a curriculum to meet them. The committee labored long on these issues, but its proposals for meaningful reform foundered on departmental fears of losing enrollment. In 1986, the Academic Requirements Committee proposed to reduce the number of courses eligible for general education distribution requirements. This effort was successful but still left as eligible 56 percent of the University's requirements. Again, little was said in the debate about the meaning of a liberal arts education or of general education within it.[14]

In 1992, Provost Michael Reardon set in motion a review of the undergraduate curriculum, including the general education program. The review was conducted by a general education working group, which produced a report in 1993 that tried again to sort out the volatile ingredients of a general education curriculum into a coherent philosophy and program. Although unable to agree on a core of knowledge that marked the classic Columbia and Harvard programs of an earlier era, the working group did extricate general education from the collection of courses that had hitherto defined it at the University. What the working group did agree to was not substance but process. It grounded its report on the premise (which always had been a component of true general education everywhere) that general education programs should assist "students in making the critical transition from being receptors of 'facts' to becoming lifelong learners."[15]

Students in the recommended curriculum, among other qualities they were to acquire from participating in the program, were to learn to think critically, explore issues of ethics and social responsibility, become cognizant of issues of diversity and multiculturalism, and write and speak clearly. They were to do so by climbing an intellectual ladder that comprised: a freshman "core," course "clusters" for sophomore through senior levels, and a senior "capstone experience" of community exposure and community service. Students were to be given choices throughout the program, although from a limited range of courses, and small classes and team-teaching marked the freshman and sophomore years of the program. The faculty senate, with surprisingly little resistance, adopted the essential components of the new general education program (renamed University Studies) on 8 November 1993, in time to begin it in fall term 1994.

There was a battle in 1982 over the effort to introduce courses in military science. The specific issue was not whether Portland State would initially have a full Reserve Officers' Training Corps (ROTC) at the institution, but whether its students could take ROTC courses at PSU through an arrangement with OSU, which did offer such a program. The Curriculum Committee and the Educational Policies Committee both recommended Portland State students be eligible to take these courses, a recommendation that set off a spirited debate in the senate. The arguments in favor were that public universities should support public policies; that students in the program would receive scholarship money from the army; that students should not be denied the option of ROTC; and that liberally educated officers would be superior to those who received their education at purely military institutions. Those in opposition declared ROTC courses were training, not education; that the professors were not appointed by the University but rather by the army; that homosexuals were not eligible for military commissions; that the University was cutting existing programs; that ROTC would be divisive; that war had been made obsolete by nuclear weapons; and (incredibly) that if the University rejected military scholarships, "It would send a message to the government that other means of financial aid to college students should be provided." After the second day of debate, the measure passed by a single vote.[16]

The senate vote did not end the controversy. Enough faculty members signed a petition to call for a special meeting of the entire faculty on 31 January 1983. When it was obvious the majority of those at the meeting opposed ROTC, the chair of the Curriculum Committee called for a mail ballot of the faculty to decide the issue. Even though the mail ballot was decided on early in the meeting, the faculty remained for some time afterward to discuss the matter with more than twenty faculty members participating in the debate. When the mail ballot was counted, the ROTC courses were approved.[17]

In 1987, ROTC came to the fore again as a curricular issue. This time, it took the form of a recommendation from the Educational Policies Committee for a full-fledged Department of Military Science to replace the adjunct status with Oregon State. The main argument in favor of becoming a "host" school was that students in the program would have a greater opportunity for financial assistance from the army—particularly in the form of four-year scholarships, as these were

only available to students at host schools. A secondary argument was
that if the institution did not accept host status at this time, the army
would not offer it again for another three to five years. A statement by
a group of students was read at the meeting in opposition to the new
department, asserting various arguments as to its undesirability. Faculty
members spoke on both sides of the issue, and, then, Rudi Nussbaum
of the Physics Department raised a procedural objection. He asserted
the proposal had not come to the senate through the proper channel
of the Curriculum Committee (or any other constitutional committee)
but rather through an administrative committee. He moved the proposal be sent back to the Curriculum Committee. His motion was defeated but so, too, was the main motion to establish the department,
by a vote of twenty-six to twenty. In ordinary circumstances, this would
have been the end of the matter, but Pres. Natale Sicuro passed the
issue on to the state board, which voted to institute the department.[18]

The religious dimension in the University curriculum was enhanced
in the 1990s through an innovative program launched through Portland
Campus Christian Ministry (PCCM). Campus Ministry had long been
involved in offering credit courses on a variety of topics. Since its early
days, the PCCM staff had wished for a more formal role in the intellectual life of the University. As early as 1963, hopes were raised when
Portland's First Christian Church discussed endowing a school of religion at Portland State, complete with a salaried professor and classroom space in a building they hoped to construct near the College.
Nothing came of this idea, as the church put its land to other use nor
was there ever the realization of a plan proposed in 1968 by some Portland State faculty members, advised by Merlyn Satrom of the PCCM
staff, to institute a religious studies department at the College.[19]

The courses dealing with religious themes at Portland State were
not presented to students in any organized fashion through a departmental major or a certificate program, and it was difficult to muster
enthusiasm to overcome the financial and bureaucratic obstacles to
establish such a program. In 1974, for example, the minutes of the
PCCM board's annual meeting recorded both encouraging and discouraging news: "The Department of Religion which has long been a
topic of discussion with the PCCM Staff and Directors must be set
aside again, but there is a possibility that there could be a 'Chair of
Religion' endowed." Again, nothing came of the professorship hope
nor of a proposal to have the University list at one place in its catalog
courses for "an area in religious studies."[20]

The idea of a Religious Studies Center was broached informally in 1978 by William Hamilton, a prominent theologian who was also dean of the College of Arts and Letters, but nothing came of it for more than a decade. A more productive step toward the institutionalization of religious studies at Portland State was taken in 1984. In that year, Rabbi Joshua Stampfer of Congregation Nevah Shalom led the organization of the Institute for Judaic Studies of the Pacific Northwest. Although housed in the Division of Continuing Education at Portland State, the Institute served as a catalyst for educational institutions in the entire region. Its work has included helping departments develop courses, co-sponsoring conferences, and publishing procedures of several of the conferences. The Institute's scholarly programs were not only impressive in themselves but helped inspire a program at PCCM.[21]

The Reverend John Rosenberg, Lutheran Campus Pastor at PSU, initiated the plan that finally brought the old hope for a religious studies program to fruition. In 1989, in discussing the future of Campus Ministry, he wrote, "One scenario is that the current ecumenical partners look into the possibility of focusing their energy on the development of an 'Institute for Religious Studies' at PSU in partnership with the University. In a sense, K-House [Koinonia] has performed this function unofficially for years. The idea here would be to formalize it and be intentional about it." Although Rosenberg soon left Campus Ministry, his successor, Harold Schlachtenhaufen, with the support of the Lutheran Campus Council, took the idea for an institute to the PCCM board, which "passed the motion to develop a proposal for a Religious Study Institute in conjunction with Portland State University."[22]

Schlachtenhaufen drafted a letter of agreement between PCCM and the University that offered credit courses as part of the Portland State curriculum in return for the University carrying out the administrative work in presenting the courses. Negotiations with the University bureaucracy proceeded for more than a year but were never completed. By summer 1991, however, proponents of an institute had moved ahead independently, and an organizing board was meeting. Portland State was unwilling to have its name in the title of the institute, so at the suggestion of Donald Moor (Philosophy), the name Portland Center for the Study of Religion was adopted. It was decided not only to have a board of directors but also an honorary board to formulate policies for the new institute. In the academic year 1992–93, the Institute offered its first course, "Religion for the New Millennium," which began one month before the first official board of directors

Koinonia House, the building of the Portland Campus Ministry

meeting on 21 October 1992. Fittingly, John Rosenberg became the first president of the board, which by 1995 included twenty-four members from the Campus Ministry staff, faculty from the Portland-area universities and colleges, and community members. Staff members Joan Hunt and Palmer Pardington were instrumental in devising the first programs of the center. Although the center embarked on an ambitious fundraising plan in September 1993 under an executive director, it was difficult to raise money—as it always has been in Portland for intellectual endeavors—but the center persisted and succeeded in laying a foundation for additional courses when funds permitted. By spring term 1995, the center was sponsoring five courses for academic credit, plus several non-credit courses and discussion groups. In 1996, the center opened an office in Koinonia House, staffed by an office manager. From its inception, the center had been a truly ecumenical effort, with participation from Christians, Jews, and Muslims. It was, thus, appropriate that Philip E. Harder, a member of the staff since 1977, served as president of the National Campus Ministry Association from 1994–96.[23]

One of the most frustrating curricular issues of the recent past was the expensive, frustrating, and fruitless attempt to institute the semester system. In spring 1977, the faculty of the University of Oregon had voted in favor of converting to the semester system, and the Portland State faculty senate in June passed a resolution in favor of a study of the advantages of such a calendar. Nothing came of the idea at this time, but it appeared again during the 1986–87 academic year. This time, the state system seemed committed to the changeover and planned to have it instituted in fall term 1990. The plan was for an "early semester," that is, for a calendar that would have the students return to work before Labor Day and begin their winter vacation before Christmas. In the spring, the semester would run from the middle of January to the middle of May. Both semesters would comprise sixteen weeks, including one week of final examinations. Each course under the semester system would carry three hours of credit.[24]

At Portland State, Michael Reardon, associate vice-president for Academic Affairs, was given the task of chairing a committee to implement this framework. It was an involved job that had ramifications ranging from dealing with the chancellor's office to the community colleges, and from revising the general education requirements to shaping a summer school calendar. Although there is no formal record of their sentiment (they were not asked as a faculty to vote on the issue), most faculty members seemed to favor the semester system on the grounds it would make for a more leisurely examination of subject matter and permit the assignment of longer research papers and fuller reading lists. By June 1987, Reardon announced to the senate that during the following fall term the conversion process to the semester system would begin at the departmental level. There was also a series of working committees that undertook different dimensions of the assignment given to a calendar conversion coordinating committee. All seemed to be on course for the implementation date of fall 1990.[25]

Over the winter of 1987–88, however, the semester plan began to lose momentum. At the February 1988 senate meeting, Jim Heath, chair of Portland State's conversion committee, summarized the opposition that had developed to the proposal in concluding, "There was much anguish and frustration....Community colleges felt they had not been properly consulted, and that OSSHE faculty also felt that they had not been allowed to give much input in the deliberations." Certain legislators were reported to be voicing their objections to the semester system based on the opposition of the food processing, tourism, and agriculture industries, all of which feared a loss of their temporary labor force because of an earlier starting date in the fall. In the end, after spending thousands of dollars and expending thousands of hours of staff and faculty time, the state system on 9 December 1988 recognized the scope of the opposition and fled the field. The plan to alter the semester system was an enormous fiasco in every respect.[26]

A compelling and novel curricular issue of these days was the attempt to add a "diversity" requirement to the undergraduate degree requirements. The issue was first raised by Darrell Millner (Black Studies) at the October 1990 meeting of the faculty senate. The senate unanimously adopted his motion that the Academic Requirements Committee investigate curricula at other universities that presented a "diverse range of ethnic, cultural, and gender based perspectives" and to report to the senate the possibility of instituting such a program at Portland State. In June 1991, the committee made its report. It stated it could not determine the effectiveness of such courses at other institutions, because no studies had been made. It did not recommend a special required course in cultural, ethnic, and gender diversity. What it did recommend was a requirement of six hours of courses in cultural, ethnic, and gender diversity chosen by a committee appointed by the faculty senate. The requirement was to be evaluated after two years.[27]

The motion was debated at some length. There was fear expressed by one senator that the whole idea was based on "political correctness" and, hence, would be counter-productive. Others wondered what the motion implied, as it was difficult to vote on it without a specific list of approved courses. The effect of the requirement on transfer students was weighed as was the result of adding another requirement for students who already had trouble fitting in existing ones. The difficulty of defining courses with "diversity" content was discussed. In the end, the motion was passed, after it had been amended to make the Academic Requirements Committee the body to select the list of appropriate courses.[28]

This committee then faced the formidable task of developing criteria for the approved courses. It called for advice from the entire University community to develop these standards, and, by January 1992, the draft statement of criteria for diversity courses was presented to the senate, based on voluntary contributions from twelve departments. Of the two courses required for fulfilling the requirement, one was based on content dealing with "racial, cultural, gender, or ethnic groups which have historically experienced oppression or discrimination." The second course focused on intergroup relations, in the context of issues such as intolerance and inequality in the context of intergroup relations. There were seven requirements to make courses in these two categories eligible for inclusion, although a course need not include all of them—for example, to "examine the historical or social origin of differentiation based on race, ethnicity, religion, social class, or gender." Based on comments made in the senate and elsewhere, the committee revised the criteria by February to incorporate a third category of courses, which included those dealing with "non-Western" societies and requiring the two courses be taken in different departments, including the gender courses in the diversity requirement. After further debate in the February meeting, during which "disability" was added as a criteria, the matter was delayed until the following month, when it was passed after engendering only one comment.[29]

Next to the faculty, the most important element in the teaching process is the library, which in the last quarter century underwent a series of successes and reverses concomitant to that of the University as a whole. Compared to Oregon and Oregon State, Portland State entered the recent era well behind these universities in library resources. Commenting on this situation in a 1971 editorial, the *Oregonian* noted, "Its shelves now hold only 26 volumes per student as compared to 42 per student at Oregon State University and 66 per student at the University of Oregon." The newspaper hoped the new Portland State University Foundation would help narrow this gap.[30]

Any optimism about great gains at the library, however, was belied by the grim realities of the State's finances and their effect on the higher education system. In October 1971, for example, 25 percent of the library's book budget was frozen by the administration to help meet cuts mandated by the state board. Cuts were sometimes delayed or reduced by outside revenues, such as a Title II grant of $77,555 in 1971, which made up for much of the aforementioned book budget loss, or another federal grant of $75,000 for programs emphasizing minority groups and the urban environment that came in summer 1973. Even when cuts were not made or when last-minute financial rescues emerged, an enormous amount of time was spent and psychic energy drained in preparing contingency plans, such as one in 1973 to cut $200,000 from the library budget in the following two years, which would have resulted in the loss of two professional librarians and fourteen members of the classified staff. A particularly appreciated effort to help the library was the organization by Kenneth Hawkins, a History undergraduate, of Students for an Effective Library, which persuaded the Incidental Fee Committee to donate $10,000 of its annual allocation for the purchase of library books.[31]

Besides the reduced services and fewer books and periodicals forced by budget cuts, patrons found other striking changes in library operations. On the positive side, the library in 1972 became the Oregon Regional Depository for federal documents. This status meant faculty and students were now able to use a vast array of materials from the United States government to facilitate their research. After January 1977, no new entries were made in the card catalog. Patrons, thereafter, were required to use motorized microfilm readers for new materials, with microfiche supplements to keep it up to date. The microform catalog was a stop gap, however, as computers were en route. In 1981, library staff were able to do computer searches of major subject indices for students returning for fall term. Other new computers permitted library staff to automate cataloging of materials through the Washington Library Network.[32]

In 1989, fall term saw the installation of computers that made it possible to locate 85 percent of the library's holdings. Bar codes were installed on books in a five-day period in September when the library was closed. The new system made holdings accessible not only to patrons in the library but also to those possessing home computers, who could access the collection by modem.[33]

The most evident change for library patrons, however, was the construction of the second addition, the east block, of the Library West building. (The third part of the original 1963 plan, as yet unaccomplished, was to place four additional stories on top of the first two buildings.) Authorization for this structure came slowly and grudgingly from the state board and the legislature. Frank Rodgers, the librarian, had hoped for it to be completed in 1974. Five years after that date, the building was made the third priority on the University's own construction list for the 1979–81 biennium. The state board did not at first include it at any place on its priority list, but President Blumel persuaded the board to accord it at least position eighteen. Seven more years passed before the state board in 1986 made Phase II its third priority, and the legislature voted on 25 June 1987, two days before adjournment and with the outcome in doubt until the last minute, to expend $11 million to build the structure. Assistance, while late, was welcome. By 1987, a library built to house 420,000 volumes was holding 750,000 books, about 10 percent of the collection was in storage, and seating was half as great as recommended by national library standards.[34]

As with the original, the Phase II addition was designed by the architectural firm of Skidmore, Owings, and Merrill. Its most evident feature was a graceful concave glass wall that enveloped the entrance elevation and preserved a 150-year-old copper beech tree of mammoth proportions. The size of the addition, seventy-two thousand square feet, nearly doubled the size of the additional Library West structure. Indeed, when members of the public attended the dedication in November 1991, they found a functional and attractive building that was a credit to all concerned with its planning and implementation, especially among Portland State staff members Mike Irish, construction project manager, and Robert Lockerby, head of readers services and engineering librarian. Not the least of their achievements was successfully scheduling the work so that the library could still serve students and faculty throughout the two years of construction.[35]

Within the new building, technology facilitated the traditional functions of the library in preserving and disseminating knowledge. The most spectacular aspect of the new technology manifested itself in fall term 1995, when a large computer laboratory went into service in a space on the first floor of Library West—fittingly, the site of the old card catalog. The new facility, comprising forty computers, enabled students to gain access to the Internet and the Portland Area Library System (PORTALS) network, which linked all major colleges and universities in the Portland metropolitan area with the Multnomah County Library.[36]

So far as faculty affairs went, the mid-1970s saw the resolution to probably the last matter remaining from the days of Vietnam War protests: Frank Giese's trial was finally held. He was convicted in October 1974 of the crime of conspiring to commit offenses against the United States and was sentenced in November to a maximum term of five years in jail. Then, the question of his suitability to continue as a faculty member was addressed. President Blumel convened an *ad hoc* hearing committee to consider the matter. The committee recommended Giese not be sanctioned by the University, contending his ability to teach had not been impaired by the conviction. After deliberating on the matter, President Blumel rejected the committee's recommendation and, in effect, dismissed Giese. There were questions raised in the senate by one faculty member, but the vast majority of the faculty acquiesced to the president's decision.[37]

Faculty members were more concerned with their benefits than with Frank Giese. There were changes made in the faculty fringe benefit system that had begun with the creation of the Public Employees Retirement System (PERS) in 1946. In 1953, PERS had been integrated with Social Security, and in 1967, the State permitted faculty members to choose between PERS and the Teachers Insurance and Annuity-College Retirement Equities Fund (TIAA-CREF), a retirement alternative with annual earnings of more than $4,800. In 1968, the TIAA-CREF option became less desirable, as it was ruled it could not be collected if members wished to protect their pre-1968 contributions to PERS. After 1973, a portion of unused sick leave benefits could be added to the retirement benefits. There was talk of creating a faculty club, but while an *ad hoc* committee resolution supporting these efforts passed the senate, nothing came of the idea. What was desirable in theory failed in practice because of the necessity of hard work and monetary contributions to make it possible, efforts most faculty members were unwilling to make. Lack of interest in realizing a faculty club, like most students' disdain for extracurricular activities, is an indication of the non-traditional nature of PSU.[38]

Other matters involved more traditional faculty concerns. The original grievance procedure for faculty members was cumbersome and time-consuming. It was replaced in 1980 by a new one formulated by the local chapter of the AAUP and the administration and passed unanimously by the faculty senate. In 1988, the grievance procedure was revised and strengthened to make it fairer for grievants: the definition of a "grievant" was made more precise; it was made a violation of the grievance procedure for an accountable administrator not to respond to the deadlines set in the procedure; the hearing committee established under the procedure had to act promptly, as did the provost and president; no action could be taken against the grievant for invoking the procedure; and the hearings committee could use a hearings officer if it chose to do so. Again, cooperation between the AAUP and the administration had resulted in a significant improvement in faculty rights.[39]

A matter fraught with malice and misunderstanding that ultimately was turned into an asset was the development of "post-tenure review." In the early 1970s, there was a hostile backlash toward faculty and faculty rights in the aftermath of the Vietnam War protests. Several politicians and many in the public were outraged that faculty who held dissenting views could not be disciplined because they held tenured positions. This was not a new complaint, but one held with especially deep and widespread fervor in these emotional days. Other citizens believed faculty were lazy and unproductive feeders at the public trough, whose workloads should be increased substantially. To strike at these faculty "undesirables," influence was brought upon the state board to develop a way to discipline or dismiss tenured faculty for their unpopular ideas or their lack of productivity. Post-tenure review was a way to accomplish these objectives.

Post-tenure review, when first conceived, was a system whereby tenured faculty members would be reviewed—by their colleagues, by administrators, or by some combination thereof—with those who did not measure up being sanctioned. It was a purely punitive device that could have led to great injustices. The state board established such a system in the spring of 1975. It met much opposition. Portland State's AAUP chapter asked the state board to repeal its regulation on the classic grounds that tenure was indispensable to protecting academic freedom. An *ad hoc* committee on post-tenure review was appointed at PSU by the provost. Its report was controversial by the very fact it saw merit in some kind of post-tenure review. The senate debated the *ad hoc* committee report carefully in early June 1975. Some took the AAUP position. Some said protest was futile, as the board would do what it liked. Others asserted even a benign system was ill-advised, because it would consume hours of faculty time. Still others declared that instead of calling for the repeal of the board system, it should be rebutted by a statement that faculty were already being reviewed annually in their departments. Another tack taken in the debate was that the existing system of departmental faculty review could be strengthened if funds were voted to improve all faculty, both those who were doing a good job and those who were doing a less than satisfactory one. The resolution to ask the board to rescind post-tenure review was adopted.[40]

But the faculty did not leave it at that. Recognizing either that there was merit in some type of properly constructed system of post-tenure review (a belief of several faculty members) or that it would be politically expedient to endorse it (or both), the senate decided, after discussing resolutions proposed by David Wrench (Psychology) and John Cooper (English), to reject the policy proposed by the post-tenure review panel and to call for a new panel to develop a plan for post-tenure review that preserved the institution of tenure as it existed, presumed that the faculty were competent teachers, did not impose an additional burden on the faculty, and made use of existing mechanisms to review tenured faculty. In the years ahead, again because of AAUP-administration cooperation, a post-tenure review policy was developed that was designed to be flexible and helpful, rather than rigid and punitive, and one that received at least a mod-icum of monetary support.[41]

Another traditional element of dissatisfaction, both internal and external to the University, was teaching evaluation. As in the days of the Mosser Plan, teaching evaluations were a recurrent topic of discussion, although little was done about making them uniform and nothing at all about requiring them of all faculty. In June 1971, the senate autho-rized the first systematic attempt to evaluate teaching since the time of the Mosser Plan when it assigned the task to the Committee on Effective Teaching (CET). The committee worked for more than two years on the matter of the evaluation of faculty and presented in May 1973 a set of "Suggested Guidelines for a Program of Student Evaluation of Fac-ulty." Later in the month, the committee sponsored an open meeting on the subject.[42]

One year later, after digesting the suggestions arising from the open meeting and other sources, the committee presented its recom-mendation to the senate. It proposed the establishment of an inde-pendent instructional rating center. The center would be operated by the Office of Institutional Planning and Research, but the form, content, and confidentiality of the evaluations it made were to be regulated by a special joint faculty-student committee. No faculty member was re-quired to use the center, and its evaluations were to be given only to the faculty members themselves. The center's tasks also would include conducting research in teacher evaluation. Although careful to specify its recommendations were not the only ways to evaluate pedagogy, the Committee on Effective Teaching declared they were a move in the direction of more objective standards for the evaluation of teaching.[43]

When CET formally moved for the establishment of the center in the senate, it occasioned a lengthy debate. A handful of members spoke in favor of the motion, some pointing out that most universities had an evaluation process, but most senators opposed it, raising objections such as cost, the danger of tailoring teaching to the evaluation form, and distrust of a quantitative instrument. Many said they favored teacher evaluation but preferred it be done by departments or through some other agency. No one stated candidly that he or she feared to be given a poor evaluation, if indeed that was a reason in the minds of some opponents. When the vote was taken, the motion for the center was defeated, twenty to sixteen.[44]

About a year and a half later, teacher evaluation again became an issue, this time because of the action of the state legislature and the state board. The legislature required student evaluations of faculty (if they were made) be made available to students and the general public. The board declared this would be done only if the institutional presidents approved of it. In other words, both legislature and board agreed such disclosure would not violate laws protecting the privacy of individuals. The student senate passed a resolution favoring the position of the board. The Committee on Effective Teaching testified on 25 November 1975 that the state board's proposal was hasty, and that at Portland State, evaluation instruments were being developed at the departmental level. Out of this series of events came again the question of whether teacher evaluation in and of itself was a worthwhile endeavor. The faculty senate, in discussing the board's suggestion about confidentiality, was forced to grapple with teacher evaluation again, with the upshot of its debate being the decision of the presiding officer of the senate to ask CET to take up the issue along with that of the public disclosure of faculty teaching evaluations.[45]

When the committee made its report in February 1976, it triggered one of the longest debates in the history of the faculty senate. The committee report and accompanying motion dealt with two intertwined subjects: whether there should be faculty evaluations by students and whether these evaluations should be published. The committee moved that "evaluations for student use should be instituted campus-wide" and that these evaluations of faculty members should be made public—even without the consent of individual faculty members—if their departments agreed the evaluations had been made for that purpose and the faculty members had consented to that use of them, or if the department had agreed the evaluations be made for that purpose and the faculty member had been asked to make the evaluation as a result of departmental authority. Almost all the arguments over the desirability and validity of teaching evaluations had been made in earlier years, going back to the time of the Mosser Plan. The one exception was a novel point raised by Ralph Smith (Education) that no teacher should be evaluated unless the students, in turn, agreed to be evaluated according to a form that comprised nine points, including the students' agreement to avoid "'conning' for a high grade with a systematic campaign sometimes starting even before enrolling in the course" and to offer "the professor constructive suggestions for the course without unleashing hostilities pent up over the years." The final vote was an overwhelming victory for the original motion, forty-four in favor and nine opposed.

In spite of this vote, no system of University-wide evaluations was ever instituted.[46]

As always, the faculty extended its teaching throughout the community in a range of public services. In the last twenty years or so, those contributions have become so extensive a complete listing cannot be included here, though a few must serve to represent the whole. One reason Gregory Wolfe was chosen to succeed Branford Millar as president was the perception he would be more "community-minded" than his predecessor. In fact, of course, Wolfe's relations with the community were largely negative, not through his own fault but because of the publicity surrounding the antiwar protests. Joseph Blumel, out of both necessity and inclination, had to work hard in the community to undo this negative portrait of Portland State.[47]

Blumel began his work at the beginning. Instead of having a traditional academic inauguration, he arranged for a series of programs, all held at the University, on the theme of "Vital Partners: University and City," to illustrate his hope for a greater connection between campus and community. Held between 23 February and 1 March 1975, the programs included departmental open houses, two musical concerts, lectures, seminars, a play, a dance performance, and the unveiling of a statue—events all open to citizens of the metropolitan area. As the years went on, Blumel continued to participate in community work, e.g., as president of the Oregon Symphony board, labor that drew some grumbling from faculty who believed his time might better be spent raising money for the University, but this view seems shortsighted.[48]

In the political realm, faculty continued to be active. The service of Frank Roberts (Speech) in the Oregon house and senate (1975–95) and Tom Mason (Administration of Justice and Political Science) in the house (1979–93) have been mentioned. Others active in the political arena included Ronald Cease (Political Science), who served in the state legislature from 1985–95, and also Keith Skelton, Finance/Law (1957–75, intermittently). Before becoming politically active, Cease had been one of the authors of the Portland Metropolitan Service District (1970); because of his suggestion, the Portland service district was the first in the nation to have directly elected officials. Illustrative of myriad non-political public service activities was the work of the faculty of the Earth Sciences Department, following one of the great natural disasters of regional history, the eruption of Mt. St. Helens in May 1980. Faculty members spent many hours in research endeavors related to the eruption and in appearing on television explaining the causes and consequences of the eruption.[49]

As throughout its history, students did not have an extracurricular life at the University that involved many of them. Family, studies, job, and non-University entertainment occupied their time away from campus. After the days of Vietnam War protests, the student government never took any particularly controversial actions, or at least any that elicited a response from more than a handful of students. Students continued to meet high standards in their music, dance, art, and theater productions. Lectures, political programs, and informal discussions of course remained important to some, and several visiting speakers reached large audiences, but the two controversial areas of student life continued to be intercollegiate athletics and the *Vanguard*.

One of the first actions taken by E. Dean Anderson in his few months as PSU's interim president was to give the football team one more season, the year 1974, to make strides toward financial solvency. He also instituted a series of financial goals that had to be met. If they were not, he proclaimed, then reductions in the intercollegiate athletics budget would occur. Not only was there insufficient money to balance the books for intercollegiate athletics, but the running sore of the University administration (using student incidental fees for intercollegiate sports, especially football, without the consent of the student senate—which was perfectly legal although unpopular) remained unhealed. Upon assuming office, President Blumel continued Anderson's football trial period and set of goals, but when the trial period ended without the goals being met, football continued. Blumel also demonstrated his interest in making sense of the intercollegiate athletics program by making the director of athletics directly responsible to him.[50]

Another important governmental change regarding athletics was the faculty senate's adoption of a constitutional amendment in 1975 to create a University Athletics Board (UAB) to replace the Intercollegiate Athletics Committee. This was an important step in fostering women's athletics and in tightening up the lines of financial responsibility for sports. Hitherto, there had been no University-wide advisory body for women's athletics, which was a part of the Department of Physical Education. In the past, also, recreational sports and intramural sports were a part of the Educational and Cultural Affairs Board under the dean of students, which was responsible for a wide range of student programs. Under the new amendment, the University Athletics

Board would be responsible for developing policies and budgets in regard to recreational (club) sports, intramural athletics, and both men's and women's intercollegiate athletics. It would now be possible, the proponents of the new board hoped, to coordinate the requests for incidental fee monies to the student senate and, thus, save money, rather than following the wasteful piecemeal approach of the past.[51]

Football was not the sole intercollegiate sport to cause controversy. In 1980, there was an investigation into charges that the basketball coach, Ken Edwards, had misapplied College Work Study funds for the benefit of his players. Concurrently, there was a set of charges that basketball players had maintained their eligibility by taking easy courses and then left school without graduating after their eligibility had run out. President Blumel appointed George Hoffmann, dean of the College of Social Science, to look into these allegations. Of equal or greater interest was the president's decision to abolish men's intercollegiate basketball. This decision, taken following the 1980–81 season, was based on the fact that PSU was not a member of any basketball conference and thus required a high transportation budget to fly to comparable independent institutions throughout the country. Thus, it would be preferable to expend the slender sports resources on football (where there was no competing program for fans' loyalty in the Portland area), rather than on basketball, where the University of Portland and the professional Portland Trail Blazers were competitors.[52]

Infinitely more controversial than the abolition of men's basketball was the issue of moving the University intercollegiate athletics program to the level of Division I of the National Collegiate Athletic Association (NCAA). An athletic fundraising consultant to the University raised the issue in 1983, basing the case for a move on "excellence." Robert Lockwood (Administration of Justice), the faculty athletic representative, wrote to President Blumel in 1985 implying a move to Division I was in order. He noted that as Portland State was attempting to attain the status of a "comprehensive research university," it should also try "to place our athletic program in a position where it can help promote a community sense of pride in this institution....Although regrettable from an academic point of view, the public perception of PSU vis a vis our sister institutions to the south may be derived as much, if not more, from our athletic successes as from our scholarly achievements." This proposal again emerged during the administration of Pres. Natale A. Sicuro who, shortly after his assumption of office in 1987, appointed a committee chaired by a Portland businessman Fred Delkin to investigate the feasibility of such a change. Almost as soon as the Delkin committee was appointed, some of the faculty was up in arms against even considering the possibility of moving to Division I status. There was a fear it would waste money and divert not only fundraising but other efforts from the true purpose of the University. Reflecting these sentiments, the faculty senate in October 1987 passed a resolution that, "The Senate views the development of a Division I intercollegiate football program at Portland State as a misapplication of University priorities." Sicuro tried to calm objections to the Delkin committee at the November senate meeting by indicating the faculty would have opportunities to make its views known to the committee and by implying Portland State would not become a "big time" sports institution.[53]

Faculty were not calmed, however, and a special senate meeting to discuss athletics was called for later in the month. Although no motion was presented to the senate, various members aired their views. A cogent point was made by Whitney Bates (History) that the decision to move to Division I was being made by an improper body. It was in the hands of the University Advisory Board, a body appointed by the president largely from community members, instead of by the senate, which had the authority to deal with intercollegiate athletics. The meeting adjourned without formal action.[54]

On 7 December 1987, the University Athletics Board reported to the senate that it wished to reaffirm its earlier support of the move to Division I. However, it qualified its support by attaching conditions, the most important of which were that the Incidental Fee Committee of the student senate "remain solely responsible for the allocation of student activity fees to athletics;" "the move shall have no negative impact on existing programs at PSU;" and there should be a major effort to obtain conference affiliation. By the time of its report to the senate, the UAB report was supported by the report of the Delkin committee that intercollegiate sports be elevated to the level of Division I, although it is questionable if this was advantageous to its cause. At this meeting, the presiding officer announced the senate would send a representative to the state board at its next meeting to convey the senate's earlier declared opposition to the change of athletic status. In spite of the senate's objections, President Sicuro two days later recommended to the chancellor and the state board the change be made.[55]

During the next two months, President Sicuro also antagonized some students and faculty concerning another matter of intercollegiate athletics. Enrollment had risen during the fall and winter terms of 1987–88 and, along with it, the income from student incidental fees. Sicuro had decided to spend all this money on intercollegiate athletics without asking the students' Incidental Fees Committee for consent. This broke his earlier promise, made in the 2 November 1987 senate meeting, not to do so. Although Provost Frank Martino interpreted this promise as not to do so "secretly," the senate was unconvinced and unanimously passed a resolution on 1 February 1988 asking the president to reconsider his action. However, the athletic deficit continued to rise from $1.2 million in June 1988 to $1.3 million in November 1988. President Sicuro's departure in October 1988 left the situation more confused. In November—after assessing these developments—the UAB voted to defer seeking Division I status.[56]

In 1995, PSU succeeded in doing what it had first attempted thirty years earlier: it joined the Big Sky Conference, attaining Division I status. This action was taken by the president (without senate consideration of the matter), after a recommendation to do so was made by a special committee co-chaired by Bernard V. Burke of the History Department and Jack Garrison, a Portland businessman. Many of the reasons given for this recommendation were similar, in some cases identical, to arguments advanced in the past. Regularly scheduled games with "natural rivals" (those in the region—broadly defined) would draw more spectators than those with unfamiliar rivals at a distance; Portland State had the use of a large stadium that could accommodate spectators drawn by these rivalries; conference affiliation would make possible the return of men's basketball; a conference would make it easier to raise money for athletic scholarships; a regional conference membership would reduce travel costs; and interest originally created by athletics would expand into support for other programs at the University. A supporting argument was that a restored men's basketball team would have a larger facility in which to play, as the Portland Trail Blazers were vacating the Memorial Coliseum for a new facility, thus making the Coliseum available to Portland State. Additionally, it was maintained conference membership would enhance both student recruitment and retention rates. Like most aspirations at Portland State in the 1990s, Big Sky affiliation was an act of great faith.[57]

The *Vanguard* continued to be a source of news, although it did not raise as many hackles as it had in the days of the controversies over the Ginsberg photographs. In 1990–91, the newspaper changed its publication schedule from twice weekly to four times a week. It won awards consistently in the annual Oregon Collegiate Press Contest; in 1991, for example, it was given seven first-place commendations and three awards of merit. There were but two serious controversies. The first occurred in 1975, when the paper accused the chair of the Publications Board of not following its regulations by appointing a non-qualified student as editor of the *Vanguard*. This classic example of yellow journalism was rightfully resented by the chair, who wrote a defense of his actions to the senate saying he would pursue legal remedies "to restore my good name and reputation," although, ultimately, he decided to drop the matter. The second controversy arose during the Sicuro presidency and will be discussed in that context in the following chapter.[58]

TWENTY-TWO

Goals and Governance · 1975–1996

T he mission of Portland State University changed dramatically during the mid-1970s. The change involved government, politics, and curriculum, and elevated Portland State closer to the status enjoyed by the University of Oregon and Oregon State University. PSU, under the leadership of Pres. Joseph C. Blumel (who took office in May 1974), moved from a university to a comprehensive university to a comprehensive research university in a comparatively short period of time. This was a liberating change, although its effects were to be felt in the longer, rather than the nearer, future.

As in the case of earlier significant changes in the life of Portland State, administrators such as Blumel did not work in a vacuum in achieving them. From the mid-1970s to 1996, the state board and the chancellor remained major influences in PSU development. The board, in turn, was not divorced from its own external forces. Foremost among these was a gradual development of an anti-tax, anti-government spirit gaining ground in Oregon from the passage of a property tax limitation measure in California (Proposition 13) in 1978. This sentiment was fueled by a depression in Oregon beginning in 1979. One way the board and chancellor could justify the actions that followed from these changes in public attitude was to fall back on the concept of "unnecessary duplication," which seemed to justify cutting the budget. This ambiguous phrase, written into the statute creating the state system in 1929, was interpreted to support the interests of the University of Oregon whenever convenient. Of course, as was seen on earlier occasions, the effect of avoiding "duplication" was to inhibit the development of institutions such as Portland State and to favor the dominance of the U of O and OSU.[1]

The position of the two lower-Valley universities was enhanced not only by able administrators but also by the composition of the state board in these years. Even though residents of Portland, the majority of the board's members and some legislators, because they were alumni, had always favored the older institutions. But in the 1970s, board members began to be appointed from the Eugene and Corvallis areas. They now became able spokesmen, in other words, of their business communities as well as their universities. For example, Loran L. Stewart was appointed from Eugene (1970); Edward C. Harms, Jr., was appointed from Springfield (1975); and Robert Ingalls, from Corvallis, (1975).[2]

Although PSU did obtain some programs in international business, engineering, and computer science, they were secured against a great deal of opposition, not only from the board and chancellor but also from powerful political leaders. U.S. senator Mark Hatfield began channeling millions of federal dollars into the Oregon Health Sciences University (OHSU). In a sense, OHSU became *the* Portland university in the eyes of many state system officials. Gov. Victor Atiyeh had a greater willingness to support funding for the state system than did his successor, Neil Goldschmidt, but neither was an enthusiast for higher education and for PSU, in particular. Thus, it was remarkable that President Blumel, and supportive board members such as Jane Carpenter and Loren Wyss, were able to accomplish what they did in raising the University's status.[3]

In his opening convocation address to the faculty in September 1974, Blumel articulated the "urban nature" of the University. By that phrase, he meant not only an institution that place-bound students had to attend and where the location could contribute to an education outside the classroom, but also a university whose research interests would focus on urban problems and that would develop ties with other urban institutions, including local governments, in the metropolitan area. Two years later, the matter of mission became pressing.[4]

There were three reasons for the increasing pressure. Blumel himself was frustrated with the lack of progress in getting his administrators and faculty to think about mission. This was one reason he supported the creation of an Educational Policies Committee to be, he declared, "a kind of on-going goals commission for the Institution." The City Club of Portland, secondly, had a committee studying the role of PSU. Finally, the recent accrediting team report of 1975 criticized the vagueness of institutional goals. "The statement of purpose as officially defined," the evaluation team wrote, "is not specific enough to be an adequate guide. The statement, as far as it goes in defining Portland State University as a multipurpose, complex institution is all right. However, it says nothing about the *unique* functions and *unique* opportunities that characterize the university. Attention to such a definition should be a great help in future planning and coordination of effort."[5]

One year later, an important legislative decision reversed a policy dating to Portland State's creation as a four-year institution in 1955. At the behest of the Associated Students, who were demanding more housing near the University, the legislature removed the constraint that PSU not be a university of "the campus type." This decision led not only to the acquisition and construction of buildings on the West Campus in subsequent years but was the first step toward the University District of the 1990s. The process of development of the West Campus began with the preparation of a plan by a campus planning committee under the chairmanship of Nohad Toulan (dean of Urban Studies), which called for a substantial upgrading of this sector of the campus.[6]

In 1978, the Educational Policies Committee submitted its draft of a mission statement for Portland State. It defined PSU as a "metropolitan" university. The committee insisted that such a university retained the learning, teaching, and research foci of traditional universities but also called for a program expansion. It wanted more emphasis on professional and graduate education, including off-campus education, and more research and other services to be provided to the metropolitan community. President Blumel concurred with this emphasis, as did the faculty senate, which adopted it in May 1978.[7]

In fall 1978, the state board was to begin a discussion of the institutional role of Portland State. Blumel hoped fervently that when the board did engage in its discussion, "It will not simply adopt what many have interpreted as a traditional posture of seeking to

PSU Educational Media Services

Nohad Toulon, father of the College of Urban and Public Affairs and chair of the campus planning committee

limit or circumvent our areas of responsibility" but instead ask "what areas Portland State University should be encouraged to pursue." He also hoped the board would "adopt that posture, rather than one which has seemed to us always to ask: 'How can we prevent Portland State from exercising a negative influence on the programs of other State System institutions?'" The board did not disappoint Blumel or Portland State when it adopted its guidelines for the institution on 30 March 1979.[8]

As the president reported to the faculty, the new guidelines statement encompassed "all the essential elements contained in the mission document drafted by the educational policies committee and unanimously adopted by the Faculty Senate." He declared, "It is, in my opinion, a landmark document in the history of the University because, while recognizing certain special responsibilities and opportunities, it acknowledges the need for a comprehensive university in Portland and points us in the direction of its development." This happy outcome was not the result of chance.[9]

It occurred because the president was able to mobilize friendly state board members and legislators to work toward that end. As a first step toward spelling out the details of the new mission, Blumel assigned a special research committee, under the chairmanship of Susan Karant-Nunn (History) to investigate the current research role at PSU and to make recommendations about improving research conditions. The committee issued a model report recommending several improvements in the research climate, the most important of which was that the University fund research at a level to support the research expectations of the faculty and "its status as a university."[10]

The mission of Portland State became entwined with that of the state system as a whole in 1982. At that time, the new chancellor, William E. "Bud" Davis, decided to have a strategic plan for the state system prepared so that the legislature might become more receptive to its needs. To oversee the development of the plan, the chancellor appointed Larry Pierce (a faculty member at the University of Oregon) as his assistant for planning. The appointment was not a happy one for Portland State, as Pierce soon demonstrated he had little conception of the role of Portland State and less interest in expanding it. In an article in the *Vanguard* in December 1982, Pierce was quoted as stating the role of research at PSU would be de-emphasized in the future because of its limited doctoral offerings.[11]

The strategic plan had to be completed in a hurry, as the chancellor wanted it ready for the opening of the legislative session in early

January. The process of forming the plan was also troublesome, as it began at the top. In late August 1982, the chancellor's staff dispatched to Portland State a brief mission statement for the University. It was reviewed by the Office of Academic Affairs and returned to the chancellor with revisions. It also was scrutinized by the Educational Policies Committee.[12]

Portland State also initiated a much more comprehensive planning effort of its own: the work of a task force of PSU administrative and academic leaders chaired by Nohad Toulan resulted in a plan entitled "Portland State University, A Strategic Plan for the 1980s." The most important (Blumel labeled it "controversial") aspect of the plan was the second goal for the institution: "Portland State University should move to become a comprehensive research university." What this meant was that doctoral offerings should be expanded, as should other areas that might enhance the economic growth of the metropolitan area and of the state. To that end, the University made proposals to the state board for a Ph.D. in Electrical and Computer Engineering and a proposal for a master's program in Computer Science to be built on the recently approved undergraduate major in that discipline. President Blumel also laid the foundation for doctoral work in the School of Social Work. He hired Bernard Ross as dean of this school, who, in turn, added additional research-oriented faculty in the years ahead. Other parts of the plan for a comprehensive research university included a baccalaureate degree in International Education and another undergraduate degree in International Business. The Institute for International Trade and Commerce, which had been funded by the legislature in 1983, was staffed, and relationships with foreign colleges and universities were expanded.[13]

These efforts to move to the model of a comprehensive research university were successful. What made the work of the administration and faculty ultimately successful was not the chancellor's strategic plan but rather Portland State's old ally, the legislature. It took an important step by including one sentence in a note accompanying the adoption of the state system budget for 1985–87: "The Board of Higher Education shall plan for a change of status for Portland State University from that of a comprehensive university to that of a comprehensive research university with the accompanying changes in admissions standards for students and faculty staffing patterns, and to be accompanied by an additional incremental state contribution to the State System of Higher Education's base budget." Among the legislators, the most effective in bringing about this happy result for Portland State were Sen. Frank Roberts (as counselor) and Rep. Tom Mason (as activist). The legislative instruction resembled closely the "Plan for the 1980s" developed at PSU. In speaking to the faculty about the budget note, Blumel said it confirmed a position about PSU's status that it had taken for more than a decade: "I think it of great consequence that while it has never received the endorsement of the State Board of Higher Education, it has now received the collective endorsement of the Legislative Assembly." The president might have gone farther and pointed out that once again, as on several occasions since 1949, the legislature had been the salvation of Portland State.[14]

Blumel continued his remarks by indicating the plan was not a self-fulfilling document—it needed careful filling out. He suggested PSU doctoral offerings needed to be expanded and that there would have to be an increased emphasis placed on research, both on the part of current faculty and those to be hired in the immediate future. Advanced graduate work and increased research efforts obviously required more money. The president was correct in all these respects. (And a decade after they were uttered, the University had attained some of these objectives, though financial problems and interinstitutional rivalry have prevented reaching others.) Blumel hastened to meet these challenges by increasing the resources of the development office, efforts spectacularly rewarded in the receipt of an $825,000 grant from the M.J. Murdock Charitable Trust to buy a building for advanced technology in 1984.[15]

In addition to guiding PSU into a category comparable to that of the U of O and OSU, President Blumel took the lead in reorganizing its internal structure. The impetus for his action was a memorandum he received from Vice-Pres. Leon Richelle in July 1978 suggesting a consolidation of the three colleges. One month later, Blumel announced to the faculty that he would ask the Educational Policies Committee to consider combining the Colleges of Arts and Letters, Science, and Social Science into a single College of Liberal Arts and Sciences; converting the Department of Engineering into a School of Engineering; and creating a separate Graduate School. Instead, Blumel decided to create a special committee chaired by James Hart (English) to study the creation of a College of Liberal Arts and Sciences. This committee favored the proposal, as did an *ad hoc* committee of deans in 1980–81. Nothing was done on either occasion, however.[16]

In 1982, the Educational Policies Committee, under the chairmanship of Roger Moseley (Business Administration), did at last take up the matter of academic reorganization. President Blumel met with the committee in March to express his interest in establishing a College of Liberal Arts and Sciences but also in creating a separate School of Performing Arts from the Departments of Music and Theater Arts and the program in Dance. In May, the committee presented a motion to the faculty senate to make several changes in the academic structure no later than 16 September of that year. The committee recommended the single College of Liberal Arts and Sciences; the elevating of the dance program to a Department of Dance; the School of Performing Arts; the subsuming of the Center for Population Research and Census, the Public Administration program, and the pre-Architecture courses into the School of Urban Affairs; and the elevating of the Division of Engineering and Applied Science to a School of Engineering.[17]

The committee did admit its proposal might have some disadvantages. Among them were reduced accessibility to a dean whose organization would then include nineteen departments; a loss of faculty loyalty and identification with the passing of the old colleges; and uncertainty about the actual savings to be gained under the reorganization. On the positive side, it predicted—among other favorable points—a greater unity among the disciplines and more effective communication among them; an academic structure more comparable to that of most urban universities; a budget savings, especially for the 1982–83 academic year; and a demonstration to the state board and the legislature that PSU was willing "to streamline or tighten its administrative structure." It recommended the reorganization be accomplished by the beginning of fall term 1982.[18]

The faculty debated the motion in two meetings in May. Many objections were raised at these sessions, mainly to the creation of a College of Liberal Arts and Sciences. Senators questioned whether the proposals would actually save money, especially since the motion did not specify how many assistant deans would be required; whether the creation of new professional schools would threaten the liberal arts; and whether it was wise to create new administrative structures just after the Journalism Department had been eliminated on financial grounds. Proponents, led by Moseley, attempted to reassure the objectors.[19]

The advocates of the changes stressed their major concern was academic not financial. They argued the autonomy of departments would increase in a College of Liberal Arts and Sciences and that a combined college would enhance the liberal arts in an era when there seemed to be a reduced emphasis on them. A student spokesman for undergraduates also endorsed the proposal as one that would strengthen the liberal arts.[20]

There was less controversy over the other parts of the motion. The faculty in Music and Theater Arts supported the School of Performing Arts, although other faculty wondered if there were indeed a demand for it and if the costs of starting the new school would not outweigh any savings gained in doing so. The Art Department objected to the proposed transfer of its pre-architecture courses to the School of Urban Affairs. This issue hinged on whether prospective architects needed a liberal arts setting or the urban environment of the School of Urban Affairs. In the end, the senate approved all the structural changes, except for the transfer of the architecture courses. The margin of the vote was convincing, forty-five in favor to ten opposed.[21]

Far less controversial than the reorganization of the structure of the University was another innovation of President Blumel. Since its beginning, there had been a female administrator at the highest levels. The first was librarian Jean Black, appointed in 1946, though none followed for almost thirty years. It took many years before the first female department head was appointed. Orcillia Forbes was the first woman to hold a dean's position, dean for students (1975), and the first female vice-president, appointed by President Blumel as vice-pres-

ident for Student Affairs in 1978. Blumel also selected Margaret Dobson as executive vice-president in 1986. PSU's female vice-presidents were the first in the State System of Higher Education.[22]

Other governance issues arose in the last twenty years. In a move reminiscent of the battles over the Law Enforcement Assistance Administration, the administration pushed through a master's degree in Public Administration in a single meeting of the senate.

PSU Office of Publications

Margaret Dobson, first female
executive vice-president

PSU Educational Media Services

Orcillia Forbes, first female dean and first female vice-president

When it was proposed the matter be discussed at a subsequent meeting, protests were made that delay would put the matter behind schedule. George Hoffmann, dean of the College of Social Science, insisted the degree be adopted immediately, citing both a grant given to OSU to develop a sub-specialty of Public Administration and plans for a Public Administration program at Lewis & Clark College. Hoffmann proclaimed, "We are in very real competition with Lewis and Clark College. We have worked closely with the governmental community and while I don't expect that they are going to call the tune (and they haven't) I think that they expect us to move since we worked with and involved them so closely." The senate approved the degree.[23]

To somewhat assert itself about its role in curricular and in other matters (especially those in regard to faculty terminations arising from financial exigency), the senate adopted in 1975 a constitutional amendment proposed by Donald Moor (Philosophy) on behalf of the AAUP chapter. The amendment stated the senate's authority depended not simply on the power of state laws and the Administrative Rules of the State System of Higher Education but also on "the need for appropriately shared responsibility and cooperative action among the components of the academic institution." The amendment went on to state that all bodies of the institution did share in policy-making powers but that the amount varied depending on each branch's particular function, with the faculty having chief responsibility in such areas as curriculum, research, and aspects of student life relating to the educational process. Introduced at the May meeting of the senate and further considered at the June session, the amendment was criticized as a "preamble," written in "barbarous" language, reminiscent of 1960s catering to students and, most nonsensically (by Edmond Gnoza of the library), as "homiletic, hortatory, and heuristic." Final passage was by an overwhelming margin, thirty-two in favor and fourteen opposed.[24]

Progress in obtaining faculty consent for new programs was demonstrated in October 1975, when the proposal for a School of Urban
Affairs came before the senate. Work toward the school had begun in
1974, when a ten-member university-community committee recommended its establishment. Early the next year, a second committee
made recommendations on the school's structure. It proposed it encompass programs in Administration of Justice, Institute on Aging,
Black Studies certificate program, Urban Studies certificate program,
Urban Studies Center, and Urban Studies graduate programs. When
the senate took up the matter in October, President Blumel reminded senators that "some years ago I assured the Senate that no academic reorganization would be undertaken without the concurrence of
the Senate." His reference was to the senate objections to the elimination of the General Science Department. Although there was some
disagreement during the next month's meeting about who would
determine the exact structure of the school, there was no doubt the
senate would have the final say in deciding for or against it. It voted
overwhelmingly in its favor. After the school was adopted in principle,
the details of its structure were worked out by the department heads
in the College of Social Science and by a special senate committee.
When the structure proposed by this committee came before the senate, it was also accompanied by a suggestion the school's progress for
the ensuing three years be monitored by another *ad hoc* committee.
With these assurances and safeguards in place, the senate approved
the structure. The relative painlessness and lack of suspicion and rancor in the establishment of this school showed what shared authority
in creating a program could accomplish.[25]

That the millennium of shared authority had been established by
this case, however, was belied by developments in later years. Two involved the library. In 1981, Thomas Pfingsten, library director, made some
administrative changes, based on suggestions from conversations he
had had with the library faculty and on an *ad hoc* review committee he
had appointed the past year. The changes were to shift the administrative responsibilities for library services to the elected head of that department and to eliminate the title of assistant subject librarian in all departments. Pfingsten maintained the changes made it possible for library
staff to communicate more effectively with the librarian and that the
removal of the title "assistant subject librarian" would foster morale by
not drawing invidious distinctions among staff members. Approached
by three faculty members who feared this was an authoritarian measure,

the senate steering committee raised their concerns in the senate, though Pfingsten was able to assuage the concerns of most members.[26]

This was not the case in developments in the School of Business and in the library in 1991 and 1992. The School of Business was reorganized by its dean in the spring of 1992. Departments were abolished effective 1 July, and new associate deans replaced them on 16 September. There were rumblings of discontent about this reorganization—because it had not gone through the usual channels—rumblings that caused the University Planning Council to look into the matter. It reported to the senate in November 1991 that it would take one year for the school to develop bylaws and guidelines for the new organization and that a telephone survey of the school faculty by the UPC found them "willing to give the new organization a chance to succeed." Nevertheless, the senate passed a resolution asking the school to present its plan of reorganization. Ansel Johnson, the senate's presiding officer, followed up the resolution with a letter to the acting dean of the School of Business asking for a proposal for its reorganization. In other words, the school was asked to do retroactively what should have been done in the first place.[27]

In November, the school sent a response to the University Planning Council, and, in December, the council discussed further information presented by the acting dean. In March 1992, the senate held a full-fledged discussion of the final report presented by the University Planning Council, which said the School of Business had not provided enough information to answer all its questions. The senate discussed the report but took no action, in effect, acquiescing—a violation of the faculty constitution.[28]

While the changes in the School of Business were being instituted, the library was also being reorganized. Questions arose about whether or not faculty participation in this reorganization followed the terms of the faculty constitution, since no faculty members had been permitted to vote on the change. In the senate, Susan Karant-Nunn of the History Department introduced a motion in April 1992 calling for "a full review and evaluation of the effects of the 1991 reorganization of the School of Business Administration and of the University Library....and that the result of this study be reported to the 1993–94 Senate so that it may then decide whether the SBA and Library reorganizations should be modified or invalidated." In the ensuing debate, some challenged the senate's right to conduct such a review, while another member said passing the resolution—in case of future financial problems—might send "the wrong message to creative reorganizations that may become necessary." Speaking in favor of the resolution, several senators refuted these arguments, making the case that matters of University governance and academic structures were clearly within the senate's purview. The senate finally decided to table the motion but asked the Advisory Council to review the constitutionality of the issue. Although it had no effect on what had been done by the School of Business and the library, the senate did try to salvage something from the dubious actions of the two units' administrators. It passed unanimously a constitutional amendment on 4 May 1992 declaring, "The University shall not establish, abolish, or effect major alteration in the structure or educational function of departments or of programs, including those of more than one department or academic unit, without prior action by the Faculty Senate on advice of the University Planning Council."[29]

A less painful governance matter was the final sundering of Portland State University from the Division of Continuing Education (DCE). On 1 July 1976, the centralized functions of DCE were abolished, and the Division's units became branches of local campuses. It took three years to complete the arrangements necessitated by this reorganization, but on 1 July 1979, PSU assumed responsibility for the DCE building on Park Avenue and for the academic records it contained. The major difficulties that remained were continuing ones: to make sure DCE offerings did not compete with those of the University; to reconcile accounting and requisition differences between the two institutions; and to prevent other state system institutions—as was their wont—from encroaching into Portland State's metropolitan area. All three were problems for PSU but also for DCE, which continued to operate on a self-supporting basis. Another lingering problem was who had final approval for courses. Although Portland State departments had the right to approve all DCE courses offered under PSU numbers, and residence credit for Portland State students was given only for such courses, there remained a certain amount of confusion because DCE still could offer courses sponsored by another institution, courses sometimes taught by PSU faculty.[30]

An important internal change in University governance was the creation of the Educational Policies Committee in 1976. Although this committee carried the same name as the administrative committee established during the presidency of Branford Millar, it was a constitutional committee and one with faculty and student, rather than administrative, membership. The committee as proposed to the senate by its Steering Committee on 12 January 1976 dealt with both procedural and substantive subjects. It was empowered to deal with the thorny matters that had arisen in the cases of the LEAA grant and the Pacific Rim Center of creating, abolishing, or altering the structure or educational functions of departments or programs. It would also make recommendations to the senate concerning educational policies, the University's long-range priorities, and related physical resources and plans. The committee was to be composed of one faculty member from each college or school and from the Department of Health and Physical Education and two students—a total of nine members.

The senate debated the amendment over three meetings. There were several concerns advanced in this debate. One was whether it might be preferable, instead of creating a new committee, to have the chairs of the Graduate Council, the Curriculum Committee, and the Budget Committee meet as a special committee to coordinate curricular proposals from their respective committees and to bring them to the senate. Another was that the proposed committee was not based on proportional representation, as both small and large units had the same number of members on the committee. A third worry was that the library was not given a seat on the new committee. Others feared the committee would deal with affairs pertinent only to a single department.[31]

At the next month's senate meeting, the amendment to the constitution was changed to permit library representation on the Educational Policies Committee and to clarify the committee's role as an advisory body while at the same time recognizing the senate as the policy-making body. An amendment was also added to make clear that the committee would decide what matters fell within its purview, a precautionary measure relating to the old dispute as to whether the LEAA program was a new program or simply a modification of an old one. The new committee was created by a substantial majority vote, thirty-seven to five, on 1 March 1976.[32]

About ten years later, another overarching committee was proposed, this time by the University's new president, Natale A. Sicuro. In the first months of his administration in the fall of 1986, Sicuro expressed concern about the committee structure, particularly what he regarded as a lack of coordination among the members of the Budget Committee, the Educational Policies Committee, and the Campus Planning Committee. He asked the Steering Committee of the

Natale A. Sicuro, president, 1986-88

senate and the Advisory Council to
draw up a plan for a University Planning Council. The council was instituted as an administrative committee, but
there was confusion about its role with
respect to the committees dealing with
the budget and with educational policies. For example, the Budget Committee, at the request of the president
(who was trying to consolidate all budget matters in the hands of the University Planning Council), did not meet
between September 1986 and March
1988. Nor did the Educational Policies Committee meet for much of
the 1987–88 academic year, because its duties had been temporarily
assumed by the University Planning Council. To clarify roles and afford the faculty a greater say in the operations of the University Planning Council, a constitutional amendment was presented to the senate that had been shaped by the Committee on Committees and by an
ad hoc committee made up in part of six past and present chairs of the
Budget and Educational Policies committees and the University
Planning Council.[33]

The proposed amendment continued the Budget Committee and
maintained its traditional role of advising the president on the preparation of budgets and recommending budgetary priorities, while also
giving that committee new authority to recommend to the president
and senate "policies to be followed in implementing any declaration
of financial exigency." The Educational Policies Committee was to be
continued and the University Planning Council was to become a constitutional committee, charged with initiating, discussing, and considering "plans and policies that have broad significance for the University." The amendment was adopted by the senate on 6 June 1988.
Its passage assured the faculty the University Planning Council would
not become an all-powerful administrative committee appointed and
directed by the president, especially one growing as unpopular as
President Sicuro.[34]

Another controversial matter appearing in the Sicuro years concerned department heads. In February 1987, the senate began con-

sidering a constitutional amendment that would require departments to elect their chairs. Under the existing constitution, the departments could decide if they wished to elect the chairs or if they preferred them to be appointed. In either case, the president made the final appointment. The amendment, in the minds of its advocates, however, would make it less likely the president would veto a nominee than under the existing provision. The amendment passed without a dissenting vote.[35]

Five of Portland State's female faculty members became involved in a long-running discrimination case against the State System of Higher Education in the 1980s. This case, *Penk v. Oregon State Board of Higher Education,* was brought against the board on 25 April 1980 by twenty-two female faculty members of the system, on the grounds they had been discriminated against in violation of the Civil Rights Law of 1972 prohibiting discrimination in employment on the grounds of gender. The women sought monetary damages in their individual claims, alleged the board engaged in a practice of sex discrimination against female faculty members as a class, and sought class-wide damages on their group claims.[36]

The five Portland State faculty members charged a variety of violations of their rights under the statute. Bernice Gilmore (Chemistry) maintained she received less pay and fewer retirement benefits than men of equal qualifications performing the same job. Betty Leonard (Social Work) argued she received lower pay than equally qualified men performing the same job. Elaine Spencer (Chemistry) contended her starting pay was lower than equally qualified men; that she was not promoted as rapidly as equally qualified men performing the same job; and that she was being evaluated on the basis of research and scholarship without being given the opportunities to perform these tasks. Barbara Stewart (Institute on Aging, who by the time the suit was filed had moved on to OHSU) claimed she was discriminatorily assigned to part-time work. Michelle Wollert (Theater Arts) claimed she was discriminated against because she was not promoted (twice), placed on tenure track, or paid equally to a similarly qualified man in the department.[37]

The trial was lengthy and complex. Don Willner represented the faculty members, while James J. Casby was the lead lawyer for the state. The case came to trial before Judge Helen J. Frye in federal district court in Portland on 8 February 1984; closing arguments were held on 20 November 1984, with Judge Frye giving her opinion on 13 February

1985. A prodigious amount of time and effort was consumed by the lawyers for both sides and by officials of the University, who amassed data from pay and promotion records in efforts to refute the women's claims. Over the nine months of the trial, the court was presented with thousands of pages of affidavits, depositions, and exhibits. Approximately 220 witnesses testified. The final trial transcript consisted of approximately twenty-five thousand pages.[38]

The plaintiffs made three main points in presenting their case: sex discrimination was commonplace in the institutions where the women taught; the board knew of this; and it did nothing to remedy the situation. In the end, the state board won almost a complete victory. Of the fifty-eight claims of sex discrimination filed by the plaintiffs, Judge Frye ruled favorably on only three, none of which were from PSU faculty. She maintained the "plaintiffs presented very little direct evidence of sex discrimination" and that "no pattern or practice of sex discrimination exists of which the Board should have been aware."[39]

The heart of the matter was the meaning of Judge Frye's phrase, "direct evidence of sex discrimination." The women's attorneys presented many witnesses who testified to the existence of discriminatory treatment in state system colleges and universities. Yet, this was not sufficient to win the case, which was a class-action suit. Such litigation requires plaintiffs "to prove their case by statistics in order to establish that the institutions had treated women, as a group, differently from men, as a group....The state responded that the plaintiffs' statistics were flawed because other factors were used in making salary, promotion, and tenure decisions, such as teaching ability and scholarship. Because these latter factors are subjective, the plaintiffs could not quantify or refute them." In a case such as this, the plaintiffs had the burden of proof of showing that the board had no "legitimate, non-discriminatory reasons for its actions." In the judge's view, she found this burden of proof was not met by the plaintiffs.[40]

In spite of the loss of this case, faculty women may have gained something from it. Many of them in time gained raises or promotions, and thus may have helped in the overall struggle for equity for female faculty members. Perhaps, too, their case contributed to the selection of Judith Ramaley as president of Portland State in 1990, the first woman chief executive in the Oregon State System of Higher Education.[41]

The great governance issue of Portland State's history, however, had nothing to do with constitutional amendments or faculty or student rights or control of the *Vanguard* but, rather, the actions of Pres. Natale A. Sicuro. After President Blumel resigned, the state board appointed a search committee to recommend his successor. It was composed of board members, faculty, students, and members of the general public. As was customary, its deliberations were secret, but its choice among the four candidates was a person already known to the chancellor—the president of Southern Oregon State College, Natale A. Sicuro, who was selected by the state board on 18 July 1986. Sicuro's selection is a matter of dispute. There were rumors at the time, and subsequently, that he was never a favorite of the selection committee but that his choice had been insisted on by Chancellor William E. Davis. The truth of this matter, given Sicuro's later unpopularity, probably will never be fully revealed.[42]

Sicuro had taken his doctorate in the field of Educational Administration at Kent State University in 1964. Before that time, he had been a secondary school teacher, coach, and university instructor in northeastern Ohio and at Kent State. Following the award of his doctoral degree, Sicuro had been an assistant school superintendent, a consultant and manager for Peat, Marwick, Mitchell & Co., and had held various administrative positions at Kent State University. From 1979–86, he had served as president of Southern Oregon State College (SOSC). At SOSC, he compiled a creditable record of achievements, although several faculty disliked his methods. Nevertheless, he was already handicapped on arrival at Portland State by rumors he had been forced on the selection committee and by the contempt of many of the liberal arts faculty for his doctoral degree in Educational Administration, which they regarded as a field without academic merit.

These difficulties were not insurmountable, but the new president became a figure of increasing controversy (and, in time, suspicion) among most of PSU's communities throughout his term in office. The first matter in which he became embroiled was the previously discussed controversy over whether or not Portland State should become a NCAA Division I member, with all the attendant ramifications of being a major intercollegiate athletic power. This measure stamped the president in the eyes of many faculty as anti-intellectual, as a person who placed emphasis on a matter either irrelevant or insignificant to the educational process. There then followed a series of disputes involving almost all groups that had an interest in the University. These controversies were sometimes distinct, sometimes interwoven, but all had the cumulative effect of isolating the president from support both within and without the University until, in the end, he had to leave his position under a cloud.

One early dispute was a charge aired in the *Vanguard* that, in planning the annual homecoming dance in the fall of 1986, some leaders of the Associated Students, including Michael Erickson (president), had planned to arrange for it to be for "whites only." The allegations were published in the student newspaper in February 1987 and led to a critical essay in the paper a month later by David Horowitz of the History Department. In the same issue of the *Vanguard*, President Sicuro was reported as nominating Erickson for one of the student body seats on the State Board of Higher Education, telling the reporter he hoped Erickson would be "propelled just as fast as possible" into the ranks of public service in the state of Oregon. When called on to investigate the charges, Sicuro moved slowly, telling aggrieved minority students they should take their case to the faculty senate or to the Minority Affairs Council. At this very time, however, before these bodies could investigate, the president summed up his judgment of the charges: "I don't see any evidence that is substantive."[43]

This controversy flowed into another. In July 1987, Sicuro ordered a review of the guidelines the Publications Board had used to regulate the *Vanguard*. He also wrote a memorandum to members of his staff that they were not to communicate directly with the newspaper. At this time, he also removed Gerald Penk as faculty adviser to the newspaper. There was some concern expressed that these events were related to the paper's articles on the dance and those critical of Erickson, and the issues were raised in the faculty senate on 2 November 1987 by Donald Moor of the Philosophy Department. Moor asked Orcillia Forbes, vice-provost for student affairs, why a review of the *Vanguard* guidelines was being instituted at this time. Forbes replied such a review was conducted periodically; that the president no longer wanted the Publications Board to report to him directly; and that a review of the position of faculty adviser was in order. When Moor asked whether the vice-provost "could deny rumors that there is a more substantial reason for the review," Forbes replied she did not know what he "was talking about."[44]

Sicuro was worried, however, and wrote a letter to his chief administrators and the members of the Publications Board on 4 November, in which he tried to allay concerns about the *Vanguard*. He pointed out the review of the Publications Board was but one of many reviews he had made since his inauguration on 15 September 1986. He stated he had informed Vice-Provost Forbes orally to review the board guidelines but was now writing this letter to set the record straight about what he was asking her to do. He was also formally asking her in writing to search for a new adviser to the *Vanguard*. Whatever value this letter might have had in allaying fears was undercut by its final paragraph: "Finally, any continuing inferences directly related to impinging on the First Amendment rights of individuals or the publications presently at Portland State University are misguided. I would like to leave you with the thought that the freedom of expression is not a license for misrepresentation." The dismissal of Gerald Penk resulted in a good deal of poor publicity for the University, with not only the *Vanguard* but the *Oregonian* expressing its displeasure.[45]

By early spring 1988, the real crisis of confidence in Natale Sicuro was at hand. This development was a rapidly growing concern about the Portland State University Foundation. Rumors spread that Sicuro was spending money at a rapid rate and that some of this money was being diverted improperly from the foundation. Specifically, it was charged that the foundation, at Sicuro's behest, was spending money from designated gifts (given for a specific purpose) for other purposes, such as, improving the president's house or meeting the travel expenses of the president's wife.

Throughout the balance of this controversy, the moving spirit in pressing the issue of Sicuro's conduct was Marjorie Burns (English), the presiding officer of the senate. For several months, she stood alone in the cause of keeping the matter before the senate and the University community and was only joined at a later time by the department heads and other faculty. As an *ex officio* member of the foundation as well as a senate officer, Burns entered the eye of the storm. As the tension mounted in the next few months, she met daily with foundation employees—and weekly with television reporter Peter Murphy.[46]

Indeed, what brought matters out into the open was a broadcast report by Murphy on 17 February that charged misuse of foundation funds. Murphy had been tipped off about foundation practices by a "mole"—one of its own employees. Murphy then called Burns for further information. In March, the faculty senate Steering Committee reacted to the report by drafting questions for the president's consideration. There was a bit of a delay in deciding which members of the administration would answer the questions and whether or not their responses would be public, but finally, Vice-Pres. for Finance Roger Edgington and Vice-Pres. for Development Judith E. Nichols ap-

Rodger Edgington, interim president, 1988-90

PSU Office of Publications

peared at a senate meeting on 7 March to
speak about the foundation, though not
to answer the Steering Committee's questions. Just prior to this meeting, on 2
March, a public meeting in opposition to
Sicuro had taken place at the University,
and the *Oregonian* carried an article critical of him on 6 March. The most important question raised at the meeting was
whether or not designated funds had
been used for undesignated purposes.
Nichols assured the senate this was not
the case—that only the interest on desig-
nated funds had been used for general purposes. Edgington said the
foundation was a private group—supervised by itself rather than the
University—and that it had been given a clean bill of health by its
auditors. As the debate wound down, a motion was introduced to
determine by mail ballot whether the faculty had "confidence in President Sicuro's continued ability to lead Portland State University."[47]

At this stage of the debate, Provost Frank Martino made two
unfortunate accusations. He said those who favored a mail ballot had
a "hidden agenda" (presumably to get rid of the president) they would
express privately but not in an open forum. He then compared the
last few months at PSU to a Greek tragedy: "a university poised almost
by accident of history and demographics on the verge of becoming
something new and different, something the vast majority of the faculty want," but stymied by "a minority group of that faculty hell-bent
to prevent that from in fact happening." Nohad Toulan, dean of the
School of Urban Studies, also spoke of the gravity of a vote of no confidence and urged it be held off until a thorough investigation of the
charges against the president had been made and proven. On the
other hand, Whitney Bates (History) challenged the belief the opponents of the president's use of foundation money composed "a small
band of inside agitators." The roll call for a mail ballot of confidence
was defeated, thirty-eight to sixteen.[48]

By April 1988, Sicuro was concerned enough about these
charges, coming in addition to the ones about football and the *Vanguard*, that he began actively to seek assistance. He quickly obtained

letters or resolutions of support and commendation directed to either the governor or the state board from the Business School Corporate Associates, the Alumni Association board, the foundation board, and the Viking Athletic Association board. Furthermore, the foundation's accountants gave it a clean bill of health. Most helpful to the embattled president, however, was a commendation from the state board, which had recently conducted a visitation to Portland State. In some of these testimonials, the need for them was implied as a tribute to a man whose performance was more than satisfactory but whose work was being undermined by (as the president of the Alumni Association board put it) "a small but vocal group of dissidents at the University, who are either afraid of or against change, [and who] have sought to discredit President Sicuro and his programs." To get to the bottom of the matter, in April the Budget Committee appointed a special task force headed by Richard Halley (emeritus professor of Economics) "to independently examine the operations of the [PSU] Foundation." Even more ominously for Sicuro, the state Department of Justice began an investigation of the foundation on 19 April, based on recent news accounts accusing it of irregularities.[49]

On 2 May, the next turn in the ongoing controversy occurred with a report to the faculty senate by Marjorie Burns (English), who, as mentioned earlier, was the presiding officer of that body and an *ex officio* member of the foundation board. She stated she had received a directive from Provost Martino to examine the records of the foundation and to make a report to the senate. She reported first that a group of faculty members had established a trust fund to receive donations to the University. Next, she called on the president of the foundation board to make a few remarks. Faculty comment of a scattered nature followed, with one member condescendingly commenting that "the Foundation Board members have high intentions, but...are being made fools of." He further stated he felt "some responsibility to give them some advice about what they are getting themselves into." Burns, however, got to the point about how the foundation board had been misled by University employees, saying that in the board meetings, "she felt like the snake in the garden" and that "jokes are made at the expense of the faculty, as if they are dusty eggheads who need to be led into the twenty-first century and that we don't know what's going on and are afraid of change. In fact, it is the Board members who don't know what is going on."[50]

Two days later, there was an article in the *Oregonian* that attempt-ed to delineate the foibles of the foundation, and Sicuro responded with a letter to its writer on the same day, maintaining that nothing untoward had taken place in foundation operations. About a month later, several developments occurred that probably were pivotal in the foundation affair and in the presidency of Natale Sicuro. The first of these was an organized revolt of the department heads. Beginning in late April, most of the College of Liberal Arts and Sciences depart-ment heads began attending what became a series of internal meet-ings to discuss what they regarded as the "breakdown of governance" under Sicuro's administration. And finally, they came publicly to the aid of Marjorie Burns, who had hitherto stood alone.[51]

On 31 May, many of them wrote a letter to President Sicuro refut-ing the notion circulated by administrators that only a small minority of the faculty were critical of the administration. Rather, said the depart-ment heads, in a not too subtle appeal for Sicuro's resignation, "We attest that the alienation from this administration is not limited to those who have already expressed it publicly, but is to be found wide-ly and at all levels of the faculty. We fear that, given the record of your administration, it will be unable to regain the support necessary for the continued growth and improvement of Portland State University." The following day, the *Oregonian* charged in a news article that the foundation failed to report the expenditure of $5,639 to the Internal Revenue Service against the advice of its auditors.[52]

Then, on 6 June, came a report from the Budget Committee Task Force highly critical of the foundation. Clear, thorough, and objective, it was certainly one of the best reports ever made at the University. In twenty-one lucid pages, it answered seven questions raised by the fac-ulty senate, and drew four cogent conclusions from its research. First, it concluded the types of perquisites and expenses provided to the president were common at other universities (and some of them had been given at Portland State in the past) and were not unreasonable in amount by national standards. Second, the rate of increase in dona-tions had fallen below the "trend line" established before the 1986–87 academic year (President Sicuro's first year). Thirdly, the foundation "has serious financial difficulties," as it was overcommitted. It would have difficulty paying for its existing obligations, such as faculty travel and money for fundraising activities. Proof of this was the administra-tion's plan to use $150,000 of State (not foundation) funds for money-raising activities.[53]

The fourth conclusion was the most serious: "The Foundation does not appear to be maintaining the proper degree of independence from the University as is required by Oregon administrative rules relating to higher education." Specifically, decisions that should have been made by the independent foundation officials were made by its executive director, who was a PSU employee. Adequate records of committee meetings had not been kept, and "there has been a lack of internal controls and insufficient accountability over Foundation accounts." All in all, the report made many of the same points that would arise in two additional investigations into the foundation's activities.[54]

The first of these followed in two days time. It was a report made by Lou R. Merrick, assistant budget director and internal auditor. This twenty-two-page document contained numerous observations and recommendations dealing with the subjects of board governance, balance-sheet reporting, suggested fund groupings, and investment policies. The Merrick report, like the task force recommendations, was critical of the lack of involvement by the foundation board in making policies and in authorizing expenditures. Among its recommendations was that the board should be involved in these two matters; that the foundation should include in its annual budget supplemental funds given to the University president or to other employees of Portland State or of the foundation; and that the number of fund groups maintained by the foundation should be reduced (among others, the category of "designated funds" should be eliminated) to a maximum of four groups: endowment and trust funds, current funds (including both restricted and unrestricted), plant funds (optional), and agency funds (optional).[55]

Within a week, the pressures on Sicuro increased. On 12 June, the *Oregonian* editorially declared, "Sicuro would help the university by stepping down voluntarily," but if he insisted on staying, "the Board of Higher Education should initiate an immediate, in-depth review of his performance." On 14 June, the department heads again wrote to Sicuro stating, "Our reservations about the internal governance of the University and about the relationships of the University with the outside community remains unresolved." The same day, a poll revealed 62 percent of the faculty were dissatisfied with Sicuro's leadership.[56]

In mid-July, the president was hit by two other blows. On 12 July, a long-awaited report of the Oregon Department of Justice concerning the foundation was presented and discussed at a meeting in Salem by Attorney General Dave Frohnmayer. In early May, the Charitable

Activities Section of the Department of Justice had begun an investigation under the attorney general's responsibility "to oversee the solvency and practices of charitable trusts and corporations." The investigation was limited to the subject of whether the foundation "may have spent restricted funds in ways inconsistent with the restrictions." Throughout its investigation, the Justice Department had the full cooperation of the foundation's board and staff. When its inquiry was completed, the investigators made ten findings and ten recommendations in its final report, which took the form of a long letter to the chairman of the foundation board.[57]

It must have been a relief to Sicuro and those of the foundation staff to hear the Department of Justice found no examples of criminal wrongdoing in the foundation's work. It did find, however, that during Sicuro's presidency from 1986–88, the amount of unrestricted funds in the foundation had declined to a deficit of $165,000. The report faulted the foundation board for not controlling the unrestricted funds expenditures that had created this deficit. It also criticized the foundation and PSU for creating an administrative structure whereby "the foundation's operations are deeply and, in many respects, inappropriately intertwined with those of the university administration. Funds occasionally are transferred between the Foundation and the university."[58]

The investigators could make no determination whether borrowing from restricted funds had occurred but indicated if this were done, then the transaction must be documented, the monies returned with appropriate interest, and invested in compliance with "prudent person" standards. The report also chastised the directors of the foundation for failure to recognize that their responsibilities included not only raising money but also overseeing its expenditure. The investigators further found the board "seriously impeded" in its ability "to undertake independent supervision" of the foundation because its employees reported to the University rather than to the board. They also criticized the board for not having proposed a budget for President Sicuro's entertainment and travel expenses related to fundraising, a matter that led to "apparent internal misunderstandings, and to substantial public confusion regarding the propriety of expenses incurred by Dr. Sicuro. It has also contributed to the unrestricted funds deficit."[59]

Obviously, the Department of Justice investigators called for remedial measures to correct these faults. Their most important recommendation was that PSU decide whether it wanted to raise money by itself or to have it done by a truly independent foundation. Implementation of all other recommendations, some of which had been made in the Merrick report, would follow from that decision. The response of the foundation, in acknowledging the report of the attorney general, was to issue a press release stating its "intent to review the audit and develop a plan for corrective measures." Similar assurances were given by the officers of the foundation to the faculty senate in September. These promises were realized in the years ahead, but the mismanagement of foundation assets was the major crisis of the Sicuro years and the ultimate cause of his downfall. The state board decided, in Sicuro's case, to hold its customary review of university presidents one year earlier than usual. To conduct the review, Chancellor W.T. Lemman named a panel of five former presidents of the state board. Although there were complaints that three of the panel were pro-Sicuro, the early review in and of itself showed a lack of confidence in the president.[60]

The conclusion of all these unhappy affairs was near at hand. The presidential review board called for written and oral testimony in September 1988. One correspondent declared the president had "victimized" PSU through the use of "arbitrary power, overriding manipulation, base intimidation, pathetic cronyism, gangster-like bullying, and gross incompetence." In a more restrained fashion, thirty department and program heads sent to the review panel a seven-point indictment of President Sicuro's stewardship. They stated PSU had lost confidence within the national educational community; that several high-ranking female administrators had departed with attendant consequences for the affirmative action program; that—in the *Vanguard* affair—the president had shown his intolerance of the principle of freedom of expression; that the University lacked administrative direction; that the president had avoided the traditional modes of university governance; that he had not taken responsibility for his own actions but had ascribed them to his subordinates; and that his actions in regard to the foundation had "severely damaged the future of the University." The conclusion was inescapable: "It is clear to us, and evidently to many long-time supporters of the university in the community, that *only* when President Sicuro steps down can Portland State begin to recover." The department heads subsequently conveyed similar comments in oral testimony to the review panel. All in all, the panel members heard forty hours of testimony and received three hundred letters representing 425 signatories.[61]

The end for Natale Sicuro came on 10 October 1988, when he resigned his office. The news was announced at a special meeting called by the chancellor. The president gave as the reason for his resignation the conclusion of the review committee that the "differences between the President and the faculty at Portland State University were such that reestablishing a satisfactory working relationship is problematical." The effective date of the resignation was 31 December 1988; however, Sicuro's duties would be immediately reassigned. The board stated its "review panel found no evidence of misuse of University or Foundation funds or of any other wrongdoing. The chancellor and Board concur in this finding....The Board believes Dr. Sicuro is a person of integrity and moral conviction. The resignation is based on our mutual recognition of the differences between Dr. Sicuro and the University faculty." There was a fatuous, champagne "victory party" in the Department of Psychology, but the *Vanguard* editorialist was correct in stating the resignation was not a cause for celebration, for "those who attended the State Board meeting Monday were witness not to a victory, but to a defeat—a defeat for all of us." In a public statement, Marjorie Burns urged a focus on the future. "The entire PSU Community," she said, "must continue to work together, as we have over the last few weeks, and heal any divisions that might remain."[62]

Although there was quite a bit of talk that the damage inflicted by Sicuro would be long-lasting, this was not an accurate estimate. That the departing president's heritage was not a more injurious one was due to two developments—one positive, one negative. His two immediate successors as president remedied many of the morale problems that remained from the Sicuro years, and memories of the negative aspects of his career were dimmed by the devastating blow struck at all of public higher education in the state by voters' passage of a property tax limitation measure in November 1990. Although not insignificant, the Sicuro legacy was also not of lengthy duration.

The first to pick up the pieces was Roger Edgington, vice-president for Finance and Administration, who was appointed executive vice-president and interim president the day Sicuro resigned in October 1988. Edgington, who held a bachelor's degree from the University of Maryland and a master's in Business Administration from Indiana University, had been at Portland State since 1976, when he was appointed director of business affairs. He was appointed interim vice-president in 1983 and, since 1985, had been vice-president for Finance and Administration. During his presidency, Edgington rightly did not regard himself as a caretaker but rather as an active advocate for the University in the metropolitan community and before the state board and chancellor.[63]

It was fortunate he did so, among other reasons because he served a long time in his new position. The state board, tarred by its appointment of Sicuro, did not hurry to select a permanent successor, taking eighteen months to complete its task. More specifically, what Edgington accomplished was to speak as frequently as possible before community groups to remind citizens Portland State was more than a victim of Sicuro—it had an important role to play in the coming years. This was an important point to make—as mentioned earlier—as Governor Goldschmidt and the electronics industry were trying to shoulder Portland State aside as a university in order to pour most of the state's limited research monies into Oregon and Oregon State.[64]

When it did make its decision, the board's choice for president was Judith A. Ramaley, an executive vice-chancellor at the University of Kansas, who had received her bachelor's degree at Swarthmore College and her doctorate in Zoology from the University of California at Los Angeles. Before coming to Portland State as the first female president of a state system institution, she had served at four universities as professor and as administrator. Intelligent, enthusiastic, and energetic, the new president would need all of these qualities, for six months after her selection, the property-tax-limitation measure (Measure Five) was adopted by the electorate. It cast an enormous pall over the future of all state services in Oregon. In spite of this ill omen, Ramaley took up her new duties with flair, and, since 1990, faculty, administration, and students have instituted changes such as the previously mentioned new general education requirements, plans to make the campus a part of a University District in downtown Portland, and the construction of Harrison (now Hoffmann) Hall, a new classroom and conference building equipped with modern multimedia facilities.[65]

PSU Educational Media Services

At the time of its fiftieth anniversary, Oregonians could look back on a remarkable set of achievements

Judith A. Ramaley, president, 1990-96

at Portland State University. Literally starting from nothing, PSU has developed from a ramshackle housing project to a university that, in 1995–96, had a faculty of more than one thousand and a student body of 14,348, who worked in forty-one buildings on a forty-nine-acre campus. What is more noteworthy is that the University's accomplishments have come in the face of daunting adversities. The forces of nature, the state board, the chancellor, the University of Oregon, international events, and the parsimony of the state's taxpayers have limited, but not crippled, the institution's rise. Throughout its turbulent history, in all the struggles with its numerous opponents, the PSU community developed a spirit of determined combat and a hope—even in the times of greatest discontent—that conditions would improve and that there will be better days ahead. The central question for Portland State's constituencies at the time of the fiftieth anniversary—a period of the most rapid withering of support for community institutions in Oregon history—is whether this spirit of resiliency, this faith in eventual progress, has any justification in the realm of fact.

TIMELINE

1942   Vanport housing project begun

1944   GI Bill of Rights law passed by Congress

1946   24 March, State Board of Higher Education authorizes the
       Vanport Extension Center
       18 June, first session begins
       First issue of student newspaper appears
       First intercollegiate game (basketball)

1947   Edwin C. Berry, first African American faculty member, appointed
       First football game played
       First yearbook published

1948   30 May, Columbia River flood destroys Vanport
       8 June, State Board allows Vanport Extension Center to continue
       14 June, summer session opens at Grant High School
       6 July, State Board approves Oregon Shipyard site for campus

1949   15 April, bill authorizing permanent center signed by governor

1950   25 June, Korean War begins

1951   First faculty constitution adopted

1952   Faculty approves creation of a President's Advisory Council
       September, first term opens at former Lincoln High School

1955   10 February, governor signs bill making Portland State a four-
       year college
       John Francis Cramer named first president of Portland State College
       Second faculty constitution adopted
       State Board authorizes construction of second building, State
       (now Cramer) Hall
       Faculty permitted to join TIAA retirement plan

1956   Campus Christian Organization created

1957 Tau Kappa Epsilon chartered, first national fraternity
      First part of State Hall completed
      Athletics Booster Club started

1959 Branford P. Millar becomes president

1960 Library moves from Old Main to Smith Center
      Middle East Studies Center opens
      Honors Program begins
      First televised courses given

1961 School of Social Work created
      Public Health Service grant for Science Building I obtained
      State Hall and Smith Center completed
      Skidmore, Owings, and Merrill draws up campus architectural plan

1962 New faculty constitution adopted

1963 Neuberger Hall completed
      Italian studies program at Pavia, Italy, begins
      MAT and MST degrees authorized
      President Millar suspends all sororities
      Northwest Interinstitutional Council for Study Abroad created
      Harry A. Scott report on athletics

1964 First dean of graduate studies appointed, Frederick C. Cox
      Free speech movement begins at Berkeley

1965 Portland Campus Christian Ministry created
      Big Sky Conference postpones application of Portland State
      Council of Academic Deans (CADS) created

1966 Mosser Plan to evaluate teaching goes into effect
      Students made eligible to serve on university committees
      Procedures for termination of tenured faculty adopted
      Student government goes on strike

1967 New library building completed
      Koinonia House building completed
      Vanguard strike
      President Millar confiscates an issue of the *Vanguard*
      New Publications Board created
      House Un-American Activities Committee accuses three students
      of being Communists

1968 Project TEACH for disadvantaged students begins

Protests against military recruiting on campus begin
April, student strike against the Vietnam War and racism
Pass-no pass grading instituted
Program for experimental college presented and rejected
First doctoral programs approved
Campus urban renewal plan begun
Gregory B. Wolfe becomes president

1969 14 February, Portland State becomes a university
Albina Education Center begun
Andrew Haynes elected, first African American student body
president
15 October and 14-15 November, moratorium against the
Vietnam War
Campus police force established
Portland State Services created

1970 Black Studies certificate program begun
Oregon State Public Interest Research Group (OSPIRG) founded
4-11 May, protests against the Vietnam War culminate in Park
Blocks confrontation
Gay Liberation Front founded
Women's Studies Program begun
Portland State Women's Union founded

1971 Student conduct code adopted
Black Cultural Affairs Board founded
Faculty conduct code instituted
Portland State Child Care Center authorized
President Wolfe declares financial exigency

1972 General Science Department abolished
HEW committee investigates employment practices
Goose Hollow apartment building completed

1973 Controversy over *Vanguard*'s "Papal Bull" edition
University's application to join Big Sky Conference tabled
Senate committee investigates collective bargaining
University joins Law Enforcement Assistance Administration
Pacific Rim Center abandoned

1974 Joseph C. Blumel becomes president
Frank Giese convicted of conspiracy for anti-war activity

1975   Orcillia Forbes becomes first female dean
        State Board approves Women's Studies certificate program
        Post-tenure review panel voted by faculty senate
        University Athletics Board created

1976   State Board approves School of Urban Affairs

1977   State Board permits Portland State to have dormitories

1978   Orcillia Forbes becomes first female vice-president
        Faculty vote for collective bargaining—AAUP chosen as agent

1979   First collective bargaining contract negotiated

1981   Men's basketball abolished
        Controversy over reorganization of library staff
        Financial exigency declared

1982   Legislature creates Oregon Council for High Technology Education
        School of Performing Arts created
        College of Liberal Arts and Sciences created

1983   Reserve Officers Training Corps (ROTC) adopted
        Budget Allocation System model adopted

1985   Legislature declares Portland State a comprehensive research university
        Case of Penk vs. Oregon State Board of Higher Education decided

1986   Natale A. Sicuro becomes president

1988   Roger N. Edgington becomes interim president
        Semester plan for State System of Higher Education abandoned

1990   Judith Ramaley becomes president

1991   Portland Center for the Study of Religion organized
        Controversy over the reorganization of the School of Business
        Second controversy over the reorganization of the library staff
        Library addition completed
        President Ramaley announces retrenchment plan

1992   Diversity requirement added to undergraduate curriculum

1994   University Studies program adopted

1995   University joins Big Sky Conference

1996   Portland State University celebrates its fiftieth year

Notes

Chapter One

1. Stephen E. Epler to Phil Putnam, 20 June 1946, Phil Putnam folder, Box 92 Portland State University Archives, Portland, Oregon (hereafter, PSUA).

2. Manly Maben, *Vanport* (Portland: Oregon Historical Society Press, 1987), 31; *Vanguard*, 17 May 1948.

3. Davis R. B. Ross, *Preparing for Ulysses: Politics and Veterans during World War II* (New York and London: Columbia University Press, 1969), 89-124, passim.

4. Maben, *Vanport*, 1-21, passim. A solid account of the Kaiser shipbuilding enterprise is contained in Mark S. Foster, *Henry J. Kaiser: Builder in the Modern American West* (Austin: University of Texas Press, 1989), 75-78, 82-85.

5. Maben, *Vanport*, 32-80, passim.

6. Ibid., 22-31, passim.

7. Ibid., 98-103, passim; (102, quotation).

8. Stephen E. Epler, interview with Gordon B. Dodds, 26 October 1990, PSUA; Joanne Reed, "Stephen E. Epler: A Short Biography" (Portland: n.p., 1995), 11-12, 18-22, in possession of the author.

9. Stephen E. Epler, interview with Gordon B. Dodds, 26 October 1990, PSUA.

10. Ibid.

11. Stephen E. Epler, interview with Gordon B. Dodds, 26 October 1990, PSUA; Stephen E. Epler, *Six-Man Football* (New York: Harper and Brothers, 1938); *Lincoln* [Nebraska] *Journal-Star*, 6 October 1991.

12. Stephen E. Epler, interview with Gordon B. Dodds, 26 October 1990, PSUA; Lawrence A. Cremin, David A. Shannon, and Mary Evelyn Townsend, *A History of Teachers College Columbia University* (New York: Columbia University Press, 1954), 149-175, 258; Reed, "Stephen E. Epler," 24.

13. Cremin, *Teachers College*, 248-255, (252, quotation).

14. *Time*, 29 June 1942, 55-56; *New York Times*, 15 January 1942, 19; Stephen E. Epler, *Honorary Degrees: A Survey of Their Use and Abuse* (Washington: American Council on Public Affairs, 1943). The last work was revised in Epler's later study written with Phil Putnam: Stephen E. Epler and P. H. Putnam, "Honorary

Doctorates Conferred by Seven Colleges and Universities," *School and Society* 73 (1951): 5-8.

15. Stephen E. Epler, *The Teacher, The School, The Community* (Washington, D.C.: The American Council on Education, 1940); Stephen E. Epler, interview with Gordon B. Dodds, 26 October 1990, PSUA; Reed, "Stephen E. Epler," 25-26.

16. Stephen E. Epler, interview with Gordon B. Dodds, 26 October 1990, PSUA; Stephen E. Epler folder, Box 89, PSUA.

17. Stephen E. Epler, interview with Gordon B. Dodds, 26 October 1990, PSUA.

18. Stephen E. Epler, interview with Gordon B. Dodds, 26 October 1990, PSUA; Oregon State Board of Higher Education, "Minutes" (hereafter, State Board), 24 March 1946; "First Annual Report of the Vanport Extension Center, 1946–47," Box 49, PSUA; John Aidan Richardson, "The Evolution of a University: A Case Study of an Organization and Its Environment" (Ph.D. diss., Stanford University, 1974), 43.

19. Stephen E. Epler, interview with Gordon B. Dodds, 26 October 1990, PSUA; Vanport Extension Center, "Announcements 1946," Box 49, PSUA; "Radio Script," Box 49, PSUA (this is the text of a radio program produced by the Center in 1952); Stephen E. Epler, "Vanport Extension Center," in John Eliot Allen, ed., "Portland State University: The First 25 Years, 1955–1980" (n.p.: n.p., n.d.), 4-5 (hereafter, Allen, "Portland State University"); Margaret Holland Gottlieb, interview with Gordon B. Dodds, 24 July 1989, PSUA.

20. Phil Putnam folder, Box 92, PSUA; Stephen E. Epler interview with Gordon B. Dodds, 26 October 1990, PSUA; May Putnam, interview with Gordon B. Dodds, 27 July 1989, PSUA; Richard B. Halley, interview with Gordon B. Dodds, 15 July 1994, PSUA; Epler, "Vanport Extension Center," in Allen, "Portland State," 4 (quotation).

21. Stephen E. Epler, interview with Gordon B. Dodds, 26 October 1990, PSUA; William Walker, interview with Gordon B. Dodds, 7 November 1990, PSUA; "First Annual Report of the Vanport Extension Center, 1946–47," 1, 7-8, Box 49, PSUA; Don R. Hammitt, "Vanport Center College," (Portland) *Sunday Oregonian*, 9 June 1946; *Time*, 29 July 1946, 51-52.

22. Vanport Extension Center, "First Annual Report, 1946–47," 10-11, PSUA.

23. (Portland) *Oregon Journal*, 29 August 1946; (Portland) *Oregonian*, 29 August, 30 August 1946 (quotations).

24. (Portland) *Oregonian*, 30, 31 August 1946.

25. "First Annual Report of the Vanport Extension Center, 1946–1947," Box 49, PSUA.

26. Maben, *Vanport*, 72-73.

27. Ibid.

28. Vanport Extension Center, "First Annual Report, 1946–47," 5-6, PSUA, Box

49; *Vanguard,* 5 November 1952; Richard B. Halley, interview with Gordon B. Dodds, 15 July 1994, PSUA (quotation); George C. Hoffmann, interview with Janet Baisinger, 12 May 1980, Oregon Historical Society, Portland.

29. Vanport Extension Center, "First Annual Report, 1946–47," 5-6, PSUA, Box 49; ibid., "Second Annual Report, 1947–48," 7, PSUA, Box 49; *Vanguard,* 28 January 1947; Stephen E. Epler, "Vanport Extension Center," in Allen, "Portland State University," 5.

30. Richard B. Halley, interview with Gordon B. Dodds, 15 July 1994, PSUA; *Vets Extended,* 6 December 1946; Vanport Extension Center, "Second Annual Report, 1947–47," 8-9, Box 49, PSUA; "Faculty Minutes," 1946–1948, passim, Box 49, PSUA; Charles M. White, "Abbreviated Constitutional History of PSC," in possession of Charles M. White.

31. Richard B. Halley, interview with Gordon B. Dodds, 15 July 1994, PSUA; *Vanguard,* 28 January 1947.

32. Margaret Dobson to Gordon B. Dodds, 5 December 1995, PSUA; Clarence A. Hubbard, *Fleas of Western North America* (Ames, Iowa: Iowa State College Press, 1947); *Vanguard,* 8 April, 11 February 1947.

33. *Vanguard,* 1 April 1947; 23 February 1947 (quotation).

34. Vanport Extension Center, "First Annual Report, 1946–47," 7-8, Box 49, PSUA.

35. Stephen E. Epler, "Vanport Extension Center," in Allen, "Portland State University," 18-19; Vanport Extension Center, "First Annual Report, 1946– 47," 8-9, Box 49, PSUA; Vanport Extension Center, "Second Annual Report, 1947–48," 12, Box 49, PSUA; Jean Black folder, Box 88, PSUA; Jean Phyllis Black, "Vanport, The College in a Housing Project," *Pacific Northwest Library Association Quarterly* (April 1948): 117-118 (117, quotation); Jean Black, interview with David H. Newhall, 3 April 1989, PSUA.

36. Stephen E. Epler, "Vanport Extension Center," in Allen, "Portland State University," 20-21; Vanport Extension Center, "Second Annual Report," 16-17 (16, quotation), Box 49, PSUA.

37. Maben, *Vanport,* 104-105.

38. Ibid., 104-122, (106, quotation).

39. "Report of Vanport Flood, May 30, 1948, As Observed by Stephen E. Epler, Dictated June 9, 1948;" *Vanguard,* 23 April 1952; Vanport Extension Center, "Second Annual Report, 1947–48," 1, Box 49, PSUA; Allen, "Portland State University," 11-12.

40. Vanport Extension Center, "Second Annual Report, 1947–48," 1, Box 49, PSUA.

41. Jean Black, interview with David H. Newhall, 3 April 1989, PSUA; Annette Bartholomae, "The Library," in Allen, "Portland State University," 127; Stephen E. Epler to Jean Black, 9 June 1948, Jean Black folder, Box 88, PSUA; Stephen E. Epler, "Vanport Extension Center," in Allen, "Portland State University,"

12-13; Stephen E. Epler, "Report of Vanport Flood," 4; Maben, *Vanport*, 128-131; Vanport Extension Center, "Second Annual Report, 1947–48," 1, Box 49, PSUA; (Portland) *Oregonian*, 18 June 1948; *Vanguard*, 15 July 1948.

42. Stephen E. Epler, "Vanport Extension Center," in Allen, "Portland State University," 13; Richard B. Halley, interview with Gordon B. Dodds, 15 July 1994, PSUA.

Chapter Two

1. Stephen E. Epler, "Vanport Extension Center," in John Eliot Allen, ed., "Portland State University: The First 25 Years, 1955–1980" (n.p.: n.p., n.d.), 13-14 (hereafter, Allen, "Portland State University"); Stephen E. Epler to George Field, 5 June 1948, Vanport Extension Center files, Oregon State System of Higher Education Archives; Oregon State Board of Higher Education, "Minutes" (hereafter, State Board), 8 June 1948; *Vanguard*, 9 August 1948; Epler to Jean Black, 14 June 1948, Jean Black folder, Box 88, Portland State University Archives, Portland, Oregon (hereafter, PSUA) (quotation); State Board, "Minutes," 7 June 1948, quoted in John Aidan Richardson, "The Evolution of a University: A Case Study of an Organization and Its Environment" (Ph.D. diss., Stanford University, 1974), 45-46; Lois Hennessey, "A College Comes Back," *Christian Science Monitor*, 24 December 1948 (hereafter, Hennessey, "College").

2. Stephen E. Epler, "Vanport Extension Center" in Allen, "Portland State University," 14-15; Vanport Extension Center, "Second Annual Report, 1947–1948," 18, Box 49, PSUA; State Board, "Minutes," 6 July 1948; (Portland) *Oregon Journal*, 8 July 1948.

3. "Faculty Bulletin," v 3, n 1, Fall Term 1949, Box 95, PSUA; Stephen E. Epler, "Vanport Extension Center," in Allen, "Portland State University," 15; *Vanguard*, 30 January 1952 (quotation).

4. Stephen E, Epler, "Vanport Extension Center," in Allen, "Portland State University," 13-14; *Viking* 1949, n.p.; Hennessey, "College," 24 December 1948.

5. Stephen E. Epler, "Vanport Extension Center" in Allen, "Portland State University," 15; Vanport Extension Center, "Second Annual Report, 1947–48," 14, Box 49, PSUA; (Portland) *Oregon Journal*, 22 August 1948; (Portland) *Oregonian*, 26 September 1948; *Vanguard*, 1 October 1948, 18 February 1949; Vanport Extension Center, *Catalog 1949–50*, 16-17; Hennessey, "College," 24 December 1948.

6. Vanport Extension Center, "Third Annual Report, 1948–1949," 14, Box 49, PSUA; (Portland) *Oregon Journal*, 7 November 1948; *Vanguard*, 12 November 1948; Jean Black, interview with David H. Newhall, 3 April 1989, PSUA. The autographed books are now in the Special Collections Room of the Portland State University library.

7. Vanport Extension Center, "Third Annual Report, 1948–1949," 13-14, Box 49, PSUA.

8. Annette Bartholomae, "The Library," in Allen, "Portland State University," 127; *Portland State Extension Center Catalog, 1953–1954*, 22; *Portland State Extension Center Catalog*, 1953–1954, 22.

9. *Vanguard*, 1 October, 5 November 1948.

10. Faculty Bulletin," v 5, n 1, Spring Term 1949, Box 49, PSUA; (Portland) *Oregon Journal*, 18 May 1949; *Vanguard*, 1 October, 5 November 1948; 16 May 1950; 14 February 1964; 15 April 1949; 3 May 1950; 18 April 1951; "Faculty Bulletin," v 3, n 1, Fall Term 1949, Box 95, PSUA.

11. *Vanguard*, 25 October 1950; *New York Times*, 1 April 1951, 1; *Vanguard*, 11 April 1951.

12. *Vanguard*, 22 November 1950; 7 March 1951; Stephen E. Epler, Diary, 24 September 1951 (hereafter, Epler, Diary).

13. "Faculty Bulletin," 26 October 1950; *Vanguard*, 10 May 1951; 20 November 1953; "Faculty Minutes," 4 February 1952, 9 December 1953, Box 49, PSUA.

14. *Vanguard*, 6 October 1950; 10 January, 4 April, 9 May 1951.

15. Stephen E. Epler to J. F. Cramer, 15 January 1951; Stephen E. Epler to James C. Caughlan, 15 July 1952, Pierson folder, Box 92, PSUA.

16. J. F. Cramer to Director, State Department of Veterans' Affairs, 11 June 1954; L.S. Cressman to J. F. Cramer, 15 March 1954; J. F. Cramer to Charles D. Byrne, 9 April 1954, all in Merz folder, Box 91, PSUA.

17. H. C. Saalfeld and Louis S. Bonney to J. F. Cramer, 5 August 1954, Merz folder, Box 91, PSUA; Epler, Diary, 4 December 1954.

18. *Vanguard*, 8 October 1952.

19. *Vet's Extended*, 6 December 1946.

20. Ibid., 13 December 1946.

21. *Vet's Extended*, 13 December 1946; *Vanguard*, 21 January 1947.

22. *Vanguard*, 25 February 1947; Reed, "Stephen E. Epler," 45.

23. Mailing List, First Annual Report, November 14, 1947, in Box 51, PSUA; Stephen E. Epler, "Do Veterans Make Better Grades than Nonveterans," *School and Society* 66 (October 1947): 270-271; *Vanguard*, 1 December 1947.

24. John W. Hakanson, Biographical Data, June 1988, in possession of the author.

25. (Portland) *Sunday Oregonian*, 1 February 1948.

26. Ibid.

27. Thomas F. Gun to John H. Hall, 14 February 1948, higher education folder, Hall Papers, State of Oregon Archives, Salem.

28. *Vanguard*, 29 March 1948.

29. (Portland) *Oregon Journal*, 8 June 1948.

30. (Portland) *Oregon Journal*, 4 June, 20 September, 1948; Vivian McMurtrey to

Edgar W. Smith, 5 June 1948, Box 49, PSUA; (Portland) *Oregonian*, 9 June 1948; Stephen E. Epler to John Hakanson, 5 November 1948, Epler folder, Box 49, PSUA.

31. *Vanguard*, 24 May 1948.

32. John Hakanson to Stephen E. Epler, 30 October 1948, Epler folder, Box 49, PSUA; (Portland) *Oregon Journal*, 10 December 1948; John Hakanson to Stephen E. Epler, 30 December 1948, Epler folder, Box 49, PSUA.

33. John Hakanson to Stephen E, Epler, n.d., Epler folder, Box 49, PSUA, although undated, its context indicates the letter was written in early 1949; John Hakanson to Stephen E. Epler, 4, 8 January 1949; Stephen E. Epler to John Hakanson, 5, 10 January 1949, all in Epler folder, Box 49, PSUA.

34. Senate Bill 9, Forty-fifth Legislative Assembly.

35. John Hakanson to Stephen E. Epler, 14 January 1949, Epler folder, Box 49, PSUA. Although not a very disciplined group, the Republicans did unite against measures that would benefit their Democratic colleagues.

36. (Portland) *Sunday Oregonian*, 16 January 1949; *Vanguard*, 21 January 1949; (Portland) *Oregonian* 23 January 1949 (quotation).

37. State Board "Minutes," 25 January 1949; (Portland) *Oregon Journal*, 27 January 1949; Oregon State daily *Barometer*, 22 January 1949; Stephen E. Epler to John Hakanson, 15 February 1949, Epler folder, Box 49, PSUA.

38. House Bill 213, Forty-fifth Legislative Assembly.

39. (Portland) *Oregon Journal*, 3 February 1949; Epler, Diary, 14 February 1949; *Vanguard*, 4 February 1949.

40. John Hakanson to Stephen E. Epler, 13 February 1949, Epler folder, Box 49, PSUA.

41. House amendments to House Bill 213, Forty-fifth Legislative Assembly, 5 April 1949; *Oregon Senate and House Journals, 1949,* 294, 592, 638; Stephen E. Epler to John Hakanson, 6 June 1950, Epler folder, Box 49, PSUA.

42. (Portland) *Oregon Journal*, 20 April 1949.

Chapter Three

1. Oregon State Board of Higher Education, "Minutes" (hereafter, State Board), 13 September 1949; *Oregon Laws*, 1951, 235.

2. *Vanguard*, 3 May 1950; (Portland) *Oregonian*, 22 August 1966; *Vanguard*, 12 March 1952.

3. State Board, "Minutes," 18 June 1952; Charles M. White to Gordon B. Dodds, 26 January 1996, Portland State University Archives, Portland, Oregon (hereafter, PSUA).

4. *Vanguard*, 8 October (quotation), 26 September 1952.

5.   Vanport Extension Center, "Fourth Annual Report, 1949–1950," 10; Vanport Extension Center, "Biennial Report, 1950–1952," 7-8, both in Box 49, PSUA; *Vanguard*, 26 September 1952; State Board, "Minutes," 28 April 1953; Faculty, "Minutes," 14 March 1955; *Vanguard*, 2 February 1955.

6.   Stephen E. Epler, Diary, 29 December 1952 (hereafter, Epler, Diary).

7.   (Portland) *Oregonian*, 26 October 1952.

8.   State Board, "Minutes," 28 April 1953; *Vanguard*, 9 April 1954; Faculty, "Minutes," 9 December 1953.

9.   Faculty, "Minutes," 2 November 1953, Box 51, PSUA; *Vanguard*, 20 November 1953; Portland State Extension Center, *Administrative Bulletin*, 20 July 1953; *Vanguard*, 12 February, 16 April, 13, 20 October 1954; Faculty, "Minutes," 8 February, 19 May, 2 June 1954.

10. "Faculty Minutes," 13 December 1951; Epler, Diary, 13 December 1951, 6 February 1952.

11. Errett Hummel to J. F. Cramer, 15 February 1951, folder "History-Vanport: Move to Lincoln H.S. (Old Main)" Box 95, PSUA. Hummel's plan is contained in the folder marked "History-Portland State Extension Center," Box 95, PSUA; J. F. Cramer to Charles D. Byrne, 24 January 1952, Oregon State System of Higher Education Archives, Box B19; the dates of the conferences are not known.

12. "General Extension Division, Administrative Council Meeting, January 18, 1952," Box 95, PSUA; J. F. Cramer to Charles D. Byrne, 24 January 1952, Oregon State System of Higher Education Archives, Box B19.

13. Epler, Diary, 13 February 1952; State Board, "Minutes," 11 March 1952; Epler, Diary, 11 March 1952.

14. *Vanguard*, 26 April 1949.

15. Ibid., 26 April 1950; (Portland) *Oregonian*, 21 May 1950.

16. (Portland) *Oregonian*, 21 May 1950.

17. Ibid., 22 May 1950.

18. State Board, "Minutes," 7 January 1951.

19. "Vanport College, Its Story," n.p., n.d.

20. (Name obscured) to Dr. Newburn, 26 February 51, University of Oregon Presidential Archives, 206-44, 1950–51; Charles D. Byrne to J. F. Cramer, 23 February 1951, Stephen E. Epler folder, Box 89, PSUA.

21. "Faculty Bulletin," 18 April 1950, Box 95, PSUA.

22. Epler, Diary, 15 March 1952; (Portland) *Oregonian*, 23 March 1952; (Portland) *Oregon Journal*, 26 March 1952; (Portland) *Oregonian*, 27 March 1952.

23. Amos Reim to Douglas McKay, 17 March 1952; Douglas McKay to Amos Reim, 31 March 1952, Douglas McKay Papers, State of Oregon Archives.

24. (Portland) *Oregon Journal,* 24 March 1952; Epler, Diary, 6 April 1952.

25. Epler, Diary, 29 April, 19 May 1952; *Vanguard,* 23 April 1952.

26. Brief for a Four-Year State College for Portland (Portland: Portland State College Advancement Committee, 1952.)

27. State Board, "Minutes," 18 June 1952; Epler, Diary, 16, 26, 27 October; 17 November; 16 December 1952.

28. Earl W. Anderson, *A Survey of Some Phases of Teacher Education in the Oregon State System of Higher Education* (Eugene: Oregon State Board of Higher Education, n.d., 118; State Board, "Minutes," 5 January 1953; (Portland) *Oregonian,* 6 January 1953.

29. Epler, Diary, 18 December 1952; "Faculty Minutes," 18 December 1952, Box 95, PSUA.

30. State Board, "Minutes," 5 January 1953.

31. Ibid.

32. Ibid.

33. (Portland) *Oregonian,* 6 January 1953.

34. Epler Diary, 22 December 1952. Like John Hakanson, Allen had once run for the legislature but was disqualified because he had given out a campaign item—an emery board with his name on it—an action in violation of Oregon law, which prohibited giving away "useful" items. Charles M. White to Gordon B. Dodds, 26 January 1995, PSUA; Travis Cross to Ed Armstrong, 7 January 1953, Oregon State Archives, Record Group Four, 56-51, carton 6.

35. Epler, Diary, 15, 18, 20, 22, 23 January 1953; (Portland) *Oregonian,* 24 January 1953.

36. Epler, Diary, 28 (quotation), 30 January 1953.

37. *Vanguard,* 10 February 1953; *Oregon Voter,* 14 February 1953; (Portland) *Oregonian,* 15 February 1953.

38. (Portland) *Oregon Journal,* 14 February 1953.

39. University of Oregon, "Faculty Minutes," 4 March 1953, Registrars Office, University of Oregon; "A Statement Concerning Recent Trends in the Oregon State System of Higher Education," in possession of the author.

40. "Faculty Minutes," 8 March 1953.

41. Epler, Diary, 4 March 1953; (Portland) *Oregonian,* 13 March 1953; Charles M. White to Gordon B. Dodds, 26 January 1996, PSUA.

42. (Portland) *Oregonian,* 13 March 1953.

43. Epler, Diary, 13, 15, 22 March 1953; (Portland) *Oregonian,* 23, 25 March 1953.

44. Epler, Diary, 29, 31 March 1953; (Portland) *Oregon Journal,* 4 April 1953.

45. (Portland) *Oregonian,* 7, 8 April 1953.

46. Ibid., 18, 19 April 1953; *Vanguard*, 22 April 1953. The Portland State law is in *Oregon Laws*, 1953, 1405; Epler, Diary, 18, 19 April 1953.

47. (Portland) *Oregonian*, 28 May 1953.

48. Epler, Diary, 19 May 1953; Oregon State Federation of Labor, *Proceedings of the Fifty-First Annual Convention*, 77-78.

49. *Opinions of Attorney General of the State of Oregon.* n 2727, 7 May 1954.

50. State Board, "Minutes," 9 March 1954.

51. Ibid., 8, 9 March 1954; (Portland) *Oregonian* 10 March 1954; *Vanguard*, 12 March 1954; Epler, Diary, 2-5 May 1954.

52. Oregon State Federation of Labor, *Proceedings of the Fifty-second Annual Convention 1954*, 121; (Portland) *Oregonian*, 27 September 1954; *Vanguard*, 3 November 1954.

53. State Board, "Minutes," 14 December 1954; Epler, Diary, 14, 16 December 1954, 6, 7 January 1955.

54. (Portland) *Oregonian*, 18 September 1955; Senate Education Committee, "Minutes," 17, 19 January 1955, State of Oregon Archives; John F. Cramer to Will Norris, 22 January 1955, Will Norris folder, Box 91, PSUA.

55. House Education Committee, "Minutes," 27 January and 1 February 1955, State of Oregon Archives; John F. Cramer to Will Norris, 28 January, 9 February 1955, Will Norris folder, Box 91, PSUA.

56. *Vanguard*, 17 February 1955.

Chapter Four

1. The Committee's decision was confirmed by the full board on 27 October. Oregon State Board of Higher Education, "Minutes" (hereafter, State Board), 27 October 1953.

2. J. F. Cramer to H. K. Newburn, 27 January, 23 February, 1953; H. K. Newburn to J. F. Cramer, 27 January 1953, Presidents Archives, n 223-46, 1952-53, University of Oregon Archives.

3. *Vet's Extended*, 6 December 1946; "Faculty Bulletin," 15 September, 26 October 1950.

4. E.g., Faculty, "Minutes," 11, 18 January, 28 September 1954.

5. Ibid., 9 December 1953.

6. Ibid., 18 January, 1 March 1954.

7. Ibid., 5 April 1954.

8. Ibid., 28 September 1954.

9. Ibid. The list of requirements that were adopted is not available in the Portland State University Archives, Portland, Oregon (hereafter, PSUA).

10. "Faculty Minutes," 1 March, 8 February 1954. There was a costume party in 1954 at which John Dart of the Geography Department dressed as a professor with a garbage can cover as a "watchfob." On the fob was written, "Just missed me in the halls." Dahlstrom always wore a fob. Charles M. White to Gordon B. Dodds, 26 January 1996; "Faculty Bulletin," 2 February 1948.

11. Stephen E. Epler, Diary, 13 May 1954 (hereafter, Epler, Diary); Faculty, "Minutes," 19 May, 2 June 1954.

12. Faculty, "Minutes," 2 June 1954.

13. Faculty, "Minutes," Charles M. White, "Abbreviated Constitutional History of PSC," in possession of the author. There is no extant copy of the 1951 constitution.

14. Faculty, "Minutes," 13 December 1951.

15. Ibid.

16. Ibid., 25 March 1952.

17. Ibid., 7 April 1952.

18. Temporary Faculty Council to All Faculty Members, 28 April 1952, PSUA.

19. *Vanguard*, 19 November 1952; Charles M. White to Gordon B. Dodds, 26 January 1996, PSUA; *Vanguard*, 23 September 1953, 7 May 1954; Faculty, "Minutes," 18 May 1953; "Faculty Bulletin," 15 September 1950; Faculty, "Minutes," 4 October 1954.

20. "Faculty Bulletin," 1 November 1949; v 7, n 1 1950; 3 March 1950; 6 October 1947; Faculty, "Minutes," 9 December 1953; 11 January 1954; 28 September 1954.

21. Faculty, "Minutes," 6 April 1953. Cramer, of course, was not referring to tenure rights, which were already protected.

22. "Faculty Bulletin," v 3, n 2 Fall Term (1948); Faculty, "Minutes," 3 November 1952; 4 October 1954.

23. Faculty, "Minutes," 6 December 1954.

24. *Vanguard*, 17 May 1948; *Vanguard*, 3 March 1950; *Vanguard*, 17 May 1948, 3 March 1950; Cecile T. Cole to John F. Cramer, 15 February 1954, Leora LaRiviere folder, Box 91, PSUA.

25. Epler, Diary, 21 December 1951; *Vanguard*, 5 November 1952; (first quotation); *Vanguard*, 12 March 1952 (second quotation); Paul Pintarich, telephone interview with Gordon B. Dodds, 12 December 1995, PSUA.

26. The issuing of the wrong robes at the commencement ceremony was not unusual; *Vanguard*, 6 February 1952, 1 December 1948. Actually, Parker was an entrepreneur and ticket seller, not a "skipper." Charles M. White to Gordon B. Dodds, 26 January 1996, PSUA.

27. *Vanguard*, 1 December 1948; 14 May 1954; Epler, Diary, 16 April 1954; Charles M. White to Gordon B. Dodds, 26 January 1996, PSUA.

Chapter Five

1. *Vanguard*, 27 August, 10 October 1945; 12 March 1952.

2. Ibid., 19 January 1949; 17 January, 31 October 1951; 14 May 1954; 23 January 1952. The Crickets was a women's club.

3. "Constitution Associated Women Students of Vanport College," Box 49, Portland State University Archives, Portland, Oregon (hereafter, PSUA); *Viking*, 1948; "Vanport Student Handbook," Box 95, PSUA; *Viking* 1952; Margaret Dobson to Gordon B. Dodds, 5 December 1995, PSUA.

4. *Viking* 1948 (quotation); *Vanguard*, 14 March, 15 April 1947; 1 March 1948; Cricket Club Charter, Box 49, PSUA; *Viking* 1953, 1955.

5. *Vanguard*, 13 October 1949.

6. *Vanguard*, 3 March 1950; Portland State Extension Center, *Administrative Bulletin*, 20 July 1953; *Vanguard*, 7 October 1953; 7 March, 4 April 1951.

7. *Vanguard*, 17, 24 April, 16 May, 1951; *Newsweek*, 23 April 1951; (Paris) *France Dimanche*, 1 June 1951; C. W. Wood to Phil Putnam, 20 April 1951, Putnam folder, Box 89, PSUA; *Vanguard*, 29 September 1955.

8. *Vanguard*, 3 October 1947.

9. Ibid., 3 October 1947; 13 October, 24 November 1954.

10. *Vanport Extension Center Catalog* 1947–48, 7; *Viking* 1947; *Vet's Extended*, 13 December 1946; *Vanguard*, 4 February 1947; 12 April 1948; 13 February 1952; Portland State University Women's Association (PSUWA), "Minutes," 29 April 1949; 30 March 1950; 8 November 1951; 17 November 1960; *Portland State Women's Association News*, Fall 1985. The last two sources are in the records of the PSUWA.

11. Folder entitled, "History—Vanport Enrollment, 1947–52," Box 49, PSUA; (Portland) *Oregonian*, 5 October 1947 (quotation); *Vanguard*, 1 December 1947.

12. *Vanguard*, 10 May 1948.

13. Grant Mumpower, interview with Gordon B. Dodds, 11 August 1989; *Viking* 1950; *Vanguard*, 3 October 1951.

14. Stephen E. Epler, Diary, 12 October, 29 December 1951 (hereafter, Epler, Diary); *Vanguard*, 30 January 1952; Janet Wasko, "Mr. Speaker," *Oregon Quarterly*, 74 (1995): 12-13; (Portland) *Sunday Oregonian*, 2 April 1995.

15. *Oregon Laws*, 1947, 881-882; 1949, 314-319; 1953, 872-873; 1957, 1333-1335.

16. *Vanguard*, 22, 29 April, 10 November 1947; 19 January 1948; 21 January, 14 February, 2 March 1949; *Vanport Extension Center Catalog*, 1950–1951, 16, 22.

17. *Vanguard*, 24 January 1951; "Faculty Bulletin," 18 January 1951.

18. The Fair Rose campaign is chronicled in the *Vanguard* in articles on 2 May; 12, 18, 24 October; 7, 14, 21 November; 5 December 1951 and in 6, 13, 20 February (quotation); 30 April 1952.

19. *Vanguard*, 20 February 1952.

20. Vern Morgus to Stephen E. Epler, 26 October 1949; Epler to Morgus, 28 November 1949, in Epler correspondence folder, Box 49, PSUA; Epler, Diary, 20 May 1954. A man of great integrity and stern morality, Epler's only character flaw was reckless driving; he once promised a colleague after running a stop sign that he would stop twice at the next one to make up. Charles M. White to Gordon B. Dodds, 26 January 1996, PSUA.

21. Stephen E. Epler, interview with Gordon B. Dodds, 26 October 1990; *Vet's Extended*, 6 December 1946.

22. *Vet's Extended*, 15 November 1946, 6 December 1946; *Vanguard*, 14 January 1947.

23. *Vanguard*, 1 April 1947; *Viking* 1947; *Vanguard*, 19 November 1948.

24. *Vanguard*, 18 May 1949.

25. Ibid., 18 May 1949; 13 November 1953; 5 February 1954.

26. *Vanguard*, 16 May 1951; *Viking* 1947, 1948, 1950, 1951.

27. *Viking* 1948, 1949, 1950; *Vanguard*, 16 May 1951; *Viking* 1948.

28. *Vanguard*, 17 May 1950.

29. Ibid., 3, 10 October 1951; Epler, Diary, 28 September 1951; *Vanguard*, 28 October 1953.

30. Vanport Extension Center, "First Annual Report 1948," 9; "Second Annual Report 1949," 13, both Box 49, PSUA; *Viking* 1947, 1948.

31. Vanport Extension Center, "Second Annual Report 1949," 14; *Viking* 1951.

32. *Viking* 1951; *Viking* 1955, 220-222.

33. *Vet's Extended*, 15, 22 November 1946; *Viking*, 1947.

34. There is no copy of the 1946 constitution available; the 1949 constitution is in the Miscellaneous Student Clubs folder in Box 49, PSUA; the 1951 constitution is in the *Vanguard*, 29 October 1952; the 1955 constitution is in the *Vanguard*, 17 May 1955.

35. *Vanguard*, 15, 22 February; 3 March, 1950; 14 May, 1954; 4, 18 May 1955.

36. "Vanport Student Handbook," 1948; *Vanguard*, 29 October 1952.

37. *Vanguard*, 8 April, 6, 20 May, 17 November 1947.

38. Ibid., 8 December 1947.

39. *Vanguard*, 2 June 1950; 7, 14 November 1951; 7 October 1953.

40. *Vanguard*, 15 October 1952; 2 February 1955.

41. Ibid., 7 April 1950.

42. (Portland) *Oregonian (Northwest Magazine)*, 15 June 1975.

Chapter Six

1. Faculty, "Minutes," 10 January 1955.

2. Ibid., 8 February, 4, 18 April, 2 May 1955; "Proposed Constitution of the Portland State Faculty" accompanying the Faculty "Minutes" of 18 April 1955.

3. Faculty "Minutes," 18 April 1955.

4. Ibid.

5. Ibid.

6. Ibid.

7. Ibid., 2 May 1955.

8. Ibid., 18 April, 2 May 1955.

9. Ibid., 2 May 1955.

10. Ibid., 18 April, 2 May 1955.

11. Ibid., 7 February 1955; *Vanguard*, 23 February 1955.

12. John F. Cramer to Will V. Norris, 17 February 1955, Norris folder, Box 89, Portland State University Archives, Portland, Oregon (hereafter, PSUA); Richard B. Halley, interview with Gordon B. Dodds, 15 July 1994, PSUA.

13. Stephen E. Epler, Diary, 24 February 1955 (hereafter, Epler, Diary); Phil H. Putnam to the State Board of Higher Education, 24 February 1955, State Board Archives.

14. (Portland) *Oregonian,* 10 February 1955; (Portland) *Oregon Journal,* 1 March 1955; Richard B. Halley, interview with Gordon B. Dodds, 15 July 1994, PSUA.

15. Epler, Diary, 9 March, 11 March (quotation), 1 May, 4 June 1955.

16. Ibid., 16 June 1955.

17. Richard B. Halley, interview with Gordon B. Dodds, 15 July 1994.

18. John F. Cramer, A Letter to My Sons, in possession of William D. Cramer (hereafter, Cramer, Letter).

19. Ibid.

20. Ibid.

21. Ibid.

22. Cramer, Letter; John Francis Cramer, *Australian Schools through American Eyes* (Melbourne: Melbourne University Press, 1936); Richard B. Halley, interview with Gordon B. Dodds, 15 July 1994, PSUA.

23. Olden Johnson to O. Meredith Wilson, 19 April 1955, presidential archives, #231-142, 154-55, University of Oregon Archives.

24. Ibid. (quotations); O. Meredith Wilson to John R. Richards, 23 April 1955, ibid.

25. Charles D. Byrne to Members of the Curriculum Committee, 8 June 1955, ibid.; Oregon State Board of Higher Education, "Minutes" (hereafter, State Board),

14 June 1955.

26. State Board, "Minutes," 14 June 1955.

27. (Portland) *Oregonian*, May 1955; Alfred H. Kreft to Clyde V. Brummel, n.d.; Clyde V. Brummel to Edwin H. Armstrong, 10 May 1955; Travis Cross to Edwin H. Armstrong, 12 May 1955, all in Gov. Paul L. Patterson papers, State of Oregon Archives.

28. (Portland) *Oregon Journal*, 24 October 1955; (Portland) *Oregonian*, 24 October 1955; *Vanguard*, 27 October 1955.

29. *Vanguard*, 27 October 1955.

30. (Portland) *Oregonian*, 30, October, 4 November 1955.

31. *Eugene Register-Guard*, 4 November 1955.

Chapter Seven

1.   Office of Institutional Research and Planning, *Statistical Portrait 1994–95*, 130.

2.   Will V. Norris, "Portland State College," July 1958, Portland State University Archives, Portland, Oregon (hereafter, PSUA); *Vanguard*, 26 October, 2 November 1956; Administrative Committee, "Minutes," 13 December 1956, PSUA. The auditorium project eventually materialized as Portland's Memorial Coliseum.

3.   Oregon State Board of Higher Education, "Minutes" (hereafter, State Board), 25 January 1955, 12 June 1956; *Vanguard*, 9 March 1956; State Board, "Minutes," 11 September 1956; Faculty, "Minutes," 22 September 1956; *Vanguard*, 1 March 1957; Norris folder, Box 91, PSUA, contains several letters from Norris to Cramer reporting on his tour. It should be noted that for lack of sufficient funding, what are now Cramer Hall, Smith Center, and Neuberger Hall had to be built in sections, rather than completed at one time, an extraordinarily noisy and distracting process.

4.   *Vanguard*, 8 November 1957.

5.   Campus Planning Committee to President Millar, 10 June 1960, Box 11, PSUA.

6.   Faculty, "Minutes," 24 February 1960; *Vanguard*, 29 January, 26 October 1960.

7.   Branford P. Millar to Arthur M. Cannon, 28 January 1960, Box 315, PSUA; Carl Abbott, *Portland: Planning, Politics, and Growth in a Twentieth-Century City* (Lincoln and London: University of Nebraska Press, 1983), 211-212; (Portland) *Oregonian*, 1 August 1960. Portland State eventually acquired Shattuck Hall in 1969.

8.   J. I. Hunderup to Freeman Holmer, 19 September 1960, Box 315, PSUA; State Board, "Minutes," 13 September 1960; "Master Plan 1961," PSU Facilities Office. In 1962, the State Board, after reviewing the plan, approved the new boundaries; State Board, "Minutes," 24 July 1962.

9.   Office of Institutional Research and Planning, *Statistical Portrait 1993–94*, 124.

10. Campbell, Michael, Yost, *Portland State Development Plan* (Portland: Campbell,

Michael, Yost, 1966), 8, hereinafter *Portland State Development Plan;* State Board, "Minutes," 24 October 1966.

11. *Portland State Development Plan,* 12.

12. State Board, "Minutes," 14 September 1964; *Vanguard,* 25 September 1964, 1.

13. State Board, "Minutes," 16 September 1966; *Vanguard,* 12 November 1965; 21 September 1966; 12 April 1968.

14. *Vanguard,* 9 February 1968.

15. Ibid.

16. Ibid.

17. Office of Institutional Research and Planning, *Statistical Portrait,* 1994–1995, 130.

Chapter Eight

1. Richard B. Halley, interview with Gordon B. Dodds, 15 July 1994, Portland State University Archives, Portland, Oregon (hereafter, PSUA); Faculty, "Minutes," 2 April 1958, PSUA; John F. Cramer, A Letter to My Sons, in possession of William D. Cramer.

2. Mabel Cramer, interview with Gordon B. Dodds, 12 July 1989, PSUA; *Vanguard,* 12 March 1958; Faculty, "Minutes," 13 June 1958.

3. J. M. Swarthout to B. P. Millar, 12 April 1963, Box 14, PSUA; (Portland) *Oregonian,* 14 October 1967; *Portland State College Bulletin,* 2 March 1959.

4. *Vanguard,* 12 March 1958; Faculty, "Minutes," 2 April 1958.

5. Faculty, "Minutes," 2 April 1958. The committee agreed, although it was never written, that the new president should be from a liberal arts field. Charles M. White to Gordon B. Dodds, 26 January 1996, PSUA.

6. J. M. Swarthout to B. P. Millar, 23 August 1961, Box 19, PSUA; John M. Swarthout to Grace M. Easton, 28 February 1963, Box 19, PSUA.

7. E.g., 5 November 1962, Box 19, PSUA; John M. Swarthout to Charles Duncan, 6 July 1966, Box 19, PSUA.

8. (Portland) *Oregon Journal,* 6 June 1981; David Newhall to Gordon B. Dodds, 22 January 1996, PSUA; (Portland) *Oregonian,* 28 March 1963; John M. Swarthout to John Coffee, 8 March 1965, Box 19, PSUA; Champaign-Urbana *News-Gazette,* 8 June 1951.

9. Howard Boroughs, "Curriculum Vitae," November 1967, Box 21, PSUA; *Vanguard,* 29 September 1967; Executive Committee, "Minutes," 30 October 1963.

10. Charles M. White to Gordon B. Dodds, 26 January 1996, PSUA; Social Science Executive Committee, "Minutes," 8 March 1960. Box 1, PSUA.

11. Willard B. Spalding to John Swarthout, 22 June 1962, Box 12, PSUA.

12. "Position Description for Dean of School or Division," "Position Description for Department Head," both 11 June 1964, Box 16, PSUA; J. M. Swarthout to

F. L. Roberts (through President Millar), 26 August 1964, Box 16, PSUA.

13. "Position Description for Dean of School or Division," "Position Description for Department Head," both 11 June 1964, Box 16, PSUA.

14. John Swarthout to Frank Roberts, 11 September 1964, Box 16, PSUA.

15. Academic Administrators Council, "Minutes," 22 April, 1965, Box 16, PSUA.

16. John Swarthout to Deans of Schools and Divisions, 24 June 1965, Box 16, PSUA.

17. Faculty "Minutes," 2 November 1960; Faculty Senate "Minutes," 5 December 1960; Faculty "Minutes," 8 February 1961.

18. Faculty, "Minutes," 3 May 1961; 17 January, 28 February 1962.

19. Faculty Senate, "Minutes," 4 April 1966.

20. B. P. Millar to the Faculty, 31 May 1966, Box 17, PSUA; B. P. Millar to the Faculty, 25 January 1967, in Faculty Senate, "Minutes," 25 January 1967; *Vanguard*, 22 February 1967.

21. Portland State College Library Report to OSSHE Library Council, April 27, 1967, in PSU Library Office; Faculty Senate, "Minutes," 6 February 1967; (Portland) *Oregonian*, 23 February 1967; *Vanguard*, 1 March 1967.

22. *Vanguard*, 1, 6 March 1967.

23. Ibid., 27 October, 3 November 1967.

24. "Constitution of the Faculty of Portland State University" (1961); *Vanguard*, 4 April 1968.

25. *Vanguard*, 4 April 1968.

26. Howard Boroughs to President Millar, 25 March 1968, Box 21, PSUA.

27. Faculty, "Minutes," 16 May 1968.

28. Ibid.

29. Ibid.

30. Faculty, "Minutes," 16, 21, 28 May, 8 October 1968; *Vanguard*, 27 September 1968 (quotation).

31. Charles M. White to Gordon B. Dodds, 26 January 1996, PSUA; "History of Departmental Majors—Portland State College," September 1967, Box 21, PSUA.

32. Educational Policies Committee, "Minutes," 11 January 1962, Box 13, PSUA.

33. Ibid., "Minutes," 26 January, 1 March 1962, Box 13, PSUA.

34. John Swarthout to Members of the Educational Policies Committee, 7 September 1962; Willard B. Spalding, "The Place of the Department in the University," 17 August 1962, both in Box 13, PSUA.

35. Educational Policies Committee, "Minutes," 12 December 1963, Box 14, PSUA.

36. Whitney Bates to Gordon B. Dodds, 1 February 1996, PSUA; Educational Policies Committee, "Minutes," 20 February, 4 June 1964, Box 14, PSUA;

Faculty Senate, "Minutes," 8 March 1971.

37. *Vanguard*, 14 November 1958; College Library Committee, "Minutes," 15 November 1960, Box 12, PSUA.

38. "Commission of the Northwest Association of Secondary and Higher Education, 1965," 12-13.

39. Curriculum Committee, "Minutes," 1 February 1966, Box 18, PSUA.

40. General Student Affairs Committee, "Report to Faculty Senate," in Faculty Senate, "Minutes," 3 October 1966; Faculty Senate, "Minutes," 3 October 1966; *Vanguard*, 5 October 1966.

41. *Vanguard*, 12 October 1966.

42. *Vanguard*, 23 November 1966; Faculty, "Minutes," 16 November 1966.

43. *Vanguard*, 25 October 1968, 25 November 1969.

Chapter Nine

1. Faculty, "Minutes," 6 November 1957; Willard Spalding to John Richards, 30 April 1958, quoted in W. B. Spalding, "Opening Remarks: Meeting of State Board of Higher Education, 20 May 1958," in Administrative Council, "Minutes," n.d.

2. Ibid.

3. Oregon State Board of Higher Education, "Minutes" (hereafter, State Board), July 1958; January 1959; John M. Swarthout to Branford P. Millar, 17 January 1962, Box 19, Portland State University Archives, Portland, Oregon (hereafter, PSUA); Faculty Senate, "Minutes," 1 May 1961.

4. U.S., *Statutes at Large*, 35th Cong. 2d Sess., 1958, 1580-1605.

5. Donald Bigelow, "American Council on Education, Report on the Middle East Studies Center, November 10, 1960;" Fred Cox to Members of the Curriculum Committee, Box 13, PSUA.

6. Fred Cox to Members of the Curriculum Committee, Box 13, PSUA; *Vanguard*, 12 February 1960.

7. Middle East Studies Center, "Technical Report, 1960–1961," Box 13, PSUA.

8. J. M. Swarthout to B. P. Millar, 25 October 1961, Box 19, PSUA.

9. Frederick Cox to John Swarthout, 17 July 1963, Box 15, PSUA; W. T. Lemman, Jr. to Allen McKenzie, 12 May 1964, Box 15, PSUA.

10. Middle East Studies Center, *Technical Report 1967–1968*, Box 15, PSUA.

11. The Honors Program Planning Committee to Dean Swarthout, 8 May 1959, Box 11, PSUA.

12. Ibid.; Faculty, "Minutes," 4 November 1959.

13. Honors Committee, "Minutes," 6 November 1959; Robert D. Clark to John M.

Swarthout, 3 December1959, both Box 11, PSUA.

14. Hoyt C. Franchere to Carl Dahlstrom, 29 January 1960, Box 11, PSUA; Hoyt C. Franchere to John M. Swarthout, 19 February 1960; Hoyt C. Franchere to Carl Dahlstrom, 19 March 1960, Box 11, PSUA; Branford P. Millar to [the five members of the committee], 10 March 1960, Box 11, PSUA.

15. John M. Swarthout to J. Richard Byrne, et al., 30 March 1960; John M. Swarthout to John F. Cramer, 31 March 1960, Box 11, PSUA; Frederick C. Waller to Division Chairmen, 9 May 1960, Box 11, PSUA.

16. Frederick Waller to Colleagues, 16 September 1960, Box 11, PSUA.

17. Faculty Senate, "Minutes," 3 April 1961; "Summary Description of an Honors Program to be Proposed for Adoption at Portland State College," with ibid.

18. *Vanguard*, 15 September 1961; 26 September 1963.

19. Faculty Senate, "Minutes," 5 April 1965, 2 May 1966.

20. *Vanguard*, 14 April 1967.

21. Howard Boroughs to Branford Millar and W. T. Lemman, Jr., 1 December 1967, Box 21, PSUA; Faculty Senate, "Minutes," 8 January 1968.

22. Charles M. White to Gordon B. Dodds, 26 January 1996, PSUA.

23. Ibid.; Charles White to Board of Directors, American Heritage Association, n.d., Box 15, PSUA.

24. Ibid.

25. J. M. Swarthout to B. P. Millar, 8 November 1961, Box 19, PSUA.

26. George Carbone to Gordon B. Dodds, 23 October 1995, in possession of the author; Dean Swarthout to President Millar, 21 November 1961; J. M. Swarthout to B. P. Millar, 10 July 1962, both Box 19, PSUA.

27. Faculty Senate, "Minutes," 1 October 1962; 5 November 1962; "A Proposal for an Italian Studies Center," 7 January 1963, Box 22, PSUA; State Board, "Minutes," 21 January 1963; George Carbone to Gordon B. Dodds, 23 October 1995, in possession of the author.

28. John M. Swarthout to Branford Millar, 21 March 1963, Box 19, PSUA.

29. *Vanguard*, 29 March 1963; Italian Studies Center, *General Information Bulletin*, Box 15, PSUA.

30. *Vanguard*, 24 May 1963; George Carbone to Gordon B. Dodds, 23 October 1995, in possession of the author; Janet Krieger to Carol Ruth Healy, 15 January 1964, Box 15, PSUA; Bonnie J. Baker, et al. to Branford P. Millar, 21 May 1964, Box 15, PSUA.

31. "Minutes of the Italian Studies Program Committee," 3 January 1964, Box 15, PSUA; Margaret R. Carbone to John M. Swarthout, 4 March 1964, Box 15, PSUA; S. D. White to 1964–1965 Italian Studies Center Students, 9 July 1964, Box 22, PSUA; *Vanguard*, 31 October 1969; Charles M. White to Gordon B. Dodds, 26 January 1996, PSUA.

32. Angelo Grisoli to J. Malcolm McMinn, 26 May 1964; Branford P. Millar to Angelo Grisoli, 4 June 1964, both Box 15, PSUA. A copy of the letter in both English and Italian was sent. Grisoli's draft constitution is in ibid.

33. John M. Swarthout to George Carbone, 16 March 1965, Box 15, PSUA.

34. P. Bolfo to John M. Swarthout, 1 July 1965; John M. Swarthout to Piero Bolfo, 30 August 1965, both in Box 22, PSUA; John M. Swarthout to Gabriele Sicurani, 2 September 1965; R. L. Merrick to John Swarthout, 10 September 1965; R. L. Merrick to Sidney White, 14 April 1966; James H. Hugon to John Dart, 15 June 1968, all in Box 22, PSUA.

35. George Carbone to John M. Swarthout, 16 April 1966, Box 22, PSUA.

36. James H. Hugon to John Dart, 15 June 1968, Box 22, PSUA; White, although he recommended dividing the position between two administrators, became director of both international programs and the summer session, Charles M. White to Joseph Blumel, 19 March 1971, Box 115, PSUA.

Chapter Ten

1. Barbara Nicholls, "Establishment of the School of Social Work," August 1962, Box 14, Portland State University Archives, Portland, Oregon (hereafter, PSUA); (hereafter, Nicholls, "Establishment").

2. "Discussion of School of Social Work in Portland," 4 May 1960, Box 13, PSUA.

3. Nicholls, "Establishment;" *Oregon Laws*, 1959, 1523; Branford P. Millar to George Hoffmann, et al., 7 July 1960, Box 13, PSUA.

4. B. P. M., "Note," 27 June 1960, Box 13, PSUA.

5. "Draft Proposal for the Establishment of a Social Service Training Program at Portland State College," 12 August 1960, Box 13, PSUA.

6. Nicholls, "Establishment;" *Oregon Laws*, 1961, 1121; J. M. Swarthout to B. P. Millar, 3 October 1961, Box 13, PSUA.

7. *Vanguard*, 20 October 1961; Nicholls, "Establishment."

8. Earl M. Pallett to Branford P. Millar, 21 September 1961; John M. Swarthout to Roy Lieuallen, 4 January 1962, both Box 13, PSUA.

9. School of Social Work, "Biennial Report: July 1960-June 1962;" Gordon Hearn to John M. Swarthout, 6 March 1964, both Box 14, PSUA.

10. Council on Social Work Education, Commission on Accreditation, "Report of On-Campus Visit School of Social Work, Portland State College," Box 14, PSUA.

11. Ibid.; John Swarthout to Gordon Hearn, 8 June 1964, Box 14, PSUA.

12. Faculty, "Minutes," 24 September 1957.

13. Ibid.

14. Administrative Council, "Minutes," 20 May 1958.

15. Faculty Senate, "Minutes," 2 June 1958.

16. Willard Spalding, "A Statement Proposing Professional Programs in Teacher Education," Box 14, PSUA; Oregon State Board of Higher Education, "Minutes" (hereafter, State Board), 22 July 1958.

17. Faculty Senate, "Minutes," 6 February 1961.

18. Willard B. Spalding to John M. Swarthout, 13 July 1961; Willard Spalding to [various committees], 31 July 1961; John M. Swarthout, "File Memorandum," 18 August 1961, all in box 14, PSUA.

19. Clarence Faust to Branford P. Millar, 6 February 1962, Box 14, PSUA.

20. Faculty Senate, "Minutes," 5 March, 7 May, 4 June 1962.

21. Graduate Council, "Minutes," 28 October 1964, Box 15, PSUA; Academic Council, "Minutes," 12 December 1963; John M. Swarthout to Division and Department Heads, 8 September 1964, Box 15, PSUA.

22. State Board, "Minutes," 15 December 1964.

23. The Graduate Council to Divisional Chairmen, et al., 1 July 1963; Willard Spalding, "Estimate of Funds," both Box 14, PSUA.

24. R. E. Lieuallen to Branford P. Millar, 3 May 1963; B. P. Millar to J. M. Swarthout, 14 May 1963, both Box 14, PSUA.

25. J. M. Swarthout to B. P. Millar, 21 March 1963, Box 19, PSUA.

26. George V. Guy to G. E. Jeub, 16 January 1964; Graduate Council to Divisional Chairmen, et al., 7 November 1963; Graduate Council, "Minutes," 1 June, 9 March, 13 January 1964, Box 14, PSUA.

27. Brock Dixon for John M. Swarthout to Whitney Bates, et al., 25 June 1963, Box 15, PSUA.

28. "Registration and Advising Procedures, MAT-MST Program," 16 August 1963, Box 14, PSUA.

29. Brock Dixon to John M. Swarthout, 7 October 1963; Academic Council, "Minutes," 19 March 1964, both Box 14, PSUA.

30. Hoyt C. Franchere to John M. Swarthout, 29 October 1965, Box 17, PSUA; Council of Academic Deans, "Minutes," 23 November 1965, Box 18, PSUA.

31. Faculty Senate, "Minutes," 17, 23 November 1964; 3 May, 7 June 1965.

32. Faculty Senate, "Minutes," 7 March 1966.

33. David E. Willis to George Hoffmann, 24 November 1964; George C. Hoffmann to Frank Roberts, 9 December 1964; Frank Roberts to George Hoffmann, 15 December 1964; B. P. Millar to F. Roberts and F. Cox, 18 December 1964, all in Box 17, PSUA.

34. F. J. Cox to Dean Swarthout, Dean Cox to Dean Swarthout and Dr. Guy, both 28 December 1964, Box 17, PSUA.

35. Fred J. Cox to John M. Swarthout, 28, 29 September 1965, Box 17, PSUA.

36. Dean Cox to Mr. Lemman, 18 October 1965; F. J. Cox to Dean Swarthout, 4

November 1965; Office of Graduate Studies, untitled memorandum, 18 April 1966; Gordon Hearn to Fred J. Cox, 20 April 1966, all in Box 17, PSUA.

37. David E. Willis to Branford P. Millar, 19 April 1966; F. J. Cox to Dean Swarthout, 28 April 1966, both in Box 17, PSUA.

Chapter Eleven

1. Oregon State became a university in 1962.

2. *U.S. Statutes at Large*, 35th Cong., 2d Sess., 1958, 1580-1605.

3. Mark O. Hatfield, *Not Quite So Simple* (New York: Harper and Row, 1968), 52-63; Gordon B. Dodds and Craig E. Wollner, *The Silicon Forest: High Tech in the Portland Area, 1945–1986* (Portland: Oregon Historical Society Press, 1990); S. Eugene Allen, "Memorandum on Oregon's Economic Problems," 30 December 1961, Box 18, Portland State University Archives, Portland, Oregon (hereafter, PSUA).

4. State of Oregon, "Governor's Committee on Science, Engineering, and New Technologies," 26 May 1961; John Swarthout to President Millar, 24 October 1961, Box 19, PSUA.

5. "Some Guiding Principles for Planning a Portland Graduate Center," 20 October 1961, Box 19, PSUA; Executive Committee, "Minutes," 6 December 1961.

6. (Portland) *Oregonian*, 8 January 1962; *Vanguard*, 2 February 1962.

7. Oregon State Board of Higher Education, "Minutes," 13 March 1962 (hereafter, State Board); "Report of the Coordinating Council for Graduate Work in the Portland Area," 8 June 1962, Box 14, PSUA.

8. Portland State College, Division of Science, "Graduate Education in Science for Portland Metropolitan Area," Box 19, PSUA.

9. Executive Committee, "Minutes," 6 June 1962.

10. J. M. Swarthout to B. P. Millar, 28 June 1962, Box 19, PSUA.

11. "Concepts and Organization of Graduate Center," 30 July 1962, Box 14, PSUA.

12. Ibid.

13. Both reports are in Box 14, PSUA. The November report was entitled, "Graduate Degree Study Opportunities in the Portland Area."

14. Ibid.

15. Ibid.

16. Miles Romney, "General Principles Relating to the General Range of Graduate Programs;" John Swarthout to Division Chairmen, 1 April 1963; J. M. Swarthout to B. P. Millar, 21 June 1963, both Box 19, PSUA.

17. "Minutes of the Board of Trustees of the Portland Graduate Center," 24 January 1963; Articles of Incorporation of Oregon Graduate Center for Study and Research, both Box 15, PSUA; The charter was approved by the State on

2 April 1963.

18. Dodds and Wollner, *The Silicon Forest*, 104-105; John Aidan Richardson, "The Evolution of a University: A Case Study of an Organization and Its Environment" (Ph.D. diss., Stanford University, 1974), 192-208 (hereafter, Richardson, "Evolution of a University").

19. *Oregon Laws*, 1963, 1376; *Vanguard*, 1 February 1963; Richardson, "Evolution of a University," 167-170.

20. Portland City Club, *Bulletin*, 10 May 1963; Richardson, "Evolution of a University," 170-174.

21. *Vanguard*, 31 January, 1 May 1964; Oregon State Board of Higher Education, "Minutes" (hereafter, State Board), 27-28 April, 8 December 1964.

22. Richardson, "Evolution of A University," 208-209; State Board, "Minutes," 26 July 1966.

23. Quoted in Richardson, "Evolution of a University," 210.

24. Richardson, "Evolution of A University," 210-214.

25. Faculty Senate, "Minutes," 6 November 1967.

26. Ibid.

27. J. C. Caughlan, "Comments Relating to a Number of Proposed Doctoral Programs," October 1967, in Faculty Senate, "Minutes," 6 November 1967.

28. Dr. F. J. Cox to Dean Swarthout, 26 March 1965, Box 15, PSUA; Portland State College, "Proposal for an Interdisciplinary Doctorate in Urban Studies, 3 November 1967, in Faculty Senate, "Minutes," 6 November 1967; "Proposed Ph.D. Program in Biophysics," October 1967, in Faculty Senate, "Minutes," 6 November 1967.

29. Richardson, "Evolution of A University," 226; Oliver C. Larson to Gordon B. Dodds, 25 November 1995, in possession of the author.

30. Faculty Senate, "Minutes," 6, 13, 20 November 1967; 8 January 1968; State Board, "Minutes," 11 June 1968; Richardson, "Evolution of a University," 223-231.

31. *Vanguard*, 8 March, 15 November 1968. Willner was under the misapprehension, shared by many, that Portland State had become a college on 14 February 1955. The confusion first arose because the College's celebration of Gov. Paul Patterson's signing the bill in 1955 (which actually occurred on 10 February) took place on 14 February.

32. *Vanguard*, 31 January 1969; *Oregon Laws*, 1969, 9-10.

33. Richardson, "Evolution of a University," 231-238.

34. Richardson, "Evolution of A University," 317-394, is an excellent analysis of the movement for university status.

35. Faculty, "Minutes," 25 February 1959.

36. Richardson, "Evolution of A University," 321.

37. Ibid., 321-322.

38. Don S. Willner to Gordon B. Dodds, 14 November 1995, in possession of the author; (Portland) *Oregon Journal*, 22 January 1969.

39. Ibid.

40. Oliver C. Larson to Gordon B. Dodds, 25 November 1995, in possession of the author.

41. Stephen Dow Beckham, *Lewis & Clark College* (Portland: Lewis & Clark College, 1991), 32-34.

42. State Board, "Minutes," 13 June 1960.

43. John B. Fenner to Roy E. Lieuallen, 21 February, 2 April 1962, B.34 a.1.5, Oregon State System of Higher Education Archives (hereafter, OSSHEA).

44. Roy M. Lieuallen, "Memorandum No. 1, No. 2, No. 3; University of Oregon Law School Situation," 13 March 1963, all in B. 34.a 1.5, OSSHEA.

45. John F. Gantenbein to Roy E. Lieuallen, et al., 28 October 1963, B. 34. a1.5, OSSHEA; R. E. Lieuallen to John F. Gantenbein, 27 November 1963, B 34 a1.5, OSSHEA; Brock Dixon, interview with Clarke Brooke, 20 June 1989, PSUA.

46. John E. Gantenbein to Charles Holloway, Jr., 15 April 1964, B 34, a1.5, OSSHEA; Charles R. Holloway, Jr. to John F. Gantenbein, 20 July 1964, B 34, a1.5, OSSHEA; The negotiations are detailed in various documents in B 34 a1.5, OSSHEA; the merger is reported in Beckham, *Lewis & Clark College*, 33; and in "Press Release, 13 September 1965," B 34 a1.5, OSSHEA.

47. Keith D. Skelton to J. W. Forrester, 10 January 1968, B 34 a1.5, OSSHEA.

48. John H. Swarthout to John H. Davidson, 8 July 1960, Box 12, PSUA.

49. Brock Dixon to John M. Swarthout, 10 October, 8 December 1960; John M. Swarthout to Clyde Johnson, 21 December 1960, Box 12, PSUA.

50. Brock Dixon to Clyde Johnson, 16 February 1961; John M Swarthout to Francis L. Schmehl, 2 June 1961; Branford P. Millar to Francis L. Schmehl, 27 June 1961; Brock Dixon to Edward F. Eldridge, 28 June 1961, all in Box 12, PSUA.

51. J. M. Swarthout to B. P. Millar, 14 February 1962, Box 19, PSUA.

52. Dr. Hoffmann to Dean Swarthout, 26 August 1965; John M. Swarthout to Robert Powloski, 31 August 1965, both Box 18, PSUA.

53. J. M. Swarthout to B. P. Millar, 22 May 1962, Box 19, PSUA.

54. Division of Science, "Graduate Education in Science," January 1965, Box 17, PSUA.

55. Applied Mathematics Institute Committee, "Minutes," 6 January 1965; Thornton Fry, "Report of Visit to Portland State College, February 18-19, 1965," 25 February 1965, both Box 17, PSUA.

56. Carl Kossack, "Graduate Education Plans at Portland State College," n.d., Box 17, PSUA.

57. Dr. Cox to Dean Swarthout, 5 March 1965; Division of Science, "Institute of Applied Mathematics," March 1965; J. M. Swarthout to T. S. Peterson, 8 March 1965, both Box 17, PSUA.

58. Council of Academic Deans, "Minutes," 16 March 1968, Box 21, PSUA.

59. Council of Academic Deans, "Minutes," 16 May 1968, Box 55, PSUA.

60. Ibid.

61. Council of Academic Deans, "Minutes," 23 May 1968, Box 55, PSUA.

62. Howard Boroughs to President Millar, 28 May 1968, Box 21, PSUA; Council of Academic Deans, "Minutes," 10 October 1968, Box 20, PSUA.

63. Council of Academic Deans, "Minutes," 10 October 1968, Box 20, PSUA.

64. Ibid.

65. Council of Academic Deans, "Minutes," 24 October 1968, Box 20, PSUA.

66. Council of Academic Deans, "Minutes," 10 October 1968, Box 20, PSUA; Howard Boroughs to President Wolfe, 11 October 1968, Box 56, PSUA.

67. *Vanguard*, 23 May 1969; Roger Jennings, telephone interview with Gordon B. Dodds, 25 June 1995.

Chapter Twelve

1. General Studies Central Committee, "Progress Report," Fall 1957, Box 13, Portland State University Archives, Portland, Oregon (hereafter, PSUA); (hereafter, "Progress Report").

2. "Joint Meeting of the PSC General Studies Committee," 22 January 1957, Box 13, PSUA.

3. Ibid.

4. "Progress Report."

5. Ibid.

6. Ibid.

7. Ibid.; Faculty Senate, "Minutes," 2 December 1957.

8. Faculty, "Minutes," 12 February 1958; General Studies Central Committee, "Report," Spring 1958; General Studies Central Committee, "Report," Spring 1958, both Box 13, PSUA.

9. Frederick Waller to the Faculty, 23 February 1968, quoted in Frederick O. Waller to All Conference Participants, n.d., in Portland State College, "General Education in an Urban College," n.p., n.d.

10. *Vanguard*, 29 March 1968.

11. Ibid.

12. Ibid., 29 March, 4, 12 April 1968.

13. Ibid. 12 April 1968.

14. Ibid., 12, 19, April 1968

15. Ibid., 19 April 1968.

16. John M. Swarthout to Bill Van Alstine, 12 December 1963, Box 19, PSUA.

17. J. F. Cramer to Charles W. Bursch II, et al., 15 December 1955, in Administrative Council, "Minutes."

18. Ibid.

19. Oregon State System of Higher Education, *Inter-Institutional Teaching by Television* (Eugene: Oregon State System of Higher Education, 1960), 1-2.

20. B. P. Millar to Dean of Faculty, et al., 17 February 1960; Lester F. Beck to PSC TV Committee, 22 February 1960, both Box 11, PSUA.

21. See TV Committee folder, Box 11, PSUA.

22. PSC TV Committee to John M. Swarthout, 11 April 1960, Box 11, PSUA; Faculty, "Minutes," 3 May 1961.

23. Charles M. White to Gordon B. Dodds, 24 December 1995, PSUA.

24. Faculty, "Minutes," 3 May 1961.

25. John E. Lallas to B. P. Millar, 3 November 1961, Box 13, PSUA.

26. "Summary of the Discussion on Television in the Institutions of Higher Education," 2 February 1962, Box 13, PSUA.

27. Lester F. Beck, "Inter-Institutional Teaching of Psychology by Television," January 1962, Box 13, PSUA.

28. "A Special Report on the Teaching of English by Television Prepared by the Television Education Committee of the English Department," March 1962; Educational Policies Committee, "Minutes," 29 March 1962, both Box 14, PSUA.

29. Hoyt C. Franchere to John M. Swarthout, 13 October 1962; D. R. Larson to D. W. E. Baird, et al., 21 November 1962; "Report on Closed-Circuit Television," December 1962; J. M. Swarthout to B. P. Millar, 11 December 1962; Branford P. Millar to Roy E. Lieuallen, 13 December 1962, all in Box 14, PSUA.

30. Brock Dixon to Division Chairmen, 31 January 1963, Box 14, PSUA; *Vanguard*, 6 December 1963.

31. *Vanguard*, 6 December 1963.

32. David Newhall to Gordon B. Dodds, 22 January 1996, PSUA; *Vanguard*, 24 April, 9 October 1964.

33. *Vanguard*, 4 March 1966.

34. Ibid., 1 April 1966.

35. Ibid., 12 October 1966.

36. *Vanguard*, 10 May 1968; Curriculum Committee, "Interim Report on Pass/No Pass Grading," in Faculty Senate, "Minutes," 6 May 1968.

37. The committee recommendation of 30 April and the debate are both in Faculty Senate, "Minutes," 6 May 1968; *Vanguard*, 18 October 1968; David Newhall to Gordon B. Dodds, 22 January 1996.

38. John M. Swarthout to The Secretary, the Ford Foundation, 17 August 1960, Box 12, PSUA.

39. Walter Nunokawa to John Swarthout, 8 June 1965, Box 16, PSUA.

40. J. M. Swarthout to B. P. Millar, 12 May 1965, Box 19, PSUA.

41. *Vanguard*, 7 March 1958.

42. John M. Swarthout to Keith Bell, 5 February 1960, Box 12, PSUA; Charles W. Bursch II to E. D. Anderson, 27 July 1960, Box 12, PSUA.

43. Brock Dixon to Charles M. White, 30 January 1961, Box 12, PSUA; *Vanguard*, 1, 8 May 1964, 26 February 1965; Executive Committee, "Minutes," 3 November 1965.

44. *Vanguard*, 15 February 1963.

45. Ibid., 12, 26, February, 2 April, 7 May, 1965.

46. Ibid., 28 May, 24 September, 8 October 1965.

47. B[rock] D[ixon] to B[ranford] P[.] M[illar], 25 March 1965, Box 16, PSUA.

48. Ibid.

49. Ibid.

50. Ibid.

51. Subcommittee No. 4 of Ways and Means Subcommittee, "Guidelines for Distributing Funds for Teaching Excellence," 29 April 1965; Miles Romney to Institutional Representatives, 29 July 1965; John Swarthout to The CADS, 3 August 1965; "Recommended Guidelines for Development of Institutional Plans...," 26 August 1965; Frank Roberts to Dean Franchere, et al., 10 September 1965, all in Box 17, PSUA.

52. "Plan for Implementing Teaching Merit Award Program at Portland State College," n.d., Box 17, PSUA; *Vanguard*, 15 October 1965.

53. Faculty, "Minutes," 3 November 1965; *Vanguard*, 5 November 1965.

54. *Vanguard*, 3 December 1965.

55. Faculty Senate, "Minutes," 3 January 1966; *Vanguard*, 7 January 1966.

56. Faculty Senate, "Minutes," 17 January 1966.

57. J. M. Swarthout to B. P. Millar, 19 April 1966; Judah Bierman to John M. Swarthout, 1 April 1966; John M. Swarthout to Judah Bierman, 26 May 1966, Box 17, PSUA.

58. *Vanguard*, 8 April 1966; Donald R. Moor to Branford P. Millar, 20 April 1966, Box 17, PSUA; Branford P. Millar to Donald R. Moor, 15, 21 April 1966.

59. J. M. Swarthout to B. P. Millar, 19 April 1966; B. P. Millar to The Faculty, 8

June 1966, in Box 17, PSUA.

60. "Report by the 'Mosser' Committee to the Faculty Senate," 3 October 1966 in Faculty Senate, "Minutes," 3 October 1966.

61. Faculty Senate, "Minutes," 3 October 1966; Faculty, "Minutes," 2 November 1966.

62. John M. Swarthout to Roy E. Lieuallen, 3 November 1966, Box 19, PSUA; *Vanguard*, 16 November 1966.

63. Faculty, "Minutes," 6 December 1966; *Vanguard*, 4 January 1967.

64. Faculty, "Minutes," 3 May 1967.

65. "Portland State Library Report to the Inter-Institutional Library Council," April 1954 (hereafter, "Library Report"), PSU Library; Ibid., 14 December 1956.

66. "Library Report 1956."

67. Ibid.

68. "Library Report, June 1958–January 1959."

69. Ibid; "Library Report, January 16–May 9, 1959."

70. *Life at Portland State*, December 1959; "Library Report, April 1961."

71. "Library Report, April 1961;" (Portland) *Oregonian*, 12 October 1961.

72. (Portland) *Oregon Journal*, 25 March 1964; Oregon State Board of Higher Education, "Minutes," 9 March 1964; 25 March 1975.

73. "Library Report, November 5-6, 1965."

74. "Library Report, October 6, 1966."

75. "Library Report, May 8, May 17-18, 1968."

76. *Vanguard*, 14 November 1969.

Chapter Thirteen

1. *Vanguard*, 8 January 1960.

2. Ibid., 4 May 1956, 26 September 1957, 8 May 1959, 7 January 1966.

3. Ibid., 13 November 1959.

4. Ibid., 25 January 1960.

5. Ibid., 12 February 1960; 20 November 1964; 16 November 1966.

6. Tom McCall, *Tom McCall: Maverick: An Autobiography with Steve Neal* (Portland: Binford & Mort, 1977), 115, 43; *Vanguard*, 11 January 1957; 16 November 1966.

7. *Vanguard*, 28 September 1966.

8. Ibid., 19 May 1961.

9. Ibid., 29 May 1964.

10. Ibid., 27 October 1961.

11. Ibid., 25 February 1966.

12. Advisory Council, "Proposed Grievance Procedures," Enclosure C, 26 October 1962, Box 13, Portland State University Archives, Portland, Oregon (hereafter, PSUA).

13. Ibid.

14. Branford P. Millar to John M. Swarthout and Egbert Oliver, 16 October 1962; Advisory Council to President Millar, "Enclosure A," 26 October 1962, both Box 13, PSUA.

15. "AAUP Executive Committee Report on Grievance and Separation Procedures," 11 April 1963, Box 13, PSUA.

16. Ibid.

17. Ibid. The correspondence regarding this case is in Box 19, PSUA, under dates of 22 October 1962 and 29 January, 1, 15, 26 February, and 18 April 1963; B. P. Millar to Executive Committee, 10 June 1966, Box 17, PSUA; Faculty Meeting, "Minutes," 3 May 1967.

18. B. P. Millar to The Faculty, 1 February 1966, Box 17, PSUA; Branford P. Millar to Dale Courtney and Mark Gurevitch, 28 February 1963, Box 13, PSUA.

19. Advisory Council, "Minutes," 18 January, 8, 27 February, 15 March 1965, Box 15, PSUA.

20. Advisory Council, "Minutes," 15 March 1965, Box 15, PSUA; B. P. Millar to The Faculty, 1 February 1966, with attached "Procedure Governing Termination of Appointment of Faculty Members on Indefinite Tenure," n.d., Box 17, PSUA; Faculty, "Minutes," 16 February 1966.

21. J. M. Swarthout to B. P. Millar, 3 March 1966, Box 17, PSUA; The teaching load in Social Science was made nine hours in 1965.; *Vanguard,* 19 November 1965; Joseph C. Blumel, interview with Gordon B. Dodds, 7 December 1995, PSUA. The formal name of the summer session was "Portland Summer Term."

22. John M. Swarthout to Dear Colleagues, 6 January 1966, Box 17, PSUA; *Vanguard,* 28 January, 4 February 1966.

23. "Retirement Planning for the State System of Higher Education," with Faculty, "Minutes," 10 February 1960.

24. Ibid.; Brock Dixon to Branford P. Millar, 25 March 1965, Box 16, PSUA; *Oregon Laws,* 1965, 1015; *Vanguard,* 21 May 1965.

25. Oregon State Board of Higher Education, "Minutes," 3 May 1961; Faculty, "Minutes," 3 May 1961. In the following year, both of these benefits were acquired; Faculty, "Minutes," 2 May 1962; Faculty Senate, "Minutes," 2 November 1964.

26. Smith's letter to Cramer is excerpted in Elmo Smith to Hoyt C. Franchere, 18 October 1956, in Faculty, "Minutes," 31 October 1956.

27. Branford P. Millar to Roy E. Lieuallen, 16 April 1963, Box 14, PSUA.

28. *Vanguard,* 20 April 1967.

29. Bob Rempfer to Offices of the Dean and President, n.d.; Branford P. Millar to Robert Rempfer, 30 January 1962, Box 13, PSUA; Branford P. Millar, untitled, n.d., Box 14, PSUA.

30. John Swarthout to Division and Department Heads, 25 August 1964, Box 15, PSUA; Joseph C. Blumel, interview with Gordon B. Dodds, 7 December 1995; Rudi Nussbaum interview with David Newhall, 11 October 1994, PSUA.

31. Branford P. Millar to Roy E. Lieuallen, 18 March 1965, Box 17, PSUA.

32. Faculty, "Minutes," 11 February 1959; *Vanguard*, 18 February 1959 (quotations).

33. (Portland) *Oregonian*, 9 October 1965; *Vanguard*, 15 October 1965.

34. *Vanguard*, 5 January 1962.

35. Executive Committee, "Minutes," 30 September 1964; *Vanguard*, 9 February, 20 April 1962; 9 October 1964.

36. R. E. Lieuallen to Leonard Alseger, 19 January 1965, Executive Committee, "Minutes," 25 January 1965.

37. *Vanguard*, 1, 15, 22 February, 24 May 1967.

38. Ibid., 12 February 1965.

39. Ibid., 22 February 1967.

40. Branford P. Millar to Grace M. Charlton, 1 December 1961, Box 13, PSUA.

Chapter Fourteen

1. Faculty Senate, "Minutes," 3 December 1956; Administrative Council, "Minutes," 6 November 1957.

2. Administrative Council, "Minutes," 6 November 1957; Erret Hummel to Ray Hawk, 15 November 1957 in ibid., 15 November 1957.

3. Faculty Senate, "Minutes," 6 April 1959.

4. *Vanguard*, 3 March 1960.

5. Faculty Senate, "Minutes," 9, 16 March, 4, 18 (quotation) April 1960; *Vanguard*, 27 January 1961.

6. Faculty Senate, "Minutes," 2 October 1961; *Vanguard*, 29 September, 12 October 1961.

7. *Vanguard*, 19 January 1962.

8. Advisory Council, "Minutes," 30 January 1962.

9. *Vanguard*, 2 February 1962.

10. Ibid., 11, 18 May 1962.

11. Executive Committee, "Minutes," 23 January 1963, Box 14, Portland State University Archives, Portland, Oregon (hereafter, PSUA).

12. *Vanguard*, 3, 11 October 1963; 8 November 1964; Faculty Senate, "Minutes,"

7 October 1963.

13. Ibid., 25 October 1963; 10 January 1964.

14. Ibid., 17 January 1964.

15. Ibid.

16. Faculty Senate, "Minutes," 20 January 1964; *Vanguard*, 24 January 1964.

17. *Vanguard*, 31 January 1964; Faculty Senate, "Minutes," 3 February 1964.

18. Faculty Senate, "Minutes," 3 February 1964; *Vanguard*, 7 February 1964.

19. *Vanguard*, 25 October 1968; 21 November 1969.

20. Ibid., 15 May 1964, 22 January 1965.

21. Ibid., 15 May 1964.

22. Ibid., 22 January 1965.

23. Ibid., 29 January 1965.

24. Ibid., 5, 19 February 1965.

25. *Vanguard*, 19 February 1965; (Portland) *Oregonian*, 8 March 1965; "They Bowled Us Over," *PSU Magazine* (Fall 1995), 17; John M. Swarthout to Ben Padrow and the College Bowl Team, 11 February 1965, Box 15, PSUA.

26. College Bowl folder, Box 15, PSUA; "They Bowled Us Over," *PSU Magazine* (Fall 1995), 17.

27. *Vanguard*, 1 November 1968; Oregon State Board of Higher Education, "Minutes" (hereafter, State Board), 18 February 1969; Charles M. White to Gordon B. Dodds, 26 January 1996, PSUA.

28. Rudi Nussbaum, et al. to All Department Heads, 6 January 1965, Box 15, PSUA.

29. Executive Committee, "Minutes," 3 February 1965.

30. Ibid., 3 February, 10 March 1965.

31. *Vanguard*, 15 January, 5 March 1965.

32. Portland Chamber of Commerce, *Commerce*, 19 March 1965; *Vanguard*, 30 April 1965.

33. *Vanguard*, 14 May, 15 October, 19 November 1965.

34. Ibid., 5 October 1966; 14 April 1967; 28 January 1966; 8 December 1967.

35. Ibid., 26 April, 3 (quotation) May 1968.

36. Ibid., 4 April, 18 October, 15 November 1968.

37. Ibid., 5 October 1966, 8 March 1967.

38. Ibid., 12 January 1968.

39. Ibid., 9 February 1968.

40. Ibid., 16 February 1968.

41. Ibid., 23 February 1968.

42. Ibid., 6 December 1968; Faculty Senate, "Minutes," 4 March 1968.

43. *Vanguard*, 2, 9 April 1965.

44. Ibid., 2 April 1965.

45. (Portland) *Oregonian*, 13, 14 April 1967; *Vanguard*, 19 April 1967.

46. *Vanguard*, 17 May 1967.

47. Ibid., 26 October 1966.

48. Ibid., 9, 16 November 1966 (second quotation).

49. Ibid., 26 April 1967.

50. Ibid., 7 October 1969.

51. Faculty Senate, "Minutes," 6 October 1969.

52. *Vanguard*, 10 October 1969; Faculty Senate, "Minutes," 6 October 1969.

53. *Vanguard*, 14, 17 October 1969.

54. Ibid.; Executive Committee, "Minutes," 29 October 1969.

55. Faculty Senate, "Minutes," 3 November 1969; *Vanguard*, 14 October, 11 November 1969.

56. Faculty, "Minutes," 7 November 1969; *Vanguard*, 11, 14 November 1969.

57. *Vanguard*, 18 November 1969.

58. Ibid., 14 February 1969.

59. Ibid., 4, 14 November 1969.

60. Charles M. White to Gordon B. Dodds, 26 January 1996, PSUA; *Vanguard*, 7 March 1969.

61. *Vanguard*, 23 May 1969.

62. Ibid., 28 May 1969.

63. Ibid., 28 May, 6 June 1969.

64. Ibid., 6, 26 June, 10 October 1969.

65. Ibid., 10 October 1969.

66. Ibid., 17 October 1969.

67. *Vanguard*, 24, 31 October 1969.

68. Ibid., 4 April 1969.

69. Ibid.

70. Ibid., 25 April 1969

71. Ibid., 2, 16, 28 May 1969; *Oregon Laws*, 1969, 1617-1618.

72. *Vanguard*, 6 May 1966.

73. Ibid., 27 May 1966; 12 April 1967.

74. Executive Committee, PSC to Executive Board, ASPSC, 7 November 1966, Box

19, PSUA; *Vanguard*, 12 April 1967; Faculty Senate, "Minutes," 1 May 1967.

75. *AAUP Policy Documents and Reports 1977 Edition* (Washington: American Association of University Professors, 1977); *Vanguard*, 29 September 1967.

76. *Vanguard*, 29 September 1967; Faculty Senate, "Minutes," 8 January, 20 May, 3 June 1968.

77. *Vanguard*, 8 March 1967.

78. Ibid.

79. Ibid., 5 April 1967.

80. David Newhall to Gordon B. Dodds, 22 January 1996, PSUA; *Vanguard*, 19, 24 May 1967.

81. *Vanguard*, 24 May 1967.

82. *Independent Vanguard*, 31 May 1967.

83. Ibid., 31 May, 2 June 1967.

84. Ibid., 2 June 1967.

85. Ibid.; Faculty Senate, "Minutes," 5 June 1967.

86. Faculty Senate, "Minutes," 5 June 1967.

87. Ibid.

88. *Vanguard*, 27 October 1967.

89. William E. Hallman to Merlyn E. Satrom, 11 April 1966, Portland Campus Christian Ministry Records (hereafter, PCCMR).

90. "Brief History of Inter-denominational Cooperation In the Christian Ministry to the Campus Communities of Oregon" (hereafter, "Brief History"); William E. Hallman to Merlyn E. Satrom, 11 April 1966 (quotation), both in PCCMR.

91. Oregon Council of Churches, "Consultation at Portland State College," 13 January 1959; "Brief History;" Robert E. Rumer to Merlyn E. Satrom, 6 April 1966; "Report to Board of Directors, Cooperative Campus Christian Ministry, 1960–1961;" William E. Hallman to Merlyn E. Satrom, 11 April 1966, all in PCCMR.

92. Robert E. Rumer to Merlyn E. Satrom, 6 April 1966, PCCMR; David Newhall to Gordon B. Dodds, 22 January 1996, PSUA.

93. Robert E. Rumer to Merlyn E. Satrom, 6 April 1966; William E. Hallman to Robert E. Rumer, 11 April 1966, both PCCMR.

94. Charles Bursch to V. N. Freeman, 20 June 1961; PCCM, "Annual Meeting Minutes," 12 March 1965; *Koinonia Courier*, Fall 1965; "Annual Staff Report," 9 March 1973, all PCCMR.

95. *Vanguard*, 4 October 1957; "Staff Report," 1960–1961, PCCCR.

96. "Annual Report of the Staff," 1971, PCCMP; Phil Harder, "Running Briefs,"

22 November 1981, PCCMR.

97. Merlyn E. Satrom, et al. to House Committee on State and Federal Affairs, 20 March 1967, PCCMR; "Annual Report of the Staff," 1969–1970; "History Portland Draft and Military Counseling Center," n.d., both PCCMR; (Portland) *Oregonian,* 6 October 1979.

98. "Annual Report of the Staff," 13 March 1970; "Portland Youth Advocates— Contact Center, 1971; PCCM Board, "Minutes," 18 November 1986.

99. Joseph C. Blumel, interview with Gordon B. Dodds, 7 December 1995, PSUA; "Report of the Long Range Planning Committee," 17 December 1963, 7 January 1964, PCCMR; (Portland) *Oregon Journal,* 23 February 1967.

Chapter Fifteen

1. Faculty Senate, "Minutes," 2 April, 4 June 1956.

2. Ibid., 4 June 1956.

3. Ibid., 3 June 1957.

4. *Vanguard,* 10 January 1956.

5. Ibid., 6 April 1962.

6. Faculty, "Minutes," 1 May 1963; Faculty Senate, "Minutes," 6 May 1963.

7. Branford P. Millar to John M. Swarthout, 12 September 1963, Box 15, Portland State University Archives, Portland, Oregon (hereafter, PSUA).

8. Harry A. Scott, "Report on A Study of the Physical Education Program at Portland State College," 30 August 1963, Box 15, PSUA (hereafter, "Scott Report"), 37 (quotation), 39.

9. "Scott Report," 48-58.

10. Ibid., 58-59.

11. Ibid., 60-63.

12. Ibid., 63-67.

13. Ibid., 67-68.

14. Faculty Senate, "Minutes," 7 October 1963.

15. Branford P. Millar to John M. Swarthout, 12 September 1963; J. M. Swarthout to B. P. Millar, 30 September 1963, Box 15, PSUA.

16. Faculty Senate, "Minutes," 1 June 1964.

17. *Vanguard,* 3, 18 October, 8 November 1963.

18. Executive Committee, "Minutes," 27 November 1963; *Vanguard,* 22 May 1964.

19. *Vanguard,* 22 May 1964; Faculty Senate, "Minutes," 1 June 1964; Executive Committee, "Minutes," 9 June 1964.

20. *Vanguard,* 29 May, 25 September 1964.

21. Ibid., 25 September, 23 October 1964.

22. Ibid., 22 January 1965 (quotation); "Intercollegiate Athletic Committee Report," n.d., in Faculty Senate, "Minutes," 5 April 1965 (hereafter, "Athletic Committee Report").

23. *Vanguard*, 26 February 1965. The Big Sky member institutions at this time were Gonzaga, Idaho, Idaho State, Montana State College, the University of Montana, and Weber State.

24. "Athletic Committee Report."

25. *Vanguard*, 23 April (quotation), 7 May 1965.

26. Ibid., 3 December 1965.

27. Ibid., 28 January 1966.

28. Intercollegiate Athletic Committee, "Report," 1 May 1967, in Faculty Senate, "Minutes," 1 May 1967; *Vanguard*, 2 February 1968.

29. Intercollegiate Athletic Committee, "Report," 1 March 1968, in Faculty Senate, "Minutes," 4 March 1968.

30. *Vanguard*, 7 May 1969.

31. Ibid., 21, 23 May 1969.

32. Ibid., 14 March 1969; Faculty Senate, "Minutes," 7 April 1969.

33. *Vanguard*, 7 November 1969.

34. Ibid., 25 November, 9 December.

Chapter Sixteen

1. *Vanguard*, 16 January 1970.

2. Faculty Senate, "Minutes," 26 January, 9 February 1970.

3. *Vanguard*, 24 February 1970.

4. Ibid., 27 February, 6 March 1970; Faculty Senate, "Minutes," 2 March 1970.

5. Faculty Senate, "Minutes," 2 March 1970.

6. Faculty, "Minutes," 15 April 1970.

7. *Vanguard*, 28 April, 1 May 1970.

8. Dory J. Hylton, "The Portland State University Strike of May 1970: Student Protest as Social Drama (Ph.D. diss., University of Oregon, 1993), 99-103. Hylton's work is a comprehensive and objective account of the strike week.

9. Ibid., 103-106.

10. Ibid., 106-109.

11. Ibid., 114-115.

12. Ibid., 118-20.

13. Ibid., 122-23; *Vanguard*, 12 May 1970.

14. Ibid., 126-31.

15. Ibid., 135-138; Charles M. White to Gordon B. Dodds, 26 January 1996, Portland State University Archives, Portland, Oregon (hereafter, PSUA).

16. Hylton, "Portland State Strike," 138-41.

17. Ibid., 145-47.

18. Ibid., 145-46.

19. "Statement to the Faculty by Gregory B. Wolfe, President" in Faculty, "Minutes," 10 May 1970 (hereafter, Wolfe, "Statement").

20. Wolfe, "Statement."

21. Faculty, "Minutes," 10 May 1970.

22. Hylton, "Portland State Strike," 153-56.

23. Ibid., 156-57.

24. Ibid., 158-59; *Vanguard*, 12 May 1970.

25. *Vanguard*, 12 May 1970.

26. Hylton, "Portland State Strike," 160; *Vanguard*, 12, 15 May 1970; David Newhall to Gordon B. Dodds, 22 January 1996, PSUA. A representative of the Mayor did address the strikers.

27. "Ad Hoc Faculty Group for Campus Safety" with Faculty, "Minutes," 12 May 1970.

28. Faculty, "Minutes," 12 May 1970.

29. *Vanguard*, 19 May 1970; Executive Committee, "Minutes," 20 May 1970, Box 490, PSUA.

30. *Vanguard*, 22 May 1970.

31. Ibid., 22 May, 2 June 1970.

32. AAUP—Horowitz folder, AAUP records, AAUP office; *Vanguard*, 2, 6, 9 October, 6 November (quotation) 1970.

33. *Vanguard*, 6 August 1970.

34. Ibid., 13 August 1970, 5 March 1971.

35. Ibid., 16 July 1970; Brent Walth, *Fire at Eden's Gate: Tom McCall & the Oregon Story* (Portland: Oregon Historical Society Press, 1995), 282-309.

36. *Vanguard*, 3 November 1970, 12 February 1971.

37. Hylton, "Portland State Strike," 165; *Vanguard*, 10 November 1970.

38. *Vanguard*, 23 July 1970, 3 December 1971 (quotation).

39. *Vanguard*, 26 February 1971.

40. The best summary of Fenyo's arguments is in Don Moor to Gordon B. Dodds, 22 November 1995, in possession of the author; *Vanguard*, 26 February 1971.

41. *Vanguard*, 12 March, 30 April 1971.

42. Faculty, "Minutes," 12 May 1971; Gregory B. Wolfe to the Faculty, 19 May 1971 (attached to the minutes of this meeting).

43. *Vanguard*, 28 March, 14 April 1972; (Portland) *Oregonian*, 24 March 1972; (Portland) *Oregon Journal*, 8 April 1972.

44. Executive Committee, "Minutes," 31 December 1969, Box 490, PSUA; *Vanguard*, 2 April 1971; Faculty Senate, "Minutes," 5 April 1971.

45. Ad Hoc Committee on Faculty Conduct, "Faculty Conduct Code," in Faculty Senate, "Minutes," 5 April 1971.

46. *Vanguard*, 12 April 1971; "Faculty Conduct Code."

47. Faculty Senate, "Minutes," 5 April, 1 June 1971.

48. Ibid., 20 February 1972.

49. Ibid., 24 May 1971.

50. *Vanguard*, 14 January, 28 April, 2 May 1972.

51. Ibid., 5, 8, 26 March 1974.

52. Ibid., 26, 29 March, 27 September 1974.

53. Joseph Blumel, interview with Gordon Dodds, 7 December 1995; Frederick E. Lockyear to President Wolfe, et al., 28 June 1971, Executive Committee, "Minutes," 28 June 1971, Box 490, PSUA; (Portland) *Oregonian*, 6 May 1990; Joseph C. Blumel, interview with Lora Meyer, 16 May 1980, Oregon Historical Society.

Chapter Seventeen

1. *Vanguard*, 23 January, 20 November, 5 January 1971.

2. Ibid., 13 March (quotation), 20 November 1970.

3. Ibid., 20, 30 April, 4 May 1971.

4. Ibid., 3 November 1972, 21 September 1973 (quotation).

5. Ibid., 17 November 1970.

6. *Vanguard*, 5, 12 August 1971; Francisco Serna to Roy E. Lieuellen, 17 August 1971; Joseph C. Blumel to Gregory B. Wolfe, 30 August 1971, Box 113, Portland State University Archives, Portland, Oregon (hereafter, PSUA); *Vanguard*, 18 April 1972.

7. *Vanguard*, 16 October, 6 November 1970.

8. Ibid., 10, 20 November 1970; 20, 30 April 1971.

9. Ibid., 6 October 1972.

10. Ibid., 26 January, 6 April 1973.

11. Ibid., 22 February 1974.

12. Ibid.

13. Ibid., 7 May 1974..

14. Faculty Senate, "Minutes," 7 October 1968.

15. Joseph C. Blumel to R. Lee Hornbake, 10 September 1968; Joseph Blumel to Gregory Wolfe, 17 September 1968; Joseph C. Blumel to Barbara Intriligator, 19 September 1968, Box 20, PSUA.

16. *Vanguard*, 3 February 1970.

17. Ibid., 3 February 1970; 9 February 1971.

18. Joseph Blumel to All Faculty, 24 December 1968, PSUA; Faculty Senate, "Minutes," 13 January 1969.

19. Faculty Senate, "Minutes," 12 January 1970; *Vanguard*, 10 April, 1 May 1970; Oregon State Board of Higher Education, "Minutes" (hereafter, State Board), 27 April 1970.

20. *Vanguard*, 1 May, 29 September 1970.

21. Ibid., 6 November 1970.

22. Ibid., 27 April 1971.

23. Ibid., 8 October 1971; 26 September 1972.

24. Ibid., 16 January 1973.

25. Ibid., 30 November 1973.

26. Ibid., 8, 22 February, 1 August 1974.

27. Ibid., 2 February 1971.

28. Ibid., 28 May 1971; 11 February 1972.

29. Ibid., 29 January, 9 November 1971.

30. Ibid., 6 October 1972; 30 October 1973.

31. Ibid., 13, 23 October 1970.

32. Ibid., 5, 12 (quotation) March 1971.

33. Ibid., 12, 30 March 1971; 23 May 1972; State Board, "Minutes," 22 May 1972.

34. Ibid., 12 April 1974.

35. Ibid., 23 April 1971.

36. Ibid., 14 January 1972.

37. Ibid., 10 March 1972.

38. Ibid., 16, 20 November 1973.

39. Ibid., 16 October 1973.

40. Ibid., 6 March 1970.

41. "Intercollegiate Athletics Committee Annual Report," 1 May 1973, with Faculty Senate, "Minutes," 7 May 1973.

42. Executive Committee, "Minutes," 6 February 1973, Box 490, PSUA; *Vanguard*, 17 November 1972; 13, 27 February 1973; *Vanguard Metropolis*, February 1973.

43. *Vanguard.*, 29 May, 27 November 1973.

44. Ibid., 6 November 1970.

45. Ibid., 8 January 1971.

46. Ibid.

47. Ibid., 29 January, 2 April 1971.

48. Ibid., 2 April, 28 September 1971.

49. Ibid., 19 November 1971; 4, 28 January 1972.

50. Ibid., 9 April, 3 December 1971.

51. Ibid., 9 (quotation), 13, 16 April 1971.

52. Ibid., 3 May 1974.

53. Ibid., 3 March 1972.

54. Ibid., 6 November 1970.

55. Ibid., 4 December 1970.

56. Ibid., 30 September 1969; Dyena Betcher, "A History of the Helen Gordon Child Development Center," term paper, June 1994, PSUA.

57. Ibid., 6 January, 29 September 1970.

58. "Portland State University Child Care Center Charter," 4 January 1971, Box 490, PSUA; *Vanguard*, 26 February, 30 March 1971.

59. *Vanguard*, 18 January 1972; Betcher, "Helen Gordon Child Development Center."

60. *Vanguard*, 20 July 1972; Betcher, "Helen Gordon Child Development Center." On 5 July 1986, the Helen Gordon Center became Portland State's only building on the prestigious National Register of Historic Places.

61. *Vanguard*, 12 January, 2 February, 5 October 1973.

62. Nancy Porter, "A Nuts and Bolts View of Women's Studies," *Vanguard*, 1 December 1970; *Vanguard*, 11 December 1970, 27 May 1972.

63. Porter, "A Nuts and Bolts View;" *Vanguard*, 27 May 1972; 27 June 1973.

64. *Vanguard*, 31 October, 5 December 1972; 13 April 1973.

65. *Vanguard*, 25 January, 15 February 1974.

66. Porter, "A Nuts and Bolts View."

67. Faculty Senate, "Minutes," 4 November 1974; State Board, "Minutes," 23 September 1975.

68. Executive Committee, "Minutes," 23 October, 18 December 1968; 1 October 1969, Box 490, PSUA; *Vanguard*, 27, 30 January, 3, 10 February 1970; Sharon Wood, telephone interview with Gordon B. Dodds, 7 February 1996; Ann Rule, *Lust Killer* (New York: Penguin Group, 1988), 94-99, 236-238.

69. *Vanguard,* 20 February 1970.

70. Ibid., 10 March, 2 July, 23 October 1970.

71. Ibid., 30 January 1970.

72. *The Shaft,* February 1970. *Shaft* was a monthly supplement to the *Vanguard.*

73. *Vanguard,* 4 June, 12 August, 9 April 1971.

74. Ibid., 16 April 1970.

75. Ibid., 16, 20 April, 7 May, 4 June 1971.

76. Ibid., 28 September 1971.

77. Ibid., 28 September, 22 October 1971.

78. Ibid., 29 October, 30 November 1971.

79. Ibid., 3 March, 12 May, 2 June, 10 August 1972.

80. Clarence Porter to Vice-President Blumel, et al., 24 May 1972, Box 113, PSUA; *Vanguard,* 2 June 1972.

81. *Vanguard,* 10 August, 21 September, 13 October, 1972; 6 April 1973.

82. Ibid., 22 February 1974.

83. Michael Keith Brewin, "Portland Student Services, Inc.: The Establishment of Student-Run Housing in Portland, Oregon, 1969–1971" (MA thesis, Portland State University, 1989), 1-4.

84. Ibid., 4-6.

85. Ibid., 4-8.

86. Joseph C. Blumel, interview with Gordon B. Dodds, 7 December 1995, PSUA; Brewin, "Portland Student Services," 9-13.

87. Brewin, "Portland Student Services," 16, 18-22.

88. Ibid., 25-32.

89. Ibid., 44-52.

90. Ibid., 52-53.

91. Ibid., 55-59.

92. Ibid., 72-76, 78, 80.

Chapter Eighteen

1. *Vanguard,* 17 November 1970.

2. "Chronology of Events," Box 114, Portland State University Archives, Portland, Oregon (hereafter, PSUA). It is doubtful that the money argument was sound, for the tuition income from General Science courses was very high; *Vanguard,* 17 November 1970.

3. *Vanguard,* 19, 26 February, 2 March, 1971.

4. Ibid., 9 April 1971.

5. Karl Dittmer to Joseph C. Blumel, 7 December 1971; Joseph Blumel to Karl Dittmer, 26 January 1972, Box 114, PSUA; *Vanguard*, 4 June 1971; 4 January 1972.

6. Faculty Senate, "Minutes," 7 February 1972.

7. Ibid., 6 March 1972.

8. Ibid., 1 May 1972.

9. Ibid.

10. Ibid., 8 May 1972.

11. "Report of Senate Committee on General Science," n.d., with Faculty Senate, "Minutes," 4 June 1972; Gregory B. Wolfe to Bruce Kaiser, 31 January 1972, Box 472, PSUA.

12. *Vanguard*, 20 October 1970.

13. The early history of the proposal is given in Faculty Senate, "Minutes," 5 November 1973.

14. *Vanguard*, 16, 19 October 1973.

15. Faculty Senate, "Minutes," 5 November 1973.

16. Ibid., 5 November 1973.

17. Ibid.; *Vanguard*, 13 November 1973.

18. A brief history of the formative stages of the Center is contained in Faculty Senate, "Minutes," 2 October 1972.

19. *Vanguard*, 31 March 1972; Oregon State Board of Higher Education, "Minutes" (hereafter, State Board), 28 March 1972.

20. Faculty Senate, "Minutes," 3 April, 1 May 1972; *Vanguard*, 5 May 1972.

21. *Vanguard*, 12, 23 May 1972.

22. K. Kim, "Pacific Rim Studies Center: A Proposal," included with Faculty Senate, "Minutes," 6 November 1972. The reports of the four sub-committees and the two full committees are all in Faculty Senate, "Minutes," 6 November 1972.

23. "Recommendations of the Advisory Committee," 29 August 1972, with State Board, "Minutes," 6 November 1972; Charles M. White to Gordon B. Dodds, 26 January 1996, PSUA.

24. State Board, Committee on Academic Affairs, "Minutes," 29 August 1972, with Faculty Senate, "Minutes," 6 November 1972.

25. State Board, "Minutes," 26 September 1972; *Vanguard*, 21, 29, September, 3 November 1972.

26. Faculty Senate, "Minutes," 2 October 1972.

27. Ibid., 6 November, 4 December 1972; 1 October 1973; Charles M. White to Gordon B. Dodds, 26 January 1996, PSUA.

28. *Vanguard*, 16 January, 2, 6, 9 March 1973.

29. Ibid., 20 April, 18 May 1973.

30. Ibid., 12 July 1973.

31. Ibid., 12 (quotation), 26 July 1973; 26 April, 28 May 1974.

32. A good summary of these difficulties is contained in a memorandum to the faculty senate from the Council of Academic Deans on 1 March 1971. Further public confusion arose from another PCC—Portland Community College.

33. Faculty Senate, "Minutes," 5 February, 15 April 1968.

34. Ibid., 4 November 1968; 11 June 1969. The section 21 and section 91 courses had been instituted in June 1964. Faculty Senate, "Minutes," 15 April 1968.

35. Ibid., 2 February, 2 November 1970.

36. Ibid., 1 March, 3 May 1971.

37. *Vanguard*, 14 May 1971.

38. Ibid., 28 September, 28 November 1971; Joseph C. Blumel, interview with Gordon B. Dodds, 7 December 1995, PSUA.

39. *Vanguard*, 29 March, 5 April 1974.

40. Charles M. White to Gordon B. Dodds, 26 January 1996, PSUA.

41. *Summer Session Catalog, 1985*; Charles M. White to Gordon B. Dodds, 26 January 1996, PSUA.

42. *Summer Session Catalog, 1970, 1990*; Charles M. White to Gordon B. Dodds, 26 January 1996, PSUA.

43. Charles M. White to Gordon B. Dodds, 26 January 1996, PSUA.

44. *Summer Session Catalog, 1985*; Charles M. White to Gordon B. Dodds, 26 January 1996, PSUA.

45. Charles M. White to Gordon B. Dodds, 26 January 1996, PSUA.

46. Don Willner to Gregory Wolfe and Robert De Luccia, 30 December 1970, Box 620, PSUA; *Vanguard*, 7, 14 May, 4 June 1971; Steve Dodge, "25 Years of Science Inquiry at OGC," *Visions* (Summer 1988), 20-21.

Chapter Nineteen

1. Robert J. Low, "The State of Financial Exigency at PSU: How it Developed," 4 January 1972, Box 472, Portland State University Archives, Portland, Oregon (hereafter, PSUA); *Vanguard*, 28 September 1971.

2. *Vanguard*, 29 October 1971; Oregon State Board of Higher Education, "Minutes," 17 December 1971; *Bulletin/72*, 3 January 1972; Robert Low, "The State of Financial Exigency at PSU: A Supplement," 17 January 1972, Box 472, PSUA.

3. *Bulletin/72*, 3 January 1972; Mark Howard to Gregory Wolfe, 19 November 1971, Box 472, PSUA.

4. *Vanguard,* 4, 7 January 1972.

5. Ibid., 23 May 1972. The list of faculty is contained in ibid., 21 April 1972.

6. Ibid., 13, 14 October 1972.

7. Ibid., 4, 8 January 1974.

8. Ibid., 15 January 1974.

9. Ibid., 8 March 1974.

10. Ibid., 5 March 1974.

11. Ibid., 29 March, 5 April 1974..

12. Faculty Senate, "Minutes," 6 May 1974.

13. Ibid.

14. *Vanguard,* 10, 17 (quotation) May 1974.

15. Ibid., 17, 31 May 1974..

16. Ibid., 21, 31 May 1974..

17. Ibid., 18 July, 27 September 1974..

18. AAUP, *Policy Documents and Reports* (Washington: The American Association of University Professors, 1977), 40-44, 56.

19. Faculty Senate, "Minutes," 6 March 1972.

20. Ibid., 1 May 1972, contains the Lovell report.

21. The report is in ibid., 8 January 1973.

22. Ibid.

23. Ibid., 2, 13 April 1973.

24. *Vanguard,* 20 April 1973; Faculty Senate, "Minutes," 23 April 1973.

25. Faculty Senate, "Minutes," 23 April 1973.

26. *Vanguard,* 15, 18 May 1973; Faculty Senate, "Minutes," 4 June 1973, erroneously records the vote as in favor of the local unit.

27. *Vanguard,* 22 January 1974.

28. *Vanguard,* 1, 5 (second quotation) March 1974; Faculty Senate, "Minutes," 4 March 1974 (first quotation).

29. *Vanguard,* 12 April 1974; Joseph C. Blumel, "Address to Faculty," 23 September 1974.

30. Dan H. Fenn and Gregory B. Wolfe, "The Pacific Rim Center at PSU," 1970.

Chapter Twenty

1. *Vanguard,* 1 March 1979.

2. Ibid. Ray was a sort of "stealth" candidate. At her request, she was interviewed without public knowledge of the fact, but the news leaked out. Whitney Bates

to Gordon B. Dodds, 1 February 1996, Portland State University Archives, Portland, Oregon (hereafter, PSUA).

3. Joseph Carlton Blumel, interview with Lora Meyer, 16 May 1980, Oregon Historical Society.

4. Ibid.; Charles M. White to Gordon B. Dodds, 26 January 1996, PSUA.

5. The Hallock bill did not pass. Faculty Senate, "Minutes," 3 February 1975.

6. Ibid., 8 January 1975.

7. Ibid., 3 March 1975.

8. *Vanguard*, 24 February 1978; *AAUP Oregon Federation Newsletter* (Spring 1977), AAUP Office Records (hereafter, Records).

9. *AAUP Oregon Federation Newsletter,* (Spring 1977). During the campaign, Vice-Pres. David Newhall (Philosophy) succeeded Bernard Burke, who had become ill.

10. *Vanguard*, 3 March 1973; Marc Feldesman to Gordon B. Dodds, 15 February 1996 (two letters), PSUA; Joseph C. Blumel, "Faculty Convocation," 21 September 1977, PSUA; Faculty Senate, "Minutes," 3 October 1977, 6 February, 6 March, 1978.

11. *Vanguard*, 3 March 1978; AAUP Executive Board, "Minutes," 3, 15 March, 9 August 1978, Records. The elections were held on 1 and 2 March, 1978.

12. Executive Board, "Minutes," 15 March, 12 April 1978, Records.

13. "*AAUP-PSU Newsletter*," 8 December 1978; January, February 1979, Records; during the course of the negotiations, Richelle resigned from the University and was replaced by Margaret Dobson, who assumed the position of acting vice-president for Academic Affairs; "Faculty Collective Bargaining Session Minutes," 1978–1979, Box 373, PSUA (hereafter, "Bargaining Minutes"); Joseph C. Blumel, interview with Gordon B. Dodds, 7 December 1995.

14. "Bargaining Minutes," 24, 31 January 1979; "*AAUP-PSU Newsletter*," 19 February 1979, Records.

15. "Bargaining Minutes," 14 March 1979; "*AAUP-PSU Newsletter*," April 1979, Records.

16. "Bargaining Minutes," 3 April 1979; "*AAUP-PSU Newsletter*," April 1979, Records. The other two campuses that were negotiating were Southern Oregon State College and Western Oregon State College.

17. "*AAUP-PSU Newsletter*," 5 June 1979, Records.

18. Don Moor to Gordon B. Dodds, 22 November 1995, PSUA; "Bargaining Minutes," 3 April 1979; *AAUP-PSU Newsletter*, 6 August 1979; "Chapter Minutes," 19 September 1979, Records; *Academe* 65 (October 1979): 372.

19. *Collective Bargaining Agreement between Portland State University Chapter, American Association of University Professors and Portland State University* (1979), Records; *Academe* (September-October 1983): 24a.

20. "Manner in Which Decision Was Made," n.d., Box 472, PSUA. This document, in spite of its title, is a chronology of the exigency crises from 3 July

1980 to 21 January 1982.

21. Faculty Senate, "Minutes," 2 March 1981.

22. Ibid.

23. Ibid., 6 April 1981.

24. Ibid., 6 April 1981.

25. Ibid., 13 April 1981.

26. Ibid.

27. Ibid. In later years, the Departments of History and Philosophy did institute plans to save junior colleagues.

28. Faculty Senate, "Minutes," 11 August 1981.

29. "Manner in Which Decision was Made;" Faculty Senate, "Minutes," 5 October 1981.

30. Faculty Senate, "Minutes," 5 October 1981; "Manner in Which Decision was Made;" Joseph C. Blumel, "Faculty Convocation," 22 September 1982, PSUA; Faculty Senate, "Minutes," 3 March 1982; John Hammond, Dick Muller, and Vivienne Olson to Colleagues, 3 June 1982, Box 472, PSUA.

31. Faculty Senate, "Minutes," 3 October 1983.

32. Ibid..

33. Ibid., 7 November 1983.

34. Ibid., 5 December 1983.

35. Ibid., 6 February 1984.

36. Ibid.

37. Ibid., 7 January 1991.

38. Ibid., 25 January 1991.

39. Ibid..

40. Ibid., 11 February, 4 March 1991.

41. Ibid., 1 April 1991.

42. Ibid., 6 May 1991.

43. Ibid., 3 June 1991.

44. Ibid., 3 February 1992.

45. Ibid., 2 March 1992.

46. Ibid., 1, 3 June 1992.

47. Portland State University, *Institutional Self-Study Report 1995*, 513-515.

48. Joseph C. Blumel, "Faculty Address," 21 September 1983, PSUA.

49. Faculty Senate, "Minutes," 3 October 1983; 5 March 1984; 3 April 1984 (wherein is included a summary of the components of the BAS model); 7 October

1985; 7 April 1986.

Chapter Twenty-One

1. For a more extended treatment of these relationships, see Gordon B. Dodds and Craig E. Wollner, *The Silicon Forest* (Portland: Oregon Historical Society, 1990), 112-115 (hereafter, Dodds, *Silicon Forest*).

2. The only state system representative on the Consortium was the president of the State Board. Ibid., 113-15.

3. Ibid., 115-116.

4. Ibid., 116.

5. Ibid., 118-119.

6. Joseph C. Blumel, "Faculty Convocation," 26 September 1985, Portland State University Archives, Portland, Oregon (hereafter, PSUA).

7. Dodds, *Silicon Forest*, 120-122.

8. Natale A. Sicuro to William E. Davis, 28 May 1987, Box 620, PSUA; Russell Sadler, "Higher Education Budget," 15 March 1987, Box 620, PSUA; (Portland) *Oregonian*, 15 December 1988.

9. Faculty Senate, "Minutes," 9 January 1989.

10. Ibid., 8 January, 6 February 1989.

11. Ibid., 6 February 1989; (Portland) *Willamette Week*, 20 April 1989.

12. Faculty Senate, "Minutes," 8 January, November 1975; Oregon State Board of Higher Education, "Minutes" (hereafter, State Board), April 1976.

13. Charles M. White to Gordon B. Dodds, 26 January 1996, PSUA; Faculty Senate, "Minutes," 3 March 1975; 7 April 1976.

14. Faculty Senate, "Minutes," 3 March 1979; 7 April 1986; 8 November 1993; Portland State University, *Institutional Self-Study Report 1995*, 517-525.

15. "General Education Working Group Report and Recommendations," 17 September 1993.

16. Faculty Senate, "Minutes," 6, 13 December 1982.

17. Faculty, "Minutes," 31 January 1983; State Board, "Minutes," 22 April 1983.

18. Faculty Senate, "Minutes," 4 May 1987.

19. Portland Campus Christian Ministry Board, "Minutes," 31 May 1963; "Annual Report of the Staff," 8 March 1968, Portland Campus Christian Ministry Records (hereafter, PCCMR).

20. Annual Meeting, "Minutes," 8 March 1974, PCCMR.

21. *Institute for Judaic Studies of the Pacific Northwest*; Philip E. Harder and G. Palmer Pardington III to Gordon B. Dodds, 7 February 1996, PSUA.

22. John Rosenberg, "The Future of Lutheran Campus Ministry in Portland," 30

April 1989; PCCM Board, "Minutes," 15 May 1990, both PCCMR.

23. "Contractual Letter of Agreement," 1990; PCCM Board, "Minutes," 15 May 1990; Portland Center for the Study of Religion Organizing Board, "Minutes," 19 September 1991; 8 April, 21 October 1992; 11 May 1993; (Portland) *Oregonian*, 30 September 1993; "Center for the Study of Religion Spring Term 1995 Curriculum."

24. Faculty Senate, "Minutes," 6 June 1977.

25. Ibid., 2 February, 1 June 1987.

26. (Portland) *Oregonian*, 15 December 1988; Faculty Senate, "Minutes," 1 February 1988; State Board, "Minutes," 9 December 1988. The rise and fall of the semester plan is detailed in Box 623, PSUA.

27. Faculty Senate, "Minutes," 1 October 1990; 13 June 1991.

28. Ibid., 3 June 1991.

29. Ibid., 6 January, 6 April, 1 June 1992.

30. (Portland) *Oregonian*, 5 April 1971.

31. "Library Report March 17-18, 1972;" "Library Report, October 19, 1973;" "Library Report, July 1972-June, 1974;" *Vanguard*, 28 April 1981.

32. The library had been a selective Regional Depository since 1963; *Vanguard*, 29 September 1981.

33. Ibid., 22 September 1989.

34. "Library Report, July, 1976-June 1978;" *Vanguard*, 1, 22 July 1987; The vote in the Legislature was very close, 17-13 in the senate and 33-27 in the house; *House and Senate Journals* 1987, S-195.

35. *Vanguard*, 1 July 1987; (Portland) *Oregonian*, 2 November 1991.

36. *Vanguard*, 7 April 1995; *Summer Vanguard*, August 1995.

37. (Portland) *Oregonian*, 22 November 1974; Faculty Senate, "Minutes," 7 April, 5 May 1975. Giese carried his case to the United States Supreme Court, which ultimately rejected his appeal in 1979. (Portland) *Oregonian*, 4 December 1979; *Giese v. United States*, 597 F 2d.1170; 444 US 979 (cert. denied).

38. A summary of fringe benefits is in Faculty Senate, "Minutes," 7 February 1977; 12 January 1981.

39. Ibid., 6 October 1980, 6 June 1988.

40. Ibid., 9 June 1975.

41. Ibid.

42. Ibid., 1 October 1973.

43. Ibid., 6 May 1974.

44. Ibid., 13 May 1974.

45. State Board, "Minutes," 25 November 1975; Faculty Senate, "Minutes," 1

December 1975.

46. Faculty Senate, "Minutes," 2 February 1976.

47. Joseph C. Blumel, interview with Gordon B. Dodds, 7 December 1995, PSUA.

48. *Vital Partners: University and the City*, Minutes 1975, Portland State Women's Association Records.

49. Joseph C. Blumel, "Faculty Convocation," 24 September 1980, PSUA.

50. Faculty Senate, "Minutes," 3 June 1974.

51. Ibid., 5 May 1975.

52. Faculty Senate, "Minutes," 7 April 1980; Joseph C. Blumel, interview with Gordon B. Dodds, 7 December 1995, PSUA.

53. Bob Lockwood to Joseph C. Blumel, 26 November 1985, Box 530, PSUA; Faculty Senate, "Minutes," 2 November 1987.

54. Faculty Senate, "Minutes," 16 November 1987.

55. Ibid., 7 December 1987; Natale Sicuro to William E. Davis, 9 December 1987, Box 621, PSUA. Technically, the football team would have been elevated to Division I-A status, while all other sports were to be at Division I.

56. Faculty Senate, "Minutes," 1 February 1988; Roger N. Edgington to W. T. Lemman, Jr., 30 November 1988, Box 621, PSUA.

57. *PSU Magazine*, Winter 1995, 5-8.

58. Faculty Senate, "Minutes," 5 May 1975; 6 May 1991.

Chapter Twenty-Two

1. Loren Wyss to Gordon B. Dodds, 7 March 1996, in possession of the author. The University of Oregon, for example, after the Second World War, obtained authorization to offer science courses that previously were believed to be duplicative of those at Oregon State.

2. "Summary of Information: Members Oregon State Board of Higher Education, 1929–Present," n.d.; *Oregon Laws*, 1955, 306.

3. Loren Wyss to Gordon B. Dodds, 7 March 1996, in possession of the author.

4. Joseph C. Blumel, "Address to the Faculty," 23 September 1974, Portland State University Archives, Portland, Oregon (hereafter, PSUA).

5. Joseph C. Blumel, untitled remarks at the Faculty Convocation, 22 September 1976, PSUA; The Northwest Association for Schools and Colleges, *Evaluation Report, October 20-22, 1975*, 1.

6. *Oregon Laws*, 1977, ch. 144, 86; Joseph C. Blumel, untitled remarks at the Faculty Convocation, 21 September 1977, PSUA; Joseph C. Blumel, Faculty Address, 19 September 1979, PSUA; Joseph C. Blumel, interview with Gordon B. Dodds, 7 December 1995.

7. Faculty Senate, "Minutes," 4 May 1978; Joseph C. Blumel, "Address to the Faculty," 20 September 1978, PSUA.

8. Joseph C. Blumel, "Address to the Faculty," 20 September 1978, PSUA; Oregon State Board of Higher Education, "Minutes" (hereafter, State Board), 30 March 1979.

9. Joseph C. Blumel, "Faculty Address," 19 September 1979, PSUA.

10. Joseph C. Blumel, interview with Gordon B. Dodds, 7 December 1995; Faculty Senate, "Minutes," 2 June 1980; "Report of the Committee on Research at Portland State University," February 1980, in possession of Susan Karant-Nunn; Joseph C. Blumel, "Faculty Convocation," 24 September 1980, PSUA.

11. Joseph C. Blumel, "Faculty Convocation," 22 September 1982, PSUA; *Vanguard*, 3 December 1982; Joseph C. Blumel, interview with Gordon B. Dodds, 7 December 1995.

12. Joseph C. Blumel, "Faculty Convocation," 22 September 1982; Educational Policies Committee, "Minutes," 18 October 1982, Box 565, PSUA.

13. Joseph C. Blumel, "Faculty Convocation," 20 September 1984; Joseph C. Blumel, interview with Gordon B. Dodds, 25 April 1996, both PSUA.

14. Joseph C. Blumel, "Faculty Convocation," 26 September 1985, PSUA; Joseph C. Blumel, interview with Gordon B. Dodds, 7 December 1995.

15. Joseph C. Blumel, "Faculty Convocation," 26 September 1985, PSUA. This is the largest private grant ever obtained by the University.

16. Joseph C. Blumel, "Address to the Faculty," 20 September 1978, PSUA; Faculty Senate, "Minutes," 17 May 1982.

17. Faculty Senate, "Minutes," 17 May 1982.

18. Ibid.

19. Ibid., 3, 17 May 1982.

20. Ibid.

21. Ibid., 17 May 1982.

22. Joseph C. Blumel, interview with Gordon B. Dodds, 25 April 1996, PSUA. Dobson was particularly helpful in documenting and assessing the new doctoral programs the University was developing.

23. Faculty Senate, "Minutes," 3 February 1975.

24. Ibid., 2 (first quotations), 9 (last quotation) June 1975.

25. Ibid., 3 November 1975; 7 June 1976.

26. Ibid., 2 February 1981.

27. Ibid., 4 November, 2 December 1991.

28. Ibid., 6 January, 2 March 1992.

29. Ibid., 6 April, 4 May 1992.

30. Ibid., 7 January 1980, 5 October 1981.

31. Ibid., 12 January 1976.

32. Ibid., 9 February, 1 March 1976.

33. Ibid., 3 November 1986; 2 May 1988.

34. Ibid., 6 June 1988.

35. *Vanguard*, 2 February, 6 April 1987; Faculty Senate, "Minutes," 6 April 1987.

36. "Opinion," *Penk v. Oregon State Board of Higher Education*, Box 463, PSUA, 4.

37. Ibid., 168-219.

38. Ibid., 3.

39. Ibid., 480-487, (480, 484, quotations).

40. Laurie Bennett Mapes, "A Period of Complexity, 1950–1991" in Carolyn M. Buan, *The First Duty: A History of the U.S. District Court for Oregon* (Portland: U.S. District Court of Oregon Historical Society, 1993.), 234-235, (235, quotations).

41. Don S. Willner to Gordon B. Dodds, 4 March 1996, in possession of the author.

42. State Board, "Minutes," 18 July 1986. The selection committee did not rank the candidates but forwarded to the chancellor an assessment of their respective strengths and weaknesses. Roderick Diman to Gordon B. Dodds, 9 February, 1996; William Savery to Gordon B. Dodds, 9 February 1996, both in possession of the author.

43. *Vanguard*, 27 February, 3 March, 7 April, 1987; David A. Horowitz to Louis B. Perry, 13 September 1988, in materials relating to Natale A. Sicuro in the possession of John R. Cooper (hereafter, Cooper Materials).

44. Faculty Senate, "Minutes," 2 November 1987.

45. Natale A. Sicuro to Frank Martino, et al., 4 November 1987, Cooper Materials; *Vanguard*, 10, 24 November 1987; (Portland) *Oregonian*, 21 November 1987. One reason for the sympathy for Penk was that the Journalism Department, of which he had been a tenured professor, had been abolished in the exigency crisis of 1982; at that time, he was given a position as a writing instructor in the English Department and the position of *Vanguard* adviser.

46. Don Moor to Gordon B. Dodds, 22 November 1995, PSUA; Marjorie Burns, interview with Gordon B. Dodds, 17 April 1996.

47. *Vanguard*, 19 February 1988; Faculty Senate, "Minutes," 7 March 1988; Marjorie Burns, interview with Gordon B. Dodds, 17 April 1996; (Portland) *Oregonian*, 6 March 1988.

48. Faculty Senate, "Minutes," 7 March 1988.

49. Jack H. Burns to James C. Petersen, 6 April 1988; Dean D. DeChaine to Gov. Neil E. Goldschmidt; "Resolution Adopted by PSU Foundation Board," 26 April 1988; John Wykoff to Natale Sicuro, 28 April 1988; Peat Marwick Main & Co. to Roger Edgington, 11 April 1988; State Board, "Minutes," 15 April

1988, all in Cooper Materials; Faculty Senate, "Minutes," 6 June 1988; (Portland) *Oregonian*, 20 April 1988.

50. Faculty Senate, "Minutes," 2 May 1988; The faculty's trust fund was a renamed summer session fund that had been in existence for about a decade. It had the advantage that the funds were within the University and, hence, expenditures were subject to all the relevant state requirements. Charles M. White to Gordon B. Dodds, 26 January 1996, PSUA.

51. (Portland) *Oregonian*, 4 May 1988; Natale A. Sicuro to Paul Koberstein, 4 May 1988, Cooper Materials; *Vanguard*, 13 May 1988.

52. The Undersigned Department Heads and Program Directors to President Sicuro, 31 May 1988, Cooper Materials; (Portland) *Oregonian*, 1 June 1988.

53. "Budget Committee Task Force Report," with Faculty Senate, "Minutes," 6 June 1988.

54. Ibid.

55. "Business and Financial Appraisal of the PSU Foundation," 8 June 1988, Cooper Materials.

56. (Portland) *Oregonian*, 12 June 1988; The Department Heads to Natale Sicuro, 14 June 1988, Cooper Collection; (Portland) *Oregonian*, 15 June 1988.

57. Dave Frohnmayer to William J. Linblad and Leigh D. Stephenson, 12 July 1988, Cooper Materials.

58. Ibid.

59. Ibid.

60. "Statement by Chancellor W. T. Lemman," 15 July 1988; (Portland) *Oregonian*, July 1988; "News Advisory," 13 July 1988, Cooper Materials; Faculty Senate, "Minutes," 23 September 1988.

61. *Vanguard*, 11 October 1988; David A. Horowitz to Louis B. Perry, 13 September 1988; Marc Feldesman, et al. to Natale Sicuro Review Panel, 2 September 1988; "Testimony Before State Board Review Committee by John Cooper.... Representing the Department Heads," n.d.; the last three references are in Cooper Materials.

62. State Board, "Minutes," 10 October 1988; Resignation, Memorandum of Understanding, Statement of the Board of Higher Education, all 10 October 1988; *Vanguard*, 11 October 1988.

63. State Board, "Minutes," 10 October 1988; *Vanguard*, 11 October 1988.

64. *Vanguard*, 11 October 1988; Jim F. Heath, interview with Gordon B. Dodds (telephone), 5 September 1995.

65. General Education Working Group, "Report and Recommendations," 17 September 1993; *Currently*, 29 January 1996.

BIBLIOGRAPHICAL ESSAY

The principal source for the writing of this book is the Portland State University Archives (PSUA). Numbering more than 700 boxes of material, they are particularly rich for their holdings of PSU's administrative offices; materials on the formative years of the Vanport Extension Center; and departmental records. They are unlocked for researchers through two documents produced by the University archivist: a shelf list and an archives subject-classification list. The student newspaper, entitled the *Vanguard* since 14 January 1947 (*Vet's Extended* before that date), gives at least a cursory view of most important events at Portland State. The minutes of the faculty senate and faculty meetings also provide a chronology of significant developments. They are available in the office of the Secretary of the Faculty (some are in the PSUA, as well.) Materials for the expansion of the buildings and grounds are contained in the files of the PSU Office of Facilities. The office of the University library maintains many scrapbooks dealing with the library's history. The Office of Institutional Research and Planning has produced many valuable statistical documents. Negatives of hundreds of photographs illuminating PSU history are stored in the holdings of Educational Media Services. The Office of Publications also has many photographs.

The records of private groups are also of great value. The files of the American Association of University Professors are held in its office. They are particularly rich since the year 1977, when it became the bargaining agent for Portland State faculty. The Portland State University Women's Association maintains its own records, which go back to 1947. Portland Campus Christian Ministry holds a particularly well-organized and comprehensive collection of its records.

The only prior history of Portland State is a booklet produced at the time of the institution's twenty-fifth anniversary of becoming a four-year college: John Eliot Allen, ed., *Portland State University: The First 25 Years,*

1955–1980 (n.p., Portland State University, n.d.). This work comprises chapters by different authors, focusing mainly on departmental histories and containing a valuable overview by Stephen Epler of the Vanport Extension Center.

Oral interviews with faculty and administrators were an important source for this work. Some are contained in the PSUA and others are in the Oregon Historical Society's Regional Research Library in Portland. The interests and experiences of both interviewers and subjects vary, but all contribute something of value to the historian.

A few graduate students have produced theses or dissertations dealing with Portland State. Three extremely valuable ones are Michael Keith Brewin, "Portland Student Services, Inc.: The Establishment of Student-Run Housing In Portland, Oregon, 1969–1971" (MA thesis, Portland State University, 1989); Dory J. Hylton, "The Portland State University Strike of May 1970: Student Protest as Social Drama" (Ph.D. diss., University of Oregon, 1993); and John Aidan Richardson, "The Evolution of a University: A Case Study of An Organization and Its Environment (Ph.D. diss., Stanford University, 1974).

Data on PSU's relationships with the State Board of Higher Education, the chancellor's office, and the other state system institutions are contained in the state board "Minutes" and the archives of the State System of Higher Education, the University of Oregon, and Oregon State University. Also valuable for these topics are the daily newspapers: the (Portland) *Oregon Journal* and the (Portland) *Oregonian.* The Oregon State Archives has legislative committee minutes and papers of individual governors, some of which bear on these matters, as well.

Two excellent works that provide valuable information about the metropolitan community, which is one context for the life of Portland State are Carl Abbott's *Portland: Planning, Politics, and Growth in a Twentieth-Century City* (University of Nebraska Press: Lincoln and London, 1983) and Manly Maben's *Vanport* (Portland: Oregon Historical Society Press, 1987).

Index

Colophon

The following typefaces were used in *The College that Would not Die*:

TEXT   DUST JACKET

New Baskerville (body)   Arquitectura
Avant Garde Gothic (display)   Castellar MT

New Baskerville was originally created by British printer John Baskerville of Birmingham in about 1752. George Jones designed this version of Baskerville for Linotype-Hell in 1930, and the International Typeface Corporation licensed it in 1982. The Adobe Type Catalog describes New Baskerville as "an excellent text typeface with a delicacy and grace that come from long, elegant serifs and the subtle transfer of stroke weight from thick to very thin."

Display type, captions, running heads, and folios in this book are set in Avant Garde Gothic (Book). Based on Herb Lubalin's logo for *Avant Garde Magazine*, the design of this geometric sans serif type is reminiscent of work from the 1920s German Bauhaus movement.

Production of this work was achieved through the professional cooperation of the following:

Editing, Design, and Production: Lori Root • Portland, Oregon

Indexing: Rick Harmon • Portland, Oregon

Scanning: Revere Graphics • Portland, Oregon

Printing: Bang Printing • Brainerd, Minnesota

Printing Consultant: Bob Smith, BookPrinters Network • Portland, Oregon